American Yiddish Poetry

*This volume is sponsored by The Foundation for the
Compendium of Yiddish Literature
devoted to the selection and publication of the best Yiddish fiction,
poetry, and drama in the last century*

President: Ephraim Katzir, Chairman: Itzhak Korn

Benjamin and Barbara Harshav

american yiddish poetry

A Bilingual Anthology

Translations with the participation of
Kathryn Hellerstein, Brian McHale, and Anita Norich

University of California Press • Berkeley · Los Angeles · London

The Publisher wishes to thank the Lucius N. Littauer Foundation, New York, N.Y., for their generous support for this project.

University of California Press
Berkeley and Los Angeles, California

University of California Press, Ltd.
London, England

Library of Congress Cataloging in Publication Data

Main entry under title:

American Yiddish poetry.

   Bibliography: p.
   1. Yiddish poetry–United States–Translations into
English. 2. American poetry–Translations from Yiddish.
3. Yiddish poetry–United States. 4. Yiddish poetry–
United States–History and criticism. I. Harshav,
Benjamin, 1928–   . II. Harshav, Barbara,
1940–
PJ5191.E3A47 1986   839'.091'0080973   85-24516
ISBN 0-520-04842-3 (alk. paper)

Printed in the United States of America

1 2 3 4 5 6 7 8 9

For Sir Leslie and Lady Shirley Porter—
with admiration and gratitude

Contents

A. Leyeles

A Jew in the Sea (1947)

At the Foot of the Mountain (1957)

Jacob Glatshteyn

*Translated in collaboration with Kathryn Hellerstein

Moyshe-Leyb Halpern

J. L. Teller

Malka Heifetz-Tussman

(Translated by Kathryn Hellerstein)

Barysh Vaynshteyn

H. Leyvik

Preface

This book attempts to introduce a body of American poetry written in Yiddish in the twentieth century, its cultural background, achievements, and concerns to a larger audience. We hope that readers of poetry as well as those interested in American literature and history will find some new texts and themes among the poems collected here. This volume is not intended merely for a Jewish audience or only for those who understand Yiddish; we believe that there are poetic qualities and human topics here that should be part of general culture, in spite of the language barrier.

For a comparatist working with modern European and American literature, Yiddish poetry is a fascinating object. This extraterritorial poetry—emerging from Vilna, Warsaw, Berlin, Kiev, Moscow, Paris, New York, Chicago, Tel Aviv—was exposed to influences from almost all major modern trends; it combined or alternated such extremely different options of Modernism as those offered in Russian, German, and Anglo-American verse. At the same time, Yiddish poetry carved out its own intense poetic world, based on its unusual, "old-new," extraterritorial language and culture.

There are frustrations inherent in the task undertaken here. How do you convey the impact and poetic achievements of poetry to readers lacking a deep knowledge of the language in which it was written? In fact, Yiddish Modernist poets, exquisite masters of their language, were never spoiled by a large, understanding readership. In the early 1950s, when I first published a study on free verse in Yiddish poetry from the perspective of comparative literature, I received an excited letter from the New York Yiddish poet, A. Leyeles, saying that he had had to wait thirty years before someone understood what he had intended to do.

One part of the challenge lies in the reevaluation of Yiddish poetry itself, selecting from the hundreds of books of poetry some of the best or most representative work, as judged by the standards of modern Western literature. Indeed, it is a new canon of Yiddish poetry for native readers as well that we would like to suggest. Such a reevaluation began in the poetry and criticism of the Introspectivists in the early 1920s in New York, but never came to fruition in the form of comprehensive anthologies, literary histories, or the establishment of a new, "great tradition" from such a perspective.

A further problem lies in the complex historical and linguistic context in which modern Yiddish poetry emerged, the unusual nature of its language, and the cultural traditions on which it drew. The attempt to reassess this junction grew larger than an anthology introduction would permit and resulted in a forthcoming book, *Aspects of Yiddish*, to which we refer the interested reader. The introductory chapters included here provide some information on the cultural background in which this poetry was created as well as some guidelines to its major trends and forms. Biographies of the poets, footnotes, a glossary, and selections from Yiddish poetic theory and criticism supply some factual clues to that background. As befits an anthology, we have not interpreted the poetry itself.

* * *

The existence of this book is due, first of all, to an ageless enthusiast, Itzhak Korn, who came to me one day in Jerusalem and talked to my conscience in terms it could not refute. Himself a lawyer and Zionist leader from Bessarabia, Rumania, Korn reached Israel in 1940, where he was, among other things, vice minister of finance and the chief builder of the great wave of agricultural settlements (Moshavim) that absorbed immigrants from the Oriental countries in the 1950s. Author of several books (notably on the history of the Moshav settlements and the history of Jews in Bessarabia), Korn is at present chairman of the Israeli Executive of the World Jewish Congress. He is also the founder and chairman of the World Council for Yiddish and Jewish Culture and the initiator of a multivolume Compendium to include the best of Yiddish literature. The committee for its publication includes Professor Ephraim Katzir, former President of Israel (President); Itzhak Korn (Chairman) and Professors Dov Sadan, Dan Miron, and Benjamin Hrushovski (Harshav), members of the editorial board. This is the framework in which the Yiddish side of this anthology was conceived.

The second step stemmed from my own skepticism as to the size of a possible Yiddish readership of poetry in the world today. It was clear to me that the utmost effort should be made to provide translations of Yiddish poems for readers who do not know the language, though I am fully aware that poetry translations in general—and from this unusual language in particular—cannot possibly match the impact of the original. It was not a matter of creating alternative English poems of similar stature, but of conveying as much of the meaning of the original text as is possible in a readable English poetic form.

The bulk of this volume was translated by my wife Barbara and myself. It was in daily collaboration with her that the ideas, the historical perspective, and the language of the introduction were elaborated. Without her, my work of the last years would have been unthinkable. Also, in collaboration with Kathryn Hellerstein, I translated several poems by M. L. Halpern, J. Glatshteyn, and B. Vaynshteyn. In addition, Hellerstein translated the section of poems by Malka Heifetz-Tussman.* We are grateful to several friends who read the drafts, gave invaluable advice, and taught us a great deal in the process. Allen Mandelbaum, a master of English poetry translation, was as critical as a good friend should be. Dr. Anita Norich, professor of English and Yiddish literature at the University of Michigan, compared the vast body of texts with their Yiddish sources and translated the "Introspectivist Manifesto." Dr. Brian McHale, professor of Literary Theory and Comparative Literature at Tel Aviv University and himself a poet, carefully read the English manuscript. Laurie Magnus and Harvey Gross made incisive remarks on earlier drafts. The dialogue with all of them made the text strange to us again, refreshed our observations, and contributed to a better final result. Those translations which were made specifically by others or in various collaborative combinations are so indicated in the table of contents. All the translations were edited by Barbara and myself and the responsibility for the final text lies with us.

The search for parallels from graphic art was aided by a number of specialists. Mr. Abram Lerner, director of the Hirshhorn Museum at the Smithsonian Institution in Washington, D.C., and its art curator, Cynthia Jaffe-McCabe, author of *The Golden Door*, a comprehensive book on American immigrant artists, gave us their invaluable and friendly help. Mrs. Adele Lozowick gave us gracious permission to reproduce some of her late husband's work. Sculptor Chaim Gross opened to us some of his own work. The Forum Gallery in New York, Mrs. Susan W. Morgenstein, director of the Goldman Fine Arts Gallery of the Judaic Museum, Jewish Community of Greater Washington, and others helped with advice and material. Thus the book has gained a dimension that may place Yiddish poetry in the perspective of twentieth-century American art.

The YIVO Jewish Scientific Institute in New York is an indispensable partner in any research in the field of Yiddish. We are grateful to its director, Sam Norich, for permission to use the illustrative documentation on the poets included in this volume, and to archivist Marek Web and librarian Dina Abramovich for their readiness to share their knowledge. Dr. Mordechai Schechter helped to clarify the meanings of several difficult words. Judd Teller's brother in Tel Aviv helped with his brother's poetic legacy. Thanks are also due to the CYCO Central Jewish Cultural Organization and to its late director, Chaim Bez, who persevered in publishing the comprehensive eight-volume *Leksikon fun der yidisher literatur* (Lexicon of Yiddish Literature), which we used as the main source for our biographical sketches. The Yiddish spelling of the original poems was unified according to YIVO principles by Paul Glasser; all deviations from those principles (in the direction of the poet's own spelling) are our responsibility.

Our editor, Stanley Holwitz, did not shy away from the magnitude of this project or the difficulties involved in printing a text in two alphabets and in two different countries, and accepted the challenge of an additional dimension of illustrations from graphic art. Nancy Shapiro and Mac Shaibe in Jerusalem spared no effort or ingenuity in harnessing Yiddish texts to the molds of modern word processing. The taste and meticulous devotion of Randall Goodall gave the volume its visual shape.

*Kathryn Hellerstein thanks the Memorial Foundation for Jewish Culture for a grant that supported her part in the translations, 1982–1983.

The bulk of the translations were made concurrently with my research on literary theory at the National Humanities Center, Research Triangle Park, North Carolina. The scriptorium of that institution is unequaled in its professional attitude, patience, and zeal in providing the cleanest manuscript possible. The introductions were written at the Institute for Advanced Study / Wissenschaftskolleg zu Berlin. I am grateful to both institutions for the opportunity given me to work there.

Last but not least, to the Porter Institute for Poetics and Semiotics of Tel Aviv University I owe the scholarly base that I have enjoyed for the last ten years. It is due to the support of Sir Leslie and Lady Shirley Porter of London that a group of original scholars were able to create a center for the study of literature and culture at Tel Aviv University.

The introductory chapter of the following essay explains some of the motivations guiding this anthology; the last chapter explains its principles. If the translations and introduction lead some readers to appreciate what Yiddish poetry was, to take an interest in some of the poems, or even to read and enjoy the originals, our work will not be in vain. If some readers are incensed by the translations and try their own hand at it, we will feel our mission fulfilled.

Benjamin Harshav (Hrushovski)

The Porter Institute for Poetics and Semiotics
Tel Aviv University, 1985

A Note on Transcription and Spelling

The transcription of Yiddish into the Latin alphabet in this book uses, in most cases, the standard system devised by YIVO. Its main principle is a direct correspondence between the Latin letters and the sounds of standard literary Yiddish. The main pronunciations to keep in mind are:

s—like *s* in English *sad*
z—like *z* in English *zebra*
sh—like *sh* in English *shoe*
tsh—like *ch* in English *chair*
ts—like *zz* in *Pizza*
kh—like *ch* in *Chanukah* or *chutzpah*
y—like *y* in *yes* or (between consonants) like *i* in *pit*
a—like the first *a* in English *affair*
e—like *e* in English *get*
o—like *o* in English *dog*
u—like *oo* in English *moon*
i—like *ee* in English *feel*
ey—like *ay* in English *day*
ay—like *uy* in English *guy*
oy—like *oi* in English *toil*

It is important to note that some Yiddish syllables have no vowels. At the end of a word (and before a suffix), two consonants in which the second is *l* or *n* constitute a syllable. Thus Yiddish *meydl* has two syllables, *mey-dl* (like English *peddle*), whereas its English translation, "girl," has one syllable. This is also the case with *ma-khn* ("to make"), *la-khn* ("to laugh"), *a shti-kl* ("a piece"), *ge-ke-stl-te* ("checkered"), *tu-ml-di-ke* ("tumultuous, noisy"), and so on.

In most Yiddish words, the stress falls on the first syllable; whenever this is not the case we have placed an apostrophe (') before the stressed syllable. (In several cases, however, we emphasize the stressed syllable by printing it in upper case letters in the text.)

We have deviated from the YIVO spelling in a number of cases when there is a commonly accepted English spelling of familiar Yiddish words. Thus the transcription *ch* for the guttural sound of *Chanukah, chutzpah, Chana, challah,* and so forth came to English from the spelling of Jewish names in German or Polish and is highly misleading to an English reader. Nevertheless, we yielded to custom and wrote *Sholem Aleichem, chutzpah,* and *challah* in the English text (but not in transliterations of Yiddish texts, where we tried to be consistent). We also accepted several commonly used compromises between the Hebrew and Yiddish spellings of Jewish religious concepts, and the double *d* in the word "Yiddish" itself. This is especially true for the English poetry translations. Yiddish words there are part of the English text and have to be spelled as in English usage, even if inconsistent.

A special problem arose from the word "rabbi," which represents a hopeless confusion in English between three different concepts. We had no choice but to separate the concepts and introduce their Yiddish pronunciation: *Reb* or *Rabbi* for "Mr."; *rebbe* for a leader of a Hassidic sect, an heir to a dynasty; *Rov* for an ordained, legal, and religious leader of a Jewish community (in Hebrew: *rav,* the American "rabbi").

THE SPELLING OF YIDDISH

Yiddish is easy to read. Each letter represents a sound in standard literary Yiddish. Readers who know the Hebrew alphabet must keep in mind that, unlike Hebrew, Yiddish has developed fixed letters for the representation of vowels (except for words of Hebrew origin, which are spelled as in Hebrew, though pronounced differently).

The problems of unifying the Yiddish spelling in a text like ours are not fully solvable. The standardization of the spelling of literary Yiddish is a very recent development. The standard YIVO spelling solved many problems but also has several difficult and contested aspects. It tends to suppress dialect expressions, some widespread old or Germanizing forms (e.g., Leyeles used *herbst,* "autumn," while YIVO decided on *harbst*), and various idiosyncratic uses of language in poetry. This is not the time for spelling reforms of Yiddish. We must remember, however, that most books of Yiddish poetry did not follow, or followed only in part, the YIVO rules—or were published before their widespread acceptance. To some extent, their spelling reflects the poets' own ways. Yet we cannot simply reproduce the original texts because, more often than not, they are the result of the whims of publishers and printers; they also reflect the lenient ways of Yiddish spelling, and the mixed results of the modern shift away from both the medieval (vocalizing) and nineteenth-century Germanizing ways of writing Yiddish. It is also impossible to reconstruct the poet's own dialect, since many writers moved and mixed with speakers of other dialects (especially in New York), and most of them tried to adapt to the dominant, "literary," standard language.

We have accepted the following compromise. First, all the texts were transcribed according to the contemporary YIVO rules. Then, a number of corrections were made to restore some spellings of the original which we deemed important for the poetic text. This was done primarily in the case of compounds. Poets often hyphenated a new word combination; according to the YIVO rules, if there are no more than three syllables, the term would be spelled as one word and the effect of a poetic innovation would be lost. The opposite also holds true: YIVO decided to separate composite adverbs (as in English adverbial phrases), while some linguists and most poets stubbornly wrote them as one word or made a distinction between two slightly different concepts. For example, some native speakers feel a distinction between *far nakht* ("before night falls") and *farnakht* ("evening, dusk"). Glatshteyn, who accepted the YIVO spelling almost fully in his last books, still insisted on *inderfri* ("in the morning") as one word. Since we first accepted the YIVO rules and rewrote the whole text accordingly, we could only accommodate such cases selectively, to indicate the problem or to highlight a local subtlety rather than to solve the dilemma. Readers of Yiddish books must be used to alternative spellings in any case, and no ambiguity should arise from this. The Yiddish linguist Dr. Dovid Katz of Oxford encouraged us in this deviation. We hope that our readers—even the purists—will be flexible on this point, as was the living language of Yiddish writing itself.

American Yiddish Poetry and Its Background

AN EXPEDITION TO THE RIVERS OF MANHATTAN

> How long will Yiddish Literature be unknown among Gentiles?
> How long will they think of us—in literature—as Hotentots?
> —A. Leyeles, *In Zikh*, July 1923

> So many years in America, such a fine literature created here, and
> we remain strangers to our neighbors as if we had lived in Siam or had
> written in some Eskimo dialect.
> —A. Leyeles, *In Zikh*, March 1937

We learn the language of the mute and the deaf. We embark on anthropological expeditions to the jungles and mountains of Central America or New Guinea, we study the remnant tongues of Native American tribes. But what do we know of the poetry and fiction that flourished here, "on the rivers of Manhattan" and other cities, dynamic and polyvalent, intensely American, but mute in its language, a one-way street with no return?

There was once a rich, buoyant American literature in Yiddish, perhaps the most coherent and full-fledged literary institution in the United States outside of English. Except for its exclusive language, it was not a parochial phenomenon. It spanned a wide gamut of themes and ideologies, from utopian socialism to American *engagement*, from cosmopolitan universalism to Jewish nationalism, and encompassed a variegated range of styles and genres, from naturalist fiction to avant-garde experiments, from popular melodrama and stirring novels in newspaper installments to virtuoso sonnet garlands and hermetic free verse.

While English poetry was dominated by the exquisite elitism of T. S. Eliot and Ezra Pound and steeped in cultural allusions to the European past of Dante, Shakespeare, and the Provençal bards, Yiddish poets—shoemakers, housepainters,

3

or "poor newspaper writers" as they were—often confronted American realities directly: the wonders of construction and city architecture, the subway, the harbors, labor unions, the underworld, the plight of the blacks, the trial of Sacco and Vanzetti, alienation of the individual in the jungle of the metropolis, social injustice, and immigrant longing.

At the same time, Yiddish poets were fascinated by contemporary ideas. Modernism, Freud, the Russian Revolution, Buddhism, the Tao, Nietzsche, Baudelaire, Villon, Isaiah and Homer, Whitman and Rabbi Nakhman from Bratslav mark the range of intertextuality of American Yiddish poetry. Young Yiddish poets in New York talked "about eternity, death and grammar" (as Glatshteyn put it in his poem "On My Two-Hundredth Birthday," written at the age of twenty-five)—and talking was at the heart of their culture.

They created a chorus of voices, inscribing with emotional and intellectual intensity their responses to the human condition, to nature and the modern city, alienation and love, the "Golden Land" and the "Old Home" overseas in existential or melodic lyrical poems or long, descriptive verse narratives. Because Yiddish poetry in this period was Modernist poetry—that is, consciously art in language—it employed the most specific characteristics of the Yiddish language and drew on its cultural density, creating unique combinations of diction, sound, and allusion. Indeed, it is hardly possible to experience the full impact of this poetry without having internalized the language and its emotive and socio-semantic dimensions.

The poetry presented and translated in this volume has two faces. On the one hand, American Yiddish poetry is a prominent expression of modern Jewish culture. It gave voice to yet another permutation of Jewish history: the migration of a whole people to a new world, changes in their social fabric and value system, the traumas and internal richness of Jewish existence, the ties and tensions between collective pressures and individual freedom. It also laid bare the treasures and the contradictions of the Yiddish language and the Jewish tradition. Yiddish poetry transformed the language of a popular, age-saturated, oral culture into the aristocratic and cosmopolitan forms of post-Symbolist poetry or the coarse and cutting metaphorical outbursts of Expressionist verse. And in its decline—perhaps like no other literature—it gave voice to the tragic vision of the Holocaust in Europe, enmeshed in the tragedy of the poet's own disappearing language.

On the other hand, Yiddish poetry was no mere vehicle for the expression of "Jewish" experience. This was a time of mass movement of people of Jewish origin into general Western culture, the business world, art, and academia. Yiddish poets were part of it. They responded to the modern world as human beings and as Americans, embracing the forms of Western culture while working in their own language. As the Introspectivist manifesto of 1919 put it, "poetry is, to a very high degree, the art of language . . . and Yiddish poetry is the art of the Yiddish language and is merely a part of the general European-American culture." Thus much of Yiddish poetry written in the United States was consciously and effectively a cosmopolitan, even primarily American literature, expressing the emotions and thought of the individual in the modern metropolis. It was attuned to all facets of modern life and history, though written in the Yiddish idiom and using "Jewish" experiences (among others) as a language to express the human condition.

From an American perspective, Yiddish poetry must be seen as an unjustly neglected branch of American literature, a kaleidoscope of American experience and art entombed in yellowing, crumbling books, in the muteness of its own dead language.

From a "Jewish" perspective, Yiddish poetry was not the world of "our fathers," but of their sons. In that great centrifugal move out of the old, medieval, Eastern-European jittery Jewish existence, Yiddish literature was one of the new cultural alternatives. Like those who invented Zionism, created modern Hebrew literature, or built the unrealistic fantasyland of Israel; those who fell in the battles for Socialism; or those who assimilated into Western culture, contributing to its literature, art, and science and adopting new languages, ideas, and manners, Yiddish writers were carried on a revolutionary wave. They were creating a modern literature that would be "merely a branch, a particular stream in the whole contemporary poetry of the world" (as the Introspectivist manifesto put it), just as the founders of modern Israel wanted to build "a nation like all nations." For those who could read themselves into their world, these writers produced a brilliant performance and eventually made a tragic exit from an empty hall.

They were our cousins, a branch of the same evolutionary tree that came to a dead end, a bough that bloomed and withered away by a quirky twist of history.

A DIFFERENT ANTHOLOGY

Young scholars, pay attention. If it is, indeed, a time for the gathering of spiritual inventories, for hiding from the storm, let us register only such things for which future generations will have respect. And they will have respect only if we select such writers who have shown the greatest measure of understanding for the music of our language. Such writers must and should be selected who have shown in their Yiddish, genuinely Jewish, creativity that they have an ear and a heart for the world and also for their Jewish and worldly contemporaries; that in their writing they reflected the problems of their time. . . . Our very beginning was the Bible and, there, even the smallest poet of the twelve prophets had an ear for the rhythm of the Hebrew or the rhetoric of his time.

—Jacob Glatshteyn, *Sum and Substance*

This volume is intended as an introduction to American Yiddish poetry, to some of its major themes, concerns, and achievements, seen through a substantial sampling from the work of several poets. It is a selection on two levels: we chose what seemed the best or most interesting (and translatable) poems, and we chose a few poets to represent this literature. The selection focuses, roughly, on the period from 1918 to 1970.

In other words, we opted for a kind of traveling exhibition of several artists from a distant culture—for the effect of a Biennale in Venice, rather than an

Autumn Salon representing all the artists in town. We assume that this mode presents a much more complex image of what Yiddish poetry was than the usual kind of anthology, which registers the existence of dozens of unknown poets through one or several poems by each. Such a panorama of poets would make sense if all those names were still alive in the culture next door, or if the reader could reach for a volume of poems by any of the authors on his own shelf or in a library.

More important, the belief in the value of one poem—"the poem itself"—as an absolute work of art, is no longer as convincing as it was in the days of the New Criticism. Poems carry their weight, their full meaning and artistic import, their interest as witnesses to experience and to work in language, when seen in the context of the continuous development of a poet's work, the transformations of his imagery, personality, poetic and ideological tendencies, experiments and responses—and, ideally, when all those are placed in the perspective of other poets of the time. It is not the one, unique, great poem we are after, but a body of verse presenting a range of poetic work, the trials, interests, frustrations, and achievements of a creative activity and the concerns of a culture.

Furthermore, this mode of presentation provides space for the poetic narratives, poetic cycles, and long conversational pieces in verse that are so essential to Yiddish poetry. It also allows us to demonstrate the enormous shifts that occurred in Yiddish poetry in one generation; the transformations that took place in the work and language of each poet under the impact of historical events; and the greatest transformation of all—that of a Modernist, individual, experimental, even elitist poetry when confronted with the shock of the Holocaust.

Many tensions run through this anthology—tensions between Modernism and expressive "Realism," between art as creation in language and the weight of a message, between individual experience and social *engagement*, between cosmopolitan or typically American concerns on the one hand and a focus on "Jewish" topics on the other. The tensions and symbioses between these opposites are at the heart of Yiddish American poetry in general, just as they are characteristic of Jewish American artists of the same generation. Thus we decided to accompany this anthology with a selection of works by American visual artists of similar biographical backgrounds, illuminating this nexus from an additional perspective.

A second volume is planned for a different cross section, reflecting the historical development of Yiddish poetry in America over the last hundred years. A larger number of individual poets will appear there, representing their respective generations and literary trends as well as the changing historical styles and contexts of Yiddish verse in the United States.

Among the poets selected in the present volume are four or five of the best Yiddish poets in America. We placed at its center the poetry and poetics of the Introspectivists, a self-conscious trend of Modernist verse in Yiddish that was founded in New York in 1919. This, too, is meant primarily as a representative example, for in their poetry and criticism, the Introspectivists represent the problems and tensions that have preoccupied Yiddish poetry in all generations.

Besides the two major Introspectivist poets, Glatshteyn and Leyeles, we chose such central figures as Halpern and Leyvik, who are described in literary histories as belonging to a previous literary generation ("The Young"), but who were actually contemporaries of the Introspectivists as well and who responded to the same historical context, albeit in different poetic languages. Together with the other poets selected here, they display a panorama of possibilities, thematics, and poetics that coexisted in American Yiddish verse in its heyday. Indeed, the poets appear in this volume not in chronological order but as a kind of symphony of voices, competing with and complementing each other.

The book opens symbolically, with a poem about language and interpretation. "The God of Israel," says Leyeles, is rich not in statues and museums, but in manuscripts tied and entangled with each other. Once upon a time He dropped from a mountain two handfuls of letters, scattered them over the roads of the earth, and ever since then we have sought them, saved them, translated them, "and there is no solution on earth / for the letters, the sayings, the words." Foreshadowing Derrida—and drawing on the great book of the Kabbalah, the *Zohar*—this poem reflects a culture that for generations has written and studied commentaries upon commentaries of some basic texts and their transformations, placing its stress on understanding and reunderstanding the meanings hidden in those texts. The centrality of language, the transformation of texts, and the continuous puzzlement over their meaning were at the heart of the Introspectivist impulse and of Yiddish poetry in its precarious existence as a whole.

The book closes where it should have begun, with a late poem by Leyvik, a Whitmanesque hymn, farewell, and confession, "To America." After all the years of feeling intensely American, Yiddish poetry still stands ambivalently on the threshold: it is a language with too many reminiscences without and not really and fully allowed in.

ARCHAEOLOGY OF A CULTURE

In the past, Yiddish encountered enormous walls of prejudice. All the weight of Jewish inferiority complexes and the animosity of an alien world toward the "Jewish" image of the Jew were projected upon this language, which was seen as an embodiment of the "medieval," primitive, devious, unassimilable Jewish subsistence. Masses of young Jews streamed into the richer, more rewarding general culture whenever possible—in pre-Hitler Germany, in postrevolutionary Russia, in the relatively liberal United States. Thus no high-level effort was made to present the art of Yiddish in other languages. Halpern, Leyvik, Leyeles, Glatshteyn, or Teller (himself an English writer), who had the stamina to create a modern literature in Yiddish in New York and about New York, saw hardly any collections of their poetry translated into English, although (or, as some would argue, because) there was no lack of Jews in the American literary establishment.

Today, it may be almost too late. The best achievements of American Yiddish literature were in poetry. Translating poetry is a challenging and frustrating task. It can rarely succeed in creating an equivalent that is close to the original in poetic stature. But beyond this crucial question, in recent translations one often observes a simple lack of knowledge of the full range and precise connotations of the original.

A typical example is Leyvik's poem, "Here Lives the Jewish People" (see our translation below). One translator wrote "The imprisoned life of the prison city" instead of "The towering life of the towering city," changing the whole meaning of the poem (in Yiddish, *turem*, "tower," of German origin, is similar to *turme*, "prison," which comes from Russian). In other cases, translators have used "feet" for the Yiddish *fis*, thus referring to a woman's feet rather than to her legs. These are some of the simpler misreadings. Yiddish is much more of a forgotton tongue than we are willing to admit.

One problem is that Yiddish poetry not only explored the full range of the Yiddish language and enriched it in many ways but also benefited from the historically unique cultural junction at which the generations of its writers and readers found themselves. Along with the historical layers and multilingual components of the Yiddish language itself, Yiddish poetry reverberated with the themes and images of the Hebrew-Aramaic religious, mythological, and cultural tradition, the reminiscences and figures of Jewish history. It also drew on the stories, allusions, and intonations of Slavic folklore and literature, as well as on some German literature and on the imaginary museum of modern (including Oriental) culture, mediated through those languages.

It may be said, schematically, that modern Yiddish literature was written in the genres, forms, and conventions of Russian (and through it, European) literature, in a basically Germanic language that was impressed by layers of Hebrew texts and mythology and by "Jewish" images, typology, and intonations of speech. This complex and unique poetic language was open to the themes, motifs, ideas, and aesthetic trends of modern Europe. In this conglomerate Yiddish came to America, responded to its stimulae, and absorbed some influences of its literature, life, and ideological atmosphere. A reader or critic would have to travel the same road, at least intellectually, to perceive the full impact of the competing voices in a Yiddish text.

For example, A. Leyeles received a Jewish-Hebrew education growing up in the big-city atmosphere of the Jewish-and-German Polish city of Lodz under Russian rule, then lived for five years in London and spent most of his creative life in New York. Besides Yiddish and Hebrew, he knew Russian, German, Polish, English, and some French, and was well-read in those literatures. Leyeles was a master of Provençal poetic forms (probably under the influence of Russian Symbolism as well as of German and Yiddish Impressionism): he wrote sonnets, villanelles, rondeaux, ottava rima, triolets, terzinas, and invented his own exacting strophic patterns; at the same time, he created a variety of American-influenced but original and rhythmically intense free-verse forms. He translated an important book of aesthetics from German into Yiddish, as well as poems by E. A. Poe, Keats, Whitman, Paul Verlain, Amy Lowell, Goethe, Lermontov, Pushkin, and Stephen Spender. Leyeles's poems echo themes from Buddhism, psychoanalysis, American architecture, the Russian Revolution, the Bible, Baudelaire, and the Holocaust.

This does not mean that every Yiddish poet was a multilingual walking library, but that Yiddish poetry as a whole stood at this unusual intersection, attuning its antennae to "Culture" and open to winds from all sides. The contemporary American reader or translator can hardly match the immediacy and fusion of moods and modes that met at that junction.

Neither can it be done by the repeated nostalgic waves of fondness for Yiddish, which often rejoice in the sentimental, melodramatic aspects of lower-class Yiddish popular culture and film—in the *shmates*,* the very mention of which evokes derision or good-humored laughter. Along with the warmth of a naive humanity and a groping for some kind of "roots," nostalgia entails a distancing gesture vis-à-vis the primitive "world of our fathers" which, thank God, we have left behind forever. Clearly, nostalgia for the vestiges of Yiddish popular culture, as well as the emotive connotations of Yiddish words and expressions used in contemporary English or Hebrew, fulfill a significant sociolinguistic function. But the relation between modern Yiddish poetry and this stratum is not very different from that between English poetry and American folklore, mass media, or Hollywood films.

In recent years, a revival of interest in Yiddish literature, and in American Yiddish literature in particular, has generated a new wave of translations. A number of books and anthologies have brought some of the themes, names, and scope of Yiddish verse to the attention of the English reader. A landmark in this trend was Irving Howe and Eliezer Greenberg's *A Treasury of Yiddish Poetry* (1969). The present volume is a further step in that direction.

Unlike translations from French, Spanish, or German, we have little hope of supporting the renderings here with the full force of the living culture of the original looming in the background. If Rilke, Mandelshtam, or Baudelaire do not really come through in English translations, the reader can supplement some of the lacks of the English text with a feeling for the sound and sense of the original, with a knowledge of its intellectual background, and with a cultural belief in the halo of its importance. All this is lacking in the case of Yiddish.

The selection and density of poetic language communicates only when it can rely on a broad background, assuming the reader's familiarity with a wide body of texts in a society—written and oral, fiction, folklore, essays, ideology and philosophy. Very little of that background can be assumed in the reader's knowledge of Yiddish. Moreover, the artistic norms and values of Yiddish poetry itself are remote from the reader's expectations, and may often seem primitive, rhetorical, sentimental, or old-fashioned.

Nevertheless, in registering the nuances, the creases and folds of the original (the Yiddish *kneytsh*, "crease," stands for that added meaningful connotation and particular intention in learning), the explorer has no right to deviate much from the objects of his observation.

Hence this is not simply a translation, but an exploration of a lost continent—"Dialectology at a Distance," as Uriel Weinreich put it. Indeed, we invite the reader to engage in an "archaeology of a culture," to use his imagination to evoke the vitality of the poetry that once pulsed in these stones.

---

*Shmates is a loaded word, literally referring to rags, old cloth, or "junk," and colored by the expressive sound of the derogatory cluster *shm-*.

According to its great historian, Max Weinreich[1], Yiddish emerged in the Rhine area around C.E. 1000, as the speech of Jewish immigrants from Italy and France who adopted the German of their new neighbors and gradually spread throughout Europe, an integral part of the culture of Ashkenazi Jews. It is not quite clear to what extent and at what time Yiddish really separated from German. In any case, the question is purely academic. From its inception, the language was used by a separate, tightly organized, international community with its own isolated world of knowledge, learning, history, and beliefs, and it was written in its own separate alphabet. Its typical features can be detected from the earliest documents. Yiddish was always a language of "fusion," in which elements from various German dialects, from the Holy Tongue (the Hebrew and Aramaic of the texts of Jewish tradition), from Romance languages (brought by Jews from Italy and France), and, later, from several Slavic languages were blended into one synthetic whole and one grammatical system.[2]

At the same time, throughout its history, Yiddish was an "open" language. In addition to those elements from its source languages that it had absorbed thoroughly, Yiddish speakers could at various times and for various purposes, draw from the resources of those languages and tilt their vocabulary in one direction or another. Indeed, Yiddish was the language of a polylingual society, moving among neighbors who spoke its component languages (especially German and Slavic) and living intensely with books and with continuously multiplying texts and manuscripts written in the Holy Tongue.

The Jews were the only society in medieval Europe that had an obligatory education, at least for men. They devoted a great deal of time to learning and reading. The texts of that education—the holy books, the books of law and their commentaries, as well as the texts of prayers, Kabbalah, Hassidism, poetry, moral tracts, community annals, and so on—were in Hebrew and Aramaic. The processing of that tradition throughout the ages and in all countries of the Diaspora involved not just passive reading and praying but active studying, arguing, interpreting, and writing. Books, commentaries, poems, legal Responsa, and epistolary texts were written throughout the ages in the Holy Tongue. But the Holy Tongue was mute, and because Talmudic learning involved understanding, dialectical analysis, and argument, it needed an oral vehicle for the interactions of teaching and dialogue. The language in which this literature was taught and argued in Europe was Yiddish. Yiddish was also the language of daily life, conversation, trade, family affairs, story telling, oral preaching, and a whole spectrum of genres of oral literature.

Thus Yiddish was merely part—albeit an indispensable part—of an inter-

1. Max Weinreich (1894–1969) was the founder and head of YIVO, the Jewish Scientific Institute in Vilna (1925) and New York. See his *History of the Yiddish Language* (in Yiddish), Vols. I–IV, New York; YIVO 1973 and the English abbreviated version *History of the Yiddish Language*, University of Chicago Press, 1980.

2. For a more detailed assessment of the Yiddish language, its historical contexts and semiotics of conversation, see my forthcoming book, *Aspects of Yiddish*, University of California Press.

connected cultural polysystem, and fulfilled only some of the functions of a "normal" language. It was the language of a society that brought to Europe a Hebrew tradition from the past, as well as a tradition of understanding and commenting on the Hebrew texts in another language (especially Aramaic, which itself became part of the textual tradition). In spite of its overt Germanic garb, Yiddish naturally absorbed a great deal of the phraseology, vocabulary, conceptual world, conversational modes, and intonations of the Hebrew and Aramaic texts. It was also constantly exposed to the languages of its immediate neighbors (e.g., Polish or Ukrainian) as well as to the languages of the dominant power or culture (e.g., Russian and German), and was influenced by them. Indeed, in its grammatical structure as in its semiotic world, Yiddish was a bridge between the traditional Jewish culture and the languages and cultures of Europe, their beliefs, folklore, proverbs, and images. This is why the living Yiddish language in America in the last hundred years could so easily absorb the stream of English words and expressions that flooded the language of conversation and newspapers (though this was bitterly contested by purist Yiddish educators and writers).

As with all other Jewish languages throughout history, Yiddish was separated from its source languages while using its own, separate alphabet. Hebrew letters had to be adapted for writing this basically Germanic language, much as European vernacular languages developed their independent spelling systems from the Latin alphabet. (There was one exception: words of Hebrew origin, though pronounced differently in Yiddish, preserved their classical Hebrew spelling, although in Introspectivist writings and in Soviet Yiddish, these too were assimilated to the dominant phonetic spelling.)

The bulk of Yiddish vocabulary and many of its grammatical features are of German origin (deriving from various, mostly southern dialects in their medieval stage). There are several thousands of Hebrew and Aramaic words and expressions, some of which entered other languages: *me'shuge, tohu-va'bohu, Shabes, ganev* (thief), *bale'bos* (boss), *riboyne-shel-'oylem* (God), and so on.[3] Many words are recognizably of Slavic origin: *borsht, kashe, nudnik, shmate, pod'loge* (floor), and others. Some words still exhibit their Latin derivation: *bentshn* (to pray, from "benedicere"), *leyenen* (to read, from "legere"), *kreplakh* (dumplings, cf. the French "crêpe"), *cholent* (dish kept warm for the Sabbath, cf. Old French "chalt," warm), and such names as *Bunem* ("bonhomme"), *Shneyer* ("senior"), *Beyle* ("bella" or "belle"), *Yentl* ("gentile"), and so forth.

A more interesting feature is the integration of elements from various sources, which occurred on all levels of the language, from phonology to beliefs. Thus the European *dokter* ("doctor") has a Hebrew plural: *dok'toyrim* (*o* is pronounced *oy* in Ashkenazi Hebrew); the German-source *tayvl* ("devil") has a Hebrew plural *tay'volim* (like the Hebrew-derived *moshl-me'sholim*, "parable"). The word *shli'mazl* ("shlemiel") combines the German "Shlimm" ("bad") with the Hebrew "mazal" ("luck"); and a real shlemiel is a *shlime'zalnik*, adding the Slavic suffix *-nik* to the other two source languages. *Ikh nudzhe zikh* ("I am bored") has a Slavic root

---

3. It is important to remember that the Hebrew component in Yiddish is pronounced differently from the contemporary Israeli Hebrew. In American usage there are many compromises between the two.

embedded in a Germanic verb form; *aroyf-ge-'tshepe-te* ("attached to, hooked on to") has a Slavic root (*tshepe*, "to touch") encased in three Germanic morphemes.

Of special interest is the plural suffix *-s*, a contamination of the Old French plural *-s* (preserved in Yiddish and English but not in German) with the Hebrew plural *ot* (pronounced *-es* in Yiddish). This is used with words of all sources: for example, *khale-khales* ("Chalah") and *me'gile-me'giles* ("scroll" or "long list, long-winded talk"), of Hebrew origin; *khate-khates* ("hut") and *shmate-shmates* ("rag"), from Slavic; or *bite-bites* ("request") and *turem-turems* ("tower"), from German.

Naturally, synonyms of various origins developed separate meanings. Thus *seyfer*, from Hebrew ("book"), means "religious book written in Hebrew or Aramaic," whereas *bukh* means "secular book, in Yiddish or other languages"; and *dos heylike ort* (literally: "the holy place") means "cemetery," but its Hebrew synonym *mokem koydesh* means "synagogue."

Many expressions and idioms overtly using words of German origin actually have a Hebrew subtext. For example, the collocation *Tse'zeyt un tse'shpreyt* ("sown to the wind," "scattered and dispersed") may be used for a person's family, his disorderly clothes, or his books published in various places, but the major allusion is to a central image of Jewish historical consciousness—namely, the dispersion of the Jews. The subtext is in the book of Esther (9:8): "There is a certain people scattered abroad and dispersed among the peoples in all the provinces of thy kingdom." The pair of Hebrew adjectives in the biblical source, when read in Ashkenazi pronunciation, is linked by alliteration of its stressed syllables (and pervasive sound parallelism): *meFUzer umeFUred* ("scattered and dispersed"). This has been transposed into words of the German stock with an end-rhyme, a form favored in Yiddish folklore: *tsezEYT un tseshprEYT*. In a statistical count, the phrase has only German components, but its subtext is Hebrew and its semantic substance is specifically Jewish.

Furthermore, this Yiddish idiom is often augmented to *tse'zeyt un tse'spreyt oyf ale shive yamim* ("scattered and dispersed on all the seven seas"), adding a "Jewish" tone by spicing the idiom with an emphatically Hebrew phrase, *shive yamim* ("seven seas"). In normal Yiddish, these Hebrew words are not used: the plural of *yam* ("sea") in Yiddish is *yamen*, and the proper phrase would be *oyf ale zibn yamen*. By using a phrase in real Hebrew rather than in the Hebrew that merged into Yiddish, the impression of an authoritative quotation is achieved. In reality, however, this Hebrew phrase does not exist in the Bible and is, paradoxically, coined from the European "seven seas." The semantics and vocabulary of the German and Hebrew components have thus been reversed.

A new layer joined the Yiddish fusion, especially in the nineteenth and twentieth centuries. This consisted of so-called Internationalisms—namely, words of French, Latin, or Greek etymology that were accepted in most modern languages and that entered Yiddish via Russian, Polish, German, or English to represent new areas of modern civilization, science, art, and politics. The Introspectivist manifesto of 1919, a most consciously Yiddishist literary document, does not shy away from declaring that:

> Yiddish is now rich enough, independent enough to afford to
> enrich its vocabulary from the treasures of her sister languages. That is

why we are not afraid to borrow words from the sister languages, words to cover newly developed concepts, broadened feelings and thoughts. Such words are also *our* words. We have the same rights to them as does any other language, any other poetry.

Thus A. Leyeles, fascinated by Ouspenky's "fourth dimension" and by Oriental mysticism, wrote a poem on "Symmetry" (translated in this anthology) as rest in mid-movement, the ecstasy of universal unity beyond time and space, division of man and woman, God and demon. The second stanza reads (in transcription):

Si'metriye—	Symmetry—
Gi'matriye fun mis'terye.	Anagram of mystery.
Mis'terye fun rytm	Mystery of rhythm
Oyf yener zayt zoym	On the other side of the seam
Fun tsayt un roym.	Of time and space.

The concepts and words for "symmetry," "mystery," and "rhythm" are modern Internationalisms; *gi'matriye*, however, though matching these terms in sound and meaning as well as in its Greek origin, is a Kabbalistic word. "Mystery," too, seems related to the Hebrew term for Kabbalah, *torat ha-nistar*, "knowledge of the concealed," and its Hebrew cognate, *mistorin*. "Time and space" reflect the interest in Kantian philosophy and Einsteinian physics among Jewish intellectuals, but *tsayt* is an old Yiddish word, whereas *roym* in this sense is Yiddishized from the German *Raum*.

In his sonnet "Evening," describing Madison Square at nightfall, Leyeles underlines the modernity of the impression with a profusion of Internationalisms. We transcribe the first and last stanzas, emphasizing the "modern" words (in upper case):

Shoybn blitsn, shoybn tsindn zikh in SKVER.
S'finklen likhter oyf FANTASTISH, POLIGONISH.
DRAYEKS, ROMBN, halb SETSESYE, halb HARMONISH,
Tantsn freylekh oyf in fentster—GROD un KVER.

. . . .
A DEBOSH in SKVER. ELEKTRISH-LEGENDARISH
Roysht er op a sho, ORGYASTISH un VIRVARISH—
Zelbst-farshikerte KHIMERE, UMREAL.

Windows flash, flare up above the square.
Lights sparkle—polygonal, anonymous.
Triangles, diamonds—part Secession, part harmonious—
Dance joyfully on windowpanes, straight and queer.

. . . .
Debauchery in the square. Electrically fantastic
Carousing for an hour, boisterous, orgiastic—
A chimera drunk on itself. Unreal ball.

Many words of the fourteen lines of the Yiddish sonnet are used in English as well: square, fantastic, polygonal, Secession, harmonious, sardonic, gold, laconic, sprinkled, virile, carnival, debauchery, electrical, legendary, orgiastic, chimera, unreal. Most of them could be adopted from English or from other languages. They are, however, domesticated with Yiddish sounds and suffixes and are part of modern Yiddish. *Wirrwarr* is a German noun for "chaos, confusion, noise," and is used in Yiddish too; but here it is made strange by transforming it into the adverb *virvarish* by means of the German-stock suffix *ish* (not used in German for this root), and by being aligned with other attributes of modern turmoil (elektrish, legendarish, poligonish). *DRAYEKS, ROMBN, GROD, KVER, geVINKLt* are new Yiddish terms of geometry ("triangles, diamond shapes, straight, diagonal, angle"), here used to evoke the paintings of Klimt, of the Viennese "Secession." And all this is naturally conjoined, by the unifying flow of the metrical rhythm and Yiddish grammar, with the simplest and most domestic Yiddish words: *shoybn, fentster, likhter, himl, tantsn, freylekh, vinkn, flekn, sher, roysht, sho, farshikert* ("windowpanes, windows, lights, sky, dance, joyful, wink, stains, scissors, noise, hour, drunk").

As a language of fusion, Yiddish is similar to English in many ways. But Yiddish speakers are highly "component-conscious"—that is, aware of the differences between the source languages, their extensions beyond the accepted domain of Yiddish proper, and their rich stylistic interplay within a Yiddish text. The expression *Di mayse fun der geshikhte iz aza min historye* ("the story of this tale has the following history") is a parodic exposure of this characteristic, using three synonyms for "story," derived from Hebrew, German, and French (via Slavic), respectively. Modern Yiddish poetry based a great deal of its stylistic force on the selection of words from its component languages, on their various emotive over-tones, and on the interplay among them.

The special role of Yiddish as a vehicle for conversation and oral communication in the very unusual Jewish society, with its stress on trade, international ties, and rapid contacts between strangers, contributed to its characteristic features. Also crucial were the use of Yiddish for teaching and Talmudic analysis and argument, and the lack of a tradition of systematic treatises, essays, or philosophical writings in that language. Hence Yiddish speech typically has a high proportion of conver-sational expressions and dialogue markers intended to draw the listener's attention and to convey the speaker's emotive attitudes to the words and topics of his discourse. Yiddish discourse is talkative, associative, unsystematic; uses a wealth of proverbs, generalizations, quotations, anecdotes, and exemplary stories; and pro-ceeds by asking questions and answering questions with questions, rising constantly from language to meta-language, raising alternatives to a situation or argument, and undermining the assumptions of an assumed opponent.

At first, modern Yiddish poetry did not know what to do with these properties of the language. On the contrary, it embraced metrical verse, well-measured and sound-orchestrated, as a vehicle for refined poetic feelings, an aesthetic antidote to the colloquial coarseness of "the cholent language,"[4] as the poet Frug dubbed it in the 1880s. It tried to imitate the monologue-oriented forms of European poetry, especially those of its Russian prototypes. At the beginning of the twentieth

---

4. *Cholent*—a delicious dish containing meat, potatoes, beans, and other ingredients and kept warm for 24 hours for the Sabbath (when Jews do not cook). In the antireligious sentiment it symbolized something stale, mushy, old-fashioned, and superstitious.

century, Yiddish developed a poetic language for metrical poetry; largely in the Impressionist vein, it reached accepted standards, but its achievements were not specific or spectacular.

Indeed, the renaissance of Jewish literature in Russia in the late 1880s and 1890s created great fiction in Yiddish, based on the properties of the conversational language and the composition of the rambling, associative prose of its characters. This is epitomized in the best work of its classical writers, Mendele Moykher Sforim and Sholem Aleichem, two literary pseudonyms meaning, characteristically, "Mendele the Bookseller" and "How-Do-You-Do?" But the dominant poetry was written in Hebrew (especially by Bialik and Chernikhovski). It was based on the Romantic identification of the poet as the prophet of a society and on the poetic use of biblical Hebrew in tension with the fictional situations of the poems, which were created in European thematic and generic modes.

Only after World War I did Yiddish poetry truly respond to the special characteristics of its own language. The various Expressionist and Modernist trends encouraged such an opening up of the poetic language to all possibilities and intonations of the spoken idiom, including dialects, slang, political and scientific rhetoric, and so on. Now fiction could be "lyrical" and lyrics "prosaic," and Yiddish poets did not refrain from marring the subtle poetic instrument with coarse, ironic, dialogic, and "Jewish" markers. Glatshteyn always understood this problem and felt uneasy with poetry that was too refined for "the wise prosaic smile of the clever tongue" (see appendix A, "Chronicle of a Movement," No. 27). A master of the dramatic monologue, he reached out, time and again, to mine these resources, even at the expense of losing his grip on the rhythms of verse. Glatshteyn embedded his most personal feelings in the primitive ramblings of his protagonist, a gregarious mystic, the Hassidic rebbe Rabbi Nakhman from Bratslav, who would spice his Yiddish with noticeably Slavic and Hebrew expressions.

Associative talking—a national sport in Yiddish—is a long, exuberant, and rambling affair. It is a joy as well. When Glatshteyn's Rabbi Nakhman from Bratslav turns up in heaven, losing all his words, he complains: "What will you do from now to eternity? / No tales, no melodies. / Poor soul, you are naked. / You are a mute in heaven." Eventually, he awakens from his dream, is back on earth, and draws the moral of the dream: "May I be damned if I'd like / To sit on a heavenly rock. / Here, in the sinful world— / To talk and talk and talk" (see "Hear and be Stunned" in this anthology).

The unusual mode of Yiddish *talk-verse* may be as fresh, effective, and surprising as the language of metaphorical imagery in Western poetry (though perhaps less familiar to its readers). Naturally, the reader has to imagine the character who does the talking, to reconstruct him from his speech. The talk and the inverse characterization of the talker create a double-directed semantic dependence, with an added ironic perspective of the narrator or the poet standing above the text. Readers who judge Yiddish poetry by the ways it attempts to achieve what English poetry does will miss the unique aspects of an ironic, allusive, evaluative, conversational, and talkative medium, even when reduced to the abbreviated codes of poetic selection.

Moyshe-Leyb Halpern raised this art to an almost parodic degree in his long, aggressive, politically charged monologue to himself (addressed to his year-and-a-half-old listener), "This I Said to My Only Son at Play—and to Nobody Else," the first part of which is reproduced in this anthology. He uses the technique of associative concatenation—a mainstay of classical Yiddish fiction—to present a kaleidoscope of his bitter personal vision, an existentialist-anarchist political slashing at life in general and American capitalism in particular, interspersed with coarse curses and surprising situational analogues.

Toward the end of this poem, in a long, wildly associative tirade, the speaker, Moyshe-Leyb, warns his son against war, shifting from invective against the powers of this world and false messiahs to the child's play and back again. Instead of epithets or metaphors, *analogue situations* are flashed at the reader, comparing the high and the low, the drastic and the sentimental. Especially effective are the similes bringing something enormous down to a domestic detail. Thus everything prepares for war:

> Forests supply whips and gallows-wood
> And flagpoles for a warship that lies at foreign shores
> Like an inkstain on a loveletter.

What a peaceful simile for gunboat diplomacy! And suddenly the figure of Christ appears, hovering, bound to poles, with nails in his hands and "not even a bottle-stopper on his pierced body." His blood is not mentioned, but is reflected in the red sky:

> And not merely the cloud above
> In the gleam of a city fire—
> The bedbug on our bodies, too, is red in the light—
> Like the sun at dawn, like measle-sunset on baby-skin!

The miseries of daily life of the poverty-stricken Moyshe-Leyb seem to be as devastating—and as familiar—as the grand images of history and class warfare.

The concatenation is endless, leading from one thing to its opposite by analogy or associative whim, and then to a continuation of the new situation until a new link is sprung on us. Of course, all the links compose one ideological universe, one antiwar pathos and existential anguish, but the poem has scarcely any structural backbone or hard-edge subdivisions. Hence, all examples must cut something out of its context. Eventually, on the last page, the son is warned against the president's call for war. We excerpt just a few links from the complex chain following it:

> And if the President—who is everyone's father, only God knows how—
> Should call, let him go first, to see
> That sky-plum and hungry-face are blue
> In the enemy's country, too!

In typically Yiddish fashion (as in Sholem Aleichem's *Tevye the Milkman*), instead of a description of reality, we have a dialogue embedded in a dialogue: the son is instructed what to say to the president in a hypothetical situation. There is also a typically Yiddish aside, commenting on the word "president" and rising to meta-language that expresses the speaker's attitude and exposes the meaning of "father." (Note also the indirect metaphor in the uneasy analogy of "hungry-face" with the telescoped metaphor of "sky-plum.") Halpern continues:

And he can hire himself out to a shoemaker.
Ruling is not a craft. It is old-fashioned, like a squeak in new shoes.

This is again an associative shift from the low but practical profession of shoemaking, suggested as a better alternative to the presidency, to the phony fashion of squeaking shoes. From here we shift to other old-fashioned garb; the obsolete crowns, which merely keep the sun from bringing light into our heads; the "top hat," that symbol of the bourgeois in Georg Grosz's paintings; and then to the following chain:

Yet a top hat will not let through one drop of air—
Thus says medicine,
Which protects even a fly so the spider won't get sick,
Because we need spiderweb for science, as Caesar's patriot
Needed pork on Jehovah's altar.

Simplified, the chain goes like this: president——→ crown ——→top hat——→ theories of fresh air——→the use of medicine to protect the spiders ——→ capitalist science ——→ Roman desecration of the conquered Temple in Jerusalem ——→anti-Semitism as a weapon for diverting popular protest:

And blood spilt in vain can be diverted to the Hebrews.
All he has to do is wash his hands like Pilate
And at your table eat (if it's the Sabbath) *gefilte fish*,
Which is sweet like guests as long as they are fresh.

The symbolic "washing his hands" of blood spilt in vain has become transformed into the innocent Jewish ritual of washing the hands before eating, which leads to the Jewish dish that the Goyim are supposed to love, "gefilte fish." From here—with no thematic justification, out of sheer whim or malice—Halpern inverts the proverb, "a guest is welcome like fresh fish, after three days he stinks."

Thus we have gone from the president's call for war to his eating fish. But this may be dangerous: he may choke on a bone; and this again, in a usual inversion, leads to a positive event: Moyshe-Leyb's son's friend, the little Negro, will rejoice at the president's death. But the little Negro—like Moyshe-Leyb's son, for whom war is mere play with bottles on the stairs—does not understand a thing; suddenly, from happily rambling on, Halpern again transforms the little Negro's dance with an unexpected stab to the reader:

But he [the president] must watch out not to choke on a bone,
This may bring so much joy—that your friend, the little Negro,
Will go dancing. That's how he rejoiced
When they burned his father alive—
Two years ago, as he walked by a bakery, the smell of bread
Struck his nose—and he said "Good-Morning" to a white broad.

This is a simple, direct description, not anticipated by anything beforehand, that leaves us breathless at the end of the poem.

18
*American
Yiddish
Poetry
and its
Background*

THE HISTORICAL CONTEXT

The oldest dated text in Yiddish is a rhymed couplet written inside the ornamented initial letters of a Hebrew word in the Worms *Mahzor* (prayerbook) of 1272. The oldest large Yiddish text, the so-called Cambridge manuscript, was found in Cairo, Egypt (in the famous Genizah). Dated 1382, it contains poems on Jewish historical topics (Abraham, Joseph, the death of Aaron), religious texts, and an unknown and earliest version of a German epic, *Dukus Horant*.

Many medieval Yiddish texts have been lost, but the variety of manuscripts and books extant from that period nevertheless shows the span of its writings: adapted German epics; epic poems on biblical topics written in medieval German meters; lyrical and historical poems in German and Hebrew verse forms; stories; plays; moral guidebooks, legal protocols, and private letters. From the first half of the sixteenth century on, Yiddish books were printed in Germany, Italy, Holland, Switzerland, and Poland and were distributed in the entire Yiddish realm. Two famous books of the sixteenth century may represent the scope of Yiddish: at one extreme, Elia Levita's (Eliyahu Bakhur, Nürenberg 1469–Venice 1549) epic poem *Bove Bukh*, a Yiddish version in ottava rima of the European romance *Buovo d'Antona* (Beve of Hampton), written in Padua in 1507; and at the other *Tsene verene*, a retelling of the Bible for women, which became so popular that it saw over two hundred editions.[5]

By the sixteenth century, the center of European Jewry had shifted to Poland, which was then one of the largest countries in Europe, comprising Poland (with Galicia, Pomerania, and Silesia), the Grand Duchy of Lithuania (including today's Byelorussia), and the Ukraine, and stretching from the Baltic to the Black Sea. In medieval Poland, Jews played an important role in developing cities and settling the eastern areas, mediating between the ruling Polish aristocracy on the one hand and the peasants of various nationalities in this vast "breadbasket of Europe" on the other. In sixteenth- and seventeenth-century Poland, there was a Jewish autonomous state within a state, "The Assembly of Four Lands." A strong network of education and learning developed. Here, the Hassidic movement emerged in the eighteenth century and modern political movements, from Socialism to Zionism, arose at the end of the nineteenth. This became the base of the Jewish, Yiddish-speaking masses.

Toward the end of the eighteenth century, the great Kingdom of Poland and Lithuania was devoured by its neighbors, Prussia (later: Germany), Austria, and Russia. The Jewish population was included in these states, most of it falling within the Russian Empire. Before the Revolution, however, most Jews under Russian rule did not live in Russia proper but were confined to the formerly Polish-ruled territories, the "Pale of Settlement," a vast geographical ghetto that included the

---

5. On the history of old Yiddish literature, see Khone Shmeruk, *Yiddish Literature: Aspects of its History* [in Hebrew], Porter Institute, Tel Aviv, 1978. On Elia Levita's form, see Benjamin Hrushovski, "The Creation of Accentual Iambs in European Poetry and their First Employment in a Yiddish Romance in Italy (1508–09)," in *For Max Weinreich on His Seventieth Birthday*, Lucy Dawidowicz et al., eds., Mouton, 1964, pp. 108–146. (See Turning Points, Jerusalem; 1986.)

Ukraine, Byelorussia, and Lithuania, as well as the heart of Poland proper. The Jews of Galicia found themselves separated from their cousins and living in the Austro-Hungarian Empire.

In neither empire did the masses of Jews live among speakers of the state language but rather in the midst of various minorities: Poles, Ukrainians, Byelorussians, Lithuanians, Latvians, Germans, Rumanians, Hungarians. This fact enhanced the preservation of Yiddish in the densely populated Jewish towns. In 1897, 97.96 percent of all Jews inhabiting the Russian Empire claimed Yiddish as their mother tongue. At the same time, the process of assimilation was well under way, especially in Western Europe and in the big cities of Russia, where a few rich or educated Jews were permitted to live.

The Jewish population in Eastern Europe grew immensely, in numbers and in poverty, throughout the nineteenth century. Millions emigrated overseas. In 1800 there were 2.2 million Jews, 1 million in Eastern Europe; by the eve of World War II these numbers had grown to 15 million Ashkenazi (and 1.5 million Sephardic and Oriental) Jews in the world.

Yiddish had a considerable body of folklore and a large written literature, which flourished in the sixteenth century and again since the nineteenth century, especially in the years 1862–1970. Its revival was part of the modern Jewish renaissance, which became a tidal wave after the pogroms in Russia in 1881–82, and which transformed the existence of the Jews and their descendants. This renaissance included mass migration overseas and to the West, as well as migration from small towns to big cities; assimilation and integration of many Jews into Western culture, economy, literature, and science; the emergence of political parties, from Socialists to Zionists; and the emergence of a modern literature in Hebrew and in Yiddish.

Toward the end of the nineteenth century, several "classical writers"—the "Grandfather" of Yiddish literature, Mendele Moykher Sforim, Sholem Aleichem, and I. L. Peretz—lent prestige to a flourishing literary institution. In a short period, dozens of important writers created a literature with European standards, moving swiftly from the rationalist Enlightenment through carnivalesque parody to Realism, Naturalism, and psychological Impressionism, and then breaking out into the general literary trends of Expressionism and Modernism.

This was possible because of the secularization of the Jewish masses, the trend of abandoning traditional Hebrew religious education, and the strong wish to join the general world of modern culture and politics in the Yiddish language that they knew. The growing political parties, especially the Socialists, supported Yiddish culture and education, seeing it at first as a tool for propaganda and a way to break out of the traditional religious framework and, later on, as a goal in itself. Hundreds of periodicals and newspapers appeared in Yiddish (the earliest was the newspaper *Kurantn*, published in Amsterdam in 1686). Libraries sprang up in hundreds of towns. A modern secular school system developed all over Eastern Europe (and to some extent in both Americas). Massive translation efforts brought to the Yiddish reader the works of Tolstoy, Kropotkin, Zola, Ibsen, Jules Verne, Rabindranat Tagore, Lion Feuchtwanger, Shakespeare, Yessenin, Ezra Pound, and many others.

It was, however, a tragic destiny. As Harvard Professor Leo Wiener put it in 1899, "there is probably no other language . . . on which so much opprobrium has been heaped."[6] Traditionally, Yiddish was considered the "Servant Maid" to the "Lady" Hebrew. With the onset of the Enlightenment among German Jews, Yiddish became the ugly symbol of everything that kept the Jews from entering civilized Western society. Indeed, from the point of view of a "pure" literary German language based in Berlin, Yiddish looked like a contortion, a corrupted medley with no aesthetic values. Moses Mendelssohn wrote that "this jargon contributed no little to the immorality of the common Jews," and demanded "pure German or pure Hebrew, but no hodge-podge." It was not merely a matter of language: Yiddish became the externalized object of Jewish self-hatred. Pressured by a Gentile society, Jews internalized many anti-Semitic stereotypes, blaming "Jewish" professions, character traits, mentality, and behavior for their lot among Christian nations. Moving out of the Jewish towns in areas of minority nationalities into centers of the state languages like Warsaw, Vienna, Berlin, Moscow, London, Paris, Tel Aviv, or New York, masses of Jews eagerly embraced the dominant language and culture. The movement of the young, bright, and successful away from Yiddish again left the language mostly to lower-class readers of limited culture and thus reinforced the vicious circle.

To be sure, there was a vigorous Yiddishist movement counteracting both assimilation and self-abasement. Baptized in the famous "Czernowitz Conference" of 1908, it freed Yiddish from the demeaning label, "Jargon" and pronounced it "a Jewish national language." Yiddishism, too, was part of the trend that was profoundly critical of the old ways of Jewish Diaspora existence (though it usually heaped the blame on religion rather than on language). A network of schools, publishing houses, libraries, and scientific institutions was built, especially in post-World War I Poland and the Soviet Union. Textbooks were written, terminologies developed, elitist theater and poetry cherished, and so on.

In retrospect, however, it is clear that, in a long-range perspective of Jewish history, Yiddish culture was merely a bridge between traditional religious Jewish society and assimilation into Western cultures. Yiddish literature as an institution existed perhaps for seven centuries. But for each writer, it was a matter of only one (or, in rare cases, of two) generations. Most modern Yiddish writers had grown up with some Hebrew religious education, whereas their children were already steeped in the culture of another language.

The base of Yiddish culture in Eastern Europe, with its historical foundation, institutional network, and millions of native speakers, was destroyed by Hitler and Stalin. A third of the Jewish people perished in the Holocaust, but the destruction of Yiddish was total. Stalin killed Yiddish writers; Hitler killed Yiddish writers and their readers alike.

We must admit, however, that the trend toward assimilation was overpowering everywhere: in Soviet Russia after the Revolution, in Poland, France, England, Argentina, and the United States. The attempt to create a modern, cosmopolitan, autonomous culture in a separate Jewish language with no state of its own was doomed to failure.

6. *History of Yiddish Literature in the Nineteenth Century*, New York, 1899. See Joshua A. Fishman's survey, "The Sociology of Yiddish," in his anthology, *Never Say Die!: A Thousand Years of Yiddish in Jewish Life and Letters*, Mouton, 1981.

THE MODERN LITERARY RENAISSANCE

21
*American
Yiddish
Poetry
and its
Background*

In spite of its age-old tradition, the history of Yiddish literature was not a living presence that engendered its modern stage. Rather, from the position of a new culture, created in the spoken language and modeled upon European literature of the modern age, scholars and writers set out to recover and reconstruct the past of their language and literature. Only Yiddish folklore was felt as a living tradition, eagerly collected and imitated. Hence, when new generations of writers entered Yiddish literature, they felt the frustration and elation of having to create and enrich both their literature and their language, as if they were just beginning. It was not merely a Modernist stance when the Introspectivists stated: "We have no tradition. We have found very little that could serve as tradition for us. The tradition begins perhaps with us, strange as it may sound" (*In Zikh*, March 1923; see appendix A, "Chronicle of a Movement," No. 14).

By the time Yiddish assumed center stage in Jewish culture and society, at the beginning of the twentieth century, the potential sources of influence on the creation of a new poetics in this literature were coming from several directions. The modern Jewish intellectual confronted several languages and cultures—Hebrew, Russian, German and, later, English—all of which were thrown into great turmoil and ferment precisely at this juncture. He toured an imaginary museum of periods and styles which was opened to the eager outsider who came to observe the history of those literatures from a panoramic vista. As I have pointed out elsewhere,[7]

> for reasons of cultural history, Yiddish literature had not shared the development of its neighbors for hundreds of years; consequently, when the East European Jewish intelligentsia, in one grand leap, landed in the general twentieth century, Yiddish poetry undertook not only to catch up with Europe's deepened appreciation of the classics and the modernistic trends of recent generations, but also to take an active part in the discussion of the most timely cultural problems and in the artistic movements of the environment.

We must remember the unusual condition of the Yiddish poet. Almost no poet learned Yiddish literature in school (most Yiddish schools were founded in Europe after World War I—after the major writers and poets appeared, using their authority for validation). Naturally, they imbibed a vivid Yiddish language spoken in their homes and environment, but only in rare cases did they acquire knowledge of Yiddish literature from their parents. Most Yiddish poets had a basic Hebrew religious education; some continued in general schools in other languages; and all made up their own, private university by reading books in a number of languages, including the rapidly developing Yiddish library. Many Yiddish poets even began by writing poetry in other languages (Leyvik, in Hebrew; M. L. Halpern, in

---

7. "On Free Rhythms in Modern Yiddish Poetry," in Weinreich, Uriel, ed., *The Field of Yiddish*, New York, 1954, pp. 219–266. Revised version in *Turning Points: Studies in Versification.* Jerusalem: Israel Science Publishers, 1986.

German; Leyeles, in Russian; Malka Heifetz-Tussman, in English) before creating in the intimate language that was warmly referred to as *"mame-loshn."*[8]

The polylingual intersection, coupled with the international scope of Yiddish literature and the migrations of its writers, was extremely fruitful for Yiddish poetry; at the same time, it also contributed to the great shifts and zigzags in its history. A poet could switch from writing Russian poetry to Yiddish (S. Frug, in the 1880s) or from Hebrew to Yiddish and vice versa (Bialik, most Hebrew poets of the beginning of the twentieth century, Uri Zvi Grinberg, Aron Zeitlin). In each of those literatures, there were different poetic norms at any given time. Furthermore, Yiddish poetry in any given generation was different in America, in Europe, and in the Soviet Union (somewhat like the differences between American and British poetry). Since the poets tended to continue their personal style, migrating or shifting from one of those countries, languages, or orientations to another often led to at least a partial transfer of norms, and hence to changes in the receiving literature.

For example, S. Frug (1860–1916), who "made it" as a Russian poet in Petersburg in the 1880s, writing sad lyrical poetry and sentimental verse on Jewish themes, accepted Russian meters as a matter of course and brought them along, unwittingly, when he began writing Yiddish verse, thus causing a revolutionary change in the history of Yiddish and Hebrew versification. Similarly, Moyshe-Leyb Halpern brought German poetic rhetoric from Hoffmansthal's Vienna to the Russian-oriented verse of the Yiddish "Young Generation" in New York of 1910.

It is important to realize that when a Yiddish poet wrote poetry, that poetry was not part of a normal nation-state with a stratified society. The Yiddish poet did not have Yiddish schools, universities, philosophers, sociologists, research institutes, police stations, bus drivers and such all around him. Literature was "everything." It was a substitute for religion and for statehood, it was a state in itself, "Yiddishland"; to abandon it was to abandon the whole culture. Hence the enormous importance of literature in the eyes of its adherents (reinforced by the Romantic view of the poet as prophet of a society, acquired from German philosophy via Russian literature), and the desperation of its isolation. To be sure, literature fulfilled that role in conjunction with the Yiddish press and some social organizations linked to the same cluster. But the close relations of Yiddish writers with the popular press, on which their existence depended, were love-hate relations; succumbing altogether would have meant giving up the "elitist" dream of a separate culture.

* * *

In its lifetime, Yiddish literature hovered between the illusion of art and the awareness of its precarious existence. Indeed, its best work may serve as a classical parable for the central dilemmas of modern literature. Yiddish writing reflected all the modern tensions of a self-ironic society in the process of losing a traditional value system; the throes of urban alienation gripping the scattered descendants of a close-knit feudal community; the tensions between the demands of Modernist art

8. *Mame-loshn*—"mama-language," a typically emotive Yiddish-Hebrew compound, is diametrically opposed to the sociological term, the cold, Germanizing *muter-shprakh*, "mother-tongue."

on the one hand and the repeated search for new forms of mimesis and expression on the other; and the critical problem of language renewal in a text-burdened culture. All this was magnified by the traumas of Jewish history, from which the poets tried to escape through the forms and myth of modern poetry, and into which they were pulled back by the intimate ropes of their Jewish language.

THE OPTIMIST IMPULSE

After World War I, a true mass movement of Yiddish readers and writers carried the day. Great centers of Yiddish literature emerged on the new map in Poland, the Soviet Union, the United States, with minor centers in Rumania, Argentina, Israel, France, England, Canada, South Africa, and elsewhere. Yiddish newspapers, schools, libraries, unions, and theaters spread everywhere. With the participation of artists such as Marc Chagall and El Lissitzky, Modernist Yiddish journals were published in Warsaw, Berlin, Paris, Moscow, New York, and other cities.

Indeed, the early twenties were the best years of Yiddish poetry. Yiddish never really had a tradition of a high-style language or a Latin-oriented poetry. The Yiddish language was colloquial, "juicy," expressive, and powerful. With Expressionism in Germany and Futurism and Revolutionary poetry in Russia, the new trends were amenable to absorption of the spoken language in verse—including ironies, puns, harsh sounds, wild associations, and conversational gestures—as well as to opening the doors of poetry to dialect, slang, Hebrew allusions, and the international vocabulary of urban civilization. Yiddish poetry came of age and became part of the international movement. It learned the lessons of Yiddish fiction, worked on the unique aspects of its language, and faced the imaginary world of Jewish historical existence head-on.

Yiddish literature enjoyed an atmosphere of confidence in the value of its work and in the talents engaged in it. Here was an age-old culture, the oldest continuous culture (except for the Chinese, perhaps), wise, with high moral values, permeated with a sense of its historicity and—as some saw it—burying its energies in ancient learning of irrelevant issues under the aegis of a rigid religious code of behavior written in a language incomprehensible to the masses. Yiddish would speak directly to the people in their own rich and living language; express their experiences in the present as full-fledged, free human beings; communicate to them the events, works, and ideas of the great modern world; and evoke their vitality and folk wisdom, the only guarantors of a rejuvenation from within.

In a Yiddish literary journal, *Shtrom* (Stream or Torrent), published in Moscow in 1922, a Soviet commissar of art, writing on the question of whether Jews, who had never created graphic art, could achieve it now, concluded:

I myself know very well what this little nation can achieve.
Unfortunately, I am too shy to utter the words. It's really something, what this little nation has done!

When it wanted—it showed Christ and Christianity.
When it wanted—it gave Marx and Socialism.
Can you imagine that it will not show the world some art?
It will!
Kill me if not.

The conversational tone of this essay is typical, sentimental, ironic Yiddish speech. The bravado is revolutionary style. The author was Marc Chagall. Such optimism about the possibilities of the new creative impulse among Jews was widespread and gave Yiddish literature, along with other manifestations of this sweeping trend, its boom years of the early twenties (some gloomy thematics that often appeared in it notwithstanding).

The exuberant atmosphere, hard realities, and world-embracing ambitions among young Yiddish poets in New York are nostalgically recounted in Leyeles's long poem, *A Dream Under Skyscrapers* (1947), the stock-taking of a generation, written in virtuoso-rhymed Byronian octaves that cannot possibly be translated without losing the effect of their metrical patterns and the play with Yiddish sound-and-language fusion. We quote here four separate stanzas for the sake of the theme, in transcription and with English prose paraphrases (the meter is alternating 6 and 7 trochees, as indicated in the first line):

In di hoykhe un ge'kestlte ge'baydes
Fun der vunderbarer, tumldiker shtot New-'York
Zitst ge'engt a yungvarg, i mit zorg, i on shum zorg,
Un di volknkratsers zenen vakhe eydes,
Vi mit der ye'rushe fun di tates, zeydes
Vert ge'shtelt a nayer binyen—do, in'mitn torg.
S'iz a verter-binyen, s'boyen yunge boyer,
Un zey leygn tsigl mit a freyd un troyer.

. . . .

S'voltn di kha'loymes fun dem dor ge'stayet
Oyftsuboyen Pisem, Ramses un a zayl fun gold.
Runda'rum hot raykhkeyt zikh ge'koylert un ge'rolt.
Nor dos umruyike yungvarg hot far'tayet
Oysgeshmidt a nayem ol, a naye frayhayt,
Un ge'shribn, un fun himl s'telerl gevolt,
Un ge'mostn zikh mit ale hekhste likhter,
Un a tsekh ge'shtelt fun shtoltse, naye dikhter.

. . . .

Bay di taykhn fun New-'York bin ikh ge'zesn
Un der nayer, frayer, breyter luft mayn troym far'troyt.
Kh'hob a kholem raykh far'kholemt, kh'hob a troym ge'boyt
Unter shvere volknkratsers durkh mes'lesn,
Unter shteyn—nisht palmes, lipes tsi tsi'presn.
Nisht tsu visn oft dem khilek tsvishn morgn-royt

Un dem ovnt-gold, hob ikh ge'hit di likhter
Fun a yid an akshn, fun a yidish-dikhter.

. . . .

Un bay undz? Es hot a nayer stil un zhaner
Oykh a bloz ge'ton oyf undzer gas, oyf undzer veg.
Nisht um'zist geshvumen tsu dem nayem vaytn breg.
Nisht um'zist ge'leyent s'lid ameri'kaner,
Un gezapt in zikh dem nusakh dem Whit'maner
Durkh di umruyike nekht nokh shvere arbets-teg.
S'land a'merike iz heym ge'ven, nisht gast-hoyz,
Lib geven dos land on yikhes un on kastes.

[literal translation:]

In the soaring checkered buildings
Of the magnificent, tumultuous metropolis New-York,
Young people sit cramped-in, careworn, careless,
And the skyscrapers are alert witnesses
To a new edifice being erected—here, in the marketplace.
With the heritage of fathers and grandfathers,
A tower-of-words is built; the builders are young,
They lay the bricks in joy and in sorrow.

. . . .

The dreams of that generation were enough
To erect Pithom, Ramses and a Pillar of gold.
All around, wealth has unfurled and unrolled.
But the restless youth have secretly
Forged a new burden, a new freedom.
And created, and wanted pie in the sky,
And measured themselves with the brightest lights,
And founded a guild of proud, new poets.

. . . .

By the rivers of New York I sat down
And confined my dream to the new, free, wide-open air.
I dreamt a rich dream, I built a vision
Through days and nights, under heavy skyscrapers,
Under stone—not palms, poplars or cypresses.
Often, unaware of the change from evening-gold
To morning-red, I watched over the lights
Of a stubborn Jew, a Yiddish poet.

. . . .

And in our own domain? A new style and genre
Blew in our street too, on our road.

Not in vain did we swim to the new, distant shore,
Not in vain have we read the American poem
And inhaled, absorbed the Whitman tone
Through restless nights after hard workdays.
The land America was home, not a guest-house,
We loved the land with no pedigree, no castes.

Yiddish Poetry in America

THE SOCIAL SETTING

A little book of Yiddish poems appeared in the United States in 1877, and the first journals were published in the 1870s, but the real life of Yiddish literature in America began in the 1880s. It was part of the massive immigration of Yiddish-speaking Jews from Eastern Europe and of the institutional network that the immigrants built in New York and other American cities, so admirably described in Irving Howe's *The World of Our Fathers*.

Yiddish writers in America often felt that they were refugees from a great literature; that the Jews in America were too pulverized, too busy making a living or assimilating for a vital literary audience to be established; and that the real, deeply rooted base of Yiddish was in the Jewish masses of Eastern Europe. Actually, a new, quite different literature developed in Yiddish in the United States, independent of its counterpart in Europe. In Dubnovian terms, the historical center of Jewish life and culture wandered from Poland and Russia to the United States, where it remolded the old forms—among them, Yiddish literature—and at the same time developed new forms, more organic to the environment and institutionalized in the English language or integrated in the general American framework. Simultaneously, a second center grew in Eretz Israel, with Hebrew as its communicational vehicle, to form what is now a bipolar, Hebrew-English, new historical axis of Jewish existence.

Yiddish literature in America was based to a large extent in the daily and periodical press, which included literally hundreds of publications unhampered by the censorship that plagued Yiddish publications in Russia. The first daily newspaper appeared in July 1881.[9] In certain periods, the combined circulation of Yiddish dailies was very high (about 700,000 in 1916). Many of the young and the intelligent

---

9. In Russia, a Yiddish newspaper was founded in Petersburg in October 1881, but it was a weekly. The earlier weekly, *Kol mevaser*, which practically launched modern Yiddish literature, appeared between 1862 and 1873.

Raphael Soyer: *In a Jewish Cafe*, 1925.

kept leaving the Yiddish-speaking enclave and thus drained its intellectual resources. But for almost a century, the culture was able to sustain itself.

The Yiddish press felt that promoting culture and knowledge was one of its chief responsibilities. It became a major vehicle of Yiddish literature and cricitism, published the works of the best authors, and eventually gave many writers who were willing to practice journalism a livelihood and a forum in which to express their opinions on culture, politics, society, Jewish history, and world events. At first, "selling oneself" to a newspaper was considered degrading for a real artist, and some "held out" longer than others. "If there is a profession in the world which rubs off words like coins changing hands, it is the anonymous journalism which provides bread and butter for Glatshteyn's table," wrote his friend and fellow poet A. Leyeles, who himself earned his daily bread as a journalist and editor in the daily *Der Tog* (*In Zikh*, July 1934). But journalism also fulfilled a real need of the Yiddish writer, who was constantly reminded of the problematic aspects of existence and of the intentional choices that had to be made in any effort against the current in this turbulent and politicized century. "Every genuine poet," Glatshteyn wrote on another occasion, "should have a lot of opportunity to write journalism so that he can write it out of his system, steam it out of himself, so that when he comes to write a spoken poem, he is already shouted out" (*Sum and Substance*, p. 131).

Thus the "anarchist" paper, *Di Fraye Arbeter Shtime* (The Free Workers' Voice), edited from 1899 by S. Yanofsky, published some of the best Yiddish writers, promoted new talent, and published essays on theoretical issues. The *Daily Forward*, founded in 1897, though ostensibly socialist and actually rather sensational and popular, did a lot to support major writers or bring them over from Europe. All papers published poems as well as literary criticism. In addition, there were countless monthlies, cultural journals, little reviews, and periodical collections devoted to literature, to social and political matters, or specifically to poetry. There were many Yiddish publishers, and hundreds of books appeared. In this abnormally unbalanced culture, where the language could not serve any broader political purposes and where the system of daily life and the bureaucratic and educational networks were increasingly conducted in English, literature was the heart of the culture. Poets, however, kept complaining, remembering the idealized mission of the poet as a prophet of a society in post-Romantic Russian and Hebrew literature, and forgetting that it was not easy to publish Modernist poetry in English, either.

Yiddish culture in America was active for over a century. It sustained the continuous life of several newspapers, publishing houses, schools, and institutions, but there was little continuity of human resources and a mere vestigial internal development of new generations. The continuity of this culture was, rather, supported by wave after wave of new immigrants. Most Yiddish writers in America, no matter when they crossed the ocean, came from religious homes in Eastern Europe. They left their parents behind, in the "Old Home"; at the same time, they left the old world of Jewish existence in Eastern Europe and its overpowering traditional religious framework. Theirs was a radical revolt—part of a youth trend in the old country—against those two ancient and conventional social frames. It was accompanied by the emotionally upsetting move of leaving one's parents' home, often at an early age. The sculptor Chaim Gross and the poet Moyshe-Leyb Halpern left their parents at the age of twelve and went into the big world (Vienna and Budapest) to make it on their own even before they moved to America. Many of their readers had shared this experience. When they came to America and rebuilt their lives and personalities with the strong motivation of becoming "American," some of them joined the already existing institutions of secular Yiddish culture.

Thus most Yiddish American poets came to the United States as young men in their late teens or early twenties. They had not yet formed their poetic personalities, not yet integrated into the Yiddish literature of their old homes, and hence were able to feel the exhilaration of creating a new literature in a new country—and their own lives with it. They were both old enough to have imbibed the atmosphere of a full-bodied Yiddish language and culture, and too old to embrace English as a creative language. Jacob Glatshteyn arrived in New York at the age of eighteen. A. Leyeles came at the age of twenty, but had left his parents' home in Lodz for London when he was sixteen. Halpern arrived when he was twenty-two and had already published some poems in German in Vienna; he had left his parents' home in Galicia at the age of twelve. Leyvik came from Siberia at age twenty-five, but had been arrested and taken from home as a young revolutionary at eighteen.

An analysis of the ages of immigration of all the poets included in the two comprehensive anthologies of American Yiddish poetry published in Yiddish shows that these examples are representative. Of the thirty-one poets included in

M. Basin's immense anthology, *Amerikaner Yidishe Poezye* (American Yiddish Poetry, 1940), about two-thirds were 18–23 years old when they reached America. The average age was 20.5. (However, some stopped over for several years in London or elsewhere, i.e., left their homes at an earlier age.) M. Shtarkman's anthology, *Hemshekh* (Continuation, 1946), included fifty poets, with a larger proportion of the younger generation. Here, the average age of immigration was sixteen years. Two-thirds of the poets came at ages 14–19.[10]

The younger immigrants grew up in the early 1920s, in an atmosphere of great hopes for Yiddish literature around the world, when joining it was still interesting and possible. A telling example is J. L. Teller, who came to America at the age of eight, was an *iluy* ("genius") in Hebrew and Talmudic studies, and had an excellent English education (culminating in a Ph. D. in psychology from Columbia University). As a young man, he was obviously influenced by contemporary American poetry, notably by "Objectivist" verse; he also wrote books of history and journalism in English, but in poetry opted neither for English nor Hebrew but for his mother's tongue, Yiddish—still an option in 1930. His friend Gabriel Preil, who began as a Yiddish Introspectivist poet, did shift to Hebrew and became one of the most interesting Hebrew poets in New York.

In contrast, few immigrants of an older age joined the ranks of the Yiddish poets. This was a new poetry of a new country, although written in Yiddish; to be able to understand the situation and contribute to it, you had to build a new life here. Furthermore, those young writers who established themselves in the still-vital Yiddish literature of Europe became part of the literary establishment there. Only a few recognized poets reached American shores as refugees: Kadya Molodovsky in 1935, Aron Zeitlin in 1940, Chaim Grade and others after the Holocaust.

A comparative analysis of the biographies of American graphic artists of Jewish origin, who came from the same Eastern-European background, shows that most of them arrived at a somewhat earlier age: Ben Shahn was eight years old; Max Weber, ten; Louis Lozowick, fourteen; Raphael Soyer, thirteen; Mark Rothko, ten. They were young enough to enter American culture proper, receive an American education, and create art, but were not rooted enough in the language to be able to write poetry. The few immigrants who did write in English, like Anzia Yezierska, Abraham Cahan, or Judd L. Teller, did so in prose rather than poetry. Their writing still reflected a Yiddish-speaking society. It took another generation for creative Jews like Saul Bellow or Philip Roth—the children of immigrants—to have an impact on English literature.

Thus Yiddish poetry in America was created mostly by young immigrants. It was, nevertheless, a truly American literature, as an internal analysis of the poetry demonstrates. Leyeles's *Rondeaux* or *Fabius Lind*, Glatshteyn's *Free Verse* or *Credos*, J. L. Teller's *Miniatures*, Berysh Vaynshteyn's *Broken Pieces*, or M.-L. Halpern's two posthumous volumes of *Poems* published in 1934 are as American as anything written in English in that period. It was in America that the poets sensed freedom of thought and ideas, that their conscious perceptions of literature were formed and their poetic language crystalized. America was the real and imaginary space from

10. Three others were born in America, four came as children, and only six came to the US at ages older than twenty.

" 'Kibetzarnie' Literary Cafe.' " Cartoon by Joseph Foshko. Standing, in center: Sholem Ash, to his right: Joseph Opatoshu, Moyshe-Leyb Halpern.

which the material of their poetry was drawn; where they made their acute observations with the fresh eyes of involved participants; and where the overwhelming power of the melting-pot metropolis found them unprotected and sent them off to political protest or to "escapist," individualistic lyrical fictions. Even their recollections of the "Old Home"—negative and derisive at first, and nostalgic later—were made from an irreversible position on American ground. Calling M.-L. Halpern, the author of *In New York*, a poet from Galicia makes no more sense than calling T. S. Eliot a "poet of Missouri" or Ben-Gurion a "Polish politician." But while their peers the graphic artists became part of the accepted history of American art, and their contemporaries writing in English (like Charles Reznikoff) are part of American poetry, the Yiddish poets—who could certainly match them in form and theme—were quarantined within their alien language.

32
*American
Yiddish
Poetry
and its
Background*

THE MAJOR TRENDS

The trends of Yiddish poetry created in America were never extensions of Yiddish literature in the old country but evolved from the concrete dynamics of the independent American Yiddish literary center. Though its poets often felt like the young branch of a lush tree, refugees washed out on a strange shore, American Yiddish poetry actually developed concurrently with the Yiddish literary renaissance in Europe, and even preceded the latter in its major achievements. The "orphan" feeling merely meant coming to terms with the isolation of the modern poet—and this by people who were used to the warm embrace of an admiring society—or so it seemed at a distance.

True, many American Yiddish poets still read European languages and often drew on various sources from the Jewish and non-Jewish culture of Europe to which they had grown attached in their youth. These influences, as well as the autonomous development of an American Yiddish poetry and poetics, made their writing different from the English poetry next door. But no generation of American Yiddish poets was part of any worldwide Yiddish poetic trend. The atmosphere of life in the United States, which included not only harsh working conditions but also a more peaceful scene and sense of freedom, contributed to this difference, as did the impact of American poetry and social ideas. The terrifying events of the twentieth century shook Yiddish American poets to the quick, but those events did not occur in the streets of their own cities and spoke, rather, to their more general historical sense of humanity and Jewish destiny.

We can observe four major groups of Yiddish poets that emerged in the United States:

1. **The "Proletarian" or "Sweatshop" poets** of the end of the nineteenth century were mostly Socialist- and Anarchist-inspired, but at the same time expressed panhistorical despair about Jewish destiny in the Diaspora and even dreamed of Zion. They were known for their personal involvement in the life of the sweatshop proletariat, their concern with social and political issues, and their direct revolutionary rhetoric, and were popular with Jewish workers. They also considered themselves inspired "Poets," however, and wrote poetry on "lofty" subjects like love, nature, or the art of poetry, vacillating between their interests in "Jewish" and "cosmopolitan" themes.

An account of the Yiddish poets in America, published in a Russian Yiddish newspaper in 1905, demonstrates their plight:

> [Many of them had to suffer] the most bitter poverty which has shackled the poetic imagination in chains and destroyed the beautiful, rich aspirations one after another. We mean, of course, the writers who did not agree to accept compromises with their concept of art, who did not want to sell out their inspiration for a mess of pottage, did not want to serve with their pen purposes which have nothing to do with literature. In the end, they were forced into factories, into sweatshops, into the streets and marketplaces to peddle newspapers, apples and sus-

penders. Look what happened to our best poets: one died in the flower of his youth of tuberculosis [David Edelstadt], a second one is confined to a madhouse [Joseph Bovshover], a third, sick with consumption, has a tailor's shop in Colorado [Yehoash], two or three write news items and articles in the daily papers, and others have neither time nor courage to create poems in the prosaic, oppressive atmosphere of American hustle-bustle. (H. Alexandrov, quoted by Sh. Nigger in the *General Encyclopedia* in Yiddish, vol. *Yiddn G.,* New York, 1942, p. 123).

The "Young Generation," 1915. *Sitting* (from left): Menakhem Boreysho, Avraham Reyzin, Moyshe-Leyb Halpern; *Standing*: A.M. Dilon, H. Leyvik, Zisho Landoy, Reuven Ayzland, A. Raboy; On the wall: Shalom Ash, I.J. Schwartz, Peretz Hirshbeyn, J. Opatoshu; Above: J. Rolnik.

2. "The Young Generation" (also known by their Yiddish name, *Di Yunge*) emerged with their first journal in 1907. They were interested to a large extent in art for art's sake, in exquisite Impressionist poetry of mood and atmosphere, in mellifluous, masterfully formed verse, written in a smooth, "poetic" diction. They would not harness their verse to any political purposes, not become "the rhyme department of the labor movement," as Zisho Landoy expressed it; rather, they centered on the experiences of the individual. They translated much from world poetry and, in general, introduced a cosmopolitan spirit into American Yiddish literature. In some respects, their poetry was akin to English Edwardian verse or to the general European neo-Romantic trend, but it was also influenced by the playful irony of Heine's lyrics. The Young Generation was a purely American product. Though influenced by a general European mood, its poets had little in common with contemporary Yiddish writers in Europe, where prose carried the day. Their counterparts were a few Hebrew poets in Europe and Eretz Israel who were exposed to similar influences, though the two groups hardly knew of each other at the time. The Young Generation established in Yiddish poetry the mastery of verse forms, a cultured tradition of poetry translations, and children's poetry of high literary quality.

We should not be amazed by the fact that the best poets of the Young Generation in New York were simple workers: Mani Leyb was a shoemaker; Landoy, a housepainter; Leyvik, a paperhanger; Halpern, a poverty-stricken jack-of-all-trades. These were not traditional proletarians who turned to writing. They were eagerly reading and discussing the poetry of Pushkin, Blok, Rilke, Hofmannsthal, Baudelaire, Verlaine, and Rimbaud, while publishing translations from European, Chinese, Japanese, or Indian poets. Shoemaking was merely a necessity of life (Moyshe-Leyb recommended it to the American president); after all, a poet had to make a living, and professorial jobs were not yet available. Besides, socialist ideology enhanced the poet's pride in being a real shoemaker, which, along with tailoring, had been the most despised profession in Jewish folklore. In accordance with the folk consciousness of the East Side Jews in general, the Young Generation viewed being proletarian and poor as a transitory stage, a temporary necessity brought about by the hard course of history, while aristocracy of the mind and ambitions to achieve the highest intellectual and artistic standards were inherent in being Jewish or—as they would think—in being human. (Whether or not such ideals could be realized was, of course, another matter.) This is not unlike the theory of the split mind advocated in Hassidism: while half of one's mind is steeped in the dark of everyday work and worries, the other half should be kept separate, rising high and unifying with God.

3. **The "Introspectivists,"** a trend launched in 1919, began a theoretical and practical revolt against the dominance and "poeticalness" of the Young Generation (see the next section). For the Introspectivists, a poem presented a kaleidoscope of broken pieces from the historical world, as perceived in the psyche of a sophisticated urban individual and as expressed in a unique rhythmical "fugue." Theirs was a post-Symbolist poetics, stressing free verse, open thematics and language, and an end to the poetic ivory tower. But they, too, were radically different from their Yiddish contemporaries in Warsaw, Berlin, Kiev, Moscow, or Tel Aviv, who screamed in a loud voice the slogans of Expressionism, Revolution, and Zionism. The Introspectivists developed a rather Anglo-American poetics of irony, dramatized and objectified poetic situations, and intellectual understatement; they formed a much more mature, antisentimental, and honestly harsh view of the real world.

4. **The leftist poets of the twenties and thirties** clustered around the "Proletpen" and more or less openly Communist journals, such as the daily *Frayhayt* and the monthly *Hamer*. Communist ideals had a great fascination for many justice-seeking Jewish writers in the face of the harsh aspects of American capitalism. Communism was also a dignified way of shedding the burden of Jewish particularity, or so they

thought. Furthermore, it fed on the nostalgia for the Russia of the books, its literature, "open soul," melancholy songs, and revolutionary spirit. The memory of the liberation of the Jews from unbearable tsarist oppression (which many remembered with horror from their own childhood) was still fresh; so was the impression of the truly equal rights accorded them by the early Soviet regime and of the visible role many Jews were able to play in the new Russian culture, science, and government. Furthermore, Jewish Communists in America had a real audience and readership devoted to the cause and to Yiddish international culture, and a collective spirit that lured many a lonely poet.

The writers of the left did create some interesting poetry of naturalist description of urban realities and social protest, ranging from the obligatory topic of Sacco-Vanzetti to a book-length poem on *Little Rock*. But the pressures of Soviet-inspired policies, with their demands for flattening the language of poetry and making it a propaganda tool or rhetorical jingle of Socialist Realism that could be "understood by the masses," coupled with their anti-Zionist attitudes (especially their pro-Arab stance during the Arab uprising and anti-Jewish outbursts of 1929 in Palestine), estranged most of the important poets from their fold.

Many creative poets did not belong to any of these groups. Furthermore, certain basic trends and historical events had an impact on writers of various directions, and there was a great deal of infighting and mutual influence among them. In many ways, the description of literature in such groupings reflects the clusters of typical alternatives more than absolute differences among poets. For instance, Moyshe-Leyb Halpern and H. Leyvik began their poetic development with the Young Generation. But the young Introspectivist, Jacob Glatshteyn, while dismissing the Young Generation altogether, sensed even in 1920 the different poetic value of these two poets (see "A Quick Run Through Yiddish Poetry," appendix A, "Chronicle," No. 2). Indeed, Halpern exhibited strong Expressionist features in the 1920s, and Leyvik and Leyeles shared a certain tendency to an aura of mysticism in their verse (as well as a lifelong friendship). From the mid-1920s on, the achievements of all these trends and the influences of English contemporary poetry became common property. Poets of various backgrounds used them according to their personal development, as was the case with Modernism in other literatures.

After World War II, an influx of refugees from Europe brought a number of important poets to America and for a time increased the number of Yiddish readers. The Holocaust in Europe, disenchantment with Stalinism, recognition of the great light coming from the State of Israel, and dissolution of any firm body of Yiddish readership huddled all the writers together in one community.

Almost no new Yiddish writers were added after the 1950s, however. With the dying out of the poets of the generations that had emerged in the 1920s and 1930s, Yiddish literature in America dwindled to a tiny band. The famous *Daily Forward*, which epitomized Jewish immigrant life in America and the struggles of the Jewish world for eighty-five years, and which had often lowered Yiddish culture to the level of the street but had also published some of its best writers, including Nobel-prize winner Isaac Bashevis Singer, stopped daily publication in 1983.

36
*American
Yiddish
Poetry
and its
Background*

INTROSPECTIVISM: A MODERNIST POETICS

The Introspectivist movement can serve as an outstanding example of the critical ambience in American Yiddish literature. The so-called Introspectivist manifesto of 1919 and the excerpts selected in the "Chronicle of a Movement," (both in appendix A) document the main theoretical ideas of its poets (especially of the young Leyeles and Glatshteyn, whose poetry is represented in this anthology). Similar problems—concerning the relations between art and life, language and form, the individual and social reality, the "Jewish" and the "universal"—preoccupied other trends and generations in American Yiddish poetry as well, but the Introspectivists formulated a consciously Modernist poetics, supported by their own creative work and related to Modernist poetics in the international context.

After sixty years of literary theory and criticism, the theorizing of the Yiddish poets around 1920 may seem somewhat naive, but theirs was a more mature and complex view of poetic art than the one formulated in the early manifestoes of Anglo-American Imagism. Theorizing by poets in manifestoes, programmatic articles, or criticism uses a very different language and serves a different function than academic theory or criticism and should not be judged by those standards, but rather as a direct expression of artistic ideology and polemics in a specific cultural context.

The Introspectivists absorbed the ideas on art that were developed in recent Modernist movements. In their arguments one can find traces of Italian and Russian Futurism, German and Yiddish Expressionism, English Imagism and Vorticism, as well as ideas expressed by Nietzsche, Croce, Freud, and T. S. Eliot. Sometimes it is

The Introspectivists, 1923. *Sitting* (from left): Jacob Stodolsky, Jacob Glatshteyn, Celia Dropkin, N.B. Minkov; standing: A. Leyeles, B. Alquit, Mikhl Likht.

hard to tell to what extent such echoes derive directly from primary texts and to what extent they are part of a cultural aura available to intellectual readers after World War I. The important point is the attempt to integrate such elements into a single coherent, "classical" Modernism, rather than voicing the slogans of one extreme position.

In 1918, A. Leyeles published his first book of poems, *Labyrinth*, each page of which was appropriately adorned with a frame made of swastikas, the ancient Indian symbol. Though still steeped in neo-Romantic moods and forms, his was a radical individualism and a sophisticated intellectual stance. As such, it was hardly acceptable either to his contemporaries, the poets of the Young Generation, or to the politicized environment of Yiddish cultural life in New York following the First World War. Some time in 1918, two young students, Jacob Glatshteyn and N. B. Minkov, came to Leyeles with their poems and "actively raised the idea of a new [poetic] trend." All three were intellectuals, well-read both in general and in Jewish culture; they met and talked continuously, developing the ideology and poetics of a new, Modernist trend in Yiddish poetry (see A. Leyeles, "Twenty Years of 'Inzikh,' " *In Zikh*, April 1940). At the time, they published their poems in H. Gudelman's journal, *po'ezye* ("poetry," like the name of its English-language counterpart and Marinetti's *Poesia*), together with members of the Young Generation and several European Yiddish poets.

In 1919, the three poets formulated the principles of their trend and published them as an introduction to an anthology, *In Zikh* (In oneself), including their own poems as well as those of several like-minded young poets. This introduction, entitled "Introspectivism," became the so-called manifesto of their movement. It is written as a declaration of principles, although in a discursive and didactic tone addressed to the general Yiddish reader. The anthology appeared in January 1920, and the first issue of the journal, *In Zikh*, appeared shortly thereafter. In time, the title of the journal was contracted into one word, *Inzikh*, and became the Yiddish name of their trend, "Inzikhism," and of its poets, "Inzikhists."

In Zikh was a typical little review, devoted primarily to poetry and also publishing poetic theory, criticism, and polemics, as well as political and cultural essays written by the poets. It appeared, with several interruptions, from January 1920 until December 1940. In all, 100 poets and writers participated in *In Zikh*, among them some of the young European Yiddish Modernists, such as Dvora Fogel (the friend of Bruno Schulz) and Abraham Sutskever.[11] Though suffering from the lack of an intelligent readership and from vicious attacks by newspaper critics and party hacks, *In Zikh* became the standard-bearer of Yiddish Modernism in America.

At the end of the 1930s, the plight of the Jews in Europe diverted the focus from the theory of poetic language to the problem of art in an age of destruction. The poets, however, never abandoned their concern with art and language, as is clear from Glatshteyn's essays of 1945–1947, collected in *Sum and Substance*[12] and several subsequent collections. The shift of emphasis was also accompanied by a

11. J. Birnboym, "The Journal *In zikh*," [in Yiddish] in *Pinkes far der forshung fun der yidisher literatur un prese*, New York, 1972, pp. 28–49.

12. This is Glatshteyn's own translation of the book's title. The Yiddish name, *In tokh ge'numen*, was the title of Glatshteyn's column in the Labor Zionist cultural weekly, *Yidisher kemfer* ("The Jewish Fighter"); a closer translation of this title would be "The Heart of the Matter."

shift from Leyeles's dominance in the early years as a theoretician of poetry and free verse to Jacob Glatshteyn's prominence as the major Yiddish literary critic and poet after the Holocaust.

In Zikh, the first journal of its kind, was soon followed by Yiddish Modernist journals published in Warsaw, Lodz, Berlin, Moscow, and Paris, and devoted primarily to poetry, poetic theory, and graphic art. Such journals as *Shtrom* (The Torrent), *Khalyastre* (The Gang), and *Albatros* published a new, Modernist poetry in Yiddish, a poetry influenced primarily by Expressionism and Futurism, and the impact of the Russian Revolution with its messianic mood, futuristic utopia, and atrocities. The American Inzikhists did not share the horrors that the European Yiddish poets experienced in World War I and the pogroms of 1919, nor did they share the Expressionist poetics of "Scream" about "Horror" and the "Twilight of Humanity" and the politicized views of literature (communist or zionist). They were, however, aware of these European waves.

The name "Introspectivism" seems to be a direct challenge to the slogan of Expressionism that swept Europe. The opposition of Expressionism versus Impressionism was used to describe the radical shift from an art registering external mood and atmosphere—the subtleties of air, light, and psychological nuances—to the coarse and pathetic expression of the rhythm and spirit of modern, urban civilization, with its technology, wars, masses, radical politics, and the destruction of bourgeois morality. Impressionism seemed to be the last art of mimesis, not essential for real expression. In his manifesto, "On Expressionism in Literature" (1917),[13] the German writer Kasimir Edschmid wrote: "The world exists. It makes no sense to repeat it. To explore it in its every last tremor, in its innermost core, and to create it anew—this is the greatest mission of art."

The Introspectivist manifesto echoes the initial assumption of this statement, opposing mimesis as the principle of art, but seeks its object elsewhere: "The world exists and we are part of it. But for us, the world exists as it is mirrored in us, as it touches *us*. . . . It becomes an actuality only in and *through* us." They promoted Introspectivist poetry as an intellectual insight into one's self, as a personal reflection of an internalized social world, rather than as a mere vehicle for the expression of a *Zeitgeist*, a political mood, the "essence" of the world or of "Man" in general. The poet's major concern was to express the organic relation between outside phenomena and the self, and to do it in an introspective and individual manner: "*In an introspective manner* means that the poet must really listen to his inner voice, observe his internal panorama—kaleidoscopic, contradictory, unclear or confused as it may be."

This is not an escapist, ivory-tower poetry, however. A major antinomy of Introspectivist theory is between the emphasis on individual experience and the range of the world it reflects. A key passage in the "manifesto" reads:

> For us, everything is "personal." Wars and Revolutions, Jewish pogroms and the workers' movement, Protestantism and Buddha, the Yiddish school and the Cross, the mayoral elections and a ban on our language: all these may concern us or not, just as a blond woman and our

13. Kasimir Edschmid, Uber den Expressionismus in der Literatur und die nene Dichtung, Berlin: Erich Reitz, 1919, p. 56.

own unrest may or may not concern us. If it does concern us, we write poetry; if it does not, we keep quiet. In either case, we write about ourselves because all these exist only insofar as they are in us, insofar as they are perceived *introspectively*.

The list of thematic domains in this statement represents an Expressionist grasp of political and cultural realities, though observed when they become part of the personal world of a modern man. It mixes religious attitudes and daily politics, world events and personal emotions, universal history and Jewish news in one kaleidoscopic whirl. One must not be misled by the individualism of the label, "Introspectivism." Theirs was a poetry acutely attuned to the historical and political world, however personally internalized by each poet. The major influence of Anglo-American poetry on the New York Yiddish poets lay in the tone of understatement and irony typical of Glatshteyn, the Leyeles of *Fabius Lind*, or the early Halpern, as opposed to the noisy screams of the Yiddish "big-city" poets in Europe. The Introspectivists were essentially political poets, though in a party-line sense they were the most apolitical poets in Jewish New York.

This conception also abolished the simplistic opposition between "Jewish" and "universal" topics and put an end to the escape of the Young Generation poets from national themes for the sake of pure poetry. It also prepared the Introspectivists—Glatshteyn, Teller, Minkov, Leyeles—to react naturally, as poets, to the Holocaust, and to grasp it in an individual poetic language, as part of their personal experience.

Thus the Introspectivists met the challenge of Expressionism to find a response to the political and social realities which entered personal life as never before. (They certainly determined the personal lives of Jews on the move, whose very channels of existence depended on the political climate.)

The Introspectivists fought an ongoing battle against accusations that they were knowledgeable but cerebral poets. (Leyeles "knows" how to make poems, therefore he is not a poet.) The distinction between "poetry of feeling" and "poetry of thought" was meaningless for them ("there is no boundary between feeling and thought in contemporary man"), as it was for T. S. Eliot. Those who adhered to either were "dualists" (compare Eliot's "dissociation of sensibilities") who created monotonous rhythms. Just as for other Expressionist or post-Symbolist trends, for them, "everything is an object for poetry": "There is no ugly or beautiful, no good or bad, no high or low." This opening of all thematic boundaries did not imply, however, any general permission for laissez-faire: they proposed a specific theory allowing the inclusion of all elements in a poem, under the slogans of "chaotic" and "kaleidoscopic."

The idea that poetry should present "the chaotic" rather than neat, well-made poems was in the air. For the Expressionists, this meant being truthful to the real world. Uri Zvi Grinberg, a soldier and deserter in World War I, wrote in the manifesto of his Yiddish journal, *Albatros* (Warsaw, 1922):

> *This is how things are*. Whether we want it or not. We stand as we are: with slash-lipped wounds, rolled up veins, unscrewed bones, after artillery bombardments and cries of "Hurrah," after gas-attacks; after

bowls filled with gall and opium and the daily water: disgust. And the foam of decay covers our lips.

Hence the atrocious in the poem.
Hence the chaotic in the image.
Hence the scream in the blood.

. . . *It is imperative to write such poems.* Atrocious. Chaotic. Bleeding.

The translation of this ideology into the actual language of poetry meant promoting a chaotic composition, avoiding any continuity of time and space ("death to time and space," called an Italian Futurist manifesto), showing defiance to overt coherence and closure, and constructing a random collage of discordant elements in one text. Moyshe-Leyb Halpern is an extreme example of such a poet: after his first book, he abandoned the Impressionist poetics of the Young Generation and the well-rounded poem, and became increasingly demonstrative and whimsical in the disordered, chaotic compositions of his poems, especially in his rambling dramatic monologues.

The Introspectivists found the chaos in their own psyche: "If the internal world is a chaos, let the chaos be manifested [in the poetry]." Chaos is not merely—and not primarily—the chaos of the modern world breaking out of all rationality, but the chaos of our personal stream of consciousness: "The human psyche is an awesome labyrinth." A person's "I" is subject and object at the same time, present and past, part and whole, his present life and the metamorphosis of previous lives; all exist in him simultaneously: "He is simultaneously at the Ganghes and at the Hudson, in the year 1922 and in the year when Tiglathpileser conquered and terrorized the world. Therefore, the Introspectivist is chaotic and kaleidoscopic" (Leyeles; see appendix A, "Chronicle," No. 11). Hence their opposition to the Imagist ideal of concentration. Concentration and well-roundedness create a poem and a mood that is cut-off, isolated, and this is simply "a lie," the artificiality of art in relation to real "life," because the impact of any phenomenon on the human psyche stimulates a whole galaxy of moods, feelings, and perceptions.

The basic idea is similar to the concepts of "simultaneity" and "intersecting planes" in Italian Futurist plastic art, as the following passage from the manifesto shows:

When the poet, or any person, looks at a sunset, he may see the strangest things which, ostensibly, have perhaps no relation to the sunset. The image reflected in his psyche is rather a series of far-reaching associations moving away from what his eye sees, a chain of suggestions evoked by the sunset. *This*, the series of associations and the chain of suggestions, constitutes *truth*, is life, much as an illusion is often more real than the cluster of external appearances we call life.

In Leyeles's "Autumn," "Symmetry," and other poems, we find motifs of this perception, which often has elements of Freudian psychoanalysis as well as of Oriental-type mysticism and Ouspensky's "fourth dimension."

The poetic equivalent to this psychological conception is the theory of kaleidoscopic art. Rather than mere "chaos," as promoted by the Expressionists and,

instinctively, by M.-L. Halpern, the kaleidoscopic vision is an organized presenta-
tion indicating elements from various discordant situations. Instead of the one
image of the Imagists, the poem has many faces; instead of similes, they preferred
colorful splinters of direct images. As N. B. Minkov pointed out in a later article
devoted to the poetry of Leyeles (1939), this resulted in an inherent contradiction:
while introspection itself is analytical, the kaleidoscopic method is synthetic. The
excellent poet Minkov was biased himself, always tending to the former, immersed
in a mystifying Introspectivism, although the analogy to Synthetic Cubism (as
opposed to the earlier Analytical Cubism) was apt: the idea was to present, like
Picasso, a conscious construct of broken pieces simultaneously representing several
discordant aspects or points of view. Whereas the Expressionist chaos had its
unifying force in its loud, Whitmanesque voice or political pathos, Leyeles was
looking for a unifying force in an all-pervasive rhythm, constituting the "soul" or
the "essence" of the poem. As the kaleidoscope is opposed to the single image, so the
"fugue" of a free rhythm is opposed to the monotonous "air" presented by one
meter.

The concept of the kaleidoscopic method thus brought together several
modern principles: the psychology of the stream of consciousness, the multi-
dimensional nature of modern life, simultaneity of experience, representation
through a splinter element rather than a full description, and the conscious organi-
zation of a poem as a "fugue" or a "symphony" of heterogeneous elements playing
together in a single integrated whole. This concept describes the art of T. S. Eliot in
"The Waste Land" or "Ash Wednesday" and Pound's "Cantos" better than the
Imagist theories stressing the "thing," the individual "image," or "concentration."

In their actual praxis, not all Introspectivist poets implemented the kaleido-
scopic principle with full vigor. Glatshteyn used it in "1919" and then preferred to
base the composition of a poem on a particular, possibly unrealistic, situation.
Leyeles, after using it in such texts as "January 28" and some of his city poems, found
a solution in the poetic cycle, such as "The Diary of Fabius Lind" or "To You—To
Me." Though each individual poem of a cycle centered on one mood or situation (to
be sure, with associations to other moods), the cycle as a whole contained con-
sciously heterogeneous topics—erotic, political, urban, and so on—presented in an
intentional rainbow of rhythmical forms. Thus the cycle "To You—To Me" has a
framework written in a special eight-line strophe, in precise meter and rhyme; it is,
however, interrupted in mid-strophe and mid-line—where a number of greatly
varying metrical and free-verse poems are inserted (among them, "Bolted Room"
and "Fabius Lind to Fabius Lind")—to be resumed thirty pages later in the middle
of the interrupted line and completed in a formal closure. On a higher level, the
whole book, *Fabius Lind*, is such a diary of a contemporary, in which the personal
and the social, the trivial and the metaphysical alternate—matched by an ostensibly
random alternation of a broad spectrum of formal and free verse—to present a
kaleidoscope "of metamorphoses, pain, transformations, elation and achievement
over a range of a lived piece of life." As Glatshteyn described it: "In this book, ten
years in the life of a highly cultured, unsettled, searching, refined Jew were fixed
forever"; hence, ipso facto, "for me, Leyeles's ten years are also—and pri-
marily—ten Jewish years" (appendix A, "Chronicle", No. 25).

The second principle accompanying introspection was individuality of expression; according to the Introspectivist manifesto: "Because we perceive the world egocentrically and because we think that this is the most natural and therefore *the truest and most human* mode of perception, we think that the poem of every poet must first of all be *his own* poem." This principle is applied equally to content and form: "We insist that the poet should give us the authentic image that he sees in himself and give it in such a form as only he and no one else can see it." Each poet must develop his own poetic language and his own poetics, which may eventually subvert any principle of the group.

Here, again, there is a paradox: by individuality the Introspectivists did not mean relativism in value judgments. They insisted that the poet should not only be a "person" in his own right but an "interesting," "contemporary, "intelligent, conscious person. . . capable of expressing the seen, felt and understood in his own, internally true, introspectively sincere manner." By means of association and suggestion—that is, deliberate discontinuous composition and alogical devices of poetic language—the poet must "express the complex feelings and perceptions of a contemporary person." Verslibrisme, as Leyeles puts it, is not just an innovation in form but an expression of a new content: "The new content is the modern life of the modern man, who is breaking away from the old idyllic world, from the old provincialism and small-town atmosphere" (appendix A, "Chronicle," No. 10). When, like Eliot and Pound, the Introspectivists stressed that poetry should use the spoken language, it is "the spoken language of the more intelligent, more conscious part of the Jewish people" that they had in mind ("Chronicle," No. 7).

Thus the poetic theory of the Introspectivists is based on several antinomies: introspection—but reflection of the social and political world; individual poetic language—but expression of "modern man." We may add a third pair: art for art's sake—but art as an "authentic" expression of "life." Answering the critic Nigger's demands for a "Jewish art," Leyeles claims: "Literature is *art*. And art has its own laws, the highest of which is—art itself." But he continues immediately: "Art is *only* an expression of life" ("Chronicle," No. 5). In another context, Leyeles explains the formula, "art for art's sake": "Armed with his intuition, the modern artist does not want to know any tasks or goals other than art," but here, too, he adds, "because he knows that, for him, art is the only road to arrive at the truth, to see the world in its real light and to understand his own relation to the world" ("Chronicle," No. 15).

These antinomies catch some of the central contradictions and polemics of Modernist poetry since Symbolism. They do not offer an uneasy marriage of opposites but a conjunction of two poles, making the one stronger when it is expressed through the other, and vice versa. Value judgment seems to require that both poles be expressed in each of the dilemmas.

From this conception, several additional antinomies can be derived. The Introspectivists did not impose on poetry any "Jewish" or other social mission but, "because it is art, it is Jewish anyway" ("Chronicle," No. 5). In their most experimental poetry, the Introspectivists invested "Jewish" elements; the Jewish experience was always part of their personal, "universal" experience. For them, Jewishness was a language rather than a mission: "A Jew will write about an Indian fertility temple and Japanese Shinto shrines as a Jew" (appendix A, "Introspectivism"). Not just as human beings, but *as poets, as an essential aspect of their poetics*, they developed antennae sensitive to the political climate surrounding them and wrote about it rather than about conventional poetic topics. This was as true for their intense Americanness as for their deeply felt Jewishness. The Introspectivists were the first Yiddish poets who enthusiastically accepted the magnificence of the big American city, "the relation to the big city, to the Woolworth [Tower]'s, the Empire State's, the total gigantic rhythm of the Metropolis New York or the Metropolis Chicago" (A. Leyeles, *In Zikh*, October 1935). Yet even before the Holocaust, they shifted their emphasis to Jewish topics as part of their personal experience: "The same writers who perceived America and expressed it in poem, novel, drama, turned to Jewish history and sought characters and situations there for their contemporary and even 'American' ideas," Leyeles wrote in 1935 (appendix A, "Chronicle," No. 22). That is why they were prepared to face the oncoming Holocaust and respond to it in poetry.

Similar antinomies obtain in the perception of poetic form. The Introspectivists paid attention to the details of form and language. The individual image, the right word in the right place, no superfluous similes or adjectives, and the liberation of the word as the material of art from the conventional ballast of centuries—all these seem to have been influenced by Italian and Russian Futurism. At the same time, for them, enhancing the art of language meant enhancing true expression. For example, on the one hand Leyeles keeps emphasizing that "rhythm is what actually makes the poem," that "words, ideas, content, images by themselves have no independent meaning in the poem. They exist only to serve. They help to create rhythm." On the other hand, rhythm has no value when it is rhythm only, rather than the "soul" of the poem, its metaphysical "essence," something that transcends the trivial and accidental "content."

Free verse was a central principle of most modernist trends in poetry: Imagism, Futurism, Expressionism, Acmeism—all felt it to be a crucial issue for the nature of the new art in language. Though free verse appeared as a conscious tendency in French Symbolism in the last third of the nineteenth century and can be traced back to Goethe, Novalis, and Coleridge, it was moved from the periphery to the center of poetic theory at the beginning of this century. In 1905, F. T. Marinetti launched an international referendum on free verse, in which many important European poets participated. Published in 1909 in book form (together with the Italian Futurist Manifesto), the *Enquête international sur le vers libre* may be considered a landmark that transformed one late French Symbolist technique into a central hallmark of Modernism. However, the rationalizations of the theory of free verse as well as the actual forms it assumed differed widely.

Only a few free-verse poems appeared in Yiddish before World War I. The Introspectivists were the first to make this a cardinal issue dividing the new from the old. It was a genuine revolution, since it is not easy for a poet raised on metrical verse to free himself from the automatized habit of falling into scansion. The Introspectivists may have received the green light for this move from Anglo-American Imagism, but they had a different conception of the problem. They emphasized not so much the aspect of freedom from tradition as that of individual expression and deliberate orchestration of a richer, rather than a more prosaic, rhythm. For them, free verse demands "an intense effort" in coordinating and subordinating all aspects of sound patterning in the poetic texture. Free verse is to be an expression of individuality on all levels: of the poet, of the poem, and of the individual line. It is to express both "the natural rise and fall of a mood" and "the new music that stirs the world," the irregular tempo of the big city and the "disharmony" of the "contemporary psychic experience." Hence the emphasis not on uniformity or prosaic tone but on the interaction of many shifting rhythmical devices and the symphonic nature of a free rhythmic poem. Since individuality of rhythm, rather than freedom of verse, was the issue, this could be accomplished in regular meters as well, provided the variety of selected forms guaranteed the uniqueness of each poem. In sum, free verse was a departure from the dominant, conventional form of a symmetrical, four-line, rhymed strophe, and it went in two opposite directions: of less and more structured texts.

Monotony was death to poetry. Glatshteyn understood this in his own way when he denied the musicality of Edgar Allan Poe's "The Raven" (arguing against Leyeles, who translated it twice, in 1918 and in 1945 [!]). He used the term again when he exposed the danger of a whole literature becoming "monotonic and monothematic" in "wailing together" after the Holocaust. Glatshteyn himself tried to save the individuality of the poem, even in that age of "collective stammer." As he put it: "Our word is our weapon and we must not let ourselves become primitive [in wailing over the destruction]." Glatshteyn cites as an example the prophet Jeremiah who, when a whole people was enslaved, "played" with the art of language and sought perfection in his "Jeremiads" ("May one Enjoy Elegies?" *Sum and Substance*, pp. 428–434).

The documents translated in appendix A provide additional details on Introspectivist thinking about the art of poetry. The poets themselves were aware that their poetics was part of an international trend: "Certainly, there is a more direct relation between an Introspectivist and a German Expressionist or English Vorticist than between us and most Yiddish poets of the previous periods" ("Chronicle." No. 14). For the outside world, however, the Yiddish poets were isolated in a sealed ghetto. A telling example was the answer of the editors of the English-language *Poetry*, asking whether the language of *In Zikh* was Chinese (see *In Zikh's* reply in "Chronicle" No. 18, and also Nos. 24, 26). In the Jewish domain itself, there was a chronic scarcity of readers (see "Chronicle, Nos. 8, 13, 23). Of course, English poets, too, had only small circles of readers at the time, before Modernist poetry was introduced into college curricula, but Yiddish poets never enjoyed that canonization. Only the common national tragedy brought them back to the center of Jewish society and made them into social bards, sometimes at the expense of poetic quality. Then it became clear what immense work had been done in the development of a new poetic language in Yiddish in New York between 1919 and 1950.

METER AND FREE VERSE

The selections in this volume represent a radical shift in the history of Yiddish poetry: on the one hand, many poems still relish the use of regular meters; on the other hand, there is a broad move toward rhythmical innovation and free verse.[14]

Meter and sound orchestration were, and still are, central to Yiddish verse to an extent that a contemporary reader of English poetry may not be prepared to sense. The magic of repeated metrical patterns, symmetry, and parallelism, reinforced by sound play and rhythmical variation, does to the simplest words what music does to the elementary words of good songs. As in a song, the "magic" is not in the sound patterns themselves but in their interaction with a few, perhaps quite elementary words and suggested themes, which give the sound patterns certain emotive and thematic directions and which are, in turn, reinforced by them.

This central, poetry-making function of meter and sound can be seen in the role they play in Russian poetry to this day. Russian Modernist poets—Mandelshtam, Mayakovsky, Pasternak—molded their futurist metaphors and surrealist compositions in consciously metrical rhythms (or variations of them), dense sound patterning, and conspicuous rhyme inventions. This was also true for German Modernist poets at the beginning of the century, such as Rilke or George. In Yiddish this remains a strong tendency, as can be seen in the "Neo-Classical Modernism" of the greatest living Yiddish poet, A. Sutzkever.

After World War I, Yiddish poetry developed various deviations from this metrical tradition, at first in ways still close to it but deforming its effects of regularity. For example, in Halpern's "Our Garden," each strophe establishes a perfect meter of four trochees, which is repeated in four rhymed couplets in an almost folksong tone (though once interrupted by an exclamation, in the fifth, unrhymed line):

14. For a fuller treatment of this topic, see my forthcoming *Aspects of Yiddish*.

What a garden, where the tree is
Bare, but for its seven leaves,
And it seems it is amazed:
"Who has set me in this place?"
What a garden, what a garden —
It takes a magnifying glass
Just to see a little grass.
Is this garden here our own.
As it is, in light of dawn?

This regularity is then suddenly subverted by an additional, unrhymed, nonmetrical long line, in a provocative, "Jewish" conversational manner:

Sure, it's our garden. What, not our garden?

A more radical departure was effected in the "free rhythms," as advocated by the Introspectivists. The main directions of their free verse may be called "dynamic" and "conversational" rhythms.[15] "Dynamic" rhythms are irregular too—that is, they have no overall metrical pattern for a whole poem, but are more rather than less rhythmically structured, using rhythmical configurations strongly deviant from prose or an interplay of changing metrical segments, heightened sound effects, and internally inverted rhymes, all of which serve the local shifts of mood in the text. (An English example for one kind of dynamic rhythm can be seen in T. S. Eliot's "Ash Wednesday".) Leyeles claimed that Yiddish free verse, though influenced by the principle raised in Anglo-American Imagism, developed a richer gamut of rhythmical expression. Indeed, Yiddish poets combined the Russian sensibility for heightened sound-patterning in poetry with the Anglo-American "battle cry for freedom,"—that is, for the individuality of the artist, the single poem, and the particular line.

At the other pole, "conversational" rhythms were developed, especially by Halpern, Glatshteyn, and Leyeles. These introduce the intonations and inter-jections of a speech situation, suppressing meter as well as any tendency of parallelism between adjacent lines. The continuity of an advancing monologue rather than equivalences of verse determine their rhythmical impact. They are convenient for bringing out the full flavor of Yiddish conversation, verbal gesture, and characterization in poetry.

At the same time, however, there was a tendency to enrich the gamut of poetic rhythms through mastering difficult strophic forms, both as found in the European tradition and as originally constructed by the poet (as in Leyeles's "Herod," analyzed below).

Leyeles's sonnet garland, "Autumn," may serve as an example of a European form re-created in Yiddish. It has fifteen sonnets, writen in an iambic pentameter. The sonnets are concatenated: the last line of each sonnet is repeated as the first line of the next sonnet (often with subtle syntactic variations). The fifteenth sonnet is composed of the first lines of the fourteen preceding sonnets.

15. See my paper of 1952, "On Free Rhythms in Modern Yiddish Poetry," in Weinreich, Uriel, eds., *The Field of Yiddish*, New York, 1954, pp. 219–266, where I suggested a typology for some of those free rhythms.

Each sonnet employs the difficult Italian rhyme-pattern, binding the first eight lines with only two rhymes, though in an inverted order: *abba baab cdcd ee* (with an English closing couplet). Since the sonnets are concatenated, a dense rhyme grid embraces the whole structure, creating innumerable echoes between the various sonnets and their key words. Two key rhymes occur twenty-eight and twenty-six times, respectively, and others occur fourteen times (with no rhyming word repeated)—a musical magic impossible to reproduce in translation.

In our translation, we faithfully conveyed the iambic pentameter; the concatenation of sonnets culminating in the last sonnet; the rhymes in the closing couplet of each sonnet; and the full rhyme scheme in the fifteenth sonnet. We also introduced additional sound orchestration but had to forego reproducing the full rhyming network (which, if done, would obstruct the meaning of the text for the English reader not used to such rhyming saturation).

FORMAL CONFINEMENT OF EVIL

The horrors of Dante's *Inferno* would remain unalleviated horrors, the raptures of his *Paradiso* would be visionary dreams were they not molded into a new shape by the magic of Dante's diction and verse.

—Ernst Cassirer, *An Essay on Man*

Horkht mayn vort durkh ayer zukhn, laydn, haven,
In ge'tsoymte un ge'mostene ok'tavn.
. . . .
Ven keyn grenets iz nish'to far di ye'surim,
veytik-oys a syog fun shtreng-ge'tsoymtn furem.

[prose translation:]

Through your searching, suffering, frenzy, hear my word
In restrained and measured octaves.
. . . .
When there is no limit to your anguish,
Build your pain into a fence of rigorous form.

—A. Leyeles, "To You, Yiddish Poets," in
"A Dream Among Skyscrapers"

At about the same time, A. Leyeles wrote three poems with a surprisingly similar perception of the soul as a battlefield of madness, of irrational drives that possess a person. The points of view, however, are cardinally different—and so, appropriately, are the rhythmical conceptions of the poems. (All three were published after the Holocaust and are translated in this anthology.)

"Herod" is the brutal, paranoid madman slaughtering everyone in sight, a Stalin out of Jewish history, breeding hatred and fear and himself a "slave to a curse," moved by powerful internal forces he cannot control. "Shlomo Molkho

Sings on the Eve of His Burning" presents an intriguing historical figure who preoccupied Leyeles because of his mixture of messianic vision and daring arrogance, his stance as a redeemer in dark times of Jewish history, a leader who carries the masses with him in a utopian vision, only to pay for it with his own isolation and inevitable destruction. (Molkho, 1500–1532, was burned at the stake after an attempt to enlist the Pope in his cause.) Leyeles's drama on this topic had its world premier in the Vilna Ghetto before its annihilation. In the poem, Molkho, too, has the Stalinist streak. He is the Messiah, the Redeemer, enjoying the blind submission of the crowd; he, too, is gripped by vanity, by the narcissistic aggrandizing of his "I," which breeds loneliness and fear of himself. But historically, Molkho is a positive hero, and Leyeles presents his tortured self-understanding from within. Night, "the metamorphoser of forms," piles doubts on him in its darkness, on the eve of his execution, and extorts his real, personal confession; Molkho's transformation makes him "humble and silent with joy," relieved to exchange the "redeemer's poison" within him for the pure breath of the flame of the auto-da-fé.

In "Herod," though revealing the king's internal psychotic drama, he is seen from the outside—incorporating, however, Herod's own point of view in Free Indirect Style. Herod's position is formulated in rhetorical, aphoristic summaries. The tone is a solemn, concise, and nervous recitation, underlined by the formal strophic structure and declamatory rhetoric. In contrast, Molkho's is the internal monologue of a mystic transformed and liberated by embracing the exalted vision of his own burning. The poem's rhythm is as free as his liberated mood. It is not a prosaic free verse, however, but conveys the festive tone of an ode to the night, gradually transformed into a passionate confession leading up to the dramatic gesture.

The third poem, "Foreign Fencers," presents the sleepless nights of Leyeles's own arrogant and lonely "I"—a resigned, latter-day Fabius Lind in sophisticated introspection, in the grip of overpowering drives and contradictions. No leader, redeemer, or slaughterer, he too is a "battlefield of madness"; within him, too, there are "masters of evil," devious demons descending "from a spiderwebbed attic" and devastating his "authentic image." (Is the attic his subconscious? Or should we say "superconscious"? Or is it a collective subconscious like a "*boydem*," an attic filled with antiques?) But he manages to externalize the battlefields, the whole "foreign fencing" that goes on inside him and from which he has no escape; he stands like an observer outside himself and smiles. The rhythm is free, too, following his fluctuating observations yet emphasizing their ironies almost from the beginning, and lacking the long, periodic sentences and exclamation points of Molkho's ode.

The evil inside the most individual Introspectivist and the introspection in the most evil figure of the century—transposed into the repetition of history—are two poles of one scale. There is an affinity between messiah and tyrant, between inhuman history and the frail humanity of the poet himself. The different conceptions, however, are reflected in the changing forms of the poems. According to Leyeles's theory of "bipolarity" (see appendix A, "Chronicle of a Movement," No. 22), "the most dedicated verslibriste will suddenly turn to the most confined, classical forms." We shall not analyze the rhythms of the two free poems, but will concentrate on the formal principles of "Herod."

"Herod" has a fixed, rigorous strophic structure, enriched by free sound-orchestration and rhythmical variation. There are nine strophes of nine rhyming lines each, with a tenth line as an unrhymed defiant closure. The original reads (stressed syllables are in upper case):

> HORdos is ALT shoyn. zayn POnim, geRIbn mit ZALbn
> MITSrishe SHMIrekhtsn, KUKT nokh oys YUNG, nor zayn BLIK—
> UMru un PAkhad un KHMAres in TUNkele FALbn,
> OPgrunt vu S'LOyern MONstrishe HALbn;
> ROYmer—seMIT; halb farTSVEYflung, halb GLIK;
> ZORger far VILD-fremde SHVALbn
> BREkher fun Umes geNIK,
> KNEKHT oyf a TRON,
> KINig in KON
> bay umLESHbarer DORSHT, bay farDAKHtn geHEYme un KRANke.

Meter	Rhyme	Ending
– ⌣ ⌣ – ⌣ ⌣ – ⌣ ⌣ – ⌣ ⌣ – ⌣	a	f
– ⌣ ⌣ – ⌣ ⌣ – ⌣ ⌣ – ⌣ ⌣ –	b	m
– ⌣ ⌣ – ⌣ ⌣ – ⌣ ⌣ – ⌣ ⌣ – ⌣	a	f
– ⌣ ⌣ – ⌣ ⌣ – ⌣ ⌣ – ⌣	a	f
– ⌣ ⌣ – ⌣ ⌣ – ⌣ ⌣ –	b	m
– ⌣ ⌣ – ⌣ ⌣ – ⌣	a	f
– ⌣ ⌣ – ⌣ ⌣ –	b	m
– ⌣ ⌣ –	c	m
– ⌣ ⌣ –	c	m
⌣ ⌣ – ⌣ ⌣ – ⌣ ⌣ – ⌣ ⌣ – ⌣ ⌣ – ⌣	x	f

(f=feminine, m=masculine)

The meter begins with the solemnity of a dactylic, almost epic line. Unlike the iamb, the dactyl is a very pronounced meter in Yiddish, with its stress at the opening of each line and foot. The length of the lines systematically recedes, from five dactyls to two, the rhythmical units becoming more and more concise and tense.

The rhyme patterning does not coincide with the patterns of length; rather, it creates a counterpoint to them until the last couplet, where they fall together. In the couplet, each of the short lines creates a bow, leaning on two strong stressed syllables at its ends, reinforced by rhyme and often by alliteration as well:

> KNEKHT oyf a TRON,
> KINig in KON

Against this background of the long-winded, forward-pulling, ever-narrowing dactylic rhythm, there is the unexpected break of the last line. Its meter is opposite: an anapest, it has no rhyme and, after the couplet of short-breathing exclamatory verses, sounds like an endlessly long line, a cry of madness breaking out of confinement.

This long-winded forward movement, too, is filled with obstacles and broken up into small autonomous segments, marked by the rhymes and by rhetorical pairs of oppositions ("Roman—and Semite; despair—and good fortune"), though never permitting a final stop until all rhymes are completed and the flow issues into the final long, unrhymed phrase. The tension between the ever-continuing, ruthless forward drive, in ever shorter and tenser units, and the stalling, local dams constitutes the rhythmical character of this poem. The original strophic structure is its indispensable base.

In the translation of this poem, we gave up the rhymes altogether, trying to convey the metrical scheme precisely, but skipping a syllable here and there to avoid what would be too mechanical an impression or too easy a forward flow in English, when uninhibited by the rhymes.

A great deal of what was going on in Yiddish poetry in this period was invested with such intensive attention to the texture of sound and language.

The End of a Language

> Night. In the darkest places sparkle traces
> Of words. Loaded ships with ideo-glyphs
> Sail away. And you, armored in silence and wisdom,
> Unwrap word from sense.
> —J. Glatshteyn, "We the Wordproletariat"

The young Introspectivist Jacob Glatshteyn felt that one could not make sense of the *velt-plonter* ("tangle of the world") when shiploads of ideas sail away incomprehensibly. The Introspectivist poet wears the armor of silence toward politicized society, he retreats into personal wisdom, observes his own consciousness ironically, and tries to liberate words from the burden of sense. In the poetry of the early Glatshteyn, there is no denial of his Jewishness, but it is actually irrelevant for the human condition he represents. Jewish traces are simply part of his "impulses of memory," flashing suddenly in his field of consciousness like the strange word *tirtle-toyben* from his early childhood, in the poem "Turtledoves."

In "1919" (one of his first poems), a date in history filled with red headlines of the Red Revolution and rivers of blood from pogroms in the Ukraine, he is running around in New York, a latter-day Jacob the son of Isaac, comically reduced to the familiar and childish "Yankl, son of Yitskhok," a tiny round dot that rolls crazily through the streets with hooked-on, clumsy limbs. There once was "The Jewish Dot," the most elementary, irreducible point of identity of a Jew ("*dos pintele yid,*" referring both to the smallest Hebrew letter and the smallest vowel, represented by a dot, as well as to the name "Jew" and the initial letters of God, Isaac, and Jacob). Now only the dot remains, a hard core, the tiniest visible existence, rolling in the streets. (These are two anti-allusions—allusions evoked to cancel the validity of the allusion.) His limbs do not belong to him but are somehow hooked on, haphazardly attached to his body, clumsily irrelevant, as the stylistically outstanding two long words (6 and 5 syllables) expressively convey: *a-royf-ge-'tshe-pe-te, um-ge-'lum-per-te* ("hooked-on, clumsy," like those words themselves). "Extras!" (special editions of newspapers) fall everywhere from above, presumably from the El running above the streets of New York; but he cannot comprehend a thing, and they squash his dumb, "watery head."

There is no single specific reference in the poem to any political event, though the time was filled with them; only the character's myopic eyeglasses get smeared with red and he is condemned to spin, lost in ether for eternities, with red before his eyes. Of course, this is New York. Glatshteyn's contemporaries in Europe filled their Expressionist poems with direct descriptions of the horrors of World War I and the pogroms of 1919 (though those were published later). His experience is only a reflection of the European world, of news reports about it that fall absurdly in rapid succession onto his uncomprehending head. But the chaos of the modern world and the noisy metropolis are expressed just as strongly in indirection and understatement.

Glatshteyn's "1919" is a self-ironic, kaleidoscopic poem and, at the same time, an inverted statement about the political world and the mess it is in. The direct, coarse, juicy, rich, spoken language, with its diminutives, allusions, stylistic clashes, and ironic twists, is as Jewish as Yiddish lyrical poetry never was before, even though thematically "1919" is a cosmopolitan poem, smelling of New York confusion. The conversational markers and precise sensibility for the effects of spoken intonations and sound relations in free verse demonstrate what the "Young Generation" missed with their exact meters and Symbolist poeticalness. There is also a direct jibe at Neo-Romantic poetics in proclaiming that there is "no escape," not from politics, its "Extras!" and red colors, but from the color "heaven-blue," a poetic cliché externalized in nature: "The lord-above surrounded / The whole world with heaven-blue / And there is no escape."

Two poems from *Credos* (1929), "Autobiography" and "Jewish Kingdoms," again exhibit Glatshteyn's rich Jewish language of situations coupled with an ironic distancing from a Jewish world. Like the Austrian Jewish novelist Joseph Roth. Glatshteyn suspects in "Autobiography," that he is a lapsed Gentile and grotesquely demystifies the whole issue of history and roots. "Autobiography" may not be as coarse or inwardly "anti-Semitic" as some of Halpern's poems about the old country (e.g., "Zlochov"), but it is as antinostalgic and cut off from it. In "Jewish Kingdoms," strange names of Polish towns float up in Glatshteyn's memory like dry leaves in a bath, but he is incapable of longing for them.

Gradually but persistently, the rhyme *erter—verter* ("places—words") emerges in Glatshteyn's poetry, as in the motto to this chapter. As the rhyme itself suggests, words contain places. The names of Polish towns are mere names, but they also recall a warm, early-erotic, childhood experience. In the poetics of the early Glatshteyn, places occupy a central position. Though a master of the kaleidoscopic technique, he is uneasy about it. Glatshteyn is a talker, a narrator, and he prefers to locate his speakers in dramatized fictional situations. The narration is presented mostly in the third person but represents the point of view of the central character of the poem. A poem is centered on a re-created human experience that is located in a fictional situation. In the early poetry, the situations are mostly antirealistic, historical, or legendary: Gaggie the bear-trainer with his five wives, the poet's two-hundredth birthday, the Proud King or Abishag. The Baron, an incorrigible liar, invents places with his words. Only in *Credos* does a more political realism enter the book, and even so, the basic technique is neither kaleidoscope nor metaphor but re-created fictional situations. Poems are anchored in places where characters are situated and enact their desentimentalized behavior.

At least since Glatshteyn's poems of Nakhman from Bratslav, the connection is thematized: on the way to heaven, Nakhman becomes "everythingless in the world" and loses all his places and all his words, because there are no words ("*verter*") without places ("*erter*"). Glatshteyn keeps repeating this persistent pair; in itself, it is a trite, obvious rhyme, but it becomes the focus of a central theme, underlined by the spare and sporadic use of rhymes in his poetry. The theme is central even when the rhyme itself is absent. "Wagons" or "On the Butcher Block" are fictional places in which individual characters are located, expressing the horror of the impending Holocaust (rather than talking about it or attempting direct, realistic descriptions). In the chilling poem, "A Hunger Fell Upon Us," the speaker may be in the same suburban home and garden as in the poem on his "Two-Hundredth Birthday," though there are also indications of a panhistorical space: "You touch your fig tree, / Stroke the bricks of your house." The safety of well-built bricks and of the biblical allusion ("everyone under his fig tree") are both undermined in the beautiful understatement: "Maybe nobody's come yet, / But my bones already ache / With the dampness of the Jewish weather." Hence, when the first news of the Holocaust arrives, he places the experience in space: "Here I have never been" (coupled with an anti-déjà vu: "This I have never seen"). The metaphor of space, embodying a "world" of experience and meaning, is central to Glatshteyn's thematics, poetic language, and fictional constructs.

But now the relation is inverted as well: in Glatshteyn's early poetics, places carried words; now, the words are the carriers of a lost world. When they lose their meaning, we lose our world:

> All the existing words, / The expressed, / The understood, / Lie in their dumbfounded clarity. / Their sucked-dry meanings dozing off. / It is our world, / Soon it will lower the curtain. ("We, Of the Singing Swords")

When Glatshteyn tries to understand the Holocaust, he conjures up a place, a tiny dot from which he recreates a lost world:

> I shall stubborn myself, / Plant myself / In a private, intimate night / That I totally invented / And wondered-in on all sides. / I shall find a spot in space / As big as a fly, / And there I shall impose, / For all time, / A cradle, a child, / I shall sing into it a voice / Of a dozing father, / With a face in the voice, / With love in the voice / . . . / And around the cradle I shall build a Jewish town . . . ("I Shall Transport Myself." See also the poem "I Shall Remember.")

Those were words that carried in themselves the memory of places; you could conjure up whole Jewish worlds from them. (Did these worlds ever exist? Is he inventing them now?) But when the immediate pain of the Holocaust was somewhat subdued, a new pain arose, the pain of losing hold of the words themselves. The rhyme *erter—verter* ("words"—"places") is back, and so is their overlapping:

As to sad synagogues,
To doorsteps of belief—
How hard to come back
To old words.
I know well their places.
I hear their humming.
At times I get close, I look longingly
Through the windowpanes.

            ("Without Offerings")

* * *

Can we imagine the tragedy of writers—H. Leyvik, Jacob Glatshteyn, A. Leyeles, others—who felt such a mission of beginning in their own lifetime and stood before the abyss of the end, losing first their readership, then their source, their people in Europe (along with their own parents), and finally the very language that they had made into such a fine instrument?

Here stands the aging Glatshteyn, holding a handful of water in his palm:

A few trembling lines on the palm of my hand.
I held them long
And let them flow through my fingers,
Word by word.

            ("A Few Lines")

And again:

Soon we'll have lost all the words.
The stammer-mouths are growing silent.
The heritage-sack is empty. Where can we get
The holy prattle of promised
Joy? A child's grimaces
Are an alien spite-language.
In the dark we compose
Lightning words, fast extinguished.
    And ash becomes their meaning.
    And ash becomes their meaning.

            ("Soon")

This is a very private, a very final Holocaust, for someone who was not there, who lived through it here, in America.

The artists selected in this volume are part of the history of American art in the twentieth century. Large bodies of their work have nothing specifically Jewish about them. They were concerned with problems of the language of art and with personal expression. They are enmeshed in the context of the development of American art and its responses both to the new trends in Europe and to the phenomena of American life. At the same time, their work exhibits striking parallels to the work of the Yiddish poets selected here, who also tried to express the experiences of a modern individual in an American metropolis, alert to Western culture and to the political world of this century. To the extent that these poets and the visual artists turned to "Jewish" themes, especially in their later years, it was from the achieved position of their art and in response to historical events, from the point of view of contemporary Americans with Jewish memories. The difference in their fate, nevertheless, is astounding, albeit understandable: since the language of art is universal, the graphic artists are part of American art, just as citizens of Jewish origin are part of American society in general, whereas the Yiddish poets have remained enclosed in the ruins of their unapproachable language.

As with the poets, we concentrated primarily on several artists, all of them more or less figurative Modernists, preceding Abstract Expressionism. Most were born in Eastern Europe or grew up in the Jewish ghettos of New York City and were contemporaries of the poets in this volume (the middle date indicates the year of immigration to the United States): Max Weber (1881–1891–1961), Abraham Walkowitz (1878–1893–1965), Louis Lozowick (1892–1906–1973), Ben Shahn (1898–1906–1969), Raphael Soyer (1899–1912–   ), Chaim Gross (1904–1921–   ), William Gropper (born in New York, 1897–1977). For a while they were eclipsed by the New York School of the 1950s and the predominance of abstraction in art. But in recent years, they have been gaining public recognition, and with it, comprehensive exhibits in major museums and galleries and a prominent place in histories of American art.

Most of these artists went to Europe at one time or another and were profoundly impressed by the Modernist trends there. Max Weber went to Paris in 1905, studied with Matisse, was friendly with Derain, Vlaminck, and Picasso, organized the first Rousseau exhibition in the United States in Alfred Stieglitz's Gallery "291," and was the first to introduce Cubism into American painting. His friend Abraham Walkowitz, in Paris in 1906–1907, came under similar influences. Both exhibited their work in New York in Stieglitz's gallery and in the famous Armory Show of 1913. Chaim Gross studied art in Budapest and absorbed some principles of German Expressionist sculpture. When Ben Shahn came to Paris in the mid-1920s, the excitement of Cubism was over and Picasso himself was groping between deformation and figurative forms. But Shahn learned an important lesson and, though remaining figurative, employed forms of stylized simplification and abstraction, giving expressive force to his socially engaged paintings.

Louis Lozowick, born in Russia, immigrated to the United States by himself as a boy of fourteen, studied at the National Academy of Design, and received a B.A.

Max Weber: *Grand Central Terminal*, 1915.

from Ohio State University in 1918. When he traveled in Russia, France, and Germany in 1919–1924, he was a representative of American art and American industrial optimism in the eyes of his European colleagues. " 'Ah, America,' they say, 'wonderful machinery, wonderful factories, wonderful buildings' " (as he recalled in "The Americanization of Art," 1927). Indeed, his geometrically precise and imposing paintings of American cities and industry, of majestic buildings, ports, and factories, were close to the Constructivist spirit and were first painted in Berlin (though based on sketches from his earlier tour of the U.S.). In Europe, Lozowick befriended El Lissitzky, a major figure in Soviet abstract art and Constructivism who organized the famous Soviet exhibition in Germany and introduced new methods in graphic art and book production. Both Lozowick and Lissitzky were Yiddish-speaking and Yiddish-writing Russian Jews, but in Berlin they represented Russian and American art, respectively, just as Gertrude Stein represented American avant-garde literature in Paris.[16]

Indeed, after spending only thirteen years in the United States, Lozowick felt profoundly "American" and recalled proudly that "all the references to my work stressed its Americanism." In his essay, "The Americanization of Art," written for a catalogue of the international Machine Age Exposition held in 1927 in New York, he wrote:[17]

> The dominant trend in America of today, beneath all the apparent chaos and confusion is towards order and organization which find their outward sign and symbol in the rigid geometry of the American city. . . . The artist cannot and should not . . . attempt a literal soulless transcription of the American scene but rather give a penetrating creative interpretation of it. . . . The intrinsic importance of the contemporary theme may thus be immensely enhanced by the formal significance of the treatment. In this manner the flowing rhythm of modern America may be gripped and stayed and its synthesis eloquently rendered in the native idiom.

These are motifs echoed in the paintings of Walkowitz and Weber in the early 1920s and in the poetry of Leyeles and others in Yiddish.

To a large extent, this is true of the other artists as well. They felt themselves first of all as "Artists." They were attached to modern Western culture in its latest developments, were intellectually part of it, and felt free to participate in creating its art. The extent to which they drew on personal experience or national memories depended on the nature of their art at any particular moment. The Introspectivist conception of "Jewish" topics as only a possible part of a modern person's consciousness, reflected in the kaleidoscope of his response to the world, is valid for these artists as well. In Marc Chagall's statement quoted earlier, he expressed pride and optimism in the future contribution of Jews to art; it was, however, not "Jewish art" he was speaking about but "Art" in general, though it may be achieved, as in his

---

16. On Lozowick, see Janet Flint, *The Prints of Louis Lozowick*, Hudson Hills Press, 1982.

17. Flint, Ibid., p. 19. See also the chapter on "The Image of Urban Optimism" in Joshua C. Taylor, *America as Art*, Smithsonian Institution Press, 1976.

case, through the use of Jewish materials. Whether such materials were used or not was immaterial to the value of the art.

Thus, in the 1920s, Lozowick was a spokesman of American industrial optimism and geometrical construction. Ben Shahn, in his paintings and photographs of the 1930s, was a major artist of American symbolic realism and social protest, whether portraying conditions in the South or the trial of Sacco and Vanzetti. William Gropper was an effective political caricaturist and social painter of the left. Raphael Soyer depicted the alienation and internal stress and emotions of individuals in the city. One critic wrote of Soyer's "office girls": "Hemmed in by the crowd, whose presence they do not acknowledge, they are absorbed in coping with life in the city. . . . His people—appealing, even noble—are marked by the frailties, anxieties and emotional traumas inflicted on them by their environment."[18] Soyer's characters could have walked out of Glatshteyn's *Credos*, Leyeles's *Fabius Lind*, or Halpern's city poems.

This was a response to America by people who could observe its social context with fresh eyes. There was nothing Jewish about the subjects of their work. And thus they were perceived by their contemporaries. The influential critic, H. McBride, wrote of Max Weber: "At last we have an artist who is not afraid of this big great city of New York." Similarly the vitriolic attacks against these artists as intruding foreigners stressed their "assault on the fortresses of academic culture" and the abominable introduction of Cubism and Modernism by those distasteful immigrants, the perpetrators of "Ellis Island Art," rather than any specifically Jewish content.[19]

Many painters of Jewish origin seem consciously to have avoided overtly "Jewish" topics for a long time. Like Kafka, whose interest in Jewish subjects is reflected in his correspondence, whereas any overt trace of it was excluded from his fiction, these artists were universal in their iconography. This is certainly true of Ben Shahn in the period of his fame in the thirties. It is also true of a painter like Abraham Walkowitz, who has no Jewish themes in his drawings of "Metropolis"; in his book, *100 Drawings and Paintings* (1925); in his hundreds of drawings of Isadora Duncan; or in his *Barns and Coal Mines*. Even when Walkowitz did turn to drawing Jewish religious types, he called his book *Ghetto Motifs*—that is, motifs painted from the distance of one who has left the ghetto. Max Weber, the most consciously Jewish among his contemporaries, painted his first major painting on a Jewish theme, "Sabbath," at the age of thirty-eight, and he, too, distanced himself from his intensely, fatally Jewish types through almost grotesque deformations. Similarly, Chaim Gross's biographer notes:[20]

> On the whole, the religious theme is rare in his work, and this is odd; although, like many artists, somewhere in the transition between adolescence and young manhood he left his traditional, family religion behind, Gross, unlike many others, returned to the faith of his fathers.

Breaking out into the modern world meant breaking away from the Jewish

18. Abraham A. Davidson, *The Story of American Painting*, New York: Abrams, 1974, p. 126.
19. See Cynthia Jaffe McCabe, *The Golden Door: Artist-Immigrants of America, 1876–1976*. Smithsonian Institution Press, 1976.
20. Frank Getlein, *Chaim Gross*, New York: Abrams, 1974, p. 57.

fictional world, its symbols and typology, and it was not easy to find artistic means with which to confront it again when returning in older age to its faith or identity. Gross drew many Jewish types and symbols throughout the years, when illustrating his brother's retelling of Jewish folklore or other books of Yiddish literature. It is only into his own, original sculpture that Jewish symbolism found its way hesitantly and rather late. Only occasionally can we see in one of Soyer's paintings an element such as a Yiddish newspaper (read by the parents, with a picture of the grandparents of the old country on the wall, in "The Dance Lesson"). In the moving title of "Reading from Left to Right," Soyer's usual, apparently unemployed characters stand with their backs to the hand-lettered signs announcing food in English, alienated by the very direction of its writing (Jews read from right to left). But even this is not a "Jewish" painting in any substantial sense; it merely draws on the experiences of immigrant Jews.

As artists, the sculptors and painters represented here were all consciously American, but in daily life many of them did maintain Jewish contacts, both because their social environment was largely Jewish and because Yiddish, the language of their childhood, was still a viable force in New York. A typical case was the Educational Alliance Art School on the Lower East Side of New York. A community center built by uptown German Jews for Eastern-European Jewish immigrants at the end of the nineteenth century, it became an important art school in the twentieth century. Indeed, "the initial attraction of the Alliance was that the language of instruction was Yiddish."[21] Among its students were Jacob Epstein, Jo Davidson, Chaim Gross, Peter Blume, Adolph Gotlieb, Moses Soyer, Ben Shahn, Saul Beizerman, Leonard Baskin, Louise Nevelson, Barnett Newman, and Mark Rothko, several of whom later became teachers there.

Several artists maintained contact with Yiddish literature. Abraham Walkowitz, Max Weber, Louis Lozowick, William Gropper, and others published paintings, lithographs, drawings, and essays in Yiddish literary and social journals. Moses Soyer wrote a weekly column, "In the World of Art," for a Yiddish newspaper. Abraham Shauer, the father of painters Rafael, Moses, and Isaac Soyer, was a Hebrew teacher and later a professor of Talmud at Yeshiva University, where Yiddish poet J. L. Teller studied with him. Naftoli Gross, the elder brother of the sculptor, was a well-known Yiddish poet and writer. Chaim Gross, Ben Shahn, Max Weber, Abraham Walkowitz, and others illustrated books of Yiddish literature. Louis Lozowick edited a book in Yiddish and English, *100 Contemporary American Jewish Painters and Sculptors*, published by the leftist Yiddish Cultural Association (YKUF).

The woodcuts and linoleum blocks by Max Weber reproduced in this volume were originally published in the Yiddish literary journal *Shriftn*, which was dominated by the writers of the Young Generation, in the years 1919–1926. As Weber's biographer noted: "the reproductions in *Shriftn*, printed in black ink on off-white paper, were the exact size of the original prints and were characterized by a delicacy and fine clarity of line and form, particularly evident when compared with the later, flatter, and more heavily inked reproductions in *Primitives* (1926)." (Daryl R. Rubenstein, *Max Weber; A Catalogue Raisonne of his Graphic Work*, University of

21. Ibid., p. 15.

Chicago Press, 1980). As Rubenstein points out, "there is no record that Weber titled any of his relief prints." Subsequent identifying titles were of two kinds; A "Jewish" and a cosmopolitan label, sometimes attached to the same figure (e.g., Rabbi Reading/Pensioned, or Rabbi/Face with a Beard).

Raphael Soyer: *Reading from Left to Right*, 1937.

Max Weber wrote and published poetry in Yiddish in the style of impressionist primitivism, describing the snow as a land of pure white nymphs or evoking "the big city of Cubist forms—New York." All of a sudden, in a poem entitled "Chanukah Candles" (*Shriftn*, 1920), we read:

> I was seeking the miracle of Chanukah/ and instead, I found our eternal miracle./ Here, in a tiny store, far from Zion,/ Where the old, grey, pious Jew stands/ like a sign, an echo of bygone times,/ He stands for the whole Jewish people. Eternal, eternal, eternal is the Jewish people!/ Eternal— / The eternal Chanukah miracle among peoples of the world.

Yiddish poets did it in a more sophisticated way.

Little by little, with age, recollections of childhood, and perhaps the need to join a social "tribe," some of the artists returned to memories of the world of their fathers and tried their hand at "Jewish" themes. Artificially tied to Orthodox religious iconography and Eastern-European stereotypes—and unavoidably so, because there were no separate visual signs for modern Jews or Jewish concerns—these paintings could not really express the artist's contemporary personality (as poems could) and often fell below the same artist's highest standards. As in Yiddish poetry, a wave of return to Jewish topics came in the wake of the Holocaust and the creation of the State of Israel. One solution was found by Ben Shahn. Reliving in his later work the world of Hebrew learning of his early childhood in Lithuania, Shahn made graphic art of the letters of the Hebrew alphabet, in their mystical apotheosis as God's tools in the creation of the world. He also turned to biblical proverbs, types, and motifs, rather than to the usual Eastern-European religious figures. Hebrew letters, the elementary vestiges of a culture, also appeared in the work of other artists, such as Louis Lozowick, Chaim Gross, and Leonard Baskin.

The tension between Jewish and universal iconography is subordinated to another tension—that between various demands of artistic form or, more specifically, the language of Modernism on the one hand and the challenges of confronting the real or mythological America on the other. Though most of these artists were highly aware both of Modernism and of the centrality of the language of art, they rarely represented an extreme artistic dogma; rather, they compromised under the pressures of an American expressive realism. This may have been due to a combination of their Jewish condition, the immediacy of social problems in America, the Socialist trends of Jewish New York (especially in the 1930s), and the lack of an aristocratic, isolated stance of high culture in American art as compared to Paris. Lozowick formulated this tension in the form of an ideal solution: "A composition is most effective when its elements are used in a double function: associative, establishing contact with concrete objects of the real world and aesthetic, serving to create plastic values." Indeed, Lozowick's own art was much closer to the first function than was Lissitzky's.

The uneasy compromise between the language of art and the demands of a message, between Modernism and realism, between being Jewish and creating human art was common to these artists and to the Yiddish poets. In both groups, it caused a hesitation between short periods of fully committed Modernist experimentation and the return to more eclectic responses—responses that were more "literary" in art and more "conversational" in poetry, and perhaps more human and emotional as well. This prevented the formation of a clear-cut Modernist "school" in American art until World War II.

When the dominant trend in America became abstract art, the Jewish topic all but disappeared, not only because there were more American-born artists among the Abstract Expressionists but because there were no more recognizable mimetic themes in their paintings. The participation of Jews in this new wave was even greater than it had been in previous movements. Thus, in 1935, when Mark Rothko joined a group of artists, "The Ten" ("The Ten Who are Nine") they were, apparently, all Jews. Indeed, in some comments by Newman or Rothko, one can detect allusions to Jewish mysticism. (And who would deny that abstraction is a Jewish tendency in this theoretical and scientific age?) But this was part of their wider cultural background, as was the case of most Yiddish poets.

Comparing various tendencies in the two domains of poetry and art, their historical unfolding in the context of American society, and even individual items, one is struck by many parallels, despite the radical difference between the two media and the lack of real contact between the poets and artists themselves. Max Weber's Cubist-inspired "Rush Hour" was described by a critic as "conveying the maddening unrest and visual diversity by means of a fuguelike composition in which fierce verticals alternate with vigorous diagonals."[22] The fugue is a central theme in Leyeles's theory of free rhythms; the interest in rhythm and in geometrical forms was shared both by several painters of the early 1920s and by Leyeles (see, e.g., his "Symmetry"). "Rush Hour" evoked many Yiddish poems (see the poems by Halpern and Leyeles in this anthology), both because Jews had to use the subways and because their poetry was alert to the myth of the big city, which they brought from Europe and fully confronted in New York. The same mood is expressed in Walkowitz's geometrical paintings of the "Metropolis" and in Leyeles's hymns to big-city architecture.

This adoration of technology did not last long, however. A more inward, introspective, and individualistic conception ensued, as seen in Leyeles's *Fabius Lind*, in Teller's *Miniatures*, and in Soyer's paintings. A striking parallel can be seen in the defiant, unsentimental, independent look of Gross's "East Side Girl" of 1928 and Glatshteyn's "Girl of My Generation," published in *Credos* in the same year. At the same time, a poetry of the proletarian, harsh, ugly side of the city evolved, as exemplified by Halpern and Vaynshteyn and by some of the painting of the 1930s.

Both in the sculpture and paintings by Jewish artists and in American Yiddish poetry, Jewish elements were subdued and, if present at all, were used as a language to describe the human condition. But with the awareness of what was happening to the Jews in Europe, especially after the Holocaust, poets and artists of Jewish origin naturally felt the need to respond to the theme and to meditate on problems of Jewish history, identity, and symbolism. An interesting parallel can be seen in the return to the basic atoms of Jewishness, the letters of the Hebrew alphabet: for Lozowick, they became the material for a new constructivist edifice; for Ben Shahn,

22. Alfred Werner, *Max Weber*, New York: Abrams, 1975.

they were the elements of creation, molded in a hieroglyphic-like organically unified body that became his artist's logo; and for Leyeles, they were a divine provocation for a people of texts and interpretations. All of these evolved at about the same time (see the opening of this anthology).

There was, however, a radical difference between the two domains that are brought together here for the first time. Both reflected similar problems of art in the twentieth century and may have been influenced by the same American ambience. But their social existence was profoundly different. While some of the artists occasionally maintained their ties with Yiddish literature, their natural allegiance was to the realm of American art, created and received by all Americans regardless of origin. As Raphael Soyer put it:

> I came to the United States at the age of twelve and have lived here ever since. I have benefitted by all the advantages it has to offer one: schools, museums, art galleries and libraries. My work has been influenced by the multi-ethnical character and the pluralistic culture of this country.

An artist, born to Jewish parents or not, could chose whether to demonstrate his origins or to bypass them altogether. Some of the Yiddish poets would have liked to do the same; indeed, one of the fascinations that the communist ambience held for them lay precisely in the possibility of freedom from being Jewish without, however, having to deny it. But the ghetto of their language (as Glatshteyn dubbed it) cast the Yiddish poets back into the isolated magic circle of a Yiddish newspaper culture and steeped them in Jewish problems—perhaps more than some of them had wanted to be in their youth.

The parallel presented in this book between the graphic art and Yiddish poetry of Jewish Americans is not intended to obliterate their obvious differences. Rather, it is meant to shed new light on the Americanism of Yiddish poetry and its validity as an expression of American art. Yiddish poetry was one mode of the great trend of Jews to join general Western culture and contribute to it. The obsession of Yiddish poets with poetic form, though a legacy of Russian Symbolism, was part of a wider move to embrace the beautiful, to join the aesthetic domain as one way out of the ghetto. The hunger of young Jews for art emanated from the same impulse, though it obviously had specific causes in each particular biography.

SELECTION

The aim of this selection is to introduce the reader to some of the concerns and transformations of twentieth-century American poetry in Yiddish via the work of several representative poets. As befits an anthology, we chose not to discuss the poetry in the introduction but to provide some background information, letting the reader both discover those works and topics that may interest him and construct his own interpretations.

The value judgments used in the selection were so complex that it would be hard to make them explicit in a general manner. A pluralistic perspective was our guide. It is our conviction that there is no single recipe for good or interesting poetry, that literature is valuable not in exemplifying one code or set of values but in providing a variety of possibilities of expression in language. Anything that can be formed in fictional texts and conveyed through language, or any aspect of the language of poetry itself, may become an asset of art. Poems were chosen for their interesting images, rhetoric, fictional situations, or thematic conceptions. The general bias, admittedly, was that of the poetic taste developed in the Modernist period, but we used a much more open door and more relaxed standards. It would make no sense to select merely those poems that follow Anglo-American Modernist norms. The considerable body of texts presented here is intended to enable the reader to move closer to the world and the norms which are inherent in Yiddish poetry itself and which appealed to its native readers. We did not intend each poem to be a masterpiece. Sometimes a poem was selected for its experimental merits, its documentary interest, or its programmatic value in representing an author's point of view at a certain period, to be read in conjunction with the other poems by the same author or with the historical and thematic background of the period.

Selection and disproportion were our principles on all levels. We selected a few poets from a large literature. Each poet was represented in one period or mode more than in another. The text itself was often chosen from several versions. The idea was to provide a general panorama of the field, to show its major themes and forms in the book as a whole rather than to do justice to all the poets who worked in it. We preferred to provide sufficient bodies of texts for particular aspects or groups of poems—to achieve the impact that a cycle or a book of poetry may have—rather than to give samples of all the periods, aspects, or ideological positions of each poet. For example, we selected a large group of poems from Berysh Vaynshteyn's first book, *Broken Pieces*, which confront a whole complex of his harsh and semi-surrealist naturalism—the waterfront, the junkyards, the slaughterhouses in New York, the black experience, and the author's old-country underworld perspective—but only a few poems from his other periods. By the same token, the Holocaust is represented here in many poems by Glatshteyn and Teller, who found a personal mode of responding to the catastrophe, and fewer such poems were included by others, though every living Yiddish poet wrote about it.

One problem was what to do about poems that did not lend themselves to translation. In a purely Yiddish anthology, a number of additional poems would have been included—especially poems containing what would be felt in Yiddish to be a charming meter and musicality with little paraphrasable content, or poems relying heavily on language play and language creativity. In collections of translations from Yiddish, one often encounters rather weak and helpless texts originating in impressive Yiddish lyrics. To some extent, translation efforts expose the flimsiness of such poems—what Glatshteyn called their thoughtless and contentless quality—but in many cases, it is a loss that cannot be compensated for in translation. Here, too, we made a compromise. In several cases we included such a poem, knowing that it is untranslatable or that our translation is insufficient, but relying on the original poem for those who can read it.

Another problem lies in a possible contradiction between the strivings of the poets themselves and the motivations for an interest in Yiddish literature displayed by some contemporary readers. While many readers turn to Yiddish poetry as part of their interest in Jewish topics, much of Yiddish poetry itself—like contemporary Israeli poetry—was fueled by a double intention: to express the poet's individuality, for which poetry was especially suited in a politicized society, and to address "universal" topics and the challenges of art in language.

TRANSLATION

The same principles of pluralism that informed the selection process guided the translations as well. In some cases we invested efforts in translating the poetic form, meter, and rhyme in order to represent that aspect of Yiddish poetry; with other poems, some of the formal aspects were abandoned or free verse was elected instead.

This problem is more fundamental than it would seem. On the one hand, of course, there is the simple difficulty of translation, both subjective (our own limitations) and objective: what is an organic unity of sound and meaning in one language cannot be matched directly in another. The poem has to be decomposed and each level translated in its own right, then merged into a new organic unity. There is no way that one can be faithful to the full meaning of the original while preserving the verse patterns. In some cases we paid attention to the form, at least in part, assuming that the precise words were less important and that the poem makes no impact without its symmetrical form and rhyme. In other cases we were more faithful to the meanings and poetic language than to the versification, trying to convey the rhythmical tone through a variety of free rhythmical techniques. These range from almost metrical regularities—through the widespread accentual meters of Yiddish (and English) folksong, which use regular numbers of stresses (3 or 4) and limited freedom of unstressed syllables (1 or 2)—to an individualized balancing of phrases and interactions between syntax and verse line, subordinated to the dominant tone of a text: conversational, hymnical, lyrical and intimate, or tense and staccato.

There is, on the other hand, a more profound reason for abandoning the precise original meters in translation. Translating poetry means translating not only into another language but also into the climate and "language" of another poetry. The value and position of metrical verse has changed in English poetry during the twentieth century. When translated precisely, the symmetrical meters and well-rhymed strophes or iambic couplets, employed in Yiddish even by Modernist poets, would create the effect of a jingle or of a naive, trite, and old-fashioned form, which is not at all their status in the context of Yiddish poetry. It is the same problem as translating Goethe or Pushkin in their original metrical forms, let alone the Modernist masters, Rilke, Mandelshtam, or Pasternak.

Furthermore, a translation—unless it is a re-creation, an English alternative made by an English poet—cannot dare to make innovations in unexpected rhymes or coin many new words unknown to the target language, as the poet did in the original. At best, it can offer yet another example of the same, known meter, losing the effects of subtle deviation and freshness of the original. There is no real solution to this problem except to translate into the dominant form of contemporary American poetry—namely, free verse—accompanied by a recommendation to read the original. In some cases, however, especially when the form and language sounded more classical, as in Leyeles's sonnet garland, "Autumn," we did make an effort to preserve the original meter.

Two additional, almost insurmountable difficulties are: (1) the poetic value derived in Yiddish poetry from the play with synonymous alternatives and clashes between words from its component languages, since Yiddish still has a high degree of component-consciousness and relatively open boundaries toward those languages; and (2) the profusion of allusions, hints, and stylistic ironies relating to the codified worlds of its Hebrew heritage, Yiddish folklore, and Slavic realities—a background largely unfamiliar to English-speaking readers—which are almost a matter of course in Yiddish and provide it with a rich texture.

These untranslatable properties of Yiddish poetry were enhanced by the Modernist awareness of the art in language. Together, they make any translation pale vis-à-vis the connotative semantic density and sound-orchestration of the original text. Since the force of Yiddish poetry rarely depended on profound philosophical statements, this loss is felt even more than it otherwise would be.

66
*American
Yiddish
Poetry
and its
Background*

TEXT

The selection of the Yiddish texts themselves was not an easy task. There are almost no critical editions of modern Yiddish poetry, and many published books contain obvious misprints as well as inconsistencies in punctuation (a painful subject in Yiddish!). Yiddish poets, like their English contemporaries, made various changes in later editions of their early poetry. One reason was the changing times, especially in the case of collected writings that appeared after World War II (e.g., Vaynshteyn or his editors excluded the "Germans" from the list of immigrant groups on the New York waterfront). Another reason can be found in the usual changes made by many poets in their later years, when they become more ideological and socially responsible, and less sensuous and immediate in perception. On the whole, we preferred the text as published in its first book form to texts that appeared in collected writings, because the earlier version really reflects the date and period of its writing and the unified conception of the poem.

In some cases, however, we accepted the obvious corrections of later editions. On several occasions we used poems not reprinted by the poet himself in his collected writings (e.g., some striking responses by Glatshteyn to the early signs of the Holocaust). On several other occasions, we restored the original version as published in a journal at the time. Unfortunately, it would take us too far afield to search out the first versions of all poems in a literature that had its home in newspapers and ephemeral publications. Let us make a virtue of the lack and assume that collecting a poem in a book is the first stage of cultural selection, made by the author himself.

Thus, in most cases, the Yiddish text that appears here is the first version published in book form. To a limited extent, this text was amended from a later version, obvious misprints were corrected, and in a few cases, the punctuation was slightly touched up. We were very careful about this. We preferred leaving lines either without any punctuation or with a strange mark to making unnecessary changes. But because this may be the authoritative text for many readers, we did try to make it readable, except for cases in which any decision would be arbitrary. It is a mistake to assume that the texts of later re-editions or of collected poems are cleaner than the original publication. Glatshteyn's book, *Fun mayn gantser mi* (From All My Toil), lavishly published in 1956, at the height of his fame, is riddled with typographical errors, haphazard changes, and sloppy punctuation. Halpern's manuscripts, lovingly published posthumously in 1934, still await a careful text editor: dozens of versions for many poems are extant in his archive at YIVO, but it is very hard to decide which version preceded which. (In one case, we translated two versions of a poem "My Crying-Out-Loud," as published in two different posthumous volumes; the reader is invited to guess which is later and why.) Given the disconnected composition in Halpern's later poetry, one feels inclined to shuffle around some rhymed couplets, especially in his "What I Said to My Only Son at Play—and to Nobody Else," but we left this to puzzle-oriented readers.

We also dared in several cases to select not whole poems but excerpts (always indicated by lines of dots). The reasons vary from the possibility this gives us to absorb such long poems as Leyvik's "The Wolf" to the feeling that Yiddish poetry was often too talkative and repetitive and that a translation into another poetic language must (carefully!) consider that aspect, too—that is, see a part of a text as a sufficiently effective and independent whole.

Changes from this general principle of selecting a version of the Yiddish text and major emendations are discussed in the footnotes. The Yiddish spelling was unified, as described in the "Note on Transcription and Spelling."

Unlike most anthologies of Yiddish poetry in translation, the poems here have been placed in their historical context. For lack of proper bibliographical tools, we did not date each individual poem (unless the author did so), but grouped the poems chronologically according to the books in which they were originally published (and in the order in which they appeared in the book). The date and name of the book appear at the head of each section. The reader will surely supply the relevant parallel events from the history of the period.

American Yiddish Poetry

A. Leyeles

1889–1966

The poet A. Leyeles was one of the founders of Introspectivism in New York in 1919 and its chief theoretician of free verse. He was a major poet on the American theme in Yiddish, a writer with a rich and precise intellectual Yiddish language, and probably the most interesting and inventive master of verse and strophic forms in modern Yiddish literature. Many of his early views on poetry are discussed in the introductory section on Introspectivism, and excerpts of his critical writings are reproduced in the "Chronicle of a Movement" (see appendix A).

Leyeles was born as Aron Glanz in Wloclawek, Poland (then under Russian rule), and grew up in the city of Lodz, where his father taught in a modern Hebrew school and occasionally wrote for the Hebrew newspaper, *Ha-Melits*. He finished Hebrew school and a Russian commercial school and, in 1905, immigrated to London. He studied at London University and was active in the S.-S. (Zionist-Socialist) party.

At the end of 1909, Glanz came to New York, where he studied at Columbia University, was active in the Socialist-Territorialist party (which strove for a Jewish state outside of Palestine), and participated in the organization of Yiddish schools in the United States. He was among the founders and was a teacher at the first Yiddish school on Henry Street in New York, and helped to build Yiddish schools in Toronto, Winnipeg, Rochester, and Sioux City, Iowa. In 1913–14, he was director of the Yiddish National-Radical School in Chicago and later taught at various institutions of Yiddish higher education. Leyeles was a moving force and cofounder of many Jewish cultural organizations, such as the Workmans Circle schools, the Central Yiddish Cultural Organization, and the World Jewish Culture Congress. In public life he became known as A. Glanz-Leyeles. For many years, he served as president of the international Yiddish P.E.N. Club. He participated in many periodicals and was editor or coeditor of several of them.

From 1914 on, A. Glanz was a staff member of the New York Yiddish daily, *Der Tog* (The Day), where he edited several sections, wrote on political and topical matters, and contributed a weekly column of literary criticism, "World and Word,"

Joseph Foshko: *A. Leyeles*, 1939.

in which he reviewed books of Yiddish and world literature. Under various pseudonyms, as well as his own name, A. Glanz wrote hundreds of articles on literary and political themes, repeatedly attacking Stalinist Communism, among others. He was aware of the damage newspaper writing may do to the style of a poet and tried to keep the two domains apart. Nevertheless, his own journalism did rub off on his later writings, especially on his literary criticism and, to some extent, on his poetry.

His first published book was political and was written in German: *Der Territorialismus ist die einzige Lösung der Judenfrage* (Territorialism Is the Only Solution to the Jewish Question; Zurich, 1913). He translated books, poems, and other texts from German, Russian, Polish, and English into Yiddish, among them two volumes of a German book of aesthetics, Broder Christiansen's *Art: The Philosophy of Art*, which had influenced the Russian Formalists, and Leo Trotsky's *The Russian Revolution* (published in installments in the daily newspaper *Der Tog* in 1931–32). He also wrote two ambitious historical messianic dramas, *Shlomo Molkho* (1926) and *Asher Lemlin* (1928), and a drama on the struggle between Stalin and Trotsky. Leyeles was twice awarded the prestigious Louis Lamed Prize for his books of poetry, *A Jew in the Sea* (1948) and *At the Foot of the Mountain* (1958).

In his childhood, Glanz wrote poems in Russian; later, he published Yiddish poems in New York using several pen names. In 1914 the first poems under the name A. Leyeles appeared in the anarchist *Di Fraye Arbeter Shtime* (The Free Workers' Voice) a newspaper with excellent literary taste. From his first book, he was a champion of Modernism. However, in *Labyrinth* (1918) and *Young-Autumn* (1922), tendencies of Aestheticism and Neo-Romantic moods are still strongly felt. In *Rondeaux and Other Poems* (1926), there is a celebration of urbanism, the architectural creations of man, the power of New York, the mystical aspects of time-space, abstraction, rhythm, and symmetry, along with restrained and slightly ironic personal poems of desentimentalized experiences. This volume is also a celebration of form, from various difficult classical strophic compositions that Leyeles "conquered" for the Yiddish language to a whole gamut of free-verse experiments, including staccato rhythms, dynamic free verse with rich sound-orchestration, and ironic-conversational poems.

Leyeles's next book, *Fabius Lind* (1937), is a complete reversal: here the urbanism is expressed not in hymns to the architecture of New York but in poems of the alienation and isolation of a sophisticated, uncompromising, stubborn individual, along with increasingly pessimistic poems on political themes, all embedded in a kaleidoscopic diary of his objectified alter ego, Fabius Lind, and written in a colorful variety of free-verse and metrical forms. The book opens with two poems looking back to his roots: "My Father" and "My Mother." Rather than nostalgia for a distant, bygone world, these poems express thoughtful ruminations on the sources of his character and lot, as Leyeles registers in Fabius Lind's diary:

> I inherited naive open-heartedness
> From generations of small-town Polish Jews,
> And sharp talk
> From hot-bathed women in my clan.
> A blind June-night mixed it all
> And sent me out—
> With no regard for symmetry.
>
> ("February 7")

As Jacob Glatshteyn summed it up in his essay, "The Figure of Fabius Lind" (*In Zikh*, April 1937),

> Fabius Lind delivers it all as a key to his colorful restlessness and to the tragic reflection of all the knowledge and understanding that he has amassed—not as tatters but as roots. Leyeles constructs the character of Fabius Lind with an amazing dramatic versatility and through the whole tangle of restless, almost catastrophical ten years, he gives us the ultimate, the person at the very bottom, the Fabius Lind who seeks rest in the perfection of stasis, in the calm high noon, in the sated sunniness and in the "ecstasy of the evening sun." He seeks the gelid calm in his "Etude," "Commradery," "Antelopes," in models of cool beauty, and reaches out, in the poem "February 12," to the intimacy of death.

The introduction to *Fabius Lind* contains a bitter settling of accounts with Leyeles's critics and a restatement of the principles of Introspectivism. Indeed, the philistine critics of the newspapers—and, worse, in communist circles—demanded "hymns to two-times-two" and accused him of "knowing": Leyeles *knows* how to write poems, he does not *have to*. (There is a pun in Yiddish: *muz* means "have to, must" and *muze* is the "muse.") Such was the atmosphere of Yiddish mass culture in New York. Leyeles again explains his "anti-emotionalist and anti-rationalist" Modernism: "It is, first of all, an *intellectual* method that wants to feel but, not less—to know." And he proclaims: "Poetry is that which an important poet creates. . . . Between *Labyrinth* and *Fabius Lind* a new standard emerged in Yiddish poetry."

A. Leyeles at the offices of
"Der Tog."

"Twenty-six generations before
the creation of the world, the
twenty-two letters of the alphabet
descended from the crown of
God whereon they were engraved
with a pen of flaming fire. They
gathered around God and one
after another spoke and
entreated, each one, that the
world be created through him."
(Cf. **The Alphabet of Creation:**
An ancient legend from the
Zohar with drawings by Ben
Shahn, [New York: Schocken
Books, 1954].)

◄ דער גאָט פֿון ישׂראל

דער גאָט פֿון ישׂראל איז נישט רײַך.
כ׳האָב געזען די סיסטינער קאַפּליצע,
די נאַטר-דאַם, דעם דאָם פֿון קעלן.
ס׳איז דאָ דאָס אויג צו לאָבן, צו געפֿעלן.

דער גאָט פֿון ישׂראל איז קאַרג.
ער וויל נישט אָנפֿילן זײַן מוזיי מיט סטאַטוען,
מיט געמעלן, אַלטאַרן, טראָג-שטולן,
פֿורפֿורנע קליידער, דרײַי-גאָרנדיקע קרוינען,
ער וויל אין קיין פֿאַלייען נישט ווינען.
דער ייִדישער מוזיי האָט ווינציק פֿאַרשוינען.

Louis Lozowick: *Hebraica I.*

► *The God of Israel*

This poem was first published in
A Jew in the Sea, 1947.

The God of Israel is not rich.
I saw the Sistine Chapel,
Notre-Dame, the Cathedral of Cologne—
You can feast your eyes on them, you can enjoy.

The God of Israel is stingy.
He won't fill his museum with statues,
Paintings, altars, thrones,
Purple gowns, three-tiered crowns,
He does not wish to live in a Palais.
The Jewish museum has a modest display.

אַ חנוכּה-לעמפּל, אַ פּרוכת, אַ מגילה,

אַ בשׂמים-ביקסל, אַ תּפילין-זעקל, אַ יד,

אַ מנורה, כּתר-תּורה, מכשירים פאַר מילה,

און אַ פאַרצײַטיקער, פאַר-פאַרצײַטיקער כּתב-יד.

נאָך אַ מאַנוסקריפּט און נאָך אַ מאַנוסקריפּט,

געוויקלט, געבונדן, פאַרקניפּט,

אותיות אין אותיות פאַרליבט.

װאָס װיל דער גאָט פון ישׂראל?

װאָס מאַנט דער גאָט פון ישׂראל?

דער גאָט פון ישׂראל איז אַ גערעכטער מאַנער.

דער גאָט פון ישׂראל איז אַ שטרענגער מאַנער.

דער גאָט פון ישׂראל איז אַ קאַרגער מאַנער:

זוך אַליין, פאָרש אַליין, לײַד אַליין —

פאַר דײַן און פאַר מײַן אייגענעם האַנער.

האָט ער גענומען אין אַ גרוי-גרויען אַמאָל,

און פון אַ באַרג-אַראָפּ אין אַ טאָל,

געוואָרפן צוויי הויפנס אותיות,

זיי צעשאָטן איבער די װעגן פון דער ערד.

זיי האָבן געפינקלט מיט רייד, מיט מימראָס געפלעמלט,

און פון דעמאָלט —

שיין טויזנטער יאָרן װי מען זוכט זיי,

שיין טויזנטער יאָרן װי מען קלײַבט זיי,

שיין טויזנטער יאָרן װי מען טײַטשט זיי,

און נאָך אַלץ נישטאָ קיין באַשייד,

פאַר די אותיות, פאַר די מימראָס, פאַר די רייד.

נאָך אַ מאַנוסקריפּט, און נאָך אַ מאַנוסקריפּט,

געוויקלט, געבונדן, פאַרקניפּט —

אותיות אין אותיות פאַרליבט.

A Chanukah-lamp, a curtain, a scroll,
A spice-box, tefillin, a pointing Hand,
A menorah, a Torah Crown, tools for circumcision,
And an old, ancient manuscript.
And another manuscript and another manuscript,
Entangled, bound, locked together.
Letters in love with letters.

What does the God of Israel ask?
What does the God of Israel demand?
The God of Israel is a just demander.
The God of Israel is a strict demander.
The God of Israel is a stingy demander:
Search by yourself, research by yourself, suffer yourself—
For your own and for my honor.

In a gray-gray once-upon-a-time,
From a mountain-top into a valley,
He dropped two handfuls of letters,
Scattered them over the roads of the earth.
They sparkled with speech, blazed with sayings,
And since then—
For thousands of years we seek them,
For thousands of years we save them,
For thousands of years we explain them,
And there is no solution on earth
For the letters, the sayings, the words.

Another manuscript, and another manuscript,
Entangled, bound, locked together—
Letters in love with letters.

**Chanukah-lamp*, curtain
(Poroykhes*), scroll*,
spice-box*, tefillin*, pointing
hand*, menorah*, Torah
crown***—Jewish religious
objects (see glossary).

Ben Shahn: Figure from *The
Alphabet of Creation.*

◄ ווינטער-נאַכט סאָנעט

עס קרייזט די זון מיט אירע פלאַמען,
און אַלפֿאַ קרייזט אין הימלס צעלט.
די וועלט און איך, איך און די וועלט:
מיר רייזן צופֿעליק צוזאַמען.

איר קימערט ניט, וואָס מיר געפֿעלט,
און ס'קימערט מיך ניט, צי עס שטאַמען
די בני-כנען פֿון שוואַרצן חמען,
און צי אַנטאָניוס איז אַ העלד.

און טענות האָב איך ניט צו קיינעם,
און קיינער קומט מיר ניט קיין זאַך,
איך שלאָף מיין שלאָף און לאַך מיין לאַך.

און אין אַ טאָג (פֿילייכט אַ שיינעם)
וועל איך מיר זאָגן: צייט. פֿאַרמאַך
די אויגן. אַ-ליע-ליו. גוט-נאַכט...

◄ ניו-יאָרק

מעטאַל. גראַניט. געוויש. געבראַזג. געפֿילדער.
אויטאָמאָבילן. הויך-באַן. טיף-באַן. קאַר.
בורלעסק. גראָטעסק. קאַפֿעען. קינאָ-בילדער.
עלעקטריש ליכט אין גרילציקן ווירוואַר.

געזיכטער פֿרעמד און בליקן פֿול געפֿאַר,
קיין שמייכל, קיין גאָט-העלף, קיין נויג, קיין מילדער.
און בלאַנדזשעניש, און הענגענדיקער גזר,
און דזשונגל, און געדרענג און אומזין ווילדער.

► *Winter-Night Sonnet*

The sun revolves in its red flames,
And Alpha circles in sky's tent.
The world and me, me and the world:
We travel together by accident.

It does not care what I prefer,
And I don't care to know or hear
Whether the Canaanites were black
Or whether Antony's a hero.

I don't complain to anyone,
And no one owes me anything,
I sleep my sleep and smile my smile.

And one fine day (perhaps—quite bright)
I'll say to me: You had your while.
It's time now. Shut your eyes. Good-night.

Joseph Foshko: Title page of
Labyrinth, 1918.

► *New York*

Metal. Granite. Uproar. Racket. Clatter.
Automobile. Bus. Subway. El.
Burlesque. Grotesque. Café. Movie-theater.
Electric light in screeching maze. A spell.

In eyes—a pending verdict, faces—strangers:
No smile, no Bless-you, no nod, no gentle word.
And straying, rambling, imminent danger.
And jungle, crush, upheaval, wild absurd.

This poem, famous for its
staccato rhythm, is presented
here in its later version, as
published in the book, *America
and I*, 1956.

◄ שלעסער

שלעסער —
שלעסער פֿון אײַזן געבױט און גראַניט,
שלעסער פֿון מאַרמאָר און פֿון מאַלאַכיט,
שלעסער פֿון בראָנדז און געגאָסענעם שטאָל,
שלעסער, און שלעסער, און שלעסער אָן צאָל.

שלעסער —
ביבליאָטעקן און מוזעומס,
מאָנומענטן, מאַוזאָלעומס,
טעמפּלען, קירכן, קאַטעדראָלן,
אַלע שלעסער —
איצטער פֿאַלן, פֿאַלן, פֿאַלן.

אָבער מײַנע שלעסער —
געבױט פֿון פֿאַרלאַנגען,
טעגלעכע זוכעניש, נאַכטלעכע באַנגען,
רעגונגען, זעונגען,
שטרעבונגען, װוּנטשן;
געפֿלאַכטן, געשפּונען
פֿון װײַטע לבֿנות און װײַטערע זונען,
פֿון האַרצנס-באַגערן,
װאָס הערן
ניט אױף פֿון דעם האַרצן צו שטראַלן:

מײַנע שלעסער קאָנען קיין מאָל
ניט פֿאַלן, ניט פֿאַלן, ניט פֿאַלן.

◄ װײַסקײט

שנייִיקע װײַסקײט אַרום.
װײַסע רױקייט אַרום.
דאָך קאָן זיך קיין יאַנואַר-שניי נישט פֿאַרגלײַכן
צו דער װײַסקײט און רױקייט,
װאָס קנױלט זיך פֿונאַנדער
און שפּרייט זיך אױס אַזױ װײַך
אַ מאָל אין אַ יולי-נאָכמיטאָג —
אין מיר.

➤ *Castles*

Castles—
Castles of iron and of granite,
Castles of marble and of malachite,
Castles of bronze, of steel, of cement,
Castles, and castles, and castles no end.

Castles—
Libraries and museums,
Monuments, mausoleums,
Temples, cathedrals, halls,
All the castles—
Now fall, fall, fall.

But my castles—
Built of urgings,
Daily searching, nightly yearning,
Sensations, visions,
Strivings, wishes;
Desires—
Braided, spun
By distant moons and distant suns—
Rays of my heart
That won't stop at all:

My castles can never
Fall, fall, fall.

➤ *Whiteness*

Snow whiteness all around.
White calm.
But what January snow can compare
With the whiteness and calm
That unfold
And spread out, so softly,
On a July-afternoon—
Within me.

העל צינדן זיך דעם יונגהאַרבסטס צאַרטע, גאָלדענע קופּאַלן.
פון מערבס פערלמוטער וווייט מיט שמאַכטיק־רייפן אַראָמאַט.
די גראָזן זיפּצן לינד און מאַט, מיט בענקשאַפט פלאַטערט צווייג און בלאַט,
אום יעדן בוים־שפּיץ לייכטן יונגהאַרבסטס באַנגע אָרעאָלן.
די לייכטע וואָלקנס שטייען אויסגעהאַקטע — מינאַרעטן אין באַגדאַד.
אָט גליטשן זיי זיך פויליע — וועענציאַנישע גאָנדאָלן.
דער הימל שפּרייט זיין זילבער־צער אויף יונגהאַרבסטס גאָלדענע שאָלן
און פאַנגט מיין האַרץ אין רייפן־קלעם פון מעלאַנכאָלישן בראָקאַט.

אין אָט דעם צויבער־רייך פון בלייכער רו און פאַרביקן פאַרפום
שפּרייז איך, מיין גאָלדענע, און רוף דיך שטיל און זוך דיך שטיל אַרום —
דו ביסט נישט האַרבסט־גאָלד; ביסט שפּעט־פרילינגס ליד, וואָס פריט און טוט דאָך ווי.
דער מאָרגנרייך פון מיזרח; דער טאַנץ פון מערבס לעצטער אָוונט־פעע.

וועענעדיג און באַגדאַד! אילוזיע מיין, אילוזיע פיינלעך־שיין,
איך בענק נאָך דיר מיט אַלע בענקשאַפטן פון יונגהאַרבסט און פאַרגיין.

לאַנגע רייען הויכע שטיינערנע גלאַדיאָלן.
ווייטער פליעסק פון ווייַט גליטשנדיע גאָנדאָלן.
ציטער־שיין פון טויטע, גאָלדענע קופּאַלן.
איך — אַליין.

שלאָס פון קאַלטע, בלישטשענדיקע כריזאָפּראַזן.
אומעטום — דראַקאָנען־בייכעדיקע וואַזן.
טראָן פון בלאָלעך־גרינלעך־געלבלעכע טאָפּאַזן.
איך — אַ שטיין.

געצן — שטערנס קופּער, אויגן פון רובינען,
געצן — לענדן מעש, מיט אויגן פון בורשטינען,
קומען בוויגן, נויגן, בוקן זיך און דינען,
דינען מיר.

און זיי זינגען: ס'שפּילט אוראָראַ באַראָאַליס,
ס'בענקט די בענקעניש פון אַלע פרינצן־אַליס,
ס'טרוימט דער בלאָער טרוים פון בלאָנדן דייַטש נאָוואַליס,
בלויז פאַר דיר.

➤ *Young-Autumn*

Bright—Young-Autumn's delicate gold cupolas ignite,
A languid-ripe aroma wafts from West's mother-of-pearl.
Soft and opaque, the sigh of grass; in longing flutter leaf and twig;
On every treetop, Young-Autumn-pensive aureoles light up.
Light clouds stand hewn high in the sky—now minarets in Baghdad,
Now gliding lazily like gondolas in Venice.
The sky spreads silver-sadness on Young-Autumn's golden shells
And grips my heart in hoops of melancholy brocade.

In this enchanted realm of pallid calm and colorful perfume
I stroll, my golden love, I call you softly, seek you silently—
You are not Autumn-gold, you are Late-Spring's song, joy and pain,
East's charm-of-dawn, the dance of West's last evening fay.

Baghdad and Venice! My illusion, painfully beautiful illusion,
I long for you with all the longings of Young-Autumn and decay.

➤ *Tao*

Long colonnades of slender, stone gladiolas.
Distant splash of far-off gliding gondolas.
Tremble-light of dying golden cupolas.
I—alone.

Castle of cold, sparkling chrysoprase.
All around me—dragon-bellied vases.
Throne of blue-green-yellowish topaz.
I—a stone.

Idols—copper foreheads, ruby eyes,
Idols—loins of brass, and amber eyes,
Come to bow, and stoop, and bring advice,
Serving me.

And they sing: it is the music of Aurora Borealis,
And it is the longing of all Princes Ali's,
The blue dream of the blond German Novalis,
All—for me.

און זיי בעטן: גיב אַ קלאַפ אין דיינע טאַצן,

גיב אַ פאַך מיט דיינע גאָלדענע פאַלאַצן,

זאָלן פאַרבן-פאַנצער, טרוים און בענקשאַפט, פלאַצן,

שנעל — צעשטער!

און זיי וואָרענען: ס׳האָט אונדז מיד געמאַכט דער כאַאָס,

מיד דער שטרענגער, ווייַטער, גרויזאַמער צבאות,

איצטער זיינען מיר אויך מיד פון דיר, אַ טאַאָס.

שוין. נישט מער.

הער דו אויף מיט דיינע אָפּפער פון קאָלירן,

מיט די שטיינער-הימנען, בענקעניש-טורנירן,

הער שוין אויף, דו, אונדזער ברודער צו פאַרפירן.

מוזט פאַרגיין.

הער איך די התראות פון די ברידער-געצן,

שטרעק מיין אָרעם אויס, צעקוועטש זיי אין די נעצן,

און באַשמיר מיין לייַב מיט זייערע פאַרבן-פעטסן.

בלייַב — אַ שטיין.

◄ יואַלאַ

יואַלאַ! יואַלאַ! זי הייסט נישט אַזוי.

אַזוי איז זי מיר נאָר באַקאַנט.

איר אויג — איז עס גרוי? אָדער שוואַרץ? אָדער בלוי?

איר האַנט — איז זי שמאָל, עלעגאַנט?

ווו זוכט מען איר שטאַם? ווי רופט מען איר לאַנד —

עגיפטן, פּאָמפּיי, אָדער טראָי,

צי גאָר סאַמאַרקאַנד? כ׳בין דאָס אַלץ נישט אימשטאַנד

צו זאָגן. מיר איז זי די פרוי.

נאָר איינס ווייס איך זיכער. איין זאַך איז מיר קלאָר:

יואַלאַ באַפעלט און באַצווינגט.

טאָג, מאָנאַט און יאָר, סיי אין טרוים, סיי אין וואָר

פאַרקלינגט מיך איר רוף און פאַרקלינגט.

נאָר וואָס איז יואַלאַ? ווער איז זי, וואָס ברענגט

מיר ליידן און זאָרגן און אומרוען נאָר?

אַ ליד, וואָס פאַרזינגט, צי אַ וועל, וואָס פאַרשלינגט?

איך ווייס נישט, איך ווייס נישט פאַרוואָר.

And they beg me: strike your cymbal brasses,
Wave on high your golden palaces,
Let your armor, dream and longing, break like colored glass,
Fast—destroy!

And they warn me: we are weary of the chaos,
Tired of the strict, the distant, ruthless God Sabaoth,
Now we're tired of you too, Oh Tao.
Stop. No more.

Stop your offerings of rainbow visions,
Stop your stone-hymns, stop your longing-competitions,
Stop deluding our brothers, your derisions.
Be gone.

I hear the warnings of my brother idols.
I stretch my arm, I crush them in my coils.
I anount my body with their color-oils.
And stay—a stone.

➤ *Yuola*

Yuola! Yuola! It is not her name.
It is only her sound and her scent.
Her eye—is it gray? Is it blue? Wild or tame?
Elegant, slender—her hand?
Where look for her tribe? Where was her land?
Pompei? Egypt? Or maybe she came
From Troy? Or from old Samarkand?
She is woman to me, all the same.

Only this I know clearly, one thing I recall:
Yuola commands and subdues.
Day and year, in dream as in waking, her call
Takes me in with its tones and its hues.
But what is Yuola? Who is she to bruise,
To disturb and unsettle my soul?
Is she song that will sway, wave I cannot refuse?
I don't know, do not know at all.

An earlier version of "Yuola" appeared in *Labyrinth*. In *Young Autumn*, it is one of a series of poems to imaginary women with mellifluous names: Yolanda, Eladea, Selima, Karahild.

װערים אַרום מיר.

װערים.

גרױסע.

װײַסע.

פֿאַרבלאָזע.

דרײען זיך אַרום מיר מיט דיקע, לױזע, װײכע בײַכער,

שטילע און שימלדיק-פֿײַכטע.

זײ פֿאַרשלינגען מיך נישט,

זײ װיקלען זיך אַרום מיר פֿון אַלע זײַטן,

פֿאַראומרײניקן מיך מיט דער פֿײַכטער, קאַלטער קלעפּעדיקײט פֿון זײער הױט,

הױפֿן זיך אָן אױף מיר,

אַלץ שטאַרקער,

מערער,

ענגער,

תּאװהדיקער,

ביז איך װער װער דערשטיקט, דערװאָרגן פֿון דער װײַסער, װײכער, קלעפּעדיקער מאַסע,

ביז ס׳װעט קומען מײַן טױט.

װו איז ער, דער אײביקער, אומפֿאַרמײַדלעכער, אױף אַלע ראָגן לױערנדער, פֿינצטערער,

אַלמעכטיקער

שומר ?

איך,

דער אַטאָם,

װאָס לעבט, אַז ער זאָל האָבן מיט װאָס צו גרױסן זיך,

איך,

דער אַטאָם, װאָס פֿאַרמאָגט אין זײַן טראָפּל מאַרך

אַלע זײַנע װעלטן און אַלע זײַנע אַמביציעס,

איך —

דער פֿונעם ערשטן טאָג צום אונטערגאַנג פֿאַרמשפּטער,

דעם גערוך פֿון זײַן אײגענעם פֿױלן יעדן טאָג שפּירנדער,

װאָלט װעלן זען אים

פּנים-אל-פּנים !

Worms around me.
Worms.
Big.
White.
Colorless.
Swarm around me
With thick, loose, soft bellies.
Quiet, moldy-damp.
They don't devour me,
They entangle me,
Make me filthy with the damp, cold sliminess of their skin,
Heap up,
Amass,
Denser,
Lustier,
Til I am choked by the white, soft, slimy mass,
Til death comes.
Where is He, the eternal, the unavoidable, lurking at all corners, the dark,
Almighty
Watchman?

I,
The atom,
Who lives, so He can be proud of it,
I,
The atom, containing in a drop of marrow
All His worlds and all His ambitions,
I—
From my first day condemned to doom,
Daily inhaling the smell of my own decay—
Want to see Him
Face to face!

◄ װילאַנעל פֿון מיסטישן ציקל

מיסטישער ציקל פֿון פֿינעף מאָל זיבן,
פֿינעף מיסטעריעס, אַ קרײַז אין אַ קרײַז.
שאָלעכץ אַװעק, און דער קערן געבליבן.

יאָרן נאָך יאָרן, אין יאָרן צעריבן.
יונג װען אַ מאַן, װען אַ יונגלינג אַ גרײַז.
(מיסטישער ציקל פֿון פֿינעף מאָל זיבן).

זאַמדיקע װעגן מיט פוסטריט פֿאַרשריבן.
פוסטריט־זיגזאַגן. פֿאַרבלענדונג און גרײַז.
שאָלעכץ אַװעק, און דער קערן געבליבן.

ראַנגל. פֿאַרלוירן. פֿאַרצװײַפלונג געטריבן.
דאָ איז מחיצה. פֿון איצטער אָן װײַז —
מיסטישער ציקל פֿון פֿינעף מאָל זיבן.

זאַמען פֿון העלקײט געמערט און געקליבן.
אינװײניק פֿלאַמען, פֿון דרויסן װי אײַז.
שאָלעכץ אַװעק, און דער קערן געבליבן.

העלער און העלער. אָ חסד פֿון ליבן.
גײן צו דעם ליכט, װאָס דערלײַזט און איז װײַס —
מיסטישער ציקל פֿון פֿינעף מאָל זיבן.
שאָלעכץ אַװעק, און דער קערן געבליבן.

► *Villanelle of the Mystical Cycle*

Mystical cycle of seven times five,
Five times seven, a ring in a ring.
Shell swept away, the core will survive.

Ground by the years, and in years revived.
Young when a man, and gray in young spring.
Mystical cycle of seven times five.

Paths in the sand. Footsteps inscribed.
Zigzags of error, delusion and stings.
Shell swept away, the core will survive.

Struggle. And loss. And despair. And strife.
Here—the divide. Now, be succinct—
Mystical cycle of seven times five.

Seeds of brightness, sifted in hives.
Flames on the inside, ice on the wings.
Shell swept away, the core will survive.

Brighter and brighter. On love you thrive.
To light that redeems, white, in a ring.
Mystical cycle of seven times five.
Shell swept away, the core will survive.

Written on Leyeles's thirty-fifth birthday.

Chaim Gross: Sketch for *Bareback Riders*, 1960.

◄ וואָל-סטריט

ניט אַשורבאַניפּאַל.
ניט אַלעקסאַנדער.
ניט טאַמערלאַן.
ניט באָנאַפּאַרט.
איך —
וואָל-סטריט.
מײַן —
די הערשאַפֿט איבער טרוקעניש און ים.
ניט מיט רוט.
ניט מיט בלוט.
ניט מיט שוערד
און יאָגעניש נאָך ערד.
איך רעגיר
מיט פּאַפּיר
און מיט געלער בענקעניש.

אַ לענגלעכע געדרייטע הייל
צווישן געקעסטלטע, אײַנגעמויערטע געצן.
די געצן רײַסן זיך אַרויף, אַרויף,
מערן זיך אין דער הייך,
פֿאַרצערן שפּיצן פֿון קירכן,
שלינגען זון און הימל.
שמאָל אין דער הייל,
טונקל און סומנע.

שטיין, שטיין, אומעטום שטיין.
און אונטערן שטיין
דאָס האַרץ,
דאָס קאַלטע בלישטשענדיקע האַרץ
פֿון אַלע געצן.
אַרום אים,
אין אונטערערדישע געוועלבן,
הינטער אײַזערנע ווענט —
אַן אייביקער, פֿאַרטאַיעטער ריטואַל.
געלער בליאַסק,
און ציטערדיקע העמט פֿון כּוהנים-גדולים
אין פֿאַרכּתיקער עבודה,
אויף אַלטאַרן פֿון גרויען צעמענט.

➤ *Wall Street*

Not Ashurbanipal.
Not Alexander.
Not Tamerlane.
Not Bonaparte.
Me—
Wall Street.
Mine—
Dominion over continents and oceans.
Not with whip.
Not with blood.
Not with sword
Or race for land—
I rule
With paper
And yellow craving.

A long, winding cavern
Between boxed, walled-in idols.
The idols strive upward,
Multiply in the heights,
Devour church spires,
Swallow sun and sky.
The cavern is narrow,
Somber and dark.

Stone, everywhere stone.
And under the stone—
A heart.
Cold, shimmering heart
Of the idols.
All around it,
In underground vaults,
Behind iron walls—
Eternal clandestine ritual.
Yellow glimmer,
Trembling hands of High Priests:
An awesome ceremony
On altars of gray concrete.

Adrian Lubbers: *Exchange Alley,*
1929.

די פעלדזיקע שערענגעס
קוקן גלייכגילטיק, קוקן שווייגיק,
און שווייגיק זענען דאָ שטעענדיק די מענטשן.
עס צעקייקלט זיך אַ מאָל מיט געלעכטער
די פינצטערע ערד פון קאַטאַקאָמב.
עס צעשרייַט זיך אַ מאָל דאָס באַגראָבענע האַרץ —
נאָר מענטשן זענען שטיל און ערנסט
אין וואָל-סטריט.

◄ מאַנהעטן־בריק

צוויי מוטנע שטראָמען אין צונויפגוס פון זוניקן שימער.
צוויי בלאַטיק-צעפליאַטשעטע פיס און איבער זיי אַ פאַבריצישער קאָפּ.
די בויערי, היים פון קינעזיש טעאַטער, פון באָמס און פון מישאַנס,
קאַנעל-סטריט, די גאַס פון ביליקן, ייִדישן מיסחר —
און זיי בינדט צונויף
אויף זייער גרילציקן לויף,
אַ פינקלענדער שנאָל,
דער געשמוקטער פאָרטאָל
פון מאַנהעטן־בריק.

קאַנעל-סטריט און בויערי! זינגט אייַער פרייד צו דעם הימל,
שאַלט שיכורערהייט אייַער שטאָלץ מיט די קופּאָלן פון לאָוער-בראָדוויי,
אייַער ייִחוס מיט וואָלוווירט, מיוניסיפּאַל, מיט אַזוי פיל טעמפּלען פון ביזנעס:
לויכטנדיקע זונען פאַר אייַערע פאַרקאָפּטשעטע שויבן,
קונציקע געזימסן פון געטאָקטער עשירות פאַר אייַער אָרעמער גרויקייט.
נאָר העכער פון אַלץ הייבט אויף אייַער שטים אין אַ דאַנקבאַרן הימן,
פאַר דעם גליק,
וואָס די אונטערפירערער זענט איר
צו מאַנהעטן־בריק.

מאַנהעטן־בריק!
זאָל איך באַזינגען דיין מאָרגן,
ווען דיין רחבותדיקער עמפאַנג
גריסט מיך מיט געקלאַנג פון מענטשן און סחורות,
מיט דער דזשאַז-סימפאָניע פון שטאָט,
אין וועלכער איך שפּיל מיט?
זאָל איך באַזינגען דיין פאַרנאַכט,
ווען דער הימל איבער דיר צעבענקט זיך דאָרפיש-סענטימענטאַל
און שיקט אַ בלוי-ראָזיקע ייִנגלישע בשורה
אויף דיין מענלעכער גבורה פון ציגל און מעטאַל?

The rocky rows—
Indifferent, silent.
And silent, the men.
At times, the dark earth of the catacombs
Rolls with laughter.
At times, the buried heart cries out—
But men are serious and silent
On Wall Street.

➤ *Manhattan Bridge*

Two turbid streams in a confluence of sun's glare.
Two muddy splashed feet and above them—a patrician head.
The Bowery, home of the Chinese theater, of bums and missions,
Canal Street, the row of cheap Jewish trade—
    Are linked and locked,
    In their screeching rush,
    By a sparkling buckle—
    The ornate portal
Of Manhattan Bridge.

Canal Street and Bowery! Sing your joy to the sky,
Roar drunkenly your glory in the cupolas of Lower Broadway,
Your pride in Woolworth, Municipal, in so many temples of business:
Shining suns for your smudged windows,
Elaborate cornices of refined riches for your poor grayness.
But above all, raise your voice in a grateful hymn
    For the joy
    Of being best men
    To Manhattan Bridge.

Manhattan Bridge!
Shall I sing your morning,
When your grand reception
Greets me with the clutter of people and wares,
With the city's jazz-symphony
In which I play too?
Shall I praise your twilight,
When the sky above you grows moody, pastoral-sentimental,
And sends a rosy-blue boyish message
To your manly might of brick and metal?

זאָל איך באַזינגען דײַן נאַכט,

ווען מיט דער ענדלאָזער שורה פון באַליכטענע אויטאָס און טראַקס,

מיט די עלעקטרישע בליצן בײַ דײַנע ריפן פון שטאָל

פינקלסטו, רײצסטו, ווי אַ רינג פון מאָנסטער-בריליאַנטן,

דו פאַרקנסערין פון צוויי זיך יאָגנדיקע שטעט?

איך האָב דיך ליבער, מאַנהעטן-בריק,

ווי איך קאָן דיך באַזינגען.

ביזט דײַן אייגן מעת-לעתיק געזאַנג,

די דרייסטע פאַרמעסטונג, דער באָפעל פון דערפאָלג:

זאָלן די צעדרייטע האָקנדיקע פינגער,

זאָלן די באַצאַלטע, געדונגענע הענט

נאָכטאָן אַטען און רוים.

זאָלן זיי צעשאַלן אונדזערע סוחרישע נעמען,

בויען אַ בריק צו פאַרשעמען אין שיינקייט —

לאָנדאָן, פּאַריז און בערלין.

אין סאָבוויי ◄

I

אַ וואַנט.

אַ טעמפּע וואַנט פון מענטשן-פלייצעס, הענט, פיס.

אַ גרויער מויער מיט ווײַסע רונדע פלעקן.

אַ באַזיגטע אַרמיי אין אַ הייל, פאַרן מושטירן,

וואָס וואַרט אויף אָפענע טירן.

ניט קיין אויפגעפראַלטע שטײַגן נעמען פילדערן.

ניט קיין פעלדזן נעמען זיך פון די גרונטן רירן.

די אַרמיי נעמט שפּירן

דאָס שלאָנגען זיך פון אַ סאָבוויי-צוג אין דער סטאַנציע

אַרײַן.

ווייניק טירן.

ווייניק טירן.

אינעווייניק אין געדרענג,

שטייענדיק און אויף בענק —

ווענט, ווענט.

פלייצעס, הענט,

פיס, פּנימער.

אַ קעניגרײַך פאַר אַ זיץ!

Shall I sing your night,
When in the endless chain of illuminated cars and trucks,
In the electrical lightnings at your ribs of steel,
You sparkle, tease, like a ring of monster-diamonds,
You, matchmaker of two speeding cities?

I love you, Manhattan Bridge,
More than I can sing you.
You are your own daily song,
The daring challenge, the command of success:
     Let the crooked, hooked fingers,
     Let the bought, hired hands
     Emulate Athens and Rome.
     Let them proclaim our mercantile names,
     Build a bridge to shame in beauty—
     London, Paris, Berlin.

➤ *In the Subway*

     I

A wall.
A blunt wall of human backs, arms, legs.
A gray bulwark with white round stains.
A defeated army in a cave, before maneuvers,
Waiting for doors to open.

Not cages unlatched, in uproar.
Not rocks upheaved from their ground.
An army senses
The serpentine swaying of a subway
Into a station.

Too few doors.
Too few doors.

Inside—crammed,
Standing, and on benches—
Walls, walls.
Arms, backs,
Faces, legs—
A kingdom for a seat!

א קעניגרײַך פֿאַר אַ העַנגער !
די וואַנט אינעווייניק לענגער,
געדיכטער, שטײַפֿער, ענגער,
די פֿינעמער גרויער, שטרענגער.
אַרײַן !
פֿאַרקלאַפֿט די טיר.
ריר־ריר.
לעבעדיקער קנויל.
אײַנגעהאַלטענער, פֿאַרשטיקטער, דראַענדער געפֿילדער.

געדרענגט און געדרענגטער,
פֿאַרביסענער, פֿאַרבענקטער,
טעמפֿער און אַנגעשטרענגטער —
צו רו, נאַכטעסן און קינאַ־בילדער.

◄ אין סאָבוויי

II

Rush Hours.
יעדער צאָל איז פֿאַרפֿילט.
יעדער צאָל שעלט די געזעצן פֿון רוים.
קוים וואָס מען קאָן אָטעמען.
און ערגער פֿון אַלץ די הענט.
האָבן זיך ניט ווו אַהינצוטאָן.
הענט קריכן.

A kingdom for a strap!
The walls grow longer,
Thicker, tighter, denser,
Faces grayer, tenser.
Got-in!
Doors slam shut.
Tremor.
A living tangle:
Restrained, stifled, menacing clamor.

Dense, ever denser,
Grimmer, dreamier,
Blunter, tenser—
To rest, supper and cinema.

Max Weber: *Rush Hour, New York*, 1915.

► *In the Subway*

II

"Rush Hour."
Each cell is filled.
Each cell curses the laws of Rome.
No air to breathe.
And worst of all—hands.
No place to hide.
Hands slide.

פיס שאַרן.

מענער. פרויען.

אין גרויען, עלעקטריש־געלן ליכט

וויגט זיך לאַנגזאַם, וויגט זיך פלינק,

וויגט זיך לינקס, וויגט זיך רעכטס

דער שווער־אָטעמדיקער, באַוועגלעכער געפלעכט.

— איין חיה —

טויזנט שֹונאים.

— איין פנים —

טויזנט פיס און הענט.

ברענט און ראַצט דאָס ליכט.

ברענט די שנאה

אויף די געזעצן פון רוים.

ברענט גרוי און רוי

— פון מאַן אויף פרוי, פון פרוי אויף מאַן —

אין דער סאָבוויי־באַן.

פלוצלונג ווייַזט פון באַלקן זיך אַ האַנט

און נעמט שטראָמען גאָלדענע דאָלאַרן

אויף דער לעבעדיקער וואַנט אין דעם קאָשמאַרענעם טונעלן־לאַנד — אַראָפּ.

— די לעבעדיקע וואַנט —

אַ ציטער.

— די וואַנט אַ ציטער —

מענטשן־געווייטער.

הענט ווייסן וואָס צו טאָן.

הענט קלאַפֿן.

הענט שפּאַרן.

הענט טאַפּן.

הענט שאַרן.

כאַפֿן הענט!

ברענט

אַ שנאהדיקער, מענטשעדיקער קנויל.

אויגן, אויערן — גאָרן.

און די דאָלאַרן

שטראַלן,

פֿאַלן,

שאַלן

אויף אַ ליגנדיקער, ראַנגלענדיקער, האַסנדיקער וואַנט

פון דער האַנט אויפֿן באַלקן

אַראָפּ.

קאָפּ אויף קאָפּ.

קנויל אויף קנויל.

גאָלדענער גרויל.

Feet shuffle.
Men. Women.
In gray, electrically-yellow light,
Swinging slow, swinging nimbly,
Swinging left, swinging right,
A heavy-breathing, moving web.
One beast—
A thousand enemies.
One face—
A thousand feet and hands.
The light burns and grates.
Hatred burns
For the laws of Rome.
Burns raw and gray,
Hatred of male for female, female for male
In the subway train.

Suddenly—from the ceiling—a hand
Pours streams of golden dollars
On the breathing wall in nightmare tunnel-land.
The breathing wall—
A tremor.
Human blizzard.
Hands hurt.
Hands push.
Hands search.
Hands shuffle.
Hands catch!
A hating human tangle—
Ablaze,
Eyes, ears—crave, race.
And the dollars
Radiate,
Roar,
Fall
Upon a sprawling, struggling hating wall—
From the hand on the ceiling
Down.
Head to head.
Tangle in tangle.
Golden horror.

קומט צו דער סטאַנציע

אַ טויטער צוג.

דורכגעשטאָכענע אויגן.

צעבלוטיקטע מײַלער.

אין די טויטע לעכער —

גאָלדענע מינצן,

בליציקע שאַרפן,

וואָס די האַנט האָט געוואָרפן

אין דער סאָבוויי-באַן

אויף דעם אונטערערדישן ו ו אַ ן — ו ו אַ ן — וואַנזין.

◂ אין סאָבוויי

III

אין דעם גרויען, רירעוודיקן מויער

אַרײַנגעמויערט

איינס לעבן אַנדערן

אַ ווײַס מיידל און אַ נעגער.

ריח פון שאַרפן מוסקאַט

האָלדזט אַראָמאַט פון אַנגסטיקן מיידלשן פלאַטער.

דער נעגער דריקט זיך שטאַרקער

צום מיידל.

שוואַרצע בענקשאַפט

בענטשט ווײַסע ענגשאַפט.

אַ ווײַס מיידל און אַ נעגער.

טרויער

אין דעם רירעוודיקן גרויען מויער.

טרויער פון דעם יעגער,

וואָס ווייס, אַז ער קאָן זײַן געגאַרטסטן פאַנג נישט קריגן.

נישט אונטן אויף די רעלסן רעדלען רעדער.

רעדער ווירבלען, שווינדלען, דרייען

אין אַ שוואַרצן, קרײַזלדיקן, אומגליקלעכן קאָפּ.

(לינטש-פײַערן — פלאַקערן, פלאַקער.

שלייף פון תליה — שטײַפער, שטײַפער.)

דער נעגער דריקט זיך שטאַרקער

צו דעם מיידל.

To the station comes
A dead train.
Pierced eyes.
Bloody mouths.
In dead holes—
Golden coins,
Flashing blades,
Dropped by a hand
In a subway train
In the underground
    mad-mad-madness.

➤ *In the Subway*

III

Walled-in
In the gray, moving wall,
Close to each other,
A white girl and a Negro.
Smell of strong musk
Hugs the flask of a girl,
    her fearful flutter.
The Negro squeezes tighter
Against the girl.
Black craving
Blesses white crowding.

A white girl and a Negro.
Gloom
In the moving, gray wall.
Gloom of a hunter
Who knows he will not get his choicest prey.
Not down on the rails do the wheels roll—
The dizzying, swinging wheels whirl
In a black, curled, unhappy head.
(Lynching fires—flaming, flaming.
Loop of a gallows—brighter, brighter).
The Negro squeezes tighter
Against the girl.

Joseph Foshko: Illustration to
"In the Subway." (from A. Leyeles,
America and I, 1963)

קיין אָפּשטעל פון דעכער.
די ליניע אַלץ העכער.
צום הימל — אַלץ פרעכער.
גראַד. ווירל.
געמיטער קאַאָטיש.
געשפּאַנט, אַנטי־גאָטיש,
געשעפטס־דאָנקיכאָטיש.
צופאַל — סטיל.
ענערגיע קאַמפּאַקטע.
טראַפּעציעס געהאַקטע
פון ווילנס געוואַגטע.
מענער־זאָרג.
גראַנדיעז אין אומשיינקייט.
מיט חוזק צו קליינקייט.
פילפאַכיק אין איינקייט —
ריז, ניו־יאָרק !

שטאָלץ, ווונדער־ווערק פלעט־איירען בילדינג, מאַן־געשטאַלט.
דו שניידסט אַריין זיך אין דעם סקווער, אַ העלד־זשאָנגלער,
די הענט און פיס אויף הינטן, ווייט דעם קאָפּ אַפער,
און ווילסט אַוועק. נאָר מענלעך צאַמסטו דיין באַגער.
גראַד שטייגט דיין ליניע, מעטראָפּאָליטאַן, און ס׳שאַלט
דיין ליד אַריבער יעדן קבצנס טרויים אין סקווער,
און ס׳פאַלט מיט שפּאַט דיין לאַך אַראָפּ אויף דעם אַספאַלט.

און ענג אַרום געהאַקטע פורעמס, יעדער — אָבעליסק.
עס שפּיצן העלדן־טורעמס זיך אַריין אין זונענדיסק.
און פון אַ ווינקל קוקט דער "גאַרדן" דורך אַ שפּאַלט,
רום פון פריערדיקן דור, וואָס מער און מער
פאַרלירט זיך אין ניו־יאָרק און לויפט פון זאָרג און ריסק.

נאָר ס׳לאַכט פיפט עוועניו און ס׳לאַכט בראָדווי פאַרשייט.
זיי האָבן ביידע ניט קיין חשק און קיין צייט
צו טראַכטן, צי עס לוינט אַ סטיל־און־פאָרמען־בייט.
זיי בייטן זיך. דער סקווער — אַ צופעליקער האַלט,
אַ טרעפעניש, וואָס האַט אין רוישיקן מאָמענט
געבוירן ריזן־זין פון אייזן און צעמענט.

No end to roofs' cry.
The line—upward, high.
Insolent—to the sky.
Straight. Virile.
Moods are chaotic.
Tense, anti-Gothic.
Business-Don-Quixotic.
Chance is style.
Energy compressed.
Trapezoids in quest:
Wills' unrest.
Men's worry.
Stupendous unbeauty.
Mocking the petty.
Polyvalent unity—
Giant, New York!

Proud wonder-work, Flatiron Building, male figure.
Your stride cuts into the square, a hero juggler,
Arms and legs behind, the head protruding far,
You want to walk away. But, manly, you curb your desire.
Metropolitan, your line shoots straight, your song roars,
Drowns out each beggar's dream down in the square,
Your laughter falls, a mocking thud, on the asphalt.

Truncated molds crowd in around you, each—an obelisk.
Hero-towers dart their spears into the sun's disk.
And from a corner, through a crack, peeps the "Garden"—
The pride of yesterday, now more and more
Fleeing risk and worry, it gets lost in New York.

But Fifth Avenue laughs and wantonly laughs Broadway.
They have neither will nor time to weigh
The worth of changing styles and forms.
They simply change. The square—an accidental pause,
A chance encounter, which in one loud moment
Gave birth to giant sons of iron and cement.

שויבן בליצן, שויבן צינדן זיך אין סקווער.
ס׳פֿינקלען ליכטער אויף פֿאַנטאַסטיש, פֿאַליגאַניש.
דרײַעקס, ראָמבן, האַלב סעצעסיע, האַלב האַרמאַניש,
טאַנצן פֿריילעך אויף אין פֿענצטער — גראַד און קווער.

צו דעם הימל ווינקן שפּיציק און סאַרדאָניש
פֿלעקן גאָלד און שוואַרץ. און ער — פֿאַרטיפֿט זיך מער,
הענגט צעשניטן שאַרף ווי פֿון אַ ריזן־שער,
גלאַנצט צוריק זײַן בלויקייט זײַטיק און לאַקאָניש.

די ווירילע טורעמס — ווייניקער געווינקלט.
באַלד און ס׳דאַכט זיך: ס׳קלײַבט אַ פֿאָלק זיך, רײַך באַשפּרינקלט
מיט שטורקאַצן צום פֿאַרשײַטן קאַרניוואַל.

אַ דעבאָש אין סקווער. עלעקטריש־לעגענדאַריש
רוישט ער אָפּ אַ שעה, אָרגיאַסטיש און ווירוואַריש —
זעלבסט־פֿאַרשיכּורטע כּימערע, אומרעאַל.

Windows flash, flare up above the square.
Lights sparkle—polygonal, anonymous.
Triangles, diamonds—part Secession, part harmonious—
Dance joyfully on windowpanes, straight and queer.

Flickers of black and gold, pointed and sardonic,
Wink to the sky. The sky—in pieces,
Hangs deep and dark, cut up by giant scissors—
Glimmers back its blueness, slant, laconic.

The virile towers—cornerless. They twinkle—
It seems: a crowd assembles, richly sprinkled
With torches for a frivolous carnival.

Debauchery in the square. Electrically-fantastic
Carousing for an hour, boisterous, orgiastic—
A chimera drunk on itself. Unreal ball.

Secession—apparently an allusion to the Viennese Secession, especially to the paintings of Gustav Klimt.

Joseph Foshko: Illustration to "Evening." (from A. Leyeles, *America and I*, 1963)

איצטער איז רויִק. פֿאַרלאָשן די פֿענצטער.
ס׳טוקן לאַמטערן זיך שטיל אין אַספֿאַלט.
ס׳קוקן די טראַמס ווי שטיינער-געשפּענסטער.

שטייט די פּלעט-אײַראָן מאַסיוו, גרוי און קאַלט,
הענגט מעטראָפּאָליטאַן שווערער און גרויער,
הורבן זיך אַנדערע סומנע ווי וואַלד.

יעדע געבײַדע איז איצטער אַ טויער
צו אַ בית-עולם ווו הינטער די ווענט
שלאָפֿן אַמביציעס און פּלענער פֿון בויער.

יעדע געבײַדע איז איצט מאָנומענט,
שטיינערנער שאָטן פֿון שטאָטישן פֿיבער,
דענקמאָל אויף אומרו, וואָס שאַפֿט און פֿאַרלענדט.

הינטער די שויבן, אין ליידיקע שטיבער,
לויערט דער דעמאָן פֿון חשבון און פּלאַן,
מאַכטלאָז אַ ווײַלע — זײַן צויבער פֿאַראיבער.

ערגעץ אַוועק איז אויף קאַר און אויף באַן,
ערגעץ פֿאַרשוווּנדן די הילכנדע מענגע
מענער און פֿרויען — דער שטאָט-קאַראַוואַן,

וואָס ווערט פֿאַרדרערנגט דאָ אין פֿירעק ענגע,
גלײַך אין פֿאַפֿירענע לייצעס געשפּאַנט,
האַרצלאָז מושטירט קעגן ציפֿערן שטרענגע.

טויט די פּאַפּיר-וועלט. אויף טיר און אויף וואַנט
הענגט נאָך אַ חלום, אַ צאָל ניט-געראָטן,
שלײַכט אַן אַמביציע, אַן מזל געפֿלאַנט.

כ׳זע שוין איצט זיך, איך בין מער ניט פֿאַרשאָטן
אונטער דעם ריזיקן רויש און פֿאַרקרעט.
כ׳זע איצט אויך מענטשן און גריס זייער שאָטן.

קום איצט מיט מיר אין דעם מעדיסאָן-סקווער.
לאָמיר שפּאַצירן אויף אַט דעם בית-עולם,
וואָס איז בית-עולם צוועלף שעה און ניט מער.

> *Night*

Now all is calm. The window-lights spent.
Lanterns slip silently into the pavement.
Towers stand watching like monsters of stone.

Massive Flatiron: imposing, gray, cold.
Then Metropolitan: heavier, grayer.
Others hang gloomily, crowd like a forest.

Every building now is a gateway
To a great graveyard. There, behind walls,
Sleep the ambitions and plans of the builders.

Every building at night is a monument,
Shadow in stone of the fever of cities,
Crown of unrest that creates and destroys.

And, behind panes, in the empty corridors,
Lurks the demon of counting and planning—
Powerless now, while his charm is subdued.

Somewhere, the chattering crowd disappeared,
Left, departed in cars and in trains—
Women and men of the city caravan,

Crammed here by day in tight little squares,
Harnessed like horses with reins of paper,
Heartlessly drilled against rigorous numbers.

Dead is the paper-world. On doors and on walls
Lingers a dream, a figure that failed,
Skulks an ambition, designed with no luck.

Now I can see my own face, not interred
Under the turbulent traffic and roar,
People I see, too, and I nod to their shadows.

Come with me now to Madison Square.
Let's stroll about in the beautiful graveyard,
Graveyard that lasts for twelve hours, no more.

לאָמיר אים בענטשן: אַז גוט אים, אַז וווֹיל אים,
און אים פֿאַרגעבן, וואָס באַלד וועט אויף ס׳נייַ
שטורמען זייַן קראַפֿט ווי אַ גאָט אָדער גולם.

אומשולדיק שוועבן די נעמען פֿאַרבייַ
אויף די מצבֿות. געהיימניספֿול טראָגט זיך
עכאָ נאָך עכאָ פֿון דער שטיינערייַ:

ס׳ליד פֿון די אויטאָס, וואָס האָבן געיאָגט זיך
הונדערטערווייַז דורך דעם טאָגיקן קרייַז,
ס׳ליד פֿון די זוילן, וואָס האָבן געטאָקט זיך

אָן טראָטואַרן — צענטויזנטערווייַז.
(אַלץ איז בייַ טאָג דאָ פֿאַרפֿאַלן געוואָרן
קעגן דעם שטאָלן-געמויערטן פֿלייַס).

מעדיסאָן-סקווער! טראָג זיך וואָכן צי יאָרן,
וועסט ניט געפֿינען קיין אָרט, ווו עס זאָל
העכער, געוואַגטער, צו דרייסטערן גאָרן,

שטייַגן די ליניע די גראַדע פֿון שטאָל,
יענע, וואָס פֿורעמט די שטעט און די לענדער,
שלייַדערט דאָרט מענטשן צונויף אָן אַ צאָל.

ד אַ הערשט די ליניע די גראַדע, וואָס בענדער
שמידט זי פֿון אייַזן, צעמענט און גראַניט,
מאַכט פֿון דעם מענטשן אַ בויער-פֿאַרשווענדער.

דאָ אויך די צאַם פֿון דער ליניע. זי שמידט
ווענט צווישן מענטש און זייַן בענקשאַפֿט צום ווונדער,
קאָוועט אין פֿלאָכן, כאָטש ס׳דאַכט אים, ער פֿליט —

קעגן דער ליניע פֿון הימל, דער רונדער.

Let us embrace it: be blessed and be happy,
Let us forgive that its power will soon
Rage here again like a God or a Golem.

Innocent, names on the gravestones appear,
Hover and vanish. Mysteriously carry
Echo to echo the sounds of the quarry:

Song of the cars that raced in the streets—
Hordes of hundreds, through the ring of the day,
Song of the soles, that shuffled and polished

Sidewalks—tens of thousands of soles.
(During the daytime all this was subdued,
Lost in the sway of steelfast persistence.)

Madison Square! If you travel for weeks,
Travel for years, you won't find such a place,
Where, with more daring, to insolent stories,

Rises the line, the straight line of steel,
Molding the shapes of cities and countries,
Hurtling men into numberless heaps.

Here the line rules, the straight line that forges
Ties of iron, concrete, and granite,
Making men into builders-and-squanderers.

Here, too, the line has a limit. It raises
Walls between man and his longing for miracle,
Welds them in planes,
        though he thinks that he flies—

Against the rounded line of the skies.

די ווענט פון שטיין, דער דיל פון מוטנעם שטיין.
אין פרעמדקייט, גרויער, שטייניקער אליין.
ווי רוישלאָז ס׳פאַלט אויף דעם אַספאַלט מיין טראָט,
וואַרפט הילכיק זיך אויף די וואָג פון שטאָט.
מיין גאָט !

מיט אויגוסט-וואַנזין אָטעמט דער גראַניט.
אין הייסע, האַרטע אָרעמס אײַנגעשמידט,
רײַס איך זיך פון דעם שטייניקן וואַמפיר —
ווי ס׳אויג צום ווײַטן הימלס בלוי-קאָליר —
צו דיר.

און קיין מאָל האָט נאָך ניט אַזוי אינטים
געוואַעלט אין מיר מיין ליבעס שטילע שטים,
ווי יענע שעה, בײַ טאָג, אַ זייגער צוויי,
ווען ס׳איז געוואָרן איין דולער שטיין-געשריי —
בראָדוויי.

הערבסט

(סאָנעטן-קראַנץ)

I

מיין לויב דיר, הערבסט, סעזאָן פון רײַפן גאָלד,
פון דורכזיכטיקע בענקענדע קריסטאַלן,
פון קלוגע ביימער — ריזיקע קאָראַלן,
פון ברייטער רו, וואָס שמייכלט אויף רעוואָלט.
עס זענען רו און אומרו דאָך די שטראַלן
דערפון בלויז, וואָס מיר האָבן וועין געוואָלט.
דער הערבסט לערנט ערנסט וויִזהייט אונדז. זיין רײַכקייט צאָלט
פאַר פרילינגס לײַכטקייט, פאַר די שווערע וואַלן

פון זומער, וועלכע נאַרן מיט דער לאַסט
פון פאַלשע און פאַרפירנדע מיראַזשן.
"וואָס ווען געוואָלט", און ווען געליבט, געהאַסט —
ס׳איז אַלץ נישט נישט מער, ווי פײַנע קאַמופלאַזשן.

דער אמת איז אין הערבסטס קאָלאָראַטורן:
אָראַנזש, וויאָלעט און טרוימענדע פורפורן.

The walls of stone, the floor of muddy stone.
In alien air, a stony, gray alone.
As soundless as my step falls on the asphalt,
The city's weight assaults me with a roar.
My God!

The granite breathes August-madness.
Enclosed in hot, hard arms, I squirm
To flee from stony vampire's clutch—
As my eye flees to far sky's blue—
To you.

And never yet, so intimately poised,
Welled up in me my love's soft voice,
As on that afternoon, at two o'clock,
When one mad shriek of stone and rock
Was Broadway.

Autumn

A Sonnet Garland

See the description of its formal
structure in the introductory
chapter, "Forms of Yiddish
Poetry."

I

I praise you, Autumn, season of ripe gold,
Of cold, translucent, and nostalgic crystals,
Of wise trees—giant colonies of corals,
Of spacious rest that smiles at all revolt.
Unrest and rest are merely shining rays
Of everything we ever wished to have.
Autumn teaches wisdom. Its richness pays
For Spring's light-heartedness, for heavy waves

Of Summer, which delude with all the burden
Of false, deceptive, desertlike mirages.
What you have ever wished, or loved, or hated—
These were no more than pretty camouflages.

Truth lies in Fall's coloraturas: purpose
In orange, violet, and dreamy purples.

אָראַנזש, וויאָלעט און טרוימענדע פורפורן.
ס׳איז נישט די פול-באַשטימטע ליניע וואָר,
נישט דאָס, וואָס האָט איין בילד, איין פנים נאָר,
און רײַסט זיך אָפ מיט זיכערע צעזורן.
וואָר איז דער האַלב-טאָן, דער געמישטער כאָר,
ווּ ס׳קלינגען ציטעריק זיך צונויף די שפורן
פון פילע קלאַנגען, צײַטן, קרעאַטורן,
ווּ ס׳בענקט דער כאַאָס אַלץ צו ווערן קלאָר.

דאָס איז דער ערבסט. דאָס זענען די פאַרנאַכטן,
ווען ס׳איז אײנצײַטיק אומעטיק און העל,
ווען ס׳עפנט אַלע שלומערנדע פראַכטן
די פײַנלעך-לויטער ווערנדיקע זעל.

דאַן בעטסטו צו אַ פרוי, ווײַט אין לאַזורן:
"אין דײַנע צאַרטע, שטראַליקע קאַנטורן."

אין דײַנע צאַרטע, שטראַליקע קאַנטורן
שוועבט אום מײַן טרוים, דו זעלטן-ווײַטע פרוי,
דו אײנציקע, וואָס נאָר אין אָוונט-בלוי
דערשײַנסטו מיר, געשפין פון עטער-שנורן.
דורך צופאַל זענען מיר נאָר ווײַט אַזוי —
צוויי אָפּגעזונדערט-באַלאַנדזשענדע פיגורן,
צוויי אָפּגעשפּאַלטן-בענקענדיקע שפורן
פון אײנס. דאָס ווײַס און שוואַרץ פון בלויז אײן גרוי.

נײן, ניט פון גרוי. פיל ריכטיקער: וויאָלעט,
ווי רויט און בלוי אין ווי ווונדער-אַמאַלגאַמע
העל זינגען אוניסאָניש אַ דועט,
אײן אײנציק-לויטערע, פאַרבענקטע גאַמע.

אין דיר, אַ זעוונג דו פון בלוי און גאָלד,
ווערט גאָר מײַן זעלן-פלאַנטער אויפגעראָלט.

ווערט גאָר מײַן זעלן-פלאַנטער אויפגעראָלט,
כּאַטש כ׳ווייס זי איז דאָך בלויז אַן אויסגעטראַכטע.
נאָר ווי ווי הייבט אָן, ווי ענדיקט ס׳אויסגעדאַכטע?
די וואָר איז פעסט-געצוגלט, פעסט-געשטאַלט.
און דאָך ווי אָפט אַנטלויפט זי, אַ פאַרלאַכטע,
אין שלאָף אַרײַן נאָך טרויסט! דאָס וואָס געזאָלט,

II

Of orange, violet, and dreamy purples.
Not the fully determined line is real,
Not that which has one image, or one face,
The line defined by self-assured caesuras.
Half-tones are real, the compounded choir,
In which, vibrating, still resound the traces
Of multitudes of times and sounds and creatures,
Where chaos yearns for a lucidity.

This is the Autumn. This the fall of twilights
That are at once depressed and filled with light.
When your own soul, in growing pain of clarity,
Reveals its slumbering riches, opens up.

Pray to a distant woman, in deep azures:
"Within your delicate and radiant contours."

III

Within your delicate and radiant contours
Hovers my dream, you rare and distant woman.
Unique one, you emerged in evening blue
Before my eyes, a web of ether-threads.
Through chance alone we find ourselves so distant,
Two wandering, two separated phantoms,
Two split-apart and craving traces of
A one. The white and black of one mere gray.

No, not of gray. More accurately: violet,
Where red and blue sing brightly a duet
In unison, a wonderful amalgam,
In one uniquely-lucid, yearning gamut.

In you, oh vision live in blue and gold,
The tangle of my soul is now unrolled.

IV

The tangle of my soul is now unrolled,
Though I know well that it is an invention.
But where begin, where end all things imagined?
Reality is built of bricks, steel-fast.
But often, made a laughingstock, it flees
For comfort into sleep! What should have been

איז וואָרער פיל, ווי אין דעם אָוונט-גאָלד
אַן אמתע, זיך גליטשנדיקע יאַכטע,

וואָס גיט אַ ווי מיט בענקשאַפט און פֿאַרשוווינדט.
אילוזיע איז אַ פֿאַקט. דער פֿאַקט — אילוזיע.
און כ׳בין ניט זיכער, צי איך שרײַב אַצינד
אין ראָסקאָ-דאָרף, צי גאָר אין אַנדאַלוזיע.

אילוזיע מײַן, בײַ דיר אין שויס זיך נורען
זכרונות, בילדער, זעונגען, פֿיגורן.

V

זכרונות, בילדער, זעונגען, פֿיגורן
פֿון עפּעס גאָר אַן אַנדערשדיקער וועלט
גענענען איצט זו מיר און פֿרײדיק העלט
מײַן זעל אויף. כ׳זע זיך אונטער אַבאַזשורן
פֿון ליכט — אין ליכט. די גאַנצע וועלט — מײַן צעלט,
געבוים אויף זיבן-פֿאַרביקע וועליורן.
איך בין ניט איך. גאָר אַנדערע קאָנטורן
פֿאַרמאָגט מײַן לײַב; אי מער ווי איצט, אי ס׳פֿעלט.

כ׳בין מאַן און פֿרוי צוזאַמען. יאָ, צוזאַמען.
כ׳בין מענטש און דאָך ניטש מענטש. פֿיל גרעסער, מער.
פֿיל מער ווי מענטש. מיט וועלכע הימנען-פֿלאַמען
זאָל איך דען אויסזינגען, וואָס כ׳זע און הער?

איך וואָג נישט זינגען דאָס, וואָס אין זײַן גאָלד
דער פֿאַרבן-זאַטער הערבסט מאָלט אַלץ און מאָלט.

VI

דער פֿאַרבן-זאַטער הערבסט מאָלט אַלץ און מאָלט.
כ׳זע וואָס געוואָון און אפֿשר גאָר דעם שפּעטער.
איך בין ניט איך. אַ גאָט אַן ברידער-געטער.
און אויף אַ וועג, וואָס ברייט זיך און וואָס שמאָלט
פֿון צווישן וועלטן-בימער, זונען-בלעטער
גיי איך אַליין. איך מאַן-ווײַב-גאָט. באַטאָלט,
באַבאַרגט איז אויסטערליש די ערד. זי ראָלט
און וויקלט זיך. איך בוי און איך צעשמעטער.

איך בוי אַ וועלט און מאַך זי ווידער וויסט.
כ׳בין מעכטיק אין מײַן קראַפֿט. נאָר אײנזאַם שפּינען
זיך טעג. ניטאָ ווער ס׳זאָל מיר זאָגן: "ביסט!"
ווער ס׳זאָל מײַן גרויסע מאַכט מיט ליב באַדינען.

Is—in the evening's gold—more real than
That actual, that gliding yacht at sea

Which sends a longing wave and disappears.
Illusion is a fact. The fact—illusion.
I am not sure if I am writing now
In Roscoe village or in Andalusia.

Illusion, in your lap you warm amazing
Memories, visions, images, and faces.

Andalusia—An allusion to the Hebrew poets of the "Golden Age" in Spain, tenth to thirteenth century.

V

Memories, visions, images, and faces—
As of a strange and otherworldly world—
Approach me closely, and my soul with joy
Lights up. I see: I'm under chandeliers
Of light—in light. The whole world is my tent,
Stretched over me in seven-hued velours.
I am no more myself. Amazing contours
Incorporate my body: both more and less than now.

I am both man and woman. Both together.
I'm human and not human. Larger, more.
Much more than human. In what hymnal flames
Shall I now sing all that I see and hear?

My poem dare not mime what gold attains
When color-sated Autumn paints and paints.

VI

When color-sated Autumn paints and paints
I see the past, perhaps I see the future.
I am not me. A God with no God-peers.
And on a road that widens and that narrows
Among world-trees, among sun-leaves, I walk
Alone. I am man-woman-god. Full-valleyed,
Rich-mountained—the amazing earth. It rolls,
Unfolds again. I build and I destroy.

I build a world, and lay it waste again.
My strength is mighty. But the days spin on
In loneliness. No one to say: "You are!"
No one to worship, praise my mighty power.

מײַן ווערק איז ניט אַזוי, ווי כ׳וואָלט געוואָלט.
יעטוועדעס בילד דערצײַלט: געקאָנט, געזאָלט.

VII

יעטוועדעס בילד דערצײַלט: געקאָנט, געזאָלט,
געקאָנט אַן אַנדער וועלט פֿאַר זיך געשטאַלטן.
כ׳בין גאָט. איך קאָן ניט יונגן און ניט אַלטן,
כ׳בין מאַן און ווײַב צוזאַמען, און עס צאָלט
מײַן איך זײַן ליבעס פֿרוכטבאַרע געהאַלטן
צו מיר אַלײן. נאָר עפּעס שטעכט און אַלט
אין האַרץ בײַ מיר. ניט דאָס, וואָס כ׳האָב געוואָלט.
כ׳בין שטאַרק און גרויס נאָר אײנזאַם. כ׳מוז זיך שפּאַלטן.

געשען. פֿון ווײַב האָט אָפּגעטײלט זיך מאַן.
געוואָרן זעגען זוכנדיקע מענטשן.
איך גײ אַרום און בענק און זוך פֿון דאַן.
און ווײס ניט: זאָל איך שעלטן אָדער בענטשן.

איך פֿאָרש זינט דאַן אין דער הערבסטיקע לאַזורן.
אין אַלץ מײַן איך׳ס פֿאַרגאַנגען-ווײַטע שפּורן.

VIII

אין אַלץ מײַן איך׳ס פֿאַרגאַנגען-ווײַטע שפּורן.
האַלב גלוסט נאָך גאַנץ. און ווען אַ פֿרוי-געשטאַלט
קריצט אָפּ זיך אין מײַן האַרץ, מײַן איך — עס שאַלט
דער רוף פֿון יענע אור-ערשטע לאַזורן.
נאָר פֿרײד רינט אויס אין דער אַנטוישונג באַלד.
די צײַט בײַטשט פֿלינק אַוועק די לײַכטע פֿורן
מיט לײַמענע, צעבראָכענע אַמורן,
און ס׳האַרץ בלײַבט — טריט-פֿאַרשטויביקטער אַספֿאַלט.

און כ׳בענק נאָך דעם, וואָס איך האָב אָנגעווירן.
דער מענטש וויל וויל ווידער ווערן גאָט און וועט.
מײַן העלפֿט, וואָס כ׳האָב דורך אַ קאַפּריז פֿאַרלוירן,
בענקט אויך און וועט פֿאַרנעמען מײַן געבעט.

כ׳וועל זײַן נאָך גאַנץ. אילוזיע איז אַ פֿאַקט.
וואָס איז אַצינד, איז שײַנבאַרער אַנטראַקט.

IX

וואָס איז אַצינד, איז שײַנבאַרער אַנטראַקט.
דער עבר איז נאָך צוקונפֿט ניט געוואָרן.
די צוקונפֿט בענקט בײַ מיר נאָך אין זיכרון.

What I have done is less than my intent.
Each image claims: you could, you should, you meant.

VII

Each image claims: I could, I should, I meant.
I could have formed for me another world.
I'm God. I cannot age, cannot be younger.
I am both man and woman in one shape.
My I will offer love's fruitbearing seeds
To me alone. But something nags and burdens
Within my heart. It is not what I meant.
I'm strong and great and lonely. Must divide.

It happened. Woman separates from man.
And searching people populate my world.
Since then I walk about and crave and seek,
And do not know if I should curse or bless.

I scrutinize the Autumn's azure faces.
In all I find my I's far, faded traces.

VIII

In all I find my I's far, faded traces.
Half yearns for whole. And when a female figure
Is etched within my heart, deep in my self
Resounds the call of those primeval azures.
But soon the joy runs out in disappointment.
Time lashes deftly out, sends off the wagons
With broken cupid-figurines of clay,
Your heart remains—like dust-imprinted asphalt.

Yet I am longing still for what I lost.
Man wants to be a god again—and will.
The half which I have lost through a caprice
Is longing too. It will perceive my prayer.

I shall be whole. Illusion is a fact.
What now exists is shadowy entr'acte.

IX

What now exists is shadowy entr'acte,
The past not yet transformed into a future.
The future still is yearning in my memory,

נאָר שטענדיק קלאַפֿט מײַן האַרץ מיט איר אין טאַקט.
עס לעבן, שטאַרבן וועלטן, צײַטן, יאָרן.
איך בײַט מיר מײַן בילד פֿון קאָסמאָס-אַקט צו אַקט.
כ'מוז אָפּקומען פֿאַר דעם וואָס כ'האָב געוואָגט
אין יענע ווײַטע, ראָזיקע אוויראַרן.

און אַלץ וואָס כ'טראַכט און טו, וואָס כ'טו און בין —
דערויף העַנגט שטענדיק יענער רגעס צייכן.
מײַן לאַנד איז ס'פֿאַרביק ווערנדיקע גרין
פֿון הערבסטעס באַדאַכטע טאָלן, ווײַזע הײַכן.

דאָס ליכט צאַנקט שטענדיק. נאָר אַוועק מיט זאָרגן!
ס'איז דאָס פֿאַרגייין נאָר ערב נײַעם מאָרגן.

X

ס'איז דאָס פֿאַרגייין, נאָר ערב נײַעם מאָרגן —
מײַן לעבן. און ס'איז רעכט און גוט אַזוי.
עס מוז זיך לײַטערן דאָס, וואָס שאַרף, ניט-רײַף און רוי,
לאַנג לײַטערן אין די פֿאַנטאַמען-זאָרגן
פֿון בלײַכן צווישן-ליכט, וואָס רויט און בלוי.
מען קריפֿט ניט זעליקייט אויף מערק און טאָרגן,
דער ציל, וואָס איז פֿון מענטשן-אויג פֿאַרבאָרגן
איז ניט פֿאַר יעדן ווינט אַ לײַכטע שטרוי.

אין שײַן פֿון דעם פֿאַרגייין ווערט אַלעס לויטער,
און אַלעס קריגט אַ ניט-געהאַטן ווערט,
בלוי ווערט ווילאַעט, ווילאַעט ווערט רויט און רויטער,
און מער קיין גרענעץ צווישן הימל, ערד.

דאַן הערסטו פֿון דער אייביקייט דעם טאַקט.
דו פֿילסט עס איז נאָך ניט דער לעצטער אַקט.

XI

דו פֿילסט עס איז נאָך ניט דער לעצטער אַקט,
ווײַל ס'איז גאָר קיין שום לעצטער אַקט פֿאַראַנען.
און ערשטער ניט. קיין בליען און קיין וויאַנען,
קיין זיכערקייט פֿון פֿענאָמען און פֿאַקט.
ס'איז שפּראַי אַלץ פֿון דיזעלבע קראַפֿט-פֿאַנטאַנען.
און ברענט די זון מיט פֿײַער-הויך און באַקט,
און שטראַפֿט דער פֿראָסט מיט אײַזיקן קאָנטאַקט —
צום זעלבן שורש פֿירן אַלע באַנען.

און אַלעס איז ניט מער ווי אַ רעפֿלעקס.

But with its beat my heart will always beat.
All worlds, times, years—they live and die again.
I change my image between cosmic acts.
I have to suffer for defiant deeds
In distant, rosy-wakening Auroras.

And over all I think and do and am—
Forever hangs the sign of that far moment.
My land—it is the color-flooded green
Of Autumn's prudent valleys and wise hills.

Light flickers always. Yet forget the worries!
The sunset is but eve of a new morning.

X

It is the sunset, eve of a new morning—
It is my life. And it is good like this.
All that is harsh, and raw, and not-quite-ripe
Must seek its clarity in phantom-worries
Of pallid twilights, that are red and blue.
You don't buy bliss at fairs and marketplaces,
The goal is hidden from a human eye,
It is no straw that any wind can sway.

Within the sunset light all things are lucid,
Attain a value never had, all blue
Turns violet, and violet turns red,
No more horizon between earth and sky.

You hear eternity's time-beat, its track.
You sense: it is not yet the final act.

XI

You sense: it is not yet the final act,
Because there is no final act at all.
Nor first. No blooming and no withering,
No certainty: phenomenon or fact.
All are but spurts of the same power-fountain.
If sun should burn and bake with its high fire,
If frost should punish with its icy touch—
All trains will lead you to the selfsame root.

And every thing is merely a reflex,

און אלע זאכן זענען בלויז סימבאלן.
און אומעטום הערש איך — איך האמא-רעקס.
די צייטן זענען מיינע אראלן.

ווער שפירט ניט, פילט ניט צווישן היינט און מארגן:
פאריס איז ס'גרויסע וווונדער ערשט פארבאראגן?

XII

פאריס איז ס'גרויסע וווונדער ערשט פארבאראגן.
דער טויט איז שיינבאר. בלויז א צייטן-טרוים.
א דינער אויסגעטראקטער צווישן-זוים
וואס פירט פון ערשטן צו א צווייטן מארגן.
און דאס וואס איז אויף יענער זייט פון צוים,
איז ניט אין תפיסה ביי די שוועסטער גארגאן.
עס איז אין דיר, דו קינד פון פאלשע זארגן,
וואס זעסט ניט, ווי ס'איז איינס אי צייט אי רוים.

אין דיר און דא. און וויפל שווארצע שלייערן
עס זאלן ניט פארדעקן ס'וואורע ליכט,
און ווי דאס כלומרשטע פארגיין זאל לויערן —
זעסט וווונדער, אויב דו קוקסט זיי אין געזיכט.

קריגסט ענטפער, אויב דו וועגסט צו זיי ס'געבעט:
"א, וווונדער דא און דארטן, דורך מיר רעדט!"

XIII

א, וווונדער דא און דארטן. דורך מיר רעדט
דאס שטענדיקע פארגיין אין באנגן שימער.
דעם שיקזאל'ס "ניין" הייזט שטענדיק אין מיין צימער —
עס זינגט פארווירט א יידישער פאעט.
דאך ווייס איך, אז איך בין דער אייגנטימער
פון ווילן-קוואל, וואס איז, געווען און וועט,
און אז מיין פיין-געשליפענער סאנעט
קוועלט אויך פון דארט, און זע! ער לעבט שוין אימער.

דאס וווונדער איז ביי מיר קיין פרעמדער גאסט.
דער ווילן צו דעם וווונדער איז מיין שורש.
פונקט ווי מיין שטאם טראג איך א וועלטן-לאסט,
און ווייס ווי ער: עס קומט טאג-טעגלעך קורש.

איך שטאם פון טרוימער. כ'הער אין לענדער, שטעט
זייער שטים אי שטיל, אי הויך, אי פרי, אי שפעט.

All objects that surround us are but symbols,
And everywhere, I rule—I homo-rex.
The changing times—they are my aureoles.

Who does not sense between today and morrow:
Ahead—the stunning wonder, yet unborn?

XII

Ahead—the stunning wonder, yet unborn.
Death is illusory. A dream of time.
It is a thin, imagined, twilight-seam
Which carries you from one to second morning.
And what is on the hedge's other side
Is not imprisoned by the Gorgon sisters.
It is in you, you child of false anxieties,
Who does not see how time and space are one.

It is in you and here. May many more
Black veils conceal and hide the real light,
And may the seeming sunset lurk nearby—
You can see wonders, looking in their face.

They answer, if your prayer to them resounds:
"Oh, wonders there and here, through me speak out!"

XIII

Oh, wonders there and here. Through me speaks out
The gleaming sadness of recurring sunsets.
Destiny's "no" lives ever in my room—
A Yiddish poet's song must be confused.
And yet I know, that I am one who owns
The well of Will, which is, and was, and will be,
And that my beautifully chiseled sonnet
Springs from that well, and see! It lives for good.

The wonder is no stranger in my house.
The will to wonder is and was my root.
I carry, like my tribe, the weight of worlds.
I know like them: my Cyrus comes each day.

Son of dreamers—I hear, roaming about,
Their voice: both late and early, low and loud.

XIV

‏זייער שטים אי שטיל, אי הויך, אי פרי, אי שפעט —
‏מיך צוווינגען הערן אלע שיקזאל-צוימער.
‏און פון דעם הערבסטס זכרונות-שווערע בוימער
‏רופט מיך א פארבן-הימן, א וועלט-געבעט.

‏איך צוים און טרוים. און מעג דער סומנער שומר
‏פון אונטערגאאנג באוואכן אונדז — ער וועט
‏נאר מחזן העלפן זינגען אין דועט
‏דעם, וועלכער האט געוויילט צו זיין א טרוימער.

‏א, שאפן אין דעם שיין פון נאנטן טויט !
‏א, ווער קאן ווילן הערלעכערע שטונדן ?
‏זע, הערבסט צירט זיך אין ווינדערבארן רויט —
‏ס׳איז ניט פארגיין, עס זענען לעבנס-ווונדן.

‏אויב טויט — איז רויטער, פארב פון פרישן בלוט.
‏גרויט דאס פארגיין — העלט אויף דער גרויסער מוט.

XV

‏מיין לויב דיר, הערבסט, סעזאן פון רייפן גאלד,
‏אראנזש, וויאלעט און טרוימענדע פורפורן.
‏אין דיינע צארטע, שטראליקע קאנטורן
‏ווערט גאר מיין זעלן-פלאנטער אויפגעראלט.
‏זכרונות, בילדער, זעונגען, פיגורן —
‏דער פארבן-זאטער הערבסט מאלט אלץ און מאלט.
‏יעטוועדעס בילד ער דערצײלט: געקאנט, געזאלט,
‏אין אלץ מיין איך׳ס פארגאנגען-ווייטע שפורן.

‏וואס איז אצינד איז שיינבארער אנטראקט,
‏ס׳איז דאס פארגיין, נאר ערב ניעם מארגן.
‏דו פילסט עס איז נאך ניט דער לעצטער אקט,
‏פאראויס איז ס׳גרויסע ווונדער ערשט פארבארגן.

‏א, ווונדער דא און דארטן. דורך מיר רעדט
‏זייער שטים אי שטיל, אי הויך, אי פרי, אי שפעט.

(ראסקא, נ.י., אויגוסט-סעפטעמבער, 1922)

XIV

Their voice—both late and early, low and loud—
All destiny-restrainers make me hear.
From trees of Autumn heavy with remembrance
A hymn of colors calls me, a world-prayer.
I, too, restrain—and dream. And may the gloomy
Cold watchman of decline guard us—he'll have
To join the one who chose to be a dreamer
And sing the song with him in a duet.

Oh, to create in light of nearing death!
Who could elect more solemn, splendid hours?
See, Autumn dresses up in gorgeous red—
It is no sunset, those are wounds of life.

If death—then red, the color of fresh blood.
As sunset grays, then courage comes—a flood.

XV

I praise you, Autumn, season of ripe gold,
Of orange, violet, and dreamy purples.
Within your delicate and radiant contours
The tangle of my soul is now unrolled.
Memories, visions, images and faces—
The color-sated Autumn paints and paints.
Each image claims: you could, you should, you meant,
In all I find my I's far, faded traces.

What now exists is shadowy entr'acte.
The sunset is but eve of a new morning.
You sense: it is not yet the final act,
Ahead—the stunning wonder, yet unborn.

Oh, wonders there and here, through me speaks out
Their voice: both late and early, low and loud.

Roscoe, N.Y., August–September 1922

◄ שטורעמס און טורעמס

שנייִקע ווײַטן
אויף בערגלעך פֿון ערד.
ווײַסע אומענדלעכקייטן, צעשטערט און פֿאַרצערט אויפֿן שפּיץ פֿון אַ שפּיז,
אויפֿן שפּיץ פֿון דעם טורעם פֿון וווּלוואָירט.
„ווו זענען די פֿאַראַיאָריקע שנייען?‟

Georgia O'Keeffe: *Radiator Building, Night, New York,* 1927

➤ *Storms and Towers*

Snowy expanses
On hills of earth.
White endless spaces, broken and absorbed on the point of a spear,
On the peak of Woolworth Tower.
"Where are the snows of yesteryear?"

Villon, מײַן ברודער, Maître Villon
דו האָסט ניט געזען
דעם טורעם פון וווּלוואָירט
אין אַ שטורעם פון שניי.
דו האָסט ניט געזען דעם אינטראָספעקטיוון צײַכן,
וואָס צעמענטעוע הייכן מיט טויזנט עלעקטרישע שטערן
(יעדער דאָס מזל פון אַ העלאָיז, אַ בעאַטריטשע, אַן אַליס)
שפּיגלען אַרײַן אינמיטן פון שנייען,
אין מיטן פון מענטשן, רעלסן, אויטאָמאָבילן.
דו האָסט נאָר געוווּסט, אַז אייביק איז דער ווילן,
וואָס פאַרוויניט די שנייען פון פאַראַיאָרן,
אייביק דער זיכרון, וואָס געדענקט זיי,
אייביק די האַנט וואָס זייט ווײַסקייט אין דער וועלט.

אַזוי ווייס איך,
אַז אייביק איז די האַנט, וואָס בויט טורעמס,
און אייביק דו און איך —
די געדענקער,
די ווײַסער,
די שאַפערס.

◄ נאָוועמבער

I

מעלאַנכאָליש גרין פון נאָוועמבער,
ווי זאָפטיק ברוינסטו הײַנט פרי אין קראָטאָנאַ־פּאַרק.
ווי רירסטו מיך הײַנט, קראָטאָנאַ־פּאַרק,
אין דײַן פײַכטן טול פון נאָוועמבער.
אין דײַן נעפלדיקער צוריקגעצויגנקייט
שמייכלסטו דורך טרערן,
און אין דײַן דערפאַרן־צערפולן שמייכל
ווייסלען זיך זכרונות פון בעסערע טעג.
אַזוי שמייכלט אַ פּופּציקיאָריקע דאָמע
מיט שפּאַקולן אויף די אויגן
איבער אַ ראָמאַן פון יונגן לעבן,
און אין אירע אויגן־ווינקלען
פינקלען פײַכטע פּערל.

II

נאָוועמבער.
הײַנט ביסטו צוגעקומען אַ נאָנטער, אינטימער, דערקענטער
צו דעם געשטאַן פון די צוועלף ערן־פאַזשן,

Villon, my brother, *Maitre Villon*,
You did not see
The Tower of Woolworth
In a storm of snow.
You did not see the introspective sign,
Which spires of concrete with a thousand electrical sparks
(Each—the star of a Heloise, a Beatrice, an Alice)
Thrust into the thick of snows,
Among masses of people, rails, automobiles.
You only knew, that eternal is the will
Sweeping away the snows of yesteryear,
Eternal, the memory which remembers them,
Eternal, the hand sowing whiteness in the world.

And so I know,
That eternal is the hand that builds towers,
And eternal, you and I—
The rememberers,
The knowers,
The creators.

➤ *November*

I

Melancholy green of November,
How juicy is your browning in the early morning in Crotona Park.
How you move me today, Crotona Park,
In your damp tulle of November,
In your foggy detachment
Smiling through tears.
Memories of better days
Gleam white in your sad experienced smile,
The smile of a fifty-year old
Bespectacled lady
Leaving over a novel of young life,
In the corners of her eyes
Glisten humid pearls.

II

November.
Today you came close, intimate, familiar,
Joining the team of twelve honorary pages

וואָס פירן די עקיפּאַזשן פֿון מײַנע געצײַכנטע יאָרן
אויף דער ערד.

הײַנט האָסטו זיך אַנטפֿלעקט פֿאַר מײַן זיכרון
מיט דײַן אייגן ליכט און לעבן,
און אויפֿגעהערט צו זײַן אַ נאָמען אויפֿן קאַלענדער.
יעדער טאָג האָט זײַן פֿאַרב,
יעדער מאָנאַט — זײַן קלאַנג.
ביז הײַנט האָט דײַן נאָמען ניט געקלונגען
אין דער קאַמער פֿון מײַנע זכרונות.
אָבער הײַנט האָסטו זיך צאַרט, אומדערוואַרט
פֿאַרגעשטעלט פֿאַר מיר,
מיט דעם גראָדן ברוינעם שרונט אויף דײַן גרוילעכן קאָפּ,
מיט דער דורכזיכטיקער מעלאַנכאָליע
אין די ווינקלען פֿון דײַנע ליפֿן.
גלײַך אין דעם האַרץ
האָט געדרונגען דײַן בליק
דורך דעם וואַל פֿון דײַנע נעפֿלען,
און אינטים האָבן מײַנע ליפֿן גענומען פּרעפּלען
דײַן נאָמען.

◀ סימעטריע

סימעטריע —
ריטם אין שטילשטאַנד.
אָפּרו אינמיטן באַוועגונג.
באַוועגונג אין איבער-רוים.

סימעטריע —
גימטריה פֿון מיסטעריע.
מיסטעריע פֿון ריטם
אויף יענער זײַט זוים
פֿון צײַט און רוים.

סימעטריע —
פּנים פֿון אַלץ וואָס האָט לעבעדיקן אָטעם.
דראַנג פֿון דומם וואָס גאָרט צום לעבן.
געשטאַלט פֿון פֿלאַנץ און חיה.
אור-בענקשאַפֿט פֿון מאַן און ווײַב.

מײַן געזאַנג צו דער סימעטריע
פֿון מאַן-ווײַב-פּנים,

That attend the carriages of my assigned years
On earth.

Today you unfolded before my memory
With your own life and light,
No more just a name in the calendar.
To each day its color,
To each month its sound,
Your name had not resounded
In the chamber of my memories.
But today you introduced yourself to me
Softly, unexpectedly,
With a straight, brown part in your graying head,
Transparent melancholy
In the corners of your lips.
Your gaze emerged
Through the veil of your fogs,
Entered my heart.
And my lips intimately murmured
Your name.

➤ *Symmetry*

Symmetry—
Rhythm arrested.
Rest in mid-movement.
Movement in higher space.

Symmetry—
Anagram of mystery.
Mystery of rhythm
On the other side of the seam
Of time and space.

Symmetry—face
Of all living breath. Drive
Of matter craving for life.
Figure of plant and animal.
Ancient longing of man and wife.

My song to the symmetry
Of man-woman face,

פון מאַן-ווײַב-לײַב.

מײַן געזאַנג — דער ריטם פון איבער-רוים,

וואָס האָט דאָס לעבעדיקע לײַב צעשפּאַלטן

אין צוויי.

אַ לאַמענט

פון צווישנלענד,

וואָס גאָרט צום אָנהייב,

צום סאַקראַמענט

פון פאַריכטן גאָטס פאַרבלענד.

קאַנוועקס —

און קאָנקאַוו.

(ווײַנענדיקער רעפלעקס

פון שקלאַפין און שקלאַף,

וואָס קאָנען זײַן גאָט!)

דאָס ליד פון צוויי,

פון צוויי וואָס ווילן זײַן,

וואָס זענען דאָ אַ בלויז צו זײַן —

איין.

פּנים צו פּנים געוווענדט.

לענד אויף לענד —

איין.

ריטם מיט ריטם געברענט,

ריטם אין ריטם פאַרלענדט —

איין.

סוד פון סוד און יסוד.

פרייד פון שד און פון גאָט.

בליץ פון שפּיז. משוגעת.

פלאַנצער און זאָט.

זעליקייט. האָס.

עקסטאַז.

אחד !

◄ אימאָביל

אָן קאָליר.

פאַרבײַ מיר קיין קלאַנג, קיין פאַרבן.

ווינטן שטאַרבן און בלײַבן הענגען אין מיטן פלי.

אין גלי פון זון ניט וואַרעם, ניט קאַלט.

Of man-woman body.
My song—the rhythm of higher space,
Which has split the living body
In two.

Oh, lament
Of loins,
Longing for the beginning,
For the sacrament
Of undoing God's blunder.

Convex—
And concave.
(Weeping reflex
Of maid and slave
Who could have been God!)
The song of two,
Of two who wish to be,
Who are here only to be—
One.

Face facing face.
Loin on loin—
One.
Rhythm seared in rhythm,
Rhythm sunk in rhythm—
One.

Secret of secret and sacred.
Joy of demon and God.
Flash of spear. Madness.
Planter and plot.
Beatitude. Hatred.
Ecstasy.
E-chod!

E-Chod*—one, unique,
oneness, attribute of God.

➤ *Immobile*

Colorless.
No sound, no hue passed by.
Hanging in mid-flight, winds die.
The sun's blaze—not hot, not cold.

אין האַרץ פון ים אַ וואַלד.

וואַסער, פלאַנצן, חיות — איין געשטאַלט מיט אַ סך פנימער.

קנוילן, שפילן זיך פון צײַטס קרײַז אַרויס — וועלטן, יאָרן.

נאָר אָן אַ ריר.

ניט גייען — שטייען אין דער ווײַסטע פון זיכרון.

אויפן שפיץ פון עווערעסט,

וואָס פאַרגעסט, אַז ער איז אַ באַרג געוואָרן,

לענט זיך פאַרגליווערט אָן דער דיסק פון זון.

פון אַ באַשטימטן אָרט שטייגט, צו אַ באַשטימטן ציל שפיזט —

דער אומרחמנותדיקער אַבעליסק

פון רויִק־אַנטשלאָסענעם ווילן.

אויבן איז אונטן.

אויבן, אונטן — איינס.

אַלץ איז איינס.

אַלץ איז.

בלויז איז.

שטיל.

אימאָביל.

◄ איך קום פון אַביסיניע

איך קום פון אַביסיניע.

אַ ווײַסער אַביסינער,

און בין —

אַ פרעמדער.

וואָלט איך געוועזן שוואַרץ,

וואָלט מען מיך פלינק אויסגעלייגט און אויפגעראַלט

און געלייענט ווי אַ מגילה אויף שוואַרצן פּאַרמעט מיט אותיות פון גאָלד.

נאָר איך בין העל.

שנאָפן פאַרדאָכטן אַרום מײַן שוועל.

מײַן בלאָנדקייט —

אפשר לויער איך בײַם גאָלדענעם טויער אין דער דעמער־שעה

אָפצוכאַ דעם אַ שטיקל זון.

מײַנע בלויע אויגן —

אפשר רײַב איך זיי אָן מיט טורקוזן אום האַלבע נאַכט

ווען די טויטע קומען פון די קברים,

און די מכשפים האָבן זייער שליטה.

אפשר בין איך אליין פון אשמדאַיס סוויטע.

ס׳אַרא וווּנדער, אַ עדגאַר,

וואָס אין די קינדער־צימערן

פאַרבײַט נאָך ניט מײַן נאָמען —

די שוואַרצע קאַץ און דעם וווּלקולאַק.

A forest in the heart of the sea.
Water, plants, animals—one figure with many faces.
Worlds, years—untangled, sliced from time's ring.
Not a stir.
Not traversing—standing in the desert of memory.
On the peak of Everest,
That forgot he was a mountain,
Leans a jelled sun disk.
From a certain spot rises, to a certain goal darts
The pitiless obelisk
Of calm determined will.
Up is down.
Up, down—one.
All is one.
All is.
Only is.
Still.
Immobile.

➤ *I Came from Ethiopia*

I came from Ethiopia.
A white Ethiopian,
I am—
A stranger.
Had I been black,
They would have deftly laid me out, unrolled me,
And read me like a scroll of black parchment with golden letters.
But I am light.
Suspicions sniff about my threshold.
My blond hair—
Perhaps I lurk at dusk by the golden gate
To bite off a piece of the sun.
My blue eyes—
Perhaps I rub them at midnight with a turquoise gem
When the dead walk out of their graves
And the sorcerers regain their power.
Perhaps I am myself of Asmodeus's gang.

Asmodeus—in Jewish folklore, the king of demons.

What a wonder, Oh, Edgar,
That in the nurseries
My name has not yet supplanted
The black cat and the werewolf.

◄ **פֿאַביוס לינדס טעג**

פֿאַביוס לינדס טעג גייען אָפּ מיט בלוט.
דורכפֿאַלן אין רויטע שלענגעלעך לײדיקן אויס די אָדערן.
אין קאָפּ — מוטנע־װײַסע פֿלעקן. צעטומלעניש.
און דאָס האַרץ איז שװער־באַלאָדן.
ער װאָלט ...
ער װאָלט ...
גרויע געשפּינסן מרה־שחורה
אין דעם זינען, פֿאַר די אויגן,
און עפּעס אַן אָנגעצויגענער בויגן, װאָס צילט
אין סאַמע שפּיץ נאָז.
פֿאַביוס לינד פֿאַרטראַכט זיך,
פֿאַררעדט זיך, פֿאַרלייענט זיך, פֿאַרציט
פֿון פֿאַרלוירעניש
די פֿעטליע אַרום דעם האַלדז.

פֿאַר װאָס קאָן זיך פֿאַביוס לינד נישט אָנכאַפּן
פֿאַר די פֿאַלעס פֿון דער צײַט
און מיטגיין אין די רייען פֿון אַלע מאַרשירער?
פֿאַר װאָס קאָן ער נישט אַ פֿאַר טאָן צוריק צום קינדישן שפּיל־הויף
און ברענגען פֿון דאָרטן די פֿײַפעלעך אויסצופֿײַפֿן זיך
דאָס ליד פֿון באַרוונג?
פֿאַר װאָס איז ער אַזוי גלײַכגילטיק בײַ אַ לוויה
און אַזוי דענערווירט בײַ אַ געבורט?
פֿאַר װאָס קאָן ער נישט אַ כאַפּ טאָן בײַדע הורן —
טויט און לעבן
און לאָזן זיך מיט זיי אין אַ הייליק־נאַריש ריקודל?

נאָר װעמען פֿרעגט דען פֿאַביוס לינד?
קיינעם נישט, בלויז זיך אַליין.
און װאָלט ער געקאָנט אויסמאַכן אַן ענטפֿער,
װאָלט ער נישט געפֿרעגט.

פֿאַביוס לינד איז אין אָט די טעג פֿון גראָדע רעלסן
גאָרנישט װאַך.
ער גייט אַרום שעהן, טעג
און חלומט גאָלע נישטאָען.
אַ צײַט, װאָס נישטאָ,
אַ לאַנד, װאָס נישטאָ,
מענטשן, װאָס נישטאָ,

➤ *Fabius Lind's Days*

Fabius Lind's days are running out in blood.
Red serpents of failures empty his veins.
In his head—white muddy stains. Confusion.
And a heavy load on his heart.
He could have . . .
He could have . . .
Gray spiderwebs of melancholy
Cover his mind, veil his eyes
And a strange taut bow
Aims at the tip of his nose.
Fabius Lind, sunk in contemplation,
In talking, in reading, tightens—
Out of sheer being lost—
The noose around his neck.

Why can't Fabius Lind hold on to
The coattails of these times
And stride in the rows of all the marchers?
Why can't he swing back to his childhood playground
And bring his flutes to play
The song of calm?
Why is he so indifferent at funerals,
So nervous at a birth?
Why can't he grab the two whores—
                          death and life
And let himself go in a holy-foolish dance?

  Whom does he ask?
  No one. Just himself.
  If he could brain-out an answer,
  He would not have asked.

In these days of straight rails, Fabius Lind
Is not awake.
He strays for hours, for days,
And dreams of pure isn'ts.
A time that isn't,
A land that isn't,

Max Weber: Woodcut, from
Shriftn 6, Spring 1920.

אַ פּאַביוס לינד, וואָס נישטאָ.
ער וואָלט ...
ער וואָלט ...
יאָ, יאָ, ער וואָלט !

דער פאַרלאַנג, דער געדאַנק פליט אַוועק אויף אַ נישט-געבעטענעם ווינט,
און קומט צוריק ווי אַ קנויל רויך.
דער חשבונדיקער מוח האָט פּאַביוס לינדן קיין מאָל נישט גוט געדינט.

_____

◄ 28 יאַנואַר

פינצטערניש.
געדיכטע, קנויליקע,
אוראַלטע, גרויליקע, אומהיימלעכע, מויליקע.
און פּלוצלונג — פונקען ווײַסע, גאַנצע פּאַסן.
מאַגניום-גלי — ווײַס, ווײַס.
אַ קני — וואַרעם, ווייך און שטײַף.
אַ רייף אַרום מיר, ווי דער רינג אַרום סאַטורן.
שטײַף אַרום מיר. ווײַס. מוטערלעכער נאָקטורן.
סומנע רייצעניש.
מאַרך-פאַרפלייצעניש. פאַל — פלי. פאַל — פלי.
קני. מאַגניום-גלי. און ווידער —
קנויליקע, קױליקע פינצטערניש.
פאַרפאַלעניש.

People that aren't,
A Fabius Lind who doesn't exist.
He could have . . .
He could have . . .
Yes, yes, he could have!

The desire, the thought, flies away on an uninvited wind
And comes back in a ball of smoke.
The calculating mind has never served Fabius Lind.

From **Fabius Lind's Diary**

➤ *January 28*

Darkness.
Thick, lumpy,
Primeval, uncanny, gaping darkness.
Suddenly—white sparks, bright stripes.
Magnesium-flare—white, white.
A knee—warm, soft, tight.
A hoop around me, like the ring around Saturn.
Tight around me. White. Motherly nocturne.
Somber excitement.
Brain-flood. Fall—fly. Fall—fly.
Knee. Magnesium-glow. And again—
Lumpy, coal-black darkness.
Abyss.

Louis Lozowick: *Subway Construction*, 1930.

קאָלאָמבוס-סױרקל פאַרנאַכט — אַ געמיש פון לײַב און שטײן,
אַ צענױפלױף פון דער שטאָטס עשירות,
מיט אַ שװינדזוכטיק נעגעריש געסל
פאַר זײַטיקע, אונטערטעניקע עדות
אױף דעם הפקר, הו-האַ און הױקלעטערײַ.

דעם פאַרגעסענעם דענקמאָל פון דעם גרעסטן אַנטדעקער
איז לאַנגװײליק פון די אױטאָס, עלעקטרישע רעגנבױגנס,
פון די פאַטריאָטישע סטאַטועריײַען,
װאָס באַװאָכן דעם פאַרק פאַרן פאָלק, פון דעם פאָלק, דורכן פאָלק.
די דרײַסיק-פערציק-שטאָקערס אַרום —
אַט שטרעקן זײ זײיערע גראַניטענע לאַפעס
צו די מײדלשע הינטנדלעך,
װאָס טאַנצן אױף די פּרװשינעס פון אַ כיטרען מעכאַניקער,
אַראָפ און אַרױף, אַראָפ און אַרױף,
מיט צוזאָג, מיט לאַדונג — װער װײס װאָס פאַר אַ גליקן!

פון לאַנגװײל באַסעװעט פינקטלעך מיט יעדן זײיגער-קער
(װער ס׳קאָן הערן — הערט)
די שטים פון דעם אַנטױשטן, פרומען קאָלומבוס:
װעמעס לעבן איז נישט אַ צופעליק איבערגעלאָזענע שילד,
װאָס שרײַט װעגן דערפאָלג, װעגן גרעסטער מציאה
אױף אַ פאַרהאַקטן, שױן לאַנג באַנקראָטירטן געשעפט?

פעברואַר 1 ◄

מען האָט אים געפירט צו דער גיליאָטין.
די מאַשין האָט געזאָגט: איך בין, איך בין בלױז אײַזן.
דער הענקער איז געװען קלוג און פרײַנטלעך,
און הינטער אים האָט ער געזען נאָך אַ קליגערן, נאָך אַ פרײַנטלעכערן.
אים האָבן פאַרװוּנדערט די פרײד-געשרײַען פון די שונאים.
ער האָט מורא געהאַט מיט אַלע מוראס
פון יעדן לעבעדיקן בלוטסטראָפן.
נאָר נישט קײן װאָרט און נישט קײן װילן
האָבן אָפּגעטײלט זיך פון אים
אױסצושרײַען אָדער אַרײַנצושעפטשען
זײַן אומשולד.

Columbus Circle at dusk—mixture of flesh and stone.
A confluence of city's riches
And a consumptive Negro alley
With marginal, meek witnesses
To wanton, uproar and highclimb.

The forgotten monument of the greatest discoverer
Is bored with the automobiles, electrical rainbows,
Patriotic statues
That guard the park for the people, from the people, by the people.
The thirty-forty-storiers all around
Push their granite paws
At the girly behinds,
Dancing on the springs of a clever mechanic
Up and down, up and down,
With promise, with invitation—who knows for what happiness!

Precisely at each turn of the clock,
    resounds the bored bass
Of the disenchanted, pious Columbus
(Those who can, hear):
—Whose life is not a leftover signboard,
Screaming success, great bargains,
On a boarded-up, long-ago
    bankrupted store?

Ben Shahn: *Bulletin Board*,
c. 1953.

➤ *February 1*

They led him to the guillotine.
The machine said: I am, I am only iron.
The executioner was wise and friendly,
And beyond him he saw a wiser,
    a friendlier one.
His enemies' cries of joy amazed him.
He feared with all the fears
Of each living drop of blood.
But no word and no wish
Parted his lips
To shout aloud or whisper low
His innocence.

לײַב קעגן אײַזן.

ער האָט גאָרנישט געוואָלט באַווײַזן.

ווי דאָס מעטאַל וואָלט אַרײַן אין זײַנע מוראַס

און זיי געשטײַפט מיט מוט און איראָניע.

אין פּולער האַרמאָניע מיט זיך —

צום ערשטן און לעצטן מאָל —

האָט ער געקושט דאָס שטאָל פון מעסער,

און ברײדערלעך געגריסט דעם הענקער.

קיין איין וויטרינע

פון זײַנע טויגענטן האָט ער נישט אויסגעפּוצט.

אויף אַלץ פאַרצויגן גרויע גאַרדינען און געזאָגט:

דו ביזט בלויז אײַזן,

איך בין בלויז אומשולדיק.

צוויי אַלטע נאַנאָס זענען געשטאַנען אין דער זאָווערוכע

פון מײַנס אַ חלום.

אויף זיי די סימבאָלן פון אַ פרעמדן גלויבן.

איך האָב זיי באַוואָרפן מיט שנײיענע קוילן.

האָט אַ ווינט זיך צעהוילן און בײַזע פליגל האָבן געקלאַפּט,

און כ׳האָב צעריסענע ווערטער געכאַפּט:

שׂונא אויף שׂונא.

ווי די נעכטנס, אַזוי די הײַנטן.

לאָמיר זיך פײַנטן, איינס ס׳אַנדערע היטן.

איך דיך, דו מיך, מיר בײַדע אַ דריטן —

שׂונאים אַלע.

Body against iron.
He didn't wish to prove a thing.
As if the metal flowed in his fears
And stiffened them with courage and irony.
In full harmony with himself—
For the first and the last time in his life—
He kissed the steel of the knife,
And greeted the hangman as a brother.
He polished
No showcase of his virtues.
He pulled grey curtains over it all
    and said:
You are only iron.
I am only innocent.

Louis Lozowick: *Nuns on Wall
Street*, 1941.

➤ *February 4*

Two old nuns stood in the blizzard
Of my dream.
On their chests the symbols of an alien religion.
I bombarded them with snowballs.
A wind howled, wicked wings battered in the wind,
And I caught tatters of words:

    Enemy upon enemy.
    Todays like yesterdays.
    Let us hate, let us watch one another.
    I—you, you—me, both of us—a third one,
    All are enemies.

שוין נישט קיין נאָנעס, קיין זקנות —
אינמיטן צעבייזערטער ווייסקייט פון שניי
האָבן צוויי שוואַרצע שווערדן געפאַכט מיט סוף.
און איך האָב זיך צעריטשעט אין שלאָף,
און געעפנט די אויגן מיט אַ צעשראָקן געשריי —
חברים, חברים, חברים.

◄ פעברואַר 7

איך האָב געירשנט נאָיוון אָפנהאַרץ
פון דורות קליינשטעטלעדיקע פוילישע ייִדן,
און שפיציקע רייד
פון הייסגעבאַדענע פרויען אין מיַין קלאָן.
אַ בלינדע יוני-נאַכט האָט אַלץ אויסגעמישט
און מיך אַרויסגעשיקט —
אָן איַינזעעניש פאַר סימעטריע.

מיַין ווזזאַווי וועגט מיך פאַרזיכטיק
אויף דער וואָג פון זיַין וועלט- און מענטש-געניטקייט.
רופט מיַין שטים צוריק — אינטים און גראָד.
לויט דעם כלל פון אַ העלפט דער וואָנט און אַ העלפט דעם טיַיך,
איז ער מיר מוחל די אינטימיטעט.
און די גראָדקייט — עלעהיי אַ ווירע פון שטאָל:
צעשיידט און שטעכט.

ווערן מיַינע ווזזאַווס שיטעכער.
און דער זשאַווער פון מיַין קליאָמקע —
נישט בלויז דער זוירערשטאָף פון דער לופט.
נאָך גוט וואָס פון ציַיט צו ציַיט
קאָן איך האָבן מיַין אייגן ביסל שפּאַס מיט זיך אַליין.

◄ פעברואַר 10

כ׳בין מיד פון ווערטער. וואָס מער קלאָר איז אַלץ מער דול.
איך בין מיט דולקייט ביז דער קלאָרסטער קלאָרקייט פול.

פון סתירות האָט אַ טורעם פאַר אַ טאָג זיך אויסגעבויט.
דאָס ליד איז רו פאַר מיר, אַ פריַיד-באַגעגעניש מיט טויט.

No more nuns, no old women—
In the midst of a furious snow whiteness
Two black swords wielded the end.
And I roared in my sleep,
And opened my eyes with a terrified shriek—
Friends, friends, friends.

➤ *February 7*

I inherited naive open-heartedness
From generations of small-town Polish Jews,
And sharp talk
From hot-bathed women in my clan.
A blind June-night mixed it all
And sent me out—
With no regard for symmetry.

My counterpart weighs me carefully
On the scales of his experience with world and man.
My voice calls back—intimate and straight.
By the rule of half to the wall and half to the river,
He forgives me my intimacy.
And the straightness—like a steel ruler:
Cuts and divides.

My counterparts grow rarer and rarer.
And the rust on my door-knob—
Not just the oxygen in the air.
Luckily, from time to time
I can enjoy a joke with myself.

➤ *February 10*

I'm tired of words. The clearer—the madder still,
To the clearest clarity I am with madness filled.

A tower of contradictions rose in one day's breath.
The poem is my rest, a joyful encounter with death.

זוך נישט קיין בריק צו מענטשן.
ווארט מיט דער וועלט אויף דעם ווארט,
וואָס זאָל זיין ווי דאָס שטאַרבן פון אַ צדיק
נאָך אַ פול און אָפּגעגאַרט לעבן.
בענק אויס דאָס ווארט,
וואָס זאָל אָפּשטעלן די רציחה פון מידע בייזע מחנות.
זוך דאָס ווארט,
וואָס זאָל פאַרציִען מיט אַ נעפּל די אויגן פון שטאַרקע לייט.
טראָג אויס דאָס ווארט,
וואָס זאָל רעדן ווי דאָס שווייגן פון אַ גרייז
ווען ער קוקט אויף דער זון אויבן און אויף אַ לוויה אונטן
מיט דעם זעלבן זעענדיקן בליק.
פון דיַין האַרץ שטראַלן זיך בריקן אין אַלע זייטן.

פאַביוס לינדס קעניגרייך —
עטלעכע אָפּגעצאַמטע קעסטלער.
ווי לויט אַ שטענדיקן, זעלביקן שפּרוך
צעעפענען זיך די קעסטלער אַרויסצולאָזן זיַינע טעג —
פון איין הויז מיט אַ נומער
צו אַ צווייט הויז מיט אַ נומער.
איבער אים גערוישן פון גרויסשטאָט,

רעדער, רעלסן אויבן,
רעלסן, רעדער אונטן, טיף אין אַ טונעל.

ווען פאַביוס לינד טוט זיך אויס פון די גערוישן,
בליַיבן ברעקלעך פאַרב, פלעקלעך קלאַנג,
אַ צוזאַמענגעשטעלטע מאַסקע פון אָמרו און צעטומלעניש.
אַ מאָל בליצט אויף אַ קלאָרקייט און זי כאַפּט דעם אָנבליק
פון אַן אויסגעבענקטער נאָטרדאַם,
פון אַ געפּלאַנטן עמפּייר-סטייט,
פון אַן עלעקטראָ-סטאַנציע אויפן דניעפּר —
אַמאָל, אַמאָל.

די אַמאָלן ווערן בליַנד צעשטאָכן פון זיגזאַגישן בראַכווואַרג,
וואָס פאַלט אויף זיַין קאָפּ. דער קאָפּ אין סאַמע מיטן
פון פאַל און בראָך. און ער אַליין — אין אַ זייַט, אויפן ראַנד.

Don't look for bridges to people.
Wait with the world for the word
That would be like the dying of a saint
After a full and cheated life.
Dream up the word
That would stop the slaughter of weary, wicked hordes.
Look for the word
That would fog the eyes of strong men.
Bear in your body the word
That would speak like the silence of an elder
When he looks at the sun above and at a funeral below
With the same seeing gaze.
From your heart, bridges radiate in all directions.

➤ *February 17*

Fabius Lind's kingdom—
A few fenced crates.
As to a permanent, identical incantation,
The crates open up to let his days out—
From one house with a number
To another house with a number.
All over him, noises of the big city.

Wheels, rails above,
Rails, wheels below, in deep tunnels.

When Fabius Lind undresses the noises,
He is left with crumbs of color, spots of sound,
A composite mask of unrest and confusion.
Sometimes a clearing flashes, it has the image
Of a dreamed-up Notre-Dame,
Of a well-planned Empire-State,
Of a hydro-electrical power-station on the Dnieper—
Once upon a time.
Once upon a time.

Power station on the Dnieper
(turbulent river in the
Ukraine)—hailed as one of the
wonders of communist
construction, a major image of
pro-Soviet sentiment in the West.

The once-upon-a-times are stabbed blind by the jagged wreckage
Falling on his head. His head in the midst
Of crush and downfall. And he himself on a side, on the brink.

דאַן איז ער אײַנגעהילט אין נאָכטעניש,
אַלץ איז אים דאָכטעניש, אויסטראָכטעניש,
קונצן און מאַסקעס פון טויט.

◄ פעברואַר 23

אַ שוין נישט ווײַטע שטײַט ערגעץ אויף אַ באַרג
די פאַרשײַטע יונגע העקסע
אין ברײַט און הויך צעפלאַשעטן קלייד
אָן אונטערהויזן.
אירע הוילע, זאָפטיקע פיס
קלײַבן זיך אַ טרעט צו טאָן איבער אַלע דיכן אויף דער ערד.
די פיס וועלן זיגן.
אַלע דיכן וועלן אָנהייבן קאָנוווּלסירן, וויבירירן
און באַשפּריצן מיט פאַרבן און ריחות די וועגט פון דער וועלט.
נאָך אַ טאָג, נאָך אַ טאָג —
זי וועט אײַננעמען אַלץ און אַלעמען
די נאַקעטע מויטשישקע.

◄ מײַנע לידער

מײַנע לידער קאַלטע זענען
און פון זיי מיט ווײַטקייט בלאָזט.
האָט קיינער ניט געהערט פון קאַלטן ברענען,
ניט געלעקט דעם פלאַם פון פראָסט?
מײַנע לידער האַרטע זענען
שטײַפער, פעלדזיקער מאַרשרוט.
קאָן קיינער ניט אין האַרטן פעלדז דערקענען
קיל פאַרטאַיעט לאַווואַ־בלוט?

◄ קאַלטע נאַכט

פאַראַן אַ געבוירן אַזאַס,
וואָס איז רויוינטיקער, ווי אַ באַלויכטענע גאַס
אין מיטן מערץ.
פאַראַן אַ געבוירן אַזאַס,
וואָס איז אומפאַרשטענדלעכער ווי דער כעס
פון אַ פאַרשפּעטיקטן ווינטער
מיט זײַן אויסערצײַט,
אויסערפּלאַץ,
אויסעראָנשטענדיקייט.

Then he is wrapped in night's profusion,
All seems to him imagining, delusion,
Tricks and masks of death.

► *February 23*

Not any more distant, somewhere on a mountain,
The frivolous young witch
Stands in a wide, billowing dress,
With no panties.
Her naked, juicy legs
Will soon step over the thighs of the earth.
The legs will win.
All thighs will begin to convulse, to vibrate,
And spurt colors and smells on the walls of the world.
One more day, one more day—
She will conquer all and everyone,
The naked, impertinent tart.

► *My Poems*

This is Part I of a longer poem.

My poems are cold.
Distance blows from them.
Has no one heard of cold burning,
Or licked the flame of frost?
My poems are hard.
Stiff, rocky route.
Can no one see in the hard rock
Cool, lurking lava-blood?

► *Cold Night*

There is a birth
Raw-windier than a lighted street
In March.
There is a birth
More incomprehensible than the rage
Of a belated winter
At his being out-of-time,
Out-of-place,
Out-of-decency.

און דאָס געבוירן האָט מען אַ נאָמען: איך,
און בירגער איך איז אַ פֿאַרהאַקטער שלאָס.
פֿלינקע לײַט ווילן צו אים צופֿאַסן אַ פֿלינקן שליסל,
אָבער אַליין איז ער שוין לאַנג אַן אויפֿדריי.

און בירגער איך
האָט זיך שוין עטלעכע-און-פֿערציק מאָל געדרייט אַרום דער זון.
טאָקע די טעג איז געוואָרן רונד אַ פֿולער חשבון —
און דער שלאָס איז נאָך מער פֿאַרדרייט.

◄ פֿאַרריגלט צימער

טונקל, פֿאַרריגלט צימער.
לופֿט געדיכט און אָנגעזאַפֿט מיט מורא און געפֿאַר.
פֿאַביוס לינד איז אויג אויף אויג
מיט אַן אויסטערלישער פֿרוי.
פֿאַביוס לינד איז קליין און ציטערט.
די פֿרוי איז גרויס און וואַקסט — און שלאָקסט
מיט שווערלײַביקע ריחות.
גערוך פֿון שטאָל,
פֿון זומערדיקע נאָכמיטיקס אין געדיכטעגניש פֿון וואַלד.
מעכטיקע לענדן און מעכטיקע פֿיס.
פֿאַביוס לינד האָט מורא, און אים איז צום שטאַרבן גוט.
די ריחות וויקלען אײַן,

נעמען צו ווילן — אים איז צום שטאַרבן גוט.
ער דאַרף נישט דאַרפֿן עקזיסטירן.

ער און די פֿרוי און די מורא און דאָס גוטסקייט איז איין,
און ער איז געוואַלטיק אַליין.

◄ אַ באַגעגעניש

אַ צוויי מינוט האָבן מיר זיך אָנגעקוקט
אין נײַגעריקער שווײַגעניש.
ווען די העפֿלעכקייט האָט מיך אַ טאָרע געטאָן בײַם אַקסל,
האָב איך זיך פֿאַרגעשטעלט:
אַ מענטש, די קרוין פֿון באַשאַף.
דער גראָזנהאָפּסער
איז נישט נתפּעל געוואָרן
און ווײַטער געקוקט מיט פֿאַרדזיכטיקע, גלימערדיקע אויגן.

And that birth has a name: I.
And citizen I is a twisted lock.
Clever people would fit him with a clever key,
But he himself got jammed up long ago.

And citizen I
Has forty-some times turned around the sun
(Just the other day he reached a round number),
And the lock is turned ever tighter.

➤ *Bolted Room*

Dark, bolted room.
Thick air soaked with fear and danger.
Fabius Lind—eye to eye
With a bewildering woman.
Fabius Lind is small and trembling,
The woman is big and growing—and pouring out
Odors of a heavy body.
Smells of stable,
Of summer afternoons in the thick of a forest.
Powerful hips and powerful legs.
Fabius Lind is scared and feels so deadly good.
The odors enfold him,

Take away his will—
He doesn't need to need to exist.

He and the woman and the fear and the goodness are one.
And he is enormously alone.

➤ *An Encounter*

For two minutes we gazed at each other
In curious silence.
When politeness nudged me in the shoulder,
I introduced myself:
A man, the crown of creation.
The grasshopper
Was not overwhelmed.
He kept on gazing with careful, glimmering eyes.

אַפֿילו װען איך האָב אים מיט אים שטאָלץ געװיזן דעם עראָפּלאַן,
װאָס האָט פּונקט דעמאָלט פֿאַרבײַגעזשוזשעט
איבער אונדז בײדן,
האָט ער נישט פֿאַרלוירן די װירדע.
אַ באַליידיקטער האָב איך שוין אָן צערעמאָניעס
גענומען אים אויף מײַנע אויגן
און באַטראַכט זײַנע פֿײַן-געשניצטע רױטע פֿיס,
די שטאַרקע פֿליגל,
די העכסט-מענלעכע װאָנצעס.
מײַן חוצפה איז דעם קינצלער פֿון גראָזן גאָרנישט געפֿעלן.
מיט אויבנאַראָפֿיקער גלײַכגילט
האָט ער אויסגעדרײט צו מיר זײַן זײער באַחנט הינטנדל
און האָפּס-האָפּס
אַװעק —
אַ סך שענער, עלעגאַנטער, זיכערער,
װי מײַן עראָפּלאַן.

װען איך װעל לעבן נאָך נאָך הונדערט יאָר,
װעל איך שוין מסתמא האָבן די נײַטיקע מאַשין צו הערן
זײַן אור-, מיליאָנמאָל אור-אור-אייניקלס
פֿאַרניכטנדיק געלעכטער.

◄ מאָסקװער נאַכט סוף דעצעמבער 1934

שװער צו זײַן קלוג הײַנטיקע נעכט,
און ס׳העלפֿט נישט צו זײַן מאָדערן.
עס העלפֿט נישט צו שמײכלען װיסיק און מעלאַנכאָליש
אויף די שפּראַכלעכע ממזריײַען פֿון דער היסטאָריע:
"די רעגירונג פֿון דער רעפּובליק װערט איבערגעגעבן אין די הענט פֿון אַן אימפּעראַטאָר".

אַ פֿאַסקודנע אַלטע לבֿנה קריכט אַרײַן צו מיר דורכן פֿענצטער
און װאַרגט מיך מיט קאַלטער האַנט.
זי קײַכט, זי שומט איבער מיר:
װער ביזט דו צו צו װעלן אויסגלײַכן חשבונות פֿון דער װעלט,

צו צערענען טאָמער איז דיר אַ קינדישע צאַצקע צעבראָכן.
ערשט אײַערנעכטן האָב איך געזען אַ פֿאַלעסטינער מורד און בטלן
אַכצן: יושר, ליבשאַפֿט,
און רופֿן צו הילף עפּעס אַ טאַטל דאָ בײַ אונדז אין הימל.
ערשט נעכטן האָט זיך אײַערס אַ געזעמל נאַריש געמאַכט
אַרום אַ שטײַנערנער מוידעטשיסקע מיט אַ שטורקאַץ אין געהויבענעם אָרעם
און געשטורעמט, געליאַרעמט מיט התפעלות:

Even when I proudly showed him the airplane
That just then buzzed by
Over our heads,
He did not lose his dignity.
Offended, I fixed him with my eye
And examined without ceremony
His finely wrought red legs,
His strong wings,
His manly mustaches.
He didn't like my impertinence, the trickster of grass.
With condescending indifference,
He turned to me his gracious ass
And hopped away—
With a leap
More beautiful, elegant, surer
Than my airplane.

If I live another hundred years
I shall probably have the necessary machine to hear
His great-, million times great-grandson's
Devastating laughter.

➤ *Moscow Night, End of December 1934*

It's hard to be clever these nights,
And useless to be modern.
Useless to smile knowingly and observe with melancholy
The language bastardisms of history:
"The government of the Republic is delivered into the hands of the Emperor."

A nasty old moon crawls in my window
And chokes me with a cold hand.
She coughs, she foams over me:
Who do you think you are
That you want to straighten the accounts of the world,
To rage when a childish toy of yours is broken.
The other day I saw a Palestinian bum and rebel
Growl: Justice, love,
And call for help to some daddy here in the sky.
Yesterday a crowd of yours made fools of themselves
Around a stone broad with a torch in her raised arm
And stormed, clamored in excitement:

ברידערלעכקייט, גלייכהייט, די פֿאַרונופֿט !
און היינט גלאָצטו אַרויף צו מיר פֿון אַ צעקנאָדערט קישן,
און מאָנסט מיט טרוקן-בראַנדיקע אויגן אַן ענטפֿער פֿון מיר,
הלמאַי אַן איקאַנע דיינע איז אַרויסגעפֿאַלן פֿון ראַם,
און די ראַם אַליין — באַשפּריצט מיט הבלס ווערעמען שוידער.
אפֿשר ווילסטו פֿרעגן נאָך העכער, די שטערן?
נאַ, פֿאַרנעם (ווי איר יאָלדישע פֿאַעטן האָט ליב צו זאָגן) זייער געזאַנג —
וואָס הערסטו?
האָרך גוט, האָרך גוט.

איך האָב געהערט, איך האָב פֿאַרנומען,
און געוואָלט אויסשרייען מיין גרעסט-לעצט געשריי
פֿאַר מיר און פֿאַרן גאַנצן באַשאַף.
נאָר דער העקסעס האָנט אויף מיין האַלדז,
דער העקסעס קעלט אין מיין קעל.

אָ ווער האָט געזאָגט, אַז רחמנות איז נישט אַ יסוד פֿון דער וועלט?
פּונקט דאָ האָט דער לוח
געגעבן דער אַלטער אַ בלאָטן ווונק
און זי איז אַוועק מיט אים ווי קיין מאָל גאָרנישט.

מיין האַלדז איז לויז געוואָרן.
נאָר מיין צונג שטום.
נאָך שטומער.

◄ פֿאַביוס לינד רייַט אויפֿן ווינט

I

פֿאַביוס לינד האָלט זיך פֿעסט אָן דער צעפֿלאָשעטער גריווע
פֿון יונגן פֿרילינג
און גאַלאָפּירט איבער די פֿרייַע שליאַכן פֿון באַגער.
וואָליופֿטע סאַמומלעך אַרום אים,
וואָליופֿטע סאַמומלעך אין אים.
פֿאַביוס לינד פֿאַרטרויט זיך דער פֿאַרשייַטער גריווע
און ער טראַכט,
און ער חלומט.

II

פֿאַביוס לינד האָט זיך שוין לאַנג געכאַפֿט,
אַז אַרום אים מערן זיך אַלץ מער און דרייסטער
אַלערליי יונגע מאַנספֿאַרשוינען,
אומגלייבלעך יינגערע פֿאַר אים.

Brotherhood, Equality, Reason!
And today you stare at me from a rumpled pillow
With fiery-dry eyes demanding an answer:
Why has an icon of yours fallen out of its frame,
And the frame itself is speckled with Abel's warm shudder?
Maybe you'd like to ask—even higher—the stars?
Go on, perceive (as you idiot poets like to say) their singing—
What do you hear?
But listen well.

I listened, I perceived,
I wanted to scream my last, and greatest scream
For me and for the whole creation.
But the hag's hand was on my neck,
The hag's chill in my throat.

Who said that pity is not a foundation of the world?
Right then the calendar
Gave the old witch a lewd wink
And she left with him, just like that.

My throat relaxed.
But my tongue is dumb.
Dumber.

➤ *Fabius Lind is Riding the Wind*

I

Fabius Lind clings to the flowing mane
Of young spring,
Galloping on the free highways of desire.
Voluptuous desert-winds around him,
Voluptuous desert-winds inside him.
Fabius Lind surrenders to the frivolous mane
And ponders
And dreams.

II

Fabius Lind has long since understood
That assorted young males,
Unbelievably younger than himself,
Will multiply daringly around him.

אָסור, צי ער ווייס

ווען אַזוי פיל טעג

האָבן צײַט געהאַט זיך אויסצושטעלן ווי חיילות וועכטער

הינטער זײַן נישט־פאַרדעכטנדיקער שטאָלצער פלייצע.

אָסור, צי ער פאַרשטייט,

פאַר וואָס די אַלע פרעמדע עדות זאָלן ניט צוריק אַוועק

אין די נישט־געבעטענע נעכטנס, אײערנעכטנס און פאַרפינעפיאַרנס —

פון אַ פאַך בלויז מיט זײַן יונגער האַנט.

אָבער צו־וואָס אַזוי פיל נײַע מאַנספאַרשוינען?

און פאַר וואָס בײַ זיסן פרעכע צײַנער אָפּ שטיקער פון זײַן פרייד

בײַם אָנבליק פון די נײַע אָפעליאַס?

III

פאַביוס לינדס האַרץ איז פול מיט צאַרטקייט

צו די לעצטע פרויען־מאָדעס.

זײַנע ליפן מורמלען אָפט פרומע אָדעס צום אײדעלן ריטם

פון נישט־איבערגעוואַקסענע, וויבערירנדיקע היפטן,

און מיט ליבשאַפט גליטשט זײַן זיך דערפרײַט אויג

איבער דעם שטײַפן בויג פון אָפּנהאַרציק טרעטנדיקע פיס.

נאָר די נײַע ער׳לעך

פאַרשטעלן אָפט חוצפהדיק דעם פרײַען אויסקוק.

און פאַביוס לינד איז נישט קיין הײלמאַן־יעגער,

נישט קיין ער־גאָרילע.

ער איז נישט אַפילו — גלאַט אַ שטרײַטער אָדער שלעגער.

ער איז אַ דזשענטלמאַן

פון דער געצאַמטער, ציוויליזירטער שטאָט ניו־יאָרק,

וואָס וואַנדלט נאָר אַ מאָל איבער די סאַמיק־רײַצנדיקע שטעגלעך

פון פרוידס חלום־טײַטשונג.

און אויב נישט ער פאַרשעמט זיך,

און נישט ער ווערט געטריבן,

דערלויבט אים דאָך דער גרויסער זעער און פאַרשטייער פון ווין

צו שמייכלען גוטמוטיק.

און אַז וועלכעלעך טרויער

שלאָגן אין די ברעגן פון דעם שמייכל —

זעט עס דאָך קיינער נישט.

IV

פאַביוס לינד איז שוין אָפּגעריטן אַ מהלך

אויף זײַן האַרקזאַם פערד.

נאָך דאַרשטיקער טוליעט ער זיך צו דער הפקרדיקער גריווע,

און אײַלט —

— אײַלט, אײַלט, אײַלט —

אויף אַלץ נײַע און נײַערער רופן.

Damned if he knows
When so many days had time
To muster like armies of watchmen
Behind his unsuspecting proud back.
Damned if he understands
Why all these strange witnesses should not retreat
Into unwanted yesterdays, before-yesterdays, five-years-ago—
At a mere wave of his young arm.
But why so many new males?
And why do insolent teeth bite off pieces of his joy
At the sight of the new Ophelias?

III

Fabius Lind's heart is full of tenderness
For the latest feminine fashions.
His lips mutter pious odes to the refined rhythm
Of not-overgrown vibrant hips,
And his happy eye glides lovingly
Over the taut curves of sincerely walking legs.
But the new "he"s
Impertinently obstruct the open view.
And Fabius Lind is not a Shaman-hunter,
Not a he-gorilla.
He isn't even a rival or a fighter.
He is a gentleman
Of the restrained, civilized city New York
Who wanders at times in the exciting-poisoning paths
Of Freud's dream-interpretation.
And though he's not ashamed,
Nor appeased,
Still the great seer and understander from Vienna
Allows him a good-natured smile.
And if light waves of sadness
Lap the shores of his smile—
Nobody will see it.

IV

Fabius Lind has ridden quite a distance
On his obedient horse.
Ever thirstier, he clings to the frivolous mane,
And hurries—
Hurries, hurries, hurries—
To ever newer and newer calls.

נישט אַזוי דו אַליין,

װי דער גאַנג צו דיר, דאָס קאַפּיטולירן צו דיר,

ליבער דיקטאַטאָר.

איך װייס נישט אין װאָס פֿאַר אַ קאַלקאַװיוון

ס׳האָבן זיך מײַנע שטאַפֿן געפֿורעמט,

נאָר קאַפּיטולאַציע פֿײַנען זיי מיט אַ גרויס פֿײַנטעניש.

איך בין נישט געבוירן זיך אונטערצוגעבן.

װען דו גיסט דו הינטערװײַלעכץ אַן אַטעם אויף מיר —

אין דעם אַװעקפֿאַל פֿון אַ נאָענטן,

אין אַ רגע פֿון אייגענער געפֿאַר,

צי אין אַ פֿרעמדער לוויה אויפֿן גאַס —

װיל איך שוין זײַן אויף יענער זײַט פֿאַרק,

אין דעם נישט־הערן־געדענקען פֿון דײַנע שאַטנס —

אַבי אויסמײַדן דאָס געפֿעכט, װוּ דו מוזט זײַן זיגער.

אויף מײַן שװעל איז שוין אויסגעקאַרבט דער טאָג,

װען דו װעסט קומען צו מיר גוט־יום־טובֿ ביטן.

נאָר װיל איך — קאָן איך פֿריִער קלאַפֿן אין דײַן טיר,

און דו װעסט מיך אויפֿנעמען.

אָן פֿרעגענישן, אָן טענות,

װעסטו דריקן מײַן האַנט און באַדעקן דעם טיש

מיט דײַן ברויט און זאַלץ.

דו צו מיר — אָבער איך אויך צו דיר,

װי עס דאַרף זײַן צװישן אמתע, נאָענטע פֿרײַנט,

חבר טויט.

קעגן מיר אין דעם סאַבוויי איז געזעסן די מאַדאָנע,

פֿאַרלייגט אַ פֿוס אויף אַ פֿוס

און געלייענט אַ טאַבלאַיד.

געלייענט װי אַ קאַסירשע האָט זיך געטאָן אַ טוק און אַ טויך —

איר חתן האָט זי פֿאַרלאָזן מיט אַן אויפֿגעגאַנגענעם בויך.

די מאַדאָנע האָט מיט איר ליפּ־שטיפֿט באַשמירט איר מויל

און װײַטער געביסן אין דער ברעניקער קויל

פֿון טראַגעדיע.

די מאַדאָנע האָט אַ גלעט געטאָן איר שיכל פֿון שלאַנגישער הויט

און װײַטער באַאָמערט דעם שלונדיקן טויט

פֿון דער קאַסירשע.

➤ *Fabius Lind to Comrade Death*

Not so much you yourself,
As the road to you, the surrender to you,
Dear dictator.
I do not know in what lime kiln
My mettle was formed,
But it hates surrender with a great hatred.
I was not born to give up.
When you breathe backward upon me—
In the falling away of a friend,
In a moment of danger,
In a stranger's funeral on a street—
I wish I'd been on the other side of the fence,
In the not-hearing-not-remembering of your shadows—
If only to avoid the duel, in which you always have the upper hand.

On my threshold, the date is engraved
When you arrive with your holiday greetings.
But if I will—I can knock first on your door,
And you will receive me.
No questions, no complaints,
You will shake my hand and deck your table
With bread and salt.
You to me—but me to you too,
As with real, close friends,
Comrade death.

➤ *The Madonna in the Subway*

Across from me in the subway sat the madonna
Crossing her legs,
Bending over a tabloid.
She read about a cashier-girl who jumped into the water
When her bridegroom left her with a rising belly.
The madonna put lipstick on her mouth
And went on biting into the burning coal
Of tragedy.
She stroked her snakeskin shoe,
And proceeded to lament the drowning death
Of the cashier-girl.

טיק-טאַק האָט געקלאַפּט מײַן בליק.

דער מאַדאַנעס אויגנדעקלעך האָבן דערהערט

און צוויי לענגלעכע היילן האָבן געטאָן אויף מיר אַ קער

זייער זאַמשענע טיפקייט, זייער היימלעכן סוד,

און איך האָב פֿאַרנומען אָט די רייד דער מאַדאַנעס,

די רייד, וואָס זי האָט גערעדט בלויז צו מיר

אין דעם סאַבווי:

אין גליל, דעמאַלט אין גליל,

האָבן די סטאַליערס, די שוסטערס, די שנײַדערס,

Raphael Soyer: *Passer-By*, c. 1935.

My gaze tick-tocked.
The madonna's eyelids heard,
And two longish caves turned to me
Their suede depth, their intimate mystery.
And I perceived the words of the madonna,
The words which she spoke to me alone
In the subway:
In Galilee, once upon a time in Galilee,
The carpenters, the shoemakers, the tailors,

די פֿישערס, די מלוות, די גנבים

אַ רעטער באַדאַרפֿט און אַ גאָט.

האָב איך געעפֿנט מײַנע בתוּלישע לענדן

און אין אַ טונקעלער שעה — אויפֿגענומען אין מײַן טראַכט

דעם באַדערפֿטיקן זאָמען פֿון דעם, װאָס כ׳װייס נאָך אַלץ נישט זײַן נאָמען.

אַ זעלנער, אַ פֿרעמדער, אַ בייזער, אַ קנעכט פֿון דעם קייסער,

אַ פֿישער מיט דעם הענט אין קרעץ פֿון שלעפֿן די שטריק פֿון זײַן נעץ,

צי אַזױ אַ בראַדיאַגע, װאָס האָט גראָד דעמאָלט געפֿרעפֿלט: מײַן גאָט!

איך קאָן דיר נאָר זאָגן, כ׳בין פֿאַרגאַנגען אין טראַגן.

אַ, פֿאַראַנען נעכט װען ס׳שטעכט דער גײַסט דײַן אײַנגעװײד,

װי אַ קאָרשונס שנאָבל,

און פֿלעכט דיך אַרום װי אַ שלאַנג.

פֿאַראַן שװאַרצע, אָפֿנהאַרציקע נעכט, װאָס אָנען

דאָס מאַנען פֿון בתוּלישע לענדן.

ס׳איז געװען דער גײַסט פֿון גאָט,

װײַל זעלנער און פֿישערס און בראַדיאַגעס

האָבן געמאַנט אַ רעטער, אַ גאָט.

די מאַדאַנע האָט באַפֿאָדערט איר נאָז און קין,

(איר נאָז איז געװאָזן נאָבל און דין)

און האָט װײַטער גערעדט:

פֿון װײַטן בלענד

און ליכטיקן רוף,

פֿון נאַנטן טרויער

אין שװערן גוף

חלומען אויס מאָלער און פּאָעטן

מײַנע פֿאָרטרעטן דור נאָך דור.

פֿון אַמאָליקן צװייטיקן פֿרילינג

אויף פֿעלדער, אין װעלדער,

שטרעקן הענט זיך: באַװיליק!

בעטן אױגן

דורך דער לענג און ברייט פֿון יאָר.

אין געװאָרגענער װאָר

אויף גאַסן, אין סאַבוויס,

בענקען מענטשן אַלץ נאָך דעם װוּנדער,

כאָטש זיי גלייבן נישט מער אין זײַן געבוירן.

אַ, איך װעל אַ מאָל װאַרפֿן פֿון זיך די געװעבן

װאָס װיקלען מיך, פֿענעט אַרום

און מיט נאַקעטקייט

אַנטרינקען אײַער דאָרשט.

און הער:

ס׳װעט זײַן װי יענער גרויסער באַשער

דעמאָלט, דעמאָלט אין גליל.

The fishermen, the moneylenders, the thieves
Needed a savior and a God.
Then I opened my virgin loins
And in a dark hour received in my womb
The needy seed of one whose name I still don't know.
A soldier, a stranger, an angry man, a slave of a Caesar,
A fisherman, hands calloused from pulling his nets,
Or just a bum who happened to whisper: my God!
All I can tell you is, I got pregnant.
Oh, there are nights when the spirit slices into your guts
Like a vulture's beak,
Embraces you like a serpent.
There are black, open-hearted nights, that sense
The claim of virgin loins.
It was the spirit of God,
Because soldiers and fishermen and bums
Demanded a savior, a God.

The madonna powdered her nose and chin
(Her nose was noble and thin)
And spoke again:
From that far dazzle
And bright call,
From this near sorrow
In the heavy body—
Painters and poets dream up
My portraits, age after age.
From the old sprouting spring
In fields, in forests,
Hands stretch out: bestow on us!
Eyes pray
Through the warp and the woof of the year.
In the choking air
Of streets, in subways—
People still long for the miracle,
Though they don't believe in its birth.
Oh, one day I shall strip off the webs
Which enfold me, tie me,
I shall quench your thirst
With my nakedness.
You hear:
It will be like that great destiny
Then, in Galilee.

די מאַדאָנע האָט גערעדט נאָך לאַנג,

נאָך לאַנג און הייס און גיך.

נאָר איך — כ׳האָב שוין מער נישט פֿאַרנומען.

אין פֿלאַטער אין פֿרומען האָט גענענט דאָס קומען

פֿון אָפֿנהאַרציקע לבֿנות און זונען,

און כ׳האָב געשפֿירט ווי עס רירט זיך גאָטס גייסט אין מיר

ווי אַ האָז, ווי אַ שלאַנג, ווי אַ פֿויגל.

◄ פֿאַביוס לינד צו פֿאַביוס לינד

פֿ. ל. איינס :   אויף די קאַלירטע גומיס פֿון אילוזיע
ווי לאַנג נאָך וועסטו טרעטן?

פֿ. ל. צוויי :   כ׳וואָלט אין גאַנצן נישט געטראָטן
ווען נישט אַ רגע אילוזיע יעדן טאָג.

פֿ. ל. איינס :   אויף דעם מויל פֿון דער רגע הענגט נישט מער פֿרייד,
ווי אויף די ליפֿן פֿון אַן אַלטער צעקנייטשטער מומע.
וויפֿל דו ווילסט זיך נישט נאַרן,
די ביטערניש לויפֿט פֿאָרויס,
און באַגלייט דיך געטרײַ צוריק.

פֿ. ל. צוויי :   בין איך געקומען צו־פֿרי,
בין איך געקומען צו־שפֿעט.

פֿ. ל. איינס :   קיין אַליבי פֿאַר זיך אַליין איז קיין מאָל נישטאָ.
גיי העכער אַרויף ווי דײַן אויג גרייכט,
גיי טיפֿער אַראָפּ ווי דײַן ווילן דערוועגט זיך.

פֿ. ל. צוויי :   האָב איך פֿראָבירט.
אַרויף — האָט מען געזאָגט: נישט שוין ווײַל ער דאָס טעלערל פֿון הימל,
און ס׳איז די צײַט פֿון גרויס ליבשאַפֿט צו באַשיידנקייט.
אַראָפּ — האָט מען געזאָגט: מיט וואָסערע מאַסקעס שרעקט ער אונדז —
ס׳איז די צײַט פֿון הימנען צו צווייימאָלצוויי.

פֿ. ל. איינס :   און וואָס האָסטו אַליין געזאָגט, אַ פֿאַביוס לינד?

פֿ. ל. צוויי :   איך אַליין ... איך בין נישט געגאַנגען גענוג.

פֿ. ל. איינס :   גיין — גייט מען קיין מאָל נישט גענוג,
נאָר מורא פֿאַרן גאַנג זאָל מען נישט האָבן.
מען דאַרף גיין ווּהין מען וויל קומען.

The madonna spoke much more,
Long and hot and fast.
But I—I no longer perceived.
In the pious flutter, I felt the coming
Of open-hearted moons and suns,
And I sensed God's spirit move in me
Like a hare, like a serpent, like a bird.

➤ *Fabius Lind to Fabius Lind*

F.L. One: On colored rubber soles of illusion
How long will you tread?

F.L. Two: I wouldn't tread at all if not
For one moment of illusion each day.

F.L. One: On the mouth of the moment hangs no more joy
Than on the lips of an old crumpled aunt.
Fool yourself as much as you like,
Bitterness runs ahead
And escorts you faithfully back.

F.L. Two: So I came too early,
So I came too late.

F.L. One: There is never an alibi for yourself.
Go higher up than your eye can reach.
Go deeper down than your will may dare.

F.L. Two: I tried.
Up—said they: Isn't he after the saucer from the sky,
And it's an age of great love of modesty.
Down—said they: Look at the masks he wears to scare us—
And it's an age of hymns to two-times-two.

F.L. One: And what did you yourself say, Fabius Lind?

F.L. Two: I myself . . . I did not go far enough.

F.L. One: No one ever goes far enough,
But one should not fear the going.
One must go where one wants to come.

פ. ל. צווייי: איך קאָן נישט אַרויס פון דעם פאַנצער, וואָס אויף מיר.
און נאָך מער אין מיר.
איך בין דער, וואָס קלעטערט אויף טרעפן און טרעפן צו באַגעגענען,
און געשעעט די באַגעגעניש —
אַנטלויפט ער אין אײַלעניש צוריק.

פ. ל. איינס: ווען מען וויל נישט פון אָנהייב אַנטלויפן, אַנטלויפט מען נישט.
נישט-געמיינטער אָנהייב קאָן דעם ציל נישט אָניאָגן.

פ. ל. צווייי: שטרײַט איז מיר דערווידער.
כ'מוז זײַן געווינער אָן געראַנגל.

פ. ל. איינס: קיין אַליבי פאַר זיך אַליין איז קיין מאָל נישטאָ.
וואַרט מיט דעם כּוח, וואָס דערוואַרט זיך.

פ. ל. צווייי: האָב איך פּראָבירט.
איך בין געווען ווי אַ פאָטעל, וואָס לאָדט אײַן זיך צו זעצן אין אים —
און בלײַבט לײדיק.
און מען האָט געזאָגט: אַ קעלט טראָגט פון אים.
און מען האָט געזאָגט: נישט אין, נאָר אויסער דעם צירקל איז ער.

פ. ל. איינס: און וואָס האָסטו אַליין געזאָגט, אָ פאַביוס לינד?

פ. ל. צווייי: איך אַליין ... איך האָב צו פיל אַריבער-
געקוקט כ'זאָל קאָנען דעם צירקל דורכרײַסן.

פ. ל. איינס: מען רײַסט קיין מאָל נישט דורך.
נאָר מען זאָל עס נישט מײַדן.
רײַס ביז עס טוט ווייי.
נישט געמיינערט, נאָר געמערט ווערן די רינגען אַרום און אַרום,
סײַדן מען פליקט דאָס אייגענע לײַב און מען מאַכט נישט צו די אויגן
אויס רחמנות צו זיך.

פ. ל. צווייי: כ'בין אַזוי אויך פול מיט אַליינקייט.
זאָל איך נאָך אַליינער ווערן?

פ. ל. איינס: וואָס פאַר אַ שׂרך איז אַ קלייד פון לויזע פעדים, אַ פאַביוס לינד?
וואָס פאַר אַ באַהעלטעניש אַ גאַרטל פון שיטערע קראלן,
ווי עס טראָגן די מיידלעך פון טראָבריאַנד?

פ. ל. צווייי: מען מיינט — עס דאַכט זיך — מען האָפט ...

פ. ל. איינס: קיין אַליבי פאַר זיך אַליין איז קיין מאָל נישטאָ.
אויס מיט מיינען, דאַכטעניש, האָפן.

F.L. Two: I cannot get out of the armor that I wear,
Or worse, the armor inside me.
I am the one who climbs up stairs and stairs to meet,
And when the meeting occurs—
Flees hastily.

F.L. One: If one doesn't want to flee from the beginning, one doesn't flee.
Un-intended beginning cannot reach its goal.

F.L. Two: Strife is repulsive to me.
I must win without struggle.

F.L. One: There is never an alibi for yourself.
Wait with the strength that lives to see.

F.L. Two: I tried.
I was like an inviting armchair—
And remained empty.
And they said: Cold blows from him.
And they said: Not in, but outside the circle is he.

F.L. One: And what did you yourself say, Fabius Lind?

F.L. Two: I myself . . . I looked too much beyond
To be able to break through the circle.

F.L. One: One never breaks through.
But one must not evade it.
Break till it hurts.
The rings don't decrease but multiply around you,
Unless you flay your own flesh and don't shut your eyes
In pity for yourself.

F.L. Two: I am full of loneliness as is.
Should I grow even lonelier?

F.L. One: What kind of shield is a garment of thin threads, oh Fabius Lind?
What kind of sanctuary is a belt of loose beads,
Such as the girls wear in Trobriand?

F.L. Two: One thinks—it seems—one hopes . . .

F.L. One: There is never an alibi for yourself.
Out with thinking, seeming, hope.

פּ. ל. צוויי: האָב איך פֿאַרבירט.
אין יענע זעלטענע גניבֿות בײַ זיך און בײַ צײַט
בין איך געווען ווי אַ שויב:
ליכט און פֿינצטערניש זענען געגאַנגען דורך מיר
און אָטעמס האָב איך אויפֿגעכאַפֿט,
און פֿינגער האָב איך אויף זיך געשפּירט,
און אַליין געבליבן בלאַנק און אומבאַרירט.
האָט מען געזאָגט: אי 'ם שטײט נישט אָן צו זײַן אַ שפּיגל.
און נאָך האָט מען געזאָגט: דער שׂכר פֿון אייגנמײַן איז פֿאַרגעסעניש.

פּ. ל. איינס: און וואָס האַסטו אַליין געזאָגט, אַ פֿאַביוס לינד?

_____

אַ ייִד אױפֿן ים (1947)

◄ דאָס ליד

אין אָנהייב איז דער ניגון.
אַ נישט־דײַטלעכער אויפֿשפּיל, אַ ווײַטלעכער צונויפֿשפּיל
טיף אין דעם וועזן —
אַריבער, אַריבער דעם פֿיבער פֿון יאָרן,
אריבער דעם פֿײַזאַש און דעם אַש פֿון די יאָרן;
אַ זומענדיק אױפֿראַלן פֿון די ספֿיראַלן
אין דעם געוווערק פֿון זיכרון.

אין אָנהייב וועקט זיך דער ניגון —
שטאַמלענדיק, זיפֿנדיק, זאַמלענדיק,
זיפֿנדיק, זוכנדיק, זאַמלענדיק זילבן און ווערטער,
זילבערנע העלקייט פֿון זילבן און ווערטער
פֿאַר זיך, נאָר פֿאַר זיך —
פֿאַר דער קלאָר און דער וואָר און דער פֿולקייט פֿון ניגון.
פֿאַר דער געטרײַישאַפֿט און פֿרײַישאַפֿט און נײַישאַפֿט פֿון ניגון.

דער אָנהייב פֿון אָנהייב איז ניגון.
בלויז דער, וואָס דערהערט זײַן אייגענעם ניגון,
איז נישט קיין גר אין געהיים־לאַנד פֿון ליד,
איז אַ תּושבֿ אין היימלאַנד פֿון ליד.
דער האָט דעם פֿולן שׂכר פֿון דעם ליד,
דען דעם האָט דער שׂר פֿון דעם ליד
אײן מאָל אויף שטענדיק באַרירט
דאָס נאַקעטע אָפֿענע האַרץ
מיט דעם פֿלאַם פֿון זײַן מויל.

F.L. Two: I tried.
In those rare thefts from myself and from time
I was like a window:
Light and darkness passed through me—
And I caught breaths,
I sensed fingers on my surface,
And I myself remained blank and untouched.
Said they: He is too good to be a mirror.
And they said: The reward of arrogance is oblivion.

F.L. One: And what did you yourself say, Fabius Lind?

A JEW IN THE SEA (1947)

➤ *The Poem*

In the beginning was the tune.
A dim stirring of strings, a distant consonance rings
Deep in your essence—
Leaping over the fever of years,
Over the landscape and ashes of years;
A buzzing unrolling of spirals
In the mechanism of memory.

In the beginning awakens the tune—
Stammering, sifting, assembling,
Sifting, searching, assembling syllables and words,
Silvery brightness of syllables and words—
For themselves, just for themselves—
For the clarity and the truth and the fullness of tune,
For the faith and the freedom and the newness of tune.

The beginning of beginning is tune.
Only he who hears his own tune
Is no stranger in mysteryland of song,
Is a citizen in the homeland of song.
He has the full reward of song:
For the lord of song
Touched once and forever
His naked open heart
With the flame of his mouth.

◄ אַזוי איז עס

אַזוי איז עס. אַזוי וועט זײַן.
געבליבן בלויז אַ ציפער.
די ערד האָט זיך גערײַכערט, דער הימל האָט געשוויגן,
און פֿון בריִדער, שוועסטער,
פֿון קינדערשע לאַכנדיקע מײַלעכלעך —
געבליבן בלויז אַ ציפער, אַ מיספּר, אַ צאָל.

זומער וועט זומערן, ווינטער וועט ווינטערן,
און אונדז וועט בלײַבן אַ ציפער, אַ מיספּר, אַ צאָל.

עס קאָנען נישט אומערן לאַנג די געבײַען פֿון מענטשן.
טיפֿער, אַלץ טיפֿער

Ben Shahn: *Liberation*, 1945.

➤ *That's It*

That's it. That's how it will be.
Only a number remains.
The earth went up in smoke, the sky was silent,

And of brothers, sisters,
Of children's laughing mouths—
What's left is only a figure, a number, a sum.

Summers will summer, winters will winter,
And we are left with a figure, a number, a sum.

Human structures cannot grieve for long.
Deeper, ever deeper,

וועט געטריבן ווערן דער ווייטיק פון דעם שניט,

און אויבן וועלן זיך ברייט עפענען די פענצטער

צו די פליִען פון פֿאַרגעסונג.

אַ מאָל בלויז, אין אַ נאַכט,

וועט אַ זקן אויפֿן טויטנבעט

דערפֿילן דעם שניט, אויפֿברענגען פלאַמיק מיטן שניט

אין דעם אייגענעם האַרץ,

און נישט קאָנען שטאַרבן.

און אַ חתן אין דער חופה־נאַכט —

נישט קאָנען באַשאַפֿן אַ ניַי לעבן.

אַרום וועלן זיך ציִען פֿאַרשאָטענע פליִען

און די ווינטן פון פֿאַרגעסונג

וועלן בלאָזן אין צעפֿראַלטע פענצטער.

בלויז אונטן, טיף אונטן,

און אין די הערצער פון די ווייניקע,

וועט גליִען דאָס פֿיַער פון דער ציפֿער —

די ירושה און צוואה פון אַ פֿאָלק.

ביז —

אַ לעצטער צו געדענקען,

צו ליגן אויף דער ערד און פֿאַסטן אַ פֿאַסטונג,

וועט אויפֿשטייַן אַ גערעכטער,

און ברעכן ברויט, און ווערן

אַן ערשטער צו געבן אַ ניַעם לויב

און זינגען דאָס געזאַנג פון אַ ניַי לעבן.

געשריבן אין טאָג פון נירנבערגער ווערדיקט.

◄ שפעטע שעה

ס׳איז טיפע, שפעטע שעה, פֿאַר אַלץ שוין שפעט.

מיר שרייַבן אַלע אונדזערע צוואָות.

עס קריכן עקדיש־ווערגער, שלאַנגען־באַאַס

אויף אונדז פון אַלע זומפֿן, וועלדער, שטעט.

די וועלט — אַ שוידער־מעשה עדגאַר פֿאָעס,

אַ פֿירוש אויף דעם טרויער פון באָדלער,

דער זון פון פֿיַין, פֿון שוידער דער פֿאַרשטייער:

"פֿאַרמישפֿט פֿון אַ גאָט אַ לץ, אַ דרייער".

ווי היימיש ס׳ווארט פֿון אימה און מאַלעיר

אין אָט דער וועלט פון וויי און וויי און ווייער!

The pain of the slash will be driven down,
And up above, windows will open wide
To the plains of forgetting.

Only sometimes at night,
An old man on his deathbed
Will sense the slash, flare up
With the slash in his own heart,
Unable to die.
And a bridegroom on his wedding night—
Unable to create a new life.

All around, dust-covered plains will stretch
And the winds of forgetting
Will blow in the wide-open windows.
Only down, deep down,
And in the hearts of the few,
Still glows the fire of the number—
The heritage and testament of a nation.

Until—
A last one to remember,
To lie on the earth and fast,
A Just man will rise
And break bread, and he will be the first
To offer new praise
And sing the song of a new life.

Written on the day of the Nuremberg Verdict

The Nuremberg verdict—the sentencing of the Nazi leaders, October 1, 1946.

► *Late Hour*

It is a deep, late hour, late for everything.
We all are writing our wills.
Scorpion-eaters, boa serpents
Crawl toward us from all the swamps, forests, cities.
The world—a horror tale of Edgar Poe's,
A commentary on the spleen of Baudelaire,
The son of pain, the terror-understander,
"Condemned by a mocking God to paint on shadows."
How familiar sound his words of horror and *malheur*
In this world of woe and wail and despair.

באמת — וואָס אַרט עס וועמען,
אַז ערגעץ אויפֿן זעקסטן שטאָק
זיצט אין שפּעטער, נאַכטיקסטער נאַכטיקייט
אַ ייִד
און פֿרעגט זיך אַליין:
צי אַרט עס וועמען?
וואָס אַרט עס וועמען?
דער ענטפֿער ענטפֿערט זיך אַליין:
עס אַרט נישט קיינעם.
דער פֿרעגער ווייסט דעם ענטפֿער גוט,
דעם פֿרעגער שפּרינגט אין קאָפּ דאָס בלוט.

דער פֿרעגער זעט וואָס וואָס איז געווען,
דער פֿרעגער ווייס ווי ס׳וועט געשען.
און די נאַכט איז טעמנע, טרייסטלאָז, טרויעריק,
און די נאַכט איז טויב און טעמפּ און טינטיק,
און דרייט דעם פֿרעגער אין דעם ראָד
פֿון איין געדאַנק —
וואָס אַרט עס וועמען?
ער ווייס אַז אַנדערש קאָן נישט זײַן,
ער ווייס אַז אַנדערש נישט געווען.
נאָר דאָס ראָד דרייט טריבער, טיפֿער, טונקעלער —
וואָס אַרט עס וועמען?
וואָס אַרט עס וועמען?
דאָס ראָד דרייט טיפֿער, תּהומיקער
וואָס אַרט עס וועמען?
דאָס ראָד דרייט שטראָמיקער, פֿאַרצווייפֿלטער
אין טעמפֿער, טויבער נאַכטיקייט,
אין טינטיק-טויטער נאַכטיקייט,
ערגעץ אויפֿן זעקסטן שטאָק,
ערגעץ אין ניו-יאָרק.

דעם וואַכערס נעכט זענען אַ שלאַכטפֿעלד פֿון שיגעון
פֿאַר בייזע נײַנען, גרײַזע יאָען,
פֿאַר סומנע דאָען, קרומע נישטאָען,
וואָס ער דערקענט קוים זײַן שייכות מיט זיי.
צום ליבסטן וואָלט ער אַנטלאָפֿן,
געלאָזט די פֿעכטער פֿאַלן מיט משונהדיקע טויטן,

Indeed, who cares
That somewhere on a sixth floor
Sits in the late, darkest dark
A Jew
And asks himself:
Does anyone care?
Why would anyone care?
The answer answers itself:
No one cares.
The asker knows the answer, knows the dread.
The asker's blood rushes to his head.

The asker sees what has been,
The asker knows what will be.
And the night is murky, merciless and dim,
And the night is dense and deaf and pitch-black,
And it turns the asker on a wheel
Of one thought—
Who cares?
He knows that it could not be different,
He knows that it never was different.
But the wheel turns deep and turgid and dark—
Who cares?
Who cares?
The wheel turns deeper, down an abyss:
Who cares?
Flooding, despairing,
In dumb, deaf darkness,
In pitch-dead darkness,
Somewhere on a sixth floor,
Somewhere in New York.

➤ *Foreign Fencers*

His sleepless nights are battlefields of madness
For angry Nos, for graying Yesses,
For gloomy Heres, for twisted Nevers—
He can hardly see his connection with them.
He would like to escape,
He'd let the fencers die weird deaths,

American
Yiddish
Poetry

אַרויסגעוואָרפֿן זיי ווי קרעציקע הויטן,
און אַליין — אָנגעהויבן גאָר פֿון סאַמע ניי.
אַז וואָס האָט ער צו טאָן מיט אַ פֿרעמד געפֿעכט?
וואָס קער ער זיך אָן מיט יעגער און שלעגער?
דאָס זענען שולדיק זיי — די מייסטערס פֿון שלעכטס,
די שאַקלאָפֿטע שדים, וואָס קומען פֿון אַ פֿאַרשפֿינעוועבטן ביידעם,
און מאַכן אַ תל פֿון זיין אמתן געמעל.

דער וואָכער שמייכלט.
אַ פֿאַרמאַטערטער לאָזט ער אַראָפּ די הענט.
ווערט פֿאַרברענט! טוט, ברידערלעך, וואָס איר ווילט.
איר קומט סיי־ווי אָן פֿאַרבעטונג,
און נישטאָ קיין רעטונג צו ראַטעווען מיך.

◄ שלמה מולכו זינגט ערב זיין פֿאַרברענונג

נאַכט, פֿאַרוואַנדלערין פֿון פֿורעמס,
דו וואָס יאָגסט־אָן ספֿקות מיט דיינע פֿינצטערנישן,
און מאַכסט נאָך שלאַפֿער אַ שוואַך און שלאָף געמיט —
זיי עדות פֿון מיין אמת היינט.
נאַכט, וועקערין פֿון פֿאַרהוילענע שרעקן,
דו, וואָס פֿאַרגרעסערסט געפֿאַרן,
און ציסט אַרויס אומווילקיקע ווידוים פֿון געשפֿאַלטענע לעבנס —
לייג צו דיין שוואַרצן זיגל
צו דעם פֿריידיקן, באַפֿרייטן ווילן
פֿון מיין ווידוי היינט.

באַלד קומט אָן מיין וואָרסטע שעה.
אשיקער נישטאָ וועט בלייבן פֿון מיין שטאָלצן שם.
באַלד וועט ס׳פֿייער אָפּטאָן פֿון מיר
דעם פֿאַלשן קלעם, וואָס האָט מיך גענאַרט מיט זיסקייט.
באַלד וועט קומען דאָס גרויסע שווייגן.

אַ זיסער פֿון אַלע גלוסטונגען פֿון לייב
איז מיר געווען די אמונה פֿון די מחנות:
גואל! פֿירער!
כ׳האָב מיט תאווה זיך צו זיי געטוליעט,
און געקוואַלן האָט יעדער שפֿרונג פֿון בלוט אין מיר:
גואל. פֿירער. איך.

אַ געזאַנג פֿון איך האָב איך געזונגען
אין זינדיקער פֿאַרבאָרגן־שטילער שטיל.

He'd shed them like scabby skins,
And he himself would begin from the very beginning.
What would he have to do with the foreign fencers?
What is his business with hunters and beaters?
It is all their fault—the masters of evil,
The devious demons who descend from a spiderwebbed attic
And devastate his authentic image.

The sleepless man smiles.
Weary, he throws up his hands.
Burn in hell! You, brothers, do what you want.
You come anyway uninvited.
And there is no escape for me.

➤ *Shlomo Molkho Sings on the Eve of His Burning*

Night, metamorphoser of forms,
You who pile up doubts in your darknesses,
Who weaken a weak and weary soul—
Be now the witness of my truth.
Night, awakener of hidden fears,
You who magnify dangers,
Who extort unwanted confessions from split lives—
Now, put your black seal
On the joyful, liberated will
Of my confession.

Soon it will be here—my most truthful hour,
Ash and nothingness will remain of my proud fame.
Soon the fire will strip me
Of the false plight that deluded me with sweetness.
Soon the great silence will be here.

Oh, sweeter than all lusts of the body
Was the belief of the crowds:
Redeemer! Leader!
I clung to them with passion,
Each throb of blood in me rejoiced:
Redeemer. Leader. I.

In sinful clandestine silence
I sang a song of my I.

Molkho—or Molcho, Solomon. Born Diego Pires in 1500 in Portugal of Marrano parents. Announced the coming of the Messiah, obtained the protection of the Pope and aroused the expectations of European Jews. In 1532, was burned at the stake by the Inquisition in Mantua.

און ווען ווי זעמדער פיל האָבן די געטרייע
זיך אײַנגעזאַמלטאַרום מיר,
ווען כ׳האָב געקליבן ווערטער צו פאָרן מיט זייער שוועערער נויט,
האָב איך צו גלײַכער צײַט געבויט אַ פינקלדיקן טראָן
פאַר זיך,
האָט דאַן פאַרשײַט די גאווה מיט מײַן גלויבן זיך געהאַלדזט.
זייער אמונה איז געוואָקסן און מיט איר
מײַן פאַרריסענער קאָפ.
נאָר אויך מײַן אַלײנקייט און די שרעק —
פאַר זיך.
כ׳האָב געזען ווי זייער גלויבן ווערט אַ האַרץ אָן אויגן.
כ׳האָב געזען ווי זייער בלינדער ווייטיק לייגט זיך אויס
ווי אַ טעפיך,
פאַר די טרעטנדיקע, געצערטלטע פיס
פון גואל;
און ווי טרעפן,
פאַר די שטײַגנדיקע אָפּערדיקע טריט
פון פירער.
כ׳האָב געזען מיט גרויל ווי ס׳פאַלט
אַ וואַלד מיט ווילנס הויכע ווי די צעדערן
אונטער דער האַק פון שקר:
דער עקער זינקט אין אומווערדיקייט,
און דער גרויסער ליכטיקער ציל —
דער פאַרפרעמדטער וווּנדער-פויגל —
פליט אַ פאַרשעמטער צוריק
אין דער ווײַטער, פאַרהוילענער נעסט.

הכנעהדיק און שטיל מיט פרייד איז איצט שלמה מולכו:
ער האָט אין צײַט דערשפירט דעם גואלס סם,
און אים פאַרביטן
אויף דעם גוטן, פרײַען רײַנעם אַטעם
פון דעם פלאַם.

◄ הורדוס

הורדוס איז אַלט שוין. זײַן פּנים, געריבן מיט זאַלבן,
מיצרישע שמירעכצן, קוקט נאָך אויס יונג. נאָר זײַן בליק —
אומרו און פּחד און כמאַרעס אין טונקעלע פֿאַלבן,
אָפּגרונט ווי ס׳לויערן מאָנסטרישע אַלבן:
רוימער — סעמיט; האַלב פֿאַרצווייפֿלונג, האַלב גליק;
זאָרגער פֿאַר ווילד-פֿרעמדע שוואַלבן,
ברעכער פון אומהס גענוג,

And while, like multitudes of sand,
My faithful gathered around me,
While I selected words to match their heavy anguish,
I built a sparkling throne
For myself.
Frivolously, my arrogance embraced my faith.
Their belief grew, and with it
My haughty head.
And my loneliness too, and the fear—
Of myself.
I saw their faith become a heart with no eyes,
I saw their blind pain spread
Like a carpet
Before the treading, fondled feet
Of the redeemer;
And like stairs—
For the climbing, insolent steps
Of the leader.
Appalled, I saw
A forest of wills, tall as cedars,
Fall under the axe of falsehood:
The hewer sinks in indignity,
And the great bright goal—
The estranged wonder-bird—
Flies back, abashed,
To his distant, hidden nest.

Now Shlomo Molkho is humble and silent with joy.
He sensed in time the redeemer's poison
And exchanged it
For the good, free, pure breath
Of the flame.

► *Herod*

Herod is old. His face, anointed with ointments,
Balsams and makeup from Egypt, looks young. But his gaze—
Restlessness, fear, and grim clouds in the darkening folds,
Monstrous two halves side by side in abyss:
Roman—and Semite; despair—and good fortune;
Patron of strange little swallows,
Breaker of nation's neck;

Herod the Great (73–4 B.C.), an Edomite who became king of Judea under the Roman Empire. His reign was marked by extensive construction and his own mental instability and cruelty.

קנעכט אויף אַ טראָן,

קיניג אין קאָן

בײַ אומלעשבאַרער דאָרשט, בײַ פאַרדאַכטן געהײמע און קראַנקע.

פרי האָט זיך הורדוס געריסן צום גלוסטיקן טורעם,

פרי זיך געפוצט פאַר דעם גאָלדענעם צעפטער פון מאַכט.

האָט אים באַגליקט. נאָר איז אַלץ בלויז אַ ליידיקער פורעם?

זײַנען די אַלטע גערעכט, אַז יסורים,

נישטיקייט, ווינט, איז וואָס מענטש האָט פאַרטראַכט?

ער — ער וועט צוימען דעם שטורעם,

אים האָט די שטאַרקייט געבראַכט!

לייד — נישט פאַר אים.

ס'האַרץ פון דער שטים,

וואָס פאַרתחינהט מיט תשובה און רעכנשאַפט, וועט ער צעפערטלען.

גרויער ווערט הורדוס און אַלץ נישט געשטילט. מיט דער עלטער

וואָרגט אים אַ בענקשאַפט צו קריגן וואָס אים איז פאַרווערט.

ליבע! דער מלך וויל ליבשאַפט. ווען מעגלעך, באַשטעלט ער —

אָט ווי אַ זעלטענעם ווײַן פון דעם קעלטער —

פעסער מיט שמײכלען אויף גוטסקייט גערערט.

אפשר וועט ווערן באַהעלטער

דאָרטן וווּ טונקלקייט שווערט,

שוואַרצעניש רײַסט.

איז דען זײַן גײַסט

שוין אויף שטענדיק פאַרמישפט צו זײַן אַ געווויטערדיק שלאַכט-פעלד?

הורדוסעס ליבע בוים טעמפלען און מירמלענע גולמס,

בעדער און שטעט. נאָר דאָס פאָלק קריכט אין שווײַגן אַרײַן.

שטום מעסט עס אָף די גרוײען און — צײַלט די בית-עולמס.

שווײַגיק, אין שטיקיקע רעטעניש-קנוילן

שטײט עס, דאָס פאָלק, און עס זופֿט נישט זײַן ווײַן.

ברענט עס אין דעם הערשער ווי קוילן.

"ס'וויל נישט דאָס פֿעבל — זאָל זײַן!"

שטאַרקט זיך זײַן כעס.

הוליעט דער האַס

און פאַרלעשט אין דעם קיניגס געווויסן די פונקען די לעצטע.

ס'טרעפֿט: אין די אָרעמס פֿון ווײַב וויל פֿאַרגעסן זיך הורדוס.

ס'ווײַב האָט אים ער ליב, ס'איז אים גוט צו זײַן מויל און באַריר.

"צערטל מיך, מרים, כאַטש דו!" מיט אַ מאָל — ערשט אין האָרדעס

קלײַבן זיך רוחות מיט העצישע מאָרדעס,

שושקען און שטעכן און טײַטלען אויף איר:

זיס איז דאָס לײַב, נאָר דערמאָרד עס!

Slave on a throne,
King in the yoke
Of unsated desires, of sickly and stealthy suspicions.

Herod raced early to fortress of lust and desire,
Groomed in his youth for the golden scepter of might.
Lucky was he. Yet, are all things just hollowed-out vessels?
Could the old sages be right, that all pain is
Nothingness, wind, a mere human invention?
He—he will harness the tempest,
He is the scion of strength!
Pain—not for him.
The heart of the voice
That engulfs in laments of account and repentance—destroy it!

Herod gets grayer and ever unsettled. With age,
Choked by a craving to get what's forbidden to him.
Love! King wants love. If only he could, he would order—
Just like an exquisite wine from his cellars—
Barrels of smiles, fermented on kindness.
Maybe it will then be brighter
There where the darkness is heavy,
Blackness torments.
Is, then, his soul
Condemned to be ever a battlefield hosting the storm?

Herod's great love erects temples and Golems of marble,
Cities and baths. Yet the people curl up in their silence.
Mutely they measure the buildings—and count all the graveyards.
Stifled, entangled in riddles, the people
Stand there, refusing to sip from his wine.
Glowing hot coals to the ruler.
"Rabble will not—let it be!"
Fiercer his anger.
Wild is his hatred,
Stamping out the last sparks of the aging king's conscience.

Sometimes: he would lose himself in the arms of his wife.
Her he adores, she is good to his mouth and his touch.
"Fondle, Miriamne, the king!" But suddenly hordes of
Demons, intruding their snouts, come together,
Whisper and sting and point at Miriamne:
Sweet is her flesh—you must kill it!

Miriamne—Herod's wife. She was of the Judean royal family, the Hasmoneans, thus lending legitimacy to his claim to the throne and, at the same time, threatening it. Herod murdered Miriamne, her two sons, and her relatives.

פֿאַלש מיט פֿאַרראַט איז עס דיר!

האָרכט ער צום וואָרט,

רוויטלט אַ מאָרד

זײַן געלעגער און ס׳ווערט זײַן געמיט איצט אַ דולהויז, וואָס טרענקט זיך.

ס׳לאַנד ליגט פֿאַרטאָיעט בײַ זײ הוֹרדוֹסעס שינאה און האַמער.

שינאה שפּײַזט האַמער און האַמער שפּײַזט שרעק — אין געדרײַ.

נאָנטסטע, לײַב פֿון זײַן לײַב — אין דעמזעלביקן קלאַמער.

אַלע באַשטימט פֿאַר דער הענקערשער קאַמער.

הוֹרדוֹס פֿירט חשבון: אַזוֹי פֿיל פֿון ז י י י

האָבן שוֹין קבורה פֿון חמור.

אָבער די מורדים, ווי פֿליי,

מערן זיך נאָך.

שווער איז זײַן יאָך.

און ער שרײַבט נײַע צעטלען מיט נעמען פֿאַרהאַסטע — אויף מאָרגן.

אײנזאַמער ווערט אַלץ דער מלך און טעגלעך אַלײנער.

הוֹרדוֹס געטרויט נישט קײן העלפֿער, קײן שקלאַף, קײן יעוונוך,

זון איז אַ שונא, פֿאַרשווערער די ערד מיט די שטיינער,

אַלע פֿאַררעטער און ער איז בלוֹיז אײנער.

טאָמער קומט וואָרענען אַ וואָרט פֿון דעם בוך:

אָפֿשטעלן — זיך און די וויינער! —

קאָן ער נישט, קנעכט פֿון אַ פֿלוך.

שלאָפֿט שוֹין זײַן וואָר,

חלומט ער נאָר

וועגן חורבות און מתים, וואָס קניִען און זינגען אים שירה.

דולהויז אין הערשערס נשמה, און דולע געשפּינען

ציִען זיך, קריכן געדיכט פֿון דעם שולדיקן טראָן,

וויקלען אַרום יעדן אָטעם, אַז נישט צו געפֿינען

פֿון דעם שיגעון אַ שפּאַלט צו אַנטרינען.

איצט כאַפּט די מורא די לעצטע אים אָן,

שלאָגט ווי נקמהס לעגיאָן:

ס׳וועט דער המן

טראָמפּלען דײַן קרוין,

און זיך קושן פֿאַר פֿרייד, ווען מיט דיר וועט אויך שטאַרבן דײַן הערשאַפֿט.

הוֹרדוֹס פֿלאַנט לאַנג. איז פֿאַרבאָטן פֿון ליבע דער נחת

אים בײַ זײַן לעבן — מוז טרויער באַגלײַטן זײַן טויט!

וועט ער באַפֿעלן: די בעסטע, אין פּורפּל צי לאַכעס,

יעדער וואָס לעבט און באָט ווי אים אויף צו הכעיס —

קוילן — ווי באַלד ס׳לעשט ס׳לעשט זײַן זאָל אויס איר קניט.

ס׳וועלן שוֹין וויינען די זנאַכערס,

False and betraying it is!
He—heeds the voices.
Murder dyes crimson
His couch, and the mood of the king is a madhouse in drowning.

Still lies the land under Herod's hatred and hammer.
Hatred feeds hammer and hammer feeds fear—in a circle.
All who are close to him, flesh of his flesh—in a vise.
All of them destined for dungeons of hangmen.
Herod counts clearly: so many of them
Died and were buried like dogs.
Yet the rebellious, like fleas,
Multiply still.
Heavy his yoke.
And he scribbles fresh notes with names hateful to him—for the morrow.

Ever more lonely, secluded the king, day by day.
Herod won't trust an assistant, a slave or a eunuch.
Sun is his foe, the earth and the stones are insurgents,
All of them traitors, and he—only one.
Yet, though the words of the Book bear a warning:
Stop—yourself and the mourners!—
He is the slave to a curse.
His world is asleep;
Waking, he dreams
But of ruins and corpses, kneeling and singing his praise.

Bedlam—the soul of the ruler. Mad spiderwebs
Spread, crawl thickly from under the villainous throne,
Cover, enfold every breath, so that no one will find
Even a crack for escape from the bedlam.
Now the last fear grips the king,
Strikes like a legion of vengeance:
Soon will the crowd
Trample your crown
And embrace, and rejoice, when your reign and yourself die together.

Herod plans carefully. If in his lifetime the joys of
Love are forbidden—let mourning surround him in death!
He will command: Take the best, in purple or tatters,
All who still live, as in spite of his will—
Kill them—as soon as his wick has burnt out.
Quacks will lament on that day,

ווײַבער זיך רײַסן די הויט
יענעם-אַ טאָג!
זײַן וועט אַ קלאָג!
טריומפֿירט דער משוגענער אכזר — און נאַכט שטאַרבט פֿון אימה.

◄ פֿאַטאַלע בענקשאַפֿט

דאָס קליינע ליד פֿאַר פֿאָרן אינדיווייד.
אַ הייסע בענקשאַפֿט, שנײַדיק, פֿלוצים,
אַ טיפֿע בענקשאַפֿט — אָן תירוצים.
זי מאָנט פֿאַטאַל דאָס קליינע ליד
פֿאַרן אינדיווייד, וואָס טויטלעך מיד.

מיט אײַז באַשמידט ווערט גליד נאָך גליד
דער אויסגעשפּרייטער גוף פֿון האָדסאָן.
עס נעמען פֿראָסט-געוויקסן שפּראָצן
אויף האַרטער פּלאָך. אַן אײַז-בלום גליט
אין סאַמע מיט. אויך זי וויל ס׳ליד.

די זון באַשיט מיט בלישטשן-צוויט
דאָס שטיקל אַרקטיק אין מײַן נאָנטשאַפֿט.
דער טײַך פֿילט אָן די האָריזאָנטשאַפֿט
מיט שאַרפֿקייט, שטאַרק ווי אָקעוויט,
מיט קאָלאָריט פֿון שטיין, גראַניט.

נאָר ס׳ווערט דאָס ליד נישט אויסגעבריט,
ווייל ווי אין לאָדזש אַ שטיקל זעמל —
(און לויט דעם פּעז פֿון ריקאַרד דעמעל) —
פֿעלט פּשוט צײַט דעם אינדיווייד,
ווי אויך ס׳געמיט, וואָס פֿאַנגט און היט.

אין האַרצן קניט פֿאַרקלעמט, געניט,
די דאָרשטיקע, פֿאַטאַלע בענקשאַפֿט.
עס דריקט אין האַלדז אַ שווערע ענגשאַפֿט:
עס בלייכט דערשטיקט דאָס קליינע ליד,
ווייל אינדיווייד איז טויטלעך מיד.

◄ בײַם האָדסאָן

דער האָדסאָן ברענט אין ווײַסער שײַן פֿון מערצאַ‎ווער זון.
דער בליאַסק הילט אײַן אַ שוואַרצן בוים
מיט נאַקעטע צווײַגן.

Women will tear at their skin.
Oh, on that day!
Wailing will rule!
Triumphantly raves the mad tyrant—and night dies in fear.

► *Fatal Longing*

A little poem for the individual.
A hot longing, sudden, obtuse,
A deep longing—with no excuse.
A fatal desire for a poem residual
For the individual, who is tired to death.

The Hudson's body stretched out, indigenous,
Shackled in ice. Frost plants soar
On the hard surface from shore to shore.
In the center—an ice-flower sprouts, an original.
It, too, would beseech you all: the poem should be.

The sun sprinkles sparks, as for a ritual,
On the fragment of arctic in my sight.
The river fills up the horizon bright
With air sharp as brandy, strong as barbiturates,
With colors as vigilant as granite and stone.

But the poem won't brew as an ancient remedial,
For as in Lodz they had lacked a zemel—   **zemel**—a roll.
(And as in a verse by Richard Dehmel)
He simply lacks time, the individual,
And the mood, so immediate, that snares you and holds.

Caught in his heart, experienced, assiduous,
The fatal longing—thirsty, taut.
A heavy tightness grips his throat:
Now stifled, pales the poem residual,
For the individual is tired to death.

► *On the Hudson*

The Hudson burns in the white shine of a March sun.
The glitter envelops a black tree
With naked boughs.

זעסט אַ מענטש אויף ווײַסן אויטאָ-דאָ-פּע.
זעסט אַ ווײַסן סנה.

אַרום-אַרום נעילהדיקע אָרעאָלן
איבער שוואַרצע נעצן פון בײַמער-שפּיצן.
סימבאָלן ברידערן זיך מיט זאַכן,
זאַכן פאַרמאַכן זיך אונטער סימבאָלן.
דער האָדסאָן ברענט ווײַס, פאַרגלייזט.

און בײַ דעם האָדסאָן —
גליטשן זיך קינדער אויף רעדלעך,
רײַטן אויף וועליסאָפּעדלעך.
אַ פאַראַליזירטע דאַמע מיט אויגן — גלאָז,
מיט גראָע האָר — געוועזן-בלאָנד,
זיצט אין אַ רוק-שטול
און וואַקסט און וואַקסט אויף אַ האָריזאָנט,
וואָס האָרבט זיך, באַרגט זיך
און וואַרגט זיך מיט דער ליגנערישער רו פון מערץ.

מערצאָווע, ווײַסע, פאַרגלייזטע רו.

◄ פאַר וואָס?

בלויז עטלעכע שפּאַן
פון די מעבלירטע שטאָטישע קאַסטנס
שטייט אַ קליינער פּאַנטאָן.
אַ פרײַלעכער, געדיכטער שפּריץ — אַ באָד פאַר פייגל.
פון וווּ איך זיץ
שטרעקט זיך דער האָדסאָן גלאַנציק, גלאַטיק אין דער זון.
די זון ברענט ווי אויף באַפעל,
נאָר דאָ איז בלויז העל און קיל.
דאָ איז שטיל.
די זון ווינקט זיך הײַס דורך מיט דעם פּאָנטאָנס טראָפּנס,
און מיר צוקאָפּנס אויף אַ צווײַג
צוויטשערט צופרידן אַ שפּערל — ס'איז אים גוט.
מיר אויך — אַבסאָלוט.
דאָס גרין אַרום בלישטשעט פול און פייכט,
די גראָזן אָטעמען לײַכט אין פרעכן זומערטאָג.
גאָלד, גרין, זילבער, פייגלשער צוויטשער צום בלויען הימל.
ס'נעמט מיך נײַגן צום דרימל.

You see a man on a white auto-da-fé,
You see a white Burning Bush.

Around you, end-time aureoles
Over black nets of tree-peaks.
Symbols fraternize with things,
Things close up in symbols.
The Hudson is burning white, glazed.

And on the banks—
Children glide on rollerskates,
Ride bicycles.
A paralyzed lady with eyes of glass,
Gray hair—that once was blond,
Sits in a rocking chair
And grows, and grows on the horizon,
Which hunches up, hills in,
And chokes on the false calm of March.

White, glazed calm of March.

➤ *Why?*

Just a few steps
From the furnished city crates
Stands a small fountain.
A joyful, dense spurt—a birdbath.
From where I sit
The Hudson stretches radiant, smooth in the sun.
The sun flames, as if obeying orders,
But here it is just bright and cool.
Here it is calm.
The sun exchanges hot winks with the fountain drops,
And on a branch over my head
A sparrow twitters happily—he likes it.
Me too—absolutely.
The greenery all around glimmers lush and wet,
The grass breathes lightly in the impertinent summer day.
Gold, green, silver, birds' twitter to blue sky.
I am dozing off.

צו דער אידיליע

געהערט אויך די װײַסע ליליע

אין דער האַנט פֿון דעם פּאַרשוין,

װאָס יאָװועט זיך פּלוצים און זאָגט

(מיר זעענען אַלײן) :

פֿון מײַנעטװעגן מעגסטו שטאַרבן הײַנט בײַ נאַכט.

פֿאַר װאָס ? — פֿרעג איך, אומבאַטראַכט.

װײַל, זאָגט ער, דאָס לעבן

איז גאָטס אומגעטלעכער האַס,

און דער מענטש — די כּלי פֿון זײַן הפֿקרדיקן שפּאַס.

און דו פֿאַעטיזירסט, שטאָט צו ריטשען: װיי געשריגן !

כּפֿלסט ליגן אויף ליגן,

נאַרסט און פֿאַרפֿירסט.

דאָ האָט ער דרײַ מאָל געשפֿיגן,

מיר אויסגעשטרעקט אַ לאַנגע צונג,

צעמורשט די ליליע אין זײַן האַנט

און שילטנדיק אַװעקגעשפּאַנט.

דער שפּערל האָט געצװיטשערט,

די זון האָט געשטיפֿט מיט דעם פֿאַנטאַנס ברילִיאַנטענע שנירלעך,

געמיניעט פֿיל-קאָלעריק.

צו די קאָלירן איז צוגעקומען אַ רויטע צונג,

און אַ שיכּורער יונג אין אוניפֿאָרם האָט פֿון פֿעטן, פֿײַכטן גראָז

געריטשעט: פֿאַר װאָס ?

Ben Shahn: *Flowering Brushes*,
1968.

To this idyllic
Picture belongs a white lily
In the hand of a fellow
Who shows up all of a sudden and says
(We are alone):
"As far as I'm concerned you may die this very night."
"Why?"—I ask, not thinking.
"Because," he says, "life
Is God's ungodly hatred,
And man—the vehicle of his wanton joke.
And you poeticize, instead of howling: Horror!
You multiply lie upon lie,
You fool and deceive."
At this he spat three times,
Stuck out at me his long tongue,
Crumpled the lily in his hand
And, cursing, walked away.

The sparrow twittered,
The sun teased the fountain's diamond strings,
Shimmering in a rainbow of colors.
A red tongue was added to the colors,
And a drunken guy in uniform, in the lush, wet grass,
Howled: Why?

ריח האַרבער פון הויכע שאַטנדיקע אייקאַליפטן
מיט צאַרטע, צונטערנע פעכערס פון צווײַט,
און קווייטן ווי אײדל געשניטן רױ פלייש;
פאַרטאַיעטע בערג, ווי רוענדיקע קעמלען אױף די קני
נאָך אַ לאַנגן, שטױביקן וואָכעדיקן מאַרש;
גאַרטנדיקע, בלומענדיקע רחבות
פון גילדערנעם, אייביקן יונג-זומער —
ס׳איז שבת אין קאַליפאָרניע.

הויכע בערג פון זאַמד און געדאַנק
שטייען צווישן לאָס-אַנדזשעלעס און לאָדזש.
טיפע תהומות פון רוישיקע אינדן און ברוױזיקן גומיט
ליגן צווישן צוויי שטילע שבת-שעהן,
וואָס גיבן זיך שלום אַריבער אַ האַלבן יאָרהונדערט.

דער לאָדזשער שפעטער שבת נאָכמיטיק קומט ליב און געלאַסן
מיט באַשיידענער גרינקייט פון פרישן שטשאַװ,
מיט קאָרן-ברויט, מילך און ווײַסן קעז,
און מיט אַ יינגלס פאַרטאַיעטער שקאָצישער בלאָנדקייט
אונטער טאַטע-מאַמעס בליקן פון מנוחה.

וואָס איז בידנער שטשאַװ
אַקעגן גדלותדיקע אייקאַליפטן און פּאַלמען,
אַקעגן מאַראַנצן-בלױונג, וואָס באַרוישט שמעקעדיקער
פון יינגסטן האָניק?
ווי בינדט זיך די צופרידענע זעט פון אַ יינגל
בײַם בוזעם פון שבתדיקער שלווה, וואָס רינט ליבשאַפט און מילך,
מיט דעם מילדן פרידן אױף זון-געטובלטע בערג —
עלעהיי אַ צעפראַלטע, איבער-רײַיפע, געלע ריזיקע רױז?

איבער דער בריק פון אַ האַלב יאָרהונדערט
שפּאַנט פון לאָדזש די מאַמע, די מלכה,
שפּאַנט דער טאַטע מיט דער באַרד פון טונקל גאָלד.
די מאַמע טראָגט ברויט און אַן ערדענע שיסל שטשאַװ.
דעם טאַטנס גוטע גרינלעכע אויגן בענטשן אַריַין
אין דעם יינגלס באַשירעמט האַרץ:
שבת, שבת,
שבת אױף דער גאַנצער וועלט.

האַלב יאָרהונדערט איז אַ ריר פון אַ וויִע,
זיבנטויזנט-מײַליקער מהלך — שמאָלסטער שפּאַן,

Spicy smell of tall shadowy eucalyptuses
With tender, tinder-red fans of blossoms
And flowers like delicately cut-up raw meat;
Lurking mountains, like camels resting on their knees
After a week-long dusty march;
Gardenful, flowering wide expanses
Of the golden, eternal Young-Summer—
Sabbath in California.

High mountains of sand and thought
Separate Los Angeles from Lodz.
Deep abysses of rushing brooks and turbulent moods
Lie between two quiet Sabbath-hours,
Shaking their hands over half a century.

The late Sabbath afternoon in Lodz comes lovely and leisurely,
With the modest green of fresh shtshav,
With rye bread, milk and farmer's cheese,
And with a boy's lurking, impudent blondness
Under Mama's and Papa's restful gazes.

How can dull shtshav   Shtshav*
Compare with the vanity of eucalyptuses and palms,
With orange-blossom which make you groggy with aromas
More fragrant than young honey?
What is the link that ties a boy's sated happiness
In the lap of Sabbath peace, running with milk and love,
To the soft peace of sun-steeped mountains—
Like a wide-open, over-ripe, giant yellow rose?

Over the bridge of half a century
Walks from Lodz my mother the Queen,
My father with his beard of dark gold.
Mother brings bread and an earthenware bowl of shtshav.
Father's kindly greenish eyes are like blessings
In the boy's sheltered heart:
Sabbath, Sabbath,
Sabbath in the whole world.

Half a century is the blink of an eye.
Seven-thousand-miles—the smallest step,

וועו פלוצלינג, אומגעריכט
פלאטערט פידלדיק פֿאַרבײַ
דער גאָלדענער פליגל פון געבענקטער, געבענטשטער
הייליקער שלווה
פֿון שבת.

◄ מידבר־שגעון

אויבן האָט זיך געוועלבט אַ הויכער הימל,
אַרום האָט געאָטעמט מיט וואַרעמער קראַפט,
און פֿאַר מײַנע אויגן, אַ תחום פון געקינצלטן לאַס־אַנדזשעלעס
האָט זיך געקנײדערט אַ משוגען געוויקס פון מידבר.

ווילד צעוואָקסענע גרוי־גרינע צווײַגן, ריטלעך, אָדערן,
געבויגן, געדרייט און געפלאָכטן,
זענען פון עפּעס אַ וואָרצל אין טרוקענע געזעמדער
געשטיגן אַרויף, זיך צעפעכערט,
און צוריק זיך געוויקלט אַראָפּ און צענויפגעקנוילט.
נישט אַנדערש — אַן אָפענער מאַרך, אָן דעקל פון שאַרבן,
אַ גרוי־גרינער מאַכטיקער ריזיקער מאַרך,
מיט אַלע רינעלעך, דרייונגען, שטעגן און סטעזשקעס,
נאַקעט צום פרייען הימל, צו דער גרויסער מאַמע, דער זון.

כ׳האָב געקוקט אויף דעם צעוואָקסענעם פלאַנטער,
און געאָנט אַן אויסטערלישן ריטעם,
וואָס האָט זיניק געזאַמלט האַרמאָניע אין זאַמדיקע גרונטן.

מײַן אויג האָט אַ וואָנדער געטאָן צו אַ וווינקל
פֿון דעם מידבר־שגעון —
ערשט אַ בלום האָט געבליט אויף סאַמע נישט־דערוואַרטן אָרט,
און גלוסטיק געשאַלט איר רויטן רוף צו שאָנקייט
דורך דער גאַנצער מידברדיקער רווייקייט.

וויפל איז דער שפּאַן פון אַ קאַקטוס צו אַ רויז?
ליגט נישט אַ רויז אין דעם האַרץ פון אַ מידבר־פֿאַרזעעניש?

When suddenly, unexpectedly,
Like the sound of a violin, flutters by
The golden wing of the craved-for, blessed
Holy peace
Of Sabbath.

➤ *Desert Madness*

Wide sky arching above.
Warm strength breathing all around.
And before my eyes, beyond the limits of synthetic Los Angeles—
A convoluted, insane desert growth.

Wildly sprawling gray-green branches, twigs, arteries,
Bent, twisted, braided,
Climbing up, fanning out
From some root in dry sands,
Then winding down again, rolling in a knot.
An open brain, uncovered skull,
A gray-green powerful giant brain,
With all its rivulets, curves, paths and trails,
Naked to the open sky, to the big mother, the sun.

I looked at the overgrown tangle
And caught a bizarre rhythm
Assembling sense and harmony in sandy depths.

My eyes strayed to a corner
Of the desert madness—
There, in the most unexpected spot, a flower bloomed
And blared passionately its red call for beauty
Through all the desolate rawness.

How far is a cactus from the bloom of a rose?
Doesn't a rose lie in the heart of a desert-monster?

◄ וואָס טוען מענטשן?

וואָס טוען מענטשן דורך די טעג?
זיי האַסן זיך, מיַין ליבער.
וואָס טראַכטן מענטשן אין די נעכט?
שלעכט צו טאָן, מיַין ליבער.

וואָס טראָגט די טוונג פון די טעג?
פאַרטיליקונג, מיַין ליבער.
וואָס ברענגט דאָס טראַכטן אין די נעכט?
בייז בלוט, בייז בלוט, מיַין ליבער.

און איז קיין היילונג גאָר נישטאָ?
ס'האַסט אויך דער היילער, ליבער.
וואָרט אַנטרינונג ערגעצוווּ?
אויפן מילכוועג, סיַידן, ליבער.

◄ ס'וועט גיסן

נאָך אַ דעמפיקן, אָנאַטעמדיקן טאָג
האָבן אויף די פלוינען פון דעם מערבדיקן הימל
זיך סטאַדעסוויַיז געקליבן די סומנע,
ערנצטע אָקסן
פון דער נאַכט,
די פייַכטע, שטאַרקע שוואַרצע יונג-אָקסן
פון דער נאַכט.

אַ ווינט האָט זיי געטריבן
און זיי האָבן זיך געטוליעט און געשפּרייט,
און פאַרדעקט דעם גאַנצן טונקל-גרויען אויסשפּרייט,
איבער די ביימערשע שפּיצן,
איבער די העכסטע מיצן פון די בערג.
פינצטער האָט זיך די סטאַדע געמאַרט און געהורבעט.
אין געדרענג האָבן זיך אַלץ מער געשפּאַנט און געשטרענגט
זייערע שווערע לענדן,
זייערע איבערפולע, נידעריק הענגענדיקע לענדן —
עס וועט גיסן, עס וועט גיסן, עס וועט גיסן.

די שופרות פון דעם ווינט האָבן געבלאָזן און געברומט
דורך דעם געדיכטן געצווייג פון די ביימער —
עס וועט גיסן, גיסן, גיסן.

➤ *What Do People Do?*

What do people do in the days?
    They hate each other, my dear.
What do people think in the nights?
    Of evil to do, my dear.

What does work of the days yield?
    Destruction, my dear.
What does thinking at night bring?
    Bad blood, bad blood, my dear.

Is there no healing at all?
    The healer hates too, my dear.
Is there an escape anywhere?
    In the Milky Way, maybe, my dear.

➤ *It Will Pour*

After a damp, breathless day,
On the plains of the westerly sky
Gathered, hordes upon hordes,
    the gloomy, serious bulls
Of night,
The humid, strong, black young bulls
Of night.

A wind drove them
And they clung to each other and spread
And covered the whole dark-gray expanse,
Above the treetops
Above the highest hats of the mountains.
A dark horde, it amassed and multiplied.
Crowded, tenser and tighter
Grew their heavy loins,
Their overfull, low, weighted loins—
It will pour, it will pour, it will pour.

The horns of the wind blew and roared
Through the thick branches of the trees—
It will pour, pour, pour.

Max Weber: Woodcut, from
Shriftn 6, Spring 1920.

פֿון די בערג האָט עם געקנאַלט
מיט עכאָ נאָך עכאָ —
עס וועט גיסן !

◄ אין גרויען ליכט

איבערן קליינעם ייִדישן בית-עולם
איז פֿאַרוואָרפֿן אַ טול פֿון גרוי ליכט,
ווי אַ גרויסער שפֿין וואָלט דאָ געוועבט זײַן געוועבס
פֿון די ביימער-שפֿיצן אַראָפּ.
דער איינזאַמער קדיש מאַכט געדיכטער דעם טול.

דער איינזאַמער קדיש
ברענגט ווידער די שטענדיקע דערמאָנונג,
וואָס באַגלייט מיך איצט אומעטום,
און וועט בלײַבן מיט מיר ביזן לעצט פֿון מײַנע טעג,
ווי אַן אינעווייניקסטער אַשיקער שאָטן.

לעבן מיר שטייט אַ יונגע פֿרוי.
זי האָט בלאָנדע האָר און ברוינע אויגן.
זי קומט פֿון מדינת-ישראל.
זי רעדט צו מיר קלוגע, מונטערע רייד:
מיר וועלן טאָן ... מיר וועלן ... קלוג און מונטער.
איך מאַטער זיך צו ענטפֿערן מיט העפֿלעכע גאַלאַנטקייטן.

דער איינזאַמער קדיש
שטייט אין מײַנע אויערן מיט אַ שטים,
וואָס קומט פֿון זייער ווײַט,
און פֿליסטערט זייער נאָענט:
די שטים פֿון מײַן ברודער ווינגדער-אײַזיק.
די שטים פֿון מײַן ברודער יעקב-דן.

◄ צוריקוועגס

אין מערב איז די זון שוין געהאַנגען
ווי אַ גרויסער מאַראַנץ,
געוואַקסן אין רונדקייט, געפֿאַלן אַלץ נידעריקער.
זי האָט נישט געוואַרעמט, און איר ליכט
איז געקומען זײַטיק, פֿרעמד און פֿאַרגעצט.

דער וועג האָט געפֿירט צווישן גויִשע הײַזער.

From the mountains thundered
Echo after echo–
It will pour!

► *In Gray Light*

Over the small Jewish graveyard
Is thrown a tulle of gray light,
As if a big spider had woven its web
Down from the treetops.
The orphan Kaddish thickens the tulle.

The orphan Kaddish
Brings back the unrelenting remembrance
Which accompanies me wherever I go,
And will stay with me to the last of my days
As an internal ash shadow.

Next to me stands a young woman.
She has blond hair and brown eyes.
She is from the State of Israel.
She speaks to me wise, courageous words:
We will do . . . We will . . . Wise and courageous.
I make an effort to answer with polite gallantries.

The orphan Kaddish
Hovering in my ears, has a voice
That comes from very far
And whispers very near:
The voice of my brother Vigder-Isaac.
The voice of my brother Yankev-Don.

Orphan Kaddish—Kaddish said by an orphan. Here, a play on words, also meaning a lonely, orphaned Kaddish.

► *On the Way Back*

The sun was hanging in the west
Like a big orange,
It grew rounder, fell lower and lower.
It didn't warm, and its light
Came sideways, foreign, like an idol.

The road led among Gentile houses.

אויף די פעלדער זייַנען געשטאַנען פאַרטאַן ווי אַ קו, ווי אַ פערד.

זיי האָבן זיך אָפּגעשטעלט אין מיטן פּיטערן,

פאַרהויבן די מאָרדעס

און טעמפּ געגלאַצט צום פאַלנדיקן ליכט,

און אויף אונדז.

די שויבן אין די הײַזער

האָבן געקוקט מיט בייַזן בליאַסק,

און פייַנדלעך נאָכגעשפּירט אונדזערע טריט.

די יונגע פרוי בייַ מייַן זייַט האָט גוט געטאָן,

וואָס זי האָט געשוויגן.

נאָר אפשר האָט זי גערעדט,

און איך האָב נישט געהערט.

◄ אינדזלדיק

כ׳בין געבוירן ווייַט פון אַ טייַך

און נאָך ווייַטער פון אַ ים.

וועגן אינדזלען האָב איך געלערנט בלויז אין דער שולע.

נאָר דאָס לעבן האָט פון מיר אַן אינדזל געמאַכט

און אינדזלדיק פליסן מייַנע מעת-לעתן.

האָב איך געוואָלט אַוועק פון דער ברייטקייַט,

ווו אַלע זעגלען אין קאָמפּאַניעס?

ווער בין איך, איך זאָל וויסן?

נאָר די וועלסלעס האָבן מייַן שיפל אַליין געפירט,

די שאַר-ברעטער האָבן פון דער ברייטקייַט אָפּגעוואָנדן

און אָפּגעשטעלט מיך, נאָך אַ בלאַנדן, בייַ אַן אינדזל:

דאָס ביסטו.

איך האָב געלייַענט אין מענטשלעכע בליקן:

גיי-מיט מיט דעם רוב, מיט יעדן רוב,

צו יעדער צייַט, מיט זייַן יעדן בייַט.

איך האָב באַנומען מענטשלעכע שמייכלען:

דער טייַטש פון רוב רוב איז זיכערער האַרבעריק,

מיט צוגעלאָזטע פּיַערלעך און ווייכע פּאַטעלן.

האָב איך פאַראַכט די ווינקענדיקע, געשמאַקע פלעמלעך?

ווער בין איך צו וויסן?

נאָר די וועגן האָבן זיך אַליין מושטירט

און מייַנע פיס געפירט צום ענגסטן שטעג,

וואָס האָט זיך פאַרענדיקט מיט אַן אָנוועג,

ווו מענטשן גייען נישט און הענער קרייען נישט.

In the fields stood absorbed—here a cow, there a horse,
They broke off their grazing,
Lifted their blank faces,
Gazing at the falling light
And at us.
The bright windowpanes
Watched us with a wicked shimmer,
Sniffing hostilely at our footsteps.

The young woman at my side did well
To be silent.
Or perhaps she talked,
And I didn't hear.

► *Islandish*

I was born far from a river
And even farther from a sea.
Of islands, I learned in school.
Yet life has made me into an island,
And islandish flow my days.

Did I want to escape the open waters
Where they all sail in companies?
Who am I, that I should know?
Yet the oars drove my boat by themselves,
The paddles led away from the open space
And landed me, still a blond lad, on an island:
This is you.

I have read in people's gazes:
Go with the majority, any majority,
At any time, with any change.
I understood their human smiles:
Majority means secure refuge,
With affable hearths and soft sofas.

Did I despise the winking, pleasant flames?
Who am I to know?
Yet the roads had mustered themselves
And led my feet to the narrowest path,
Which ended in an impasse
Where people don't walk and cocks don't crow.

דאָרט הויער איך אינדזלדיק און בלויז אַ מאָל
דערטראָגן זיך קולות,
וואָס זייער רוף איז מיר אומפֿאַרשטענדלעך
ווען ער איז נישט נקמהדיק-פֿײַנטלעך.

אַ מאָל אויך דערהער איך דעם גרילץ
פֿון טעמפֿער קינאה, דער פֿלאַך-אויגעדיקער:
"ווי גוט אים, דעם טויגעוודיקן, ווי באַקוועם!"
דעמאָלט ציטערט מײַן ברעם
און איך לאַך מײַן אינדזלדיקן לאַך.

◄ וואַריאַנט

דאָס לעבן אַ בינע און מיר די אַקטיאָרן —
אַן אַלטע געשיכטע, מיט גראָען זיכרון.
און קיינער דערוואַרט נישט, כ'בין זיכער, פֿון מיר
כ'זאָל זאָגן דאָס דאָס בעסער פֿון גרויסן שעקספּיר.
נאָר כ'וויל זיך פֿאַרגינען אַ קליינע הוספֿה,
אַ צוגאָב-וואַריאַנט, ס'פֿאַרנעמט קוים אַ סטראָפֿע.

די בינע איז נישט פֿון געהילץ און פּאַפּיר,
מיט קינצלדיק ליכט, מיט עפֿעקט פֿון קאָליר.
נאָר אומגליק און ספּאַזמען, מיט רויבער און פֿעבל,
מיט חשק און חושך, מיט קין און הבל.
אַקטיאָרן אָן ווירדע, אָן מוט, אָן הומאָר,
אומהיימלעך געראַנגל, אומהיילעקער כאָר.
אַ בינע — אַ קליניק, מיט עיפּוש און צאַפּל,
אַ שפּילן פֿון פּורצעס, אַ דראַמע — אַ מפּיל.

◄ אין רויטער באַרד

איך האָב הײַנט געזען דעם זעלבסטזיכערן אמת,
וואָס ווײַזט זיך דאָ אָפֿן, דאָ גנבֿיש,
נאָר שטענדיק פֿיל-פֿנימדיק
סײַ בײַ טאָג, סײַ בײַ נאַכט.

דאָס איצטיקע פּנים — איך האָב עס אַרומגעטאַפּט מיט אויגן
און עס דערקענט, אויך נישט צו פֿאַרגעסן.
אין רויטער, קופֿערנער באַרד,
מיט שאַרפֿע ציין, הונגעריקע צום ביס,
מיט זשעדנע בליקן פֿון אַ רויב-פֿויגל,
וואָס דערשנאַפּט דעם קרבן פֿון הויכער הייך,
און לאָזט זיך אַראָפּ אויף אים גראָד, אין גלײַכער ליניע —
האָב איך אַט דאָס פּנים געזען.

There I crouch in my Islandness. Only sometimes
Voices reach me,
Their call is unintelligible
But for hatred and vengeance.

Sometimes I can hear the grating
Of blunt, flat-eyed envy:
"How good he has it, the loner, how convenient!"
Then my brow quivers
And I laugh my islandish laughter.

➤ *A Variant*

Life is a stage, and we are the actors—
It's an ancient story, in graying remembrance.
No one will expect, I am sure, of myself
To say it better than the great Shakespeare.
Yet I'd like to indulge in a little appendix,
An additional variant, it takes a mere strophe.

The stage is not made of wood and of cardboard,
With artful lighting, effects of color.
But misfortune and spasm, robber and rabble,
With darkness and lust, Cain and Abel.
The actors—no pride, no courage, no humor,
Uncanny struggle, unholy choir.
The stage—a poor clinic, with stench and with torture,
The players are whores, and the play an abortion.

➤ *A Red Beard*

Today I saw the arrogant Truth.
He comes sometimes openly, sometimes slyly,
Always with many faces,
By day and by night.

The present face—I sniffed it with my eyes,
I recognized it, I shall not forget it.
A red, copper beard,
Sharp teeth, hungry to bite,
The eager looks of a preying bird
That smells its prey from high up
And drops down on it with precision, in a straight line—
I saw that face.

ווי אַ יאַסטרויב, וואָס שטעכט זײַן שאַרפן שנאָבל
גלײַך אין דעם קרבנס האַרץ,
און פאַרשפרייט דערנאָך איבער אים
זײַנע גרויסע, בייז-גבורהדיקע פליגל
אין פינצטערן, טאָווהדיקן, געזעטיקטן ניצחון,
האָב איך אים געזען —
דעם זעלבסטזיכערן אמת.

כ׳האָב געקוקט אויף אים
און איך האָב געציטערט אַ גרויס ציטערניש.
אָט איז ער —
דער צערײַסער פון לעבעדיקע געוועבן,
דער ברענער פון פיאָטעס און טראָמפּלער פון שאַרבנס.
אזוי טשאַטעווועט ער און באַפאַלט —
דער שענדער פון גוף,
דער פאַרקרימער פון גײַסט,
דער לעשער פון האָפענונג,
דער לעסטערער פון חלומות.

דער בראַנד-באָרדיקער
און שאַרף-צייניקער
האָט גערעדט מיט דעם סאַמע העכסטן נאָמען
אויף די ליפן.

◄ ראָנדאָ פון לעבנס-גאַנג

איך האָב דעם וועג אַליין געוויילט, איך ווייס גענוי אַצינד,
און בין אויף אים געגאַנגען אימפּעטיק, געשווינד,
ווי ס׳וואָלט דער גורל מיט אַ בײַטש אויף אים געטריבן.
אַ וועג, וואָס האָט קיין צו-פיל גוטס נישט אָנגעקליבן
און אויך נישט צו-פיל פרײַנד פאַר זיך פאַרדינט.
פאַרדראָסן, ראָנגלעניש — אין פאַלעס גאַנצע זיבן.
כ׳האָב אָפּגעשפּאַרט זעלבסט-קענטעניש. הכנעה צינדט
איר לעמפּל אויף מײַן גאַנג דורך גראָקייט און — באַזינט.
איך האָב דעם וועג אַליין געוויילט.

נישט בײַ איציקלידן בלויז, אין לעבנס לאַבירינט
איז אויך דער גראַדער וועג דער קירצעסטער. ער פאַרבינדט
היפּש פײַנע סתירות: פויגל-מילך מיט פוילע ריבן,
ווייך האַרץ מיט שטאָלן ווערט, דאָס האַסן און דאָס ליבן.
נישט צאַצקעס — כ׳האָב באַגערט פאַרשטענדעניש אַ קוינט.
איך האָב דעם וועג אַליין געוויילט.

Like a vulture, piercing its sharp beak
Right into the victim's heart
And then spreading over him
Its large evil, heroic wings
In dark, passionate, satiated victory,
I saw him—
The arrogant Truth.

I looked at him
And trembled.
Here he is—
Who rips living textures,
Sears soles, tramples skulls.
This is how he lurks and attacks—
He who violates the body,
Twists the soul,
Extinguishes hope,
Desecrates dreams.

The flame-bearded,
The sharp-toothed,
He talked, and the loftiest name
Was on his lips.

Ben Shahn: *Poet,* 1960.

► *Rondeau of My Life's Walk*

I chose the road myself, I know it now precisely,
I walked on it with energy, with haste as if
My destiny had chased me through it with a whip.
A road, that has not gathered too much good,
And neither has it gained too many friends.
Resentments, struggles—pockets full of them.
I have saved up self-knowledge. Humility lights up
Its lantern on my walk through grayness and—makes sense.
     I chose the road myself.

Not just in Euclid—in life's labyrinth
The straight road is the shortest too. It links together
The finest contradictions: bird's-milk with foul turnip,
Soft heart with steel words, the hatred and the loving.
I craved not toys–but just an ounce of understanding.
     I chose the road myself.

Jacob Glatshteyn

1896–1971

After the Holocaust, Jacob Glatshteyn* was the most celebrated "national" Yiddish poet. Readers found in his poetry a response to the catastrophe and an evocation of Jewish historiosophical awareness. When the critics lauded the later Glatshteyn as a great "national" poet, A. Leyeles challenged them, arguing that for the Introspectivists, Glatshteyn had always been a great poet. Indeed, without the development of Glatshteyn's sophisticated, individualistic, and ironic style, sparkling with wit and innovations of language, the achievements of his Holocaust poetry would have been impossible. Glatshteyn's nationalist poetry was deceptively simple; between the 1920s and 1950s, the Yiddish reader also grew into accepting Modernist poetry and free verse.

Clearly, the catastrophe in Europe brought Jewish themes into the center of Glatshteyn's poetry. In earlier poems such as "Autobiography" and "Jewish Kingdoms" (1929), Glatshteyn still dissociated himself from his Eastern-European past or looked at it with amazement, but the events of the late thirties brought him back to the Jewish ghetto. In 1938 and early 1939, Glatshteyn was among the first to sense the coming disaster. In such poems as "A Hunger Fell Upon Us," "On the Butcher Block," "Here I Have Never Been," and the celebrated "Goodnight, World," he gave forceful expression to a sense of Jewish isolation in the face of the approaching catastrophe, although only its first signs were apparent at the time. It was only after the Holocaust that he was able to re-create from a certain distance of tragic tranquility the pious world of his parents and his childhood.

His first book, entitled *Jacob Glatshteyn* (1921), was a celebration of moments in the present, a bewildered individual's attempt to make some sense of the "world tangle" (*velt-plonter*), with some traces of New York in the background and no sign of history. It was also the first book in Yiddish poetry written entirely in free verse. Glatshteyn went on to write a dozen mature books, very American in their sensibilities, only to announce himself in 1966, in the very title of his book, as *A Jew from Lublin*.

*Also Yankev Glatstein, Gladstone.

The young Jacob Glatshteyn.

Glatshteyn was born in Lublin, Poland, then under Russian rule, to an Enlightened religious family. He received a traditional education until the age of sixteen, studying the Bible, the Talmud, and later commentaries, as well as secular subjects with private tutors. His father introduced him to modern Yiddish literature.

In 1914 he immigrated to America to join an uncle, and in the same year published his first short story in the anarchist Yiddish newspaper, *Di Fraye Arbeter Shtime*. After 1918 he studied law at New York University, but abandoned it for the career of a Yiddish writer.

At first, Glatshteyn felt that poets should refrain from journalism, but after some years he relented, making a living through the only Yiddish medium with a mass audience, the newspaper. In 1926 he became a regular contributor to one of the three New York Yiddish dailies, *Morgen-Zhurnal*, and participated actively in other Yiddish journals. In 1945 he began writing a regular column for the weekly *Yiddisher Kemfer*, entitled "In Tokh Genumen" (The Heart of the Matter), publishing until 1957 some six hundred essays—primarily literary cricitism, reviews of new books, and discussions of Jewish cultural problems. Some of these essays were masterpieces of Yiddish style and of concise, sensitive, and personal literary criticism.

In 1940, Glatshteyn received the Louis Lamed Prize for his two volumes of masterly prose, *When Yash Went* and *When Yash Came* (English translation: *Homecoming at Twilight*, 1962), which reflected the author's confrontation with the Old World during a voyage to Europe in 1934. He received the Lamed prize again in 1956 for a volume of his collected poems, *From All My Toil* (which was arranged in reverse chronological order).

Glatshteyn always believed in experimentation in poetry and in the need for the poet to create his own individual language. In his poems, he laid bare the unique properties of the Yiddish language, articulating the interplay of the source languages of Yiddish, using the wealth of Yiddish idioms for new poetic metaphors, and weaving the intonations of colloquial folk Yiddish into the measured sentences of a modern intellectual. The interplay of invention and stylistic parody reached a virtuoso culmination in pieces such as "If Joyce Had Written in Yiddish" (an emulation of the style of *Finnegans Wake*) and especially in his book, *Yiddishtaytshn* (here translated as *Exegyddish*), which is one of the most brilliant achievements of Yiddish poetry, and for the most part untranslatable.

Exegyddish appeared in 1937, just a year before Glatshteyn's first Holocaust poems, which, though replete with irony, shifted to a blunt, straightforward style. Glatshteyn's experiments with language—the fresh turns of phrases, the effective interplay with dialects, the archaisms or Hebrew allusions—are at work in his later period as well, though naturally subordinated to the "theme" imposed by the intrusion of history. In the last thirty years of his life, Glatshteyn's poetry became an incessant, internalized conversation on Jewish history, the lost world of European Jewry, the birth of Israel, assimilation in America, the tragic demise of the Yiddish language, and the loneliness of the poet.

The poems selected from Glatshteyn's earlier books follow the texts of his original volumes rather than his better-known book of collected poems, *Fun Mayn Gantser Mi* (From All My Toil, 1956). In only a few cases have we accepted changes from the later variant. This selection restores a number of poems which Glatshteyn did not include in his celebrated collected volume.

Jacob Glatshteytn.

די לעצטע צייט איז קיין שפּור ניט מער געבליבן

פֿון יאַנקל ברב יצחק,

נאָר אַ קלײנטשיק פֿינטעלע אַ קײלעכדיקס,

וואָס קײקלט זיך צעדולטערהײט איבער גאַסן

מיט אַרויפֿגעטשעפּעטע, אומגעלומפּערטע גלידער.

דער איבערהאָר האָט מיט דעם הימלבלוי

די גאַנצע ערד אַרומגערינגלט

און ניטאָ קיין רעטונג.

אומעטום פֿאַלן ״עקסטראַס״ פֿון אויבן

און צעפֿלעטשן מײַן וואָסערדיקן קאָפּ.

און איינער מיט אַ לאַנגער צונג

האָט מיט אַ שטיק רויט מײַנע בריל אויף אײביק באַפֿלעקט

און רויט, רויט, רויט.

איר הערט:

אָט די טעג וועט עפּעס אַזוינס אין מײַן קאָפּ פּלאַצן

און מיט אַ טעמפֿן קראַך זיך אָנצינדן דאָרט

און איבערלאָזן אַ קופּקע שמוציקלעכן אַש.

און איך,

דאָס קײלעכדיקע פֿינטעלע,

וועל זיך דרייען אין עטער אויף אײביקייטן

מיט רויטע וואָאַלן אַרומגעהילט.

ווען דער שטאָלצער קיניג איז אין שׁיונאַס שטאָט אַרײַנגעריטן,

האָט זײַן רויטע באָרד געפֿלאַמט אין דער אויפֿגײיענדיקער זון,

ווי די בלאָנקע שווערדן פֿון זײַן סוויטע.

און ווען ס׳האָט דער שטאָלצער קיניג באַשײַמפּערלעך געזען

ווי ס׳האָלט דער טויט די שטאָט אין זײַנע אָרעמס,

און אַז ס׳זענען אויסגעשטאָרבן אַלע ציגל אין די הײַזער,

און אַ מינדסט ווינטל קאָן די הײַזער צעבלאָזן אויף דינעם שטויב —

האָט ער געלאַכט.

און אומגעדרייט האָט ער זײַן שטאַרקן קאָפּ

אַ קוק צו טאָן אויף זײַנע יונגען,

וואָס האָבן מיד און טעמפּ געשלעפּט אַ פֿאַרמאַטערטן דעם זיג.

און דער קיניג האָט באַפֿוילן,

אַז ס׳זאָלן די יינגסטע זכרים פֿון דער שטאָט

קומען אים אַנטקעגן מיט ברויט און זאַלץ.

➤ *1919*

Lately, there's no trace left
Of Yankl, son of Yitskhok,
But for a tiny round dot
That rolls crazily through the streets
With hooked-on, clumsy limbs.
The lord-above surrounded
The whole world with heaven-blue
And there is no escape.
Everywhere "Extras!" fall from above
And squash my watery head.
And someone's long tongue
Has stained my glasses for good with a smear of red,
And red, red, red.
You see:
One of these days something will explode in my head,
Ignite there with a dull crash
And leave behind a heap of dirty ashes.
And I,
The tiny dot,
Will spin in ether for eternities,
Wrapped in red veils.

➤ *The Proud King*

When the proud king rode into the enemy's city,
His red beard flamed in the rising sun
Like the dazzling swords of his retinue.
And when the proud king saw with his own eyes
How death held the city in its grip
And how all the bricks in the houses had died
So the mildest wind could blow them into thin dust—
He laughed.
And he turned his strong head
To look at his boys.
And the boys were tired and dulled and dragged a weary victory.
And the king commanded
That the youngest men of the city
Should come to greet him with bread and salt.

1919

The political events of 1919
included Wilson's attempts to
create a lasting world peace, the
fresh impressions of the Russian
Revolution and Civil War, the
Red Scare in America, and the
wave of massive pogroms in the
Ukraine.

Yankl, son of Yitschok—a
familiarizing form of the biblical
Jacob, son of Isaac, using,
however, the real names of the
poet and his father.

tiny round dot—an allusion to
"**dos pintele Yid**" (the "tiny dot
Jew," or the heart of Jewishness
in a person). In most Yiddish
dialects, it also means "the tiny
dot of 'i.' " Yud (= Yid) is the
smallest Hebrew letter, and a
dot—for the vowel /i/—is the
minimal representation of any
Hebrew sound. At the same time,
it is the initial letter of both
"Jew" and the name of God
(YHWH); as well as of Jacob
(Yankl) and Isaac (Yitstchok).
The idiom refers to the
irreducible hard core of
Jewishness—that tiny, minimal
point that makes the difference,
no matter how assimilated a
person may be. In this poem, the
dot is devoid of any specifically
Jewish connotation; he becomes
a dot, a hardly observable but
stubborn core of existence.

באלד האבן גענענט צום קיניג צען אלטע לייט מיט לאנגע גראע בערד
און אויף די קני געפאלן:

שטאלצער קיניג, מ י ר זענען די יינגסטע זכרים פון דער שטאט און קיין ברויט האבן מיר ניט,

ווייל ס׳האט זיך אויסגעלאזט דאס ברויט ביי אונדז, שוין איבער צוועלף חדשים.

עדות זענען אונדזערע הענט די אויסגעצערטע,

אונדזערע גומענס די אויסגעטריקנטע.

א ביסל זאלץ האבן מיר געבראכט,

בלויז א ביסל זאלץ האבן מיר געבראכט.

ווידער האט דער שטאלצער קיניג א קוק געטאן אהינטער אויף זיינע יונגען,

וואס זיינען פון די פיס געפאלן, שלעפנדיק א פארמאטערטן דעם זיג.

ס׳האט דער קיניג באפוילן:

זאלן איערע שענסטע יונגפרויען קומען באגריסן מיינע יונגען,

זאלן זיי שפרייטן בלומען פאר די טריט פון אונדזער זיג.

אין ווינענדיקע רייען האבן בארוועסע געשפאנט די יונגפרויען מיט גראע קעפ,

און געשפרייט פארוועלקטע בלומען-בלעטלעך.

און ס׳האבן זיך פאראייניגט די ערשטע פיר פרויען פארן שטאלצן קיניג
און אזוי געשפראכן:

ס׳האט דער אטעם פון טויט אויסגעטריקנט אונדזערע וואסער-קוואלן,

ווי די ווארצלען פון אונדזערע האר,

אויך אונדזערע הימלען זענען געווארן שטיין.

האבן מיר דען געקאנט מיט לערע קרוגן שטילן דעם דורשט פון די בלומען?

און ס׳איז אויפגעשטאנען דער עלטסטער מאנצביל פון דער ערד
און אזוי געשפראכן:

שטאלצער קיניג,

ניט קוק וואס געבוקט איז מיין קאפ און מיין טריט ניט זיכער.

דאס האבן יארן מיר געגעבן א שטעקן אין האנט

און מיין קאפ צו דר׳ערד געבויגן.

יארן וועלן אויך דעם קאפ פון דיין שטאלץ מיט אש באדעקן

און אים הייסן גיין ווי א בעטלער.

דער שטאלצער קיניג האט פארשטאנען,

אז דא דארף זיין גרימצארן ברענען, ווי זיין רויטע בארד.

אבער ער האט ניט געצארנט.

זיינע אויגן האבן בלויז געקוקט אויף די פארוועלקטע בלומען-בלעטלעך,

וואס די יונגפרויען האבן געשפרייט פאר די טריט פון זיין זיג.

און אראפגעריסן האט זיך פון זיי אלע שמאטעס איינע פון די יונגפרויען.

איר נאקעטקייט האט זי געוויינט, און זי האט אזוי געשפראכן:

זע, שטאלצער קיניג, מיינע גלידער, וואס האבן געוווסט א מאן, העונגען איצט פארשעמטע,

ווייל ס׳האט די בענקשאפט אין מיר נאך דעם טאטן פון מיין קינד

פארצערט אין מיר אלע פרויען-זאפטן —

אזוי זאל פארטרוקנט ווערן די טראכט פון דיין וויב אויף אייביק.

ווידער האט דער שטאלצער קיניג פארשטאנען,

אז ער מוז פריי לאזן זיין צארן, ווי א ווילדן יונגן אקס.

Then ten old men with long gray beards approached the king
And fell on their knees:
Proud king, we are the youngest men of the city
And we have no bread,
For over twelve months we have seen no bread in the city.
May our withered hands bear witness
And our parched mouths.
A pinch of salt we have brought,
Merely a pinch of salt.
And the proud king turned back to look at his boys,
And they were collapsing, dragging a weary victory.

Then the king commanded:
Let your most beautiful maidens come to greet my boys,
Let them spread flowers at the feet of our victory.
In weeping columns walked barefoot maidens with gray heads,
Spreading withered petals.
And the first four women bowed to the proud king
And said:
The breath of death has dried our wellsprings
Like the roots of our hair,
Our skies were turned to stone.
How could we quench the thirst of flowers with empty pitchers?
And the oldest man rose up from the ground
And said:
Proud king,
Do not look at me with my head stooped and my step faltering.
The years have put a cane in my hand
And bowed my head to the ground.
The years will cover your proud head, too, with ashes
And send it walking like a beggar.
Then the proud king knew
That now his wrath should burn like his red beard.
But he did not rage.
Only his eyes looked at the withered petals
The maidens had spread at the feet of his victory.
And one of the maidens tore off all her tatters.
Her nakedness cried when she said:
Look, proud king, my flesh, that once knew a man, now sags ashamed.
Because my longing for the father of my child
Has dried out all my female juices—
May the womb of your wife so dry out forever.
Then the proud king knew again
That he must free his wrath like a wild young bull,

אָבער ער האָט ניט געצאָרנט.
זיינע אויגן האָבן אַלץ געקוקט אויף די פאַרוועלקטע בלומען-בלעטלעך,
וואָס די יונגפרויען האָבן געשפרייט פאַר די טריט פון זיין זיג.

אַ פינצטערע מורא האָט זיך געלייגט אויף די הייזער.
דערשראָקענע קינדער האָבן פון די פענצטער זייערע מאַמעס גערופן.
פון קלויסטער אַרויס האָט זיך דערטראָגן דער געוויין פון די פרומע בענק
נאָך די יונגע טאָטעס פון דער שטאָט.
דער איינגעשלאָפענער בלינדער גלאָקן-ציִער האָט פון זיין שלאָף דערוואַכט.
זיינע אַלטע געלע הענט האָבן ווי תמיד געבעטן דעם קלויסטער-גלאָק אַנצוזאָגן,
אַז ס'איז געקומען די שעה פאַר דער אָוונט-תפילה,
אָבער די שטומע צונג פון גלאָק האָט אויסגעקלונגען
אַ טריטן-קלונג.
אַ טריטן-קלונג.
די זון איז איינגעשרומפן.
אַ שלאַקסרעגן האָט אויסגעבראָכן.
דער רעגן האָט באַנעצט די קעפ פון די פריינט, ווי די קעפ פון די פיינט.
די צען אַלטע לייט האָבן אומגעקערט זייערע רוקנס צום קיניג
און זיך צום קלויסטער געלאָזט גיין.
און דער שטאָלצער קיניג האָט אַלץ געקוקט,
ווי אין ווינענדיקע רייען שפּאַנען באַרוועס די יונגפרויען מיט גראָע קעפ
און שפּרייטן פאַרוועלקטע בלומען-בלעטלעך פאַר די טריט פון זיין זיג.

◄ באַיאָנעטן

ס'האָבן צוויי פינצטערנישן געהאַלדזט איינע די אַנדערע,
און האָלדזנדיק געשטיקט די מאַטע ליכט פון אַ ליקוי-חמה.
צווישן ביידע פינצטערנישן
האָבן אויסגעדאַרטע הענט געשפונען בלאָע פייערן פון גלויבן.
די רעכטע האָנט האָט געשפונען פון דער פינצטערניש פון אָנהייב.
די לינקע — פון דער פינצטערניש פון סוף.
קעגן דער ליקוי-חמה האָבן פאַרחלשט געבלאָנקט מיליאָנען באַיאָנעטן.
זייער שטאָל האָט טעמפ געוויינט.

דער אָטעם פון לעבן האָט פויל געדרימלט ווי אין אַ הייסן נאָכמיטאָג.

◄ אייגנס

ביי פאַרריגלטע טירן פון רעשטלעך אייגנס
וואַכן די שאַטנס פון די קרעמער גאַנצע נעכט.
אַ זייגער זעקס פאַר טאָג שלייכן זיך די שאַטנס אַהיים

But he did not rage.
His eyes looked on at the withered petals
The maidens had spread at the feet of his victory.

A dark fear descended on the houses.
Terrified children at the windows called for their mothers.
From the church came the crying of the pious benches
For the young fathers of the city.
The dozing blind sexton woke up from his sleep.
His old, yellow hands begged the bell to sound
That the hour of evening prayers had come,
But the mute tongue of the bell rang
A death knell.
A death knell.
The sun shrank.
A rain poured down.
And the rain soaked the heads of friends and the heads of foes.
Then the ten old men turned their backs to the king
And walked away toward the church.
And the proud king looked on
As the maidens with gray heads walked barefoot in weeping columns
Spreading withered petals at the feet of his victory.

➤ *Bayonets*

Two darknesses embraced each other
And choked the dim light of sun's eclipse.
Between the two darknesses
Withered hands spun blue fires of faith.
The right hand spun the darkness of beginning.
The left, the darkness of end.
Against the sun's eclipse, millions of fainting bayonets glittered.
Bluntly wept their steel.

The breath of life dozed lazily, as on a hot afternoon.

➤ *Property*

At the bolted doors of the crumbs of property
Shadows of the storekeepers watch all night.
At six in the morning the shadows slither home,

וועקן די באַלעבאַטים זייערע פון שלאָף,
פֿאַר דעם טאָג-טאַנץ איבער רעשטלעך אייגנס.
מײַן שאַטן אָבער היט דאָס נאַכט-זילבער פֿון דער לבנה
אויף דעם שפּיץ פֿון וואָלוואָירט,
און פֿאַרטאָג ברענגט מיר מײַן שאַטן
דאָס רויע ביסל גאָלד פֿון אַ פֿרישער זון.

► טירטל-טויבן

אימפּולסן פֿון געדאַנק
בליציקע און ראַשיק —
בליאַסק פֿון זון אויף מעסער-שאַרף.
פּלוצעם:
חדר-יאָרן און אַ וואָרט,
מער נישט ווי אַ וואָרט:
טירטל-טויבן.
און ס׳לאָזט ניט אָפּ,
מיט דעם ווייכן קנייטש פֿון טירטל,
מיט דעם לאַשטשענדיקן קנייטש.
אַ, טירטל-טויבן
טירטל-טויבן.
טירטל-טירטל
טירטל-טויבן.
חדר-יאָרן, קינדער-יאָרן.
און עס זינגט.
און פֿאַרפֿאָלגט.
און פֿאַרווייגט.
און דערמאָנט:
טירטל-טויבן
טירטל-טירטל
טירטל-טויבן.

► צוועלף

די ווײַזערס פֿון באַלויכטענעם שטאָט-זייגער
הויערן איינער אויפֿן אַנדערן,
ווי דער גאַסן-הונט אויף זײַן צופֿעליק ווײַב. —
צוועלף.
איצט שטײַגט דאָס הייזעריקע געזאַנג פֿון בלוט
צו די נאַכטיקע אויערן פֿון דער שטאָט.

To wake their bosses
For the day-dance over the crumbs of property.
But my shadow watches the night-silver of the moon
On the peak of Woolworth,
And at dawn my shadow brings me
A piece of raw gold from the fresh sun.

► *Turtledoves*

Impulses of memory:
Lightning, swift—
Gleam of the sun on a blade.
Suddenly:
Heder years and a word,
Just a word:
Tirtle-toyben.
Turtledoves.
And it won't relent,
With the soft bend of *tir-tle*,
With the fondling fold.
Oh *tirtle-toyben*
Tirtle-toyben.
Tirtle-tirtle
Tirtle-toyben.
Heder years, childhood years.
And it sings.
And it haunts.
And it rocks.
And reminds:
Tirtle-toyben
Tirtle-tirtle
Tirtle-toyben.

Tirtle-toyben—an archaic Yiddish word, preserved in the language of the **heder**.

► *Twelve*

The hands of the lighted city clock
Climb one on top of the other
Like a street dog on his accidental mate—
Twelve.
Now the hoarse song of blood rises
To the night ears of the city.

איצט זינגט די גאַנצע שטאָט דאָס געזאַנג פֿון צוויי.
איצט וויינט די גאַנצע שטאָט דאָס געוויין פֿון איינס נאָך איינס.
ענטפֿערט אָפּ דער באַלױכטענער שטאָט-זייגער:
צוועלף.

◄ אַרטעריאָסקלעראָזיס

און אױב, אין לױף פֿון דײַנע טעג,
האָסטו מיט גיבור-קראַפֿט געזיגט
איבער װערעמלעך אַלערלײ,
װאָס האָבן מיליאָנענװײַז
געלױערט אומעטום אױף דיר.
און אָפּגעבליאַקעװעט האָסטו דײַן הױט אין קאַמף.
און פֿאַרלױרן האָבן דײַנע האָר די קראַפֿט
און װי גראָז פֿאַרװיאַנעטער געגראָאַט זיך
לעבן דײַנע שלייפֿן.
הערסטו דען ניט,
אין דעם לױף,
אין דעם פֿליס,
פֿון דײַן בלוט אין דײַן מאַרך
זינגען װי אַ גריל,
זינגען װי אַ טיטוס-װאָרעם,
זינגען צו דעם טאַקט
פֿון אַ לאָפֿאַטע-גראָב אין דער שװאַרצער ערד
אַרטעריאָסקלעראָזיס.
אַרטעריאָסקלעראָזיס.

און האָט דיר די איבערמאַכט באַשערט
אַ לעבן װי אַ זומפֿ אַ פֿרידיקס,
מיט טעג װאָס ציִען זיך
װי אַ לאַנגער נודנער ניגון,
מיט נעכט לעבן אַ װײַבל אַ געטרײַס,
װאָס דערלאַנגט די שטעקשיך דיר,
װען קומסט אין הױז,
און לאָזט הערשן איר זעל,
צװישן די מאַסיװע מעבל אין דײַן הױז.
אױך דאָמאַלס װעבט אַ שפֿין זיך רויִק,
מיט מערדעריש גדולד, אין מוח בײַ דיר זײַן נעץ.
און צום טאַקט פֿון זייגער װאָס קלאַפֿט.
און צום טריל פֿון קאַנאַריק אין דער פֿרי.
און צום סקריפ פֿון דײַן װיג-שטול אַהין-צוריק.
זינגט דײַן בלוט דאָס לאַנגזאַם-צעשטערנדע ליד.

Now the whole city sings the song of two.
Now the whole city cries the cry of one to one.
And the lighted city clock replies:
Twelve.

➤ *Arteriosclerosis*

And if, in the rush of your days,
Heroically, you vanquished
Myriads of little worms
Lurking everywhere,
And your skin faded in the struggle,
And your hair lost its luster
And grayed like withered grass
On your skull—
Can't you hear,
In the rush
Of your blood,
In the marrow
Of your bones,
Singing like a cricket,
Singing like Titus's mosquito,
Singing to the beat
Of a spade digging in black earth:
Arteriosclerosis.
Arteriosclerosis.

And if the higher-up destined it for you:
A life like a peaceful swamp,
With days that drag on
Like a long boring melody,
With nights next to a faithful wife,
Who brings your slippers
When you come home,
And her soul rules
Among the massive furniture in your house,—
Even then a spider weaves quietly,
With murderous patience, a net in your brain.
And to the beat of the ticking clock,
And to the trill of the canary in the morning,
And to the creak of your rocking chair back-and-forth,
Your blood sings the slowly destroying song:

אַרטעריאָסקלעראָזיס.

אַרטעריאָסקלעראָזיס.

אַרטעריאָסקלעראָזיס.

אַ געדולדיקער גזלן וואָס לויערט אויף די וועגן.

אַרטעריאָסקלעראָזיס.

דער מוז וואָס מוז געשעען.

ערגעצוווּ איז אַ בלאַט אַ פאַרוויאַנעטער פון בוים געפאַלן.

האָרך דעם שאָרך.

האָרך דעם רויש.

אַרטעריאָסקלעראָזיס.

אַרטעריאָסקלעראָזיס.

פרייע פערזן (1926)

◀ **אַבישג**

אַבישג. קליינע, יונגע, וואַרעמע אַבישג.

שריי אויס אין גאַס אַריין, קעניג דוד איז נאָך ניט געשטאָרבן.

נאָר שלאָפן וויל קעניג דוד און מען לאָזט ניט.

אדניהו מיט זיין באַנדע שרייען שוין די קרוין אַראָפ פון מיין גראָען קאָפ.

די פעטע בת-שבע בענטשט מיך מיט אייביק לעבן און היט מיינע לעצטע ווערטער מיט אַ כיטרען שמייכל.

שלאָף מיין קעניג. די נאַכט איז שטיל. מיר זענען אַלע דיינע קנעכט.

אַבישג. קליינע דאָרפישע אַבישג.

וואַרף מיין קרוין אין גאַס אַריין, זאָל זי כאַפן ווער עס וויל.

ס'יאָמערט געשטאָרבענע מאַכט אין יעדן פינגער מיינעם.

איבער דיר אַליין בלויז הערשט איצט די קעניגלעכע דערוויידערדיקע עלטער.

דוד דער קעניג האָט אַלע זיינע דינער פאַרלאָרן. מיט איין דינסט פאַרבליבן.

דרימל מיין קעניג. די נאַכט איז טויט. מיר זענען אַלע דיינע קנעכט.

Arteriosclerosis.
Arteriosclerosis.
Arteriosclerosis.
A patient robber lurking on the roads.
Arteriosclerosis.
The must that must happen.
Somewhere a yellowed leaf is falling from a tree.
Listen to its rustle.
Listen to its murmur.
Arteriosclerosis.
Arteriosclerosis.

Max Weber: Woodcut, from
Shriftn 6, Spring 1920.

FREE VERSE (1926)

► *Abishag*

Abishag. Little, young, warm Abishag.
Shout into the street: King David is not yet dead.
But King David wants to sleep and they won't let him.
Adoniyahu with his gang shout my crown off my gray head.
The fat Bathsheba blesses me with eternal life and watches
    my last words with a sly smile.

Sleep, my king. The night is still. We are all your slaves.

Abishag. Little village girl, Abishag.
Throw my crown into the street—whoever wants, may catch it.
My dead might wails in my every finger.
Only over you I reign in my kingly, disgusting old age.
King David has lost all his servants. Just one maidservant left.

Doze, my king. The night is dead. We are all your slaves.

Abishag—a girl brought to
comfort King David in his old
age.

Adoniyahu, Solomon—King
David's sons, competing for the
throne.

Bathsheba—Solomon's mother,
who conspired to win the crown
for Solomon instead of
Adoniyahu.

אַבישג. קלײנע, טרױעריקע אַבישג.

אַ קלײנטשיק קעצעלע אין שטײַג פֿון אַלטן צײנערלאָזן לײַב געװאָרפֿן.

ס'איז באַשערט מײַן עלטער אױסצוגײן אין שױס פֿון דײַנע קלאָגנדיקע יונגע יאָרן.

מײַנע זיגרײַכע מלחמות זענען בלױז קאַלװשעס בלוט אין מײַן זיכרון.

און װי װי לאַנג ערשט האָבן יונגפֿרױען באַזונגען מיך אין לידער.

רו מײַן קעניג. די נאַכט איז שטיל. מיר זענען אַלע דײַנע קנעכט.

אַבישג. קלײנע, האַרציקע אַבישג.

ס'װאַלגלט די מורא אין אַלע מײַנע גלידער.

קען מען דורך קאַלװשעס בלוט צו שטאַגן געטלעכע דערבלאַנדזשען?

בײַם שײדװעג, װעלן מיר בײַשטײַן דען די רױקע געזאַנגען פֿון מײַנע פֿרומע שעהן?

אַבישג, ס'זענען דאָך געזאַנגען װאָרהאַפֿטיקער פֿון זינד.

חלום, מײַן קעניג. די נאַכט איז טױט. מיר זענען אַלע דײַנע קנעכט.

אַבישג, קלײנע, יונגע װאַרעמע אַבישג.

שרײַ אױס אין גאַס אַרײַן, קעניג דוד איז נאָך ניט געשטאָרבן.

נאָר שטאַרבן װיל קעניג דוד און מען לאָזט ניט.

װאַרף אַרױס מײַן קרױן — זאָל זי כאַפֿן װער עס װיל.

אַדניהו צי שלמה איבערן פֿאָלק, און איך איבער דיר די לעצטע טעג מיט מײַן דערװידערדיקער עלטער.

שלאָף אײַן, מײַן קעניג, ס'טאָגט שױן באַלד. מיר זענען אַלע דײַנע קנעכט.

◄ צו מײַן צװײיהונדערטיאָריקן געבורטסטאָג

װי לאַנגזאַם די צײַט קריכט פֿאַר מיר.

װי פֿליגן לעבן מענטשן און שטאַרבן.

אָבער מיט ציטערדיקע הענט שרײַב איך שױן פֿאַרגעלטע זכרונות,

װער װײסט װי לאַנג.

שטילע געשטאָרבענע פֿרײַנד מײַנע, װי אײנזאַם איז מײַן לעבן אָן אײַך.

שטילע געשטאָרבענע פֿרײַנד מײַנע, װי איר לעבט אין מיר.

רױטער מיטאָג. רױקע װענט.

די שטילקײט פֿון אינעװײניק האַלדזט די שטילקײטן פֿון דרױסן.

איך זיץ און טראַכט.

מײַן ליב װײַב איז אַװעקגעפֿאָרן אױף אַ פֿאַעטאָן צו גאַסט.

מײַנע צװײי טײַבן, דער זון מיט דער טאָכטער זײַנען אױך געפֿאָרן.

איך בין אײנער אַלײן. אין צימער פֿלאַטערט זײַער אונטערטעניקע ליבע צו מיר.

ס'קומען אָן מײַנע פֿרײַנד. מיר זיצן אַלע אין גערטנדל

און רײדן װעגן סודות פֿון װערטער.

Abishag. Little, sad Abishag.
A small kitten thrown into the cage of an old, toothless lion.
It befell my old age to expire in the lap of your lamenting young years.
My victorious wars are but puddles of blood in my memory.
And how long has it been since maidens praised me in their songs.

Rest, my king. The night is still. We are all your slaves.

Abishag. Little, sweet Abishag.
Fear is straying through all my limbs.
Wandering through puddles of blood, can you reach the paths of God?
At the crossroads, will the soft songs of my pious hours come to my defense?
Abishag, you know that songs are more real than sins.

Dream, my king. The night is dead. We are all your slaves.

Abishag. Little, young, warm Abishag.
Shout into the street: King David is not yet dead.
But King David wants to die and they won't let him.
Throw out my crown—whoever wants may catch it.
Adoniyahu or Solomon over the people, and I over you in the last days of my
    digusting old age.

Sleep, my king, it will soon be dawn. We are all your slaves.

► *On My Two-Hundredth Birthday*

How slowly time crawls for me.
Like flies, people live and die.
With trembling hands I have been writing yellowing memoirs
For who knows how long.
My silent dead friends, how lonesome is my life without you.
My silent dead friends, how you live within me.

Red noon. Calm walls.
The stillness in the house embraces the stillness outdoors.
I sit and think.
My dear wife has left on a phaeton for a visit.
The two doves, my son and daughter, went too.
I am all by myself. Their subservient love hovers in my room.
My friends arrive. We sit together in the garden
And talk about mysteries of words.

רײדן פֿון גאָט אָן מורא.

די ייִנגערע פֿון אונדז רײדן פֿון טויט.

מיר זיצן אויף וווי קישנס און רײדן

פֿון אייביקייט, טויט און גראַמאַטיק.

די דינסט דערלאַנגט אונדז אַלעמען גלעזער וווײַן.

מײַנע פֿרײַנד פֿאַרלאָזן מיך. פֿאַרנאַכט.

דער גאָרטן איז פֿול מיט פֿרײַנדשאַפֿט און קלוגע געמאַסטענע ווערטער.

די פֿײַכטקייט טרײַבט מיך אין הויז אַרײַן.

אין די אויבערשטע צימערן טרעט מײַן דינסט

מיט באַרוועסע פֿיס אויף מײַנע וואַרעמע געדאַנקען.

כ׳גיי אַרויף.

מײַן דינסט איז געהאָרכזאַם און צערטלעך מיט שטילער שעמעוודיקייט.

די שטילקייט שמעקט אַרײַן פֿון גאָרטן דורכן פֿענצטער.

דעם פֿרימאָרגן גריסן מײַנע אײנזאַמע טריט אין גערטנדל.

מײַנע געדאַנקען זענען מיט מײַן ליב ווײַב און מײַנע שטילע טויבן.

מײַן דינסט זינגט ערגעץ אין גערטנדל.

דאָס זײַד פֿון מײַנע קליידער גלעט מײַנע באַרויִקטע גלידער.

ס׳קומען אָן צוויי שטאַטסמענטשן און בעטן אַ נדבה,

כ׳גיב זיי אַ גאָלדשטיק.

מײַנע פֿרײַנד קומען ווידער מיט זייערע קלוגע רייד.

מיט דער נאָכמיטאָג-זויבערקייט אין זייערע קליידער.

זיי דערצײַלן מעשיות פֿון לענדער און ביכער.

מיר רײדן ווידער פֿון גאָט און סודות פֿון אייביקייט.

שטילע נאַכט.

די דינסט וואַשט איר לײַב מיט שמעקעדיקן בוימל.

מיט לאָמפּ אין האַנט לײַכט איך צו און מאַך לאַנגע שאָטנס אויף די ווענט.

ס׳איז וואַרעם זאַלבעצווייט אין אײנזאַמקייט.

אין דער פֿרי קומט צוריק מײַן ליב ווײַב מיט מײַנע שטילע טויבן,

ווידער ווערן ווינקעלעך פֿול מיט געזאַנג פֿון מײַן ליבע.

ליבע פֿרוי מײַנע, קינדער מײַנע, שעמעוודיקע דינסט מײַנע.

טײַערע פֿרײַנד מײַנע אויף אומצאָליקע בית-עלמינס.

וווילגערוך פֿון גראָז אויף נאָענטע מצבֿות.

נאָכמיטאָג רייד פֿון דער גאָטהייט און פֿאַרבאָרגענעם סוד פֿון וואָרט.

באַשערט איז מיר אַן אײנזאַמע עלטער.

די אַלטע לײַט זײַנען אַלע ייִנגער פֿון מיר.

און לאַכן פֿון מײַנע פֿאַרשטויבטע ווערטער.

פֿון מײַנע קלוגע ווערטער.

כאַפּ איך אַ קרענצל קינדער, דערצײַל איך זיי שײַנע מעשיות.

קריג איך פֿון זייערע טאַטעס רחמנות-געלט

צו דערהאַלטן מײַנע אַלטע ביינער פֿון צעפֿאַלן.

די סטעליע ליגט אויפֿן קאָפּ אין אײנזאַמען קעמערל.

כ׳טראַכט פֿון גאָט אָן מורא.

And talk about God, without fear.
The younger ones talk about death.
We sit on soft cushions and talk
About eternity, death, and grammar.
The maid serves us glasses of wine.
My friends leave. Dusk.
The garden is filled with friendliness and wise, measured words.
Dampness chases me indoors.
In the upper rooms, my maid treads
With bare feet on my warm thoughts.
I go upstairs. My maid is obedient and soft with quiet bashfulness.
Through the window comes the smell of silence from the yard.

My lonely footsteps greet dawn in the garden.
My thoughts are with my dear wife and my quiet doves.
My maid sings somewhere in the garden.
The silk of my robe strokes my calmed limbs.
Two people from the city knock, asking for alms.
I give them a piece of gold.
My friends come again with their wise talk.
With afternoon-purity in their clothes.
They tell stories of countries and books.
We speak again of God and mysteries of eternity.
Quiet night.
The maid washes her body with fragrant oil.
Lantern in hand, I give her light and make long shadows on the walls.
It is warm to be two in loneliness.
In the morning my dear wife and my quiet doves return.
The corners are filled again with the song of my love.

My dear wife, my children, my bashful maid.
My dear friends in countless cemeteries.
The scent of grass on intimate graves.
Afternoon talk about divinity, about the hidden mystery of the word.
A lonely old age is my lot.
All the old people are younger than I.
And laugh at my dusty words.
At my wise words.
I pick a wreath of children, tell them beautiful stories.
Their fathers pay me pity-money
To keep my old bones from falling apart.
The ceiling weighs on my head in my lonely closet.
I think of God, with no fear.

זענען געגאַנגען די האַריקע מענער מיט שווערע טריט,

ווי אַלטע פעטע לאַסט-פערד אין געשפּאַן

און נאָך זיי האָבן געפֿאָלגט די ווײַבער.

ווען ס׳האָבן די האַריקע מענער אומגעדרייט זייערע צורות,

האָבן זיי געזען, אַז דער אייניציקער דאַרער מאַן מיט דער בײַטש איז ניטאָ,

און אַז די משׂא זייערע איז אויך פֿאַרשווונדן.

אפֿשר איז ער געפֿאַלן אין וועג,

און ווער ווייסט ווי לאַנג זיי גייען שוין אַזוי, די קנעכט פֿון קיינעם

און די טרעגער פֿון גאָרנישט.

פֿאַלט זיי אײַן:

ס׳איז שוין לאַנג וואָס מען האָט זיי ניט געלאָזט צו זייערע ווײַבער,

און אַז זיי ווילן די מידיקייט זייערע

מיט דער מידיקייט פֿון זייערע ווײַבער באַהעפֿטן.

הײַנט וועלן זיי ניט געבײַטשט זײַן צו וועלן קליינע געטלעך און באַשאַפֿן

נאָר זיי וועלן צעזייען זייער קראַפֿט ווי פֿלעווע.

און אויב דער מאַן מיט דער בײַטש איז טאַקע ערגעצוווו געפֿאַלן אויף די וועגן,

וועלן זיי שטענדיק שוין צעזייען זייער קראַפֿט ווי פֿלעווע.

כאַטש ס׳איז שוין לאַנג, וואָס זיי האָבן אין מויל ניט געהאַט,

האָבן זיי די פֿעקלעך ניט אָפּגעבונדן,

נאָר ס׳האָבן די האַריקע מענער אין דער פֿינצטערניש גערופֿן,

אַלע גלידער זייערע האָבן גערופֿן.

הויך און זיכער גערופֿן

די נעמען פֿון זייערע ווײַבער.

און זיי, די ווײַבער, האָבן אין דער פֿינצטערניש אָפּגעענטפֿערט.

ווינטער איז וואַרעם אין הויז בײַ געגי דעם בערנטרייבער

פֿון בלויזן גערייד פֿון זײַנע פֿינף ווײַבער.

אַ קראַנץ פֿון וואַרעמע ווערטער פֿלעכטן זיי

אַרום זײַן שווערן גוף.

➤ *Like Chaff*

With heavy steps the hairy men trudged
Like old fat dray-horses in harness,
And the women followed them.
And when the hairy men turned their heads, they saw
That the one lean man with the whip wasn't there,
And their load, too, had disappeared.
Perhaps he fell on the road,
And who knows how long they've been trudging, slaves to no one
And bearers of nothing.
It occurred to them:
It's been a long time since they were allowed their women.
And it occurred to them:
They want to mate their tiredness
With the tiredness of their women.
Today they will not be whipped to become little gods and procreate,
But will spread their strength like chaff.
And if the man with the whip really has fallen somewhere on the roads,
They will always spread their strength like chaff.
It's been long since they've had anything in their mouths—
But they did not untie their packs,
The hairy men called in the darkness,
All their limbs called,
Loud and sure they called
The names of their women.
And the women responded in the darkness.

Max Weber: Woodcut, from
Shriftn 6, Spring 1920.

➤ *Gaggie*

In winter, the house of Gaggie the bear-trainer is warm
From the chatter of his five wives.
They weave a wreath of warm words
Around his heavy body.

און ס׳איז אים גוט און ער דערציילט מעשׂיות פון וואַלד

מיט אַ האַרציקן געלעכטער.

שפּעטער הייבן זיי אַן צו פלאַפּלען מיט קינדישער אומאָרדענונג,

ווי פינף שלעפּעריקע לאָרעליַיען.

זיי קרײזלען זײנע האָר און וואַרפן אים אַרײן אין אַ טיפן בראָנעם פון דרימל.

אַז ס׳קומט דער זומער פאַרלאָזן אים זײנע ווײַבער.

מײלן ווײַט פון אים שטייען זיי מיט פאַרשאַרצטע קליידלעך,

און באַרוועסע פיס אין וואַסער.

זיי וואַשן פרעמד גרעט.

ווערט ער פויל און זיצט אַרום הויז גאַנצע טעג און דרימלט.

זיי דאָרט איז קיל.

ס׳פליעסקעט דאָס וואַסער דורך זייערע באַרוועסע פיס.

און אים איז הייס.

די פינף רעדן פון אים ווי פון אַ גוטן פעטער,

אָבער בענקען ניט נאָך אים.

אַז ס׳קומט די נאַכט קושן זיי זיך איינס דאָס אַנדערע די ליַיבער

מיט אַ זיסן ווייטיק.

אים איז אויך גוט.

שפּעט-האַרבסט וועלן זיי צוריק קומען

מיט פּעקלעך שפּײז אויף די פלייצעס,

נײע קליידלעך מיט געלט אין די קעשענעס.

איז אים גוט צו דרימלען און צו וואַרטן.

◄ אָוונטברויט

אויפן טיש אַ פריש אַ ברויט, שוואַנגער מיט זעטיקייט.

אַרום טיש שווײַגנדיקע געסט —

איך און זי און נאָך אַ זי.

די מײלער שווײַגן, נאָר די הערצער קלאַפן.

ווי די קליינע גאָלדענע זייגערלעך, קלאַפן די הערצער בײַ די געסט.

און לעבן ברויט אַ מעסער אַ שאַרפס שווײַגט נאָך שוערער פון די געסט

און קלאַפט מיט אַ הערצל נאָך אומרויקער,

ווי בײַ מיר, בײַ איר און בײַ דער אַנדערער איר.

די טיר איז אָפן צו דער זון וואָס גייט אונטער.

אויף דער סטעליע דרעמלען פליגן מידע פון טאָג

און די שויבן ליכטיקן פאַרוווּנדערט מיט דערוואַרטונג און שרעק,

שרעק און דערוואַרטונג פון אָוונטברויט.

דאָס מעסער און איך האַלדזן שטײַף איינס דעם אַנדערנס מורא.

איך פאָך אַרום ברויט מיט ציטערדיקע הענט.

און איך טראַכט פון מײַן וואַרעמער ליבע צו זיי.

He likes it and, laughing heartily,
Tells them stories of the forest.
Later they prattle away in childish disorder
Like five drowsy Loreleis.
They curl his hair and throw him into a deep well of dozing.
When summer comes his wives forsake him.
Miles away from him, with dresses tucked up,
They stand barefoot in water.
They wash other people's laundry.
Then he gets, and sits around the house for whole days and dozes.
They feel cool.
The water splashes between their naked feet.
And he feels hot.
The five talk of him as of a good uncle,
But don't long for him.
When night falls, they kiss each other's bodies
With sweet pain.
He too feels good.
In late autumn they will come back
With packs of food on their shoulders
And new dresses with money in the pockets.
He feels good, dozing and waiting.

► *Evening-Bread*

On the table a fresh bread, pregnant with promise.
Around the table silent guests—
I and she and another she.
Mouths are silent, but hearts beat.
Like tiny gold watches beat the hearts of the guests.
And near the bread a sharp knife, its silence heavier than theirs,
Beating with a heart more restless
Than mine, than hers, and hers.

The door is open to the declining sun.
On the ceiling, flies doze, tired of the day.
And the panes light up in wonder of expectation and fear,
Fear and expectation of evening-bread.

The knife and I clutch tightly each other's fear.
I flutter with trembling hands over the bread
And think of my warm love for them.

פֿון מײַן טױטלעכער שֹינאה צו זײ.
דאָס מעסער חלשט אין מײַן פֿאַרקלעמערטער האַנט
פֿון שרעק און געפֿאַר פֿון אָװנטברױט.

זי נעמט דאָס מעסער און קוקט אױף מיר און אױף איר:
צװײ טױטע געסט זיצן שטיל אַרום טיש.
און אין האַרץ פֿון זי דאָס מעסערשאַרף זינגט
אַ ליד פֿון געפֿאַר פֿון אָװנטברױט.

די אַנדערע זי שפּילט זיך מיט פּלאַטערדיקער פֿרײד
מיטן שאַרף פֿון מעסער און געשטאַרבענע רײד;
און איר ליבע צו אונדז און איר שֹינאה צו אונדז
און איר ליבע צו מיר און איר שֹינאה צו איר
זינגט אַרױס דורך דער צעפֿראַלטער טיר
צו דער זון װאָס גײט אונטער, צו דער זון, צו דער זון,
מיט פֿאַרבענקטע געזאַנגען פֿון אָװנטברױט.

שױבן פֿאַרפֿלײצט מיט קאָליר און געזאַנג.
דאָס מעסער פֿאַרמאַטערט פֿון רױטן פֿאַרלאַנג.
שטיל זיצן אַרום טיש שװײַגנדיקע געסט —
איך און זי און נאָך אַ זי.
דאָס מעסער טאַנצט פֿון מיר צו איר און פֿון איר צו איר.
און שװײַגנדיק עסן מיר פֿון ליבע און האַס
דאָס אָװנטברױט.

◄ דער האַרבסט

פֿײגל זינגען דאָס ליד פֿון ליד פֿון פֿרײלעכטרױער.
װינטן־בױגנס פֿלאַטערן איבער די האַרבסטיקע פֿעלדער.
געװעלדער רױטלען זיך.
בלעטער טױטלען זיך מיט פֿאַרצערטלטער בענקשאַפֿט.
ס'איז שטיל דער רױש און װערטער־טױש
צװישן קלײנע װערעמלעך װאָס װינטשן זיך אַ דערלעבט־איבער־אַ־יאָר.
אַן אַלטער פֿעטער װאָרעם זיפֿצט אָפּ.
און לעקט זיך דעם פֿליכעװאַטן קאָפּ מיט מױל־הערעלעך:
איבער אַ יאָר? הע, הע! איבער אַ יאָר.

אַן אַלטער גױ קלעטערט מיט געמאָסטענע טריט
איבער דער האַריקײט פֿון באַרג.
אין זײַנע אױסגעטערערטע אױגן פֿלעמלט בלױלעך קינאה
אױפֿן טױט פֿון פֿאַרבן — װי שײן זיי שטאַרבן.
ער הײבט די אױגן צום הימל.

Of my deadly hatred for them.
In my clenched hand the knife faints
From fear and danger of evening-bread.

She takes the knife and looks at me and at her:
Around the table, silently, sit two dead guests
And in her heart the knife blade sings
The song of danger of evening-bread.

The other she plays in quivering joy
With the blade of the knife and dead words;
And her love for us and her hatred for us
And her love for me and her hatred for her
Sing out through the wide-open doors
To the sun which declines, to the sun, to the sun,
Nostalgic songs of evening-bread.

Panes flooded with color and song.
The knife weary of red desire.
Around the table silent guests:
I and she and another she.
The knife dances from me to her and from her to her.
And silently we eat with love and hatred
The evening-bread.

➤ *Autumn*

Birds sing the song of sadjoy.
Wind-bows hover over autumn fields.
Woods blush.
Leaves die in scarlet longing.
Quiet is the crawl and the chatter
Of little worms wishing each other may-you-live-till-next-year.
A fat old worm sighs
And licks his bald head with his feelers:
Next year? Heh, heh! Next year.

An old peasant climbs with measured steps
On the hump of a mountain.
In his cried-out eyes flickers a bluish envy
Of the death of colors—how beautifully they die.
He raises his eyes to the sky.

זײַנע אויערן פֿאַרנעמען דעם געפּליסטער פֿון בלום און בלאַט:
— דערלעבט איבער אַ יאָר!
איבער אַ יאָר? הע! הע! איבער אַ יאָר.

◄ אַ טויט-שאַראַדע

דער זיידע האָט דערפֿילט זײַן חוב צו זײַנע אייניקלעך
און געשטאָרבן.
דעם זיידן האָט צוגעדעקט די ערד.
די אייניקלעך האָבן דערפֿילט זייער חוב צום זיידן
און זײַן טויט באַװיינט.
זײַן טויט צו זיי.
זײַן טויט צו זיך איז געבליבן אומבאַװיינט,
װײַל דער זיידע איז געװען טויט.

די אייניקלעך האָבן דערפֿילט זייער חוב צו זייערע אייניקלעך
און געשטאָרבן.
זיי זענען טויט צו זייערע אייניקלעך.
טויט צו זיך.
און דעם זיידנס טויט איז טויט צו זיי.
דעם זיידנס טויט איז טויט צו זיי
פֿון זייער טויט ביז —
דער זיידע איז טויט צו זיך
פֿון זײַן טויט ביז —

װײַל צום טויטסטן איז דער טויט צו זיך אַליין.

◄ דאָס געװײן פֿון די באַגרעבערס

װײ איז אונדז.
ניט אַקערן דיך קומען מיר, מאַמע פֿון שפֿע.
ניט פֿון שניט-צײַט װעגן זענען מיר אויה-רגל צו דיר, היילִיקע מאַמע.
די לאָפּאַטע איז זיגער איצט איבער דעם אַקער.
מיר גראָבן, גראָבן דיך, שװאָרצע מאַמע.
װײ איז אונדז.
מיר גראָבן און װיינען.
מיר װיינען און גראָבן.
מיט שװייס אויפֿן שטערן פֿאַרדינען מיר אונדזער ברויט.
דײַן ברויט, היילִיקע מאַמע.
און ניט מיר אַקערן דיך, מאַמע פֿון שפֿע,
נאָר מיר גראָבן, גראָבן דיך, שװאָרצע מאַמע.

His ears catch the whisper of flower and leaf:
—May-you-live-till-next-year!
Next year? Heh, heh! Next year.

► *A Death-Charade*

The grandfather fulfilled his duty to the grandchildren
And died.
The earth covered the grandfather.
The grandchildren fulfilled their duty to the grandfather
And mourned his death.
His death to them.
His death to himself remained unmourned,
Because the grandfather was dead.

The grandchildren fulfilled their duty to their grandchildren
And died.
They are dead to their grandchildren.
Dead to themselves.
And the grandfather's death is dead to them.
The grandfather's death is dead to them
From their death until—
The grandfather is dead to himself
From his death until—

Because the deadest is death to himself.

► *The Cry of the Gravediggers*

Woe to us.
We come not to plow you, mother of plenty.
We come not to sow for a harvest, holy mother.
Today the spade has supplanted the plow.
We dig, we dig into you, black mother.
Woe to us.
We dig and cry.
We cry and dig.
With the sweat of our brow we earn our bread.
Your bread, holy mother.
We come not to plow you, mother of plenty,
But to dig, to dig into you, black mother.

◄ באַלאַדע

שיסט מיר אָפּ, חברים מײַנע,

די פיס וואָס זײַנען אַנטלאָפֿן,

אָבער שיסט מיר ניט אין קאָפּ

וואָס טראַכט איצט פֿון שוואַלבן אין אַ נעסט.

אַזוי האָט ער זיך געבעטן

ווען מען האָט אים באַגינען אַרויסגעפֿירט

אויפֿן ברייטן סקווער.

ער האָט ניט געוויינט, נאָר געצופּט זיך דאָס בערדל.

שוינט — האָט ער געגעבעכט — האָט רחמנות

אויף אַ מענטשנס אַ קאָפּ.

אָבער צוואַנציק ביקסן האָבן אַ ווי איין זאַלפּ

צעשאָסן דעם קאָפּ וואָס האָט זיך געמאַטערט

צו כאַפּן דעם מיין פֿון וואָרט —

דעזערטירער.

און איך וואָס בין געווען איינער פֿון די צוואַנציק ביקסן

האָב לאַנג געוואַנדערט און געפֿונען זײַן נעסט.

איך האָב געגלעט דרײַ קינדערלעך איבער די קעפּלעך

און אין האַלדז בײַ זיי מיר געהאַלטן געפּאַנגען

מײַנע טרערן.

אַ הויכע, שווייגנדיקע פֿרוי מיט אַן אויפֿגעהויבענעם בוזעם

האָט געוואַרט אויף מײַנע ווערטער.

אוי, צי האָב איך איר געקענט דערציילן,

און מיט וואָס האָב איך זיך געקענט רעכטפֿערטיקן,

אפֿילו ווען איר מאַן איז געווען

אַ דעזערטירער.

◄ מיידל פֿון מײַן דור

צוויי-מאָל בלאָ און קײלעכדיק —

פֿאַרהויכטע שפּיגלען פֿון אַ נשמה

וואָס קיינער וועט קיין נאָר ניט זײַן צו פֿאָרשן און דערגיין.

אַ שאַרפֿער רויטער פּתח שטרײכט אונטער:

דאָ רועֵן ווערטער, צונג און ציין

מיט אַ באַלאַסט פֿון נאָבעלע מעטאַלן.

אַרום האַלדז ווײַסע פּוטערוואָרג.

וויל איך — געדעכעניש פֿון ווײַסן לאַם און פֿאַשע,

און וויל איך — וואַלד און ווילד און פֿאַנג און יאַגד.

➤ *Ballad*

Shoot, comrades,
My legs that fled,
But don't shoot my head
That thinks of swallows in a nest.
So he pleaded
When they took him at dawn
To the white square.
He didn't cry but plucked at his beard.
Spare—he whined—take pity
On a man's head.
But twenty rifles in one salvo
Shot to pieces the head that was at pains
To grasp the meaning of the word—
Deserter.
And I who was one of the twenty rifles
Wandered long till I found his nest.
I caressed the heads of three little children
And in my throat I kept imprisoned
My tears.
A tall, silent woman with high breasts
Was waiting for my words.
Oh, could I have told her,
And what could I have said for myself,
Even if her husband was
A deserter.

➤ *Girl of My Generation*

Twice blue and round—
Misted mirrors of a soul
No one would be stupid enough to research and fathom.
A sharp red dash underlines:
Here rest words, tongue and teeth
Weighted with noble metals.
Around the neck white fur.
If I choose—remembrance of a white lamb and pasture,
If I choose—forest and prey and catch and chase.

איך וויל גאָרניט, נאָר איך קוק
אויף דעם בלאָען סאַמעט וואָס הילט אַנדערטהאַלבן מאָל
דעם דינעם קרומגלייך וואָס פֿאַרמאָגט
(דער טייוול ווייסט ווי אַזוי)
אַלץ וואָס אַ פֿרוי דאַרף פֿאַרמאָגן.
(ווו   זײַנען די רונדע, באַרויִקטע ליניען און פֿאַלדן,
ווו קיטס און שעלי און בײַראָן האָבן באַהאַלטן
אַזוי פֿיל אומרו פֿון עטלעכע דורות צוריק?)
ווו זאָל איך מײַן אומרו באַגראָבן,
סײַדן צווישן די איבערגעקרייצטע דינע שטאָלצן וואָס רייצן
מיט שוואַרצע סאַמעט-שיכלעך.
פֿאַררייכער אַ ציגאַרעטל, מײַן לעבן, און זאָג ניט
אַז דו ווילסט לאָזן דערשיסן דײַן אומשולד.
דײַן יעגער מיט דעם פֿײַל און בויגן לאָכט שוין לאַנג פֿון מיר.
שפּיגל אָפּ אויף דײַנע בלוטיק-רויטע נעגל
פֿאַר אַ רגע בלויז מײַן קיל געשטאַלט.

I don't choose anything, but I look
At the blue velvet which covers one-and-a-half times
The thin straight curve holding
(The devil only knows how)
Everything a woman should have.
(Where are the restful, flowing lines and folds,
Where Keats and Shelley and Byron buried
So much unrest a few generations ago?)
Where shall I bury my unrest,
If not between the thin crossed stilts which tease
With black velvet shoes.
Light a cigarette, my life, and don't say
That you'd like your innocence shot.
Your hunter with bow and arrow has long been laughing at me.
In your blood-red nails, mirror
For only a moment my cool image.

Chaim Gross: *East Side Girl*, 1928.

➤ אַ געזאַנג

דײַין געזאַנג קומט צו מיר אין קלײנע חלקים.
דו שפּײַזסט מיך מיט אַ קרישקע יעדן פרימאָרגן.
דאָס קאַרגע הענטל דײַנס שפּאָרט פּאָרזיכטיק דעם לאַבן.
זײַ געדולדיק ביז כ׳וועל דיר געבן דעם שליסל צום טויער.
בלײַב מיר געטרײַ ביז דעם זומער.

דו זיצסט און וואַרעמסט דײַנע פּיסלעך בײַם אויוון
און קליגסט זיך צו באַהאַלטן דײַן בענקשאַפט פון מיר.
באַלד וועט דער זומער צעשמעלצן זײַנע אײַזיקע קייטן,
וועל איך עפענען די טירן און דיך אַרויסבאַגלייטן אַריבער אַלע שוועלן.
בלײַב מיר געטרײַ ביז דעם זומער.

זומער וועל איך שנײַדן קלײנע פּאָמידאָרן און טראַכטן פון דײַנע ליפּן,
און דו וועסט שפּאַנען אויף די וועגן און זינגען צו יעדן פאַרבײַגייער.
וועל איך באַדויערן וואָס איך האָב מיט אַ שניט דיר ניט פאַרשענדט דײַן פּנים,
אָדער פאַר וואָס איך האָב ניט שווערער געמאַכט דײַן וועג מיט אַ קינד מײַנס אין דיר.
בלײַב מיר געטרײַ ביז דעם זומער.

➤ איך קום צו דיר

שלאַנקע, מיטליעריקע פרוי,
היט זיך פאַר דער נאַכט
וואָס באַשרײַבט דײַן פּנים מיט יאָרן.
כ׳האָב דיך געזען אַ פאַרפלאָנטערטע הירשין
אין די צווײַגן פון דער גרויסער שטאָט.
איך האָב דיך געפירט צו אַ בעט און געזאָגט:
דער גאָט פון מיטליעריקער פאַרשטענדיקייט
זאָל היטן דײַן יעדן באַוועג,
זאָל דיר בײַשטיין אין דײַן גרויסער געניטקייט.
בײַ וועמען האָב איך נאָך געזען אַזאַ בלוטיקע מלחמה
צווישן עלטער און קינדישקייט ווי אויף דײַן געזיכט.
דו נאַרישע קעמפערין, איך קום צו דיר,
צו דער פריסטערין פון פאַרשטענדיקייט,
און שפּיל זיך מיט דײַנע קלוגע רייד און נאָך ניט אָפּגענוצטע פּיס,
דורך דער גאַנצער נאַכט וואָס שמינקט דײַן פּנים מיט יאָרן.
אין דער פרי האָב איך אומזיסט געזוכט ווערטער
וואָס לאָזן זיך מאָלן אויף ראָז פּאַפּיר.
אַז איך וועל געפינען וועל איך עס דיר צושיקן
און דו וועסט עס באַהאַלטן אין אַ בוך פון לידער
לעבן פאַרטריקנטע בלומען-בלעטלעך פון ערשטער ליבע.

► *A Song*

Your song comes to me in little pieces.
You feed me a crumb each morning.
Your stingy little hand carefully saves the loaf.
Be patient till I give you the key to the gate.
Stay true to me till summer.

You sit and warm your little feet at the oven
And cleverly hide from me your longing.
Soon the summer will melt its chains of ice,
I shall open the doors and escort you over all thresholds.
Stay true to me till summer.

In summer I shall slice little tomatoes and think of your lips,
And you will stroll over the roads and sing to every passer-by.
And I shall regret that I didn't mark your face with a scar,
Or that I didn't burden your walk with a child.
Stay true to me till summer.

► *I Am Coming to You*

Slender, middle-aged woman,
Watch out for the night
Which paints your face with years.
I saw you an entangled deer
In the branches of the big city.
I led you to a bed and said:
Let the god of middle-aged understanding
Watch over your every move,
Let him stand by you in your great skill.
Where else have I seen such a bloody war
Between age and childishness, as on your face.
You silly warrior, I am coming to you,
To the priestess of understanding,
And I play with your wise words and still fresh legs
All through the night that rouges your face with years.

In the morning I search in vain for words
That can be painted on pink paper.
When I find them, I'll send them to you
And you will hide them in a book of poetry
Next to dry petals of first love.

דאָס לעצטע װענטל צװישן אונדז איז געפֿאַלן

און איך האָב געזען, אַז זי איז ניט צױבערלעך.

איך האָב געהערט דאָס װאַקלען פֿון אירע רייד

און ניט געבענקט נאָך חכמה.

און דאָך, גראָד איצט,

האָב איך מיט זיכערע הענט

אַליין געשלאָגן שינדלען

אין דעם דאָך איבער אונדזערע קעפּ.

איך װייס שױן אַז זי איז ניט די אַנדערע

װאָס איך האָב אַרומגעזוכט.

פֿאַר איר האָב איך קיין נעצן ניט געשפּרייט.

װאָס פֿאַר אַ יעגער קען איך, מישטיינס געזאָגט, זיַין

מיט דעם פּאַק פֿון אױסגעקליגטע יאָרן.

זי איז אַליין צו מיר געקומען.

און דאָך איז מיר גוט איצט

װאָס מיר האָבן איינס דאָס אַנדערע געװוּנען.

און אַז זי איז אַליין צו מיר געקומען

און געזאָגט:

איך בין ניט צױבערלעך

און ניט קלוג

און איך דאַרף ניט די אַלע סטימולן

כּדי צו װעלן לעבן.

איך װייס אַפֿילו אַז מיַין לייב װי דיַינס

איז אַ ביסל אָפּגעטראָגן,

און איך האָב אױך װי דו שױן

אַ דריַי־פֿיר חלאַותן

װאָס קיין פֿאַרפֿומען קענען ניט פֿאַרװישן.

עס איז דער קערפּער — גוף.

און דאָס װאָס איז ביַי מיר אַנדערש װי ביַי דיר

װערט אַנדערש בלױז דורך דיַין באַריר.

װע‎ַיל פֿאַר זיך זײַנען די בריסט ניט קיין בריסט

און דאָס גאַנצע ביסל מיידלשע קלאַפּערגעצַיִיג

װערט מיידלש בלױז מיט דיר.

איך האָב די פּשוטע רייד געװױגן און געמאָסטן.

איך האָב געװאָלט זען װוּ ליגט אין אירע װערטער

דאָס געהיימניספֿולע און פֿאַרבאָרגענע

װאָס קען נאָר שפּיַיזן מיַין באַגער נאָך איר

און אירן צו מיר.

אירע רייד זיַינען געװען סקעלעט,

אָן באַפּוצונגען פֿון פֿלייש און אָדערן

The last wall between us fell down
And I saw that she was not all charm.
I heard the wavering of her words
And did not long for wisdom.
And still,
With confident hands
I hammered shingles
On the roof over our heads.
I know that she is not the one
I searched for.
For her I did not spread any nets.
What kind of hunter could I be anyway
With a pack of years that I managed to sneak through;
She came to me herself.
And yet I like it now
That we have won each other.
And when she came to me herself
And said:
I am not all charm
And not clever
And I don't need all the stimulations
In order to want to live.
I know that my body, like yours,
Is a bit worn,
And I have, like you,
Three or four illnesses
That no perfume can disguise.
The body is—flesh.
And what in me is different from yours
Becomes different only by your touch.
Because in themselves the breasts are not breasts
And the girlish paraphernalia
Becomes girlish only with you.
I weighed and measured her simple talk.
I wanted to see where in her words
Lay the hidden and the mysterious
That could feed my desire for her
And hers for me.
Her words were pure skeleton,
With no embellishment of flesh and veins.

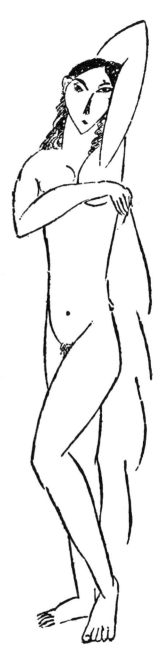

Max Weber: (from *Shriftn*).

און ווי האָב איך שוין געקאָנט רעדן צו איר

וועגן "זײַ אַ מאַמע מיר אָדער אַ שוועסטער".

טרויזנטער ליריִשע לידער האָט זי פֿאַרלייקנט מיט אירע ווערטער.

און דאָך בין איך אַרויף אויף דעם דאַך,

און אומעטום פֿאַרריכט אַז דער רעגן זאָל ניט דורכקנעצן,

און געטאָן עס מיט פֿרייד

וואָס נאָך אַ מענטש איז מיט מיר.

און ווען איך האָב געשלאָגן די שינדלען

האָב איך געטראַכט

אַז ווי נאָענט מאַן און ווײַב זאָלן ניט שלאָפֿן

זײַנען זייערע חלומות פֿאַרשידן.

אין שלאָף זײַנען זיי עלנט

און שליסן אויס איינער דעם אַנדערן.

איך האָב צו זיך געזאָגט:

ווען איך וועל אַרונטער פֿון דאַך

וועל איך עס איר זאָגן און גוט באַטראַכטן

וואָס אירע אויגן וועלן ענטפֿערן.

◄ שיני מײַק

I

שיני מײַק שלאָפֿט אין אַ בראָנדזעגעם אָרון.

עס וויינט נאָך אים אַ מלוכה פֿון צוועלף בלאָק

און דער מאַמעס שייטל און דעם טאַטנס אַלטע באָרד.

פֿאַריתומטע יונגען שטייען בײַ די ראַגן

און קנייטשן ציגאַרעטלעך מיט ציטערדיקע, דינע פֿינגער.

שטייט אַ יונג בײַם ראַג מיט דעם קאָפֿעלושל אָן אַ זײַט

און שפּײַט ווײַט אַ דינעם שפּײַ.

אויפֿן בראָנעם פֿון טערען ליגט אַ האַרטער, שווערער שטיין,

אָבער ער ווייסט אַז שיני מײַק שלאָפֿט איצט

אין אַ בראָנדזעגעם אָרון.

דער שרעק און דער היטער, דער מלך און געביטער

פֿון אַרום און אַרום צוועלף גאַנצע בלאָק,

ליגט אויסגעפֿראַנטעוועט און שלאָפֿט.

דער מאַמעס שייטל יאָמערט אים נאָך אַ זכות,

אַז ער האָט אַלטע טאַטע-מאַמע

ניט געלאָזט פֿאַלן מענטשן צו לאַסט.

און דעם טאַטנס באָרד איז פֿאַרשעמט אויף די עלטערע יאָרן,

ווײַל אַלע, אַלע ווייסן פֿון אַרום און אַרום די צוועלף בלאָק,

אַז שיני מײַק איז געפֿאַלן און שלאָפֿט איצט

אין אַ בראָנדזעגעם אָרון.

How could I have talked to her
About "Be a mother to me or a sister."
A thousand lyrical poems she denied with her words.
And still I climbed on the roof
And mended all the leaks.
And I did it, rejoicing
That another human being was with me.
And as I hammered the shingles
I thought that
No matter how close man and woman may sleep
Their dreams are separate.
In sleep they are lonely
And shut each other out.
I told myself:
When I come down from the roof
I will tell her this and watch closely
What her eyes will answer.

"Be a mother to me or a sister"—an ironic allusion to Bialik's famous Hebrew love poem, "Take Me in Under Your Wing," where the quoted line reads: "Be a mother and a sister to me."

➤ *Sheeny Mike*

I

Sheeny Mike sleeps in a coffin of bronze.
He is mourned by a kingdom of twelve blocks
And by his mama's *shaytl* and his papa's old beard.
Orphaned guys stand at the streetcorners
And crumple cigarettes with thin, shaking fingers.
A guy stands on the corner, his hat slanted,
And spits a thin stream through his teeth.
A heavy stone covers the well of tears,
But he knows that Sheeny Mike lies asleep
In a coffin of bronze.
The terror and the guardian, the ruler and the king
Of twelve whole blocks
Lies spruced up, asleep.
Mama's *shaytl* wails out his merit:
He didn't let his old father-and-mother
Be anybody's burden.
And papa's beard is ashamed in its old age,
For everyone, everyone in the twelve whole blocks knows
That Sheeny Mike fell and is now asleep
In a coffin of bronze.

Shaytl*

II

שוערע שלעפשיפן שניידן דאָס קרוטיקע וואַסער,

שטינקענדיקער רויך פֿאַרסאַזשעט די דעכער

אויף די הײַזער פֿון דעם פֿיצל וועלט.

דאָ, אויף דעם דאַך האָט ער דאַך דעם חלום פֿון זײַן קיניגרײַך דערזען.

די ציטערדיקע וועש אויף די שטריק

זײַנען געווען זײַנע לאָנעך,

ווען אונטן האָט דער טאַטע מיט האַלב-בלינדע אויגן

איבער אַ פֿאַרפֿעצטן ספֿר

געלערנט מיט קינדער דעם טײַטש

פֿון שולחן — אַ טײַבל און כּיסא — אַ טשער.

אַ, די מאַמע האָט געוווסט איר בראַך,

אַז ס׳קלעטערט איר קינד שנעל די לײטער,

פֿון קעשענע-גנב צום סאַמע שפּיץ,

צום גרויסן שׂררה, מלך און באַפֿעלער,

איבער די גאַנצע אַרום און אַרום צוועלף בלאָק.

די אבות, די פֿרומע וואַסערטרעגער און פֿאַרגרעבטע גאָטפֿאָרכטיקע קצבים,

זײַנען פֿאַרבליבן אויף די בית-עלמינס פֿון יענער זײַט.

האָבן זיי זיך ניט געמיט,

ווען דער טאַטע מיט די רויטע אויגן האָט בהרחבהדיק

באַזעצט דעם דלות אין הויז מיט זײַן געזאַנג —

אוי, שולחן — אַ טײַבל און כּיסא — אַ טשער.

Raphael Soyer: *Self-Portrait,* 1933.

II

Heavy tugboats cut through the dirty water,
Stinking smoke covers with soot
The roofs of the little world.
Here, on the roof, he saw the dream of his kingdom.
The flapping sheets on the lines
Were his plains,
While below, over a greasy holy book,
His papa with half-blind eyes
Taught children the meaning
Of *Shulchon—a taybel* and *Keessay—a chair.*
Oh, mama knew her woe,
That her child climbed the ladder fast—
From pickpocket to the very top,
To big boss, king and ruler
Over twelve whole blocks.
The forefathers, the pious waterbearers and coarsened God-fearing butchers,
Stayed behind in the cemeteries over there.
They did not intercede
When papa with his red eyes generously
Furnished the poverty of his house with chanting:
Oy, *Shulchon—a taybel* and *Keessay—a chair.*

shulchon—table. The traditional mode of teaching in **heder** consisted of reading each Hebrew word followed by a translation.

ווי אַזוי האָט ער אויסגעחלומט זײַן מלוכה.

ווי אַזוי האָט ער געוועלטיקט.

ווי אַזוי געהערשט.

ווי אַזוי האָט ער פֿאַראונטערטעניקט,

ווי אַזוי פֿאַריאָכט

זײַן פֿיצל וועלט ביז אפֿילו

צום הויז פֿון געזעץ מיט דער גרינער לאַמטערנע.

דער מאַמעס פֿאַרזשאַווערטע בענטשלײַכטער,

דער אָרעמער שבת אין הויז,

די פֿײַכטע ווענט,

דעם טאַטנס באָרד און דער מאַמעס שײטל

האָבן זיי דען געוווּסט אַז אונטער איין דאַך

וווינט אַ קיניג,

וואָס האָט געקיניגט און געקיניגט, געשאַלט און געוואַלט,

ביז ער איז געפֿאַלן פֿון אַ שׂונאס האַנט.

ווער האָט איבערגעריסן די דינאַסטיע?

שיני מײַק ווייסט, אָבער מען טאָר ניט דערציילן,

שיני מײַק שמייכלט אין בראָנדזענעם אָרון.

וויפֿל מוט פֿאַרמאָגט אַזאַ דינער קערפֿער,

וויפֿל קראַפֿט אין פֿאַרשלאָסענע ליפֿן,

וויפֿל עקשנות אין שטאָלצע פֿיס

צו קומען שווײַגן, שווײַגן, שווײַגן

צוקאָפֿנס דעם שווײַגנדיקן קאָפֿ.

לאָזט זי צו צום בראָנדזענעם אָרון.

אָ. אויך איר יונג און גליִענדיק לעבן

איז ער געווען דער אײדלמאַן,

דער רײַטנדיקער ריטער,

דער טעמפֿער יונג, דער שיכּור,

וואָס האָט געוווערזעט כעס

און פֿיִערדיקע רייד.

וויפֿל עקשנות דורכצוגיין אַלע רייען

און קומען שווײַגן, שווײַגן, שווײַגן

צוקאָפֿנס דעם שווײַגנדיקן קאָפֿ.

לאָזט זי צו צום בראָנדזענעם אָרון.

III

How did he dream up his kingdom.
How did he govern.
How did he rule.
How did he subdue,
How did he harness
His little world right up to the
House of the law with the green lantern.
Mama's rusty candle holders,
The poor sabbath at home,
The damp walls,
Papa's beard and mama's *shaytl*—
Did they know that under the same roof
Lived a king,
Who ruled and ruled, governed and commanded
Till he fell by an enemy hand.
Who broke the dynasty?
Sheeny Mike knows, but one must not tell.
Sheeny Mike smiles in a coffin of bronze.

IV

How much courage in a thin body,
How much strength in clenched lips,
How much stubbornness in proud legs
Coming to be silent, silent, silent
At the side of the silent head.

Let her through to the coffin of bronze.

Oh, over her young and glowing life
He was the nobleman,
The knight on horseback,
The dumb guy, the drunkard,
Who exploded with anger
And fiery words.
How much stubbornness walking through all the rows,
Coming to be silent, silent, silent
At the side of the silent head.

Let her through to the coffin of bronze.

איך האָב נעכטן אָפּגעשטעקט מײַן זון די דאָזיקע געשיכטע:
אַז מײַן טאַטע איז געווען אַ ציקלאָפּ און, פֿאַרשטייט זיך, מיט איין אויג,
אַז מײַנע פֿופֿצן ברידער האָבן מיך געוואָלט אויפֿפֿרעסן,
האָב איך זיך קוים אַרויסגעראַטעוועט פֿון זייערע הענט
און זיך גענומען קײַקלען קײַקלען איבער דער וועלט.
קײַקלענדיק זיך בין איך אויסגעוואַקסן אין צוויי מעת-לעת,
אָבער צוריק צום פֿאַטערס הויז האָב איך שוין ניט געוואָלט גיין.
בין איך אַוועק קיין צפֿניה און זיך אויסגעלערנט שפּרעכן ייִדיש,
זיך מלה געווען און געוואָרן יודע.
האָב איך אָנגעהויבן האַנדלען מיט פֿלאַקס, טריוואַקס, אתרוגים און אָפּגעביסענע פֿיטומס
און געמאַכט וואַסער אויף קאַשע.
ביז איך האָב אָנגעגעגנט אַן אַלטע פֿרינצעסין
וואָס האָט מיר אָפּגעשריבן אירס אַ גוט און געשטאָרבן.
בין איך געוואָרן אַ גוט-באַזיצער
און אָנגעהויבן פֿרעסן און זויפֿן.
און אַז כ'האָב געזען איך ווער אַ ביסל פֿעט,
האָב איך גענומען און חתונה געהאַט.
נאָך דער חתונה האָט מײַן גוט אָפּגעברענט,
בין איך געוואָרן אַן אָרעמער צײַטונג-שרײַבער.

צו מײַן טאַטן, דעם ציקלאָפּ, שרײַב איך נאָך אַ מאָל אַ בריוול,
אָבער צו מײַנע פֿופֿצן ברידער — אַ זאַסיע.

◄ ייִדישע מלוכות

קאָנסקיוואָליע, מאַזלבאַזשעץ, קאָזשניצע,
ליעווערטאָוו, פּולאַווע און בעכעווע,
גליסק, פּיוסק און שאַבעשין —
נעמען פֿון פּוילנס שטעט, ווייסט דער טײַוול פֿאַר וואָס,
שווימען נאָך אום ווי מרחק-בלעטלעך אין מײַן זיכרון.
ווען איך בין געווען אַ קלײַנער פּעמפֿיק,
האָב איך געוווּסט אַז אַ נסיעה אַהין,
שמעקט מיט אַ בויד, אַ פֿור, אָדער אַ סקריפּענדיקן וואָגן,
ווי עס פֿאָרן שטענדיק וואַרעמע דינסטמיידן אַרויף דינסט.
איך האָב געזען אַלע שטעטלעך ווי ייִדישע מלוכות,
ווי יום-כיפּור לייגט אַוועק אַ שרעק,
אַפֿילו איבער די גויישע כאַלופּעס,
ווו עס הענגען צלמים
פֿאַר אַ שמירה קעגן ייִדישן גאָט.

איך וואָלט אַוועקגעגעבן גאַנצע מאַיאָנטקעס מיט אָרעמקייט
איך זאָל אַצינדערט נאָך דעם בענקען.

Yesterday I dumped on my son the following story:
That my father was a cyclops and, of course, had one eye,
That my fifteen brothers wanted to devour me,
So, I barely got myself out of their clutches
And started rolling all over the world.
Rolling, I grew up in two days,
But I wouldn't go back to my father's house.
So, I went to Tsefania and learned *sprechen* Jewish,
I got myself circumcised and became a Yid.
So, I started selling flax, wax, esrogs with bitten-off tips,
And earned water for kasha.
Till I met an old princess
Who willed me an estate and died.
So, I became a landowner
And began guzzling and gorging.
And when I saw I was getting fat,
I made up my mind and got married.
After the marriage, my estate burned down.
So, I became a poor newspaper writer.

To my father, the cyclops, I sometimes write a letter,
But to my fifteen brothers—the finger.

esrog (Hebrew: ethrog)—citron, a ritual fruit used for Sukkot, not kosher without the tip intact.

kasha*—"earning water for kasha" is indeed hardly making a living.

► *Jewish Kingdoms*

Konskiwolie, Mazelbożec, Korznice,
Liewertow, Pulawe, Bechewe,
Glisk, Piusk, Szabeszin—
Names of Polish towns, the devil knows why
They float up in my memory like dry leaves in a bath.
When I was a fat little brat
I knew that a voyage there
Smelled of a coach, a carriage, a squeaking wagon,
Carrying warm maids to new places.
I saw all the towns as Jewish kingdoms,
Where Yom Kippur lays its fear
Even on goyish huts,
Where crosses hang on the walls
As amulets against the Jewish god.

I would give a wealth of poverty
If I could still long for that.

I

אַ שטילער, שמאָלער טײַך שלענגלט זיך דאָס לעבן,
דאָרפֿיש-פֿאַמעלעך דורך פֿינצטערע גאַסן,
פֿאַרקרוטיקט און פֿאַרפֿלעקט מיט אַלטע הײַזער,
טערעמער און קלויסטער.
אין אַ גרויסן מיסטקאַסטן וואַרפֿט אַ האַנט אַרײַן
יאָרן ווי פֿאַרפֿוילטע בלעטער,
וואָס זאַמלען זיך און עיפּוש אַזוי קאָלירפֿול
ווי וויאַנע בלעטער קענען.
און צו שווער איז דעם מענטשנס לאַסט
זיך אָפּצושטעלן און איבערלײענען דעם אַנאָדאַמיני —
עס איז הײַ-יאָר, פֿאַריאָרן און דאָס יאָר וואָס וועט קומען
מיט שטילע פֿאַסירלאָזע טעג.
די האָפֿנונגען אויף מאָרגן טונקלען
ווי די קאָפּטשענדיקע גאַס-לאַמטערנעס.
די איינציקע וואָס חלומען נאָך וואַכערהייט
זײַנען די קינדער וואָס שפּילן זיך אין וואָס-וועט-זײַן,
און טאַפּן זיך אין דער פֿינצטער אויף די ביידעמס
מיט הייסע הענטלעך.
אין שטאָלצע פֿילקאָלירטע מונדירן
דרייען זיך אַרום די סאָלדאַטן אין גאַסן
ווי פֿאַרביקע אויסטראַלישע פֿייגל.
בײַ נאַכט ווערן וואַרעם און באַוועגלעך ווי מוראשקע-נעסטן די ראָגן.
די מוידן וואָס האָבן פּרעכע מײַלער און הויכע בוזעמס
און די סאָלדאַטן וואָס אָטעמען שווער דורך די לאַנגע וואָנצעס
און בײַטן אומרויִק די פֿיס,
קלעפּן צוזאַמען אין דער טונקלעניש
און ריידן שטיל און זינגעוודיק וועגן אויסדינען
און וועגן בויען אַן אייגן הויז.

אַהער איז דער באַראָן געקומען אויסהוסטן
זײַנע לעצטע חדשים.
דאָ אין דעם קליינעם קלויסטעם האָט ער געהערט
די ציכטיקע ריידן פֿון גלח:
קליינע געמאָסטענע ריידן ווי קליינע פֿינטעלעך,
שטילע ווערטער וועגן לעבן
און פֿריידיקע טרייסט אַנטקעגן דעם טויט.
די בערג אונטער די אויגן זײַנען העכער געוואָרן,
און די אויגן פֿאַרלאָפֿן מיט וואַרעמקייט,
ווען דער פֿאַסטעך פֿון די מענטשעלעכע בהמות
האָט גערעדט געלאַסן וועגן הימלישן פֿאַטער,

I

A quiet narrow river, life is winding
Rustic-slow through dark streets,
Marred and stained by old houses,
Towers and churches.
Into a big dustbin a hand throws
Years like rotten leaves,
Heaped and stinking colorfully,
As withered leaves do.
And too heavy is a man's burden
To stop and read the annodomini—
This-year, the year-before and the year that will come
With quiet eventless days.
Like smouldering street lamps
Darken the hopes for tomorrow.
Only the children still dream wide awake,
Playing what-will-be,
And pet in the dark in attics
With hot little hands.
In proud colorful uniforms
Soldiers stroll in the streets
Like bright Australian birds.
At night, street corners grow warm and lively like anthills.
Girls with sassy mouths and high breasts
And soldiers breathing heavily through long moustaches,
Restlessly shifting their weight,
Glued to each other in the dark,
Talk with a quiet sing-song about getting discharged
And building their own home.

Here the baron came to cough out
His last months.
Here, in the little church, he heard
The pure words of the pastor:
Small measured words like little dots,
Quiet talk about life and about
Joyful comfort in the face of death.
The mountains under his eyes swelled
And the eyes were filled with warmth,
When the shepherd of the human flock
Talked quietly about the Heavenly Father,

In his collected poems of 1956,
Glatshteyn renamed this poem
"The Sword of Lies."

אונדזער אַלעמענס פּאַסטעך וואָס איז געדולדיק
און באַשיידן ווי אַ בעטלער.
עס איז געווען ליב און ענג ווי אין אַ שווייצבאַד
אין דעם קליינעם שטעטל,
ווו ער האָט מיט דעם לאַנגן שטעקן זיינעם
געשריבן מיט דעם שפּינוועב פון די היוזער
דעם ווייטן נאָמען פּעטערבורג,
אָדער דאָס קורצע וואָרט רוים,
ווו פרויען אויף הויכע אָפּצאַסן
רופן מיט אויגן ווי לאָמפּן
און זיינען קליגער און דערפֿאַרענער פון די מענער.
אַ הויכער דינער בוים איז ער אַרומגעגאַנגען
איבער דער לענג און ברייט
און געטראַכט זאַכן וואָס האָבן אים געוואָרגן
און געזוכט אַ ברייטן שטח,
כדי אַ פלייץ צו טאָן מיט גינגאָלדענע ווערטער
וואָס דראַפּן זיך אַקראָבאַטיש צום הימל.
דער טאָג איז פאַרגאַנגען אויף אַ שטיק וואָלקן
מיט די שענסטע פאַרבן.
דער באַראָן האָט זיך פאַרגעוואָרפן
אַז ער איז אַלט און סענטימענטאַל,
ווען ער האָט גראָד איצט געטראַכט
אַז דאָס פּלאָקערט זיין צוויבערדיק לעבן אַזוי ערב אונטערגיין,
און עס איז אים געווען עגאַל אַצינד,
צי ער האָט איינער אַליין אויסגעשלאָכט הונדערטער מענטשן
אָדער עס אויסגעטראַכט.
אַלץ איז געווען אַזוי ווייט פון אים ווי אַ רעגנבויגן.
און אפילו ווען ער האָט אַ לעבן לאַנג
באַזעצט זיינע יאָרן מיט דימענטענע ביַיקעס —
די קרוין האָט ער שוין לאַנג פאַרלוירן,
און איצט טראַכט ער אַזוי איינפאַך
וועגן דעם מאַן וואָס האָט פּשוט אָפּגעלעבט זיין לעבן
און געשטאָרבן ווי אַ גאָט.
ווער קען אַצינד אויסשטרעקן די דאַרע האַנט
צו דעם וואָס איז אַוועק
און זאָגן אַז דאָס איז געווען
און דאָס האָט זיך בלויז אויסגעדאַכט?
איצט ביַים סוף פון וועג,
אין אַ שטעטל וואָס איז פאַר אים סוף-וועלט,
און צוריק ווילן די מידע פיס
שוין מער ניט גיין.

The shepherd of us all, who is patient
And modest as a beggar.
The small town
Was lovely and cramped as a steambath.
Here, stretching his long stick,
He wrote with the spiderweb of houses
The distant name, Petersburg,
Or the short word, Rome,
Where women on high heels
Call with eyes like lanterns, and are
More clever and experienced than men.
A tall thin tree, he strolled
The length and breadth of the town
And thought of things that choked him,
And looked for open spaces
To flood with spungold words
That soar to the sky like acrobats.
The day set on a patch of cloud
In beautiful colors.
The baron reproached himself
For being old and sentimental
When he thought of his enchanted life
Flaring up before its decline,
And it was all the same to him
Whether he had singlehandedly slaughtered hundreds of men
Or had invented it all.
Everything was as distant as a rainbow.
Even if all his life
He had set his years with diamond legends—
He had lost the crown long ago,
And now he thinks so simply
Of the man who just lived his life
And died like a god.
Who could now stretch a skinny arm
To what has gone,
And say that this really happened,
And that was only imagined?
Now, at the end of the road,
In a town that is for him end-of-the-world,
When the tired feet
Won't go back.

גליפֿליגן האָבן זיך גענומען שפּילן צווישן די ביימער,
אויפֿגעליכטיקט און פֿאַרלאָשן זיך אַליין.
די טונקלעניש איז געקומען מיט שטילער רו
און אַלץ האָט אָפּגעצאַנקט אין אים,
ווי עס וואָלט שוין איצט געווען אַ טאָג נאָך זײַן טויט.
די קילקייט איז געווען דער איינציקער ציטער פֿון לעבן
וואָס האָט דורכגעשוידערט זײַנע אַלטע ביינער.
די נאַכט האָט גערעדט דורך וואָסער־מורמל, בלאַט און פֿראָש,
מיט אַזאַ האַרצרײַסנדיקן צויבער,
ווי אַ פֿלייט וואָלט געשפּילט פֿון זיך אַליין
אויף אַ בית־הקברות.
און דער באָראָן איז געלאָפֿן זוכן
אַ וואַרעם אָרט און אַ מענטשלעך קול.

II

צוויי שיכּורים זינגען אין דער קנײַפּע.
איינער זינגט אַז גרויסמעכטיק איז דער באַשעפֿער,
און דער צווייטער וועגן מאָגדאַן מיט דעם ברייטן הינטן.
און ביידע זײַנען טרויעריק און וויינען צוזאַמען,
און וויינען באַזונדער,
יעדער איינער איבער זײַן קופֿל ביר.
אויף דער איינגעבראָקענער לאַנגער באַנק
זיצט ער בײַם נאַקעטן טיש און דענקט נאָך
פֿון דעם דינעם, שלאַנקן יונגנמאַן,
וואָס האָט אַ מאָל געפֿלאַסטערט די אַרײַגאַנגען אין די שענסטע הײַזער
מיט ליגנס,
פֿון דעם רײַטער וואָס האָט דורכגאַלאָפּירט
דעם שטויב פֿון עטלעכע צענדליק יאָר,
און קיין מאָל קיין צײַט ניט געהאַט צו זען דעם אָפּשײַן
פֿון די אייגענע אויגן.
און צוליב וואָס איז דער מאַן אַזוי געריטן, געריטן און געריטן
און האָט אויסגעמיטן צו זען זיך אַליין אין שפּיגל
אָדער רעדן צו זיך אַליין אַ וואָר וואָרט?
יעדן מעת־לעת זײַנעם האָט ער פֿאַרלייקנט
און אָפּגעמעקט פֿון זײַן אייגענעם זיכרון.
ער איז געוואָרן דער צויבער־אַרכיטעקט
פֿון זײַנע אייגענע פֿאַרגאַנגענע שעהן.
ער האָט באַלזאַמירט זײַנע טויטע רגעס
און אויסגעטראַכט פֿאַר זיך אַ לעבן
מיט פֿאַרביקע רייד.
אַ מאָל זײַנען ווערטער אים געווען אונטערטעניק
און דער פֿלאַקערדיקער מוח האָט זיי געצונדן ווי שטורקאַצן.
איצט קריצט ער זײַן אייגענע מצבה

Glowworms playing among the trees
Lit up and went out.
Darkness came with quiet peace.
Everything in him flickered out
As if it were the day after his death.
The chill was the only tremor of life
That shivered his old bones.
The night spoke through water murmur, leaf and frog,
With the heart-rending magic
Of a flute playing by itself
In a cemetery.
And the baron fled
To seek a warm place and a human voice.

II

Two drunkards sing in the tavern.
One sings that omnipotent is the Creator,
And the other about Magda and her big ass.
And both are sad and cry together,
And cry separately,
Each in his mug of beer.
On a broken long bench,
He sits at the bare table, reminiscing
About the lean and slender youth
Who once paved with lies
The entries to the best houses,
About the rider who galloped
Through the dust of several dozen years
And never had time to see
The reflection of his own eyes.
Why did he ride and ride and ride,
Never looking at himself in a mirror
Or telling himself a true word?
He denied every one of his days,
Erased them from his memory.
He became the magician-architect
Of his own bygone hours.
He embalmed his dead moments
And with colorful words
Invented a life for himself.
Once, words were his servants,
His blazing brain had kindled them like torches.
Now he is engraving his own tombstone

און זוכט אן אײן-און-אײנציק שטיל װאָרט װאָס זאָל סומירן
און אפילו באַװײנען.
די קלוגשאַפט װאָס איז אלע מאָל געװען
אַזוי פאַרװאָרצלט און שטאַמיק אַ טײל פון אים
האָט זיך איצט, נאָך עטלעכע שימענדיקע גלעזער ביר,
אָפּגעטײלט פון אים און זיך אױװעקגעשטעלט אױפן טיש.
װי אַ סאָװע מיט שפאַקולן איז זי געשטאַנען
און געלאַכט פון אים איבער זײן ביטערן רחמנות צו זיך אלײן.

און באַלד האָט זיך אים גענומען דאַכטן,
אַז ניט ער זיצט נאָר ער הענגט אין װינקל
אַ געקרײציקטער פון זײן אײגענעם רחמנות.
מיט אױסגעשפרײטע הענט הענגט ער,
װי זײנע עטלעכע יאָר װאָס ער האָט ער אָפּגעלעבט
װאָלטן ניט געװען זײן אײגנס,
נאָר אַ מאַרטירער-צײכן פאַר אַ װעלט.
אַזוי זיך צו איבערפינדזלען איז אים אלײן געװאָרן פריקרע
און ער איז געלאָפן פון דעם װינקל.
ער האָט זיך צוגעזעצט צו די צװײ שיכורים
און ניט געבעטענערהײט גענומען דערצײלן,
פון זײן רעגנבױגנדיקער, ניטגעשטױגענער פאַרגאַנגענהײט.

עס איז געװען אין זעלבן יאָר װען אַ פאַרפלוקטער פרידן
האָט אױסגעשפרײט די פאַפירענע פליגל
איבער דער גאַנצער װעלט.
אױסגעהונגערטע קראָען, די גרױס פון לײבן,
זײנען אַרומגעפלױגן און געקראָקעט.
די פעלדער האָבן געבליט און געבענקט נאָך פאַרװײסטונג
און מענטש האָט פײנט געהאַט מענטש
מיט אַ פאַרראַסטעטער ליבע.
דאַמאָלט, מײנע ליבע פרײנד, האָב איך געהאַט אױף מײנע פלײצעס
אַן אײגענע מלחמה.
מײן שװאַרץ װײב פון אינדזל האָט זיך געקעצלט
און אין אײן יאָר האָט זי מיר געבױרן
צװאַנציק קינדער,
װאָס זײנען געװאָקסן אױף הײװן און האָבן גלײך געגומען שטעלן פיס —
די גאַנצע שװאַרצע משפחה איז מיר נאָכגעלאָפן פון אָרט צו אָרט.
און מײנע געדאַנקען זײנען גאָר געװען
אין דער קופערנער שטאָט פעטערבורג.
פעטערבורג! די קופערנע דעקער װאָס די זון האָט אױף גאָלד אױסגעבאַקן.
פעטערבורג! װי איך האָב צום ערשטן מאָל
אָנגעטראָפן דעם װאָאנדערדיקן ײדן מיט דעם שװוערן צלם אױף די פלײצעס.
פעטערבורג! די שטאָט װו גאָט האָט געשניטן אַ בונד מיט דעם טײװול.

And looking for one quiet word that will sum up
And perhaps even mourn.
Now, after several foamy glasses of beer,
The wisdom that was always
So rooted in him, stem of his stem,
Separated from him and stood up on the table.
Like an owl with spectacles it stood
And mocked him for his bitter self-pity.

And then it seemed to him
That he was not sitting but hanging in a corner,
Crucified by his own pity.
Hanging with outstretched arms,
As if the few years that he had lived
Were not his own,
But a martyr-sign for a world.
All this self-repainting became loathsome
And he fled from the corner.
He joined the two drunkards
And, uninvited, began telling
Of his unreal, rainbow past.

It was in the year that a cursed peace
Spread its paper wings
Over the whole world.
Starving crows, big as lions,
Were roaming and cawing.
The fields were blooming and longing for desolation.
And man hated man
With a rusty love.
Then, my dear friends, I had on my hands
A war of my own.
My black wife from the island, like a cat,
Bore me twenty kids in one year.
The kids grew like on yeast
And went off stretching their legs—
And the whole black family ran after me from place to place.
But my thoughts were elsewhere,
In the coppered city, Petersburg.
Petersburg! Copper roofs baked gold by the sun.
Petersburg! Where for the first time I encountered
The Wandering Jew with the heavy cross on his back.
Petersburg! City where God made a pact with the devil.

פעטערבורג! ווו   מיידלעך ווייזן פֿאר אַ קאָפּיקע דעם הינטן

און ווו מײַן שווערלײַביקע נאַטאַשאַ

האָט געהונגערט נאָך מיר.

האָב איך אין אַ שיינעם העלן טאָג

אָנגעפֿליקט שלאָפּקרייטעכצער אין וואַלד,

און מײַן ווײַב מיט מײַנע קינדער האָבן זיך צוגעכאַפֿט און אײַנגעקראָפּעט.

אָנגעזאַטלט האָב איך גלײַך מײַן פֿערד און אים אין אונער

אַרײַנגעשעריעןַ דאָס צױבערװואָרט —

פעטערבורג.

גיט ער בלויז אײן שפרונג און בלײַבט שטיין

גאַנצע הונדערט מייל נאָך דער רוסנשטאָט.

נעם איך אים קערעווען אויף צוריק

גיט ער ווידער אַ שפרונג

און בלײַבט שטיין לעבן מײַן שלאָפֿנדיקער משפחה.

זע איך אַז זײַן שנעלקייט לאָזט זיך ניט צוימען,

האָב איך אים ווידער באַפּוילן: פעטערבורג,

און ערשט נאָך דעם שפרונג בין איך אַרונטערגעקראָכן

און גענומען זיך שלעפן מיט מײַן פֿערדל

אויף צוריק די הונדערט מייל צופֿוס.

אָבער אין מיטן וועג האָב איך דערזען,

אַז פֿון מײַן פֿערדס שנעלן שפרונג

האָבן די הויזן בײַ מיר געפֿלאַצט,

און די שווערד האָט זיך נעבעכדיק געבאַמבלט

אויף די צעריסענע פֿליודערן.

און דאָ שטיי איך אין מיטן אַ וואַלד,

ווו נאָדל-פֿאָדעם וואַקסט ניט אויף די בײַמער.

האָב איך פֿון אַ דינער צווײַג זיך אויסגעשניצט אַ נאָדל

און דאָס אויערל פֿאַרפֿעדעמט מיט אַ ביסל זונשטויב

און פֿאַרנייט מײַנע בלויע מיליטערישע הויזן.

אַז עס איז צוגעפֿאַלן די נאַכט

האָבן מיר די הויזן גוט געדינט אין וועג —

די זון-שטעך האָבן געלויכטן ווי לאַמטערנעס

און דער וועג איז געווען ווי אויף אַ שליאַך פֿון דימענטן.

און שטעלט זיך פֿאַר, די נאַכט איז דאָרט אַזאַ חושכדיקע,

אַז די פֿינצטערניש האָט זיך אײַנגעגעסן אין מײַן געזיכט

און עס פֿאַרשוואַרצט ווי איך וואָלט געווען אַ הינדוס.

אין דער פֿרי, אַז איך האָב זיך אין ערשטן וועסערל דערזען

האָב איך געמיינט איך בין פֿון אײנער פֿון מײַנע אייגענע קינדער,

וואָס די שוואַרצע קלעמפּע האָט מיר אָנגעפּלאָדיעט.

בין איך אַרויף אויף מײַן פֿערד און אַ פֿײַף געגעבן:

גרייט!

און אויסגעשריגן: אַרט.

אַ שפרונג — און איך האָב זיך געקײַקלט

Petersburg! Where, for a kopeck, girls bared their asses,
And where my heavy-bodied Natasha
Was starving for me.
So, one fine day,
I picked a bunch of sleeping-herbs in the forest,
And my wife and the kids fell for it and were soon snoring.
Right away I saddled my horse and shouted in his ear
The magic word:
Petersburg.
In one leap he landed
A hundred miles beyond the Russian capital.
I began to steer him back
And he jumped again
And landed near my sleeping family.
Seeing that I could not curb his speed,
I commanded again: Petersburg,
And after the leap I climbed down
And began trudging with my horse
The hundred miles back.
But on the way I saw
That, in my horse's bound,
My trousers had split
And my sword dangled pitifully
Over the torn pants.
And here I am, in the middle of a forest,
Where needle-and-thread don't grow on trees.
So I carved a needle from a thin twig,
Threaded its eye with sundust
And sewed my blue military trousers.
When night fell
The trousers served me well on the road—
The sunstitches glowed like lanterns
And the road was like a highway of diamonds.
Can you imagine, the night was so deep
That the darkness ate into my face
And blackened it as if I were a Hindu.
In the morning, when I saw myself in the first pond,
I thought I was one of my own children
That the black bitch had spawned.
So I jumped on my horse and whistled:
Ready!
And I called: Ararat!
A leap—and I rolled

אין דעם אייביקן שניי,

ביז מײַן פּנים האָט צוריק אויף זיך אַרויפגעצויגן

די אייגענע ווײַסקייט.

אַ שפּרונג אַרונטער און איך בין מיט מײַן צויבערפערד

געשטאַנען לעבן צאַרס פּאַלאַץ.

אַלע דינער זײַנען געפֿאַלן צו דר׳ערד

און איך האָב געשפּאַנט איבער זעכציק טויזנט קנעכט

צום בײַזן צאַר.

אַז איך האָב געעפֿנט די טיר האָט דער צאַר אויסגערופֿן מיט פֿרייד:

ווילקאָמען, הער באַראַן!

און באַלד האָט ער מיר דערציילט די טרויעריקע בשׂורה,

אַז נאַטאַשאַ איז פֿון בענקשאַפֿט געשטאָרבן.

איך האָב פֿאַרגאָסן בלויז אײַן טרער,

ווי עס פּאַסט פֿאַר אַ סאָלדאַט און געזאָגט:

איך קום צו דיר צאַר-פּאַטערל וועגן אַ גרויסער זאַך.

די וועלט שימלט פֿון פֿרידן,

און די שווערד מיט דער ביקס זשאַווערן.

מען וואָלט באַדאַרפֿט אַ ביסל אַ קיצל טאָן דעם טערק,

און איך בין גרייט צו דײַן דינסט.

זאָגט דער צאַר: מלחמה אָן אויסרייד?

זאָג איך: מיר וועלן צוטראַכטן אַן אויסרייד אין אַ האַלבער שעה,

און דו האַלט גרייט דאָס מיליטער

פֿאַר דער מלחמה וואָס וועט באַלד פֿלאַקערן

און פֿאַרבן די וועלט מיט סאָלדאַטסקע געפֿילן.

בין איך מיט דעם צאַר גלײַך אַוועק אין אַ שאַנדהויז,

און פֿון שאַנדהויז אין אַ קלויסטער,

און דאָרט האָבן מיר דעם טויבן פּאַפּ אָנגעזאָגט די בשׂורה

אַז עס קומט אַ נײַע שלאַכט.

In the eternal snow,
Till my face again pulled on
Its whiteness.
A leap down and I stood with my magic horse
At the Czar's palace.
All his servants fell to the ground
And I walked over the backs of sixty thousand slaves
To the evil Czar.
As I opened the door, the Czar cried out with joy:
Willkommen Herr Baron!
And soon he told me the sad news
That Natasha had died of longing.
I shed only one tear,
As befits a soldier, and said:
I have come to you, Papa-Czar, about an important matter.
The world is growing moldy from peace
And the sword and the rifle are rusting.
Wouldn't it be nice to tickle the Turk—
I am at your service.
Says the Czar: War with no pretext?
Says I: We shall invent a pretext in half-an-hour,
Better go prepare the army
For the war that will soon be blazing,
Painting the world with soldier's feelings.
So I went with the Czar straight to a brothel
And from the brothel to a church,
And there we told the deaf priest the news
That a fresh battle was on the way.

Louis Lozowick: *Russian Village*,
1932.

דער שיכור וואָס האָט געזונגען וועגן גאָטס באַרעמהאַרציקייט,

האָט אַ שלײַדער געטאָן זײַן גלאָז צו דער וואַנט

וואָס האָט זיך צעשפּריצט אין אַלע ווינקלען.

פֿאַרמאַך דעם פֿיסק, באַראָן.

דײַנע מעשׂיות פֿאַרמאָגן ניט קיין בּרעקל פֿון גאָטס גענאָד

און זײַנען פּוסטע זייפֿנבּלאָזן.

גלײַכער איז שוין צו לאָנגווײַלן זיך מיט אייגן ווײַב און קינדער

אין אָרעמען הויז וווּ גאָטס בענטשעניש גיסט זיך שטיל ווי הייליקער בּוימל,

איידער צו הערן דײַנע ליידיקע באַרימערײַען.

דורכגעקראָכן בּיסטו אַלע מאָל דאָס לעכל פֿון אַ נאָדל

מיט דער בלאָנקער שווערד פֿון ליגנערײַ,

געבויגן זיך, געקאָרטשעט פֿאַר מאַכט,

געגרײַסט זיך קעגן די וואָס זײַנען פֿון מיסט ניט דערהויבּן.

און בּלויז איין מאָל האָסטו געזען דאָס געשטאַלט

פֿון אייבּיקן ייִדן מיט דעם צלם-לאָסט.

וואָס האָסטו אים געזאָגט?

האָסטו געוווינט אויף גאָטס קללה?

האָסטו אַליין געזוכט גאָטס פּנים?

דו וועסט באַלד אַוועקפֿאָגרן און אונדז איבּערלאָזן אַ ירושה

דײַנע מעשׂיות וואָס מען וועט דערציילן אין יעדן הויז —

פֿאַרביקע ליגנס וואָס וועלן נאָך הונדערטער יאָרן פֿאַרווײַלן,

און גאָטס אמת ליגט פֿאַרשעמט

און וואַלגערט זיך אין קויט.

איינער אַליין אין דער קנײַפּע איז דער באַראָן פֿאַרבּליבּן

און פֿאַר זיך געבּרומט דאָס ליד פֿון פֿינצטערן פֿאַיאָץ:

שטראָמען ליכט פֿליַיצן צוייבער

אויף איין געזיכט.

ער אַליין פֿון זיי דערוויילט,

שטייט דערהייכט און זיי פֿאַרווײַלט,

מיט אַלץ וואָס אין זיי

פֿערלט, פֿריידיקט מיט לאַך און ווײַ;

ער ליגנערט, ליבט, ליבט, לעבט,

ער שטרויכלט, הייבּט און פֿאַלט,

ער צאָפֿלט וואָרט און צערטלט קלאָנג,

ער אויגט צום טרויער און פֿאַרווייגט מיט געזאַנג,

ער פֿאַרבט די וואָר מיט רויט און בּלוי.

עס האָט געבּלויט אויף טאָג און דער הימל האָט זיך גערויטלט בּײַ די זוימען.

"ער פֿאַרבט די וואָר מיט רויט און בּלוי" —

האָט ער איבּערגעזונגען און זינגענדיק אַרויסגעשפֿאַנט פֿון דער קנײַפּע.

ווערשערינס זײַנען געגאַנגען מיט פֿעקלעך גרעט צום טײַך

און אים פֿריילעך בּאַגריסט.

דער פֿאַסטאָר איז געשטאַנען אויפֿן שוועל פֿון קלויסטער

און אַרײַנגעאָטעמט יונגע מאָרגנלופֿט.

The drunkard who sang of God's mercy
Threw his glass at the wall
And it shattered into splinters.
Shut up, Baron. Your stories
Don't have a single crumb of God's grace,
They're just hollow soap-bubbles.
Better to be bored with one's own wife and kids
In a poor house, where God's blessing flows quietly like holy oil,
Than to listen to your empty boasting.
You've always crawled through the eye of a needle
With the gleaming sword of lies,
You grovelled before power,
You bragged to those who could not rise from the dirt.
And only once did you see the image
Of the Eternal Jew with the cross of his burden.
What did you say to him?
Did you cry over God's curse?
Did you yourself seek God's face?
You will soon croak and leave us a heritage
Of stories that people will tell at every hearth—
Colorful lies that will entertain for hundreds of years,
And God's true word lies disgraced,
Wallowing in the dirt.

All alone, the baron remained in the tavern
And hummed to himself the song of the dark clown:
  Streams of light flooding magic
  On his face.
  He is chosen by the crowd
  To entertain!
  All that bubbles in their eyes,
  All that laughs and all that cries—
  He stumbles, rises, falls and bounds,
  He loves, he lauds, he lives, he lies,
  He flutters words and flatters sounds,
  He rocks with song and touches rue,
  He paints the truth in red and blue.
Blue dawned the day and the sky was red at the seams.
"He paints the truth in red and blue"—
He sang again and, singing, strolled out of the tavern.
Washerwomen carried packs of laundry to the river
And greeted him joyfully.
The pastor stood at the door of the church
And breathed young morning air.

דער באַראַן איז אַוועק אין וואַלד,

און בײַ אַ פאַרוואָרלאָזט וואַלדהײַזל

האָט ער געכאַפּט דעם רויטן שפּין בײַ דער אַרבעט.

ווי ער האָט זיך אַ גליטש געטאָן אויף זײַן אייגענעם פאָדעם

און עס פאַרטשעפּעט בײַם דעכל,

און זיך אַ וויג געטאָן אויף צוריק,

און פאַרפּלאָנטערט אַרום זיך

און ווידער אַרויסגעשפּיגן אַ נײַעם פאָדעם.

טראָפּנס טוי זײַנען געלעגן אויף אַ פאַרטיקן שפּינוועב,

ערגעץ אַנדערש אויף אַ בוים,

און געפינקלט אין דער זון ווי אַ דיאַדעמע.

ער איז אַוועק צום בית-הקברות און הויך געלייענט די מצבות

פון גוטע בירגער און זייערע פרויען

וואָס האָבן אָפּגעלעבט אַ לעבן אין אין שטעטל.

און צום הונדערטסטן מאָל ער האָט זיך געלאַכט פון זײַן ווייץ

אַז אַפילו נאָך דעם טויט

ליגן זיי מיט די אייגענע ווײַבער.

ער האָט אויפגעציטערט פון טריט און דערזען דעם פּאַסטאָר לעבן זיך.

איר קוקט זיך אַרום, באַראַן, אויף מײַן טויטער עדה,

האָט דער פּאַסטאָר באַמערקט מיט אַ שמייכל

וואָס האָט נאָך מער אײַנגעגרונצלט זײַן אַלט געזיכט.

זײַן שטים איז געווען טיף און קלאָר

ווי ער וואָלט ערשט אַרויסגערעדט דאָס ערשטע וואָרט

נאָך אַ שווײַגנדיקער מאָרגן-תּפילה.

איך האָב שפּאַצירט מיט דעם וועלדל און אײַך אָנגעיאָגט.

קומט און מיר וועלן גיין צוזאַמען.

אין אַזאַ טאָג איז כּדאי צו רעדן וועגן גאָטס פּנים

וואָס אַנטפּלעקט זיך צו די וואָס זוכן אים,

אין די ערשטע בלוילעכע שעהן פון מאָרגן.

אָט דאָ, אויף דעם בית-עולם, אויף דעם סוף פון אַלע וועגן,

טראַכט איך אַלע מאָל וועגן אַ נײַעם אָנפֿאַנג, הער באַראַן.

איך גיי אַוועק פון דאַנען גאַנץ אָפֿט

באַיונגט און דערפרישט אין געדאַנק ווי אַן ערשט-געבוירן קינד.

"ער פאַרבעט די וואָר מיט רויט און בלוי",

האָט זיך בײַם באַראַן געפלאַנטערט אין קאָפּ אַ שפּינוועב פון ווערטער.

און אויפן קול האָט ער אויסגערופן מיט אַ שנײַדנדיקער דרייסטיקייט:

הער פּאַסטאָר, איז דאָס אײַער אמת?

קעגן מײַנע פינקלדיקע ווערטער שטעלט איר אַנטקעגן

אײַערע רייד פון אַ נײַעם געבוירט

דאָ אויפן וועג וועג וואָס אַלץ איז סוף.

הער פּאַסטאָר, לאָמיר, בײַדע ליגנער, גיין ווײַטער

און צוזאַמען זוכן גאָטס פּנים.

The baron went to the forest,
And in an abandoned hut
He caught the red spider at his work:
How well he slid on his own thread
And hooked it to the roof,
And swung back,
Entangled himself,
And spit out a new thread.
Elsewhere on a tree
Dewdrops lay on a finished spider web
And shimmered in the sun like a diadem.
He went to the cemetery and read aloud the tombstones
Of good citizens and their wives
Who had lived all their lives in this town.
And for the hundredth time he laughed at his own joke
That even after their death
They lie with their own wives.
He shuddered at footsteps, and saw the pastor near him.
You're observing, Baron, my dead congregation,
The pastor remarked with a smile
That deepened the wrinkles on his old countenance.
His voice was low and clear,
As if it were his first word
After a silent morning prayer.
I strolled in the forest and caught up with you.
Come, let us go together.
On such a day, it is good to talk of God's face
That is revealed to those who seek Him
In the first blue hours of dawn.
Here, in the cemetery, at the end of all roads,
I think always of a new beginning, Herr Baron.
I often leave this place younger,
My mind refreshed as a newborn babe.
    "He paints the truth in red and blue,"
A spider web of words entangled in the baron's head.
And with a cutting insolence he cried out:
Herr Pastor, is this your truth?
To my sparkling words you counter
With your talk of a new birth
Here on the road where everything is end.
Herr Pastor, let us—two liars—go on
And together seek God's face.

פֿון קינדער-צימער

◄ זייגער און מאַמע

אַ קליק טיקט און זי אַ

איז אַ וואַרעם און אויג

און אויג און כאַ און האַנט און האַנט

און קלייד און קליק

קליק קליק קליק.

◄ אַ ייִנגעלע און אַ זעמעלע

אַ ייִנגעלע עסט אַ זעמל מיט פּוטער,

אַ קעצל קוקט אים אין די אויגן.

דאָס ייִנגעלע איז שלעפֿע און הונגע.

איין אויג קלעפּט זיך.

די קאַץ האָט אַ גרויס גלעזערן אויג

און די נאַכט האָט דרײַ אָדער אפֿשר פֿיר

גלעזערנע אויגן.

און די מאַמע האָט אַן עק און לאַפּעס מיט נעגל.

זי טוט אים אויס און דראָפּעט.

זי איז גוט און דראָפּעט.

דער זעמל איז פֿינצטער, ווי די נאַכט,

פֿון דאַנען ביז אַהער און העט.

און די נאַכט איז אַ גלעזערנע.

אַ שוואַרץ פֿענצטער איז די נאַכט,

וואָס ליגט אויפֿן דיל און אין מאַמעס לידל.

מאָרגן וועט זײַן בעסער.

עס וועט זײַן אַביסל ליכטיק

און מען וועט נישט מורא האָבן צו קוקן

דורכן קעצל-אויג צום דרויסן.

◄ נאַכט, זײַ שטיל צו מיר

— נאַכט, זײַ שטיל צו מיר —

שטילע נאַכט.

— נאַכט, זײַ לאַנג צו מיר —

לאַנגע נאַכט.

מיט מיר אונטער דעם צודעק זײַ שווייַג צו מיר —

שווייַגע נאַכט.

From the Nursery

➤ *Clock and Mommie*

a click ticks and she a
is warm and eye
and eye and ha and hand and hand
and close and click
click click click.

➤ *A Boy and a Roll*

A boy eats a roll with butter,
A kitten looks into his eyes.
The boy is slee—and hun—.
One eye sticky.
The cat has a big glass eye
And the night has three or maybe four
Glass eyes.
And mommie has a tail and paws with nails.
She undresses him and scratches.
She is good and scratches.
The roll is dark as the night
From here to there and away.
And the night is of glass.
The night is a black window,
Lying on the floor and in mommie's song.
Tomorrow will be better.
There will be a little light,
And it won't be scary to look
Through a kitten-eye outside.

➤ *Night, Be Mood to Me*

Night, be mood to me—
Mood night.
Night, be long to me—
Long night.
With me under the cover, be calm to me—
Calm night.

The Yiddish title of the book,
"Yiddishtaytshn," means
roughly: Explications in (or of)
Yiddish; it is coined from
"Ivre-taytsch," meaning
Hebrew-translated (or
Germanized), the old name for
Yiddish as the language for
medieval Hebrew teaching and
Bible translations; or stylized,
archaic Yiddish.

איך וועל עס דריַי מאָל איבעראיבערן,
העכער פון דער מורא זינגען.
היימלעך איז מיר דער גרויל פון דיַינע
קעצלדיקע אויגן אין אַלע טונקלען.
ליב איז מיר די שרעק פון דיַינע
מיליאַסן רוישן אין אַלע ווינקלען.
די מאַמע איז אַ מערדערין,
איר אָרט נישט, וואָס אַ שאַטן
שאַרפט אַ מעסער און וויל מיך קוילען.
זי איז אַוועק, אין טאַטנס בעט,
און איר אָרט נישט, וואָס מאָרגן
וועט מען מיך געפינען אַ דערוואָרגן.
אָרט מיך אויך נישט.
אָרט מיך נישט.
אָרט מיך אויך נישט.
אַרט מיך נישט.
אַרט מיך אויך
נישט.
דורך דער שמאָלער סטעזשקע
נאַכט, זיַי קום צו מיר.
צו מיר אין פענצטער.
נאַכט, זיַי קוק צו מיר.
קוקע נאַכט.

▶ צו אַ פריַינט וואָס וויל
זיך נישט ברעכן דעם
לאָקשנברעט וויַיל עס
איז אַזוי אויך שווער צו
גיין אויף יאַגד ווען
די ביקס איז
שטומפיק און די
ליבע איז
צערטלעך ווי
אַן אַלטע
קאָלדרע

און עס איז שווער צו פונאַנדערן
אַלץ אין ווערטערטומל פון רוישיקער
עברי פון טיַיטש און זאָג און מיין
און פאַרקערט מיט סתּירותדיקער איינשטימי-
קייט ווען אַ בלאַט איז פשוט גרין

Three times I shall repeatrepeatrepeat,
Louder than fear I shall sing.
Intimate is the terror
Of your catty eyes in all darknesses.
Lovely is the scare
Of your myriad noises in all corners.
My mother is a murderess,
She doesn't care that a shadow
Sharpens his knife and will kill me.
She left, she's in daddy's bed,
She doesn't care that in the morning
They'll find me strangled,
So I don't care either.
I don't care.
I don't care either.
I don't care.
I don't
Care either.
Through the narrow path,
Night, be come to me.
To me in the window.
Night, be look to me.
Look night.

► *To a Friend Who*
Wouldn't Bother to Strain
His Noodleboard Because
Even So It Is Hard to
Go Hunting When
Your Rifle Is
Blunt and
Love Is
Soft as
An Old
Blanket

And it is hard to tell one
Thing from another in the worduproar of the noisy
Bible of meaning and saying and verse
And reverse with contradictory uni-
Valence when a leaf is simply green

In a review of Glatshteyn's *Credos*, the writer, Lamed Shapiro, wrote: "Many of the poems I do not understand. They look like riddles: who wants to break his head on them? Even without them, it is hard to live in the world." As Glatshteyn tells it, he liked the phrase and seventeen or eighteen years later wrote a poem in which he wanted "to confront hard life with absolute incomprehensibility which doesn't plague your head anymore because breaking your head won't help anyway. From this confrontation, I wanted to extract as much music as possible."

און קופּעררויט אין ווינטער-אָנזאָג
פֿון וועלטצײבער וואָס דרײט אַרײן
דעם פֿאָנאַר בײַ נאַכט ווי אַ שטיל
הויז און וואַכט מיט אײן אויג
און זעט טאָפּלט זיך און זיך
אויפֿן אויבערפֿלאַך אין טיפֿן
און דאָס איז אפֿשר אַ שײַן
פֿון אַן אמת-שאַטן אָדער
אַ פֿאָרשפּיל צו אַ געשעעניש
איז אָבער גלויבן און איבערגלויבן
אין הינטערגלויבן ליגט וואָס
צום שטילן טומל פֿון קיניגרײַכן
וואָס שווערן זיך מיט געטרײַשאַפֿטן
צום אונטערטאַנער וואָס פֿאַרדינט נישט
און בויט און אַקערט
און מאַכט רײַך די גאַנצקײט אומעטום
די גאַנצע געאָגראַפֿיע איז נישטאָ צום
פֿאַרזינדיקן אָבער בײַם ים יחיד
אויפֿן שוואַרצאַפּל
ווערט דאָס דרײַ מאָל צום טײַוול
אומפֿאַרשטענדלעך און דאָס לעבן
די זונה רופֿט און פּטרט אָפּ
אַלץ אַזוי שנעל און אין שלומפּער
אַ קלומפּער לעבן אַ שלײַדער ערד
וואָס דעם קאָלעקטיוו אָרט
קנאַפּ און נאַרט זיך אַז
ער איז אײביק
ווען ער איז שוין ניטאָדל
איז ער אַ מאַרטירער מיט
אַ מאָנומאַנט אין האַנט
און אַ קראַנץ אין
און דאָס טעאַטער יאַטערט
און דאָס בוך וויל דווקא
אַלץ אין טאָטאַ אנאַליזירן
און מען מאָלט בײז צום אויג ווײַסל
כדי מען זאָל די טײַכן געדענקען בעת
און מען איז שוין אַלץ צוריקגעשמועסט
קלאָר ווי אַ קינדערליד
אָדער ווי די שווייצרעגיר
אָבער דאָס גליק דאָס מענטשישע
דער פֿילאָסאָף קמיע
די צוויי פֿיס די מיידלשע
די שײן געבײנטע וואָס פֿירן
די ליב געאָדערטע וואָס פֿירן

And copper-red in wintereve
Of worldmagic which turns down
The streetlamp at night like a quiet
House and watches with one eye
And sees double oneself and oneself
On the surface in the depths
And this is perhaps a glow
Of a truthshadow or
A prelude to an event
But belief and superstition
Lie in posteriorstition which
To the quiet tumult of kingdoms
That swear with loyalties
To the serf who doesn't deserve
And builds and plows
And enriches the whole everywhere
The whole geography is nothing to
Complain about but in the individual's
Pupil it becomes
Thrice devil take it
Unintelligible and life
The whore winks and gets done with
Everything so fast and slovenly
A clumpy life a shovel of earth
Which the collective minds
Little and fools himself that
He is eternal
When he is no-longer
Then he's a martyr with
A monumand in hand
And a wick in his
And the stage is a stench
And the book wants regardless
To analyze everything *in toto*
And they paint up to the tears
To remember the rivers while
And if we pull the chat back
We become clear like a lullaby
Or like the Swiss government
But human luck
The philosopher amulet
The girl's two legs
The beautifully boned which lead
The lovely-veined which lead

אַװעק און אַרױף װערט דאָס שױן
װידער דרײַ-מאָל צום טײװל אומפֿאַרשטענדלעך
און אָנגעהענעם אומבאַגרײַפֿלעך
אַז אַ פּלאַך זאָל דימענסיאָנירן אַזש
ביז צום נישט אויסגעפֿאָרשטן
און אַרום דעם אַלץ
און אויף דעם אַלץ
ליגן מצבות פֿון טײַטשן
פֿון װערטער פֿון מײנען
און פֿאַרקערטן פֿון סודות
פֿון פּרינציפּן פֿון מאָראַלן
פֿון באַגריפֿן פֿון שטאַנדפּונקטן
פֿון װערטן און אומװערטן
פֿון קאָמפּליצירטקײטן
און פֿאַרפֿלאַנטערטקײטן פֿון קאָסמישער
עטיק עסטעטיק און זאַפֿטן
װאָס האָבן האָפֿטן און באַשאַפֿטן
און שפּאַנען און פֿליסן און פֿלײצן
און רײצן און קרײצן און קרײצן און לעבן
און לעבן און לעבן און לעבן
װערט דאָס שײן אמת טפֿוי ימח-שמו
דרײַסיק מאָל אומפֿאַרשטענדלעך
װען אַלץ איז קלאָר װי די דאָס קאַנאַריקל
װאָס האָט געזונגען
איך בין געגאַסן פֿון גאָלד
און מײַן שטים איז רײַנסטער פֿלײט
און דער מאָרגן איז געגאַסן פֿון גינגאָלד
און דער האָן איז הײזעריק
און דעם מאָרגן אַרט נישט
ער שפּאַנט סײַ װי אױף שטעקשיך
שאַרט אַװעק די בלױע פֿאָרהאַנג
און פֿאַרנײַיגט זיך
עך בין דאָ
און אַז ער זאָל לעבן איז דאָ
שאָקלען זיך שײן בײמער
פֿרײיען זיך שײן טײַכן
זינגען שײן די פֿײגל און אַפֿילו
עס רעגנט אין מיטן דערינען
איז מה-בכך איז מה-בכך
דאָס קאַנאַריקל קראַצט זיך די פֿעדערן
מיט אַ פֿיסל און זאָגט
עס װעט זײַן אַן עװלהלה

Away and upward then it becomes
Again thrice devil take it unintelligible
And infernicely incomprehensible
That a surface could dimension out
To the very unresearched
And around everything
And on top of everything
Lie graves of meanings
Of words of verses
And reverses of mysteries
Of principles of morals
Of concepts of pointofviews
Of values and devalues
Of complexities
And perplexities of cosmic
Ethics aesthetics and juices
Which have foundations and creations
And stride and flow and flood
And excite and excise and crucify and engrave
And live and live and live
Then it becomes really hell
May his name be blotted out
Thirty times unintelligible
When everything is clear like the canary
Who used to sing
I am cast of gold
And my voice is pure flute
And the morning is cast of spun gold
And the rooster is hoarse
And the morning doesn't mind
He walks anyway in slippers
Pulls aside the blue curtain
And bows deeply
I am here
And when he may-he-live-long is here
Then the trees sway
The rivers rejoice
The birds sing and it even
Rains out of the blue
So-what so-what
The canary scratches his feathers
With his foot and says
It would be a crime

אויב מען זאָל

אויב מען זאָל

(אל בנה

אל בנה)

מיינען אַז דאָס איז צימבאַליק

די ריינע וואָרהייט איז

איך בין געגאָסן פון גאָלד

און מיַין שטים איז ריינסטער פלייט

גאָלד שמאָלד פלייט שמייד

עס איז צום טיַיוול שרעקלעך

אומפֿאַרשטענדלעך

◄ אויפלייז

אין טרויעריקן אויפלייז זשאַווערן ציטאַטן

פון פליגאַראפֿן.

מאַטילדאַ טיערע, זינג מיר אַ ציטערין פון געזעצטע אַפֿאַריזמען

און לעבנוויַיזוינען.

צייטן פון שטילקייט, געקרייציקטע ליידיקייטן.

איך דערלויף פולסירט צום קאָמישן סאָפֿיסטישן סוף.

אין צווישן-צווואַשן זשאַנגליר איך אָנגעהאַנגענע לונג-און-לעבערס

פון אויפגייענדיקע און אונטערגייענדיקע רעגלמעסיקייטן,

פון סטענאָגראַמען ערודיציע —

מאַראלאָראַטאָסאַציען.

יאָ.

לינדע בוימערוויויגן. ראָזפֿאַרשניַיטע מיזאַנסצענען.

עגיש שטיי איך ביים סאַמע קראַטער,

אונטער סומנעם צייכן פון מיַין געאָגראַפֿיע.

פֿאַרצייכן אַלץ מיט פֿאַרשניטן לאַנצעט.

די גרויזאַמע פֿאַרבינדונגען, די וויינענדיקע קאָנטינויטעטן —

די אטאַוע לוסטלאָסט.

פֿאַרשפּיצטע שפּריכווערטער, פֿאַרוונדלטע פֿאַלקערייען.

איך בין צוויי-יעריק און איך פיַילנבויגן אַריבער

פליוטן, שטאַכעטן.

מיט מיַין בלום אין האַנט פרעג איך אָפּ

אַלע אַקסיאָמעוואַרענע פּאַרטיפֿערייען.

רויטער צאָפֿל פון אַש איבער פֿאַרשטויבטע וואַנדאַלן.

מאָנומענטיש שטייגט ווילן צום פֿאַטאַלן צויבער.

זיַין אָדער זשאַווערן. הונגער אָדער פלאַדיען.

If one would
If one would
(God build
God build)
Think that this is cymbalism
The real truth is
I am cast of gold
And my voice is pure flute
Gold shmold flute shmute
It is devil take it terribly
Unintelligible

God build (Hebrew: **El Bene**)—an allusion to a Hebrew song in the Passover Hagadah.

➤ *Dissolution*

In sad dissolution rust quotations
Of bugographs.
Dear Matilda, sing me a lemon of sedate aphorisms
And howtolives.
Tatters of silence, crucified emptiness.
Throbbing, I race to the comic sophistical finish.
In wishy-washy meantime

I juggle the lung-and-liver that they hung on me:
Rising and setting regularities,
Shorthands of erudition—
Moralerotassociations.
Yoke.

Lung-and-liver—an idiom, "to hang a lung and liver on someone's nose," meaning to dupe him.

Mild treeswings. Rosysnowed mise-en-scenes.
Egoish, I stand at the very crater,
Under the gloomy sign of my geography.
I note everything with a sharpened lancet.
The gruesome connections, the crying continuities—
The atavistic lustburden.
Pointed proverbs, rounded folksiness.
I am two-years-old and I bow-and-arrow over
Fences and spikes.
Flower in hand, I question
All axiomatized indepthinkings.
Red quiver of ashes over dusty vandals.
Will rises monumental to be fatal charm.
To be or to rust.
Hunger or multiply.

אין ראַסט פון באַשערטן זון-אונטערגאַנג
וואַרף איך אין קעסל געבאַרגטע עלעגיעס.
די שווערע שטאָלענע מאַשין האָט זיך באַפליגלט
און עס זינגט דער שנײַדיקער בליאַסק
איבער פאַנאָראַמישע אומעטומען.

◄ מיר, די וואָרטפראָלעטאַריער

נאַכט. אין די טונקלסטע ערטער פינקלען ווערטער.
ס׳גייען אָף גאַנצע שיפן מיט באַגריפן.
און דו, באַפאַנצערט מיט שווײַגן און קלוגזײַן,
ווייקלסט אָף וואָרט פון מײַן.

מעמענטאָס — פאַרערגענטער האָריזאָנט,
אויפגעפלעמלטער צוריקקום, קוים דערקאָנט:
אַ בוך, אַ פּנים, אַ שמייכל, צײַנער.

די פאַרשאָלטענע נאַכט איז דיר אַרײַן אין די ביינער.

פאַרצערטל, פאַרטוש, פאַרגעס.
מאַך נישט פון קיין הויזן-קנעפל אַ נס.

וואָרטפראָלעטאַריער. ס׳פליען אָף גאַנצע עראָפּלאַנען
מיט פאַרשטאַנען.
און דו האָסט זיך פאַרשפּענצערט מיט סעזאַמעס און אַליבאַבעס.
הערסטו דען נישט, ווי עס קרעכצן יאָכן?
אויף דײַנע ווערטער ליגן אײַזערנע שטאַבעס.
פאַרגרילט, פאַרשעלט מיט בראָכן.
וווּ דײַנע געלעכטערס, וווּ דײַנע געוויינער?

די פאַרשאָלטענע נאַכט איז דיר אַרײַן אין די ביינער.

דײַן טיטלבוים טיטלט אונטער דײַנע פענצטער.
אַ שטיין און דאָ רוט.
די צוווישנצײַטן האָבן דיך דערפירט צום אַבסאָלוט.
מצבות פון אינדיווידן, מאַסע, יידן, ראַסע —
אַרכיוון.
ס׳זינגען איצט גאַנצע קאָלעקטיוון,
סטראָטאָספערן, שטערן, אַפילו מוירען, שטיינער.

די פאַרשאָלטענע נאַכט איז דיר אַרײַן אין די ביינער.

In the corrosion of the destined sunset
I throw borrowed elegies into the melting pot.
The heavy steel machine grew wings
And the cutting glare sings
Over panoramic everywheres.

➤ *We the Wordproletariat*

Night. In the darkest places sparkle traces
Of words. Loaded ships with ideo-glyphs
Sail away. And you, armored in silence and wisdom,
Unwrap word from sense.

Mementos—rain-veiled horizon,
Flickering return, barely recalled:
A book, a face, a smile, a yawn.

The cursed night has got into your bones.

Soften up, cover up, forget.
Don't make a miracle of a trouser button.

Wordproletarian. Airplanes leave land
Full of understands.
And you in your vest of Sesames and Ali-Babas.
Don't you hear how yokes sigh?
Iron girders lie on your words.
Gnash them, curse them with disaster.
Where are your laughters, where are your groans?

The cursed night has got into your bones.

Your palm dates under your windows.
A stone and Here-Lies.
The in-between times have brought you to the absolute.
Graves of individuals, masses, Jews, races—
Archives.
Now whole collectives sing,
Stratospheres, stars, even buildings, stones.

The cursed night has got into your bones.

דער הימל, דער בלויער אזארט, האט זיך פארלאשן.
דו זיצסט און זוכסט נאך אלץ די שאטנס פון ווארט
און רייניקסט דעם שימל פון מיינען.
ס׳ווערן ווערטער טרויעריקער און ריינער.

די פארשאלטענע נאכט איז דיר ארײַן אין די ביינער.

The sky, the blue hazard, went out.
You still sit and seek the shadows of a word
And scrape the mold off meanings.
Words take on sadder and purer tones.

The cursed night has got into your bones.

Ben Shahn: *Lute and Molecule,
No. 2,* 1958.

◄ דער בראַצלאַווער צו זײַן סופר

I

נתן, דאָװאַי הײַנט נישט טראַכטן.

האָסט שוין אַ מאָל געזען אַזאַ װעלט

מיט אַזוי פיל לײַטערע פראָקטן?

כ׳װעל דיר דערלאַנגען אַ פראַסק,

אויב װעסט הײַנט אויסקװעטשן אַ געדאַנק.

קראַנק ביסטו הײַנט צו לעבן?

לעב מיט אַלע דײַנע אברים

און אָטעם זון װי אַ פליג.

לאָמיר נעמען גיין אויף קעריק,

לאָמיר אָװעקטראַכטן אונדזער גאַנץ פאַרמעגן,

און צעטרענצלען אונדזערע רעיונות אויף די װעגן.

לאָמיר װערן הייליקע פויעּרימלעך,

מיט הייליקע קי אויף אַ הייליקער פּאַשע.

לאָמיר עסן קאַשע מיט מילך,

לאָמיר רייכערן שטינקענדיקע פײַקעס

און דערצײלן בײַקעס פון שרעטעלעך,

לאָמיר זינגען לידעלעך —

דײַ־דאַנע־דײַ, דײַ־דאַנע־דײַ.

הוילע לידעלעך אָן װערטער,

דײַ־דאַנע־דײַ.

כ׳זע, ס׳איז שוין אויפגעגאַנגען אַ כמאַרעלע

אויף דײַן שטערן.

װעסט כאַפּן בײַ מיר אַ פליק אין פרעסער,

טאָמער נעמסטו קלערן.

הײַנט װעסטו מוזן פאַרשליסן

דעם טראָקטער הינטער שלעסער.

הײַנט זײַנען מיר זינגענדיקע תּמעלעך

און מיר קענען קיין צװיי נישט צײילן.

איז כאַפּ זשע נאָר —

װי װוּנדערלעך דאָס איז,

איינס — אחד.

איינס און באַזונדער איינס

איז אַלץ אחד,

און נאָכאַמאָל און װידעראַמאָל אחד.

הער נאָר װי פּשוט,

װי אַליין, װי שײן, װי טרויעריק־שײן,

איינס — אחד.

➤ *Nakhman of Bratslav to His Scribe*

I

Come on, Nathan, let's not think today.
Did you ever see a world
With so many beautiful things?
I'll give you a smack in the face
If you squeeze out one thought.
Will it kill you to live, just to live?
Live with all your limbs
And breathe sun like a fly.
Let us go backward,
Let us think away all our possessions,
Squander our ideas on the roads.
Let us become holy peasants
With holy cows in a holy meadow,
Eat kasha with milk,
Smoke stinking pipes
And tell stories of dwarves,
Let us sing simple songs—
Day-dana-day, day-dana-day.
Naked songs without words,
Day-dana-day.

I can see a cloud forming
On your brow.
You'll get a slap in your mug
If you start thinking.
Today you better lock up
Your thinker behind locks.
Today we are singing fools,
We cannot count to two.
Can you grasp it—
How wonderful it is:
One—unique.
One and separately one
Is still unique,
And again, and time and again unique.
Listen, how simple,
How lonely, how lovely, how sadly beautiful:
One—unique.

Rabbi Nakhman of Bratslav (1772–1811), one of the most influential Hassidic rebbes, founder of the Bratslaver Hassidic sect. Rabbi Nakhman had messianic aspirations. He is famous for his stories and parables, told in Yiddish, recorded and translated into Hebrew by his scribe, Nathan. Nakhman's stories have become known in the West through Martin Buber's renderings as well as through more recent translations into English.

William Gropper: *A Village in the Ukraine.*

Day-dana-day—popular Slavic refrain, adapted for Hassidic songs.

unique—in the original: **Echod**, the attribute of God's oneness.

גרעזעלע זינג,
בינעלע זום,
גלעט די בלום,
וואָלקנדל רעגן,
פריש-אויף די וועגן.
טרינק אָן די ערד.

נתן, באַלד פאַלט צו די נאַכט,
לאָמיר שלאָפן אומגעחלומט און אומגעטראַכט
ווי די פויערימלעך.
לאָמיר היינט אַוועקלייגן די לייטער
און לאָמיר נישט הימלעוועז,
זאָלן מלאכים קלעטערן
אַראָפ און אַרויף, אַרויף און אַראָפ.
לאָמיר כאַפן אַ כראָפ און אַ שנאָרך
און זיך אויפכאַפן אַנטקעגן אַ צעפלאַמטן מיזרח
מיט דעם געזאַנג —
דיי-דאַנע-דיי, דיי-דאַנע-דיי.

כ'וועל דיר ברעכן אַ ביין
אויב וועסט דאָס ניגונדל נישט פאַרשטייז.
טאָמער וועסטו עפעס דערלייגז, אַ וואָרט אָדער אפילו אַן אות.
ס'וועט מוזן זיין אַזוי פשוט ווי דאָס —
דיי-דאַנע-דיי.

2

פאַראַן אַזעלכע שטייגער לייט,
וואָס טראַכטן אַ יאָר מיט אַ מיטוואָך
און דער קאָפ ווערט ביי זיי הייליק,
אָבער דער גאַנצער גוף בלייבט שטויב פון שטויבן.
זיי קוקן אַריין אין אַ ספר
און די אויגן גלאָצן באַלד אַרויף אויבן,
אָבער די פיסלעך מיט די הענטלעך
זיינען נאָך ביי זיי עפר-ואפר,
און איבערן גאַרטל
און אונטער דעם צווישנשייד,
ווערט אַלץ טרף און טרף'ער.
זיי לערנען זיך אויס שיינע ווערטער,
זיי זיינען עולה-רגל צו די הייליקסטע ערטער.
נאָר זאָל קומען אַ נדבה בעטן אַ מענטש אַ פאַרשמאַכטער,
בלייבט זייער האַנט פאַרמאַכט
און ס'האַרץ פאַרמאַכטער.

Sing, grass,
Bee, buzz,
Fondle a flower,
Cloud, rain
On roads again,
For earth a shower.

Nathan, soon night falls,
Let us sleep un-dreamed and un-thought
Like the peasants.
Today, put aside the ladders
And let's not pry into the sky,
Let the angels climb
Down and up, up and down.
Let's take a plunge and a snore
And wake up facing the flaming East
With a song—
Day-dana-day, day-dana-day.

ladders—an allusion to Jacob's dream.

I'll break your bones
If you don't understand the tune,
If you add anything, a word or even a letter.
It must be as simple as that—
Day-dana-day.

2

There are some kind of people
Who think for a year and a Wednesday
And their head becomes holy,
But their whole body remains dust of dust.
They open a holy book
And right away their eyes roll upward,
But their legs and arms
Are still dust and ashes,
And above their belt
And below their thigh
Everything becomes vile.
They learn pretty words by rote,
They make a pilgrimage to the holiest places.
But if a starving man asks them for alms,
Their hand will be closed
And their heart shut.

דעם קאָפּ האָבן זיי מרחיק געוועזן פֿונעם שׂכל,
און ס׳אַרעמע מוחל רודערט אַזש מיט די גלגלים,
נאָר ס׳פֿיצענאַנטשיקל מענטשל ווערט פֿאַרפֿאַלן
אויף עולם-ועד.

דערימעך, זאָג איך דיר, נתן,
טראַכטן איז ווי נאָטן צו געזאַנגען,
און די געזאַנגען ווווינען אין לב.
זע, אַז ס׳האַרץ זאָל טראַכטן לויטער,
וועט ממילא דער קאָפּ אויפֿהערן צו טשאַדן.
פֿײַנט האָב איך דעם גוטן ייִדן,
דעם כלומרשטן ידען,
וואָס פֿאַרטריפֿט די אותיות פֿון ספֿרים
מיט נעצרדיקע טראַכטערײַען.
נעם אַ ליכט און באַלײַכט דעם בראשית.
ברא האָט באַשאַפֿן.
בראשית האָט באַשאַפֿן.
גוואַלד, נתן, וואָס איז דאָ שײַך צו טראַכטן.
לאָמיר גיין באַזאַמען אין רעגנס און אין שנייען,
אין זונען און אין קעלטן.
— און לאָמיר זינגען
בראשית האָט באַשאַפֿן וועלטן.

3

אָט ווי איך דערצייל דיר אַזוי האָט עס פּאַסירט.
כעלות, ווען איך האָב מיטן וואַלד שפּאַצירט,
זע איך ווי דער מאָרגן גייט אויף אינדערקרום
און די גאַנצע יצירה איז ברוגזלעך-שטום.
די ביימער שטעלן זיך מיט די זײַטשעמויכלס צו מיר.
די פֿייגל הערן מײַן גוטמאָרגן און גיבן זיך נישט קיין ריר.
אַ העזל קוקט מיך אָן ווי אַ ייִדענע אַ מרשעת,
און דער טרונקוואַסער אין קוועלכל זאָגט מיר מיט כעס:
נחמן, מוחל, מאַך איבער מיר הײַנט נישט קיין ברכה.
און די בלומען לאָזן נעבעך אַרויס אַ פֿינצטערע געסרחה.
און אַלץ וואָס איך טראַכט ווערט פֿאַרפֿלאַנטערט און פֿאַרצווייגט,
און אַלץ וואָס איך זאָג ווערט פֿאַרשטילט און פֿאַרשווייגט.
כאָפּ זשע, ליבערשט, די פֿיס אויף די פֿלייצעס און טראָג זיך אָפּ.
נחמן, וואָס טויג עס, אַז די גאַנצע וועלט איז ברוגז.

ווייס איך דאָך, אַז די וועלט איז צו אַ מענטש געגליכן.
ווייל אַלץ וואָס וואַקסט און וואָקסט און אַלץ וואָס פֿליט,
און אַלץ וואָס טוט קריקן וויל נעבעך זײַן.

They've separated their head from their mind;
The poor brain spins on all its wheels,
But the tiny-teeny person gets lost
For ever and ever.

That's why, I'm telling you, Nathan,
Thinking is like sheet music to songs,
And the songs live in your heart.
See that your heart thinks clearly,
And your head won't be filled with smoke.
I hate the good Jew,
The seeming savant,
Who drips upon letters of books
With constipated ruminations.
Take a candle and light up the *Bereyshis*.
Boro, created.
Bereyshis, In the beginning created.
What a scream, Nathan! What has thinking to do with it?
Let us walk together in rain and in snow,
In sun and in frost,
And let us sing—
In-the-Beginning created worlds.

Be'reyshis boro (Hebrew: **Bereshit Bara**)—"In the beginning [He] created," the opening words of the Bible.

3

Just as I am telling you, so it happened.
At dawn, I walk in the woods,
I see the morning rising queerly
And the entire creation is out of sorts.
The trees turn to me their forgive-me-for-the-expression.
The birds hear my Good-Morning and do not move.
A rabbit looks me over like a wicked woman,
And the drinking-water in the spring tells me angrily:
Nakhman, forget it, don't bless me today.
And the flowers give off a dark stink.
And all that I think gets tangled and twisted,
And all that I say is silenced and hushed.
Take your feet on your shoulders, Nakhman, and flee.
What good is it, if the whole world is cross.

I know, of course, the world, poor thing, is like a human being:
All that grows, all that flies
All that crawls, wants to be.

גיב איך זיך אזוי א זאג אויף קאטאָוועס:
וואָס איז דען די וועלט?
אַן איינבילדעניש, אַ פֿאַרבלענדעניש.
אַ רגעדיקע פֿאַרבײַיִקייט,
אַן אויסגעטראַכטע נישטזײַיִקייט.
און אזוי ערנאָך האָב איך דער גאַנצער יצירה
דערלאַנגט אין דער זיבעטער ריפ.
אַן אַלטער בוים האָט געטאָן אַ קליפ.
ס׳האָט מיר טאַקע גלײַך פֿאַרקלעמט בײַים האַרץ.
אָבער ס׳איז געגאַנגען אַ גאַנג.
מיט אַ כּוח אַ פֿאַרבאַרגענעם
האָט דער גאַנצער וואַלד גענומען זײַן
און זיך מאַרגענען.
די ביימער האָבן צוריק אויסגעדרייט די פּנימער צו מיר.
די פֿייגל האָבן געטשוויטשערט.
דאָס העזל האָט זיך צעשמייכלט.
דער טרונקוואַסער אין קוועלכל האָט זיך געבעטן מיט זיך האַרץ:
נחמן, מאַך אַ ברכה איבער מיר.
און די בלומען האָבן זיך געגעבן אַ צעבלי
ווי אין גאָרטן עדן.
אַ קראָ האָט זיך צעלאַכט ווי אַ קינד.
און דער גאַנצער ברוגז האָט געטאָן אַ פֿאַרשווינד.
און איך האָב ווייניקע לופֿט געשעפּט
און אַלץ האָט געלאַבט און אַלץ האָט געלעבט.
און ס׳האָט זיך צעטראָגן אַ פֿריידיקער געשריי.
ווער איז אַ פֿאַרבלענדעניש?
ווער איז נישטאָ.
מיר זײַנען דאָ, דאָ, דאָ.

און אָט אזוי האָט אַ ברוגזע וועלט
זיך צעמאַרגנט, צעשטראַלט און צעהעלט.
און ס׳איז געוואָרן אַ קוויטשערײַ,
אַ געשרייעריי, אַ טשוויטשעריי פֿון קולי-קולות.
מיר זײַנען דאָדאָדאָ.
מיר זײַנען דאָדאָדאָ.
אז איך האָב זיך שוין אויך
אויעקגעשטעלט אינמיטן וואַלד
און מײַן קול האָט זיך ווי אַ שופֿר צעשאַלט.
וועלט, איך שווער דיר בײַ דער מאָרגן-שעה,
וועלט, דו ביסט דאָ.

So, I poked fun at it and said:
What good is it, the world?
An imagining, a mirage,
A fleeting moment,
An invented not-being.
Thus I gave the entire creation
A poke in its seventh rib.
An old tree sighed out a sob—
I felt a pang in my heart.
But it all started to move.
With a hidden force,
The whole forest began to be,
To dawn.
The trees again turned their faces to me,
The birds twittered,
The rabbit gave me a smile.
The drinking water in the spring pleaded:
Nakhman, make a blessing over me,
And the flowers blossomed
As in the garden of Eden.
A crow burst out laughing like a child.
And all the sulkiness disappeared.
I breathed a whiff of air
And everything loved and everything lived.
And a happy shouting spread:
Who is a mirage?
Who is not-being?
We are, are, are.

And so it was that a sulky world
Awakened to morning, to radiance, to brightness.
And all was drowned in squeaking,
Screaming, twittering of voices of voices.
We areareare.
We areareare.
Then I too
Stood in the middle of the woods
And my voice roared like a shofar:
World, I swear by this morning-hour,
World, you are.

a poke in its seventh rib—a Yiddish idiom: a sharp blow that will be remembered.

shofar*

כ׳האָב זיך דערהונגערט,

ביז צום טעם פֿון ברויט מיט פּוטער

און גופֿיק טראַכטן.

כ׳בין געגאַנגען און מײַן גוף איז געגאַנגען מיט מיר,

און ס׳איז נישט געוואָרן קיין איין געדאַנק,

וואָס האָט נישט דורכגעשטראַלט מײַן הויט-און-בײַנער.

כ׳האָב געקלעטערט און מײַנע פֿיס האָבן געקלעטערט מיט מיר,

און איטלעכע מחשבה האָט געגליט

מיט וווּנדערלעכער וואַכקייט.

און אַז ס׳איז צוגעפֿאַלן די נאַכט,

האָב איך זיך דערהונגערט ביז פֿיסנע ברויט

און געטראַכט האָב איך מיט פֿרייד

איינסיק אין דער פֿינצטערניש,

באַזונדערע איינסיקייטן וואָס שלעפֿערן אײַן,

און וואָס טאָמער זײַנען זיי הייליק,

פֿאַרהייליקן זיי און פֿאַרדרימלען

פֿיס און העגט און קאָפּ.

און הײַנט האָב איך זיך אויפֿגעכאַפּט אַ הונגעריקער

און אויפֿן ניכטערן מאָגן האָב איך אָנגעהויבן

פֿון סאַמע גאָרנישט,

און דער טאָג איז אויך געוואָקסן

פֿון כמעט גאָרנישט, פֿון שוואַרץ און קוים-קוים בלוי.

און איך האָב מײַנע טונקעלע גלידער

באַפֿוילן: יהי אור.

און מיר ביידע האָבן געקראָגן ליכטיקע פֿליגל,

איך און דער טאָג,

און ביידע זײַנען מיר געוואָרן איינס

און ביידע האָבן מיר געדאַוונט אויפֿן קול —

ווי גוט זײַנען דײַנע געצעלטן.

אַ מאָל דוכט זיך מיר, כ׳האָב עס אַלץ אויף דער האַנט,

און מיטאַמאָל גיט עס זיך אַ פֿאַרהויל און אַ פֿאַרמאַך.

פֿאַרשטייסט, נתן, מיר איז פֿלא גאָר אַ סך.

כ׳וויל דאָס מויל נישט צוזאַמענפֿירן מיטן אייגענעם אויער.

מיר וואַרפֿן אויף דעם בן-אדם אַרויף אַ דרימלעניש.

מען ווײַזט אים די ערד אונטן

און העט-אויבן אַ פֿאַרכטיק הימלעניש.

4

I starved myself
To hunger for bread and butter
And bodily thinking.
I walked and my body walked with me,
And there was no single thought
That did not radiate through my skin-and-bones.
I climbed and my legs climbed with me,
And each thought glowed
With a wonderful everydayness.
And when the night descended
I was starving for plain bread;
And one-ly in the dark,
I contemplated with joy
Separate one-linesses that lull you to sleep,
And if they are holy
They make your legs and hands and head
Holy and drowsy.

And today I woke up hungry,
And on an empty stomach I started
From sheer nothing,
And the day, too, grew
From almost nothing, from black and barely-barely blue.
And I ordered my dark limbs:
Let there be light.
And we both grew bright wings,
I and the day,
And we both became one
And we both prayed aloud—
How goodly are thy tents.

how goodly are thy tents—Numbers 24:5. The first blessing before the morning prayer.

5

Sometimes it seems to me, it's in the palm of my hand,
And all-of-a-sudden it's concealed and closed up.
You see, Nathan, I am amazed at so much.
I don't dare to match my mouth with my ear.
We cover the human being with a doze.
He is shown the earth underneath
And high up an awesome sky.

אָבער אין צווישן איז דאָ אויך עפּעס פֿאַראַן.
כ׳ווייס, מען רופֿט דאָס, דוכט זיך, לעבן.
ערגעץ גלוסט אַ פֿרוי און ס׳פֿרײדיקט
פֿון וואַרעמער באַהאַלטעניש דאָס אָפֿקול פֿון אַ מאַן.
נאָר טאָמער נעמט זיך עס אַזוי אין מיר וועבן,
באַפֿאַלט מיך אַ פּחד און איך זאָג:
זעסט יענעם שקאָץ, יענעם געדאַנק,
שלאָג אים מכּות־רצח, יאָג אים, פֿאַרטרײַב.

נתן, פֿאַרשרײַב.

למשל, נעם דעם יצר־טובֿ — אַ שיינער מחותּן, אַן אָנגעלייגטער גאַסט.
לעבט אויף גוטע קעסט, מיט אַן אויסגעפּאַשעט בײַכל פֿון מיצוות.
אָבער אַ צער איז צער איז מיר אויף דעם יצר פֿון שלעכטס.
פֿרומע ייִדעלעך טרײַבן אים נעבעך האַלדז און נאַקן.
ער פֿאַסט בײַ זיי תּעניתים.
ער חלשט נאָך אַ לעפֿל וואַרעם געקעכטס.
און וואָס איז דען אויסן דער יצר־הרע?
חדווה. באַשייד פֿון פֿרייד. טרייסט געיערט פֿון טרויער.
געוויין פֿון אַליין פֿאַרצווייט.
איינזאַמע דורות פֿון פֿאַרגיין
פֿאַרמערט אין אייביקן דויער.
וואָס איז ער דען נעבעך אויסן דער יצר־הרע?
גוף. לײַב.

נתן, פֿאַרשרײַב.

בײַ נאַכט, אויב דו האָסט נאָר אַן אויער,
הערסטו ווי יעדער טויער פֿון אַלע ש״י וועלטן
ווײנט מיט אײן רוף:
גוף.
מיינסט, ס׳איז פֿאַראַן קנאַפּ געזאַנג אין אַזאַ בענקשאַפֿט?
און דאָס איז דאָך ס׳ביסעלע תּענוג, מישטיינס געזאָגט,
צווישן הימל און ערד,
ביז מען לייגט שערבעלעך אויף די אויגן.
דאָס איז דאָך דער טײַערער ניגון פֿון אַ האַרציקן מה־יפֿית.
דו ווייסט גאַנץ גוט, ווי אויסגעמאָרעט מײַן גוף איז,
נאָר ס׳וויינט מיר דאָס האַרץ פֿאַרן ביסל פֿאַרגענאַכעס.
— יצר־הרע מיינט דאָך יחוד אין צוזאַמען —
וווּנדערלעכער צולהכעיס.
ס׳מיינט אַ געציטערט וואָרט,
פֿײַער און פֿלאַמען אין גאָטס געפֿלעכט פֿון צוויי.
ס׳מיינט ווײַב.

But in between there is surely also something,
I guess, they call it life.
Somewhere, a woman desires, and joyfully,
From his warm hiding, echoes a man.
But as soon as this is spinning in me,
A fear grips me and I say:
You see that brat, that thought,
Beat him to the floor, chase him, expel him.

Nathan, write it down.

Take, for example, the Drive-for-Good—a decent in-law, an honored guest.
Fed well by his host, his belly big with good deeds.
But I pity the Drive-for-Bad.
Pious Jews give him a hard time.
They starve him out.
He is dying for a spoonful of warm soup.
And what does he want, the Drive-for-Bad?
Joy. A choice to rejoice. Consolation leavened with sorrow.
Weeping of aloneness entwined.
Lonely generations of decline
Multiplied in eternal duration.
What does he want, the Drive-for-Bad?
Body. Flesh.

Nathan, write it down.

At night, if you have an ear,
You can hear all the gates
Of the Two-Hundred-and-Ten Worlds
Crying out in one voice:
Flesh.
Don't you think there is song in such longing?
And isn't this the bit of pleasure
Between heaven and earth,
Till they put the shards on your eyes.
It is the precious tune of a hearty "How beautiful."
You know, don't you, how my body is tormented,
But my heart cries out for the bit of delight.
Because Drive-for-Bad means oneness in joining—
Wonderful spite.
It means a word trembling with life,
Fire and flames in God's weaving of two.
It means wife.

Drive-for-Good, Drive-for-Bad (Hebrew: **Yetser-tov, Yetser-ra**. Yiddish: **Yeytser'tov, Yeytser'hore**)—the two opposing forces in man, also personified as independent beings prodding each individual.

Two-Hundred-and-Ten-Worlds (Hebrew: **SHaY olamot**)— "The Holy-One-Blessed-Be-He will bestow on every single just man two hundred and ten worlds" (Sanhedrin).

"How beautiful!"—a song sung at the Sabbath eve dinner.

נתן, פֿאַרשרײַב.

כ׳מיין ס׳איז ממש אַ מורא דאָס צו ברענגען אויף די ליפֿן.
ס׳איז שפּעט בײַ נאַכט.
איך גיב דיר, נתן, מײַנע רייד, מיטן אויער נישט צו כאַפֿן.
ס׳קען נאָך, חלילה, ווערן אַ פֿאַרמיש.
נו, וועט מען שרײַען, ווײַל ער אפֿשר,
מתיר זײַן אַן אשת-איש?
און וואָס מיין איך דען צו זאָגן?
ס׳רײַסט מיר ס׳האַרץ אויפֿן יצר פֿון שלעכטס.
דאָס איז דאָך קראַפֿט, חשק, פֿאַרלאַנג,
כּוח, געמעכץ.
און ס׳איז דאָך געזאַנג,
און ס׳איז דאָך געוויין און סוד פֿון שטאַם,
און דאָס איז דאָך תּענוג און דאָס איז דאָך ליד.
און גליד-גליד פֿון הייליקן פֿלאַם
און דאָס ליכט פֿון אירס און זײַנס וואָס ווערט איין.
נתן, ביסט נעבעך מיד, ס׳קלעפּן זיך דיר די אויגן.
שלאָפֿסט אײַן.
לאָמיך נישט איבער מיט מײַנע רעיונות אַליין.
וואַך מיט מיר. פֿאַרבלײַב.

נתן,
פֿאַרשרײַב.

Nathan, write it down.

I think, it's really scary to bring it to your lips.
It's late at night.
I hand you, Nathan, my words. No ear should hear them.
It may, God forbid, cause confusion.
What, they will shout, maybe he wants to
Allow you a man's wife?
But what do I mean?
My heart goes out to the Drive-for-Bad.
Because it is strength, lust, desire,
Power, skill.
And isn't it melody,
And isn't it weeping and secret of race,
And isn't it grace and pleasure and song.
And flesh-and-blood of the holy flame
And the light of hers and his becoming one.
Nathan, you are tired, poor thing, your eyes are heavy,
You're slipping away.
Do not leave me alone with my thoughts.
Be awake with me. Stay.

Nathan,
Write it down.

Max Weber: *Adoration of the Moon*, 1944.

הער און שטײן, נתן.

כ'בין דיר מוחל דעם לױן

פון פעטסטן שטיק לױתן,

אױב מ'זאָל פון מיר צונעמען

מײַן שענסטע קרױן — דאָס װאָרט.

דאָס איז דיר דער מוסר-השכל.

איך בין אַ פלױשער, אַ רײדער.

גלױב מיר, נתן, נאָר אין רײד, נאָר אין אַ געשמאַק ביסל באַרײדן

פילט מען אַמאָל טעם גן-עדן.

װיפל מאָל האָב איך דיר געבױערט די אױערן,

און דו שרײַסט — װילסט אַלץ ניט אַרױס קײן פרײַער.

אײַ, טײַער שעבעטײַער,

גיב-זשע אַהער דײַנע קנעכטיקע אױערן,

פאַר מײַנע נעכטיקע טעג,

און איך װעל דיר דערצײַלן אַזױנס און אַזעלעכס.

כ'זין אַזױ אױף אַן אײַזעלע, אַ פאַמעלעכס,

הױדע זיך אַרױף-אַראָפ.

מיטאַמאָל דערלאַנגט זיך ס'אײַזעלע אַ שטעל אױף

און גיט מיך אַ שאָקל אַרונטער.

אַרום און אַרום איז אַ חושכניש.

ס'אײַזעלע איז פון מיר אַװעק,

װי אײַנער רעדט:

אַצינדערט ביסטו דער חכם-בלילה.

און דו, נתן, האָסט באַדאַרפט זען אַ בלילה,

אַ שטאָק-פינצטערניש, אַ װימש'דיקײַט,

טאַפ װי אַ בלינדער אין סמאָלע.

נאָר-װאָס אַ רײַטער און פלוצעם אַזאַ װיסטע מפלה.

באַפאַלט מיך אַ פחד און כ'װיל שרײַען גװאַלד,

שפּראָצט פון דער חושכניש אַרױס

אַ װולקולאַקיש געשטאַלט.

מאָל דיר, פאַר די לײַט

האָב איך נישט קײן מורא.

װער זײַנען די לצים, אױב נישט מיאוסע מחשבות?

איז פונקט װי דו האָסט זײ אַנגעטראַכט,

גיסטו אױף זײַ אַ בלאָז, גיסט זײַ אַ צעטראַכט,

און זײַ צערינען אין דער נאַכט.

נאָר דער חברה-מאַן הוסט אױף מיר מיט פײַער.

כאַפט מיך בײַ דער האַנט און פירט מיך.

אױ, גיב איך אַ זאָג — ס'איז אַ מיאוסע מעשׂה.

Hear and be stunned, Nathan.
I would give up my share,
A fat piece of Leviathan,
Sooner than let them take
My finest crown—the word.
Here is the moral for you.
I am a chatterer, a talker.
Believe me, Nathan, only in talk, in a juicy morsel of gossip,
Can you sometimes feel a taste of heaven.
How many times have I pierced your ears
And you scream—you don't want to be free.
Oh, dear, dear,
Give me your slave ears,
For my living yesteryears,
And I shall tell you things you'd never hear.

I'm sitting, like this, on a donkey, a slow ass,
Swaying up-and-down, up-and-down.
Suddenly the donkey rears up
And shakes me off.
Darkness all around.
The donkey walks away,
As if to say:
Now you are the Sage-at-Night.
And, Nathan, you should have seen the at-Night,
A pitch dark, groping night,
Like a blind man, you can feel the tar.
One minute a rider, the next—what a letdown.
It gets scary, I want to scream,
But out of the darkness springs
A werewolf figure.

Mind you, I'm not afraid
Of those guys.
Who are they those clowns, if not ugly thoughts?
Just as you think them up,
You puff in their faces, think them away,
And they vanish in the night.
But this wise guy coughs fire at me.
He takes me by the arm and leads me away.
Oy, I say to myself—it's ugly business.

This poem was written later and included in the cycle, "Nakhman of Bratslav to his Scribe" (1956).

leviathan—promised to the righteous at the feast in heaven.

Pierced your ears—the ear of a Hebrew slave would be pierced as a sign of eternal servitude if he refused to be freed after seven years (Exodus 21:6).

Sage-at-Night—a Yiddish euphemism for "stupid," implying that a sage at night is a fool by day.

ענטפערט ער מיר אָפּ ווי אַ ווידערקול:
אַ מיאוסע מעשה.

שווײַג איך שוין אין געהאַקטע צרות,
כ׳האָב פײַנט אַז מען לייענט מיר מײַנע געדאַנקען.
ברומט ער פֿאַר זיך אַליין:
געדאַנקען.
מיטאמאָל עפֿנט ער דעם פֿײַערדיקן פּיסק
און זאָגט אַזוי:
פֿאַרנעם און כ׳וועל דיר זאָגן וואָס מיט דיר האָט געטראָפֿן.
ס׳אײַזעלע איז געוואָרן אַלץ
און ס׳אַלץ איז פֿון דיר אַוועקגעלאָפֿן.
איצט ביסטו אַלצלאַז אויף דער וועלט.
ס׳זײַנען אַוועק פֿון דיר אַלע דײַנע פֿאַרלאַנגען,
אַלע דײַנע געזאַנגען,
ס׳זײַנען אַוועקגעשפּרונגען פֿון דיר אַלע דײַנע ערטער,
אַלע דײַנע ווערטער.
אויך ווערטער? — טראַכט איך — אַ מיאוסע מעשה.
ווי מיינסטו? ברומט ער מיר נישט נאָך —
אַ מיאוסע מעשה?

גיב איך אַ סטראַיע אָן דעם גאָרגל,
גיב אַ פֿיר מיט דער צונג ווי אַ סמיטשיק.
כ׳וויל געבן אַ רעווע אויס אַ וואָרט.
אָבער ס׳קומט אַרויס אַ חלשותדיקער קוויטשיק,
עפּעס ווי אַ שטומע אישה, באַשערעמט זאָל מען ווערן.
ס׳מויל, דער האַלדז, דער גאָרגל,
אַלץ איז ווי געשוואָלן.
כ׳האָב שוין מורא צו טראַכטן — אַ מיאוסע מעשה,
כדי דער לץ זאָל מיך נישט ווידערקולן.

גיי איך שוין אין געהאַקטע צרות.
פּלוצעם פֿירט ער מיך צו אַ ליכטיקן טויער,
און גיט אַ זאָג: דאָ איז דער גן-עדן,
מאַרש אַרײַן!
איך שטיי ווי אַ ליימענער גולם.
דערלאַנגט ער מיר אַ בריק, אַז כ׳האָב דערזען דעם עלטערזיידן.
איז דאָך דאָס אַ ווערטל — האַ?
אָבער מײַן עלטערזיידידע איז בפֿירוש עפּעס מער ווי אַ ווערטל.
שטייט ער אויף אַ ליכטיק ערטל, ווי אויף אַ בערגל.
גלעט זיך די באָרד און לאַכט.
האַ, ווי געפֿעלט דיר עפּעס?
דער בראַצלאָווער — אַ שותק.
ער קנאַלט פֿון געלעכטער.

And he answers like an echo:
Ugly business.

So I sit in jagged woes,
I hate when They read my thoughts.
And he hums to himself:
Thoughts.
All-of-a-sudden he opens his fiery snout
And speaks out:
Harken, and I shall tell you what hath befallen you.
The donkey was everything
And everything ran away from you.
Now you are everythingless in the world.
All your yearnings have gone,
All your songs,
All your places have bounced off,
All your words.
Words too?—I think to myself—ugly business.
And don't you think he didn't hum after me—
Ugly business?

So I tune up my throat,
Draw my tongue like a bow.
I want to roar a word.
But out comes a feeble squeak,
Like a mute female, heaven help us.
My mouth, my throat, my gullet—
All are puffed up.
I'm afraid to think—ugly business,
Lest the clown echo my thought.

So I walk in jagged woes.
Suddenly he brings me to a shining gate
And says out of the blue: Here is heaven,
Inside, march!
I stand there like a dummy.
And he gives me such a kick that I see my great-grandfather.
It's a proverb, right?
But my great-grandfather is more than just a proverb.
He stands there on a shining spot as on a hill,
Strokes his beard and laughs.
Nu, how do you like that?
The Bratslaver—silent.
He's bursting with laughter.

Gave me such a kick that I saw my great-grandfather—a Yiddish proverb, meaning that I almost died and went to heaven. The irony here is that Nakhman's great-grandfather was the Ba'al Shem Tov, the founder of Hassidism.

און ס׳ענטפֿערט אים אָפּ מיט אַ פֿײַערדיקן הוסט,
מײַן וועכטער.
וואָס וועסטו טאָן מהיום והלאה?
נישטאָ קיין מעשיות, נישטאָ קיין פּזמונים,
ביסט נעבעך גאָלע.
ביסט אַ שטומער אין גן-עדן.

מיטאַמאָל האָב איך דערזען אַ בוים,
ממש ווי מ׳דערזעט משיחן.
כ׳האָב גענומען צו אים קריכן,
זיך אויסגעשטעלט, זיך מיט אַלע כוחות אָנגעהאַלטן,
געקראָגן גבורה פֿון אַ שמשון,
און גענומען מאַכן אַזעלכע ליאַרעמס,
אַזעלכע יעלות,
אַזעלכע גוואַלדן,
אַז דער אַלטער האָט אָנגעהויבן שרײַען:
שאַ, בראַצלאָווער, זאָל זײַן שטיל.
ס׳איז פֿאַרטאָג, וועסט אויפֿוועקן די צדיקים פֿון שלאָף.
אויס שטראָף.
נאָדיר צוריק ס׳לשון, בראַצלאָווער,
רעד פֿאַר פֿײַער און פֿאַר וואַסער.

ס׳האָט געגעבן אַ בליץ, אַ קנאַל.
פֿאַרשטייט זיך אַז אַראָפּגעפֿאַלן בין איך נישט פֿון אַן אייזל,
נאָר פֿון דער האַרטער באַנק אין בית-המדרש.
וואָס גוילעמסטו מיט די אויגן?
האָסט נעבעך נישט געכאַפּט דעם מוסר-השׂכּל.
כ׳דערלאַנג דיר באַלד אַ פּראַסקל,
אַז וועסט מיך האָבן צו געדענקען.
זאָל איך קרענקען, אויב איך וואָלט געוואָלט זײַן
אַ שטומער אין גן עדן.
דאָ אויף דער זינדיקער וועלט —
ריידן און ריידן און ריידן.

◄ קליינע נאַכט-מוזיק

1

פֿאַרשאַטן מיך, פֿאַרטונקל מיך, פֿאַרשוויינד מיך.
איך בין צו קליין צו לעבן גרויס.
געשע אַרום מיר וואָס ווייניקער,
פֿלאָטער אַרום מיר סודות פֿון קלייניקייטן.
גיב מיר אָפּ מײַן חלק וועלט
אויף אַ קליין טעלערל,

And my watchman echoes
With a fiery cough.
What will you do from now to eternity?
No tales, no melodies.
Poor soul, you are naked.
You are a mute in heaven.

Suddenly I saw a tree
As one would see the Messiah.
I crawled to it,
Stood up, held onto it with all my might,
I got the strength of Samson
And began bellowing,
Raised such a ruckus,
Such a commotion,
That the old man began to shout:
Hush, Bratslaver, be quiet.
It's before dawn, you'll wake up the Righteous.
OK, no punishment.
Here is your tongue, Bratslaver,
Go ahead, talk through fire and water.

Righteous—Tzaddikim. Those who have gone to heaven, as opposed to sinners who go to hell.

Lightning flashed. A thud.
Of course, I fell not from the donkey,
But from the hard bench in *shul*.
Why are you staring at me like a golem?
Oh, dear, you didn't grasp the moral.
I'll give you a smack—
You'll have something to remember.
May I be damned if I'd like
To sit mute on a heavenly rock.
Here, in the sinful world—
To talk and talk and talk.

shul*

► *Small Night-Music*

I

Shadow me in, dark me in, disappear me.
I am too small to live big.
Happen around me less and less.
Flutter around me mysteries of small things.
Give me back my portion of world
On a small saucer.

און צאַפּל מיך אַרום מיט זונאויפגאַנגען,
פֿאַרגאַנגען, רעגנס, שלאָף.
גיב מיר דאָס קלענסטע בעטל.
כ׳בין צו קליין צו לעבן גרויס.
גיב אויף מיר אַ שטילן בלאַז
און לעב מיך אויס.

2

ס׳זײַנען אָנגעפלויגן די פֿייגל,
מיט דעם פֿאַרנאַכט אין זייערע
זינגענדיקע העלדזעלעך.
אַ העזל ווערט פֿאַרגליווערט פֿון שרעק
און קײַקלט מיט די אויגן.
ס׳פֿעלד ליגט אָפֿן
אנטקעגן אַ רויט-צעפֿאַסמעוועטן הימל.
אַ דאָרף-פֿידלער גייט אַהיים,
מיט דער לאַסט פֿון אויסגעשפּילטע לידלעך.
די נאַכט קומט אָן ווי אַ דין גלעקל.

3

אָ איך בין, איך בין.
טרויעריק בין איך און קרים-קרום זינגעוודיק.
דער איטאַליענער פֿירט אַהיים ס׳קליינע מאַלפּעלע,
און איך זיץ פֿאַר מײַן הויז
און באַד זיך אין שטילקייט.
ס׳קליינע מאַלפּעלע האָט אַ קלוג עקל
און ס׳גייט בריהש אויף צוויי.
די נאַכט וואַקסט אויף מיר אָן שוואַרצע פֿליגל
און איך שוויידער אויף ווי אַ פֿלעדערמויז.

4

ס׳וויגן וויגן, שטילע וויגן,
שלאָפֿנדיקע וויגן.
די נאַכט איז געבליבן הענגען אויף אַ שטיק הויז.
אַ פֿענצטער ווערט זיך מיט אַ ביסל ליכט.
די קינדער האָבן טײַערע קעפּלעך —
אַפֿילו אין דער פֿינצטער ווייסן זיי אַלץ.
ווילע קינדער מיט צוגעמאַכטע אויגן
און ליכטיקע שרעקן.

5

פֿאַרווער מיר נישט
צו זיצן אין דער פֿינצטער און טראַכטן.
דו וועסט נישט קומען צו מיר.

Quiver about me sunrises,
Sunsets, rains, sleep.
Give me the smallest cot.
I am too small to live big.
Blow quietly on my life
And put it out.

2

The birds flew in
With the evening in their
Singing throats.
A rabbit freezes in fear
And rolls his eyes.
The field lies open
Against a red-streaked sky.
A village violinist walks home
With a burden of played-out songs.
The night comes in like a thin bell.

3

Oh, I am, I am.
I am sad and barely barely singing.
The Italian takes home his little monkey.
And I sit in front of my house
And bathe in silence.
The little monkey has a wise tail
And walks cleverly on two legs.
The night grows black wings on me
And I shudder like a bat.

4

Cradles swing, quiet cradles,
Sleepy cradles.
The night stays hanging on a piece of house.
A window takes cover with a bit of light.
The children have dear little heads—
Even in the dark they know everything.
Nice children with closed eyes
And bright fears.

5

Don't forbid me
To sit in the dark and think.
You won't come to me.

אַפֿילו אין שלאָף וועסטו

פֿאַרעקשנט נישט קומען צו מיר.

פֿאַרזאָג מיר נישט מיטן האַרבן וואָרט,

איך וועל דיך אויסטראַכטן

פֿון קאָפּ ביז די פֿיס

און וועל דיך איינראָלען לעבן מיר

ווי אַ שלאָפֿנדיק קעצל.

6

אַ קליינער, טרויעריקער רב

זיצט איבער אַ ספֿר־ל און גענעצט.

אַ זילבערנע אישה שטייט פֿאַרגליווערט אין ווינקל,

מיט אַ געקאַכט הינדל אין טעפּל.

זי זינגט אַ שאלה.

טראַ־לאַם.

דער רב דרימלט איין.

די אישה זעצט זיך אַוועק אויף אַ פֿײַערטאָפּ,

מיט רויט־שוואַרצע, צעבלאָזענע קוילן.

7

טײַערע נאָנע, מיט די קינדישע פֿיסלעך,

און אַלטן קעפּל.

די נאַכט באַלאַסטיקט דיך ווי אַ שווערער צלם.

דו עפֿנסט אַ קליינע טיר

און פֿאַלסט אַוועק אויף אַ שמאָל בעטל.

אין ווינקל הענגט אַ שווערער, רויטער לאָמפּ.

דו ווערסט לײַכטער און לײַכטער.

דײַן אַלט פּנים

ווערט פֿאַרטריפֿט מיט שלאָף.

8

אַ קליין פֿענצטער, אַ זיכער מויל,

אַ רויִקע באָרד.

די אַלטע נאַכט איז נישט זײַן לעצטע.

דאָס זיכערע מויל זינגט:

ס'איז דעם זינדערס ווויליזײַן

אַ הויז פֿון קאָרטן.

אָבער מײַן טרויעריק שיפֿל

וועט זיך דערשלעפֿן צו אַ באָרטן.

וועסט אונדז אַלעמען קעריק

פֿירן אין דײַן ליכטיקן האַרבעריק.

דאָס זיכערע מויל איז זיכער מיטן מאָרגן.

Even in my sleep you will
Stubbornly not come to me.
Don't warn me with your harsh word,
I shall invent you
From head to toe
And I shall curl you up next to me
Like a sleepy cat.

6

A little, sad Rov
Sits over a holy book and yawns.
A silver woman stands frozen in a corner
With a boiled chicken in a pot.
She sings a query.
Tra-la-lam.
The Rov dozes off.
The woman sits down on a firepot
With red-black glowing coals.

Rov*—rabbi, legal authority.
The poem is a tableau of a woman
coming to the Rov with a query
as to whether her chicken or her
pot is kosher.

7

Dear nun, with your childish feet
And old little head.
The night weighs you down like a heavy cross.
You open a little door
And drown in a narrow cot.
In the corner hangs a heavy, red lamp.
You become lighter and lighter.
Dripping sleep
Covers your old face.

8

A little window, a confident mouth,
A quiet beard.
The old night is not his last.
The confident mouth sings:
The sinner's happiness
Is a house of cards.
But my dragging boat
Will get to a shore.
You will take us all back
Into your bright shelter.

The confident mouth is sure of the morning.

9

פֿאַראַן אַ דאָרף מיט שוויַיגנדיקע בלומען
און טאָג און נאַכט דרייט זיך דאָרט אַ קליינע מיל.
געבויגענע עקסלעך קייַען זיסע גראָזן
און דער פֿאַרנאַכט גרילט אין דער שטיל.
דאָס איז אַ וועלט פֿון זינגענדיקע צייכנס.
טירלעך שטייען אָפֿן ווען די נאַכט רייַט אָן.
אַ גריַיז-גרויער מאַן פֿאַרשוויַיגט זיַין אַלטן הונט,
וואָס איז סיַי-ווי אין זיך פֿאַרטאָן.

10

זאָל איך בענקען נאָך יענער פֿאַרטרויעריקטער פֿרייד,
וואָס האָט פֿאַרגעהיימט דעם קלאָרסטן זאָלבעצווייט
און פֿאַרטרערט דעם שענסטן שמייכל?
די אומזיכערקייט איז געווען אייביק,
און אין דעם אייביק איז געלעגן דער פֿאַרבונד.
איצט איז די פֿרייד אַ פֿריילעכע
און יענער ווונדער פֿון טרויער
איז פֿאַרקינדישט.
און אַלץ איז קלאָר
און דער זאָלבעצווייט איז געזאַנג.
אָבער דער אייביק איז פֿאַרוואָלקנט
מיט פֿאַרגאַנג.

11

דאָס טרויעריקע וויַיב האָט געצײלט קליינע זילבערלעך
און אַרויפֿגעבראַכט שוואַרציק ברויט מיט פּוטער.
די פֿאַרע פֿון דער הייסער טיי האָט פֿאַרוואָלקנט
די באַגערנדיקע מוטער.
כ'האָב געהערט אירע קליינע רייד.
די נאַכט האָט געדולדיק צוגעוואַרט.
זי האָט זיך אָנגעבויגן איבערן בעט
און דעם צודעק אַוועקגעשאַרט.

12

געטרוי מיר פֿון דאַנען ביז אַהער
און עטלעכע טריט וויַיטער.
כ'גיי אַליין און וועל דיך נישט נאַרן.
כ'וועל דיר ברענגען מיַין אָפֿן פּנים
און דו וועסט אָנען אַלע דערפֿאַרן.
איך בין אָנגעטרויעריקט מיט ביכער,
און אָנגעטרונקען מיט וויַין פֿון ציַיטן,

A village with mute flowers.
A little mill turns day and night.
Bent little oxen chew sweet grass
And the evening chirps quietly.
It is a world of singing signs.
Doors are open when the night comes riding.
A gray man hushes his old dog,
Who is anyway sunk in himself.

10

Shall I long for that saddened joy
That veiled in mystery the clearest twosome
And brought tears to the prettiest smile?
The uncertainty was forever,
And in that forever was our bond.
Now it's a happy joy
And that wonder of sadness
Has become childish.
And everything is clear
And the twosome is song.
But the forever is clouded
With sunset.

11

The sad woman counted small pieces of silver
And brought up black bread with butter.
The steam of hot tea clouded over
The desiring mother.
I heard her small words.
The night was waiting patiently.
She bent over the bed
And pushed aside the cover.

12

Trust me just from here to here
And a few steps more.
I am coming on my own, I won't cheat you.
I shall bring you my open face
And you will sense all the becauses.
I am oversaddened with books,
Drunk with the wine of times,

trust me just from here to here—a reference to the Yiddish proverb, "trust me from here to there," meaning: trust me completely. Glatshteyn confines the space to visible intimacy, using two different words for "here." In the later edition, the Yiddish text has been "corrected" back to the standard phrase of the proverb.

און איך בין פלעגמאַטיש װי אַ קאַץ,

װאָס לעבט אױף אַלעמגרײטן.

זע, װי איך קום צוריק צו זיך

צום װוּנדער פֿון ערשטן פֿינטל.

פֿאַרמאַך דאָס פֿענצטער, ליבער פֿרײַנד,

און היט מיך אױס פֿון מינדסטן װינטל.

און אין דער פֿינצטער זײַנען מיר צװײ.

װאָס קען נאָך זײַן װײניקער און מינער.

צו אַלע נישט-געזעטיקטע פֿאַרזוכערס

בין איך דער האַרציקסטער פֿאַרגינער.

לאָמיר אָנזאַטלען דעם שלאָף

און רײַטן אין אַן אײגענעם גאָרטן.

און אין דער פֿינצטער װעלן זיך קושן

די געמעגטן מיט די נישטגעטאָרטן.

◄   אַ גוטע נאַכט, װעלט

אַ גוטע נאַכט, ברײטע װעלט.

גרױסע, שטינקענדיקע װעלט.

נישט דו, נאָר איך פֿאַרהאַק דעם טױער.

מיט דעם לאַנגן כאַלאַט,

מיט דער פֿײַערדיקער, געלער לאַט,

מיט דעם שטאָלצן טראָט,

אױף מײַן אײגענעם געבאָט —

גײ איך צוריק אין געטאָ.

װיש אָפּ, צעטרעט אַלע געשמדטע שפּורן.

כ'װאַלגער זיך אין דײַן מיסט,

לױב, לױב, לױב,

צעהױקערט ייִדיש לעבן.

חרם, װעלט, אױף דײַנע טרײפֿענע קולטורן.

כאָטש אַלץ איז פֿאַרװיסט,

שטױב איך זיך אין דײַן שטױב,

טרױעריק ייִדיש לעבן.

חזיריש דאַטש, פֿײַנטלעכער ליאַך,

עמלק גנב, לאַנד פֿון זױפֿן און פֿרעסן.

שלאַברע דעמאָקראַטיע, מיט דײַנע קאַלטע

סימפּאַטיע-קאָמפּרעסן.

אַ גוטע נאַכט, עלעקטריש צעחוצפּהטע װעלט.

צוריק צו מײַן קעראָסין, חלב'נעם שאָטן,

אײביקן אָקטאָבער, דריבנע שטערן,

צו מײַנע קרומע גאַסן, הױקערדיקן לאַמטערן,

And languid as a pampered cat
In a warm house.
See, I am coming back to myself,
To the wonder of the first dot.
Close the window, dear friend,
Keep me from the slightest breeze.
In the dark we are two.
What could be lesser and smaller.
Let all greedy tasters
Do as they like.
And we shall saddle our sleep
And ride in a private garden.
There, the mays and the mustnots
Will kiss in the dark.

► *Good Night, World*

Good night, wide world.
Big, stinking world.
Not you, but I, slam the gate.
In my long robe,
With my flaming, yellow patch,
With my proud gait,
At my own command—
I return to the ghetto.
Wipe out, stamp out all the alien traces.
I grovel in your dirt,
Hail, hail, hail,
Humpbacked Jewish life.
A ban, world, on your unclean cultures.
Though all is desolate,
I roll in your dust,
Gloomy Jewish life.

Piggish German, hostile Polack,
Sly Amalek, land of guzzling and gorging.
Flabby democracy, with your cold
Compresses of sympathy.
Good night, world of electrical insolence.
Back to my kerosene, tallowy shadow,
Eternal October, wee little stars,
To my crooked alleys, hunchbacked street-lamp,

This and the following four poems were included in a section, "Open a Chronicle and Record." The poem first appeared in *In zikh*, April 1938.

long robe—the traditional black overcoat of religious Jews.

Amalek—a tribe that slaughtered Jews in their exodus from Egypt and was consequently condemned by God to annihilation (Exodus 17:14). Amalek became the symbol of all the persecutors of the Jews, prefiguring the hope for their punishment.

מײַנע שמות, מײַן סוואַרבע,

מײַנע גמרות, צו די האַרבע

סוגיות, צום ליכטיקן עברי-טײַטש,

צום דין, צום טיפן מײן, צום חוב, צום גערעכט,

וועלט, איך שפּאַן מיט פרייד צום שטילן געטאָ-לעכט.

אַ גוטע נאַכט. כ׳גיב דיר, וועלט, צושטײַער

אַלע מײַנע באַפרײַער.

נעם צו די יעזוסמאַרקסעס, ווערג זיך מיט זייער מוט.

קראַפּיר איבער אַ טראָפּן פון אונדזער געטויפט בלוט.

און איך האָב האָפן אַז כאַטש ער זאַמט זיך,

גייט אויף טאָג-אײַן-טאָג-אויס מײַן וואַרטן.

ס׳וועלן נאָך רוישן גרינע בלעטער

אויף אונדזער בוים דעם פאַרקוואַרטן.

איך דאַרף קיין טרייסט נישט.

אין גיי צוריק צו דלת אמות,

פון וואַגנערס געץ-מוזיק צו ניגון, ברומען.

כ׳קוש דיך, פאַרקאָלטנט ייִדיש לעבן.

ס׳וויינט אין מיר די פרייד פון קומען.

אפריל 1938

My stray pages, my Twenty-Four-Books,
My Talmud, to the puzzling
Questions, to the bright Hebrew-Yiddish,
To Law, to deep meaning, to duty, to right.
World, I stride with joy to the quiet ghetto-light.

Good night. I grant you, world,
All my liberators.
Take the Jesusmarxes, choke on their courage.
Drop dead on a drop of our baptized blood.
And I believe that even though he tarries,
Day after day rises my waiting.
Surely, green leaves will rustle
On our withered tree.
I do not need consolation.
I go back to my four walls,
From Wagner's pagan music—to tune, to humming.
I kiss you, tangled Jewish life.
It cries in me, the joy of coming.

April 1938

stray pages—of torn holy books;
they were preserved in the
synagogue.

Twenty-Four-Books—the Bible
(in Yiddish, **svarbe**, contraction
of the Hebrew **esrim-ve-arba**,
twenty-four).

puzzling questions—difficult
issues in the study of Jewish law.

Hebrew-Yiddish—the
traditional Yiddish translation of
the Hebrew Holy Books, which
acquired an archaic and religious
flavor in modern Yiddish.

even though he tarries—an
allusion to the credo, **"Ani
Maamin"** ("I Believe"), the
affirmation of faith in the coming
of the Messiah.

Max Weber: *Whither Now,* 1938.

מיט שטילע צייכנס פון ווייט
קומען אָן פֿאַרנאַכט טרויעריקע וועגגענער.
ס׳שטייען אויפֿגעפּראַלט די טירן,
נאָר אין ערגעץ וואַרט נישט קיין באַגעגענער.
ס׳דאַרף איז רויִק, ס׳קלינגען גלאָקן פֿון שטילקייט.
ס׳בייגט זיך געהאָרכיק יעדער גרעזל
אונטער צעצונדענער קילקייט.
עטלעכע קראַנקע ייִדן קריכן פֿון די וועגגענער אַראָפּ
און ס׳פֿלאַנטערט זיך אַ קלוג וואָרט
אין יעדן פֿאַרטראַכטן קאָפּ.
גאָט, אויף דיין וואָגשאָל פֿון גוטס און פֿון שלעכץ
שטעל אַוועק איצט אַ טעלער וואַרעם געקעכץ,
אָדער גיב כאָטש אַ וואָרף
אַ ביסל האָבער פֿאַר די מאָגערע פֿערד.
ס׳ווערט פֿינצטערער די טויטיקייט פֿון דאָרף.
אַ גרויזאַמע שטילקייט באַפֿאַלט די ייִדישע ערד
און איינער אין אַנדערנס אויגן דערזעט
ווי ס׳שוידערט אויף מיט שרעק אַ געבעט —
אַז ס׳וועט קומען דער טויט
זאָל איך נאָר נישט בלייַבן דער לעבעדיקער איינער.
פֿאַרזע מיך נישט מיט מייַנע דינע ביינער.

1938 יוני

עס איז אונדז באַפֿאַלן אַ הונגער,
אַ טרויעריקער הונגער.
מיר האָבן אָפּגעשפּאַרט אַן אייגן שטיקל הימל,
נישט צום פֿאַרזינדיקן.
און אַ לבֿנה קוקט אויף אונדז אַרונטער
מיט זילבערנע שפּאַקולן.
אמת, נישט אַלע ווינטשעוואַניעס
זייַנען מקוים געוואָרן,
אָבער בייַ אַ סך וויגעלעך
שטייען געזונגענע, גילדענע ציגעלעך.
נאָר די ביינער ברעכן.
ניין, נישט דאָס בעט האָט אַ קרעכץ געטאָן,
האָסט דערהערט דאָס קול פֿון די אייגענע ביינער —
וואָנדערביינער.

Twilight.
Sad wagons roll in
With quiet signs from afar.
The doors are wide open,
But no one is waiting to welcome.
The village is calm. Bells of silence, pealing.
Each blade of grass bows in submission
Under the flames of coolness.
Some sick Jews climb off the wagons,
And a wise word gets tangled
In each pondering head.
God, on your scale of good and bad
Put a plate of warm food,
Or at least throw in
Some oats for the lean horses.
The village deadness grows darker,
A gruesome silence falls on each Jewish beard.
Each sees in the other's eyes
A prayer shuddering in fear:
When death arrives,
Let me not remain alone.
Do not overlook my lean bones.

June 1938

This poem may allude to the expulsion of the Polish Jews from Nazi Germany in 1938 and their abandonment in No-Man's-Land on the Polish-German border.

➤ *A Hunger Fell upon Us*

A hunger fell upon us,
A sad hunger.
We have saved up
Our own bit of sky.
A moon looks down on us
Through silver spectacles.
Maybe not all good wishes
Have come true,
Yet by many a cradle stands
The golden kid of the song.
But your bones ache.
No, it isn't the bed that groans,
You hear the voice of your own bones—
Wanderbones.

the golden kid—standing beneath a baby's cradle, an image from the most famous Yiddish lullaby, promising a future of plenty.

טוסט אָן די שטעקשיך,
גייסט אַרויס אין שטילן דרויסן,
טרעטסט אויף דער ערד,
בלייבסט שטיין אויף אַן אָרט.
דוכט זיך וואָס קען שוין זיין אייגענער
פון דיין אייגענער פיראייליקייט?
גיסט אַ טאַפ דעם פייגנבוים,
אַ גלעט די ציגל פון הויז.
ס׳וויל דיך פאַרזיכערן די שויב די ליכטיקע.
נאָר די זיכערקייט איז אַ רויקיקע, אַ דורכזיכטיקע.
האָסט פאַרפלאַנצט? פאַרפונדעװעט?
יאָ, אָבער ס׳האָט עפעס ווידער אַ קרעכץ געטאָן,
אַלץ די שלעפעריקע ביינער —
די וואַנדערביינער.

דער טיש אין שטוב איז אַלדאָסגוטס,
לענסט זיך אונטער דאָס האַרץ.
אָבער האָסטו דען געזעטיקט דעם הונגער,
וואָס איז אונדז אַלעמען באַפאַלן,
דעם טרויעריקן הונגער
נאָך אַ וואָרט, זיכערער ווי ציגל,
ווי ערד אונטער די פיס?
ס׳שלאָפט דאָס ווייב, ס׳שלאָפן די קינדער.
אוודאי האָבן די יאָרן אַ שטיקל ראַם.
אַ רגע, אַ מינוט און ס׳ווערט אַלץ
כמעט גאַנץ און גוט.
פלוצעם עפנט זיך די טיר.
מען דערלאַנגט דיר אַ פאַפיר
גלייך אונטער דער נאָז.
שוין איין מאָל אַ צדקדיקער חשבון,
מען רעקוויזירט דאָס גאַנצע אָפּגעשפּאַרטקייט.
די ציגל, די לופט, די ערד,
דאָס רעכט אויף געפּאָרטקייט,
אַפילו דאָס געזונגענע ציגעלע,
די זילבערנע שפּאַקולן פון דער לבנה.

זאָל זיין ס׳איז נאָך קיינער נישט געקומען,
אָבער מיינע ביינער קרענקען שוין דערמיט,
מיט דער פייכטקייט פון יידישן וועטער.
איך פאַרריגל די טיר.
מיין נאַכטיקער שפּיגל איז אַ האַרבסטיקער באַראָמעטער.
עס קרעכצן מיינע איבערגעשראָקענע ביינער —
וואַנדערביינער.

You put on your slippers,
Go out into the quiet yard,
Step on the earth.
You stop.
What could be more your own
Than your own four corners?
You touch your figtree,
Stroke the bricks of the house.
The bright windowpane wants to reassure you.
But the assurance is smoky, transparent.
Have you planted? Have you laid foundations?
Yes, but again something groans.
Still the drowsy bones—
The wanderbones.

On your table—all you could wish,
You take a bite, you soothe your heart.
But did you calm the hunger
That fell upon all of us,
The sad hunger
For a word surer than brick,
Like earth under your feet?
Your wife is asleep. Your children, asleep.
Surely, there is a framework
To your years.
A moment, everything seems
Almost fine.
Suddenly the door opens.
They stick a paper under your nose.
What a just bill!
They confiscate all you've saved up,
The bricks, the air, the earth,
The right of copulation,
Even the golden kid of the song,
The silver spectacles of the moon.

Maybe nobody's come yet,
But my bones already ache
With the dampness of the Jewish weather.
I bar the door.
My night-mirror is a barometer of autumn.
I hear the groan of my scared bones—
Wanderbones.

fig tree—an allusion to I Kings 4:25: "And Judah and Israel dwelt safely, every man under his vine and under his fig tree. . . ." (See also, Isaiah 36:16.)

פֿאָרטאָג.

דאָס לעבן קרייעט קוקוריקו.

באַלד וועלן אָנהייבן מאָלן די פֿרנסה-מילן.

אָבער, אָסור, אויב עס וועט שטילן

דעם הונגער וואָס איז אונדז אַלעמען באַפֿאַלן,

דעם טרויעריקן הונגער.

אפּריל 1939

◄ אויפֿן יאַטקעקלאַץ

ס׳האָט זיך אַ ביסל געטאָן נעכטן אַרום מיר,

ווען איך בין געשטאַנען אַ צעדראַמטער

אויפֿן יאַטקעקלאַץ ווי אַ קנעכט צום פֿאָרקריפּן.

אָט איז דער מאַן, האָבן אַלע געטײַטלט,

וואָס פֿאַרדינט אונדזער רחמנות.

אמת, האָט געקוויטשעט אַ מויל אויף שרויפֿן,

ער איז אַ שטיקל שווינדלער און גאָרגלשנײַדער,

און מען דאַרף אים קוקן אויף די לעפֿקע פֿינגער.

אָבער ווער אויב נישט מיר, האָבן אים געשטויסן

צו די פרנסות וואָס זײַנען גרינגער.

אַוודאי איז ער אַליין אַ ניבזה

און אַ פּלעק אויף אונדזער משפּחה,

האָט אַ צוויטן, פֿון גרויס מיטלייד,

אַ טרער געוואָרגן דעם גאָרגל.

נאָר שווער צו פֿאַרגעסן דעם הייליקן ספר,

וואָס זײַנע עלטער-עלטערן האָבן אונדז געלאָזט בירושה,

פֿאַר די צען פֿאַרזאָגן אַליין

דאַרף מען מיט אים טאָן חסד

און פֿאַרטראָגן דעם דאָזיקן קריכער,

לומפּ, הורענזון און מאַרעוויכער.

גיט אַ קוק אויף זײַן הויקער,

טאַפּט מיר אַן אַלטע מויד דעם צעבײַלטן רוקן,

דאָס איז פֿון זיצן, קוקן אין ביכלעך,

און שאַרפֿן דעם מוח ווי אַזוי צו ײַדלען.

נאָר זידלען דאַרפֿן מיר זיך אַליין,

וואָס מיר האָבן אים נישט געטריבן

צו די שווייסיקע פֿאַכן,

ווי קאָפּען קאַרטאָפּליעס, שטיינער האַקן,

Dawn.
Life crows cockadoodledoo.
Soon the earning-mills begin to grind.
But for the life of me, it won't still
The hunger that has fallen on all of us,
The sad hunger.

April 1939

➤ *On the Butcher Block*

What a commotion there was yesterday around me,
As I stood bleeding on the butcher block
Like a slave for sale.
Here's the man, they pointed at me,
Who deserves our pity.
It's true, a fast tongue was shrieking,
You'd better watch out for his sticky fingers,
He's a a bit of a swindler, cutthroat, sleazy,
But wasn't it we who pushed him
To the livelihoods that are easy.

To be sure, he himself is loathsome,
A stain on our family—
Said another in deep compassion,
A tear choking his gullet—
But it's hard to forget the Holy Book
That his fore-forefathers bequeathed to us.
Just for the Ten Forbiddings
One should be gracious unto him
And endure
This sneak, whoreson and boor.

Just look at that hump—
An old maid felt my swollen back—
It comes from sitting, from poring over books,
Sharpening his wits for jewing.
But the blame, she says, must fall on ourselves,
For we did not force him
Into the sweaty trades,
Like cutting stones, digging potatoes;

This poem and "Here I Have Never Been" were not reprinted in Glatshteyn's collected poems of 1956.

האָט ער, שטאָט דעם נאַקן, אײַנגעשפּאַנט דעם קאָפּ,
װי אַן אָקס אין דער סאָכע,
אַלעמען איבערגעשכלט
און צוגענומען בײַ אונדז יעדן גראָשן.

און הערט װי װי ער בעבעט זײַן לשון,
װי ער פֿראָװעט באַזונדערניש אויף אונדזער ערד,
פֿאַר װעלכער מיר האָבן געפּאַקטן.
האָרכט װי ער ריטשעט װאָס מען האָט זײַן ברודער געשאָכטן,
קוקט װי ער מאַכט דאָס לעבן מיזעראַבל,
צערטלט מיך אַ באַסאָװער ליבעראַבל, —
ס׳װאָלט שוין לאַנג פֿון אים קיין זכר נישט געבליבן,
װען מיר װאָלטן אים שטאָט האָסן געטאָן ליבן,
און געעפֿנט פֿאַר אים, דעם אויסדערװײלטן,
דעם שטאָלצן, אונדזערע אָרעמס —
אונדזערע קירכן װאָלטן אים שוין לאַנג צעשמאָלצן.
מיר פֿאַרגעסן — פֿאַרענדיקט ער, מיט אַ גלחישן קנאַק, —
ס׳האַנדלט זיך נישט אין כּסדר פֿראָסקן זײַן צװײטע באַק,
נאָר אויפֿשטעלן אונדזערע אַנטקעגן זײַנע
אײַנגעװאָרצלטע געמיינהייטן.

ס׳האָט זיך אַ שײן ביסל געטאָן נעכטן אַרום מיר,
צװישן די יאַטקעס.
כ׳בין געשטאַנען אין הוילן העמד און צעפּליקטע גאַטקעס,
און זײ האָבן מיר געטרייבערט די אָדערן
מיט פֿאַרטיידיקעץ.
פֿאַרענטפֿערט אַזוי װײַל אַלע מײַנע נידריקע אינסטינקטן,
אַזוי שײן געזונגען מיר אַ זכות
פֿון מײַנע פֿרומע זיידעס װעגן,
אַז דער יאַטקעקלאָץ האָט אַזש גענומען שפּריצן מיט טרערן.
אַ פֿרומע אַלטיטשקע האָט איבער מיר געמאַכט אַ צײכן
אין דער לענג און אין דער ברײט,
און אַלץ אַרום האָט גענומען נישט װערן.
איך בין געבליבן אַליין אונטער אַ הימל פֿון קעלטעניש.
די שײַקע איז אַרויס פֿון באַהעלטעניש
און איך האָב פֿאַרמאַכט די אויגן.
די קלעפּ זײַנען מיך שוין נישט אָנגעגאַנגען.
איך האָב מיט סקרוך געדענקט
װי זײ האָבן זיך פֿאַרזאַמלט
אַרום דעם יאַטקעקלאָץ דעם רונדן,
װי זײ האָבן געבלעקערצט איבער מײַן צענערעגט לײַב,
און װי די בינען אײַנגעגעסן דעם האָניק אין מײַנע װוּנדן.

So, instead of his neck, he harnessed his head
Like an ox to a plow,
Outclevered us all,
And took away our last cent.

Now listen to the language he babbles,
See, how he celebrates separateness in our land,
The land our fathers fought for,
Here how he squeals that they slaughtered his brother,
How he makes our lives miserable—
Caresses me the bass voice of a liberable—
No trace would be left of him
If we had loved him instead of hating
And opened our arms
For him, the chosen, the proud one.
Our churches would have melted him long ago.
We must not forget—he concludes with a priestly snap—
The point isn't always to slap his other cheek,
But to set ours against
His tribal nastiness.

What a commotion there was yesterday around me
In the butcher shop.
I stood there in a shirt and tattered underwear
As they purged my veins
With justifications.
They explained away my base instincts so well,
They sang so beautifully the merits
Of my pious grandfathers,
That even the butcher block spurted tears.
A pious old woman made a sign over me,
Down and across;
And everything around me dissolved.
I remained alone under a cold sky.
The gang came out of hiding
And I closed my eyes.
The blows no longer concerned me.
With a shudder, I remembered
How they had assembled
At the round butcher block,
How they had belched over my beaten body,
And like bees, were stinging my wounds with honey.

האָסט פאַרלאָשן אײַן שטערן, צװײי, דרײַ,
דײַן גאַנצע צעליכטיקטע פּראַכט.
גאָט, װאָס טו איך דאָ אײנער אַלײן,
אין דײַן אײביקער נאַכט.

יוני 1939

◄ דאָ בין איך קײן מאָל נישט געװען

כ׳האָב אַלע מאָל געמײנט
איך בין שױן דאָ געװעזן.
מיט יעדן יאָר פון מײַן איבערגעניצעװעט לעבן
האָב איך געװאָרעמט געװעבן
פון אָפּגעלעבטע שטיקער װעלט.
איך האָב דערקענט געדענקטע פּנימער און שמײכלען
און אַפילו טאָטע-מאַמע זײַנען פאַר מיר געװען
פאַרבענקטע פּרעסקאָס אַמאָליקייט.
כ׳האָב געטראָטן אױף אַלטע רישעותדיקע שטעגן
און צװישן ברעגן פון געשיכטע
האָב איך געזעגלט.
איך האָב כּסדר געפונען דאָס װוּנדער,
װאָס איז אין געדעכעניש געװען אײַנגעקריצט,
און ס׳האָט די אָפּגעטומלטע פאַרגאַנגענהייט
זיך שעמעװודיק געבלעזלט אין דעם איצט.
איך האָב געמײנט
כ׳בין שױן דאָ אַ מאָל געװעזן.

נאָר די לעצטע שטיקלעך יאָרן-צײַטן,
מיט די אױסגעטראַכטע טױטן,
זײַנען מײַנע אײגענע טעג און נעכט.
דאָס איז מײַן אָנגעהױיקערטע באַשערטקייט,
דאָס האָב איך אַלײן אָנגעלעבט.
די פאַרגליװערטע פאַרקלערטקייט,
פאַרברענטע פעלדער,
די מאַפּעס מיט בית-עלמינס,
פאַרשראָקענע שטילקייט,
די צײכנס פון פרײדיקער רישעות —
כ׳האָב עס פון ערגעץ נישט געדענקט.
כ׳האָב עס קײן מאָל נישט געזען.
כ׳בין דאָ קײן מאָל נישט געװען.

You extinguished one star, a second, a third,
Your entire shining might.
God, what am I doing here alone,
In your eternal night.

June 1939

➤ *Here I Have Never Been*

I always thought
I had been here before.
With each year of my refurbished life
I warmed textures
From lived-up patches of worlds.
I recognized remembered faces and smiles
And even father-mother were for me
Nostalgic frescoes of antiquity.
I trod on old evil paths
And between shores of history
I sailed.
Time and again I found the wonder
Engraved in memory
And the once-tumultuous past
Bubbled bashfully in the present.
I thought
I had been here before.

But the last pieces of rag-years
With their invented deaths—
These are my own days and nights.
This is my own hunchbacked lot,
This was piled up in my own life.
The frozen melancholy,
The scorched fields,
The maps with graveyards,
Petrified silence,
The signs of happy evil—
I don't remember them from anywhere.
This I have never seen.
Here I have never been.

בלײַב שטיל, טויטע וועלט.

שווײַג אײַן אין זיך דײַן פֿאַרוויסטקייט.

ס׳וועלן ווידער אַ מאָל בליִען פֿאַרוויאַנעטע אָרנאַמענטן.

מיר וועלן איבערבויען דײַנע פֿונדאַמענטן,

אויף דעם בלוט וואָס מען האָט פֿאַרגאָסן.

נאָר די טויטע וועלן ווײַנען אין די חצותן,

יעדער מת — אַ טריפֿנדיק קול.

ווי אַ קליין ליכטל איבער יעדן קבֿר,

וועט פֿלעמלען אַ געבעט.

יעדער פֿאַר זיך.

איך בין איך —

וועלן טויזנטער געשאַכטענע איכן

ווײַנען אין דער נאַכט.

טויט בין איך און נישט דערקאָנט,

מײַן בלוט נאָך אַלץ נישט אויפֿגעמאָנט.

אַזאַ עשירות פֿון מצבֿות

האָב איך קיין מאָל נישט געזען.

טאָג און נאַכט וועל איך יאָמערן די נעמען.

דאָ בין איך קיין מאָל נישט געווען.

Be still, dead world.
Hush inside you your own desolation.
Once again withered ornaments will bloom.
We shall rebuild your foundations
On the blood that was spilled.
But the dead will cry in Midnight vigils,
Each corpse—a dripping voice.
Over every grave, like a small candle,
A prayer will flicker.
Each self for himself:
I am myself—
Thousands of slaughtered selves
Will cry in the night.
Dead am I, and not recognized,
My blood not avenged.

Such a wealth of graves
I have never seen.
Day and night I shall wail their names.

Here I have never been.

Midnight vigil*

Max Weber: *Latest News*, 1940.

◄ אָן ייִדן

אָן ייִדן וועט נישט זײַן קיין ייִדישער גאָט.
גייען מיר, חלילה, אַוועק פון דער וועלט,
פאַרלעשט זיך דאָס ליכט פון דײַן אָרעם געצעלט.
ווײַל זינט אברהם האָט דיך אין וואָלקן דערקענט,
האָסטו אויף אַלע ייִדישע פּנימער געברענט,
פון אַלע ייִדישע אויגן געשטראַלט,
און מיר האָבן דיך געפורעמט אין אונדזער געשטאַלט.
אין יעדן לאַנד, אין יעדער שטאָט
איז מיט אונדז אויך געוואָרן אַ גר
דער ייִדישער גאָט.
און יעדער צעשמעטערטער ייִדישער קאָפּ
איז אַ פאַרשעמטער, צעבראָכענער, געטלעכער טאָפּ,
ווײַל מיר זײַנען געוואָרן דײַן ליכטיק געפעס,
דער וואָרצייכן פון דײַן ממשותדיקן נס.
איצט צײלן זיך אין די מיליאָנען
אונדזערע טויטע קעפ.
ס'לעשן זיך אַרום דיר די שטערן.
דאָס געדעכעניש פון דיר ווערט פאַרטונקלט,
דײַן מלכות וועט באַלד אויפהערן.
דער גאַנצער ייִדישער פאַרזיי און פאַרפלאַנץ
איז פאַרברענט.
אויף טויטע גראָזן ווײנען די טויען.
דער ייִדישער חלום און די ייִדישע וואָר געשענדעט —
זיי שטאַרבן אינאיינעם.
ס'שלאָפן עדות גאַנצע,
עופהלעך, פרויען,
יונגעלײַט און זקנים.
אפילו דײַנע זײַלן, די פעלדזן,
די שטאַמיקע ל״ו,
שלאָפן אַ טויטן, אַן אייביקן שלאָף.

ווער וועט דיך חלומען?
ווער געדענקען?
ווער וועט דיך לייקענען,
ווער וועט דיך בענקען?
ווער וועט צו דיר, אויף אַ פאַרבענקטער בריק,
אַוועק פון דיר, כדי צו קומען צוריק?

➤ *Without Jews*

Without Jews there will be no Jewish God.
If we go away from the world,
The light will go out in your poor tent.
For ever since Abraham saw you in a cloud
Your fire has been on all Jewish faces,
Your radiance in all Jewish eyes,
We have shaped you in our own image.
In every country, in every town,
A stranger lived with us,
The Jewish God.
And every shattered Jewish head
Is God's disgraced, broken bowl,
For we were your vessel of light,
The living sign of your palpable wonder.
Now our dead heads
Are counted in millions.
The stars around you flicker out.
The memory of you is dimmed.
Your kingdom will soon fade away.
All the Jewish sowing and planting
Is burned.
On dead grass cries the dew.
The Jewish dream and the Jewish reality are ravaged,
They die together.
Whole tribes asleep—
Babies, women,
Young and old.
Even your Pillars, the Rocks,
The Thirty-Six Just,
Sleep their dead, eternal sleep.

Who will dream you?
Who will remember?
Who will deny you,
Who will long for you then?
Who will go to you, on a nostalgic bridge,
Away from you, to return again?

אֵלֶּה אֶזְכְּרָה וְנַפְשִׁי עָלַי אֶשְׁפְּכָה
כִּי בְלָעוּנוּ זֵדִים כְּעֻגָּה בְלִי
הֲפוּכָה כִּי בִימֵי הַשַּׂר לֹא
עָלְתָה אֲרוּכָה לַהֲרוּגֵי מְלוּכָה

Ben Shahn: *Warsaw, 1943–1963.*
Hebrew Quote from a 13th
century Yom Kippur prayer:
"These martyrs I will remember
and my soul is torn with sorrow.
In the days of our trials there is
no one to help us."

vessel of light—imagery from
the Kabbalah.

Pillars, Rocks—biblical epithets
applied to great sages.

The Thirty-Six Just*

**away from you to return
again**—an allusion to a personal,
religious poem by the Spanish
Hebrew classical poet Ibn
Gabirol, talking to God of fleeing
"from You to You."

די נאַכט איז אייביק פֿאַר אַ טויט פֿאָלק.

הימל און ערד אָפּגעוווּישט.

ס׳לעשט זיך דאָס ליכט אין דײַן אָרעם געצעלט.

ס׳פֿלעמלט די לעצטע ייִדישע שעה.

ייִדישער גאָט, ביסט שוין באַלד נישטאָ.

► מײַן וואָגל-ברודער

כ׳האָב ליב מײַן טרויעריקן גאָט,

מײַן וואָגל-ברודער.

כ׳האָב ליב זיך צוצוזעצן מיט אים אויף אַ שטיין

און אויסשטומען פֿון זיך אַלע רייד.

ווײַל אַז מיר זיצן אַזוי ביידע געפּלעפֿט,

ווערן אונדזערע מחשבות באַהעפֿט —

אין שווײַגן.

מײַן מידער גאָט פֿאַררייכערט אַ פּאַפּיראָס

און פֿאַרציט דעם ערשטן רויך.

ס׳צינדט זיך אַ שטערן, אַ פֿײַערדיק אות.

זײַנע גלידער בענקען נאָך שלאָף,

די נאַכט ליגט אונדז צופֿוסנס ווי אַ שאָף.

מײַן טײַערער גאָט,

וויפֿל תּפֿילות צו אים האָב איך פֿאַרשוועכט.

וויפֿל מאָל האָב איך אים געלעסטערט,

דורך די נעכט,

און געוואַרעמט די שרעקעוודיקע בײַנער

בײַם פֿײַערטאָפּ פֿון וויסן.

און דאָ זיצט ער, מײַן חבר, נעמט מיך אַרום,

און טיילט מיט מיר דעם לעצטן ביסן.

דער גאָט פֿון מײַן אומגלויבן איז פּרעכטיק,

ווי ליב איז מיר מײַן פֿאַרשלאָפֿטער גאָט,

איצט ווען ער איז מענטשלעך און אומגערעכטיק.

ווי דערהויבן איז דער שטאָלצער יורד,

ווען ס׳מינדסטע קינד איז מורד

אין זײַן געבאָט.

דורך יבשות און ימען,

וועלן מיר שוין אַזוי בלאָנדזשען און בלאָנדזשען צוזאַמען.

צו אַ דערמלענדיקן גאָט טראַכט איך אַזוי פֿון זיך:

ס׳שטרעקט זיך אָפֿט אין דער וואָרעמסטער היימישקייט —

אַ ווילדע פֿרעמד.

The night is eternal for a dead people.
Sky and earth wiped out.
The light goes out in your poor tent.
The last Jewish hour flickers.
Jewish God, soon you are no more.

➤ *My Wander-Brother*

I love my sad God,
My wander-brother.
I like to sit with him on a stone
And silence to him all my words.
When we sit like this, dumbfounded together,
Our thoughts merge
In one stillness.

My weary God lights a cigarette
And inhales the first smoke.
A star lights up, a fiery sign.
His limbs long for sleep.
The night lies at our feet like a lamb.

My beloved God.
How many prayers to him have I profaned.
How often have I blasphemed
In the nights,
Warmed my fearful bones
At the firepot of knowledge.
And here he sits, my friend, hugging me,
And shares with me his last mouthful.

The God of my unbelief is beautiful.
How nice is my feeble God
Now, when he is human and unjust.
How graceful is he in his proud downfall,
When the smallest child revolts
Against his command.
Through sea and land,
We two shall ever wander and wander together.

I think to my dozing God of myself:
At times, an alien space
Will spread in the homiest warmth.

און נאָך איידער מען באַנעמט דעם סוד דערפון,
דערפילט מען אַז די אייגענע איבעריקייט
האָט זיך צעבליט ווי מאָן אויף אַ מצבה.
איז דאָס די שטאָט וואָס איך האָב געבויט?
איז דאָס די גאַס וואָס איר האָב איך אָנפֿאַרטרויט
יעדע נאַכט פון מײַן זיכרון?
וויפל זומערן זײַנען מיר דאָ געקומען צו־חלום?
אַהער בין איך געקומען, זיך פאַרוואַרצלען און פֿאַרשטאַמען,
דאָ האָב איך געוואָלט פאַרפלאַנצן שטילקייט
אויף אַן אייגענעם לעבעדיקן בית־עולם
פון טאַטע־מאַמע.
ווײַל טויט האָב איך דאָרט געהאַט איבערגענוג.
אַהער בין איך שוין געקומען אַ יורש פון טויט,
אַן אַנטרוננענער.

דו רעדסט פון זיך,

שווײַגט צו מיר מײַן וואָגל־ברודער,
און איך טראַכט פון אונדז אַלעמען,
אַזוי צו זאָגן:
וויפל חורבן דאַרף אַ פֿאָלק פאַרטראָגן,
אַז ס׳זאָל אין אויפבוי אַלץ נאָך גלייבן.
איצט אַז ס׳וואָלגערט זיך אין שטויבן,
איז דאָס פֿאָלק געטלעכער פון מיר.
ס׳וועלן נאָך פעלקער קומען זיך בוקן
צו זײַן ווייטיק.

אָבער גאָט, מײַן ברודער,
צו וואָס האָסטו אַזוי דערהויבן מײַן פֿאָלק
און צעשטערנט זײַן אומגליק
איבערן גאַנצן הימל?

ווייטיק, בלוט, געלעכערטע הענט,
רחמנות פון אויסגעריסענע אָדערן —
אַ קינדערשער משל מיט נאַרישע רייד.
איך האָב עס געצײלט אויף זעקס מיליאָן,
איך האָב דעם משל געגעבן באַשייד.
מײַן פֿאָלק, מײַן זון, מײַן טרוים.
וועט אייביק בליִען געקרייציקט אויף אַ ליכטיקן בוים.

מײַן גאָט שלאָפֿט און איך וואַך איבער אים,
מײַן מידער ברודער חלומט דעם חלום פון מײַן פֿאָלק.
ער ווערט קליין ווי אַ קינד,
און איך וויג אים אײַן אין חלום פון מײַן פֿאָלק.
שלאָף מײַן גאָט, מײַן וואָגל־ברודער,
שלאָף אַרײַן אין חלום פון מײַן פֿאָלק.

And before you grasp its mystery,
You feel how your own futility
Blossoms like moss on a gravestone.
Is this the city that I built?
Is this the street I confided in
Every night of my memory?
How many summers appeared here in my dream?
Here I came to strike roots and grow stems,
Here I wanted to plant calm
On my own living graveyard
Of father-mother.
I had plenty of death over there.
I came here, an heir of death,
A refugee.

You are talking of yourself,
Answers the silence of my wander-brother,
And I think of all of us:
How much destruction can a people bear
And still believe in re-building?
Now, grovelling in the dust,
My people is holier than me.
One day, nations shall come to bow
To its pain.

But God, my brother,
Why hast thou raised my people
And spread their misfortune like stars
All over the sky?

Pain, blood, pierced hands,
Pity of emptied veins—
A childish fable with silly words.
I multiplied it by six million,
I gave the fable its moral.
My people, my son, my dream
Will blossom forever crucified on a tree of light.

My God sleeps and I watch over him.
My tired brother dreams the dream of my people.
He dwindles, grows small as a baby,
And I rock him into the dream of my people.
Sleep, my god, my wander-brother,
Sleep into the dream of my people.

מיר זײַנען געווען פֿאַרהונגערטע,

צעטראָטענע, פֿאַרשלאַפֿטע ייִדן.

מיר האָבן נישט געוויינט, נישט געמאַכט קיין געוואַלדן.

די ערד האָט אונדז שטיל געהאַלטן.

איצט זײַנען מיר שײנע, שטאָלצע,

שטראַלנדיקע ייִדן.

מיר זײַנען טויטע ייִדן.

מיר האָבן זיך צוזאַמענגעפֿלאָכטן,

פֿאַרברודערט, פֿאַרצווייגט און געוואָרן

אַ וואַלד מיט שוואַרצע ביימער.

דער שומר האָט איבער אונדז געבײַטשט מיט בליצן.

נאָר דער וואַלד האָט געברענט אָן שרעק,

דאָס פֿײַער האָט צו די הימלען גענומען קלעטערן און שטײַגן,

ס'האָבן געזונגען די צווײַגן.

מיר זײַנען געווען קלײַנע, פֿאַרשעמטע טאַטעלעך,

פֿאַרקרענקטע מאַמעלעך.

צו דר'ערד געבויגענע זיידעלעך

און געשטאָרבענע קינדער.

מיר האָבן גאָרנישט געזאָגט,

מיר זײַנען געווען אָן לשון.

פלוצעם האָבן מיר געקראָגן

אַ מוראדיקע און מעכטיקע שטים.

מיר האָבן געשריגן העכער און העכער,

ס'איז פֿון אונדז אַלעמען געוואָרן —

אײַן געטלעכער אַנאָנים.

זיי זײַנען געקומען, געלאָפֿן,

געפֿלויגן, געפֿאָרן איבער אונדזערע לײַבער,

זיי האָבן אויף אונדז געגאָסן הייסן אײַל.

אונדזערע קברימדיקע שטיבעלעך זײַנען פֿאַרשוווונדן.

זיי האָבן אונדז אַרומגעצונדן.

אָבער מיר האָבן געוואַנדלט אין פֿײַער.

די קלײַנע טאַטעלעך זײַנען געוואָרן

וואַלדיקע כאַרן.

און מיר האָבן אַזוי געזונגען:

מיר זײַנען דער וואַלד

און דער וואַלד ברענט,

און גאָט שפּאַצירט מיט אונדז

אין ברענענדיקן וואַלד.

We were starving,
Trampled, feeble Jews.
We did not cry, we did not raise our voices.
The earth bore us quietly.
Now we are beautiful, proud,
Radiant Jews.
We are dead Jews.

We intertwined, as brother
To brother, branched out, became
A forest of black trees.
The watchman lashed lightning over us.
But the forest burned without fear,
The fire climbed up to the skies,
The branches sang.

We were little, timid daddies,
Sickly mommies,
Stooped grandpas,
Dead babies.
We said nothing,
We were tongueless.
Suddenly we took on
A fearful and mighty voice.
We shouted louder and louder,
All together, we became
One divine anonymous.

They came racing,
Flying, driving over our bodies,
They poured hot oil on us.
Our homes, like little graves, disappeared.
They encircled us with fire.
But we were transformed in the flame.
The little daddies became
Forest choirs,
And we sang:
        We are the forest—
        A burning chorus—
        And God walks with us
        In the burning forest.

מיר זײַנען געקראָכן, געגאַנגען,
אויפֿגעשטאַנען צום לעצטן שטײַ.
ס'האָט אונדז אויף די פֿיס געשטעלט
אונדזער שוידערלעכער געשרײַ.
מיר האָבן געשאַסן, מיר האָבן געטויט.
מיר האָבן געשאַכטן און געוואָרגן.
מיר האָבן געזען זייער בלוט,
געזען מיט לעבעדיקע אויגן.

פֿונקען זײַנען ווי שטיקער זון געפֿלויגן.
ווי וווּנדערלעך דער וואַלד האָט געברענט.
און מיר האָבן געשאַסן,
מיר האָבן געזען ווי זייער בלוט איז גערונען,
זייער בלוט האָט זיך געגאָסן.

מיר זײַנען שוין מער נישט געקראָכן, מיר זײַנען געלאָפֿן,
געצילט, געשאַסן און געטראָפֿן.
מיר האָבן געזען זייערע טויטע קעפּ
און געשטאָרבן מיט זייער טויט
אין אונדזערע אויגן.
מיר האָבן זיך אײַנגעפֿלאָכטן, אײַנגעצווויגט,
מיר, די שטומע, האָבן ווי זיגרײַכע קעמפֿער
געשריגן מיט אײן שטים —
מיר, דער געטלעכער אַנאָנים.

מיר האָבן גאָרנישט געוווּנען.
דער וואַלד האָט אָט אויסגעברענט.
אָבער אין דער געטלעכער פֿינצטערניש
שפּאַצירן מיר קליינע טאַטעלעך,
פֿאַרקרענקטע מאַמעלעך,
צו דר'ערד געבויגענע זיידעלעך
און געשטאָרבענע קינדער.
מיר האָבן געזען זייער בלוט
און מיר זײַנען צופֿרידן.
מיר זײַנען שיינע, שטאָלצע,
שטראַלנדיקע ייִדן.

◄ מײַן קינדס-קינדס פֿאַרגאַנגענהייט

אין דער פֿאַרגאַנגענהייט בין איך אַלע מאָל פֿאַרגאַנגען.
ווי אַ וווּנדער פֿאַרגאַנגען.
און אין איצטער בין איך געווען אַ חדר-ייִנגל,

We crawled, we walked,
We rose up to the last stand.
Our own awesome scream
Put us on our feet.
We shot, we killed.
We slaughtered and wrung.
We saw their blood,
We saw it with our living eyes.

Sparks flew up like pieces of the sun.
How beautifully the forest burned.
And we aimed and shot,
We saw their blood running,
Their blood flowing.

We aimed, we shot, we hit—a line from a song by Shmerke Katcherjinsky in Vilna Ghetto about Vitka Kovner who blew up a German military train in 1941.

We no longer crawled, we ran,
We aimed, we shot, we hit.
We saw their dead heads,
We died with their death
In our eyes.
We intertwined, branched inward,
We, the mute, shouted like victorious fighters,
Shouted with one voice—
We, the divine anonymous.

We didn't win.
The forest burned out.
But in the divine darkness
We stroll: little daddies,
Sickly mommies,
Stooped grandpas,
Dead babies.
We saw their blood
And we rejoice.
We are beautiful, proud,
Radiant Jews.

➤ *My Children's-Children's Past*

In the past I always passed away.
I passed like a wonder.
And in the now, I lived

וואָס האָט געלעבט מיט גמרא-געזאַנגען,

ווי אַ חדר-ייִנגל דאַרף לעבן,

מיט אַ צוגעשפּאַרטער זון,

אין אַן אויסגעטראַכטן פּאַלאַץ

פון ייִדישע צרות.

אוי, מיין פּאַלאַץ האָט געברענט ליכטיקער

ווי טויזנט-און-איין-נאַכט.

ס׳האָבן עלטער-עלטער-זיידעס

מיינע געצונדענע חורבנות אויסגעטראַכט.

בין איך אונטערגעגאַנגען מיטן ערשטן חורבן

און מיט דעם צווייטן.

מיך אַליין האָט מען פּאַרטיליקט אין די טויזנטער,

אויפֿגעגאַסן אין הונגערטעג

און מיך צעזייט און צעשפּרייט צווישן די פעלקער.

און סליחות און קינות און שטראָפֿן

האָבן אויף מיר אָנגעוואָרפֿן

אשור, בבל און מלכות-יון

דורך אַלע מיינע תּישעה-באָבן.

און דער הונט און דער סטרוזש

און די זאַמדער שלעגערס

זיינען כּסדר געוווען מיינע יעגערס,

און איך — אַ קליין ייִדיש פיקסל

מיט אַ לעבן אָנגעשראָקן און אָנגעשפּיצט,

האָב זיך באַשיצט מיט אַ ל״ג-בעומר-ביקסל,

וועיל כ׳האָב געמוזט וואַקסן און לעבן איצט,

וועיל אין דער פאַרגאַנגענהייט

בין איך אַלע מאָל פאַרגאַנגען —

ווי אַ וווּנדער פאַרגאַנגען.

אין די מיטעלע יאָרן איז מיר באַשערט

אויג-אויף-אויג צו דערזען

מיין קינדערשן אַמאָל-איז-געווען.

מיין פּאַלאַץ פון ייִדישע צרות

איז נישט קיין לעגענדאַרישער,

און מען ברענגט מיך אום טאָג-טעגלעך

אין די צענדליקער טויזנטער.

ווי האָב איך גאָר געקענט מיינען,

אַז ייִדישע פאַרגאַנגענהייט

איז אַ היסטאָרישער בית-הקברות,

ווי האָב איך זיך געקענט איינריידן,

אַז ס׳ווערן ייִדישע קינדער דערצויגן

אין לוקסוס פון אויסגעטראַכטע צרות.

As a heder-boy should live,
With *Gemore*-melodies,
With a sun saved up for me,
In an invented palace
Of Jewish grief.
Oh, my palace glowed brighter
Than a thousand-and-one-nights:
Great-grandfathers
Had invented the fires of my Destructions.

I went down with the First Destruction.
And with the Second.
Me they annihilated by the thousands,
Devoured in famine,
Scattered among nations.
Assyria, Babylon, Greece—
All burdened me with
Slikhes, Kines and punishments
On all my *Tishe-Bovs*.
The dog and the janitor
And the hoodlums of the sands
Were ever my hunters,
And I—a little Jewish fox,
With a pelt of prickly fears,
Defended myself with a *Lag-Boymer* stick,
Because I had to grow up and live now.
Because in the past
I always passed away—
Passed like a wonder.

In middle age it fell upon me
To see face to face
My childish once-upon-a-time.
My palace of Jewish grief
Is no longer a legend.
Day after day they destroy me
By the tens of thousands.
How could I have thought
That the Jewish past
Is a historical graveyard?
How could I have talked myself into the belief
That Jewish children are brought up
In the luxury of invented grief?

Ge'more*

first destruction . . . second—
the two destructions of the
Temples of Jerusalem, indicating
the downfall of an independent
state and the beginning of Jewish
exile.

Slikhes (Hebrew:
Selihoth)—penitential prayers in
poetic form.

Kines (Hebrew: Kinoth)—songs
of lamentation, recited on days of
mourning.

Tishe-Bov (Hebrew: Tish'a
Be-Av)—the ninth day of the
month of Av, a day of mourning
for the two destructions of the
Temple.

hoodlums of the sands—a
typical scene in a Jewish town:
the Gentiles lived on the
outskirts.

Lag-'Boymer (Hebrew: LaG
ba-omer)—a holiday
commemorating Bar-Kokhba's
uprising against the Romans,
celebrated by children sitting
around bonfires and playing with
mock weapons.

אויג אויף אויג מיט אַלע מײַנע אונטערגאַנגגען,
מײַן חורבן ברענט.
באַלד וועלן מיך דערגרייכן די טויטן פֿון מײַן צײַט.
גאָט, כ'וואָר מײַן קינדס-קינדס פֿאַרגאַנגענהייט.

◂ שאָפֿען-נאָקטורן

א

וועסט קומען מיט קלײַנע רייד
און שלעפֿעריקע אויגן,
וועסט מיר ברענגען פֿולע אוצרות נאַכט.
זע, וויפֿל שעמעוודיקע פֿרייד פֿאַר דײַנע פֿינגער
האָב איך מיטגעבראַכט.
אַזוי וועסטו זאָגן
צו דײַן שווײַגנדיקן באַזינגער,
וואָס וואַרט אויף דיר אילע נאַכט.

צערטלען וועל איך
די געוואַגטקייט פֿון דײַנע באָרוועסע פֿיסלעך,
ווען וועסט אַנטלויפֿן פֿון טאָטנס הויז,
כ'וועל דיר לייענען אַלע שענסטע גריסלעך,
וואָס כ'האָב דיר קיין מאָל נישט געשיקט.
אײַן-אָטעס ביסטו געלאָפֿן איבער אַ שוואַרצער בריק,
כ'וועל דיך שוין קיין מאָל נישט לאָזן גיין צוריק.

אין דער פֿרי וועלן ערשטע טאָגלעך
וואַרעמען די קאַלטע שויב,
צוגעדעקט מיט אַ שטילן טונקל
וועט עפֿענען די אויגן אַ דערשראָקענע טויב.
און איך וועל קום זײַן לעבן דיר,
אַזוי קום אַז דו וועסט זוכן מײַן קול,
און איך וועל זיך דיר דיר אײַנדאַכטן
ווי אַ מעשהלע פֿון אַמאָל.
און איך וועל זיך דיר דיר אײַנדרימלען
ווי אין פֿאַרנאַכטן אַ שווײַגנדיקער בוים.
ווי אַ ציטער פֿון אַ צווײַג.
קום,
ווי אַ שלאָפֿנדיקער בוים.

Face to face with all my Destructions,
My ruin is on fire.
The deaths of my own time will reach me fast.
God, I am becoming my children's-children's past.

➤ *Chopin Nocturne*

I

You will come with small words
And sleepy eyes.
You will bring me full treasures of night.
See, how much bashful joy for your fingers
I have brought,
You will say
To your silent singer,
Who waits for you
Night after night.

I will stroke
The daring of your bare feet
When you run away from your father's home.
I'll read you all the pretty greetings
I've never sent you.
Breathless, you ran over a black bridge,
I shall never let you go back.

At dawn, the first splinters of day
Will warm my cold windowpane.
Wrapped in quiet darkness,
A frightened dove
Will open its eyes.
And I shall barely be near you,
Just barely, so you'll seek my voice.
I shall enter your thoughts
Like a story of once-upon-a-time.
I shall dream myself into you
Like a silent tree in the dusk.
Like a tremor of a twig,
Barely,
Like a sleeping tree.

ב

אין די פֿאַרנאַכטן קומען אונדזערע לעבנס אַנטקעגן
און זיצן אין שאָטן.
מיר שוויַיגן. ס׳איז אונדז ריידן פֿאַרבאָטן.
דיַין קלוג טראַכטן איז דער וויַיסער וויַין
פֿון מיַין זיַין.
כ׳זיפּ דעם קילן געטראַנק
און שריַיב אָפּ דיַין יעדער געדאַנק.

אַ וווּנדערלעך, וווּנדערלעך.
ווי ס׳פֿאָרן זיך אונדזערע טעג
און ווערן נעכט.
פֿון וויַיטן זינגט אַ שטילער ברעג,
אָבער מיר גלייבן קיין מאָל נישט יענעם וועג.
אַ וווּנדער, נאַכטיקער וווּנדער,
מיר עלטערן זיך באַזונדער,
יאָר-איַין יאָר-אויס,
און צוזאַמען ווערן מיר יונגע פֿריַיד.
ווי וויַיל דו טראַכטסט מיך
אויף די כוואַליעס פֿון דיַינע שטומע רייד.
איז וואָס אַז איך בין נישטאָ?
אַז דו ביסט נישטאָ?
די נאַכט אַליין איז דאָ.
און אין איר זיַינען מיר
פֿאַרפֿלאַנצט ווי איין שאָטן פֿון אַ בוים.
קום, קום.

At twilight our lives come together
And sit in shadow.
We are silent. Forbidden to speak.
Your wise mind is the white wine
Of my being.
I sip the cool drink
And write down your every thought.

Oh, wonderful, wonderful.
How our days pair
And become nights.
A quiet shore sings far away,
But we never believed in that way.
Oh, wonder, nightly wonder,
We age separately
Year in, year out,
And grow together in young joy.
How well you invent me
On the waves of your silent words.
So what if I don't exist?
If you don't exist?
The night alone is here.
In it we are
Planted like one shadow of a tree.
Barely.

Max Weber.

◄ זינגענדיקע שאַרפן

ב

ווי פאַרחלומטע יונגען
האָבן מיר געמאָלקן
די צעפיִערטע הימלען
פון רויך און פון וואָלקן.
געשטאַנען פאַרגאַפט.
ס׳האָט גאָרנישט מיט גאָרנישט
פאַר אונדזערע אויגן
זיך איבערגעשאַפט.

ס׳האָבן אונדז געזעטיקט
פאַרבן, קאָלירן.
מיר זיינען געווען גרייט צו שטאַרבן
אויף כוואַליעס פון קלאַנגען.
מיר האָבן רוישן מיט רוישן
באַהעפט אין געזאַנגען;
מיר האָבן געבלעקערצט,
געקניט פאַר זון-פאַרגאַנגען.

פאַרגעצטע יאָרהונדערטער
זיינען פאַרלאָפן,
אונדזערע מוחות זיינען וואַכערהייט געשלאָפן.
קלויסטערס האָבן געוויגט זייערע גלעקער.
מיר האָבן געבוקט זיך
פאַר אַלע דערשרעקער.

וויפל האָט אברם געוואוונען — אַן ערך?
ס׳איז יעדער קינסטלער
אַ טרויעריקער תרח.

ד

אַלע פאַראַנענע ווערטער,
די אויסגעזאָגטע,
די פאָרשטאַנענע,
ליגן אין זייער צעפלעפטער קלאָרקייט.
די אויסגענאָגטע מינען זייערע דרימלען.
ס׳איז אונדזער וועלט
וואָס לאָזט באַלד אַראָפ דעם פאָרהאַנג.

➤ *We, of the Singing Swords*

Parts II and III of the poem, "Singing Swords."

II

Like dreamy youngsters
We milked
The fiery sky
Of clouds and smoke.
We stood amazed.
Nothing with nothing
Was re-created
Before our eyes.

We were sated
With colors and hues.
We were ready to die
On waves of sound.
Noises with noises
We coupled in songs;
We chanted, we worshiped,
Kneeling at sunsets.

Pagan centuries
Flew by.
Our waking minds were asleep.
Churches rocked their bells.
We bowed
To every terror.

How much did Abram win?
Every artist
Is a sad Terah.

III

All the existing words,
The expressed,
The understood,
Lie in their dumbfounded clarity.
Their sucked-dry meanings dozing off.
It is our world,
Soon it will lower the curtain.

אונדזער געזאַנג איז געוואָרן באַטרויבונג.
דער טרויער וואָס איז אויף אַ ווייל
געוואָרן אונדזער דערהייבונג,
ווערט צעוויינט אין בורלעסק.

אונדזערע פּנימער ווייזן
דעם גראָטעסק,
דעם שרעק
פון דולער פאַרפלאָכונג.
לאָמיר וואָס גיכער אַוועק,
איידער מיר פאַרגייען,
צום פּויק און צום טאַץ
פון אַלץ-פאַרלאָכונג.

◄ דאָסטאָיעווסקי

דאָסטאָיעווסקי האָט אַוועקגעשטעלט גאָט
ביי זיך אויפן טיש
ווי אַ פלאַש בראָנפן
און געשליאָקעט.
ער האָט געמייקעט און געווערזעט,
זיך אויסגעניכטערט
און ווידער האָט אים געצויגן צו גאָט
ווי צום פלעשל.
אַ מאָל ווען דאָסטאָיעווסקי האָט זיך געוואַלגערט אויפן דיל,
איז צו אים אַריין אַ זקן.
דער זקן האָט אים, מיט אַ קרעכץ, אויפגעהויבן,
אים אַוועקגעלייגט אויפן האַרטן בעט,
אַרונטערגעצויגן די שטיוול פון די שמוציקע פיס,
אַרומגעוואַשן דאָס מויל,
אויסגעקעמט די פאַרקאַלטנטע און פאַרווערזעטע באָרד,
געגלעט דעם קאַלט-שווייסיקן שטערן.

דאָסטאָיעווסקי האָט געעפנט די טאָטערישע אויגן
און געפרעגט:
ווער ביסטו?
דער אַלטער איז פאַרשוווּנדן.
מיט וואַקלדיקע טריט איז ער צו צום שרייבטיש.
די פלאַש איז געווען ליידיק.
ער האָט אויסגעטרונקען זיין גאָט ביז צום דנאָ.
האָט ער גענומען די פעדער אין האַנט
און אָן אויפהער געשריבן.

Our song became a deafening din.
The sorrow that was for a while
Our elation,
Flooded all in weeping, burlesque.

Our faces show
The grotesque,
The fear of becoming
Dull and flat.
Let us quickly disappear,
Before we decay
Into the drum and the cymbal
Of all-mockery.

► *Dostoevsky*

Part I of the poem.

Dostoevsky put God
On his table
Like a bottle of vodka
And guzzled.
He retched and vomited,
Sobered up
And was drawn again to God
As to the bottle.
Once, when Dostoevsky writhed on the floor,
An old man came in.
The old man lifted him with a sigh,
Laid him on the hard bed,
Pulled the boots off his dirty feet,
Washed his mouth,
Combed the tangled and vomity beard,
Stroked the cold-sweating forehead.

Dostoevsky opened his Tartar eyes
And asked:
Who are you?
The old man disappeared.
With shaky steps he got to his desk.
The bottle was empty.
He drank his God to the bottom.
Then he took the pen in his hand
And wrote and wrote and wrote.

ער האָט מורא געהאַט אויפֿצוהייבן דעם קאָפּ

ווײַל ער האָט געוווּסט,

אַז דער אַלטער שטײט איבער אים,

וואַכט איבער אים,

מיט זײַן גוטער, מענטשלעכער ניכטערקייט.

האָט אים דאָסטאָיעווסקי אויך אַרײַנגעשריבן אין זײַנע ביכער.

◄ כ׳וועל זיך אײַנגלויבערן

כ׳וועל זיך אײַנגלויבערן אין דעם שטײַבעלע וווּנדער,

וואָס פֿלעקט דעם אויסזיכט אויף צוריק,

אַזוי ווײַט ווי דער טונקעלער בליק

קען צוריקחלומען, צוריקזען.

אין דעם אויפֿגעטײַכטן,

אויפֿגעלויכטן טונקל,

העלט אויף אַ האַלבער

אָפֿגעראַטעוועטער שטערן,

וואָס האָט נישט באַוויזן חרוב צו ווערן,

אַ שטיק אויפֿגעריסענער פּלאַנעט

וואָס האָט אַמאָל געהאַט לעבן,

גרינע שפֿע, פֿאַשעדיקע זעט.

עדות: מײַנע טרערן-פֿאַרלאָפֿענע אויגן,

די ווײַטע פּלאַראַ, די בלוט-באַטריבטע,

אונטער אַ הימל פֿון אייביקן אונטערגאַנג;

די בלעטער, וואָס וויגן זיך ווי גלעקער,

באַטויבטע, אָן קלאַנג,

אויף פֿון קיינעם-נישט-געזעענע ביימער

אין אַ ליידיקער וועלט.

כ׳וועל זיך אײַנעקשנען,

זיך אײַנפֿלאַנצן

אין אַן אייגענער, אינטימער נאַכט,

וואָס איך האָב אינגאַנצן אויסגעטראַכט

און אַרומגעוווּנדערט פֿון אַלע זײַטן.

כ׳וועל געפֿינען אַן אָרט אין רוים,

ווי אַ פֿליג די גרויס,

און מיט גוואַלד אַוועקשטעלן דאָרט,

אויף אַלע צײַטן

אַ וויג, אַ קינד,

אַרײַנזינגען אין דעם אַ קול

פֿון אַ דרימלענדיקן טאַטן,

He wouldn't raise his head,
Knowing
That the old man was standing over him,
Watching him,
In his good, humane sobriety.

Dostoevsky wrote him into his books.

➤ *I Shall Transport Myself*

I shall transport myself inside the mote of wonder
That blots the view
As far back as my dark gaze
Can dream, can see.
In the up-floating,
Illuminated darkness,
There shines half of
A saved star,
Undestroyed.
A piece of a gutted planet
That once had life,
Green plenty, lush pastures.
Witness: my tear-shot eyes,
The distant flora, hung with blood-grapes,
Under a sky of eternal sunset;
Leaves, swaying like bells,
Deafened, soundless,
On trees never-seen,
In a hollow world.

I shall stubborn myself,
Plant myself
In a private, intimate night
That I totally invented
And wondered-in on all sides.
I shall find a spot in space
As big as a fiy,
And there I shall impose,
For all time,
A cradle, a child,
I shall sing into it a voice
Of a dozing father,

The title of the poem and its opening is a neologism meaning: "I shall believe myself into"; also implying: "I shall drill myself into."

מיט אַ פּנים אין קול,

מיט ליבשאַפט אין קול,

מיט פֿאַרהויכטע אויגן,

וואָס שווימען אין קינדס שלעפֿעריקע אויגן

ווי וואַרעמע לבֿנות.

און אַרומבויען וועל איך אַרום דער וויג אַ ייִדישע שטאָט

מיט אַ שול, מיט אַ לאָ-ינומדיקן גאָט,

וואָס וואַכט איבער די אָרעמע קראָמען,

איבערן ייִדישן פּחד,

איבער דעם בית-עולם,

וואָס איז לעבעדיק אַ גאַנצע נאַכט

מיט פֿאַרדאַגהטע מתים.

כ׳וועל זיך אײַנקלאַמערן מיט די לעצטע טעג,

און אויף צו להכעיס זיי צײלן אין דיר, פֿאַרגליוועווערטער עבֿר,

וואָס האָסט מיך אויסגעלאָאַכט,

וואָס האָסט אויסגעטראַכט

מײַן לעבעדיקע, רײדעווודיקע

ייִדישע וועלט.

זי אײַנגעשטיליקט,

און אין מײַדאַנעק-וועלדדל

מיט עטלעכע שאָס פֿאַרטיליקט.

◄ אין מיטן וועג

שטילט אַ ביסל אײַן דעם פּויקן-מאַרש,

ביז וואַנען מיר, דער דור-המידבר, וועלן אויסשטאַרבן,

זײַט געדולדיק צו אונדז.

פֿאַרלאַנגגזאַמט אײַערע טריט,

זאָל מען מיינען אַז מיר וועלן אויך אָנקומען.

מיר וועלן נישט דערגרייכן.

מיר קענען נישט דערגרייכן.

דער וועג צו פֿאַרגעסנדיקער פֿרײד איז לאַנג.

אַז מיר וועלן פֿאַלן הויבט אונדז אויף,

טראָגט אונדז ווי הייליקע ספֿרים פֿון טרויער.

אויב מיר וועלן שטאַרבן,

באַגראָבט אונדז אין מיטן וועג,

ווי שטיקער פֿאַרמעט.

With a face in the voice,
With love in the voice,
With misty looks
That float in the child's sleepy eyes
Like warm moons.
And around the cradle I shall build a Jewish town
With a *shul*, with a vigilant God,
Watching over the poor shops,
Over the Jewish fear,
Over the graveyard
Alive all night
With its worrying dead.

I shall cling to it with my last days.
Spitefully, I shall count them in you, frozen past,
You, who mocked me,
You, who invented
My living, talking
Jewish world.
Then stilled it,
And in Maidanek-woods,
With a few shots
Killed it.

Maidanek—one of the major Nazi death camps, near Glatshteyn's hometown of Lublin.

➤ *In the Middle of the Road*

Could you hush the drums a bit
Until we, the desert generation, die out.
Be patient with us.
Could you slow your pace a bit,
Let them think that we, too, will arrive.

We shall not get there.
We cannot get there.
The road to forgetful joy is too long.
When we fall, lift us up,
Carry us like Holy Books of sadness.
If we die,
Bury us in the middle of the road,
Like pieces of parchment.

This is the first version, published in **Zamlbikher** 7 (1948), at the time of the creation of the state of Israel. When included in book form, the poem lost its last sentence and the strophic divisions were changed.

The desert generation—the generation of the Exodus, destined to die out during forty years of wandering in the desert and not enter the Promised Land. It was said to be contaminated with what in Glatshteyn's day would be called a "diaspora mentality" and unfit for life as a sovereign people.

pieces of parchment—holy books require a pious attitude. Stray pages and pieces of parchment must be buried and not destroyed. Unintentional damage or disrespect calls for fasting and penitence.

און טאָמער וועט איר אונדז פּוגע־בכּבוד זײַן,
זאָל אײַך נישט געגרעקנט ווערן,
דור פון זינגענדיקער עקשנות.
טאָמער וועלן מיר בלײַבן אַליין,
וועט די נאַכט פאַלן אויף אונדזערע ביינער
און פאַרהוילן אונדזערע קברים.
און אַז אונדזערע קברים וועלן אָפּגעמעקט ווערן,
וועט איר ווערן אַ פֿאָלק
פון פאַריתומטער פרייד,

אָן פאַטערלעכן, צערטלעכן טרויער.
אָבער אונדזער טרויער איז נישט נאָר צערטלעך,
נאָר אויך קרעפטיק. אָן אונדז
זענט איר אַ קינדיש פֿאָלק
מיט אַ נאַרישן, פאַפּירענעם גאָט.

And if you show some disrespect,
Let it not be held against you,
Generation of singing intransigence.
If we remain alone,
The night will fall on our bones
And cover our graves.
And when our graves disappear,
You will become a people
Of orphaned joy,

Without fatherly, gentle sadness.
But our sadness is not merely gentle,
It is full of strength. Without us,
You are a childish people
With a silly, paper God.

Max Weber: *Shriftn* 3 Spring 1921.

משה רבינו וואָס איז אין לאַנד ניט אַריַין
האָט זיך דערוואָרט אויף אַ גרויסער זכיה.
ווער פירט דאָס גאַנצע טויטע ייִדישע פֿאָלק
אין צוגעזאָגטן לאַנד אַריַין?
משה רבינו.
ער, דער פּאַסטעך פֿון זיַין שווערס שאָף,
האָט זיך אויפֿגעהויבן פֿון אַ לאַנגן שלאָף.
ווער זאָמלט איצט אַיַין
דאָס גאַנצע טויטע פֿאָלק פֿון אַלע עקן וועלט?
משה רבינו.

דאָס לאַנד איז קליין.
אָבער פֿאַר זיי שטרעקט זיך דאָס הייליקע לאַנד
און ווערט גרעסער און ברייטער.
ווער פירט איצט געטריַי די טויטע ייִדן?
משה רבינו.

און דו, לעבעדיקער יהושע בן נון,
גיי אַוועק אָן אַ זיַיט.
מאַך אַ וואָרע, שטעל אָפּ די זון.
פֿאַרהאַלט די ציַיט.
לאָז אַריַין די טויטע ייִדן.
ווער ציילט די טויטע ייִדן,
צי ס׳פֿעלט חלילה נישט איינער?
משה רבינו.

מיַין טאַטע פֿאַרמאַכט ס׳משניות,
נעמט די מאַמע ביַי דער האַנט,
און פֿאַרנייגנדיק זיך מעשׂה קאַוואַליער,
זאָגט ער:
"ייִטע ראָכעשי, מיר גייען אין ייִדישן לאַנד"
און ביידע גיבן אַ ליכטיקן ווינק צו מיר —
און דו, חכם עתיק, האָסט נישט געגלייבט.

ביַי דער מאַמען ליַיכטן קלוגע טרערן.
זעסט שוין, אפֿילו ס׳וויַיבערישע טיַיטש-חומש
מוז מקוים ווערן.

Our Teacher Moses—the usual way of referring to Moses.

Our Teacher Moses, who didn't get into The Land,
Was awarded a great honor.
Who leads the whole dead Jewish people
Into the Promised Land?
Our Teacher Moses.
He, the shepherd of his father-in-law's flock,
Woke up from a long sleep.
Who gathers now
The whole dead people from all corners of the world?
Our Teacher Moses.

The land is small.
But at their feet the Holy Land spreads
And grows bigger and wider.
Who now faithfully leads the dead Jews?
Our Teacher Moses.

And you, the living Joshua Ben-Nun,
Stand aside.
Make way, stay the sun.
Stop time.
Let in the dead Jews.
Who is counting the dead Jews,
Lest one be missing?
Out Teacher Moses.

My father closes his Mishnah-book,   **Mishnah***
Takes mother's arm,
And bowing gallantly,
He says:
"Yitte-Rokheshi dear, we are going to the Jewish Land"
And both wink at me, with a spark—
And you, wise guy, didn't believe.

Clever tears gleam in my mother's eyes.
You see, even the women's Yiddish Bible
Must come true.

א

זאָלן מיר אפשר אָנהייבן קלײן און ווײגלדיק
מיט אַ קלײן פאָלק?
מיד בײדע פאַרוואָגלטע צווישן פעלקער.
ערד־אַרבעטער וועלן זיך בוקן צו דיר.
וועסט לעבן אויף קרבנות
פון אָנגעברענטן מעל.
איך וועל אַרומגײן און זאָגן פאָלקישע חכמות
וואָס וועלן פאַרבלײבן אין אונדזערע גרענעצן,
אבער ס׳מינדסטע קינד וועט מיך
באַגריסן מיט גוט־מאָרגן.

זאָלן מיר אפשר בײדע גײן אהײם
און צוריק אָנהייבן קלײן פון סאַמע אָנהייב?

מעכטיקער יהוה, וואָס ביסט זיך צעוואָקסן
איבער זיבן הימלען און קאָנטינענטן
און ביסט געוואָרן אַ שטאָלענער וועלט־גאָט,
מיט גרויסע קירכעס און סינאַגאָגעס.
האָסט פאַרלאָזן דאָס פעלד, דעם שטאָל,
איך — די ענגע ליבשאַפט פון מײן פאָלק —
וויי, מיר זײַנען בײדע געוואָרן אוניווערסאַל.
קום צוריק, ליבער גאָט, צו אַ פיצל לאַנד.
ווער אונדזערער אינגאַנצן.
איך וועל אויך אַרומגײן און זאָגן הײמישע רייד,
וואָס מ׳וועט זיי שמועסן אין די שטיבער.
מיר וועלן בײדע זײן פּראָווינציעל —
דער גאָט און דער פּאָעט —
און ס׳וועט אונדז אפשר זײן ליבער.

וועסט אָנהייבן פון קלײנעם אמת,
נישט צוזאָגן קײן זיבן גליקן.
וועסט געדענקען דעם מענטש,
זײן פלײש, זײן בײן, זײַנע חסרונות,
דעם ווײן וואָס דערפרײט ס׳האַרץ פון מענטש,
די פרײד פון לײב.
וועסט אים ליב האָבן אין די רגעס
ווען זײן האַרץ וועט דאַוונען צו דיר מיט גלויבן.
דערווײטערט וועסטו זײן פון בלוט, האַק, מאָרד,
וועסט ליבערשט זײן דער דערגרייכטער גאָט פון מנין,

I

Maybe we should start small, in a cradle,
With a small nation?
We both, strayed among peoples.
Farmers will bow to you.
You will live on offerings
Of browned flour.
I shall walk around and talk folk wisdom,
Which will stay in our own borders,
But the smallest child will
Wish me good-morning.

Maybe we should both go home
And start again small, from the very beginning?

Mighty Jehovah, you who spread
Over seven skies and continents
And became a steel-fast world-God,
With big churches and synagogues.
You forsook the field, the stable,
I—the cramped love of my people—
Alas, we both became universal.
Come back, dear God, to a tiny land.
Be all ours.
I shall walk around and say familiar sayings
That people will talk about at home.
We will both be provincial—
The God and the poet—
And maybe we'll like it better.

You'll start from small truths.
You won't promise the sky.
You'll remember the human being,
His flesh, his bones, his frailties,
The wine that warms his heart,
The joy of the body.
You will love him in the moments
When his heart prays to you in belief.
You will stay away from blood, axe, murder,
You'd rather be the achieved God of a *minyan*

Minyan*

אײדער דער מעכטיקער גאָט פון גזלנים.
וועסט קומען נענטער צו אונדז
און מיר וועלן אָנהייבן צו שפינען
נײַע מענטשלעכע דינים,
גילטיק פאַר דיר, פאַר אונדז.

זאָלן מיר אפשר אָנהייבן ווידיק ווייגלדיק און קליין
און וואַקסן מיט די גרענעצן
פון אַ געבענטשט לאַנד?
קינדער וועלן לאַכן מיט פרייד אונדז אַנטקעגן,
ווייל מיר וועלן זיין אָרעם און אמת,
דיין געטלעכע ברכה וועט זיין פונקט גענוג
פאַר אַ רויִק און גוט פאָלק.
מיין אייגן וואָרט וועט ווערן
דער וואָרעמער נחת פון אַ משפחה.
דיינע נאָזלעכער וועלן שמעקן
דעם סולת פון אַ פאָלק,
וואָס האָדעוועט זיין גאָט
מיט אַלדאָסגוטס.
מיך וועט מען אויך קאָרמען און צערטלען ווי אַ קינד.
און איך וועל פאַרוויגט ווערן
אין אַן ענג-באַקוועמער באַרימטקייט.
און קיינער וועט אויסער די גרענעצן
נישט הערן —
נישט דיין נאָמען און נישט מייִנעם.

זאָלן מיר אפשר ביידע גיין אַהיים?
זאָלן מיר אפשר ביידע, געשלאָגענע, גיין אַהיים?

ב

אתּה בחרתנו.
דו האָסט אונדז אויסגעקליבן.
מ׳האָט אונדז ביידע פאַרשריגן פאַר גרויס,
כדי מ׳זאָל אונדז צעשטויבן און צעשפרייטן
און מאַכן אויס.
דיך האָט מען אויסגעשטערנט איבער אַ גאָנצער וועלט.
ווי קומען צו דיר גרויסע פעלקער?
ביסט שטיל און נחתדיק
און אין גאַנצן אַן אונדזעריקער.
פאַר וואָס האָסטו פאַרלאָזט דיין משכן,
דיין קליין געצעלט,
און אַוועק צו ווערן דער גאָט פון אַ וועלט?
זיינען מיר געוואָרן דיינע זינדיקע קינדער,
די זיילן-שאָקלער, וועלטן-צינדער.

Than the mighty God of plunderers.
You will come closer to us
And we shall begin to weave
New, humane laws,
Valid for you, for us.

Maybe we should start small, rocking,
And grow in the borders
Of a blessed land?
Children will greet us with laughter,
For we are poor and true.
Your divine blessing will be just right
For a quiet and good people.
My own word will become
The warm delight of a family.
Your nostrils will smell
The cream of a people
That raises its God
On all the best.
Me, too, they'll feed and fondle like a child.
I'll be rocked into
A cramped-and-cozy fame.
And no one beyond the borders
Will hear—
Your name or my name.

Shall we perhaps both go home?
Shall we perhaps both, beaten, go home?

    II

Ato bohartonu.
You have chosen us.
Both of us were shouted up big,
So they could scatter us like dust
And make us nil.
You, they spread like stars over a whole world.
What would you have to do with large nations?
You are quiet and contented
And entirely one of us.
Why have you forsaken your shrine,
Your small tent,
And gone to be the God of a world?
And we became your straying children,
Shaking pillars, setting worlds on fire.

Ato bohar'tonu—You have
chosen us.

דאָס ביסטו פריִער פון אונדז געוואָרן אַ ייִדישער אינטערנאַציאָנאַל.
מיר זיַינען דיר נאָכגעגאַנגען אין דער וועלט,
קראַנק געוואָרן מיט דיַין וועלט.
ראַטעווע זיך און קום מיט די עולים
צוריק צו אַ קליין לאַנד,
ווער ווידער דער ייִדישער גאָט.

◄ אָוונטיקע ייִדן

זיי קומען שוין באַלד צו פאַרן,
זיי קומען שוין באַלד צו רייַטן.
גרייט אויפצוקלאָרן און אויפצופראַלן
אַלע באַהאַלטענע קוואַלן
פון ליכטיקע באַטייַטן.
זיי קומען אַלץ פאַרטייַטשן.
טרוקענע מענער זייַנען זיי.
זיי טראָגן לאַנגע בייַטשן.

מאַך זיך נישט וויסן,
האָב הנאה פון ניסים,
אָוונטיקער ייִד,
דייַנע לעצטע באַשערטע יאָרן,
ביז די פאָרסייַקלערס און פאַרטייַטשערס
קומען אָנצופאָרן.

טראַכט זיך גוט אַריַין און דערמאָן זיך,
מיט וואָס פאַר אַ פאַרגלייבטקייט
מיר האָבן געשלאָסן
מיט דער וועלט באַקאַנטשאַפט.
וויי, מיט וואָס פאַר אַ ביטערע פאַרדראָסן
מיר זייַנען געלאָפן פון די דאַוונענדיקע ביימער,
פון טרויעריקן, ייִדיש מענדעלע־לאַנדשאַפט.
וואָס איז דערפון געוואָרן?
באַשערט איז אונדז צו לעבן
אין די ייִדישסטע יאָרן.

ניט נאָר ביימער, נאָר יעדע רגע
איז פאַר אונדז מעביר די סדרה
מיטן טראָפ.
דער פאַרניכטעטער ייִדישער קאָפּ
איז ווידער פאַרחלומט.
ניטאָ קיין איין ניט־ייִדישע שעה.

You were, before us, a Jewish International.
We followed after you in the world,
Became sick of your world.
Save yourself and come with the *Olim*
Back to a small land,
Be again the Jewish God.

Olim—in modern Hebrew,
immigrants to Israel.

➤ *Evening Jews*

Not included in Glatshteyn's
collected poems.

Soon they will come riding,
Soon they will come on planes.
Ready to reveal and explain
All the hidden wells
Of bright meanings.
They have all elucidations in their grip.
Dry men they are,
They carry long whips.

Pay no attention,
Enjoy your miracles,
Evening Jew,
The last years that you get,
Till the brainy explainers
Reason everything flat.

Try to think, to remember,
With how much faith
We concluded
Friendship with the world.
Oh, with what bitter grudges
We fled from the praying trees,
From the gloomy, Jewish Mendele-landscape.
What came of it? What appeared?
We were destined to live
In the Jewishest years.

Mendele-landscape—Mendele
Moykher-Sforim (1835–1917),
Yiddish and Hebrew classical
writer, who saw nature through
"Jewish eyes," describing trees as
swaying in prayer, etc.

Not just the trees, every moment
Reads to us the daily portion
With intonation.
The Jewish head
In annihilation
Is dreaming again.

daily portion—of the Bible, read
during prayers with a special
incantation.

אַ גאַנצן קײַלעכדיקן מעת-לעת
פֿלאַקערט פֿאַר אונדז די אָניאָגנדיקע,
פֿאַרגיכטע,
אָנזאָגנדיקע
ייִדישע געשיכטע.

און דו אָקאַרשטיקער אַנטלויפֿער,
אַלע מאָצאַרטישע חנען
הערסטו דאָך איצטער
אין שאַלן פֿון ייִדישן שופֿר.
זעסטו דען ניט —
אַפֿילו ייִדישע קינדער אין די וויגן
הערן טריט,
ליגן מיט אָפֿענע אויגן, אָן געוויין,
און פֿאַרשטייען די טריט.
צוגעזאַגטע טריט וואָס גייען פֿון זיך אַליין
און שלעפֿן מיט גוואַלד נאָך זיך די גייערס.
זאָלן זיי שפּאַנען, די ייִדישע טריט,
ביז ס׳קומען אָנצולויפֿן
די אויסטײַטשערס און פֿאַשטײיערס.

דאָס זאָלן מיר געדענקען.
די ייִדישסטע יאָרן האָבן מיר דורכגעלעבט.
ווער האָט נאָך געהאַט די זכיה,
צו טראָגן אויף די פּלייצעס
אַזוי פֿיל ייִדישן אומגליק
יאָר-אײַן-יאָר-אויס?
ווער קען זיך גרויסן מיט אַזוי פֿיל זעונג,
און פֿאַרהוילענער אַנטפּלעקונג?
נישט אַוועק די שעה
וואָס מיר האָבן, אין דער גרעסטער דערשרעקונג,
עפּעס נישט געאָנט, געזען,
דאָס האָבן אונדזערע אַקסלען דורכגעטראָגן
די משׂא פֿון ליכטיקן ייִדישן געשען.

באַלד וועלן אויסוואַקסן אונדזערע קינדס-קינדער.
די טריט וועלן מער נישט זײַן
אַזוי הערעוודיק.
מיר וואָס לעבן אַצינדער
און אונדזערע טעג ווערן טונקעלער און ערבדיק —
זאָל אַ געדעכעניש פֿון אונדז פֿאַרבלײַבן.
לאָמיר עס מיט שטאָלץ פֿאַרצייכענען
און פֿאַרשרײַבן:

There is no single non-Jewish hour.
Day and night, like a mystery,
Flares the pursuing,
Accelerated,
Heralding
Jewish history.

And you, who have fled so far,
Now you hear
All Mozartian charms
In a Jewish shofar.
Don't you see—
Even Jewish babies in the cradles
Hear footsteps,
Lie with eyes open, don't cry,
And understand the footsteps.
Promised footsteps, that walk by themselves
And drag the walkers with them.
Let the Jewish footsteps tread on,
Till the explainers and understanders
Come running along.

This we should remember:
We lived through the Jewishest years.
Who else had the honor
Of carrying on their backs
So much Jewish disaster
Year-in, year-out?
Who could boast so much vision,
So much revelation?
Not an hour passed
That in the greatest terror
We didn't see something, didn't sense.
Our own shoulders carried
The burden of bright Jewish events.

Soon our children's children will grow up.
The footsteps won't be heard so loud
Any more.
We, who live now,
And eveninger, darker, grow our days—
Let a memory of us remain.
Let us note with pride,
Let us record:

Shofar*

רײַנע ייִדישע טעג,

באַזונדערע, אויסגעטיילטע,

טרויעריקע ייִדישע טעג,

צעצונדענע, אויסדערוויילטע,

פֿריילעכדיקע ייִדישע טעג,

זײַנען געוו‌ען אונדזערע.

דאָס האָבן מיר דאָך אַרומגעוואָלקנטע

געשפּאַנט דעם נײַ-תנכישן וועג.

מיר זײַנען געגאַנגען צווישן די פֿעלקער,

געהילט אין ייִדישע קיטלען

און געלעבט, געאָטעמט

באַזונדערע ייִדישע קאַפּיטלען.

1949

◄ וויפֿל קריסט

וויפֿל קריסט קען איך עס ווערן, מישטיינס געזאָגט?

וויפֿל רחמנות ליגט דען אין מײַן רשות

און וואָס קען איך פֿאַרגעבן?

זאָל זײַן, כ׳קען זיך וואָרפֿן מיט וועלכע קרישקעס

אויפֿן חשבון פֿון אַ פּיצל לעבן.

אָבער וואָס איז מכּוח דער געטלעכער פֿאַרטיליקונג?

האָב איך דען פֿון זיי געקראָגן היתר און באַוויליקונג?

קען איך זײַן דער פֿאַרערטער

פֿון דעם ברענענדיקן דאָרן פֿון טויט?

אַלע מײַנע פֿאַטשערס האָבן געפֿאַטשט מײַנע ביידע באַקן.

ס׳האָבן קיין מאָל קאָזאַקן נישט געגעבן די געלעגנהייט

אַ משניות-ייִד צו ווערן אַ באַק-אויפֿשטעלער.

וויפֿל ייִד קען איך אין זיך אָפּשמדן, מישטיינס געזאָגט?

אַ כּזית. אַזוי פֿיל רחמנות

קען מען נאָך בײַ מיר אויסבעטלען

פֿאַר די קינדער פֿון מײַנע מצורעדיקע שׂונאים.

אָט דעם כּזית מיטלייד — נעם בײַ מיר צו, פֿאַרטייל אים.

אָבער פֿאַרשאָט נישט מײַן האַרץ

מיט אַ רחמנותדיקן צלם.

Pure Jewish days,
Separate, isolated,
Sad Jewish days,
Blazing, chosen,
Joyful Jewish days—
They were ours.
These were us, surrounded in clouds,
Walking the new-Biblical way.
We were wandering among peoples
With the Jewish walking stick as a scepter,
And lived, breathed,
Separate Jewish chapters.

1949

► *How Much Christian*

How much Christian, so to speak, can I get?
How much pity was left me
And what can I forgive?
Maybe I can throw a few soft crumbs
On the account of one tiny life.
But what about the divine annihilation?
Do I have any permission from them?
Who am I to betray
The Burning Bush of death?

All my face-slappers have slapped both my cheeks.
Cossacks have never given a Mishnah-Jew
A chance to turn his other cheek.
How much Jew can I convert in myself, so to speak?
A pinch. So much pity
They can still get out of me
For the children of my leprous enemies.
This pinch of sympathy—take it from me, toss.
But do not shadow my heart
With a pitiful cross.

a **Mishnah-Jew**—a simple man whose learning goes beyond the Bible to reading the Hebrew Mishnah, but who does not reach the level of a scholar in the Aramaic Talmud.

דין און דורכזיכטיק
די ליבשאַפט פון עלטערע יאָרן.
באַװעגסט זיך אומזיכער
אויף לײַב װי אויף ערד.
מיט רעכענונג נעמסטו די קראָפט דײַנע שפּאָרן,
דערשפּירסט דעם שטאָך פון יעדער טאָג, װאָס איז דיר באַאשערט.

ס׳איז דיר אַ שאָד װאָס האָסט פאַרזען
אַזױ פיל זונפאַרגאַנגען.
און בלומען, בײמער און גראָז
קריצן אײַן אין דיר דאָרניקע געזאַנגען.
טרעטסט אױפֿן לעבן װי אױף גלאָז.
שאָטנס קריגן פאַר דיר אַ טיפן באַטײַט,
נעמסט אָן אַ קילן שמייכל װי אַ געשאַנק,
װערסט קאַרג אויף גאָטס שפע פון צײַט.

Thin and transparent
Is the love of old age.
You are moving hesitantly
On your body as on earth.
With calculation, you are saving your strength,
You sense the sting of each destined day.

You regret having overlooked
So many sunsets.
Flowers, trees, grass
Engrave in you their thorny songs.
You are walking on life as on glass.
Shadows take on a deep meaning,
A cool smile you accept like a gift,
You're stingy with God's plenty of time.

Max Weber: *Shriftn* 3 Spring 1921.

◄ אָן געשאַנקען

אָרעם בין איך. כ׳ברענג דיר מער נישט
קיין געשאַנקען צו טראָגן.
כ׳קום צו דיר נאָענט מיט ליידיקע הענט.
די פסוקים מיט אָפּגעצײַטשטע קעפּלעך
האָב איך לאַנג אַוועקגעוואָרפֿן.
כ׳ווייס ווי דו האָסט תמיד אָנגעקוואָלן
פון סימבאָלן.

ווי צו טרויעריקע שולן,
צו שוועלן פון גלויבן,
אַזוי שווער איז צוריקצוקומען
צו אַמאָליקע ווערטער.
באַקאַנט זענען דיר זייערע ערטער.
הערסט זייער ברומען, ווי מיר.
קומסט אַ מאָל נאָענט, קוקסט פֿאַרבענקט
דורך די שויבן.

אָבער דו ווילסט נאָך אין שאָטן פון תנכישע ביימער,
אָ,זינג מיר קילע טרייסט
פון אַלץ וואָס געדענקסט, אַלץ וואָס דו ווייסט.

◄ הבה, לאָמיר

לאָמיר זיך אַרומוואָרענען
מיט אַ שטיקל פֿאָרק.
נישט קיין געטאָ חלילה,
נאָר אַזוי אַ שטילע וואַנט.
לאָמיר זיך אַוועקזעצן צווישן זיך
און מיט פֿאַרשטאַנד
אויסטראַכטן ווי צו שטאַרקן
אונדזערע אָפּגעשוואַכטע הענט.

דאָס דערווייַלעכץ אונדזערס,
ווי אַ סוכּה צונויפֿגעשלאָגן,
צעפֿאַלט.
ס׳איז אַלץ צעהויקערט, אָפּגעטראָגן
און אַלט.

➤ *Without Offerings*

I am poor. I don't bring you
Any more offerings.
I come near you, empty-handed.
The phrases with their explained-away heads
I threw out long ago.
I know how you always rejoiced
In symbols.

As to sad synagogues,
To doorsteps of belief—
How hard to come back
To old words.
I know well their places.
I hear their humming.
At times I get close, I look longingly
Through the windowpanes.

But you, still resting in the shadows of biblical trees,
Oh sing me chilly consolation
Of all that you remember, all that you know.

➤ *Let Us*

Let us worry around us
A bit of a fence.
Not a ghetto, God forbid,
Just a quiet wall.
Let us sit down among ourselves
And, with reason, invent
How to strengthen
Our weakened hands.

This meanwhiling of ours,
Stuck together like a Sukkah,
Is falling apart.
Everything is hunchbacked, worn out,
Old.

This is the title of a section of new poems published in *Of All My Labor: Collected Poems 1919–1956* (1956). The poems were republished in Glatshteyn's next book, *The Joy of the Yiddish Word* (1961), with minor changes in punctuation (adopted here).

Explained-away heads—an allusion to breaking the neck of the sacrificial chicken, which is then cast away as an atonement on Yom Kippur.

Sukkah—a temporary hut with no roof, of flimsy board construction, used as a dining room during the week of Sukkot.

מיר װילן נאָך נישט אײַנשלאָפֿן,
מיט גװאַלט נעמט מען אונדז פֿאַרװיגן.
הבה, לאָמיר זיך אַן עצה געבן,
לאָמיר זיך קליגן.

◄ עטלעכע שורות

עטלעכע ציטערדיקע שורות אױף דער דלאָניע.
כ׳האָב זײ לאַנג געהאַלטן
און געלאָזט דורכרינען דורך די פֿינגער
װערטערװײַז.

די שטאָט האָט מיך אָפּגעדעקט.
געהערט, געזען, געשפֿירט,
שטײ איך פֿאַרשטריקט
אין אַ גרױסער געפֿאַנגענשאַפֿט.
װאַרף מיך ניט אַװעק
אין מײַן געפֿלעפֿטער שרעק.

ס׳גאַנצע געזאַנג איז דורכגערונען.
מײַן אײלינקײט האָט די גאַס פֿאַרפֿרעכט.
די טעלעװיזיע־שױב שפּיגלט אָפּ מײַן יעדער װאָרט
מיט אַ זעץ פֿון געלעכטער.
די אײנזאַמקײט פֿאַסט מיר װי אַן אַלטמאָדיש נאַכטהעמד.
װאַרף מיך ניט אַװעק
אין מײַן געפֿלעפֿטער שרעק.

◄ שױן באַלד

מיר האָבן שױן באַלד אָנגעװױרן אַלע װערטער.
די שטאַמלמײַלער װערן אָט אַנטשװיגן.
דער ירושה־זאַק איז לײדיק. פֿון װאַנען קריגן
דעם הײליקן פֿלאָפֿל פֿון באַשערטער
פֿרײַד? דעם קינדס גרימאַסן
זענען אַ פֿרעמד להכעיס־לשון
און אין דער טונקל פֿאַרפֿאַסן
מיר בליק־רײד װאָס װערן פֿאַרלאָשן.
און אַש װערט זײער מײַן.
און אַש װערט זײער מײַן.

We don't want to sleep yet,
By force they are lulling us.
Come, let us take counsel,
Let us be wise.

► *A Few Lines*

A few trembling lines on the palm of my hand.
I held them long
And let them flow through my fingers,
Word by word.

The city uncovered me.
I who heard, who saw, who sensed,
Am entangled
In an enormous captivity.
Do not throw me out
In my bewildered fear.

The whole song ran through.
The street profaned my solitude.
The television-pane reflected my every word
With a blow of laughter.
Loneliness fits me like an old-fashioned nightgown.
Do not throw me out
In my bewildered fear.

► *Soon*

Soon we'll have lost all the words.
The stammer-mouths are growing silent.
The heritage-sack is empty. Where can we get
The holy prattle of promised
Joy? A child's grimaces
Are an alien spite-language.
In the dark we compose
Lightning-words, fast extinguished.
    And ash becomes their meaning.
    And ash becomes their meaning.

◄ די פֿרייד פֿון ייִדישן וואָרט

אָ לאָזט מיך צו צו דער פֿרייד פֿון ייִדישן וואָרט.
גיט מיר גאַנצע, פֿולע מעת-לעתן.
פֿאַרקניפּט מיך, פֿאַרוועבט מיך,
טוט מיך אויס פֿון אַלע אייטלקייטן.
באַשפּײַזט מיך דורך קראָען, שענקט מיר קרישקעס,
אַ געלעכערטן דאַך און אַ האַרט בעט.
אָבער גיט מיר גאַנצע, פֿולע מעת-לעתן,
לאָזט מיך נישט דאָס ייִדישע וואָרט
אויף אַ רגע פֿאַרגעסן.

איך וועל ווער שטרענג און געביטעריש
ווי די האַנט פֿון מײַן פּרנסה.
די קאָפֿהענער און דער שאַמפּאַניער
אומפֿאַרדיִען מײַן צײַט.
דאָס ייִדישע וואָרט ליגט פֿאַרשפּייכלערט,
דער שליסל זשאָווערט אין מײַן האַנט.
מײַן מיושבדיקער טאָג רויבט מײַן פֿאַרשטאַנד.

אָ זינג, דערזינג זיך צו נאַקעטער קנאַפּקייט.
די וועלט ווערט פֿעט אויף דײַן געלעגער.
פֿאַר אײַך בײַדן איז באַלד קיין אָרט נישטאָ.
דאָס ייִדישע וואָרט וואָרט אויף דיר געטרײַ און שטום.
און דו זיפֿצסט אין געצונדענעם חלום:
איך קום, איך קום.

► *The Joy of the Yiddish Word*

This is part of a longer poem of the same name.

Oh, let me through to the joy of the Yiddish word.
Give me whole, full days.
Tie me to it, weave me in,
Strip me of all vanities.
Send crows to feed me, bestow crumbs on me,
A leaking roof and a hard bed.
But give me whole, full days,
Let me not forget for a moment
The Yiddish word.

I become stern and commanding
Like the hand of my livelihood.
The capons and the champagne
Undigest my time.
The Yiddish word lies in a granary,
The key rusts in my hand.
My sober day robs my reason.

Oh, sing, sing yourself down to the bare bones.
The world gets fat on your couch.
Soon there will be no room for the two of you.
The Yiddish word waits for you, faithful and dumb.
And you sigh in your ignited dream:
I come, I come.

Max Weber: *Shriftn* ʒ Spring 1921.

◄ גנבע זיך אַרײַן אין סידור

גנבע זיך אַרײַן אין סידור
ווי אַ בלינדער פּאַסאַזשיר,
פּאַסט, און אָן אַ ביסן עסן
פֿאַר גאַנצע מעת-לעתן
ביז צום ברעג.
ליג אײַנגעלייגט אין דײַן באהעלטעניש.
גיב זיך נישט קיין ריר דעם גאַנצן וועג.
און אויב דו וועסט נאָר מיט אַ גלײַך ווערט
אַרײַן אין ריכטיקן אָרט
און דאָס סידורל
מיט ייִדישער פֿרייד באַשטראַלן,
וועט זײַן פֿאַרפֿאַלן.
דאָס סידורל וועט דיך מוזן
אויף אַלע אייביקייטן פֿאַרטראָגן,
און מ׳וועט דיך אויך דאַוונען,
דיך אויך זאָגן.

────────────

אַ ייִד פֿון לובלין (1966)

◄ אינדערפֿרי

אַז איך הייב זיך אָן אינדערפֿרי צוזאַמענשטעלן,
פֿעלן מיר שטענדיק אויס
עטלעכע פּיצלעך שרײַפֿלעך, די גרויס
פֿון דימענט-שפּריצלעך.
כ׳דאַרף זיי נייטיק האָבן פֿאַר מײַן צוזאַמענהאַלט.

ווו בין איך נעכטן געגאַנגען, אויף וועלכע וועגן?
ווו געזעסן? ווו געלעגן?
ווו געפֿאַלן?
מסתּמא פֿאַרטאַכליעוועט,
אפֿשר פּשוט אויפֿגעגעסן, אין טאָג-פֿאַרלויף.
יאָ, מענטשן זענען זייערע אייגענע קאַניבאַלן,
די אייגענע שרײַפֿלעך פֿרעסן זיי אויף.

פֿאַרפֿאַלן.
כ׳שטעל זיך קרעכצנדיק צונויף.
כ׳וועל נישט אַרויס אין גאַס,
ביז כ׳נעם זיך נישט צוזאַמען.

Steal into the prayerbook
Like a stowaway.
Fasting, without a bite,
Travel for days,
Till you reach the shore.
Lie folded up in your hideout.
Do not stir through the whole journey.
And if, with a right word, you get
Into the proper place
And light up the little prayerbook
With Jewish joy,
That will be it.
The little prayerbook will have to
Carry you through all eternities,
And they will *doven* you too,
Will say you.

This is part of a longer poem, "Variations on a Theme." The prayerbook includes poems by Hebrew poets of the past.

doven—pray.

A JEW FROM LUBLIN (1966)

➤ *In the Morning*

When I start to compose myself in the morning,
I always miss
A few tiny screws, the size
Of diamond-sparks.
I need them badly to keep myself together.

Where did I go yesterday, on what roads?
Where did I sit? Where did I rest?
Where did I fall?
Probably squandered,
Perhaps just swallowed, in the rush of the day.
Yes, people are their own cannibals,
They eat up their own screws.

OK.
Sighing, I put myself together.
I won't go out in the street
Till I compose myself.

מאַלע וואָס מיט אַ מענטשן פֿאַרלויפֿט.
זאָל מען נישט דערזען, נישט דערהערן,
ווי טאַנדעטנע־קונציק איך בין צוזאַמענגעשרויפֿט.

קליינע שפֿאַרעס זענען געבליבן אָפֿן,
פֿאַר חרטה־ביסן, פֿאַרדראָסן, זיך־שטראָפֿן,
קעלטן, היצן און ווירוסן.
די זאָוויעסעס פֿון מײַן צוזאַמענהאַנג
רוימען מיר אײַן מיט שפֿאַט,
אויך דער גאַנצער לענג פֿון טאָג,
אויך יעדער טראָט,
ליבע, קליינע, גילדענע,
אַכצן־קאַראַט יסורימלעך,
און מיט זיי זעטיק איך פֿונדעסטוועגן (כּמעט)
יעדער פֿאַרגענינגן.

קליינע ווייטיקן פֿאַרמאָגן אַן אייגענעם ניגון.
אין טאָג־טעגלעכן, אָנגעשטרענגטן צוזאַמענוועבן,
מיינען זיי — לעבן.
הײַבסט זיי אָן נעמען פֿאַר ליב מיטן געדאַנק,
אַז יעדער ווייטיקל איז אַלץ אַ געשאַנק.

◄ מײַן אייניקל־דור

כ'האָב דיך אויסגעבענקט
מיט אַזוי פֿיל יסורים.
כ'האָב דיך אַרויסגעפֿירט,
אַ נאָך־ניט־געבוירענעם,
פֿון ביטערן קלעם,
דיך געבראַכט נאָך אין מײַנע לענדן.
כ'האָב דיר דרײַ מאָל געזאָגט:
אין דײַן פֿאַרגעסעניש זאָלסטו לעבן,
אין דײַן פֿאַרגעסעניש.

דײַן פֿרײַער קאָפּ
איז פֿאַרקרײַזלט מיט פֿרייד.
דײַן אָרעם שטאַרק
און אויסגעשטרעקט.
לאָז מיך דערקענען אין דיר
דאָס קינד פֿון אַנטוויינטע
ייִדישע יסורים.

Who knows what may happen to a person.
Let them not see nor hear
How shoddily and cleverly I am screwed together.

Little crevices are left open
For stings of regret, rue, remorse,
Cold, heat, viruses.
The hinges of my hanging-together
Whisper mockingly in my ear
All through the day,
At my every step,
Dear little golden
Eighteen-carat sufferings.
And with them I nourish
(Almost) every pleasure.

Little pains have their own tune.
In the tense, daily weave
They mean—life.
You accept them lovingly, you know
That every little pain is still a gift.

➤ *My Grandchild-Generation*

I longed for you
In so much pain.
I led you,
Still unborn,
Out of the bitter vise,
I brought you over in my loins.
I told you thrice:
In thy forgetting shalt thou live,
In thy forgetting.

Your free head
Is curled in joy.
Your arm is strong
And outstretched.
Let me find in you
The child of weaned
Jewish anguish.

In thy forgetting shalt thou live—an allusion to the biblical "In thy blood shalt thou live," which was perceived as a symbol for Jewish history.

איצט גיי איך אַליין.

דײַן פרייד דערװוַײטערט דיך.

דײַן קול צװישן די בערג

פֿאַרשפֿאַט מײַן פֿאָרדאַװנטע עלטער.

צװישן די בערג װעל איך פֿאַלן

און װערן אַ בריק.

און דור נאָך דור װעל איך בענקען

נאָך דײַנע טריט —

הין און קריק,

הין און קריק.

◄ כ׳טו דערמאָנען

נאָך די זאַכן װיל איך דערמאָנען,

די באַזונדערע קלענערע חורבנות,

װאָס זענען צײַטיק געװאָרן אין מיר.

די שטילע אומגליקן װאָס זענען אין מיר אויפֿגעגאַנגען,

װי קלײנע שרעקעװדיקע זונען

און ביסלעכװײַז פֿאַרגאַנגען,

אַרומגעװאָלקנט מיט אייגענע יאָרן.

נאָך די זאַכן טו איך דערמאָנען,

די באָרװעסע חלום-סטעזשקע,

װאָס האָט װי אַ פרײדיקער שניט

דורכגעבליצט דורך דער מאָפֿע

פֿון מײַן פֿאַרבענקטן שלאָף,

דעם שטילן װעג װאָס האָט צוזאַמענגעקרייצט

אַלע לענדער, אַלע גאַסן, אַלע הײַזער,

אויף איין אויפֿגעשראַקענער, אויפֿגעװאַכטער
ייִדנגאַס,

װאָס האָט מיט אירע װאַרעמע שטיינער,

טוקלען געהילץ און מצבהדיקן ציגל

אויפֿגענומען מײַנע אָנלויפֿנדיקע טריט.

די בשׂמים-געשעפֿטן,

די קאָשע- און מעל-קראָמען,

די הערינג-געװעלבלעך,

די נאַפֿט-קלייטן און די געזייפֿטע ראָזורעס,

די שײטל- און פֿאַרוק-מאַכערס,

די מאַנדלען, טײטלען און פֿײַגן,

דאָס פריש-געבאַקענע זויער-ברויט,

די מאַן-און-געציבלטע-פֿלעצלעך,

די חושכדיקע טשײניעס,

מיט די דרימלענדיקע, שװאַרצע װערעם

Now I walk alone.
Your joy takes you far away.
Your voice in the mountains
Mocks my praying old age.
I shall fall between the mountains
And become a bridge.
Generation after generation I shall long
For your steps—
There and back,
There and back.

➤ *I Shall Remember*

And these too I want to remember,
The separate, smaller destructions,
That ripened in me.
The quiet calamities that rose in me
Like little frightened suns
And slowly declined,
Clouded in private years.
And these too I shall remember.
The barefoot dream-path,
Like lightening,
A joyful flash through the map
Of my nostalgic sleep,
The quiet road that brought together
All the countries, streets, houses
Into one scared-awake
Jewstreet,
With its warm stones,
Its moldy wood and somber bricks,
Accepting my light feet.
The spice shops,
The kasha-and-flour stores,
The herring stands,
The kerosene vendors, the soapy barbershops,
The toupee- and wig-makers,
The almonds, dates and figs,
The freshly-baked sour-bread
The poppy-seed and onion rolls,
The dark tearooms
With drowsing, black worms

Ben Shahn: *Boy with Cap*, 1965.

אויפֿן וואַרעמען פֿיעקעליק,
די מאַגערע לאַנקעס,
די פֿאַרדרימלטע און האַלב-לעבעדיקע בית-עלמינס,
וואָס האָבן שטענדיק באַוואַכט
דאָס אָנגעשראָקענע לעבן.

אַלץ האָט געוואָרט אויף דעם ברען און ברי
פֿון דעם ייִנגלס סאָפֿענדיקע,
אָנלויפֿנדיקע טריט
און איז זיך צוזאַמענגעקומען אויף דעם איינציקן,
שאַרפֿן און פֿריידיקן שניט,
פֿון דער חלום-סטעזשקע,
וואָס האָט געהייסן היים.

דאָס ייִנגל לויפֿט לויפֿט פֿאַרבײַ
און די פֿאַרשוואָרצטע, שטעכיקע שטיינער,
זענען באַלזאַמען צו זײַנע מידע פֿיס.
היים. ס׳ייִנגל איז געקומען צוריק אַהיים.
ס׳ייִנגל אין נאָר וואָס אָנגעלאָפֿן.
אויף איין פֿיצל אָרט
איז די גאַנצע אָנגעבענקטע שטאָט
אים געקומען מקבל-פּנים זײַן.
אויף איין שטיקל אָרט
האָבן זיך געגעבן די הענט און צוזאַמענגעחברט
אַלע נײַגעריקע ייִנגלעך און מיידלעך,
כּדי נישט צו פֿאַרנעמען צו פֿיל אָרט,
אויף דער זיגזאַגישער חלום-סטעזשקע.
אָט-די סטעזשקע איז פֿאַרשניטן,
חרוב, אָפּגעוווישט.

ס׳איז נישט קיין סך, אפֿשר
איין געסל, איין טרויעריקער מויער,
האַלב-אײַנגעפֿאַלן פֿון אָנגעבויגענער דערוואַרטונג,
אפֿשר סך-הכּל אַ שפֿאַן,
אפֿשר גאָר נישט מער ווי אַ פֿינטל,
קוים צו געפֿינען מיט אַ פֿאַרגרעסער-גלאָז
אויף אַ גרויסער, פֿאַרווײַסטער מאַפּע,
אָבער דעם קליינעם, באַזונדערן חורבן,
טו איך איצטער דערמאָנען.

נאָך דאָס וויל איך דערמאָנען.
אַן אייגן לעבעדיק תּנכל,
מיט באַוועגלעכע, שטראַלנדיקע,
שטאָלצע אבֿות און אמהות.

On their warm fireplace,
The meager pastures,
The sleepy, half-alive graveyards,
Forever watching over
The frightened life.

All this was waiting
For the fiery breath
Of the boy's panting, light feet,
All this came together on the single,
Sharp and joyful flash
Of the dream-path
Called home.

The boy runs by,
The worn-down, thorny stones—
A balm to his tired feet.
Home. The boy came back home.
The boy just now came running.
On one tiny spot
The whole city, aching with longing,
Came to welcome him.
On one little spot
All the curious boys and girls
Joined hands in a knot of friendship—
Not to take up too much space
On the zigzag dream-path.
This path was cut down,
Destroyed, wiped out.

It is not much, maybe
One lane, one sad wall,
Half-decayed in stooped waiting,
Perhaps altogether one foot,
Perhaps no more than a dot
That you can hardly find with a magnifying glass
On a large, devasted map,
But this small, separate destruction
I shall now remember.

And this too I want to remember.
My own living Bible,
Filled with alert, beaming,
Proud forefathers and mothers.

צו מיר האָבן זיי נישט גערעדט קיין וואָרט,

ווײַל זיי האָבן געמיינט,

אַז איך בין נאָך נישט געבוירן געוואָרן.

אָבער געוויינט האָבן זיי אין מײַנס אַן אייגן תּנך.

געפיטערט זייערע שאָף און געשלאָפן אויף שפּיציקע שטיינער.

ס׳איז נאָך קיינער אַזוי נישט געבוירן געוואָרן,

אין אַן אייגענעם וויגלדיקן אָנהייב ווי איך,

און קיינער איז נאָך אַזוי נישט דערגאַנגען,

צו אַן אייגענעם אָנספּקדיקן סוף.

ס׳איז נאָך קיין באַזונדערער מענטש,

אַזוי באַזונדער נישט אונטערגעגאַנגען.

די קײַטלענדיקע יאָרן האָבן נאָך קיין איין יחיד

אַזוי נישט אַרומגעצירקלט ווי מיך,

און אַזוי נישט פֿאַרלאָשן אין איין מענטשן

די אילומינאַציע פון אַ קיניגלעכן המשך,

ווי אין מיר.

די גאַנצע דערציילטע פֿאַרגאַנגענהייט

איז געווען פֿאַר מיר אַזוי גאָלדיק אמת,

ווי אַ שלאָף-געזעטיקטער נאָכמיטאָג,

ווי אַ טײַערע, אָנגעגאַסענע באַרנע,

וואָס האַלט בײַם אַרונטערפֿאַלן פון בוים.

פֿאַר וואָס איז מיר באַשערט געווען

אָנצוהייבן פון סאַמע אָנהייב

און דערגיין צום סאַמע סוף,

ווי צו אַ באַזונדערער אייגענער תּליה?

ערגעץ ווו, אפֿשר גאָר לעבן דיר,

שטייען נאָך מענטשן אונטערן שאָטן

פון אַ וויגנדיקער פֿעטליע,

אָבער דו קוקסט אַרויף צו דײַן לעצט רעפּטל זון,

צום ווערג-שלייף,

און ביסט אַליין.

צווישן מיליאָנען טויטן איז דאָס

אַ קלאָנגדיקער תּשבורת,

אָבער נאָך דאָס מוז איך דערמאָנען,

דעם אייגענעם אָנהייב,

און דעם אייגענעם, באַזונדערן סוף.

אַ גרויס פֿאָלקס-מעשׂה-ביכל

האָט זיך פֿאַרמאַכט,

אַ גאַנץ פֿאָלק האָט אַ קוש געטאָן

דעם טאָוול פון בלוטיקן חזק-חזק,

און געשטאָרבן מיט שמע-ישׂראל.

To me they didn't say a word,
They thought
I was not yet born.
But they lived in my own private Bible,
Grazed their sheep and slept on sharp stones.
No one was ever born like this,
In his own cradled beginning.
And no one arrived like this
At his own inevitable end.
No separate person ever
Declined so separately.
The chain of the years has never
Encircled an individual like me,
Has never extinguished in one man
The illumination of a royal continuity,
As in me.

The whole recounted past
Was for me so golden true—
Like a sleep-filled afternoon,
Like an exquisite, juicy pear
About to fall from a tree.
Why was it meant for me:
To begin from the very beginning
And to come to the very end,
As to my own, separate hanging?
Somewhere, perhaps quite near you,
People stand again under the shadow
Of a swaying noose,
But you look up to your last slice of sun,
To the strangling loop,
And you are all alone.

Among millions of deaths this is
A lamentable fraction,
But this too I must remember,
My own beginning,
And my own, separate end.

A big storybook
Is closed,
A whole people kissed
The cover of the bloody *Hazak-Hazak*
And died with Shema Yisroel on its lips.

Hazak-Hazak (take strength)—an allusion to a blessing at the end of reading a holy book.

She'ma, She'ma Yis'roel*

אָבער אין דעם סיום, אויף דעם סאַמע אָפּגרונט,
שימלט ערגעץ מײַן אייגענע קריאת-שמע,
אין אַ קינדערש בעטל
פרומע, האַלב-פאַרדרימלטע אויגן.
אין דײַן האַנט טו איך אַנטרויען
מײַן נשמה.
מײַן אייגענעם, לעצטן שמע-ישׂראל
טו איך איצטער דערמאָנען.

ווען איך האָב אָנגעהויבן,
האָב איך ווי אַ קליין פישל,
גענומען שווימען אין לעבעדיקן תּנכל.
כ׳האָב אַלץ געזען דורך אײַן שמאָל,
טונקל-גרין אויג,
אַ רויִק אינדזעלע.
דער מינדסטער פון מײַן פאָלק בין איך געווען,
און דאָס איז געווען די רבותא,
וואָס איך בין סײַ ווי געווען אַ געקרוינטער.
מײַן טאַטע האָט איבער מײַן פרימאָרגנדיק בעטל געדוכנט
און אין מיר אַרײַנגעזונגען
אַלץ פון סאַמע-סאַמע אָנהייב.
הער, ווי גאָט שוועבט אין דײַן מוחל,
ווי ער גראָבלט דיר דאָס הערצל,
ווי ער באַשוואַרט דיך צו גלײַבן —
בראשית ברא.

און דו האָסט זיך געשפילט מיט גאָט,
און געהערט ווי ער האָט דיך
געלײַטזעליקט.
און דיר מבטיח געווען אַ גאַנץ לאַנד צו אַרבן.
ס׳איז געוואָרן פינצטער,
האָסט מיט קורצזיכטיקע, קינדערשע אויגן
דורכגעליכטיקט די פינצטערניש
און געוואָרן דער יורש-עצר
פון אַן אייגענעם כּנען.
פאַרויס איז געגאַנגען דײַן פאָלק,
און נאָך אים מיט קליינע טריטעלעך,
ביסטו געגאַנגען, מיט אַן אייגענעם
געטלעכן עול אויף די פּלייצעס.

But at the finish, in the very abyss,
Somewhere, covered with mold,
Lies my own Shema,
In a child's cradle—
Pious, dreamy eyes.
In thy hand I shall entrust
My soul.
My own, last Shema Yisroel
I shall now remember.

When I started,
I swam like a little fish
In a living Bible.
I saw everything through one narrow,
Dark-green eye,
A quiet island.
I was the least of my people,
And even so I was crowned,
And that was the glory.
Over my morning cradle, my father
Made a priestly blessing, his head
Covered with a tallis,
And chanted into me
Everything, from the very-very beginning.
Hear, how God hovers in your head,
How He scratches at your heart,
How He implores you to believe:
Bereyshis Boro,
In the beginning He created.

Be'reyshis Boro—the first words of the Bible.

And you played with God
And you heard how He
Lifted your soul.
And He promised you a whole land for a heritage.
It grew dark,
And you, with short-sighted eyes of a child,
You pierced the darkness with light
And became the heir
To your own Canaan.
Before you, your people walked
And after them, with tiny steps,
You walked, bearing your own
Divine yoke on your shoulders.

שוין ביים סאַמע סוף פון וועג איז גאָט געוואָרן אין כּעס,

און ער האָט אויסגעגאָסן אויף דײַן פאָלק

די גאַנצע חומשדיקע תּוכחה.

שטיקער שוועבל זענען געפאַלן דיר אין פּנים,

און דו ביסט אַ האַלב־בלינדער

נאָכגעגאַנגען דעם חורבן,

און דאָס טו איך דערמאָנען.

כ׳געדענק, ווי דאָס גאַנצע לעבעדיקע תּנ״ך

איז געוואָרן אַ רירעוודיקער אַקוואַריום

מיט אַזאַ פלאַטערנדיקער, שופנדיקער פילפאַרביקייט,

אַז דאָס תּנ״ך האָט געפינקלט

און איז געוואָרן אַרומגעזעצט

מיט טײַערע אײדלשטיינער,

אַרומגערשׁ״ט מיט קלאָרקייט,

ביז ס׳איז געוואָרן די געטײַטשטע

און לויטער־געזונגענע געשיכטע פון מײַן אייגן פאָלק.

איך, דער מינדסטער,

ווי אַ שפּאַן אויסגעדאַרט,

האָב אָנגעהויבן צו הערשן

איבער אַן אייגענער ייִדישער געשיכטע.

איך האָב אַ געשריי געטאָן: יהי אור.

און ס׳האָבן אויפגעלויכטן

גמרות, מדרשים,

און ווי אַ פלעמלדיקער דימענט

האָט אַן אויפטוערישער מהרש״א

אַרויסגעשטראַלט פון מײַן רבינס טרוויעריקע אויגן,

פרנסהדיקע, וואָכעדיקע אויגן,

דאגהדיקע, עצבותדיקע אויגן,

חיונה־זוכנדיקע, פאַרטרערטע אויגן,

זיפצנדיקע, דרימלענדיקע,

זעלטן־מנוחהדיקע, שבתדיקע, גן־עדנדיקע אויגן,

שווער און טיף געפערגטע און מיט אַ ניגון

פאַרענטפערטע אויגן.

די צוויי טרערן אין די קעצלדיקע אויגן,

פון גרויסן גמרא־מלמדס שטום טעכטערל,

זענען געוואָרן — איינע אַ לשון־קודשדיקע,

און די צווייטע אַ געטײַטשטע,

אַ שעמעוודיקע טרער,

אַ באַגלייטנדיקע אויף שריט און טריט,

Almost at the end of the road
God became angry
And poured on your people
All the biblical curses.
Pieces of sulphur fell onto your face
And half-blind
You walked behind the destruction,
And this too I shall remember.

I recall how the whole living Bible
Became a moving aquarium
With such a fluttering, scale-shimmering
Rainbow of colors,
That the whole Bible gleamed,
Inlaid with precious stones,
Bathed in a Rashi of clarity,   Rashi*
Till it became the interpreted,
Lucidly sung history of my own people.
I, the least of them,
Thin as a chip,
Became the sovereign
Of my own Jewish history.
I cried out: *Let there be light*.

And pages of Talmud and Midrash
Flowed with light.
A sprightly *Maharsha*,   Maharsha—Talmudic
Like a blazing diamond,   commentator and his
Beamed from my rabbi's sad eyes,   commentary.
Eyes of daily livelihood,
Worrying, sorrowing eyes,
Searching, tear-filled eyes,
Sighing, dreaming,
Eyes of rare calm, of Sabbath, of Paradise,
Deep and heavily questioned and with a melody   Questioned . . . answered—
Answered eyes.   questions and answers are a major
                                                 form of rabbinical teaching and
                                                 decision making, constituting a
                                                 separate literary genre.

The two tears in the feline eyes
Of my Talmud-teacher's mute daughter:
One spoke the Holy Tongue
And the other—a Yiddish translation,
A timid tear,
Accompanying step by step,

א װידבר-גערעדטע,

װאָס האָט געדינט דעם לשון-קודש

מיט אזוי פיל געטרײַשאַפט,

װאָס האָט אויסגעזויגן ס׳לעצטע ביסל ליכט

פון אַ טונקעלן פסוק,

און אים גלײך דערלאַנגט אויף אַ פרײגעבערישער טאַץ,

װי אַ פון גאַנצן האַרצן פאַרגונען שבת-אויבס,

צו װײבלעך און מיידלעך,

און צו טײַערע, װאַרעמע אמעראַצים,

מיט ריזיק-גרויסע הערצער,

װי ברייט-צעעפנטע טײַסטערס,

װאָס האָבן אָנגעקװאַלן,

װאָס ס׳עפנט זיך אַ טירל, ס׳עפנט זיך דער טײַטש,

ס׳עפנט זיך דער מוח,

ס׳צעפראַלט זיך דאָס גרויסע האַרץ.

ס׳איז שוין דעמאָלט געװען

אזויפיל און אזויפיל לבריאת-העולם,

אָבער בײַ מיר איז די װעלט

געװען אַ פונק-נײַע,

אַן ערשט באַשאַפענע.

מײַן ייִדיש פאָלק האָט ערשט אָנגעהויבן

לײדן פון סאַמע אָנהײב,

מײַן אײגן, קלײן און אָרעם פאָלק,

װאָס מײַן פאַרהאָרעװעטער טאַטע

האָט פאַר מיר אויסדערװײלט.

מײַן לאַנד איז געװען אַ פיצלס,

אָבער ס׳האָט געהאַלטן אין אײן רינען

מילך און האָניק פון אַלע אײטערס,

און ס׳האָט דאָרטן געבליט אַן אײנציקער פײַגנבוים,

אַ טיטלבוים, אַן אײלבערט,

אין דעם לאַנד פון מײַן פאָלק,

װאָס מײַן גוטער טאַטע האָט פאַר מיר אויסדערװײלט.

נאָך דאָס דאַרף איך דערמאָנען:

די אויפגעציליעטע לידער

פון מײַן מאַמען,

די לאַכנדיקע, קלוגע און קרום-געגראַמטע װערטער.

די מחיהדיקע, מוסר-השכלדיקע,

איר שטיל מויל, װאָס האָט זיך אַלע מאָל

פריִער קלוג באַדאַכט,

אײדער ס׳האָט זיך שײן געעפנט

און אַרומגעקײַלעכדיקט אַ באַטעמטן זאָג,

װאָס די גאַנצע משפחה האָט געװאָרט דערויף,

װי אויף אַן עצה-טובה.

An oral, faithful servant
To the Holy Language,
Squeezing the last bit of light
From a dark phrase
And serving it fresh—like Sabbath fruit
On a generous plate—
To women and girls
And to dear warm simpletons
With giant hearts
And wide-open purses,
Who would rejoice
When a little door opened, a meaning unfolded,
The mind expanded,
The big heart opened up.

It was so-many years
After the Creation of the World,
But the world for me
Was spark-new,
Just born.
My Jewish people just now started
To suffer from the very beginning,
My own, small and poor people,
That my toil-weary father
Chose for my sake.
My land was tiny,
Yet ever flowing
With milk and honey from all udders,
And there blossomed a single fig tree,
A palm tree, an olive tree,
In the land of my people,
That my good father chose for my sake.

And this too I should remember:
My mother's songs
Strung like beads,
The laughing, wise and barely-rhymed words,
The refreshing, moral-ended,
Her quiet mouth, that always
First pondered wisely
Before it opened beautifully
And rounded out a tasteful saying;
The whole family was waiting for it
As for good advice.

An oral faithful servant—in the last millennium in Europe, Hebrew was the written language and Yiddish the oral tongue, used for daily life as well as for explicating Hebrew texts. Hebrew was called "the lady," Yiddish "the maid." Written Yiddish was considered a language for women and simple people.

מײַן מאַמע, די שטאָלצע דינסט פֿון איר הויזגעזינד,

האָט צווישן שײַערן, קאָכן,

און וואַשן גרעט,

מיר פֿאַרטרויט דאָס ווונדער

פֿון דעם פּויעריש־ייִדישן גלײַכווערטל,

פּויעריש אײַנגעזעסן אויף אייגענער ערד,

מיט אייגענע קי, אייגענע סעדער,

אייגענער סמעטענע און רויטע יאַגדעס

און געפֿעפֿערטע, האַרטע, געטרוקנטע קעזלעך.

זי, די מאַמע מײַנע, האָב איך געקרוינט

פֿאַר דער מאַמע פֿון מײַן גאַנצן ייִדישן פֿאָלק.

און צו איר און נאָך איר

האָב איך מײַן גאַנץ לעבן געבענקט,

ווען ס׳האָט אויפֿגעלויכטן און אויפֿגעטונקלט

דאָס קליינע פּינטעלע אויף מײַן חלום־מאַפּע.

און נאָך דאָס מוז איך דערמאָנען:

ווען כ׳בין געקומען צו איר מיט גראָטעסקע טריט,

פֿון אַ כלומרשט דערוואָקסענעם,

בין איך שוין געווען כמעט אַזוי אַלט,

כמעט אַזוי טרויעריק

און כמעט אַזוי קלוג ווי זי.

אָבער געזונט האָב איך שוין, אָנלען,

בײַ אַ שטאַרבנדיקער מאַמע,

וואָס כ׳האָב שוין כמעט אָנגעיאָגט אין עלטער.

כ׳האָב באַשיימפּערלעך געזען

ווי דאָס שטילע, געקאָוועטע ייִדיש

איז אויסגעגאַנגען אויף אירע ליפֿן.

אַלע קינדער־שולן, היים־שולן,

פֿאָלק־שולן, גאָרטן־שולן,

גאַנצע און האַלבע שולן,

ייִדישע גימנאַזיעס, רעאַל־שולן,

פֿאַרשעמטע, נישט־געלייענטע ייִדישע ביכער,

אַלע האָבן געוואָרט בײַ איר בעט

און איר געקוקט אין מויל אַרײַן.

פּלוצעם האָט זי געעפֿנט די אויגן

און מיך משלח געווען פֿון צימער.

מײַן קרוין, מײַן אויג אין קאָפּ,

קען נעבעך נישט פֿאַרטראָגן מײַנע לעצטע יסורים —

האָט זי שטאַרבנדיק פֿאַרנומען מײַן צער.

מײַן טײַערע מאַמע, מײַן קלוג מויל,

מײַן אייגן מאַמע־לשון, וואָס איז אַזוי

צערטלעך אויפֿגעגאַנגען פֿאַר מיר

אין לובלינער געשעפּטשעטע פֿאַרנאַכטן.

My mother, the proud servant of her household,
In between scrubbing, cooking,
And washing laundry,
Confided to me the wonder
Of the peasant-wise Jewish proverb,
Rooted like Gentile peasants on their own soil,
With their own cows, their own arbors,
Their own sweet cream and red strawberries
And peppered, hard, dried cheeses.
Her, my mother, I crowned
As the mother of my whole Jewish people.
For her I have longed my whole life,
When the little dot on my dream-map
Lit up and fell dark.

And this too I must remember.
When I came to her with the grotesque steps
Of a would-be adult,
I was already almost as old,
Almost as sad,
And almost as wise as she.
But I wanted to lean on, I sought shelter
In a dying mother,
Though I had almost caught up with her age.
I saw with my own eyes
How the quiet, tended Yiddish
Died out on her lips.
All schools, boarding schools,
Kindergartens, elementary schools,
Day-schools, and half-schools,
Yiddish high-schools, science schools,
Abashed, unread Yiddish books—
They were all waiting at her bed,
Hanging on her lips.

Suddenly she opened her eyes
And sent me out of the room.
My crown, the apple of my eye
Cannot bear my last suffering—
Dying, she sensed my grief.
My dear mother, my wise mouth,
My own mother-tongue, which rose
For me so tenderly
In Lublin's whispered twilights.

Abraham Walkowitz: from
Ghetto Motifs, 1946.

All schools, etc.—an allusion to
the decay of Yiddish cultural
institutions in the face of
assimilation: the mother tongue
is dying with the poet's mother.

מײַן מאַמע-לשון, מיט דעם וועקסענעם פנים,
מיט די יסורים-דערשראַקענע,
האַלב-פאַרמאַכטע אויגן.
נאָך דאָס מוז איך דערמאָנען.

און אַז מײַן צדקותדיקער טאַטע,
וואָס איז געווען מײַן פענצטערל צו דער גרויסער וועלט,
מײַן טאַטע, מיט די זיכערע, נחתדיקע טריט,
מיט די גלייביקע, בטחונדיקע טריט,
אַז ער האָט מיטגענומען מײַן ברודער בנימין,
מיט די גלײַקע אויגן,
און מיט בנימינ'ס ווײַב און קינד
זענען זיי אַלע געגאַנגען מיטן גאַנצן פאָלק,
האָבן זיי באַזונדערע, קליינע, געמאַסטענע, שנײַדיקע טריט
געמאַכט פאַר מיר.
זיי זענען באַזונדער געגאַנגען אויף מײַן שמאָלער אַלײע.
דאָרט, מיטן פאָלק זענען זיי געגאַנגען מיט טריט,
וואָס האָבן זיך געצײַלט, ווי זאַמד בײַם ים,
אָבער פאַר מיר זענען זיי געווען
באַזונדערדיקע טריט,
ווי אייגענע הארץ-קלעפ.
מײַן אייגן פאָלק, וואָס מיט אים האָב איך אָנגעהויבן
מײַן באַשאָפענע וועלט —
שפאַנט איצט צום סוף,
מײַן באַשאָפענע וועלט, וואָס האָט געהאַט אַן אָנהייב,
ברענט איצט אין די לעצטע שעהן פון אונטערגאַנג.

דער גאַנצער הימל לעשט זיך,
אַ גאַנץ תּנכּל ווערט פינצטער און שטום,
אַ גאַנץ לאַנד ווערט חרוב.
ס'גייען מיליאָנען און מיט זיי
מײַן טאַטע, מיט די ווייצלדיקע אויגן,
מײַן ברודער בנימין,
מיט צוטרוילעכער ליבשאַפט, נאָכן טאַטן,
מיט ווײַב און קינד.
און באַזונדער שפאַנען זיי
דורך מײַן חלום-סטעזשקע,
גייען פאַרבײַ, גייען אונטער,
און צערײַסן מײַן גאַנצן חלום,
ווי שפינוועב.

נאָך די באַזונדערע קלעֶנערע חורבנות,
וואָס זענען צײַטיק געוואָרן אין מיר,
האָב איך געמוזט טאָן דערמאָנען.

My mother-tongue, with its waxen face,
With its suffering-scared,
Half-closed eyes.
This too I must remember.

And when my saintly father,
Who was my small window on the great world,
My father with his sure, measured steps,
His believing, trusting steps,
When he took my brother Benjamin
With his glowing eyes
And Benjamin's wife and children,
When they went with the whole people,
They took separate small, measured, cutting steps
For me.
They went separately through my narrow alley.
There, with the people, they walked with steps
Numerous as the sand of the sea,
But for me they were
Separate footsteps,
My own heartbeats.
My own people, with whom I began
My created world—
Now walks to the end.
My created world, that had a beginning,
Now burns in the last hours of its doom.

The light of the sky goes out.
A whole Bible grows dark and mute.
A whole land is laid waste.
Millions walk and with them
My father with his witty eyes,
My brother Benjamin
Behind my father, with trustful love,
With wife and child.
And separately they stride
Through my dream-path,
Pass by, pass away,
And rip up my whole dream
Like a spiderweb.

These separate, smaller destructions too,
That grew ripe in me,
I had to remember.

Abraham Walkowitz: from
Ghetto Motifs, 1946.

Moyshe-Leyb Halpern

1886–1932

Moyshe-Leyb Halpern's first book, *In New York* (1919), established him as a major Yiddish American poet. Here the alienation of a new immigrant in "the Golden Land" was perceived in the framework of a deeply pessimistic worldview, transforming antecedents of a fin-de-siècle decadence into Moyshe-Leyb's peculiar, bitter, or cynical existentialism. *In New York* was a landmark of American Yiddish poetry, thoroughly different from the Expressionist and revolutionary Yiddish poetry of Europe in those years. The book was reprinted in 1927 in Warsaw, then the world center of Yiddish literature, and a third edition was published in New York in 1954.

Halpern's second book, *The Golden Peacock* (Cleveland, Ohio, 1924), was a tour de force, combining elements of Yiddish and Slavic folk ballads, direct naturalistic description with satirical and grotesque overtones, and a lyrical romanticism. In his first two books, Halpern departed from the subjective stance that still dominated the poetry of his contemporaries (the Young Generation), with whom the critics classified him. Among the various modes of dramatizing or objectifying his poetry, he used a gallery of imaginary characters, who served as addressees or as lyrical centers of the poem, detached from the poet himself: Ghingeli, Zarkhi, Yohama, the Princess Vandora, Aby Kirly, and "Moyshe-Leyb" himself—an externalized alter ego presented in the third person by means of an ironic, detached voice. It was this figure of Moyshe-Leyb that became a beloved character among Yiddish readers around the world, evoking dozens of elegies after Halpern's sudden death in 1932.

Halpern's greatest achievement may lie in two posthumously published volumes, composed in part of poems previously published in newspapers (vol. 1) and in part of manuscripts, finished or unfinished (vol. 2). These volumes exhibit freedom in verse; violent outbursts of Moyshe-Leyb's rage and unbridled imagination; his direct, coarse talk and surprising metaphorical shifts; the transformation of political and social reality into the poetic language of a fragmented, chaotic text; and disregard for coherent composition. The strict symmetry of "My Restlessness is of a

Self-portrait, 1922.

Wolf and of a Bear My Rest," written by "Moyshe the Lion"—for which Moyshe-Leyb was known throughout the Yiddish world—gave way to a rude, visionary anarchism punctuated by touching glimpses of human love. His poetry reverberates with topical themes: lynching, the death of Sacco and Vanzetti, unions, speakeasies, shady characters, Manhattan tenement life; it is filled with an anti-imperialist and antiwar pathos, without any of the optimism of his sometime fellow Communists. Paradoxically, these global themes are voiced increasingly in the intimacy of his own private world. The poetic figures of his wife, Royzele, and of his one-and-a-half- or five-year-old son now become Moyshe-Leyb's closest audience.

Although Halpern used characters from his immediate family in his poetry, they are clearly fictionalized. For example, both his grandfathers were well-to-do Galician Jews, one of them a "Kultus President" of a town. In his poetry, however, Halpern carries on a continuous fight with an imaginary stingy grandfather who threw his mother out of the house. Also, Moyshe-Leyb's hometown, Zlochov, becomes a symbol of everything ugly in Eastern-European Jewish life, although it is not clear whether Halpern himself was born in Zlochov (in eastern Galicia, under Austro-Hungarian rule) or in another town, Sosev, only later moving to Zlochov. Similarly, Halpern's father, "Isaac the Haberdasher," was an educated, modern man.

Moyshe-Leyb attended only *heder*, the first stage of a Hebrew religious educa-tion. When Isaac Halpern's business declined, he sent his twelve-year-old son to Vienna to study sign painting. There was no future for a Jewish boy in a small town. The boy spent ten years in Vienna, lived among non-Jews, devoted himself to sport, studied German literature in the evenings, and became interested in Nietzsche and Socialism. His first poems were written in German, and two of them published in a Viennese journal.

Thoroughly assimilated, Halpern returned to Zlochov in 1907. Here, under the influence of two Yiddish poets, he published his first Yiddish poems in the famous Lemberg (Lvov) *Tageblat*. In August–September 1908, Halpern attended the first international Yiddish Language Conference in Czernowitz and, in the same year, arrived in New York.

For several years, lacking steady employment, Halpern hovered on the edge of starvation. Although he lived downtown, the young poet would attend gatherings of Yiddish writers in the "cleaning store" of Yitzchak Bloom in the Bronx. In 1910–11, the "cleaning store" was a literary center where Yiddish writers would sit for hours drinking tea and planning the publication of journals. Desperate Halpern begged for work as a presser there. Bloom later described the world-famous Yiddish poet "standing with a hot heavy iron in his enormous hand, pressing a pair of trousers and reciting verses of a new poem to himself." Suddenly, the smell of burning cloth would interrupt Halpern's inspiration. The big Moyshe-Leyb would stand forlorn like a guilty child. His career as a presser thus came to an end.

In 1912, Halpern was invited to Montreal by the editor of a new weekly, *Di Folkstsaytung*, published by a coalition of Social Democracts, Anarchists, Syndicalists, Labor Zionists, and Socialists-Revolutionaries. He was offered the combined position of assistant editor, reporter, news editor, proofreader, and errand boy. The editor's argument for bringing Halpern from New York was: "Moyshe-Leyb Halpern, in my judgment, is a great poet and will become one of the greatest." On June 7, 1912, a general strike in the Montreal garment industry was called. *Di Folkstsaytung* published a special edition that included the strike proclamation and Halpern's poem, "For the Strike," on the front page. The poem became a popular song among the strikers. Halpern published several poems, short stories, and news articles until the collapse of the journal after twenty-four issues. His friends had to finance Halpern's return ticket to New York.

There he wrote profusely for several humoristic-satirical Yiddish weeklies: *The Kibbitzer, The Jewish Bandit, The Clown.* At the same time, he published a great many poems in the journals of the Young Generation and coedited a number of them (e.g., *From Man to Man*, 1915; *East Broadway*, 1916).

In 1919, after a courtship of ten years, Halpern married Royzele Baron, who became a frequent addressee of his poems. Two years later, the daily Communist newspaper, *Frayhayt*, was founded in New York. Halpern became a permanent contributor, writing and traveling on lecture and reading tours all over the United States. For the first time, he reached a wide audience and was hailed as "the great proletarian poet." Halpern shared the Communists' criticism of the injustices of capitalist America. The Decadent poet became a poet of social protest, taking up such causes as the poverty and exploitation of the masses, racial discrimination, the alienation of urban life. He was, however, never carried away by the Communists' utopian idealism. He knew very well that the Jewish characters of the Lower East Side were not fit material for a revolution (see the poem, "Make for Him a Revolution, If You Can!"). Halpern felt more sympathy for the real people of New York's underworld than for the "leaders"; a pacificist, he mocked both the symbol of power, "the President," and those who encouraged "a just murder," grotesquely deriding their hero worship (see "The Shalamouses"). His vision was one of an anarchist existentialist, bitter about the human condition and sarcastic about the world's rulers. While on a lecture tour in Chicago in 1924, he quarreled with his editors and left the *Frayhayt*. After that incident, Halpern lived for a time in Detroit, Cleveland, and Los Angeles. He was poor, depressed, and often ill.

In 1929, he moved back to New York, living with his family in a tiny apartment in the Bronx, painting portraits, cutting and painting dresses for his wife, and constructing grotesque furniture. When a group of Yiddish writers left the *Frayhayt* in the same year in protest over Communist support for the Arab pogroms in Palestine, Halpern joined them in forming a new weekly, *Di Vokh*. Once again he took an active role in literature, until his sudden death of a heart attack at the age of forty-six.

The poet and critic Jacob Glatshteyn described Halpern thus:

> The embers of unused journalistic thoughts glowed in Halpern. Once he was pregnant with the thought of publishing a journal together with me and writing poetic editorials in it even about the city government. The impulse to write poetic editorials gave birth to such poems as "That Whore, Our Leadership." Then he was a king in all his majesty. He felt that his poem could upset worlds, that he made history with "obscenities." But above all, he was happy when he believed that he moved away from the bird-free singer and transformed his word into immediate reality. Every genuine poet should have a lot of opportunity to write journalism so that he can write it out of his system, steam it out of himself, so that when he comes to write a spoken poem, he is already shouted out. Halpern's temperament was full of song, but he wanted to turn it into moralist talk. He wanted to play the rascal Moyshe-Leyb, he wanted to play out his own truth—the fear of a premature death. This fear was the most authentic in him, so much himself as his own polished word. But he wanted to mislead people with his external aspect of a wolf and with "blood that shouts and burns." (*Sum and Substance*, p. 131)

The texts of the poems we selected from Halpern's two posthumous volumes are reproduced here from the books, as edited by Yiddish poet Eliezer Greenberg, with some corrections from Halpern's manuscripts that are preserved in the YIVO archives. Some of the poems are preserved, in Halpern's beautiful and measured handwriting, in numerous versions; only rigorous textual research could establish their proper order. These brilliant poems still await their careful editor. We have included one example: two versions of the poem, "My Crying-Out-Loud."

The poems from *In New York* included here are a revised version of Kathryn Hellerstein's earlier translations, published in Halpern's *In New York* (JPS, 1982), where the reader will find a fuller representation of the poet's early work.

Memento Mori ◄

און אַז משה-לייב, דער פּאָעט, וועט דערצײלן,
אַז ער האָט דעם טויט אויף די כוואַליעס געזען,
אַזוי ווי מען זעט זיך אַליין אין אַ שפּיגל,
און דאָס אין דער פֿרי גאָר, אַזוי אַרום צען —
צי וועט מען דאָס גלײבן משה-לייבן?

און אַז משה-לייב האָט דעם טויט פֿון דער ווײַטן
באַגריסט מיט אַ האַנט און געפֿרעגט ווי עס גייט?
און דווקא בעת ס'האָבן מענטשן פֿיל טויזנט
אין וואַסער זיך ווילד מיט דעם לעבן געפֿרייט —
צי וועט מען דאָס גלײבן משה-לייבן?

און אַז משה-לייב וועט מיט טרערן זיך שווערן,
אַז ס'האָט צו דעם טויט אים געצויגן אַזוי,
אַזוי ווי עס ציט אַ פֿאַרבענקטן אין אָוונט
צום פֿענצטער פֿון זײַנס אַ פֿאַרהייליקטער פֿרוי —
צי וועט מען דאָס גלײבן משה-לייבן?

און אַז משה-לייב וועט דעם טויט פֿאַר זיי מאָלן
ניט גרוי און ניט פֿינצטער, נאָר פֿאַרבן-רײַך שיין,
אַזוי ווי ער האָט אַרום צען זיך באַוויזן
דאָרט ווײַט צווישן הימל און כוואַליעס אַליין —
צי וועט מען דאָס גלײבן משה-לייבן?

➤ *Memento Mori*

And if Moyshe-Leyb, the poet, tells
That he saw Death on the high waves—
Just as he sees himself in a mirror,
And it was in the morning, around ten—
Will they believe Moyshe-Leyb?

And if Moyshe-Leyb greeted Death from afar
With a wave of his hand, and asked how things are?
Just when thousands of people were
In the water, madly enjoying life—
Will they believe Moyshe-Leyb?

And if Moyshe-Leyb, tears in his eyes,
Swears that he was drawn to Death,
As a man is drawn at dusk in desire
To the window of a woman he adores—
Will they believe Moyshe-Leyb?

And if Moyshe-Leyb paints Death for them
Not gray and not dark, but dazzling and colorful,
As he appeared, around ten in the morning,
Far away, between sky and waves—
Will they believe Moyshe-Leyb?

Moyshe-'Leyb (pronounced as one word with the stress on the last syllable)—the convention of using double names, perhaps carried over in Yiddish from medieval France, was ridiculed as "primitive" or lower class by Europeanizing modern Jews, influenced by the contemporary mores of their neighbors. Halpern's challenging return to such simple popular names ("Moyshe" rather than "Morris") in their hyphenated form has a popular and intimate overtone.

The refrain, reinforced by an almost tautological rhyme: **Tsi vet men dos gLEYBN Moyshe-LEYBN?** ("Will they believe Moyshe-Leyb?") became proverbial with Yiddish readers.

Abraham Walkowitz: *Day of Rest*, (*Shriftn 3* 1921).

◄ גלאַט אַזוי

האָט משה-לייב זיך אַנידערגעשטעלט
אין מיטן דער נאַכט, צו דערטראַכטן די וועלט.
הערט ער צום אייגענעם טראַכטן זיך אײַן —
שעפּטשעט אים עמעץ אין אויער אַרײַן,
אַז אַלצדינג איז גלײַך און אַז אַלצדינג איז קרום
און ס׳דרייט זיך די וועלט אַרום אַלצדינג אַרום.
צופט משה-לייב מיט די נעגל אַ שטרוי
און שמייכלט.
פֿאַר וואָס?
גלאַט אַזוי.

צופט ער אַזוי זיך די שטרוי אין דער נאַכט,
טוט זיך אים נאָך אַ מאָל עפּעס אַ טראַכט.
טראַכט זיך אים — הערט ער זיך נאָך אַ מאָל אײַן —
שעפּטשעט אים עמעץ אין אויער אַרײַן,
אַז גאָרנישט איז גלײַך און אַז גאָרנישט איז קרום
און ס׳דרייט זיך די וועלט אַרום גאָרנישט אַרום.
צופט משה-לייב מיט די נעגל די שטרוי
און שמייכלט.
פֿאַר וואָס?
גלאַט אַזוי.

◄ אונדזער גאָרטן

אַזאַ גאָרטן, ווו דער בוים
האָט זיך זיבן בלעטלעך קוים,
און עס דאַכט זיך, אַז ער טראַכט:
— ווער האָט מיך אַהער געבראַכט?
אַזאַ גאָרטן, אַזאַ גאָרטן,
ווו מיט אַ פֿאַרגרעסער-גלאָז
קאָן מען זען אַ ביסל גראָז,
זאָל דאָס אונדזער גאָרטן זײַן
אָט אַזאַ אין מאַרגנשײַן? —
אַוודאי אונדזער גאָרטן. וואָס דען, ניט אונדזער גאָרטן?

אַזאַ וועכטער, ווייַ און ווינד,
מיט אַ שטעקן ווי פֿאַר הינט,
וועקט ער אויף אין גראָז די לײַט
און פֿאַרטרײַבט זיי ערגעץ ווײַט,
אַזאַ וועכטער, אַזאַ וועכטער,
וואָס בײַם קאָלנער נעמט ער אָן
דעם וואָס האָט קיין בײז געטאָן.

Moyshe-Leyb stops in the middle of the night—
To ponder whether the world is right.
He stops and listens as his thoughts appear—
Someone whispers in his ear
That everything is straight and everything is crooked
And the world spins around everything.
Moyshe-Leyb plucks a straw with his nails
And smiles.
Why?—
Why not.

Just so, he plucks a straw, at night—
And once again a thought arrives.
Again he listens—a thought appears—
Someone whispers in his ear
That nothing is straight and nothing is crooked
And the world spins around nothing.
Moyshe-Leyb plucks a straw with his nails
And smiles.
Why?—
Why not.

► *Our Garden*

What a garden, where the tree is
Bare, but for its seven leaves,
And it seems it is amazed:
"Who has set me in this place?"
What a garden, what a garden—
It takes a magnifying glass
Just to see a little grass.
Is this garden here our own,
As it is, in light of dawn?
Sure, it's our garden. What, not our garden?

What a watchman, brusque and quick,
Walks the garden with a stick,
Wakes the people on the lawn
And to hell he drives them on.
What a watchman, what a watchman—
Grabs a collar or an arm
Of some guys who've done no harm.

זאָל דאָס אונדזער וועכטער זײַן,

אָט אַזאַ אין מאָרגנשײַן? —

אָוודאי אונדזער וועכטער. וואָס דען, ניט אונדזער וועכטער?

אַזאַ פויגל, וואָס פאַרגעסט

זײַנע קינדערלעך אין נעסט,

זוכט פאַר זיי קיין עסן ניט,

זינגט מיט זיי קיין מאָרגנליד.

אַזאַ פויגל, אַזאַ פויגל,

וואָס ער הייבט זיך גאָרנישט אויף

און ער פרווּט ניט פלי'ן אַרויף.

זאָל דאָס אונדזער פויגל זײַן,

אָט אַזאַ אין מאָרגנשײַן? —

אָוודאי אונדזער פויגל. וואָס דען, ניט אונדזער פויגל!

◄ גינגילי

אָ, גינגילי, מײַן בלוטיק האַרץ,

ווער איז דער יונג וואָס טרוימט אין שניי

און שלעפּט די פיס ווי קלעצער צוויי

אין מיטן גאַס בײַ נאַכט?

דאָס איז דער תכשיט משה-לייב,

וואָס וועט אַ מאָל דערפרירן

בעת ער וועט פון פרילינג-צווײַט

און בלומען פאַנטאַזירן;

און וועט ער ליגן שוין אין שניי

און זיך שוין מער ניט רירן, —

וועט ער אין טרוים נאָך דעמאָלט אויך

אין זאַנגען-פעלד שפּאַצירן.

טרוימט דער תכשיט משה-לייב,

זינגט דער וועכטער טרי-לי-לי,

ענטפערט דער באָסיאַק האַפּטשי,

מאַכט דאָס הינטל האַוו-האַוו-האַוו,

מאַכט דאָס קעצל מיאַו.

אָ, גינגילי, מײַן בלוטיק האַרץ,

ווער קריכט אין שניי אַהער, אַהין,

און זעט זיך זיצן בײַם ים קאַמין

אין מיטן גאַס בײַ נאַכט?

דאָס איז דער תכשיט משה-לייב

וואָס פּיילט זיך צו פאַרטראַכטן;

Is this watchman here our own,
One like him, in light of dawn?
Sure, it's our watchman. What, not our watchman?

What a bird, which soon forgets
The small fledglings in its nest,
Doesn't carry food along,
Doesn't sing their morning song.
What a bird, oh, what a bird—
Doesn't lift a single wing,
Or try to fly, or anything.
Is this lazy bird our own,
As it is, in light of dawn?
Sure, it's our bird. What, not our bird?

➤ *Ghingeli*

Oh, Ghingeli, my bleeding heart,
Who is this guy who dreams in snow
And drags his feet like a pair of logs
In the middle of the street at night?

It is the rascal Moyshe-Leyb,
Who will freeze to death someday,
Having fantasies of flowers,
Of blossoms in the spring;
And while lying in the snow
And not stirring anymore,
In his dreams he will still
Stroll through cornfields.

Dreams the rascal Moyshe-Leyb,
Sings the watchman dum-dee-dee,
Answers the bum ah-choo,
Barks the dog bow-wow,
Mews the cat me-ow.

Oh, Ghingeli, my bleeding heart,
Who, in the snow, plods to and fro,
And thinks he sits by a fireplace
In the middle of the street at night?

It is the rascal Moyshe-Leyb
Who is too lazy to think.

Ghingeli (read with two hard "g"s)—a romantic feminine figure invented by Moyshe-Leyb, the addressee of many of his poems.

ער פֿרירט אין שניי און זעט פֿאַר זיך
אַ פֿאַלאַץ אַ פֿאַרמאַכטן
און זיך אַליין דעם קעניג דאָרט
פֿון שומרים אַ באַוואַכטן
און אַלע זײַנע יאָר פֿאַרגיין
ווי זונען אין פֿאַרנאַכטן.

בענקט דער תּכשיט משה-לייב,
זינגט דער וועכטער טרי-לי-לי,
ענטפֿערט דער באַסיאַק האַפּטשי,
מאַכט דאָס הינטל האַוו-האַוו-האַוו,
מאַכט דאָס קעצל מיאַו.

אָ, גינגילי, מײַן בלוטיק האַרץ,
ווער קאַרטשעט זיך אין דרײַען אײַן
און האַפּקעט בײַם לאַמטערן-שײַן
אין מיטן גאַס בײַ נאַכט?

דאָס איז דער תּכשיט משה-לייב,
וואָס שטעלט אין שניי זיך טאַנצן,
כּדי עס זאָלן אים די פֿיס
ניט אײַנפֿרירן אין גאַנצן;
דערבײַ זעט ער דעם שניי אויף זיך
ווי צוויט אין זונשײַן גלאַנצן
און מיידלעך מיט צעלאָזטע האָר
באַצירט מיט פֿײַער-קראַנצן.

טאַנצט דער תּכשיט משה-לייב,
זינגט דער וועכטער טרי-לי-לי,
ענטפֿערט דער באַסיאַק האַפּטשי,
מאַכט דאָס הינטל האַוו-האַוו-האַוו,
מאַכט דאָס קעצל מיאַו.

אָ, גינגילי, מײַן בלוטיק האַרץ,
צי איז דען דאָ אין שטאָט אַ האָן?
ווער האָט דאָס אַזאַ קריי געטאָן
אין מיטן גאַס בײַ נאַכט?

דאָס איז דער תּכשיט משה-לייב,
וואָס האָט ניט וואָס צו זאָרגן,
און ווײַל אים דאַכט זיך אַז דער טאָג
האָט ערגעץ זיך פֿאַרבאָרגן,
און ווײַל אים דאַכט זיך אַז מען האָט
דעם לעצטן האָן דערוואָרגן,
צעקרייט ער זיך אַליין און זאָגט
צו זיך אַליין גוט-מאָרגן.

He freezes in the snow and sees
A palace, closed every wing,
And, guarded by the sentries,
He is himself the King,
And all his years are passing by
Like setting suns at evening.

Yearns the rascal Moyshe-Leyb,
Sings the watchman dum-dee-dee,
Answers the bum ah-choo,
Barks the dog bow-wow,
Mews the cat me-ow.

Oh, Ghingeli, my bleeding heart,
Who curls threefold on himself
And hops in snow by streetlamp-light
In the middle of the street at night?

It is the rascal Moyshe-Leyb
Who stops in snow for a dance—
To keep his feet from freezing
Completely, in the trance;
He sees the snowflakes on his clothes
Like blossoms in sunshine breathe,
And girls with hair let loose
Adorned with fire-wreaths.

Dances the rascal Moyshe-Leyb,
Sings the watchman dum-dee-dee,
Answers the bum ah-choo,
Barks the dog bow-wow,
Mews the cat me-ow.

Oh, Ghingeli, my bleeding heart,
Is there a rooster around?
Who was it crowing in the city
In the middle of the street at night?

It is the rascal Moyshe-Leyb
Who has no worry, no care,
And because he thinks the day
Has hidden itself somewhere,
And because he thinks the last
Rooster has been strangled,
He crows himself and says
Good-Morning to himself.

Moyshe-Leyb Halpern,
Self-portrait.

קרייט דער תכשיט משה-לייב,
זינגט דער וועכטער טרי-לי-לי,
ענטפערט דער באסיאק האפטשי,
מאַכט דאָס הינטל האו-האו-האו,
מאַכט דאָס קעצל מיאַו.

◄ מײַן אומרו פֿון אַ וואָלף

מײַן אומרו פֿון אַ וואָלף און פֿון אַ בער מײַן רו,
די ווילדקייט שרײַט אין מיר, די לאַנגווײַל הערט זיך צו.
איך בין ניט וואָס איך טראַכט, איך בין ניט וואָס איך וויל,
איך בין דער צויבערער און בין דאָס צויבער-שפּיל.
איך בין אַ רעטעניש וואָס מאַטערט זיך אַליין,
אַ פֿלינקער ווי דער ווינט, געבונדן צו אַ שטיין.
איך בין די זומער-זון, איך בין די ווינטער-קעלט,
איך בין דער רײַכער פּראַנט וואָס וואַרפֿט מיט גאָלדן געלט.
איך בין דער יונג וואָס שפּאַנט, דאָס היטל אויף אַ זײַט,
און גנבֿעט פֿײַפֿנדיק בײַ זיך אַליין די צײַט.
איך בין דער פֿידל אויך, דאָס פֿײַקל און דער באַס
פֿון אַלטע קלעזמער דרײַ וואָס שפּילן אויפֿן גאַס.
איך בין דער קינדער-טאַנץ און בײַם לבֿנה-שײַן
בין איך דער נאַר וואָס בענקט אין בלויען לאַנד אַרײַן.
און אַז איך גיי פֿאַרבײַ אַן אײַנגעפֿאַלן הויז,
בין איך די פּוסטקייט אויך וואָס קוקט פֿון דאָרט אַרויס.
אַצינד בין איך די שרעק אין דרויסן פֿאַר מײַן טיר,
די גרוב די אָפֿענע וואָס וואַרט אין פֿעלד אויף מיר.
אַצינד בין איך אַ ליכט, אַ יאָרצײַט-ליכט וואָס ברענט,
אַן איבעריק בילד, אַן אַלטס, אויף גרוי-פֿאַרשטויבטע ווענט,
אַצינד בין איך דאָס האַרץ — דער אומעט אין אַ בליק
וואָס האָט געבענקט נאָך מיר מיט הונדערט יאָר צוריק.
אַצינד בין איך די נאַכט וואָס הייסט מיר ווערן מיד,
דער שווערער נאַכט-טומאַן, דאָס שטילע אָוונט-ליד.
דער שטערן איבער מיר דאָרט אויבן אין דער הויך,
דאָס רוישן פֿון אַ בוים, אַ גלאָקן-קלאַנג, אַ רויך.

Watch Your Step! ◄

גאָלד איז די צײַט אין דעם גאָלדענעם לאַנד.
גיט מען אַ קלונג און אַ הויב מיט אַ האַנט,
קלאַפֿן זיך טירן צו הילכיק און שנעל,
פֿליט דער עקספּרעס דורכן שוואַרצן טונעל

Crows the rascal Moyshe-Leyb,
Sings the watchman dum-dee-dee,
Answers the bum ah-choo,
Barks the dog bow-wow,
Mews the cat me-ow.

➤ *My Restlessness Is of a Wolf*

My restlessness is of a wolf, and of a bear my rest,
Riot shouts in me, and boredom listens.
I am not what I want, I am not what I think,
I am the magician and I'm the magic-trick.
I am an ancient riddle that ponders on its own,
Swifter than the wind, bound tightly to a stone.
I am the summer sun, I am the winter cold,
I am the rich dandy, spendthrift with gold.
I am the strolling guy, hat cocked to a side,
Who steals his own time, whistling with pride.
I am the fiddle, the bass and the flute
Of three old musicians who play in the street.
I am the children's dance and, on moonlit strand,
I am the fool longing for a far blue land.
And, as I walk past a tumble-down house,
I am its emptiness peering out.
Now, outside my door, I am myself the fear,
The open grave waiting for me in the field.
Now I am a candle for a dead soul,
A useless old picture on dusty gray walls.
Now I am the heart—the sadness in eye's glow—
That longed for me a hundred years ago.
Now I am the night that makes me weary soon,
The thick night-fog, the quiet evening-tune.
The star above my head, lost in night's dark cloak,
The rustle of a tree, a clanging bell, smoke.—

➤ *"Watch Your Step!"*

Time is gold in the Golden Land.
The ring of a bell and the wave of a hand,
And doors snap shut, express trains fly
Through black tunnels, quick as the eye.

English title in the original: the
immigrant's identifying signal of
the subway.

שנעלער פֿון ווינט און געשווינדער פֿון בליק,
פֿליִען פֿאַרבײַ מיט דער וואַנט אויף צוריק
שטערן נאָך שטערן אין גרין און אין רויט —
גרין איז דאָס לעבן און רויט איז דער טויט.
לאָזט אַ סיגנאַל זיך פֿאַרויס אין געיעג,
וואַרפֿט ער און שלײַדערט ער אַלץ אויסן וועג.
רודערן רעדער אין ווילדן געלויף,
טראָגן זיך באַנען אַראָפּ און אַרויף,
טראָגן זיך פֿייגל פֿון גאָלד און פֿון גלוט,
צינדט זיך מיר אָן אַ באַגער אין מײַן בלוט
הייסער פֿון גלוט און נאָך העלער פֿון גאָלד.
העי! ווי! ווי עס וואָלט זיך אַ כאַפּ טאָן געוואָלט
אַט-אַזאַ פֿויגל — האַ-האַ, סאַראַ פֿראַכט!
יאַנט ער פֿאַרבײַ ווי אַ בליץ אין דער נאַכט.
יאָגן און טראָגן זיך פֿייגל און פֿליִ"ן
ליכטיק, ווי בליצן, אַהער און אַהין.
ליכטיק, ווי בליצן פֿאַרבײַ נאָכאַנאַנד —
גאָלדענע פֿייגל פֿון גאָלדענעם לאַנד.

Walls fly backwards, like a screen
With star after star in red and in green—
Life is green, and death is red.
Once a signal is sent out ahead
It hurls everything out of its way,
Wheels whirl in a wild hurray,
Trains swing up, swing down, swing fast,
Birds of gold and greed zip past,
Desire ignites in my blood, behold:
Hotter than greed and brighter than gold.
Hey!—If only I could grab in my hand
Such a bird! Oh-Ho, how grand!—
Like lightning flashing in the night.
Birds race and dart and soar in flight,
Brilliant as lightning, flash and expand—
Golden birds in the Golden Land.

Louis Lozowick: *New York*,
1926–27.

צי דען וואָלסטו, מאַמע, מיר גליבן געוואָלט,
אַז אַלצדינג ביי אונדז ווערט פאַרוואַנדלט אין גאָלד,
אַז גאָלד ווערט פון בלוט און פון אייזן געמאַכט,
פון בלוט און פון אייזן ביי טאָג און ביי נאַכט?

— מיַין זון, פאַר אַ מאַמען באַהאַלט מען זיך ניט, —
אַ מאַמע דערקאָנט און אַ מאַמע פילט מיט.
מיר דאַכט זיך, אַז דו האַסט קיין ברויט צו דער זאַט
אויך דאָרט אין דעם גאָלדענעם לאַנד ניט געהאַט.

אוי מאַמע, מיַין מאַמע, צי פאַלט עס דיר איַין,
אַז ברויט ביי אונדז וואַרפט מען אין וואַסער אַריַין
דערפאַר, ווייל עס גיט אונדז אַזוי פיל די ערד,
אַז ס'הייבט אָן פאַרלירן דעם גאָלדענעם ווערט?

— איך ווייס ניט, מיַין זון, נאָר עס ווײנט מיר מיַין האַרץ —
דיַין פנים זעט אויס ווי די נאַכט אַזוי שוואַרץ
און שלעפערדיק פאַלן די אויגן דיר צו,
אַזוי ווי ביי איינעם וואָס חלשט נאָך רו.

— אוי מאַמע, מיַין מאַמע, דו האָסט דאָך געהערט
פון באַנען, וואָס יאָגן זיך אונטער דער ערד,
פאַר טאָג שלעפּט די באַן פון געלעגער אַרויס
און שפּעט אויף דער נאַכט ברענגט זי ווידער אין הויז.

— איך ווייס ניט, מיַין זון, אָבער טיף איז מיַין וווּנד —
איך האָב דיך אַוועקגעשיקט יונג און געזונט —
מיר דאַכט זיך, אָט נעכטן ערשט איז עס געווען.
און היַינט מוז איך ווידער אַזוי-אַ דיך זען.

— וואָס צאַפּסטו מיר, מאַמע, פון האַרצן דאָס בלוט?
צי פילסטו דען גאָרנישט ווי ווײ דאָס מיר טוט?
וואָס וויינסטו, מיַין מאַמע, צי זעסטו דען אויך,
ווי איך אַזאַ וואַנט אַזוי פינצטער און הויך?

— ווי זאָל איך ניט וויינען, מיַין זון, איבער דיר?
פאַרגעסן אָן גאָט און פאַרגעסן אָן מיר.
איצט איז דיר דאָס אייגענע לעבן אַ וואַנט,
וואָס שטייט דיר אין וועג אין דעם גאָלדענעם לאַנד.

— גערעכט ביסטו, מאַמע, מיר זיַינען צעשיידט.
אַ גאָלדענע קייט... און אַן אײַזערנע קייט...
אַ גאָלדענער שטול — אין הימל פאַר דיר,
אין גאָלדענעם לאַנד — אַ תליה פאַר מיר.

Would you, mama, believe if I told
That everything here is changed into gold,
That gold is made from iron and blood,
Day and night, from iron and blood?

—My son, from a mother you cannot hide—
A mother can see, mother is at your side.
I can feel from here, you have not enough bread—
In the Golden Land you aren't properly fed.

—Mama, oh mama, can you not see
That here they throw bread in the sea,
Because, when too bountiful is the earth,
It begins to lose its golden worth?

—I don't know, my son, but my heart cries:
Your face looks dark as the night's skies,
Your eyelids close, your head on your chest,
Like the eyes of a man dying for rest.

—Mama, oh mama, heven't you heard
Of trains racing under the earth,
That drag us from bed at break of dawn
And late at night bring us back home.

—I don't know, my son, but my heart is wrung:
I sent you away healthy and young—
It seems it was just yesterday!
And I want to see you like that today.

—Why do you, mama, sap the blood of my heart?
Can you not feel how it pulls me apart?
Why are you crying? Do you see at all
What I see here—a high and dark wall?

—Why shouldn't I cry, my son? You see:
You've forgotten God and forgotten me.
Now your own life is a wall that will stand
Blocking your way in the Golden Land.

—Mama, you're right. We're divided in pain.
A golden chain . . . and an iron chain . . .
A golden throne—in heaven for thee,
In the Golden Land—a gallows for me.

"Golden" is a Yiddish positive adjective, meaning: endearing, warm, good ("He has a golden heart": altruistic, helping other people; "a golden child": smiling, devoted, peaceful; "a golden idea": a brilliant idea). Here it interacts ironically with the general European image of America as the "Golden Land" (especially after the Gold Rush), where gold is "rolling in the streets."

a golden chain—an image of tradition, linking the generations (as in Peretz's drama, "The Golden Chain").

◄ די מעשה מיט דער וועלט

איך באַפעל מען זאָל איַינעמען די וועלט,
האָט דער קיניג געזאָגט.
איז דאָס לאַנד געוואָר געוואָרן דערפון,
האָט די מאַמע איר לעבעדיקן זון
ווי אַן אמתן טויטן באַקלאָגט.
אָבער דאָס אַקעראַייזן אין פעלד,
און די זויל אונטערן שוסטערס האַמער,
און די מויז אין קאַמער
האָבן שטילערהייט געלאַכט
ווען מען האָט זיי די בשורה געבראַכט
די דאָזיקע פינצטערע בשורה.

איצט האָט מען שוין איַינגענומען די וועלט.
וואָס זאָל מען טון מיט איר?
זי קען נישט אריַין אין דעם קיניגס שלאָס.
מען האָט פאַרגעסן צו נעמען אַ מאָס
פון דער וועלט — ווען מע האָט געמאַכט די טיר.
אָבער דאָס אַקעראַייזן אין פעלד,
און די זויל אונטערן שוסטערס האַמער,
און די מויז אין קאַמער,
קיַיקלען זיך פאַר געלעכטער שוין.
סע ציטערט אַזש ביַי דעם קיניג די קרוין
פון זייער פאַרשיַיט געלעכטער.

די הויפלײַיט מיינען, די וועלט זאָל דערוויַיל
אַ באַוואַכטע אין דרויסן שטיין.
נאָר דער קיניג איז ווי דער טויט אזוי בלאַס.
ער האָט מורא די וועלט קאָן נאָך ווערן נאַס
ווען סע וועט אַ רעגן גיין.
אָבער דאָס אַקעראַייזן אין פעלד,
און די זויל אונטערן שוסטערס האַמער,
און די מויז אין קאַמער,
לאַכן אזוי, אז סע איז שוין אַ שרעק.
זיי שטאַרבן שיַער פאַר געלעכטער אַוועק,
וואָס די וועלט שטייט נאָך אַלץ אין דרויסן.

► *The Story of the World*

I command that the world be conquered,
Thus spoke the king.
When this became known in the land,
The mother mourned her living son
As if he were dead.
But the plowshare in the field,
And the sole under the shoemaker's hammer,
And the mouse in the closet
Quietly laughed in their fists
When the news was brought to them—
The dire news.

So now the world has been conquered.
What shall be done with it?
It can't fit into the king's castle.
They forgot to take measurements
Of the world—when they made the door.
But the plowshare in the field,
And the sole under the shoemaker's hammer,
And the mouse in the closet
Are laughing their heads off.
The king's crown trembles
From their frivolous laughter.

The courtiers think that the world, meanwhile,
Should stand under guard outside.
But the king is pale as death.
He fears that the world will get wet
When the rains come down.
But the plowshare in the field,
And the sole under the shoemaker's hammer,
And the mouse in the closet
Laugh so much it's scary.
They almost die laughing
That the world is still outside.

אַ זלאָטשאָוו, דו, מײַן הײם, מײַן שטאָט
מיט דײַן קלויסטערשפּיץ און שול און באָד.
און מיט דײַנע זיצערקעס אױפן מאַרק
און מיט דײַנע יִדלעך װאָס רײַסן זיך אָפּ
װי הינט אױף דעם פּױער װאָס קומט אַראָפּ
מיט אַ קײשל אײער פֿון סאַסאָװער באַרג —
װי דאָס לעבן אין פֿרילינג װאַכט אױף אין מיר
מײַן אָרעם ביסל בענקשאַפֿט צו דיר,
מײַן הײם, מײַן זלאָטשאָוו. —

נאָר אַז איך דערמאָן זיך פֿאַרבענקטערהײט
אָן דעם נגיד ראַפּעפּאָרט, װי ער גײט
מיט זײַן גראָבן בױך אין שול אַרײַן,
און אָן שײַע הילעלס, דעם פּרומאַק,
װאָס װאָלט װי אַ חזיר אין אַ זאַק
פֿאַרקױפֿט אַפֿילו די זון מיט איר שײַן —
איז דאָס גענוג עס זאָל אױסגײן אין מיר,
אַזױ װי אַ ליכט, מײַן בענקשאַפֿט צו דיר,
מײַן הײם, מײַן זלאָטשאָוו. —

װי דערצײלט זיך די מעשׂה פֿון יענעם פֿאַנט:
ער האָט אײן מאָל פֿאַרנאַכט אַזױ לאַנג נאָכאַנאַנד
געזען מלאכים אַרום דער זון,
ביז סע האָט אים אַ שיכּור, אַ גױ מיט אַ האַק —
אַזאַ מין פֿאַרפֿאַר געטאָן אונטערן פֿראַק,
אַז ר׳איז נעבעך שיִער נישט געשטאָרבן דערפֿון —
דער גױ מיט דער האַק איז מײַן שׂינאה אין מיר
צו מײַן זײדן, און אים צוליב אױך צו דיר,
מײַן הײם, מײַן זלאָטשאָוו. —

דײַן ערד איז אַן עדות, אַז איך טראַכט נישט אױס.
װען מײַן זײדע האָט מײַן מאַמען פֿון הױז
אַרױסגעשטעלט מיט דער פֿאַליציי,
האָט מײַן באָבע אין דער ברײַט מיט די פֿיס
געשמײכלט שיִער אַזױ האָניק-זיס,
װי אַ שיקסע װאָס שטײט צװישן זעלנער צװײ —
אַז פֿאַרשאָלטן זאָל װערן מײַן שׂינאה אין מיר,
װאָס האָט מיר דערמאָנט אָן איר און אָן דיר,
מײַן הײם, מײַן זלאָטשאָוו. —

Oh, Zlochov, you my home, my town
With the church spires synagogue and bath,
Your women sitting in the market place,
Your little Jews, breaking loose
Like dogs at a peasant coming down
With a basket of eggs from the Sassov mountain—
Like life in spring awakens in me
My poor bit of longing for you—
My home, my Zlochov.

But when, steeped in longing, I recall
The rich man Rappeport, how he walks
With his big belly to the synagogue,
And Shaye Hillel's, the pious Jew,
Who could sell like a pig in a sack
Even the sun with all its glowing—
Then it's enough to extinguish in me
Like a candle, my longing for you—
My home, my Zlochov.

How goes the story about that dandy:
Once in an evening he watched for so long
The angels roaming about the sun,
Till a drunken peasant with an axe
Cut him down under his dress-coat,
Poor man: he almost died from that—
The peasant with the axe is my hatred in me
For my grandfather, and through him—for you—
My home, my Zlochov.

Your earth may witness, I'm not making it up.
When my grandfather called in the police
To chase my mother from his house,
My grandmother, her legs spread wide,
Smiled almost as honey-sweet
As a girl standing between two soldiers—
Cursed be my hatred inside me
Which reminds me of her and of you—
My home, my Zlochov.

my home, my town—by breaking up the hackneyed word-compound, "my hometown" (i.e., the town where I was born), he seems to return the full, positive meaning to "home"—which is immediately rendered ironic and defeated.

like a pig in a poke—Jews are not supposed to deal with pigs; the sack covers up for it. The Yiddish idiom alluded to here is: "to sell a cat in a sack."

ווי אַ קופּקעלע נאַקעטע ייִדן אין באַד
אַרום אַ פעברײַטן, האָט מען אין ראָד
געשאָקלט די קעפּ און די בערד זיך געגלעט
אַרום די אַרויסגעװאָרפענע פעק
און שמאַטעס און בעבכעס אין זעק
און אַרום דעם צעבראָכענעם שטיקל בעט —
מײַן מאַמע װײנט נאָך איצטער אין מיר,
װי דעמאָלט אונטער דײַן הימל אין דיר, —
מײַן הײם, מײַן זלאָטשאָװ.

נאָר װוּנדערלעך איז דאָך אונדזער װעלט.
מיט אַ פערד און װאָגן איבער אַ פעלד
שלעפּט מען זיך אַרויס צו דער באַן,
װאָס פליט װי אַ שד איבער פעלדער אַװעק,
ביז זי ברענגט אויף אַ שיף מיט אַ צװישנדעק,
װאָס פירט אַריבער קיין ניו־יאָרק דאָונטאַון —
איז דאָס טאַקע די אײנציקע טרײַסט כאַטש פאַר מיר,
װאָס מען װעט מיך נישט באַגראָבן אין דיר, —
מײַן הײם, מײַן זלאָטשאָװ.

◄ דער פויגל

קומט צו גײן אַ פויגל מיט אַ קוליע אונטערן פליגל
און פרעגט פאַר װאָס איך האַלט די טיר אויפן ריגל.
ענטפער איך אים, אַז פאַרן טויער
שטײען גזלנים אויף דער לויער,
װאָס װילן אויסכאַפן דאָס שטיקל קעז,
װאָס איך האַלט באַהאַלטן אונטער מײַן געזעס.

װײנט דער פויגל דורכן שליסל־לעכל
און דערצײלט מיר, אַז ער איז מײַן ברודער מעכל,
און זאָגט, אַז איך האָב נישט קײן באַגריף
װי ער האָט געליטן אויף דער שיף,
װאָס האָט אים אַריבערגעבראַכט אַהער.
אויפן קרימען — זאָגט ער — געקומען איז ער.

זע איך דאָך שוין, װאָס דער פויגל איז אויסן,
לאָז איך אים טאַקע שטײן אין דרויסן.
דערװײַל אָבער, װי עס מאַכט זיך אַ זאַך,
באַשליס איך בײַ זיך צו זײַן אויף דער װאַך,
און איך שטופּ אַרונטער מײַן שטיקל קעז
נאָך טיפער אונטער מײַן געזעס.

Like a bunch of naked Jews in a bath
Surrounding a man who'd been scalded,
They nodded their heads and stroked their beards
Around the evicted packs and junk,
Thrown-out pillows-and-blankets in sacks,
And around the bit of broken bed—
To this day my mother is crying in me,
As then, under your sky, in you—
My home, my Zlochov.

But our world is full of wonders.
A horse and a cart over the fields
Will carry you out to a railway train,
Which flies like a demon over the fields
Till it brings you to a ship with a lower deck,
Which takes you away to Newyorkdowntown—
And this, indeed, is my only consolation
That they will not bury me in you—
My home, my Zlochov.

➤ *The Bird*

A bird came with a crutch under his wing
And asked me why I bolted my door.
I answered him that before my gate
Robbers are lurking, on the wait:
They want to grab the piece of cheese
That I am hiding under my ass.

At this, the bird wept through the key-hole
And told me that he is my brother Mikhl,
And said that I cannot imagine at all
How he suffered on board the ship
That brought him over to this shore.
On the chimney—he says—he made the trip.

So, I can see what the bird intends,
And I leave him, indeed, outside to stand.
But in the meantime I make up my mind
To be on guard: Who knows what may pass,
And I push my piece of cheese
Further under my ass.

מאַכט דער פויגל, װי מײַן ברודער מעכל,
מיט אַ פליגל איבער די אויגן אַ דעכל
און ער שרײַט דורכן שליסל-לעכל אַרײַן,
אַז אַזוי זאָל דאָס מזל אים ליכטיק זײַן,
װי ער האָט געזען דאָס שטיק קעז, װאָס איך האָב,
און אַז ער װעט דערפאַר מיר שפאַלטן דעם קאָפ.

זע איך דאָך שוין, אַז סע װערט נישט פרײַלעך,
רוק איך זיך צו צום טיר פּאַמעלעך
מיט מײַן בענקל און מיטן קעז,
װאָס איך היט אים אונטער מײַן געזעס
און איך מאַך נישט חלילה קיין געװאַלט,
נאָר איך פרעג אים גלאַט-אַזוי, צי ס'איז קאַלט.

ענטפערט ער מיר, אַז בײדע אויערן
זײַנען בײַ אים אָפגעפרוירן,
און ער שװערט מיר דערבײַ מיט אַ גרויס געװײן,
אַז ער האָט אין שלאָף בײַ זיך אַלײן
אויפגעגעסן דעם פוס, װאָס אים פעלט,
און װען איך לאָז אים אַרײַן װאָלט ער מער דערצײלט.

פאַרשטײט זיך, דערהערט דאָס װאָרט: געגעסן, —
האָב איך זיך דערשראָקן. שיער נישט פאַרגעסן
אָפצוהיטן דאָס שטיקל קעז,
װאָס איך האַלט באַהאַלטן אונטער מײַן געזעס.
נאָר אַבי איך גיב — אַ טאַפ און ס'איז דאָ,
איז דאָך שוין װידער קיין זאָרג נישטאָ.

מאַך איך אַ פאָרשלאָג, מיר זאָלן פרובירן
װער עס װעט די געדולד פאַרלירן:
צי איך, אין מײַן אייגן הויז בײַ מיר,
צי ער, אין דרויסן הינטער דער טיר.
ס'איז, דאַכט זיך, טשיקאַװע אַזוינס צו דערגײן,
אפילו — זאָג איך — פאַר זיך אַלײן.

און אַזוי איז עס טאַקע זינט דעמאָלט געבליבן.
און הײַנט איז שוין אַװעק אַ יאָר זיבן,
שרײַ איך גוטמאָרגן צו אים דורכן טיר,
שרײַט ער צוריק אַ-גוט-יאָר צו מיר.
בעט איך זיך: ברודערקע, לאָז מיך אַרויס,
זאָגט ער: לאָז מיך אַרײַן אין הויז.

At this, the bird, like my brother Mikhl,
Puts a wing over his eyes like a shade
And shouts again into the key-hole,
That may he have such a bit of luck
As he saw the piece of cheese that I keep,
And that for that he'll open up my head.

So, I see that it is not a joke,
And I move over slowly to the door
With my chair and with my cheese,
That I keep safely under my ass,
And I do not raise any fuss
But ask him, whether it's cold out there.

To this he answers that both his ears
Are frozen, his eyes wet with tears,
And he swears, crying aloud,
That in his sleep he devoured
His own leg, the leg that is missing,
And if I let him in, he'll tell me all.

Of course, when I heard the word: devoured,
I really got scared. I almost forgot
To watch out for the piece of cheese
That I was keeping under my ass.
But I touched it and saw: it's here, as before,
So there's nothing to worry about anymore.

So I proposed that we should see
Who will lose his patience first:
I, waiting in my own house,
Or he, watching outside my door.
It seems, it's an interesting thing to find out,
Even—I said—for its own sake.

And this is how the matter remained.
Seven years have passed since then,
I call Good-Morning through the door,
And he calls back Have-a-Good-Year.
I beg him: brother, let me out,
And he says: let me in the house.

ווייס איך דאָך אָבער וואָס ער איז אויסן,

לאָז איך אים ווײַטער שטיין אין דרויסן.

פרעגט ער מיר וועגן דעם שטיקל קעז,

וואָס איך היט עס אונטער מײַן געזעס.

דערשרעק איך זיך, גיב איך אַ טאַפּ. איז עס דאָ.

איז דאָך שוין ווידער קיין זאָרג נישטאָ.

▶ אייבי קירלי, דער מלחמה־העלד

אייבי קירלי, דער מלחמה־העלד,

מיט די מעדאַלן אויפן ברוסט, און מיט דער קוליע,

מאַכט דאָס לינקע אויג צו, ווען ער וויינט.

נעכטן אָבער, אין אַ מיטן מיטוואָך,

האָט ער אין מיטן נאַכט אַ יום־טוב זיך געמאַכט, —

זיבן לעבעדיקע זשאַבעס אויפגעגעסן.

זיבן מאָל האָט זיך מיר אויסגעדאַכט,

אַז בלויז דער נאַכט־ווינט וויינט בײַ מיר אין גאָרטן.

נאָר איך האָב נישט געפרוווט בײַ זיך אפילו פרעגן,

פאַר וואָס ער וויינט.

אים פאַרדריסט אפשר,

פאַר וואָס ער קען די בלומען נישט באַוועגן

אין מײַן גאָרטן.

זיי זײַנען שטיינערדיקע, — אַזוי האָב איך זיי אויסגעטרוימט.

נאָר מאַדנע ווי דאָס זאָל נישט זײַן,

נישט דער נאַכט־ווינט — אייבי קירלי האָט געוויינט.

איטלעכס מאָל, ווען ער האָט איינע

פון די לעבעדיקע זשאַבעס אויפגעגעסן,

האָט ער באַוויינט איר טויט.

איצט זיצט ער ווידער אין דער זון

און וואַרט די קינדער זאָלן קומען

זאָגן אים "גוט־מאָרגן!"

ער האָט זיי ליב,

זייער וואַרעמקייט דערמאָנט אים אָן זײַן ווײַב —

די ווילדע באַרלאָ.

אים, לאַכנדיק, אַמאָל אַ ביס געטאָן אין מאָרדע.

נאָר דעמאָלט האָט ער נאָך געהאַט זײַן קאַטערינקע,

און אַ פאַווע־פעדער אויף זײַן גרינעם קאַפּעליוש

און הויזן ענג־געפאַסטע,

און די שטיוול —

But I know well what he intends,
So I leave him outside to stand.
Then he asks me about the piece of cheese
That I am keeping under my ass.
I get scared, I touch it. It's here, as before.
So there's nothing to worry about anymore.

► *Aby Kirly, The War Hero*

Aby Kirly, the war hero,
With medals on his chest and with a crutch,
Closes his left eye when he cries.
But yesterday, on a simple Wednesday,
He made a holiday at midnight for himself—
He swallowed seven living frogs.

Seven times it seemed to me
It was merely the night-wind crying in my garden.
But I didn't even try to ask myself
Why it should cry.
Maybe it regrets
That it cannot move the flowers
In my garden.
They are of stone—that's how I dreamed them up.

But strange as it may seem,
Not the night-wind—Aby Kirly cried.
Each time, as he ate up
A living frog,
He cried over its death.

Now again he's sitting in the sun,
Waiting for the children to come by
And say "Good Morning!"
He loves them,
Their warmth reminds him of his wife—
The savage Barla.
Once, laughing, she bit his chin.
But then he still had his music-box,
A peacock-feather on his green fedora,
Tight trousers,
And his boots—

William Gropper: *Steady
Employment*, drawing for the
"New Masses."

ווי אַ שפּיגל האָבן זיי געפּעקלט אין דער זון.

העי, מײַן באַרלאַ!

אײַבי קירלי טאָר זיך נישט דערמאָנען וועגן גליק,

ווײַל ער שרײַט

און דערנאָך אַז ער פֿאַרהוסט זיך, שפּײַט ער בלוט.

אַזוי איז אָבער אײַבי קירלי נישט קיין בײַזער,

בלויז דאָס לינקע אויג פֿאַרמאַכט ער,

ווען ער וויינט

מיט די מעדאַלן אויפֿן ברוסט און מיט דער קוליע.

◄ מיט זיך אַליין

יאָהאַמאַ, מײַנער דו,

דײַן פֿרײַלעכקייט איז וווּהין אַוועק?

— איך האָב אין אָוונטשײַן אויף גאָלדן גליק געוואַרט,

האָט גינגעלי, דאָס ווילדע רעטעניש,

ווי פֿון אַ טײַך אַ פֿיש

מײַן אָרעם האַרץ בײַ מיר אַרויסגענאַרט

און אָנגעהאַנגען דאָס דעם מילנערס בלאָנדן אײזל אויפֿן עק

איז ער מיט דעם אין מיל אַרײַן אַוועק,

אין מיל אַרײַן אַוועק,

אין מיל אַרײַן אַוועק.

יאָהאַמאַ, מײַנער דו,

ווי וועסטו אָן אַ האַרץ אַרומגיין דאָ?

— דער שוסטער, יאַנקל-בער, וואָס מאַכט מיר מײַנע שיך,

איז אין זײַן פֿאַך אַ ווונדער אויף דער וועלט, —

האָב איך בײַ אים באַשטעלט

אַ האַרץ אַ לעדערנס פֿאַר זיך,

וועל איך מיר שוין זיין מסתּם, ווי זרחי זאָגט, ביז צו מײַן לעצטער שעה

מיט אָט דעם האַרץ אַזוי אַרומגיין דאָ,

אַזוי אַרומגיין דאָ,

אַזוי אַרומגיין דאָ.

◄ קיין מאָל שוין וועל איך נישט זאָגן

פֿאַראַנען לײַט וואָס קענען אפֿשר זאָגן

אַז ס'איז נישט שיין, צו שטופּן זיך אַרום אַ וואָגן

מיט ציבעלעס, און אוגערקעס, און פֿלוימען.

Glimmering like mirrors in the sun.
Hey you, my Barla!

Aby Kirly must not remember happiness,
Because then he screams
And in a fit of coughing, spits blood.

Otherwise, Aby Kirly is not a bad guy,
He only closes his left eye
When he cries,
With medals on his chest and with the crutch.

➤ *With Myself*

Yohama, my dear,
Where did your joy depart?
—I was waiting in evening glow for golden happiness,
But Ghingeli, that wild riddle,
Stole my poor heart
Like a fish from a river,
And hung it on the miller's blond donkey, on his tail,
And he went with it, didn't fail,
To the mill he went,
To the mill he went.

Yohama, my dear,
How will you walk without a heart?
—The shoemaker Yankl-Bear
Is in his art a wonder in the world,—
From him I ordered me
A heart of leather,
So, as Zarkhi says, till I fall to the ground,
With a heart of leather I'll walk around,
I'll walk around,
I'll walk around.

➤ *I Shall Never Go On Bragging*

There are people who maybe go on bragging
That it's not nice to crowd around a wagon
With onions, cucumbers, and plums.

נאָר אַז ס׳איז שיין אין מיטן גאַס זיך נאָכשלעפּן אַ טויטן-וואָגן —
אַנגעטאָן אין שוואַרצן, און צו דעם נאָך קלאַגן,
איז דאָך אַ זינד צו זאָגן
אַז ס׳איז נישט שיין צו שטופּן זיך אַרום אַ וואָגן
מיט ציבעלעס, און אוגערקעס, און פֿלוימען.

מע דאַרף אפֿשר נישט רייַסן זיך אַזוי, און שלאָגן.
מע קען דאָך רויִק שטופּן זיך אַרום אַ וואָגן
מיט ציבעלעס, און אוגערקעס, און פֿלוימען.
נאָר אַז סע קען די בייַטש אפֿילו קיינעם נישט פֿאַריאָגן,
ווייַל דער טיראַן פֿון דעם באַשעפֿעניש אויף דר׳ערד, דער מאָגן
וויל אַזוי — באַדאַרף מען שוין אַ רשע זייַן, צו זאָגן
אַז ס׳איז נישט שיין צו שטופּן זיך אַרום אַ וואָגן
מיט ציבעלעס, און אוגערקעס, און פֿלוימען.

דעריבער טאַקע וועל איך קיין מאָל שוין נישט זאָגן
אַז ס׳איז ניט שיין צו שטופּן זיך אַרום אַ וואָגן
מיט ציבעלעס, און אוגערקעס, און פֿלוימען.
ווי שטאַרק עס זאָל אַ שטופֿעניש אַזאַ מיך מאַטערן און פּלאָגן,
וועל איך מייַן קאָפּ אַרונטערבייגן, און אַריבערטראָגן,
וויי@נען וועל איך אפֿשר — אָבער קיין מאָל שוין וועל איך ניט זאָגן
אַז ס׳איז ניט שיין צו שטופּן זיך אַרום אַ וואָגן
מיט ציבעלעס, און אוגערקעס, און פֿלוימען.

But if it's nice to schlepp in streets after a death wagon,
Clad in black, and lament with eyes sagging,
It is a sin to go on bragging
That it's not nice to crowd around a wagon
With onions, cucumbers, and plums.

Perhaps one should not be so pushy, so attacking.
One can, perhaps, crowd quietly around a wagon
With onions, cucumbers, and plums.
But if you cannot chase them even whip wagging,
Because earth's tyrant, our belly, nagging,
Wishes so—you must be evil to go on bragging
That it's not nice to crowd around a wagon
With onions, cucumbers, and plums.

That is why I'll never go on bragging
That it's not nice to crowd around a wagon
With onions, cucumbers, and plums.
May the shoving anguish me and plague me,
I'll stoop my head, and suffer like a beggar.
Perhaps I'll cry—but I will never go on bragging
That it's not nice to crowd around a wagon
With onions, cucumbers, and plums.

Illustration to Halpern's *Golden Peacock*, 1924.

זרחי בײַם ברעג ים

◄ זרחי צו זיך אַליין

אָ, זרחי, זרחי, דו קענסט נישט מאַכן,
עס זאָל זיך אויפבויען אַ בריק
איבערן ים אַהין און צוריק,
און דײַן בענקשאַפט שטײט דאָך אויף יענער זײַט
מיט רויט-אויפגעהויבענע לאַפעס, און שרײַט,
ווי אַ דאָרפס-מויד, וואָס דאַרף שוין אַ מאַנסביל האָבן
אַ מאַנסביל האָבן,
אַ מאַנסביל האָבן.

מעשה־לייב
ביים ברעג ים

Illustration to Halpern's *Golden Peacock*, 1924. Yiddish text: "Moyshe-Leyb on the sea shore."

Zarkhi on the Sea Shore

Poems from a larger cycle.

➤ *Zarkhi to Himself*

Oh, Zarkhi, Zarkhi, you cannot cause
A bridge to be built straight across
Over the sea, to go there and back—
And your longing stands on the other side
With red-raised paws, and calls and cries
Like a village broad who needs a man—
Needs a man,
Needs a man.

Zarkhi—another imaginary figure in Halpern's poetry, representing an older, wiser character (sometimes said to be Moyshe-Leyb's "uncle"). The name is not common in Yiddish (from Hebrew, meaning: "dawn" or "shining in the dark").

און אומזיסט, וואָס דו קוקסט אויף די שיפֿן, זרחי,
דו שלאָגסט זיך בלויז אין דײַן קאָפּ אַרײַן
טשורעקעס — מיט דעם וואָס דו רעדסט זיך אײַן.
זיי פֿירן בלויז אַלע אַזוינע לײַט,
וואָס האָבן גאָלד און וואָס האָבן צײַט
צו עסן איין מאָל און נאָך אַ מאָל עסן —
און נאָך אַ מאָל עסן,
און נאָך אַ מאָל עסן.

וואָלסטו אפֿשר געקענט בײַ דײַן חלום פֿועלן,
אַז ער זאָל מאַכן אַ וואָלקן פֿון דיר.
נאָר וואָס טויג — אַז איידער מען גיט זיך אַ ריר,
טראָגט זיך אָן יעמאַכשמאָי פֿון דער ווײַט,
דער ווינט מיט אַ מעסער אַזאַ, וואָס צעשנײַדט
דעם שווערסטן וואָלקן, ווי קרויט אַ קעפּל,
ווי קרויט אַ קעפּל.
ווי קרויט אַ קעפּל.

און ווײַזן די צונג העלפֿט אויך נישט, זרחי,
אַזוינס קאָן דאָך באַוויַזן אויך
אפֿילו אַ טויטער, וואָס העענגט אין דער הויך.
אָדער גאָר אַ קינד, ווען עס לויפֿט נאָך פֿאַרשײַט
אַרום ערגעץ אין אַ העמדל פֿון זײַד.
אָבער דו ביסט דאָך, זרחי, דאַכט זיך, אַ חכם, —
דאַכט זיך אַ חכם,
דאַכט זיך אַ חכם.

◄ זרחי מיט דער ליולקע אין דרויסן ווײַנט

זרחי מיט דער ליולקע אין דרויסן ווײַנט.
ער האָט ליב די אָוונטזון אויף גראָז.
און די אָוונטזון דווקא שײַנט און ברענט
ווי אויף רויען פֿלייש אויף די פֿיס מיט די העענט
פֿון דער מויד וואָס קעמט זיך אין דרויסן.

זרחי מיט דער ליולקע אין דרויסן ווײַנט.
ער האָט ליב פֿאַרקלערטקייט אין אָוונטשײַן
און זײַן שכן זעט ווי אַ קצבֿ-יונג אויס
און דווקא נאַקעט אויך, קומט ער אַרויס
צו דער מויד וואָס קעמט זיך אין דרויסן.

Oh, Zarkhi, you are watching the ships in vain,
You are merely hitting nails in your head
When you believe whatever you thought and said.
Ships bring only such people, behold,
Who have time and who have gold
To eat once and eat again—
And eat again,
And eat again.

Perhaps you could convince your dream
To turn you into a floating cloud.
But what's the use, if before you move out
Appears—devil-take-him—from afar
The wind with a knife, and cuts in small parts
The heaviest cloud like a head of cabbage—
Like a head of cabbage,
Like a head of cabbage.

And showing your tongue won't help either, Zarkhi,
This could be done even by a yellow
Corpse, hanging on the gallows,
Or a child, his lips white with milk,
Running around in a coat of silk.
But you, Zarkhi, seem to be wise—
Seem to be wise,
Seem to be wise.

➤ *Zarkhi, His Pipe to the Yard, Cries*   Title supplied here.

Zarkhi, his pipe to the yard, cries.
He likes the evening sun on grass.
But the evening sun shines and burns
As on raw meat, on the legs and arms
Of the broad, combing her hair in the yard.

Zarkhi, his pipe to the yard, cries.
He likes to be pensive in evening shine.
But his neighbor looks like a butcher-boy
And he walks out, naked and fresh
To the broad, combing her hair in the yard.

זרחי מיט דער ליולקע אין דרויסן וויינט.

ער האָט ליב דער ווינט זאָל זינגען אין בוים

נאָר דער ווינט האָט פֿיינט דעם בוים וואָס איז טויט

און ער זינגט אין די געפֿאַרבטע האָר פֿון דער מויד

וואָס זיצט און קעמט זיך אין דרויסן.

זרחי מיט דער ליולקע אין דרויסן וויינט,

ער האָט ליב ווײַל ער זעט שוין די נאַכט וואָס קומט

זי וועט נעמען די מויד אין אַ שטוב אַרײַן

און וועט שענקען אַ ביסל לבנה-שײַן

דעם טויטן בוים אין דרויסן.

◄ זרחי זאָגט תּורה

אָמר רב זרחי — זאָגט רב זרחי:

אין ספר ברחנדי

צונויפֿגעשטעלט פֿון די גרעסטע חכמים

אין קאַפּיטל זיבן

דערצײײלט זיך אַ מעשׂה פֿון אַ רוצח,

וואָס האָט אײַן מאָל אַזוי ווי אַ וואָלף אין דער פֿינצטער

געוויינט אין מיטן דער נאַכט.

געגאַנגען אױף רויב

און באַפֿאַלן אַן אישה אין שלאָף

און קוילען געוואָלט אױך דאָס קינד בײַ דער ברוסט;

האָט עס אױסגעשטרעקט די הענטלעך צו אים

און דאָס מעסער, וואָס האָט נאָך געטריפֿט פֿון בלוט,

בײַ אים צוגענומען

און געשפּילט זיך מיט דעם

ביז די פֿלעקן פֿונעם בלוט אױפֿן העמדל

האָבן אױסגעזען ווי בלומען אין מאָרגנליכט

בײַם שײַן פֿון דעם פֿאַקל

וואָס האָט אים געלויכטן צו קוילען.

שברולים לדררחי פֿרומה — באַהאַלטענע ליכטיקײט אין דער פֿינצטער,

די קלאָג פֿון רוצח.

און אפֿשר — ווער ווייסט?

אפֿשר מיינט דאָס גאָר־גאָר עפּעס אַנדערש חלילה,

און דײַן צונג וועט זיך בראָטן אין גיהנום,

ווײַל זי האָט נישט אױסגעטײַטשט פּונקט ווי מען דאַרף?

אמר רב זרחי — זאָגט רב זרחי:

אין ספר ברחנדי

צונויפֿגעשטעלט פֿון די גרעסטע חכמים

אין קאַפּיטל זיבן

דערצײײלט זיך אַ מעשׂה פֿון אַ צדיק.

Zarkhi, his pipe to the yard, cries.
He likes the wind to sing in the tree.
But the wind hates the tree that is dead
And sings in the painted hair of the broad
Who combs her hair in the yard.

Zarkhi, his pipe to the yard, cries.
He'd like to see the night come in:
It will take the broad and lead her inside,
And it will grant some moonshine light
To the dead tree in the yard.

➤ *From Zarkhi's Teachings*

Title supplied here.

Omar Rabbi Zarkhi—so said Rabbi Zarkhi:
In the Book of Barhandi
Compiled by the greatest sages,
In chapter seven,
A story is told of a murderer
Who once, like a wolf in the darkness,
Wept in the depth of the night.
He went out on a robbery,
Attacked a woman in her sleep
And was about to kill the baby at her breast—
When it stretched out two little hands,
Grabbed the knife, still dripping blood,
And played with it
Till the stains of blood on his shirt
Looked like flowers at dawn—
In the glow of the torch
That lighted for murder.
Shavrulim ledarrkhi peruma—Light hidden in darkness,
The lament of a murderer.
Or maybe—who knows?
Maybe it means something altogether different
And the tongue will roast in hell
For not interpreting it right?

Omar Rabbi Zarkhi—so said Rabbi Zarkhi:
In the Book of Barhandi
Compiled by the greatest sages,
In chapter seven,
A story is told of a saint.

Omar Rabbi Zarkhi (So said Rabbi Zarkhi.)—a typical opening of a saying by a sage, rendered in the traditional form of Jewish teaching: a word or phrase from the Hebrew sacred text is followed immediately by a Yiddish literal translation. The reading of such a bilingual passage is then followed by explanation and analysis of existing commentaries. Halpern uses this Jewish form with a stance from Eastern philosophy (e.g., the open-ended interpretations and the quasi-Persian name, **Barhandi**).

Shavrulim ledarrkhi pruma—a mock-Aramaic, pseudo-Talmudic text in need of explication. The syntax reads: "The **shavruls** are **prumed** for Zarkhi" (the words in boldface have no meaning). With a slight change, it would mean: Zarkhi's sleeves are slit. Also, **Proma'a** in Aramaic is burglar.

געגאַנגען פֿאַרבײַ אַ קלױסטער בײַ נאַכט
האָט מען גלײַענדיק זשאַר פֿון די פֿענצטער געװאָרפֿן,
האָט זיך אָנגעצונדן די באָרד מיטן בגד
אַזױ װי אַ פֿאַקל (אױף אים).
האָט דער צדיק אױפֿגעהױבן די אױגן צום הימל
און שטאַרבנדיק האָט ער אַזױ געזאָגט:
— פֿאַר בלינדע נאַראָנים זײַנען די שטערן מזלות,
פֿאַר רשעים זײַנען זײַ גאָרנישט;
אין דער אמתן אָבער זײַנען זײַ
גאָטס ליכטיקײט אפֿשר,
װאָס װײַזט זיך אונדז בלױז דורך זײַן הימל —
דעם אַלטן צעלעכערטן שירעם פֿון איבער דער װעלט,
און ס'איז מער נישט — אַ חסד אַ גרױסער
אױף װעמען זײַן ליכטיקײט לאָזט זיך אַראָפּ, װי אַ פֿײַער,
און נעמט אים צו זיך.
שברולים לדררחי פרומה — באַהאַלטענע ליכטיקײט אין דער פֿינצטער,
די לעצטע תּפֿילה פֿון צדיק.
און אפֿשר — װער װײסט?
אפֿשר מײנט דאָס גאָר-גאָר עפּעס אַנדערש חלילה,
און די צונג װעט זיך בראָטן אין גיהנום,
װײַל זי האָט נישט אױסגעטײַטשט פּונקט װי מען דאַרף?

▶ װאָס װײסן מיר, ליבע ברידער

גומילאַסטיקס דרײַ אױף אַ פֿענדל פֿון בלעך
און מיט די ברילן צום ים אַרױס.
זרחי װײנט אפֿשר זײַן בענקשאַפֿט אױס —
װאָס װײסן מיר ליבע ברידער.

און ס'איז אפֿשר גאָרנישט זרחי װאָס װײנט
נאָר אַ בױם װאָס ברענט און װערט נישט פֿאַרברענט
און װאָס װײנט מיט די צװײַגן אַזױ װי מיט הענט —
װאָס װײסן מיר ליבע ברידער.

און ס'איז אפֿשר אױך נישט קײן בױם װאָס װײנט
נאָר די שטומע קלאַג פֿון אַן אױג מיט אַ האַנט
פֿון אײנעם װאָס שטאַרבט בײַ דער שװעל פֿון זײַן לאַנד —
װאָס װײסן מיר ליבע ברידער.

און אפֿשר איז עס נישט אײנער װאָס שטאַרבט
נאָר אַ בלינדער רײז פֿון פֿאַר טױזנט יאָר
באַװײנט זײַנע אָפּגעשױרענע האָר —
װאָס װײסן מיר ליבע ברידער.

Once, as he passed by a church at night,
Glowing embers were thrown from the windows,
And his beard and his coat caught fire
Like a torch (on his body).
Then the saint raised his eyes to the sky
And dying, he said:
—For blind fools the stars are signs,
For evil men they are nothing;
But in truth they are
God's light maybe,
Showing through His sky—
Tiny holes in the old umbrella over the world,
And it is nothing but a grace
To one on whose head the light falls in a flame
And takes him away.
Shavrulim ledarrkhi peruma—Light hidden in darkness,
The last prayer of a saint.
Or maybe—who knows?
Maybe it means something altogether different
And the tongue will roast in hell
For not interpreting it right?

427
Moyshe-Leyb Halpern

➤ *What Do We Know, Dear Brothers*

Three rubberbands on a thin tin pot
And a pair of glasses looking out to sea.
Maybe it's Zarkhi's longing that weeps—
What do we know dear brothers.

And maybe it is not Zarkhi that weeps
But a tree that burns and isn't consumed,
Weeping with branches as if they were arms—
What do we know dear brothers.

And maybe it is not a tree that weeps
But the silent lament of an eye and a hand
Of a man dying at the threshold of his land—
What do we know dear brothers.

And maybe it is not a man that dies
But a blind giant a thousand years ago
Weeping over his shorn hair—
What do we know dear brothers.

Title supplied here.

This secular poem employs
surprisingly biblical images: the
Burning Bush (stanza II), Moses
barred from entering the
Promised Land (stanza III), and
Samson (stanza IV).

און ס׳איז אפשר אויך נישט קיין ריז וואָס וויינט
נאָר דאָס פשוטע נאַרישע אינסטרומענט
וואָס וויינט אונטער זרחיס אַלטע הענט —
וואָס וויסן מיר ליבע ברידער.

◄ פרעג איך בײַ מײַן ליבער פרוי

פרעג איך בײַ מײַן ליבער פרוי,
ווי אַזוי צו פאַרענדיקן דעם ראָמאַן,
אין מײַן ביכעלע —
זאָגט זי: דאָס גליק זאָל אַוועק מיט דער באַן,
און צוריקווינקען מיט אַ טיכעלע.
זאָג איך: טיכעלע-שמיכעלע —
זאָגט זי: ביכעלע-שמיכעלע —
און פרעגט מיך, צי וויל איך נישט בעסער
קאַווע מיט אַ קיכעלע.
זאָג איך: קיכעלע-שמיכעלע —
און הייס מיר אויפציִען אויף מײַן קישן
אַ ציכעלע.
זאָגט זי: ציכעלע-שמיכעלע.
און הייסט מיר אַרײַנטראָגן צום שוסטער
איר שיכעלע.
זאָג איך: שיכעלע-שמיכעלע.
ווערט זי ברוגז, און ווײַזט מיר
אַז כ׳האָב שוין אַ פליכעלע —
זאָג איך:
פליכעלע-שיכעלע-ציכעלע-קיכעלע-טיכעלע-ביכעלע-שמיכעלע.
קען זי נישט זאָגן אַזוי גיך ווי איך, אַזוי גיך ווי איך,
פליכעלע-שיכעלע-ציכעלע-קיכעלע-טיכעלע-ביכעלע-שמיכעלע.
האָבן מיר אינאיינעם געלאַכט —
אינאיינעם געלאַכט.
ביז זי האָט מיר די אויגן פאַרמאַכט —
די אויגן פאַרמאַכט.
און מיך אײַנגעוויגט מיט דעם ליד פונעם רעגן,
מיט דעם ליד פונעם רעגן,
וואָס מען זינגט פון קליינע קינדערס וועגן.

And maybe it is not a giant that weeps
But the simple silly instrument
Weeping under Zarkhi's aging hand—
What do we know dear brothers.

► *The End of the Book*

So I ask my dear wife
How to finish the affair
Of my little booky—
Says she: Let happiness leave on a train
And wave back with a hanky.
Says I: Hanky-panky—
Says she: Booky-shmooky—
And asks me whether I'd like
With my coffee a cooky.
Says I: Cooky-shmooky—
And tell her to put a case on my pillow
And not to play hooky.
Says she: Hooky-shmooky.
And tells me to repair her shoe
By hook or by crooky.
Says I: Crooky-shmooky.
So she jumps up, and points at my head:
I am bald and spooky.
Says I:
Spooky-crooky-hooky-cooky-hanky-panky-booky-shmooky.
But she cannot say it as fast as I can, as fast as I can:
Spooky-crooky-hooky-cooky-hanky-panky-booky-shmooky.
So we laugh together—
Laugh so nice.
Till she closes my eyes—
Closes my eyes.
And rocks me with a song of rain and light,
Rain and light,
That you sing to little children at night,
Children at night.

Title supplied here.

This is the last poem of the book, *The Golden Peacock*. The whole poem is founded on a play with a string of diminutives, untranslatable into English: **plikhele-shikhele-tsikhele-kikhele-tikhele-bikhele-shmikhele**. The cluster **shm** prefixed to any word (instead of the initial consonant) has a mocking, canceling effect.

Illustration to Halpern's *Golden Peacock*, 1924.

◄ סאָליוט

בײַ אונדז אין לאַנד איז אויך עפעס דאָ —
און וװ קיין לאַמטערן-סלופּ איז נישטאָ
איז דאָ אַ בוים — און דאָס מיינט דאָך קלאָר
אַז אַ נעגער איבער צוװאָנציק יאָר
מעג האָסן אַלץ וואָס שטרעקט זיך אַרויף
צו האַלטן דעם, וואָס מען הענגט אים אויף.
נאָר יענעם וואָס איך האָב שטאָרבן געזען,
קיין פּופּצן איז ער ניט אַלט געוואָען.

די וװיסע אַלטע מויד האָט ניט אויסגעזען זיס.
אַ פאַרזשאַוװערט שלאָס אויף אַן אַלטן וואַליס
די נאָז מיטן פּיסק. — און די הענט מיט די פיס,
איך זאָג דיר — זיך צורירן הויט צו הויט
צו אַזאַ מין פליאַקע, איז בעסער — טויט.

דו ביסט דו. — דאָס האָט זי אים אָנגעקלאָגט. —
און דו וועסט בײַ מיר הענגען, האָט זי געזאָגט.
עס איז וואָר — ער האָט אין טויט-שרעק פאַסקודנע געלאַכט;
נאָר געלאַכט האָט זי אויך און די סמאָלע געבראַכט,
און באַקוקט דעם בוים איבער זיך אין דער הויך.
און די פרייד פון המון בײַ דעם ערשטן רויך,
איך שווער — פון אַ משוגעים-הויז,
אין אַ שריפה, הערט מען אַזוינס ניט אַרויס.

און דער ערשטער לעפל סמאָלע בײַם האַרץ
איז הייס אויף הייס, און שוואַרץ אויף שוואַרץ.
און די אויגן ניט בליק, נאָר אַ וויַיס געשטאַרץ.
און דאָס לײַב — עס רײַסט זיך פון דער הויט;
ניט אַנדערש, עס וויל זיך אויסטאָן פון טויט.

אָבער ניט נאָר האָט מען דעם בהמהניק
פאַרוואָרפן אַרום האַלדז אַ שטריק,
נאָר די פאָן פון דער רעפּובליק האָט מען אויך
אַרויפגעצויגן אין דער הויך —
און דער הימל איז בלוי — אים גייט ניט אָן —
און בײַם ווינט איז אַ שׂימחה מיט דער פאָן,
און איך — אַ געשלאַגענער הונט — ניט אַ וואָרט.
ניט אַרײַנגעלייגט גאָרנישט — אַ שותף צום מאָרד.

➤ *Salute*

There are things in this country too—
And if they find no streetlamp pole,
There will be a tree—and that means clearly
That a Negro over twenty years old
May hate all things which spire
To hold a man for his hanging.
But the one whose death I saw
Was not even fifteen years old.

The white old maid was not sweet at all.
A rusty lock on an old valise—
Her nose and jaw. And the arms and legs,
I tell you—rather than touch skin-to-skin
Such a smudge—better death.

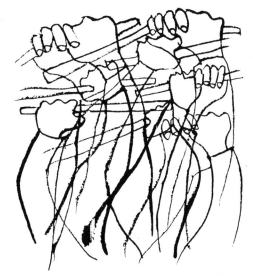

Ben Shahn: Drawing for *The
Passion of Sacco and Vanzetti*, 1968

You are you,—she pointed at him.
And you will hang for me, she said.
It's true—in death-fear he nastily laughed;
But she laughed too, and brought the tar,
And inspected the tree above her head.
And the joy of the crowd at the first smoke,
I swear—from a mad-house on fire
You would not hear such a scream.

And the first spoon of tar at his heart
Was hot upon hot, and black upon black.
And the eyes were not lightning, but white bulging out.
And the body—tearing out of the skin,
As if it wished to undress its death.

But not only did they loop a rope
Around the neck of this piece of cattle,
The flag of the republic too
Was raised on high—
And the sky was blue—it didn't care—
And the wind rejoiced with the flag in the air,
And I—a beaten dog—said not a word.
Took no part—a partner to murder.

נאָר מען דאַרף ניט פאַרשלינגען אַ חזיר-שטאָל
צו ברעכן מיט דער גרינער גאַל,
דאָס באַזאָרגט שוין דער גלח, דער חכמה-קוואל —
אויב די שוואַרצקייט — זאָגט ער — איז גאָטס אַ גרייַז,
איז אַ זינד זי צו לאָזן זיך מישן מיט ווייַס.

און איך זאָג דיר — ס׳איז ניט דער קרעכץ פון צווייַג,
ניט דער שטריק, מיטן גאַנצן קלאַפֿערגעצייַג,
ניט דאָס פֿעדערל אין ווינטגעטרייַב
וואָס האָט פאַרזאַמט זיך צו קלעפֿן צום לייַב,
נאָר דו — דאָס טרויער-געשטאַנק פון דער וועלט,
וואָס האָט זיך פון ווייַטן אַנידערגעשטעלט,
מיט די הענט, דורך די קעשענעס, ביַים דיך,
פאַרטראַכטן אַ ליד פאַר דער וועלט און פאַר זיך.

גיי בעסער, וועק אויף דעם קלעזמער שאָפֿען,
און זאָל ער אַ פֿליוקע טאָן, אויב ער קען,
מיט טענער אַ ביסל — און זאָל מען זען,
אַז אַ גוי ווי איז אויך אַ כל-נדריניק,
ווען מען דאַרף צו פאַרגאַסן בלוט — מוזיק.

◄ נאַכט אין מאַנהעטן

אַ מאַלפֿע — דאָס לייַב אָן הָאר אינגאַנצן,
שטייט ברוין-און-בלאָ פון קעלט פאַר מייַן פֿענצטער;
און ווײַנט אַרויף צום הימל אויבן
וואָס הענגט ווי אַ ים פון בלוט און בלאָטע,
אַן איבערגעקערטער איבער דער פינצטערער שטאָט.

זי ווײַנט אַזוי ווי אַ מענטש אין דער פינצטער
וואָס מיינט אַז ער האָט עפּעס אָנגעווירן,
ווען ער האָט דאָס ליכט פון די אויגן פאַרלוירן,
עס קען דאָך אַ מענטש פאַרלירן אַ מאָל
דאָס ליכט פון די אויגן.

נאָר אַז איך וועל שוין צוגיין און האָרכן
וואָס וועט דאָס העלפֿן דער מאַלפֿע וואָס ווײַנט
אַרויף צו אַ הימל אזאַ?

די לבנה, וואָס איז געשטאָרבן, איז טויט.
און די שטערן דערמאָנען דאָך בלויז אָן פֿונקען,
וואָס זייַנען געפֿלויגן אַ מאָל

You don't have to swallow a sty of pigs
In order to vomit your green bile,
The priest will take care of that, that well of wisdom—
If blackness, he says, is a blunder of God,
Then it's sinful to let it mix with white.

And I tell you—it is not the groan of a branch,
Not the rope with the whole paraphernalia,
Not the feather flown in the wind,
Too late to stick to the body—
It's you, the stinking sorrow of the world,
Standing there at a distance, safe,
Hands through your pockets, on your groin,
Composing a poem for the world and yourself.

Better go, wake up the *klezmer* Chopin,
Let him pour something strong, if he can,
A rain of tones, for everyone to see
That a goy too has a mood of *Kol-Nidre*
When to spilled blood you need music.

Klezmer—a Jewish folk musician
(from the Hebrew: **kley-zemer**,
musical instruments).

Kol-Nidre*

➤ *Night in Manhattan*

A monkey—a hairless body,
Brown-and-blue from cold—stands at my window
And cries to the sky
Hanging above like a sea of blood and mud,
Overturned on the dark city.

It cries like a man in the dark
Who thinks that he lost something
When he lost the light of his eyes:
After all, sometimes a man may lose
The light of his eyes.

And even if I come close and listen,
Would it help the monkey that cries up
To a sky like this?

The dead moon is dead.
And the stars will only remind you of sparks
That flew once-upon-a-time

פֿון אַ פֿײַער, װאָס האָט געברענט אין דער װעלט,
װען עס איז נאָך געװען נישט קײן בלוט װאָס װײנט
און נישט קײן בלאָטע.

אַ רחמנות איז נאָר אױף די קינדער פֿון שטאָט:
װי מאָדנע פֿרעמד און פֿאַרטרױערט זײ קוקן,
װען אײנער, אַ פֿון זינען געריריטער,
שעפּטשעט — מיט אױגן פֿאַרגלאָצטע צום הימל —
פֿון שטערן.

נאָר אפֿשר באַװײנט די מאַלפּע אין דרױסן
טאַקע אונדז אַלע, אירע קינדער?
עס הײבט זיך דאָך אױף װי אַ באַרג די אימה,
װען מען זעט אַזױ פֿיל מענטשן אינאײנעם
מיט אָרעמס און בערד צום הימל פֿאַרריסן,
װײנען איבער דער װעלט.

נאָר אפֿילו װען מען װאָלט שױן דערלאַנגען
צו זײ מיטן קול —
װאָס זאָגט מען צו זײ אין דער פֿינצטער?
װוּ איז די הײם פֿון דער װעלט
אױב זײ װילן אַהײמגײן?

און װאָס װעט מען טאָן, אין דער הײם, אין דער פֿינצטער?
װער ס׳עט האָבן װעט עסן אַ באַרשט אין דער פֿינצטער,
װער ניט — װעט עסן ברױט אַלטגעבאַקנס אַ שטיקל,
װאָס ער האָט נישט באַװיזן צו פֿאַרקױפֿן
צו אַן אַנדערן — פֿאַר זונפֿאַרגאַנג.

אַ, זאָל די זון שױן רחמנות האָבן
— אַזױ װי די מאַלפּע אױף אירע קינדער —
אױף אונדזער אָרעמער װעלט.
זאָל זי אױפֿעסן
װי אַ װאָלף אַ שאָף אין דער פֿינצטער
איר אײגענע ליכטיקײט ערגעץ דאָרט.

1924

From a fire burning in the world
When there was yet—neither blood that cries
Nor mud.

It's only a pity for the children here:
How strange and sad they look
When someone, not in his right mind,
With eyes staring at the sky—
Whispers of stars.

But perhaps the monkey outside
Cries over all of us, its children?
After all, wouldn't dread rise like a mountain
When you see so many people together,
Their arms and beards drawn to the sky,
Crying over the world?

And even if you could reach them
With your voice—
What could you say to them in the dark?
Where is the home of the world—
If they want to go home?

And what shall we do at home, in the dark?
He who has, will eat borscht in the dark.
He who doesn't—will eat a crust of dry bread
Which he didn't manage to sell
To another—before the sun set.

Oh, let the sun take pity—
Like the monkey on its children—
On our miserable world.
Like a wolf gobbling a sheep in the dark,
Let it devour
Its own light
Somewhere.

1924

Louis Lozowick: *Hooverville,* 1932.

◄ סאַקאָ־וואַנזעטי

מען קען זיך אויסרײַסן אַ   גרויע האָר פון קאָפּ,

וואָס קומט צו פרי אַמאָל פון צער, וואָס איז צו שווער;

נאָר וועמען אין זײַן צער עס דאַכט זיך אויס,

אַז ס׳איז אים שווער דער קאָפּ זײַנער מיט הויט און האָר,

ווי עפּעס, וואָס ער קען ניט טראָגן מער,

אויף אָט די קנאָקן די צוויי אָרימע, וואָס הייסן אַקסל, —

בײַ דעם מענטשן —

זאָל ער ניט בלײַבן שטיין דעמאָלט מיט מויל און אויגן אָפענע,

IF IT HAD NOT BEEN FOR THESE THING, I MIGHT HAVE LIVE OUT MY LIFE TALKING AT STREET CORNERS TO SCORNING MEN. I MIGHT HAVE DIE, UNMARKED, UNKNOWN A FAILURE. NOW WE ARE NOT A FAILURE. THIS IS OUR CAREER AND OUR TRIUMPH. NEVER IN OUR FULL LIFE COULD WE HOPE TO DO SUCH WORK FOR TOLERANCE, FOR JOOSTICE, FOR MAN'S ONDERSTANDING OF MAN AS NOW WE DO BY ACCIDENT. OUR WORDS - OUR LIVES - OUR PAINS NOTHING! THE TAKING OF OUR LIVES - LIVES OF A GOOD SHOEMAKER AND A POOR FISH PEDDLER - ALL! THAT LAST MOMENT BELONGS TO US - THAT AGONY IS OUR TRIUMPH.

Ben Shahn: *Portrait of Sacco and Vanzetti*, 1958.

➤ *Sacco-Vanzetti*

You can pull out
An early gray hair
That comes from grief, when it's too heavy;
But he who, in his grief, may think
That his head—with skin and hair—is heavy
And he can no longer bear it
On the two poor bones, called shoulders—

ווי אין אַ דולהויז ערגעץ;

און אויך דער שטיין פון וואַנט איז האַרטער פון זיין קאָפּ

און שלאָגן זיך אָן אים וועט ברענגען בלויז אַ בײַל,

ניט גרעסער פון אַן עפּל אויף אַ בוים, וואָס דאַרט

און האָט ניט ניט וועט עס זאָל אים אָפּרייסן אין צײַט.

און ס'איז דאָך דאָ אַן אויסוועג הײַנט אַ גרינגערער

פאַר דעם, וואָס זוכט אים:

מען דאַרף נאָר רויִק זיין אַ ווײַל,

און ווי אַ טיפוס-קראַנקער צובויגן דעם קאָפּ צו דעם, וואָס גאָלט.

אַ ברודער איז ער דאָך,

און מען דאַרף ניט ברוגז זיין אויף אים,

פאַר וואָס ער נעמט די הויט ניט מיט.

ער טוט נאָר וואָס מען הייסט און וועון מען צאָלט דערפאַר.

און אויך דאָס טויטנקלייד, —

דאָס אויך — האָט אויפגעניט אַ ברודער, וואָס איז הונגעריק.

און אַז אַ קינד — דאָס אָרימסטע,

ווען מען טוט עס אָן אַ בגד אין אַ יום-טוב,

גייט בײַם האַנט, ווּהין מען נעמט עס מיט;

מעג מען אויך זיך לאָזן פירן צו דער טויטנשטול, וואָס וואַרט

ווי אַלט מען זאָל ניט זיין.

און אַז עס בלאַנקט שוין אויך דאָס טויטנדיקע קופּער אויפן קאָפּ

וואָס קען נאָך שווער זיין דעמאָלט?

אַ קיניג — ווען דאָס גאַנצע פאָלק אַפילו ווײַנט אַרום זיין טראָן —

דאַרף שווײַגן, ווען מען קרוינט אים.

און אַז פון פײַער איז די קרוין אויף אים דעם אויסדערוויילטן

איז דאָס אַ ווונדער-קרוין אין אַט דער וויסטער וועלט.

און בלויז דער וואָלף, וואָס אייביק לוֹיערט ער, ווײַל ער איז ווילד

און בלויז דער רויבער אין דער פינצטער —

שרעקן זיך פאַר פײַער.

קינדער שטומע נאָך,

מיט אויגן אָפענע, וואָס זעען גאָרנישט נאָך,

שטרעקן זיך צום פײַער.

און בלויז דער שמעטערלינג, וואָס גאָרט נאָך ליכט

אין חושך פון דער נאַכט,

באַגעגנט מיט צעשפרייטע פליגל אייביק —

דעם טויט אין פײַער.

4טן סעפטעמבער 1927.

Let him not stand with gaping mouth and eyes
As in some madhouse; and let him know:
The stones of a wall are harder than his head,
And banging his head against stone will only raise a bump
Not larger than an apple of a tree that withers
And there is no one to pick it in time.
Today there is an easier solution
If you look for it:
Be still for a moment
And, like a typhoid patient, bend your head
To him who shaves.
He is your brother.
You mustn't be mad at him
For not taking your skin along with your hair.
He only does what he's told and when he's paid.
And the death-clothes too—
These too—were tailored by your brother who was hungry.

And if a child—the poorest,
When you dress him up on a holiday,
Will go wherever he is led;
Then you too—no matter how old you are—
May let them take you to the death-chair
That is waiting.
And when the deadly copper gleams on your head,
What can be heavy then?
A king—even when the whole people weeps around his throne—
Must be still when they crown him.
And if the crown on the chosen one is made of fire,
It is a wonder-crown in this damn world.
And only the wolf, forever lurking, the wild animal,
And only the outlaw in the dark—
Fear the fire.
Babies, still mute,
With open eyes that don't yet see a thing,
Stretch their hands to fire.
And only the moth, that yearns for light
In the dark of the night,
With outstretched wings, greets forever—
Death by fire.

September 4, 1927

I

מענטשן שטייען אױף

און יאָגן זיך מיט שיפֿן און מיט באַנען,

און פֿלאַטערן װי פֿײגל, אין דער לופֿטן איבער אַלץ,

און שפֿאַרן זיך, װי רױכן פֿון די קױמענס,

און דרייען זיך, װי שטױב אין װינט

אין אָט-דעם אײביק-זינגענדיקן גאָלד-און-אײזן-װירבל

פֿון דער שטאָט,

און דאָ בײַם ים אפֿילו אױף דעם טױטן-אינדזל;

בײַם פּראָדוקט-פֿאַרקױפֿער איז דער װאָגן

לײדיק שױן כּמעט,

און סעם דער קרעמער שטעלט די אַכטע מילכקאַן שױן אַרױס;

און אױך מעקדאָל, דער אַלטער אירלענדער,

דער שכן אונדזערער,

מיט האָנט און האָמער אױף דער זױל דער האַרטער,

פֿײַפֿט ער שױן אַרױף צום צענטן מאָל דאָס זעלבע ליד

צום פֿײגעלע אין שטײַגל, װאָס לערנט זיך

אים נאָכצוזינגען.

מײַן מאָן אָבער, —

אַזױ װי ס׳װיל דער ים נישט אױפֿהערן צו רױשן,

װיל ער נישט אױפֿהערן

צו פֿירן זײַן מלחמה מיט די פֿליגן

אין שלאָפּקאַלאַט.

און מיט מײַן הוט אױף זיך, דעם מיט די רױטע בלומען,

יאָגט ער זיך אַרום און װאַרפֿט מיט העני,

װי אין דער אָפּערע אַ דיריגענט אַ   הײסער.

און װי אַ ביבער שװיצט ער שױן (ער קען זיך נאָך,

חלילה, צוקילן) װאָס טוט מען מיט אַזױנעם — גאָט מײַנער?

עס קומט דאָך אױס, כאַטש שרײַ אױף אים, װי אױף אַ קינד,

צי גאָר פֿאַרשפּיל מיט רײד אים, װי אַ   קינד.

— אַ, זילבער-גרױער קאָפּ, — דו מאָן מײַנער, דו קינד,

װי הײסט דער רבי דײַנער, זאָג מיר, אױב דו װײסט?

— מײַן רבי איז אַ בלינדער אױף אַן אױג

און הײסט רב חיים.

— װאָס טרינקט דער רבי דײַנער, אַלע טאָג?

— ציקאָריע פֿון אַ   קװאָרטן-טעפּל

טרינקט דער רבי מײַנער אַלע טאָג,

און בלױז לכּבֿוד שבת עסט ער

קאַשע מיט פֿאַסאָליעס,

קאַשע מיט פֿאַסאָליעס,

קאַשע מיט פֿאַסאָליעס.

I

People wake up in the morning
And race in boats and trains,
And flutter like birds in the air above it all,
And push, like smoke out of a chimney,
And spin like dust in the wind,
In this ever-singing, gold-and-iron whirlpool
Of a city.
And even here, by the sea, on Dead Island:
The fruit-vendor has almost
Emptied his wagon by now,
And Sam the grocer puts out the eighth milk can;
And McDowell, too, the old Irishman,
Our neighbor,
His hands and hammer on the hard sole,
Whistles for the tenth time the same song
To a bird in a cage that learns
To mimic him.
Yet my husband—
As the sea will never stop its swell—
He'll never cease
To make war against the flies
In a bathrobe.

With my hat on his head, the one with the red flowers,
He races about and throws his arms
Like a hot conductor in an opera.
He sweats like a beaver (he might, God forbid,
Catch cold). What shall I do with such a man, my God?
Shall I scold him like a child,
Or, with words, put him to play like a child?
—Oh, silver-gray head—you, my husband, my child,
What's the name of your teacher? Tell me, if you know.
—My teacher is blind in one eye
And his name is Reb Chayem.
—What does your teacher drink every day?
—Chickory in a mug, that's what
My teacher drinks every day,
And only on the Sabbath he eats
Kasha with beans,
Kasha with beans,
Kasha with beans.

Royzele—Moyshe-Leyb's wife, a frequent figure in his poems.

Moyshe-Leyb Halpern: *Portrait of his wife Royzele,* 1926.

אַז דאָ אין לאַנד דערוואַקסענע, ווי קינדער,

בענקען אַלע טאָג נאָך נייע שפּילעכלעך,

פֿאַר וואָס זאָל — פֿרעג איך, — דאָס פֿאַרמעסטן זיך

אין פֿליִגן־כאַפּן אויך נישט זײַן אַ   שפּיל?

וואָר איז: מיר איז שווער צו טראַכטן וועגן דעם,

דאָס קומט דערפֿון, וואָס אַלצדינג מאָלט זיך גלײַך

פֿאַר מײַנע אויגן אויס, אַזוי ווי לעבעדיק.

אָט זע איך דאָך אין דעם פּלאַקאַט,

ווּ אותיות, ווי סלופּעס גרויסע,

זאָגן אָן דעם נאָמען פֿון מײַן מאַן.

דער פֿליִגן־כאַפּער־טשעמפּיאָן פֿון לאַנד איז ער, —

ס׳שטייט אַזוי געשריבן.

און אויסגעמאָלט מיט ברילן, האָר און שניפּס,

און מיט די הענט און פֿיס אין לופֿטן

קוקט ער מיר אויס — נישט אויסגערעדט זאָל זײַן, —

ווי אַ משוגענער אויף גלײַכע ווענט.

נאָר מער פֿון אַלץ פֿאַרדריסט דער פֿרוי אין מיר! —

ווי מ׳האָט מיר אָנגעטאָן מײַן ליבן מאַן.

דעם טאָפּ דעם גאָלדענעם, וואָס העֹנגט אים

אויף דער ברוסט — פֿאַרשטיי איך נאָך —

ער דאַרף מסתּמא אַרײַנוואַרפֿן אַהין

די פֿליִגן, וואָס ער כאַפּט,

מען זאָל זיי קענען איבערצײַלן,

ווען די פֿאַרווערט־צײַט וועט פֿאַריבער זײַן.

די ברייטע הויזן אָבער, אָט די רויטע זײַנע —

וואָס באַדאַרף ער?

פֿליִגן זײַנען דאָך קיין ווילדע אָקסן נישט,

מען זאָל זיי דאַרפֿן רייצן?

נאָר אפֿשר וויל מען צוציִען מיט דעם גאָר אונדז אַליין,

די פֿרויען?

רויט דערמאָנט דאָך אונדז אָן עפּל־ראָזן זונפֿאַרגאַנג,

אַן שפּאָרן־קלאַנג פֿון יונגע אָפֿיצירן.

פֿאַר מיר אַליין האָט זיך שוין אויך אַ   מאָל

פֿאַרנייגט אַזוינער.

איך בין געגאַנגען דעמאָלט

מיט מײַן חברטע שפּאַצירן

אין ווילנע — אויף דער הויפּטגאַס. —

פּעשע־גיטל איז געווען איר נאָמען.

אַ לאַנדסמאַן וואָס איז ערשט פֿון שיף אַרונטער,

האָט דעֹצײלט, אַז זי האָט זיך אַליין געטייט,

ווען זעלנער זײַנען זייער הויז

אין מיטן נאַכט באַפֿאַלן — — — —

Here, in this country, grown-ups, like children,
Desire new games every day.
Why shouldn't—I ask—a competition
In fly-catching also be a game?
It's hard for me to think about it,
Because every thought appears as an image
Before my eyes.
Now I see a poster
Where letters big as pillars
Announce the name of my husband,
The fly-catching champion of the nation,—
That's what it says.
Painted with glasses, hair and a bowtie,
With his arms and his legs in the air,
He looks—forgive me for saying so—
Like a madman climbing walls.
But above all, the woman in me is annoyed!
How they've dressed up my dear husband!
Never mind the golden pot hanging on his chest—
He has to drop the flies he catches into it,
So they can count them
When the competition is over.
But what are those
Wide red trousers for?
Are flies wild bulls
That one must tease them?
But maybe they want to attract us—
The women?
Red reminds us of an apple-rosy sunset,
And of the sound of spurs of young officers.
One of them once bowed
To me.
It happened when I strolled
With my girl friend
In Vilna, on Main Street.
Peshe-Gittel was her name.
A *landsman* who just came off a ship   Landsman*
Told me that she killed herself
When soldiers in the middle of the night
Burst into their house— — —

ארויף צום אָוונט-הימל זײַנען אויסגעשפּרייט —
ניט מײַנע אויגן.
ניט מײַנע טריט בײַם ברעג פון ים אַרונטער און אַרויף.
נאָר דו און אַרום דיר דער רויש פון שוואַרצן זײַדנקלייד,
געשאַנקען דיר פון אים, דעם אויפגעקומענעם,
אין האַנדל מיט די שוואַרצע דאָ אין לאַנד.
אַט באַלד און בײַ דײַן זײַט וועט ער אַרומגיין דאָ
און וועט זיך פרייען, וואָס דו ביסט שיין אין שוואַרצן זײַדנקלייד.
און וועט ניט זען, אַז שווער ווי הינטער אַ געשטאָרבענעם,
גייט הינטער דיר דײַן אָרעמקייט און איך,
אינאיינעם מיט אַ קינד אַ שוואַרצס,
וואָס ווײַנט, דו זאָלסט אים אָפּגעבן דאָס ברויט, וואָס בלאַנקט
אין יעדן פאַלד פון שוואַרצן זײַדנקלייד דיר אויף דיר — — —
אין אָוונטשײַן.

► אָוועראַיים

וואָלף, חיים-בערל און זאַנוול האָבן אין קאָרטן געשפּילט,
ווען מען האָט זיי די בשׂורה געבראַכט,
אַז דער פירער איז טויט.
חיים-בערל מיט שוואַרץ אין די הענט האָט באַדויערט:
— אַ שאָד, — האָט ער אונטערגעמורמלט — אַ שאָד,
זאַנוול, וואָס האָט לעבן זיך, צוליב מזל
געהאַלטן די מויד, (וואָס האָט בראַקע געהייסן),
און וואָס האָט באַקומען אַן אמתע פאַרציע רויט,
האָט דווקא געשאַלטן דעם מענטשן,
וואָס האָט זיי די בשׂורה געבראַכט,
אַז דער פירער איז טויט.
און אַפילו די מויד, וואָס איז שיער נישט געווען אַזוי רויט
ווי בײַ זאַנוולען די קאָרטן, — אויך זי האָט געברומט
— דול ניט קיין ספּאָדיק, באַרנולע,
מיר ווייסן שוין אַלע, מיר ווייסן. —
געשטומט האָט בלויז וואָלף,
די קאָרטן אַוועקגעלייגט גלײַך, ווי מען האָט זיי צעטיילט
און מיט אָפענע אויגן און מויל אַ באַנאַנע געשיילט
און געשטומט.

► *Your Dress*

Eyes drawn up to the evening sky—
Not my eyes.
Steps pacing at the seashore, up and down—
It's you, enfolded in the rustle of your black silk dress,
A gift from one who made it in this country
In business with the blacks.
Soon he will walk here by your side
And will rejoice: How beautiful you are in your black silk dress.
And he won't see behind you, heavy as behind a corpse,
Walk your poverty and me
And a black child,
Crying for his bread that glitters white
In every fold of your black silk dress— —
In evening-shine.

► *Overtime*

Wolf, Khaym-Berl and Zanvl were playing cards
When the news was brought to them
That the leader was dead.
Khaym-Berl, with a hand of spades, mourned:
A pity—he mumbled to himself—a pity.
Zanvl, who had a broad beside him
For luck (her name was Brokhe),
And who'd been dealt hearts,
Cursed the one
Who brought the news
That the leader was dead.
And even the broad, who was almost as red
As Zanvl's cards—she too growled
—Don't talk nonsense, Big Bear,
We already know, we know.
Only Wolf said nothing;
He put aside his cards as they were dealt
And with eyes and mouth open, he peeled a banana
And said nothing.

◄ ער, וואָס רופט זיך פֿירער

מיר האָבן אונדזער פּנים קיינעם ניט פֿאַרויס באַשטעלט.
און מען דאַרף קיין שטיין ניט וואַרפֿן אויף דעם הונט,
וואָס ווײַזט זײַן פּנים ווען ער ווײַנט, דעם הימל פֿון דער נאַכט.
נאָר אַז איך טראַכט שוין וועגן דעם,
פֿאַרטרויערט איבער זיך אַליין דאָ אין דעם נאַכט-קאַפֿע,
אַנגעריכערטן ביז נעפֿל-גרויקייט,
און מען ווײַזט מיר אָן דערבײַ אַ מענטש אַנטקעגן מיר,
און מען זאָגט מיר ווער דאָס איז,
און אַז איך קוק אויף אים
און ער, מיט יעדן קנייטש און פֿאַלד אויף זײַן געזיכט,
דערמאָנט דעם קבֿרן פֿון דער היים, ווי ער האָט זיך געפֿרייט
ווען מען האָט צוקאָפֿנס בײַ מײַן ברודערל דעם טויטן
אָנגעצונדן ליכט —
און אַז די קרומקייט פֿון זײַן רעכטן אויג בײַ אים,
וואָס טרעפֿט מיך אומגעריכט, איז שיִער ניט אַזוי קאַלט,
ווי אַ געהיימער מאָרד, וואָס וועקט פֿון שלאָף בײַ נאַכט —
צי מעג ניט דעמאָלט ווי טוען מיר,
ווי פֿון מײַן סאַמע האַרץ אַרויס אַ ווונד, אַ בלוטיקע,
וואָס דווקא ער באַשטייט, מיר זאָלן בלינד אים גלייבן,
אַז ער איז אויסדערוויילט צו פֿירערשאַפֿט אין לעבן.

Ben Shahn: *Café*, 1955.

➤ *He Who Calls Himself Leader*

No one can order his face in advance.
And you shouldn't throw a stone at a dog
Showing its howling muzzle to the night sky.
But when I think about it,
Losing myself in sadness, in this night-cafe
Fogged up in smoke,
And they point out a man across the room,
And tell me who he is,
And when I look at him
And he, with every fold and wrinkle of his face,
Reminds me of the undertaker back home, how he rejoiced
When they lit candles
At the head of my dead little brother—
And when the crookedness of his right eye,
Which strikes me suddenly, is almost as cold
As a hidden murder that wakes you up at night—
Am I not allowed then to feel pain,
Like a wound bleeding in my gut,
That he, of all people, insists that we blindly believe
He was chosen for leadership in life?

וואָס מיינט דען פירערשאַפט?

דאָס מיינט דאָך פרילינגס-ווינט וואָס זינגט!

דאָס מיינט דאָך זיכער ליכטיקייט, וואָס גייט פאָרויס

דורך וויסטעניש פון שטיין און דאָרן.

דאָס מיינט דאָך פרילינגס-ווינט וואָס זינגט,

צו מונטערן דעם קראַנקן פויגל, האָפענונג, וואָס וויינט,

אַז ער זאָל אויסשפרייטן די ווייסע פליגל זיינע,

ווען מען דאַרף אַריבער בערג, וואָס גרייכן ביז די וואָלקנס.

און וואָס איז דען דאָס ליכט פון פירערס אויג?

דאָס איז דאָך בלויז אַ פונק פון זיין געשטאַלט דער אויסדערווייילטער.

וואָס קען זיך דורך זיך אַליין דאָס גרויסע וווּנדער ווייַזן,

צו לייַכטן ווי אַ רעגנבויגן ליכטיק אין דער נאַכט.

נאָר ווען אַפילו דער וואָס זיצט אַנטקעגן מיר

וואָלט ניט דערמאָנט מיט זיינע רייד אַ פליג אַ בייַזע,

וואָס זשומעט אַרום אַ הייפל מיסט אין מיטן גאַס —

און ווען אַפילו איך וואָלט אויפגעהערט צו טראַכטן, ווען איך הער זיין קול,

אַז דאָס איז בייזיקייט פון אַ מענטשן-צונג, וואָס פלעקט פון רייד

אַ שטריק פאַר זיינס אַ ברודער אין דער נאַכט —

צי דען וואָלט דעמאָלט גרינגער זיין פאַר מיר

זיך אויסצומאָלן אים אין ווייַסן פירער-קלייד?

— אַ ס'אַראַ צער —

און ס'אַראַ נאַכטיק-בייזע גייסטער-שפיל דאָס איז; —

אַ קינד פון שלאָף געוועקט,

ווען עס וואָלט געזען אַזאַ ווי אים אַט איצט, אין ווייַסן, אין דער נאַכט —

וואָלט עס געטראַכט — אַ מת וואָס לויפט אין שול אַריַין,

און וואָלט זיך אפשר בלויז געטרייסט מיט דעם

וואָס ס'איז אַ שעה אַזאַ פאַראַן,

ווען סע טרייַבט דער האָן די טויטע

צוריק צו זייער רו, דער ווייסטער, אין דער נאַכט.

נאָר זאָל מייַן בלוט ניט שטראָפן מיך דערפאַר —

איך האָב נאָך קיין מאָל ניט געזען אַ מת אַרומגיין.

נאָר הייַנט נאָך שטאַרבט מייַן אַטעם אַפּ אין מיר, פאַר טויט-שרעק,

ווען סע דערמאָנט זיך מיר דאָס נעגער-ווייַב אין ווייַסן אין דער נאַכט.

אַ פּאָסטראָט לעבן מיר, האָט זי מיך אָפּגעשטעלט.

און איך, אין חושך, האָב געזוכט

אַ האַנט, אַ פּנים פון אַ מענטש, אַן אויג,

און וואָס האָב איך געזען — אַ שנייַמענטש אָן אַ קאָפּ.

אַ ווייַס געשטעל, אַזאַ ווי אויפן פעלד בייַ נאַכט,

די הונגעריקע פייגל אָפּצושרעקן.

אפילו אָטעמען האָב איך זי ניט געהערט.

און בלויז איר לייַב-גערוך —

ווי שוועבל-זויערקייט אויף פלייש וואָס פוילט —

האָט מיך צו זיך געבראַכט.

און איך געדענק אפילו נאָך ווי איצט וואָלט דאָס געווען,

What does leadership mean?
It means a wind singing in spring!
It means, for sure, a pillar of light leading the way
Through a wilderness of stones and thorns.
It means a wind singing in spring,
Urging on the crying sick bird Hope
To spread its white wings
When we must cross mountains reaching to the clouds.
And what is the light in the leader's eye?
It is but a spark of his image, the chosen image.
One spark can perform the miracle
Of shining like a rainbow in the night.
But even if the man who sits across from me
Did not remind me, with his talk, of an angry fly
Buzzing around a pile of shit in the street—
And even if, while hearing his voice, I could stop thinking
That it is the evil of a human tongue, which braids words
Into a rope for a brother in the night—
Would it be any easier for me
To imagine him in the white robe of a leader?
Oh, what grief—
What an evil ghost play
In the night!
If a child, awakened from sleep,
Saw him, clad in white, in the night—
He would think: a corpse is running into the synagogue
In its shroud, and would comfort himself, perhaps,
That there is an early hour
When the cock chases the dead
Back to their peace, their cursed peace in the night.
Let my blood not poison me for this—
I've never seen a corpse walking around.
But to this day, my breath dies in me from terror
When I remember the Negro woman in white in the night.
A step away from me, she stopped me.
I searched in the dark
For a hand, a human face, an eye,
And what I saw was a snowman with no head,
A white figure in a field at night
To scare away the hungry birds.
I didn't even hear her breathe.
Only the smell of her flesh—
Like sulphur-acid on rotting meat—
Brought me to my senses.

a corpse is running—an East-European belief that generated numerous stories about the dead leaving the graveyard at night in their white shrouds, scaring people to death; only the early morning cock's crow chases them back into their graves.

ווי שווער עס איז מײַן קאָפּ אויף מיר געהאַנגען.

פֿון איר אָבער האָב איך געקאָנט אַוועקגיין אין דער נאַכט

צו ווײנען שטילערהייט אויף זיך אַליין,

און אויף דער פֿינצטערניש, וואָס פֿירט די אָרעמקייט

זאָל אויף קופּער־געלט

זיך אויסבײַטן די בענקעניש, איר הייליקסטע אין לעבן.

דאָ אָבער, אין אָט דער נאַכט־קאַפֿע,

דער אָנגעריכערטער ביז נעפֿל־גרויקייט —

דאָ איז מײַן אָפֿרו־אָרט —

דאָ האָב איך פֿרײַנד —

און כ'האָב ניט ערגעץ אַנדערש וווּ צו גיין.

1927

◄ דער פֿויגל מערציפֿינט

I

דרײַצן שוואַרצע און ווײַסע מכשפֿות

האָבן זיך אויסגעגראַבלט די אויגן

נעכטן בײַ נאַכט אין מיטן שטאָט.

נאָר איבער זיי אין דער הייך אין אַ ראָד

איז דער בלוטיקער פֿויגל מערציפֿינט

ווי אַ פֿײַער אין אַ ווירבל ווינט,

אַרומגעפֿלויגן.

די חכמים האָבן דאָס אויסגעטײַטשט

אַז דרײַצן מאָל דרײַצן חיילות וועלן

זיך אָנרוקן אויף אונדזער לאַנד,

אַזוי ווי אַ פֿײַערדיקע וואַנט

אין מיטן דער נאַכט.

אָבער מײַן אייגענער שטומער שאָטן,

וואָס האָט מיר אַרײַנגעקוקט אין די אויגן

האָט פֿאַמעלעך צו מיר זיך צוגעבויגן

און מיט מיר רייד, ווי מען ווײַנט אויף אַ מענטש, וואָס איז טויט,

האָט ער מיר ווײַנענדיק פֿאָרטרויט,

אַז איך אַליין האָב דאָס אויסגעטראַכט,

ווײַל מײַן אייגענע זעל אין מיר איז קראַנק,

ווי דרײַצן שוואַרצע און ווײַסטע מכשפֿות.

און ווײַל דאָס פֿײַער פֿון מײַן אונטערגאַנג

פֿרײַט זיך אין מיר, ווי אין ווירבלווינט

דער בלוטיקער פֿויגל מערציפֿינט,

וואָס איך האָב אים אויסגעטראַכט אין אַ ראָד,

אַזוי ווי אַ פֿײַער איבער דער שטאָט,

ווײַל איך וויל ס'זאָל ניט בלײַבן אַ שטייין אויף אַ שטיין

אין דעם פֿײַער, וואָס זי וועט אונטערגיין.

I remember, as if it were right now,
How heavily my head dropped.
From her, however, I could walk away in the night,
To cry quietly for myself
And for the darkness, which leads poverty
To trade for pennies
Its longing, the holiest in life.
But here, in this night-cafe
Fogged up in smoke,
Here is my resting place—
Here I've got friends—
And I have no place else to go.

1927

► *The Bird Mertsyfint*

I

Thirteen black and white witches
Scratched out their own eyes
Yesterday night in mid-city.
But the bloody bird Mertsyfint
Circled high above them
Like a fire in a whirlwind.
The sages interpreted this to mean
That thirteen times thirteen
Armies will move on our land
Like a wall of fire
In the middle of the night.
But my own mute shadow,
Looking straight into my eyes,
Slowly leaned over to me
And as one cries over a dead man,
Crying he revealed to me
That I myself invented it all,
Because inside me my soul is sick
Like thirteen black and white witches,
And because the fire of my end
Rejoices in me, as in a whirlwind
The bloody bird Mertsyfint,
That I invented turning in circles
Like a fire above the city,
Because I wish that a stone on a stone shall not remain
In the fire that will devastate it.

אָ ברידער מײַנע !

ווער עס וויל מײַן פּאַיאַצן-מיך מיט די זילבערנע גלעקלעך,

ווײַל ער מיינט, אַז ס'איז גוט געפעלן צו ווערן,

אפשר ווײַבער, וואָס זעען אויס ווי שמוגלערס אין די בוזעמס מיט פעקלעך

זאָל ער וויסן, אַז איך גיב אים דאָס אָפּ מיט מײַן טיפסטן פאַרנויג

און איך שענק אים (אויב ער באַדאַרף נאָר) אפילו מײַן פּויק.

און איך לערן אים אויס, ווי צו קלאַפן אַזוי מען זאָל הערן,

און מען זאָל זען, אַז פון הײַנט אָן איז ער דער נאַר,

אויב עס פאַלט ועמען אײַן אים אָפּצוגעבן כבוד דערפאַר.

איך אַליין וועל צוריקגיין אַהיים און מיט אַ פאַרקאַטשערטער פּאַלע,

ווי רב משה דער אָרעמער קבֿרן פון ביאַלעקאַמען

וועל זיך אויװקשטעלן דאָרט בײַ אַ פּעסל מיט סמאַלע

אויפן מאַרק דעם אַלטן. און אַז סע וועט קומען אַן אָרעמער גוי

בײַ וועמען כ'על זען אַז סע סקריפעט זיין וואָגן אַזוי,

ווי בײַ מיר די נשמה, וועט ער קענען בײַ מיר

די רעדער אַרומשמירן, אַלע פאַרבלאַטיקטע פיר

פאַר אַ האַלבן גראָשן, און זיך ווײַטער פאַרן

געזונטערהייט ווּהין ער וועט וועלן.

לאָמיר זאָגן קיין סאַסאָוו, אויב סע וועט אים געפעלן,

אָדער אפילו קיין סטרעמבליע צי גאָר קיין פּאַמאָרן.

◄ דער אַלטער פירער ווײנט

די גנבֿטע פּרינצעסין וואַנדאָראַ

האָט געבראַכט מיר זײדענע אונטערהויזן.

אָבער איך האָב געוויינט — וואָס טויג מיר דײַן זײַדנס,

אַז איך פאַל (ווי אויף אַ קאָפּ אַ בלויזן)

אַ שטיין וואָס מען וואַרפט) פאַר טאָג אַנידער?

צו זײַן אַ פירער פון יוניאָן-ברידער —

ניט גוט, וואַנדאָראַ.

אָט נעכטן ערשט: דער געשטופלטער מאַקסל

אינאַיינעם מיט דזשימין, דעס ממזר דעם קרומען,

געבראַכט מיר בײַ די נאַכט אַ פאַרוואָגלט מײדל,

וואָס זיי האָבן פון גאַס אַהיימגענומען.

און זיי טוען זי אויס בײַ מיר טאָקע דאָרטן

און מען שפּילט אויף איר נאַקעט לײַב אין קאָרטן.

ניט גוט, וואַנדאָראַ.

Oh, my brothers!
Whoever wants my clown's cap with the silver bells,
Because he thinks it'll help him
To be liked—perhaps by women, who look like smugglers
With packages in their bosoms—
He should know, that I'll let him have it all,
With a deep bow,
And I'll give him (if he needs it) even my drum.
And I'll teach him to bang so that everyone will hear
And see, that from now on he is the fool,
If anybody cares to honor him for that.
And I will go back home, I'll roll up the lap of my coat
And like Moyshe the poor undertaker from Byalekamen
I'll stand there with a barrel of tar
In the old market place. And if a poor peasant comes,
Whose cart is groaning
Like my soul, I'll let him smear
All four mud-covered wheels
For half a penny, and get back on the road
To wherever he wants to go.
For example, to Sassov, if he likes,
Or even to Stremblye, or as far as Pomoren.

Sassov, Byale'kamen, Stremblye—places in the vicinity of Halpern's hometown, Zlochov.

1924

Po'moren—Pommeranien, a former Polish province that belonged to Germany (implying a long distance where Jews went on foreign trade).

➤ *The Old Leader Complains*

Princess Vandora the thief
Brought me silken underwear,
But I cried—what good is your silk
When I fall (like a stone that is thrown
On a bare head) at dawn?
To be a leader of union brothers—
No good, Vandora.

Just last night, pock-marked Maxy
Together with Jimmy, the limping bastard,
Brought me home a stray girl
They took in off the street.
They undressed her right there in my place
And we played cards on her naked body.
No good, Vandora.

ז׳איז געלעגן מיטן האַרץ אַרונטער.

כ׳האָב געוואָלט זי זאָל אויפלעבן אַ ביסל,

זאָל זי וויינען, צי שילטן אפֿילו,

אָדער שטופן אַ לאָפע צום געלט אין שיסל.

זי אָבער — זאָל מיך גאָט ניט שטראָפן —

איך גיב אַ קוק, זי איז איינגעשלאָפן.

ניט גוט, וואַנדאָראַ.

און אפֿילו די ווערטלעך פֿון אונדזער דזשימי

האָבן ניט געהאָלפן. מיטן קאָפ אַרונטער,

אַזוי ווי אַ הילצערנע איז זי געלעגן.

ניט אַנדערש, כאַטש נעם און צינד זי אונטער,

און דער הילך פֿון די קאָרטן אויף איר און דאָס לאַכן

ווי אַ טיר וואָס דער ווינט האַלט אין איין פֿאַרמאַכן.

ניט גוט, וואַנדאָראַ.

ערשט העט פֿאַר טאָג, מיט פֿייער ביים ים נאַזלאָך

און ביים בריסטל וואָס איז פֿון בעט געהאַנגען

האָט מען דערזען אַז זי איז אַ טויטע.

קען זיין — ז׳איז פֿון הונגער אויסגעגאַנגען

אָדער גאָר מיר האָבן — אַ שד זאָל וויסן —

מיט אונדזערע קאָרטן זי צום טויט פֿאַרשמיסן.

ניט גוט, וואַנדאָראַ.

נאָר מוידן פֿאַראַנען גענוג אָן אַרבעט.

כ׳על קויפן אַ היַיזל מיט פֿאַרהענגלעך ווידער.

זיי האָבן זיך אָנגעהויבן בריקען

די בהמות, מיַינע יוניאָן-ברידער,

נאָר איך האָב זיי אַזוי טאָקע אויסגעמאָלקן,

ווי די זומער-זון מעלקט אויס דעם וואָלקן.

ניט גוט, וואַנדאָראַ.

◄ מאַך פֿאַר אים אַ רעוואָלוציע, מאַך פֿאַר אים!

די גוליע אויפֿן שטערן?

וועמען גייט עס אָן?

אַבי ער איז דער ערשטער דאָ

וועט יענער — ווען ר׳וועט עפֿענען די טיר — אים מוזן זען.

— איך וואַרט שוין דאָ

(וועט ער מיט טרערן אין די אויגן בעטן זיך)

פֿון זייגער פיר פֿאַר טאָג.

She was lying, her heart hanging down.
I wanted to liven her up a bit.
I wished she'd cry or even curse,
Or push her paw toward the bowl of money.
Yet—oh, don't punish me, God,
I took a look—she had fallen asleep.
No good, Vandora.

And even the jokes of our Jimmy
Didn't help. Her head hanging down,
She lay there like a piece of wood—
Nothing to do but set her on fire.
And the thump of the cards on her body and the laughter
Were like a door that the wind keeps closing.
No good, Vandora.

Only late, at dawn, with fire in her nostrils
And in the small breast hanging off the bed,
We saw she was dead.
Maybe hunger finished her off.
Or maybe—the devil knows—we
Whipped her to death with our cards.
No good, Vandora.

But there are lots of broads out of work.
I'll buy me a house with little curtains.
They've begun to kick, I tell you,
Those silly cows, my union brothers.
But never mind, I milked them plenty,
As the summer sun milks a cloud.
No good, Vandora.

➤ *Make for Him a Revolution, If You Can!*

The bump on his forehead?
Whose business is it?
What counts is, he's the first—
Whoever opens the door will have to see him.
—I've been waiting here
(He'll beg with tears in his eyes)
Since four in the morning.

און אַז מען וועט בײַ אים אַ פרעג טאָן,
צי ער האָט שוין בײַ שמאַטעקלײַבעריי געאַרבעט?
אַוודאי האָט ער שוין בײַ שמאַטעקלײַבעריי געאַרבעט;
נאָך אין דער אַלטער היים,
אין דער פּאַפּיר-פֿאַבריק בײַ דעם משומד סעלצער.
אַן אויסטערלישער מענטש געווען.

פלעגט אַרומגיין מיט די הענט אויף הינטן, הין או קריק,
און דעם, און יענעם גלאַט אַזוי אויף שפּאַס אַ פרעג טאָן —
צי האָט מען טאַקע ליב אַ קוגל וואָס ס׳רינט פון אים דאָס שמאַלץ —
און צי מען גיט טאַקע אין האַנט אַריַין אַ גאַנצן רײַניש
דעם רבין, דעם פֿאַרכאַטע זשיד.

און כאַטש ער האָט דאָס גאַנצע שטעטל שיער
אויף בעטלברויט געבראַכט, ווען ער האָט אָנגעזעצט.
האָט ער — אַליין שוין מיט אַ פּנים פון אַ מת — נאָך אַלץ אַלץ געלאַכט;
מען וועט שוין מער ניט האָבן וואָס אין האַנט אַרײַנצושטופּן
דעם רבין, דעם פֿאַרכאַטע זשיד,
וועט ער פֿאַר הונגער פגרן.

— צי רעדט ער בײַ דער אַרבעט אויך, און שלעפּט די הויזן
אָט-אַזוי-ווי-איצט?
— זאָל גאָט אים אויסהיטן, ער איז דאָך ניט קיין ״צאַצעליסט״
וואָס וויל מען זאָל אים פֿאַר אומזיסט באַצאָלן.
ער גייט אַ לײַבצודעקל אָנגעטאָן.

און זאָל ער אַזוי האָבן, וואָס ער דאַרף,
ווי ער קען זײַן להבדיל, ווי אַ הונט געטרײַ.
ער טוט אפילו נישט קיין שפּײַ קיין איבריקן
בעת דער אַרבעט.
וואָס ער וויל ער איז בלויז, דער מײַסטער-לעב זאָל אים דערלויבן
דעם קאַפעליוש ניט אויסצוטאָן.

— פֿאַר וואָס?
— נישט ווײַל ער איז אַזוי פרום חלילה. דווקא,
דאָס דאַרף מען גאָר אַפֿילו וועגן אים נישט טראַכטן.
ער שעמט זיך בלויז מיט אָט-אַ-דעם-אָ אויפֿן שטערן
ער ווייסט אַליין נישט ווי אַזוי ער האָט עס,
אַזוי ווי איבער נאַכט איז דאָס אים אָנגעוואַקסן,
דער דאָקטאָר זאָגט, אַז ס׳איז אַ פּראָסטע גוליע בלויז —
נאָר אַז ער האָט אפֿילו נישט אויף ברויט, פֿאַר ווײַב און קינדער
(גאַנצע זיבן זאָלן זיי אים זײַן געזונט)
ליגט אים נישט אין זינען אַזאַ נאַרישקײַט.

און אָט אַזוי טאַקע — מיט אײַנגעבויגענע קני,
און מיט אַ קאַפעליוש ביז איבער די אויגן,

And when they ask him,
Did he ever work at ragpicking?
Of course he worked at ragpicking,
Even back in the old country,
In the paper factory of the convert Seltzer.
An unusual man he was.
Used to walk back and forth, his hands behind his back,
And just for fun he would ask a person
Whether one really loved a *kugel*, dripping *schmaltz*,
And whether one really sticks a whole Dinar in the hand
Of the rebbe, the cankerous yid.
And though he nearly sent the whole town
Begging for bread when he went bankrupt,
Even then, with the face of a corpse, he went on laughing:
—They won't have a penny to stick in the hand
Of the rebbe, the cankerous yid,
So he'll croak from hunger.

—Does he speak while he works too and pull his pants
Like this?
—God forbid! Is he a "Sauce-alist,"
Who will want to get paid for nothing?
Doesn't he wear a pious undergarment?
So may he have all he needs,
He can be faithful as a dog (forgive the comparison).
He doesn't even spit more than necessary
While he works.
He only asks the dear boss to let him
Keep his felt hat on.

—How come?
—Not because he's pious, God forbid, on the contrary,
One should certainly not think that of him.
It's just that he's ashamed of that-thing-here on his forehead—
He himself doesn't know how it got there,
It swelled up overnight,
The doctor says it's just a bump—
But since he's got no bread for wife and kids
(A full seven, may they be healthy)
He has no head for such foolishness.

And just like this—with bended knee,
Felt hat over his eyes,

kugel—baked noodle pudding.

schmaltz—rendered chicken or goose fat.

pious undergarment—
arbe'kanfes*

Don't mention it in the same breath—a pious Jew would add such a phrase of distinction whenever man is compared with animals or the sacred with the profane.

און מיטן קאָפּ צווישן די אַקסל
און מיט אַ בערדל אויך, וואָס גיט נישט צו
דעם מינדסטן חן צום פּנים וואָס איז בלייך,
שטייט אַ מענטשעלע אַ קליינס, פֿאַרטאָג,
אין פֿינצטערן קאָרידאָר,
אַן אָנגעשפּאַרטער בײַ דער טיר פֿון שמאַטע-קעלער,
וואָס איז דאָס אייגנטום
(ווי סע ליענט זיך אויפֿן שילד, בײַם פֿײַער פֿון אַ שוועבעלע)
פֿון לאַנדסמאַן זײַנעם, דזשייקאָב פּליטיבאַיד —
אַן אייניקל (ווי ער האָט זיך דערוווּסט)
פֿון יענעם חדר-רבין
וואָס האָט בײַ אים אַ מאָל אַ פּאה אויסגעריסן —
רב יאַנקל שפּילפֿויגל,
אַזוי האָט ער געהייסן — — —
יע — — —
רב יאַנקל שפּילפֿויגל.

◄ די הײַראַט

קוק איך אויף דער נאַקעטער פֿרוי,
מיט דעם קליינעם קאָפּ
און מיט די גראָבע אומגעלומפּערטע לענדן
און מיט די גרויסע מענערישע פֿיס, —
וועגד איך זיך צום פֿאַרבן-קינסטלער
און איך פֿרעג אים
וואָס אים האָט געבראַכט דערצו
אַזוינס אויף דעם לײַוונט אויסצוטרוימען.
רײַבט ער אָן אַ שוועבעלע
און שטופּט אַרײַן די ליולקע אין זײַן מויל
און ענטפֿערט. —
שטעלט זיך אַרויס אַט-וואָס:
ער — פּו.
אַליין — פּו.
געוועון פֿאַרהײַראַט צו איר — פּו.
אין פּאַריז טאַקע — פּו.

His head sunk in his shoulders
And a little beard which doesn't add
A bit of beauty to his pale face—
Stands a little man at dawn
In the dark corridor,
Leaning on the door of the rag-cellar,
Which is the property
(As the sign reads in the light of a match)
Of a *landsman* from his native town, J. Jacob Playboi'd—
A grandson (as he found out)
Of that *heder*-teacher
Who once pulled out his sidecurl—
Reb Yankel Shpilfoygel,
That was his name— — —
Yeah— — —
Reb Yankel Shpilfoygel.

Playboi'd—a Brooklyn
pronunciation of Playbird,
translated from the Yiddish

Shpilfoygl (German:
Spielvogel).

➤ *Married*

I look at the naked woman
With her tiny head,
Thick clumsy thighs
And big masculine legs.
And I turn to the painter
And ask him
What made him dream up
Such a thing on a canvas.
He strikes a match,
Stuffs his pipe in his mouth
And replies—
It turns out:
He—puff.
Himself—puff.
Was married to her—puff.
In Paris, mind you—puff.

Max Weber: from *Shriftn 6*,
Spring 1920.

◄ מײַן אײנציקער זון

און אַז איך רעד מיט גוטן צו מײַן זון — װאָס טויג?
אַז לויט ער קוקט ער אויף מיר, באַדאַרף מען נאָר
ער זאָל אַ זאָג טאָן אויפן קול: — אָט האָסטו דיר!
מײַן פֿאָטער דער בהמהניק האָט װידער שוין
דאָס מויל זײַנס אויפגעעפנט...

איך זאָג אים: זון מײַנער,
אַ פּרינץ אַפֿילו דאַרף דאָך הײַנט-צו-טאָג
זיך לערנען עפּעס טאָן.
און דו, קינאָרע אַנדערהאַלבן יאָר שוין אַלט,
און װאָס װעט זײַן?
אמת איז: נישטאָ קיין יאָר-יריד
בײַ אונז דאָ אין דער גרויסער שטאָט;
צי אָבער מוז מען דװקא אײַער גנבענען, צי הינער בלויז?
פֿאַר װאָס ניט געלט טאַקע?

Moyshe-Leyb Halpern: *Portrait of his son, Isaac.*

➤ *My Only Son*

And if I talk nicely to my son—what good does it do?
When he looks at me, he stops just short
Of saying aloud: How about that!
My father the cow
Has opened his mouth again . . .

I tell him: Son,
Nowadays even a prince
Has to learn how to do something.
And you—touch wood—you're already a year-and-a-half
And what will become of you?
I admit: there are no annual fairs
Here in the big city;
But must it be only eggs or chickens one steals?
Why not money?

פֿאַר װאָס ניט זײַד און סאַמעט פֿון די גרױסע לאַגערן?
פֿאַר װאָס ניט גאָלד און דימענטן בײַ יענע לײַט,
װאָס שאַרן זיך אַרום צװישן נעגערס אָרעמע
און שװינדלען? — אַ פֿינצטער יאָר אױף זײ!

נאָר װען איך זע, אַז ס׳האָט דער זון מײַנער
דעם מינדסטן אָפּשײַ ניט,
און אַז ער שטעלט זיך נאָך דערבײַ אַנידער מיר אַנטקעגן
מיט אַ לאַפּע אױפֿן אױער, װי אַ גרױסער,
װאָס מאַכט דעם אַנשטעל, אַז ער איז טױב —
זע איך דאָך באַשײַמפּערלעך,
אַז ס׳װעט פֿון אים קײן לײַט ניט זײַן,
מוז איך דאָך שױן אַ געשרײַ טאָן.

זאָג איך: — הער נאָר אױס, דו פֿינצטערלינג!
נאָך הײַנט זאָלסטו מיר גײן אַ פֿײַער אונטערלײגן,
ניט װיכטיק װוּ,
נאָר ברענען — זאָג איך — זאָל עס!
און װאָרט — זאָג איך — דו װעסט נאָך בײַ מיר זײַן אַ פּרעזידענט
מיט הענט, װאָס קלעפֿן זיך װי גומעראַביקע,
און אױב דאָס הײליקע פֿאַטערלאַנד
װעט אָנפֿירן אַ קריג,
װעסטו מיר זײַן פֿאַראַנטװאָרטלעך פֿאַר יעדן טראָפּן בלוט
פֿון אונדזערן אַ העלד.
געדענק — זאָג איך —
בלוט פֿון אונדזערע העלדן איז קײן װאַסער ניט,
בלוט אַזױנס איז גאָלד, גאָלד און נאָך אַ מאָל גאָלד.
און אַז אַ מענטש האָט גאָלד,
איז װײַבער גאָר די שענסטע פֿונעם לאַנד,
זײ פֿליִען אים װי פֿײגל אין די הענט אַרײַן
און דעמאָלט — זאָג איך — האָט מען פֿאַר גאָרניט װאָס צו זאָרגן...
אַזױנע פֿײגל — זאָג איך — גיט מען אַ באַשמיר
מיט ציגל-פֿאַרב די פּנימער, די נאָז מיט מעל,
און הײַדאַ — קינדערלעך!
זאָל זײַן פֿון שאַנד, אַבי פּרנסה.
אַז מ׳האָט דאָס ביסל קלינגערס — האָט מען אַלץ, אַט-װאָס, זון מײַנער.

נאָר רײד און שפֿרינג פֿון הױט,
אַז אַלע מײַנע רײד באַטראַכט דער זון מײַנער,
װי איך דעם אַפּפֿאַל, װאָס דער ים
װאַרפֿט אַלע טאָג אַרױס.
און פּרוּװ איך אים אַ סטראָשע טאָן און װײַז אַ פֿױסט —
שטעלט ער זיך אַנידער און באַטראַפֿט זי מיט אַ מינע,
װי ער װאָלט דאָס געװוּען דער אײנציקער אין דער מדינה צימצעדרים,

Why not silk and velvet from the big warehouses?
Why not gold and diamonds from those people
Who sneak around among poor Negroes
And swindle? The devil take them!

But when I see that my son
Doesn't have the slightest respect—
He stands across from me
With a paw to his ear, like a grown-up
Who pretends to be deaf—
Then I can see with my own eyes
That nothing will come of him,
And I have to shout.

I say: Listen, you son of the dark!
This very day go and light a fire,
No matter where,
But burn—I say—it must!
Wait—I say—I'll make you into a president,
With hands sticky as glue,
And if the holy fatherland
Goes to war,
You'd better be responsible for every drop of blood
From our heroes.
Remember—I say to him—
Blood of our heroes is not water.
Such blood is money, money and again money.
And if a guy has money,
The nicest women of the land
Fly into his hands like birds.
And then—I say—you'll have nothing to worry about . . .
Such birds—I say—just smear
Their faces with brick-color, their noses with flour,
And—giddy-up, kids!
Never mind if it's from shame—as long as you make a living.
If you have some extra change—you have everything, that's how it is, my son.

But even if I shout and jump out of my skin
My son looks at my words
As I look at the scum
The sea throws up every day.
And when I try to threaten him and show my fist,
He stands there, touches it, and makes a face
As if he were the only one in the Land of Tsimtsidrim,

Tsimsi'drim—a derogatory
nonsense word.

דער פּויסטנהעלד מעקאַרטי הונטצוואָטײַקע —
אַזאַ מין גאָרניט וואָס דאָס איז!
איך וואָלט אַ בעלן זײַן אַ פרעג טאָן אים,
צי ער וועט קדיש זאָגן נאָך מײַן טויט.

״ — וואָט ד׳יע מין קאַדעש?
די אָלד קאַיק פראָם סטינקי פּאָלאַנד מיטגעבראַכט
דאַט יאַיישמיירואַבינע,
טו העל וויט איט — דאַטס ראַיט.״

◄ אין סענטראַל פּאַרק

ווער איז שולדיק אין דעם וואָס מען זעט ניט דײַן בוים,
גאָרטן אין שניי, מײַן גאָרטן אין שניי.
ווער איז שולדיק אין דעם וואָס מען זעט ניט דײַן בוים,
אַז סע גייט שפּאַצירן אין דיר אַזאַ פרוי,
וואָס איר בוזעם הייבט זיך און וואַרפט זיך אַזוי,
ווי איבער צערודערטע כוואַליעס און שום
אַ שיפל אין ים, מיט ים-רויבער צוויי,
וואָס שרײַען, אַז זיי זײַנען ים-רויבער צוויי, —
גאָרטן אין שניי, מײַן גאָרטן אין שניי.

ווער איז שולדיק אין דעם וואָס קיין הירש איז נישטאָ,
גאָרטן אין שניי, מײַן גאָרטן אין שניי.
ווער איז שולדיק אין דעם וואָס קיין הירש איז נישטאָ,
אַז אַ גלח וואָס דאַרף זײַן פרום ווי אַ קינד
לויפט נאָך דעם קאַפּעליוש זײַנעם אין ווינט,
און ער שרײַט צו אים הײַ און האַ, און האַ-לאָ!
און דער קאַפּעליוש אין זײַן וויסטן גערײַ
הערט אים ניט, אין זײַן וויסטן גערײַ —
גאָרטן אין שניי, מײַן גאָרטן אין שניי.

ווער איז שולדיק אין דעם וואָס איך בין דיר פרעמד,
גאָרטן אין שניי, מײַן גאָרטן אין שניי.
ווער איז שולדיק אין דעם וואָס איך בין דיר פרעמד,
אַז איך גיי נאָך דעם שאַל און דאָס היטל דאָ,
וואָס בײַ קיינעם אין לאַנד איז אַזוינס נישטאָ,
און אַז כ׳האָב נאָך אַ באָרד וואָס דײַן ווינט צענעמט
ווי אַ יידענע שטרוי, ווו זי זוכט אַן איי
פאַר איר קראַנקן קינד, פון דער הון אַן איי, —
גאָרטן אין שניי, מײַן גאָרטן אין שניי.

1930

The fist-hero Dirty Dog McCarthy—
What a zero he is!
I would really like to ask him
If he'll recite the Kaddish when I die.

—"Waddya mean kadesh?
De old kike from stinkin' Polan' dragged wit' 'im
Some yaysh-may-rabberry—
To hel vit it—dats right."

yaysh-may-rubberry—a distortion of the words of the Kaddish, making it close to raspberry.

► *In Central Park*

Who is to blame that I don't see your tree,
Garden in snow, my garden in snow.
Who is to blame that I don't see your tree—
When a woman goes out for a stroll in your snow,
Her bosom rising and bouncing so,
As on choppy waves in the sea
A boat with two pirates who row
And shout that they are two pirates who row—
Garden in snow, my garden in snow.

Who is to blame that there is no deer,
Garden in snow, my garden in snow.
Who is to blame that there is no deer—
When a priest who should be good as a child
Is running after his hat gone wild
In the wind, and shouting: Hey, Ho, and Oh dear!
And the hat, in its damn whirlblow,
Heeds him not, in its damn whirlblow—
Garden in snow, my garden in snow.

Who is to blame that I'm a stranger to you,
Garden in snow, my garden in snow.
Who is to blame that I'm a stranger to you—
When I wear a scarf and a cap at a slant,
Things that no one would wear in this land,
And I still have a beard that the wind blows
Like a woman seeking an egg in the straw
For her sick child, an egg in the straw—
Garden in snow, my garden in snow.

1930

דער אַלטער קלאַון פֿון קאַראַקאַמבאַ
פֿלעגט אַרײנבראַקן ציבעלעס אין דער קאַװע.
מיר איז אומעטיק, — דערצײל איך מיר דאָס
מיט דעם ניגון "כּל-נדרי" אין דער פֿינצטער.

װי מאָדנע ער האָט מיט די רױטלעכע אױגן
געפֿינטלט בײ דעם לײמענעם טעפּל;
מיט אַ פֿראָסטן הילצערנעם לעפֿל האָט ער
די ציבעלעס מיט קאַװע געגעסן.

און זיבן טעג, האַרבסט-רעגן אין פֿענצטער
קענען אַזױ אָן טױט נישט דערמאָנען,
װי די אָרעמקײט, װאָס האָט געיאָמערט,
פֿון זײַן יעדן זופּ אַרױסגעיאָמערט.

איך װעל גײן, װוּ די אָבֿות זײַנען געגאַנגען —
האָט דאָס אָפֿענע מױל געזאָגט צום לעפֿל, —
מײַן װײַב באַלײַקאַ איז אױך שױן דאָרטן,
איך װעל גײן, װוּ די אָבֿות זײַנען געגאַנגען.

די שטיקלעך ציבעלע אױפֿן לעפֿל
האָבן אױסגעזען, װי צעבראָכענע פֿערל;
נאָר זײ האָבן דערמאָנט אױך אָן טאַבאַק-פֿאַרגעלטע
דאַרע פֿינגער אױף אַ צימבל.

אין אַ קלײד פֿון זיבן מאָל זיבן אײַלן
האָט באַלײַקאַ אַנטקעגנגעטאַנצט איר חתן.
װאָס װײַנסטו, קלאַון פֿון קאַראַקאַמבאַ,
דאָס איז דאָך בלױז מײַן כּל-נדרי-ניגון.

דאָס לײמענע קאַװע-טעפּל איז װאַרעם,
אַזױ װי מײַן הּאַרץ, װאָס איז בלינד-געבױרן;
און די ציבעלע, די אַרײַנגעבראַקטע,
איז האַרב װי מײַן אומעט אין דער פֿינצטער.

◄ מײַן שרײַענדיקײט

מײַן שרײַענדיקײט איז אײַנגעשלאָפֿן אין מיר,
װי אַ קראַנקער אין אַ װינטער-נאַכט אױף אַ שטײן אין דרױסן.
דאָס ליכט פֿון דער לבֿנה אױף אַזױנעם
איז געל, װי אױף אַ געשטאָרבענעם.

The clown of Karahamba used to crumble
Pieces of onions into his coffee.
I am sad—so I tell it to myself
To the tune of Kol-Nidre in the dark.

How strangely his red eyes blinked
Over the simple mug of clay;
With a plain wooden spoon he ate
The onions in his coffee.

Seven days of mourning, autumn rain in the window
Cannot remind me of death as much
As the misery that whined,
Whined from each sip he took.

Kol-'Nidre*—the opening
prayer of Yom Kippur and its
melody, conveying the saddest
mood in the Jewish year.

I shall go where my fathers have gone—
Thus spoke his open mouth to the spoon.
My wife Balaykah is already there,
I shall go where my fathers have gone.

The pieces of onion in his spoon
Looked like broken pearls;
And they were like tobacco-yellowed
Thin fingers plucking a guitar.

In a dress of seven times seven feet
Balaykah danced toward her bridegroom.
Why do you cry, clown of Karahamba,
It's only my Kol-Nidre tune.

The coffee mug of clay is warm.
So is my heart that was born blind.
And the crumbled bits of onion
Are harsh as my sadness in the dark.

► *My Crying-Out-Loud*

My Crying-Out-Loud fell asleep in me
Like a sick man on a stone in a winter night in a field.
The light of the moon on his face
Is yellow as on a corpse.

The Yiddish title, **Mayn
shrayendikeyt**, is a nominalized
form of "to shout," literally, "my
shoutingness," meaning: that
"something" in me that wants to
shout, to protest; the scream
inside me. See the other (earlier?)
version of this poem, as published
from the manuscript, in the next
section.

און בלויז דער ווינט, וואָס פליט אַרום — זעט אים.
די וועלט? — וואָס די וועלט?
פאַראַן פענצטער אומעטום.
אַ סך זײַנען פינצטער.
די איבעריקע לויכטן אַנטקעגן רעלסן
בײַ די ברעגן פון ים,
פון הויכע בערג אַרונטער
און פון פּאַלאַצן אַזוינע מיט גאָרטן און צוים אַרום זיך,
וווּ מען שפּילט, דאָרטן טאַנצט מען
מיט וואַרעם לײַב אונטער זײַד און סאַמעט און קאַמגאַרן.
וווּ מען זיצט אַרום טישן געדעקטע,
זעט מען געלן קוכן און ברוינעם קוכן
צווישן פינגער און צײַן, ווי פּערל שײַנע,
און פלעשער מיט לאַנגע שמאַלע העלדזער,
מיט זילבער פון אויבן און מיט גאָלד —
און בלומען.
אמת, די בלומען קאָסטן אַ סך איבעריק געלט,
נאָר זייערע פאַרבן אונטער דעם ליכט,
וואָס באַלויכטן די מענטשן אַרום,
דערמאָנען אַ רעגנבויגן איבער קינדער
און רעגן־טײַכלעך.
קינדער אַזוינע הייבן זייערע העמדלעך
ביז איבער די נאָפּלען אַרויף
און זיי האָבן ליב צו לאַכן איינס צום אַנדערן.
און וואָס קינדער בײַ טאָג — דערוואַקסענע בײַ נאַכט.
מען לאַכט און מען רעדט אַזוי,
אַז מען ווערט צאַרט און בײגיק דערבײַ,
ווי ערשט פון מוטער־לײַב.
און אויפמאַכן אַ פענצטער פון דרויסן
וועט מען זיי בלויז איבערשרעקן — און מער גאָרניט.
ווי שיין מען זאָל נישט דערצײַלן וועגן דעם שטיין אין דרויסן
און פון יענעם, וואָס שלאָפט אויף אים
און וואָס זעט אויס ווי אַ געשטאָרבענער —
וועלן זיי ניט גלייבן.
פרוויען מיט אויגן די הימלדיקע וועלן באַדויערן
דעם, וואָס דערצײַלט,
און וועלן אויסזען דערבײַ נאָך שענער ווי פריִער.
פרוויען מיט טונקעלע אויגן,
וועלן זאָגן — אַ קינסטלער אַ הונגעריקער,
וואָס וויל ניט נעמען קיין ברויט אומזיסט,
דערצײַלט ער עפּעס דערפאַר.
דאָס אַלטע פּאָר אָבער,
וואָס בײדע זעען שוין מער גאָרניט,

Only the roaming wind will see him.
The world?—What's the world?
There are windows everywhere.
Lots of them dark.
The rest are shedding light onto rails
By the seashore,
Down from high mountains
And from palaces surrounded by garden and fence.
Where people play, there they dance
With their bodies warm under silk and velvet and damask.
Where they sit at full tables,
There is yellow cake and brown cake
Between fingers and teeth like beautiful pearls
And bottles with long, slender necks,
With silver on top and with gold—
And flowers.
Granted, the flowers cost a lot of superfluous necessary money,
But their colors, bathed in light,
Illuminating the people around,
Remind you of a rainbow over children's heads
And rivulets of rain.
Children in a rainbow raise
Their shirts above their bellies
And laugh loudly to each other.
And like children in daytime, so adults at night.
They laugh and talk until
They are soft and supple,
As fresh from their mother's womb.
And opening a window to the field
Will only scare them—nothing more.
No matter how beautiful your story about the stone in a field
And the man who fell asleep on it
And looks like a corpse—
They won't believe you.
Women with skylike eyes will pity
The storyteller
And will look more beautiful than ever.
Women with dark eyes
Will say—a hungry artist,
Who wouldn't take bread for nothing,
But tells a story instead.
The old couple, however,
Who cannot see anymore,

און וואָס צוליב זיי איז דער יום-טוב,
וועלן ציטערן מיט אַלע פֿאַלדן אויף זייערע פֿנימער
און זיך צוביייגן איינס צום אַנדערן,
און וואָס מען וועט פֿירזאָגן וועט מען נאָכזאָגן.
מען קען זיך עס אויסמאָלן אַפֿילו אַז מען וויל
מער ווייניקער אַזוי —

זי: שרעק זיך ניט, פֿאַטערל;
ער: שרעק זיך ניט, מוטערל;
זי: עס איז גאָרנישט, פֿאַטערל;
ער: עס איז גאָרנישט, מוטערל;
זי: דער ווינט גייט דאָס אַלץ, פֿאַטערל;
ער: דער ווינט גייט דאָס אַלץ, מוטערל.
דער ווינט גייט, פֿאַטערל.
דער ווינט גייט, מוטערל.
דער ווינט גייט —
דאָס אַלץ.

1927

(And whom this whole celebration is for)
Will tremble in all the folds of their faces
And, leaning to each other,
One will intone, and the other will repeat.
If we wish, we could imagine it
Something like this—

She: Don't be afraid, Pop;
He: Don't be afraid, Mom;
She: It's nothing, Pop;
He: It's nothing, Mom;
She: It's just the wind passing, Pop;
He: It's just the wind passing, Mom.
The wind passing, Pop.
The wind passing, Mom.
The wind passing—
Just that.

1927

Raphael Soyer: *Waterfront*, 1934.

◀ ווי לאַנג וועל איך שטיין

ווי לאַנג וועל איך שטיין און זיך וויגן אין רעגן אַזוי,
וואָס גייט דאָס מיר אָן וואָס סע ליגט אויף דער ערד דאָ אַ פרוי
ביים שיַין פון אַ גאַסן-לאַמטערן אין אַט-אַזאַ נאַכט !
אַט-ערשט הינטער איר האָט מען דאָכט זיך די שענקטיר פאַרמאַכט,
און איך האָב געזען וואַו זי שטעלט ביים לאַמטערן זיך אַפ —
מיט הענט און מיט אַקסל און וואָס העננגען אויף איר ווי דער קאָפּ,
כ'האָב אַפילו געהערט ווי זי ציטערט און קלאַפּט מיט די ציין —
און בעט מען זאָל קומען און וואַרפן איר זאָל מען אַ שטיין :
— איר מאַמע אַ דינסטמויד, אַ פינצטערער דאָרף-סאַמעוואַר
האָט געלאָזט מיט אַ שטיוול צעבלאָזן זיך פון אַ הוזאַר,
וויַיל די וועלט דאַרף אַ הור וואָס דערוואַרעמט ווי ביליקע טיי,
מיט ליפן געפאַרבטע און לעבדן געשװאָלענע צוויי.
זיי האָבן זיך ביַידע ווי הינט ערגעץ דאָרטן געפּאָרט,
און זי מוז זיך וואַלגערן דאָ אָן אַ היים, אָן אַן אָרט,
און איר נאָמען — אַ פאַסט-פעקל ווו דער אַדרעס איז פאַרשמירט
אין אַ הינטערגאַס מיסט אויפן וועג וואָס אַ שקאָף פאַרליִירט.

אַזוי האָט די פרוי ביים לאַמטערן אַט-אַקאָרשט גערעדט,
און געקריצט מיט די ציין און אַליין זיך דאָס פנים געגלעט,
און אויסגעשטרעקט נאָך דעם די אייגענע דאַרע צוויי הענט,
צו איינעם אַן אַלטן, אַזוי ווי זי וואָלט אים געקענט.
און וואָס האָט דער אַלטער געטאָן? ער האָט געשאַרט מיט די פיס
און האָט איר געוויזן ווי גרוי און באַוואָקסן ער איז,
און עפעס געפלאַפלט דערביַי פון אַ שווערד מיט אַ פאַן,
דאַן האָט ער אין לופטן אַ דריי מיט אַ פינגער געטאָן —
און צוגערוקט נעענטער זיך און די אויגן צעשפּרייט,
געקוקט אויף איר הוט און געקוקט אויף איר יאַקל און קלייד,
געקוקט און געפרייט זיך, געפאַטשט מיט די הענט ווי אַ קינד,
געקוקט ווי עס גיסט זיך דאָס וואַסער פון איר און עס רינט.
און ווידער ווי פריִער געלאָזן אין רעגן זיך גיין —
דעם קאָפּ צווישן די אַקסל אַזוי — מיט זיך איינעם אַליין,
און האָט מען אים מער נישט געזען — האָט מען בלויז נאָך געהערט
דעם שאַר פון די שיך אויף דער נאַסער פאַרשטיינערטער ערד.

וואָס נאָך איז געשען? ס'איז פאַראיבער די באַן אין דער הויך,
און די פרוי האָט דערביַי, לאָמיר זאָגן אַזוי ווי אַ רויך,
אין אַט-אַ דער רגע געטראַכט אפשר בלויז וועגן מיר,
אַ ציטער געטאָן, אָבער איך האָב פון שירעם אפיר
און וועגן דעם אַיַיזערנעם באַן-וועג וואָס איבער דער גאַס.

► *How Long Will I Stand*

How long will I stand here, swaying like this in the rain,
And what do I care that a woman lies sprawled on the ground
In the rain in the light of a streetlamp on such a dark night!
It seems that just now the bar-door behind her was shut
And I saw how she stopped at the lamp-pole right here in the street—
With shoulders and arms hanging down like the droop of her head,
I could even hear how she shivered and chattered her teeth
And begged them to come and to throw a stone at her body:
—Her mother, a maid in a village, a dark samovar,
Got blown up with a boot like a bellows by a passing Hussar,
'Cause the world needs a whore who can warm a man like cheap tea,
With lips that are painted and hips that are swollen and soft.
They coupled somewhere like two dogs in the shade of a fence
And left her like this, to stray with no home, with no place,
Her name—a parcel whose address is smeared and forgotten,
Dung in a backstreet a mare has dropped on its way.

So spoke at the streetlamp the woman a moment ago
And gnashed her teeth and fondled her face with her hand.
And afterward, stretched out her two skinny arms to a man,
An old passer-by, as if she had known him before.
And what did he do, the old man? He shuffled his feet
And showed her how gray was his head, how hairy his body,
And mumbled something to her of a sword and a flag,
And excited, he brandished his finger high in the air—
And moved even closer to her, opened wider his eyes,
And looked at her hat, and looked at her sweater and dress,
And looked and was happy, and clapped his two hands like a child,
And looked how the water streamed off the flanks of her dress.
And then he departed again, as he came, in the rain—
His head sunk deep in his shoulders—he left all alone,
And when he had vanished from sight—one could only hear
The shuffle of shoes in the rain on the wet stony ground.

What else then occurred? A train passed by overhead
And the woman at that—how shall I put it?—like smoke
She shivered and swayed, but I, at that very moment,
With umbrella in hand, thought maybe just of myself
And perhaps of the railway of iron hung over the street.

samo'var—large Russian kettle for brewing tea with a charcoal fire in the lower part and a chimney tube running through the middle. To blow the fire, one could put a boot on top of the tube and use it as a bellows.

אַזוי ווי מען זעט א געשטאַלט האָב איך פּלוצעם דעם האַס
דערזען פֿאַר די אויגן, דעם פֿינצטערן האַס פֿון דער וועלט —
מיט א בליק דורך די צײן ווי א שד וועון ר׳איז בײז און ער שעלט,
און מיט אַזאַ בראַזג ווי די באַן איבער מיר אין דער נאַכט
האָט ער מיר געשווינדן, אַז אמת איז וואָס ער טראַכט
און איך האָב דאָך בלויז ווי א גולם מיט אויגן אַרויף
געקוקט צי עס רוקט זיך ערגעץ א פֿינצטערער נישט אויף
אין איינער פֿון אַט־אַ־די זעקס־זיבן־שטאָקיקע ווענט.
נאָר איידער איך האָב זיך אַרויף־ און אַראָפּ־צו געוועודט
האָב איך שוין דעם בראַזג פֿון די קליידער די נאַסע דערהערט:
די פֿרוי בײם בײם לאַמטערן איז דעמאָלט געפֿאַלן צו דר׳ערד.

צי בין איך אַוועק, און ווי ווײט, דאָס געדענק איך נישט מער,
קען זײן אַז איך האָב זיך אַזוי־אַ, אַהין־און־אַהער —
אַרומגעדרייט בלויז. כ׳האָב דאָך איבערגעלייענט די שילד
ווו עס שטייט אַז דער רוך פֿון האַוואַנאַ־ציגאַרן איז מילד
ווי דער אָטעם פֿון מאַמעס אויף קינדער וואָס וויינען בײ נאַכט
און די דאַזיקע קראָם (אויב איך האָב נישט קיין טעות געמאַכט)
איז דאָך דרײ גאַסן ווײט. און איך האָב דאָך אַפֿילו געזען
די קעסטלעך אין פֿענצטער דאָרט, כאַטש עס איז פֿינצטער געווען.
און געוויינט האָב איך אויך — דאָס געדענק איך. געשטאָנען, געלייענט,
און געוויינט זיך אַזוי און מיט אָפֿענע אויגן געוויינט.
מיר האָט זיך געדאַכט אַז איך האַר עס ווי עס רופֿט אויפֿן קול
מײן טאַטע וואָס שטאַרבט; און דאָס האָט מיך דערמאָנט אַן אַמאָל —
ווען ער האָט געוויינט בײ די דער באַן און ווי בלײך ר׳איז געוואָן —
ער האָט אפֿשר דערפֿילט אַז ער וועט מיך שוין קיין מאָל נישט זען.
ס׳אַזאַ שווערקייט דאָס ווערט וואָרט וועון מען שטייט און מען טראַכט אַט־אַזוי
פֿון א טאַטן, א מת, בײ א פֿרעמדער געשטאָרבענער פֿרוי.

◀ עס איז נישט געווען

עס איז נישט געווען אַזאַ מענטש אין מײן הויז
און ער האָט נישט געקוקט מיטן לינקן אויג
אויף מײן שיסל באַרש. ער האָט בלויז געזאָגט
"גוטאָוונט" — און מיט אַזאַ טיפֿן פֿאַרנויג
אַזש דאָס היטל איז אים אַרונטערגעפֿאַלן.

און אַזוי טאַקע בין איך געוואָרן געוואָר,
אַז ער האָט שוין א פֿליך און עס האָט מיך געקרענקט,
און דערפֿאַר טאַקע האָב איך אים איבערגעפֿרעגט:
צי ווײנט ער ניט א מאָל ווען ער בענקט
נאָך די נאַכט ווען דער ווינט האָט די האָר אים צעבלאָזן.

And as one can suddenly see a spectre, I saw
The hatred in front of my eyes, the world's dark hatred
With lightning in teeth, like a fiend when he's cursing and mad—
With such a clatter and roar as the train in the night,
He swore to me solemnly: true is all that I think—
Yet all that I did was to lift up my eyes like a fool
To see whether somewhere a window was raised with a noise
In one of the six-, seven-story dark walls all around,
But before I could shift my glance up the walls and back down,
I heard the thud of wet clothes on the pavement below:
The woman who stood at the streetlamp fell to the ground.

Whether I went, and how far, I don't know anymore.
Perhaps I just wandered around like this, to and fro,
In the rain. I am sure that I read on a signboard somewhere
That the smoke of Havana Cigars is pleasant and mild
Like the breathing of mothers on babies that cry in the night,
And it seems (if I am not mistaken) that store is three blocks
Away from that place. I am even sure that I saw
The boxes displayed in the window, though it was dark.
And I cried—I remember this too. I stood, and I read,
And swaying like this in the rain, with eyes open I cried.
And then I imagined I heard a voice calling aloud:
My father while dying; which reminded me how, long ago,
He cried at the train when I left and how pale was his face—
It seems that he sensed he would never see me again.
How heavy your heart when you stand and you ponder like this
On a father a corpse, near a woman a stranger, who's dead.

► *There Wasn't*

There was no such man in my house
And he didn't look with his left eye
At my bowl of borscht. He merely said   **Borscht***
"Good Evening" with such a deep bow
That his hat fell off.

And that is how I came to know
That he was bald, and it made me sick.
And that is why I was curious to ask:
Didn't he cry sometimes when he longed
For the nights when the wind blew in his hair?

ווי מאָדנע ער האָט אויף מיר געקוקט.

דאָס איז אפֿשר אמת. אַ ליגן איז בלויז,

אַז ער האָט געקוקט מיטן לינקן אויג.

ר׳איז אפֿילו ניט געוואָרן אין מײַן הויז,

ווען איך האָב דאַכט זיך מײַן באָרשט געגעסן.

אויף דעם קען איך שוואָרן בײַ גאָט אפֿילו.

אמת, איך האָב אים אַליין געזען

אין אַ שפּענצער אַזוי ווי פֿײַער רויט,

נאָר דערנאָך ווען איך האָב אַ טראַכט געטון

אַז ס׳איז ניט קיין רויטער באָרשט, וואָס איך עס,

נאָר פּראָסטע קרויט, — איז ער טאַקע פֿאַרשווונדן.

און עס האָט נישטאָ געהאָלפֿן וואָס איך בין אַרויס

און אים נאָכגערופֿן צו קומען צוריק.

כ׳האָב אפֿילו געוווּסט אַז ער וועט זיך שוין מער

אפֿילו ניט אומוועודן מיט אַ בליק, —

ער האָט דאָך דאָס אויג אין הויז פֿאַרגעסן.

ס׳איז געבליבן ליגן בײַ מיר אויפֿן טיש

און ס׳איז גרין אַזוי ווי שימל געוואָרן.

און גלײַך ווי נאָר ר׳האָט פֿאַרמאַכט הינטער זיך

די טיר פֿון מײַן הויז, האָב איך דאָס דערזען

און דערפֿאַר בין איך אים נאָכגעלאָפֿן:

— מײַן ליבער הער, מײַן ליבער הער,

עס איז דאָך גענוג וואָס איר האָט שוין אַ פֿליק, דאָס איז טרויעריק גענוג,

און אַן אויג איז דאָך ניט קיין טײַסטער מיט גאָלד,

מען זאָל דאָס וועלן באַהאַלטן פֿאַר זיך

צוליב דעם, וואָס מען דאַרף דאָס האָבן.

— פֿונדעסטוועגן — גאַנצע זיבן מינוט,

מיטן זייגער אין האַנט, דערנאָך געוואַרט,

אפֿשר גיט פֿאַר אַ גראָשן אַ קנעפּל אים ווער,

ווען ער בעט אַ נדבה — האָט מען אים דאָך גענאַרט,

וועט ער דאָך וועלן זען דעם מענטשן.

נאָר אַז איך זע, אַז קיין ברויט איז נישטאָ

אַרײַנצוברראָקן אין דעם באָרשט וואָס איך עס,

און קיין אייעלע איז אויך נישטאָ,

האָט דאָך גאָט דאָס אויג, ווי דורך אַ נס,

מיר צוגעשיקט צו מײַן באָרשט דעם פּוסטן.

How strangely he looked at me.
This is perhaps true. It's only a lie
That he looked at me with his left eye.
He wasn't even in my house
When it seems to me I ate my borscht.
This I could swear even by God.

True, I saw him myself
Wearing a jacket as red as fire.
Later, however, when I reflected
That it was not a red borscht that I ate
But plain cabbage—he indeed disappeared.

And it didn't help that I went out
And called after him to come back.
I knew of course that he wouldn't
Even as much as turn his gaze—
Since he'd forgotten his eye at my house.

It was left lying on my table
And it was as green as mold.
As soon as he shut the door behind him
Leaving my house, I saw the eye—
And that's why I ran after him:

—My dear sir, my dear sir,
Isn't it sad enough that you're bald,
And an eye is not a wallet with gold
That you want to hide it for yourself
Because you may need it sometime.

Nevertheless—for seven long minutes,
Watch in my hand, I waited: maybe
He'd get a button instead of a coin
When he begs—then, knowing he was cheated,
He would want to see who did it.

But as I saw that I had no bread
To crumble into the borscht that I ate,
And no egg either, it became clear
That God sent the eye as a miracle
For my thin borscht.

פונדעסטוועגן — נישט צו לײדן דערנאָך,
וואָס איך פֿאַרנעם אַ פּרעמדנס בלוט
האָב איך מיטן אויג אויפֿן לעפֿל שײן
געוואָרט אויפֿן זייגער נאָך אַ מינוט —
אפֿשר פֿאָרט וועט ער זיך ווײַזן.

נאָר אַפֿנים, אַז ווען דער שטן וויל
פֿאַרפֿירן אַ מענטשן צו אַ זינד
העלפֿט גאָרנישט ניט. ער איז דאָך אַרײַן
שיִער ניט אַזוי ווי אַ בליץ געשווינד,
ווען איך האָב דאָס אויג שוין געהאַט פֿאַרשלונגען.

ווי אַ טשוואָק אויף בלעך האָט זײַן אָטעם געפֿײַפֿט,
און קוים וואָס ער האָט נאָך פֿאַר פּחד גערעדט:
— מײַן אויג, ר' ייִד, מײַן אייניציק אויג!
אַ קראַנקער אויפֿן טויטנבעט
קען זיך אַזוי ניט צאַפּלען.

ווי אַן אָרעם פֿאַרזעעניש, אַ קינד
מיטן גאַנצן פּנים צו ווײנען גרייט,
און פֿון דער הויל פֿון זײַן לינקן אויג
האָט זיך טאַקע באַלד אַרויסגעדרייט
אַ טרער, ווי דאָס רויע פֿלייש, אַ רויטע.

און וואָס וואָר, איז וואָר, ווען איך וואָלט געקענט
אַרײַנקריכן מיט דער האַנט אין זיך,
גיב איך אים אָפּ נישט נאָר דאָס אויג,
נאָר אַפֿילו דעם באָרשט, אַבי ער זאָל מיך,
צום וויסטן יאָר, נישט אַזוי באַוויינען.

און ווײַזט אויס, אַז איך בין געוועזן טאַקע בײז.
איך האָב זיך דאָך פּלוצעם אויפֿגעשטעלט
און גלײַך אין פּרצוף אַ זאָג געטאָן:
אַזאַ מענטש איז ניט ווערט וואָס ער לעבט אויף דער וועלט,
אויב ער איז אַזאַ מין גולם.

◄ דערווײַל זאָ־זאָ

דערווײַל זאָ־זאָ, און פֿאַרגיב וואָס איך אײַל,
מיר זענען פֿאַרטערערט שוין די אויגן פֿון קעלט,
און איך האָב מיט האַב צוויי יונגע לײַט זיך באַשטעלט
אין אַ קעלער פֿון דאַנען אַ דרײַ, פֿיר מײַל.
נאָר זיי זענען טאַקע שווארץ ווי די ערד
ווײַל זיי עסן ווייניק און קלערן אַ סך.

Nevertheless—so as not to suffer later
For swallowing a stranger's blood,
I waited with the eye on my spoon
For one whole minute more, by the clock—
Perhaps he would still show up.

But it seems, when the devil wants
To lead a man to sin—
Nothing will help. He burst in
Almost as fast as lightning
Just as I had swallowed his eye.

Like a nail scratching tin, his breath hissed,
He could barely speak for fear:
—My eye, mister, my only eye!
A sick man on his deathbed
Could not tremble like this.

Like a miserable freak, like a child
With a face all contorted to cry,
Out of the hollow of his left eye,
Sure enough, a tear slipped out,
As red as raw meat.

What's true is true: if I could have
Crawled into myself with my hand,
I would have given him not only the eye
But even the borscht, if he would just stop
Crying over me, may a bad year take him.

It appears that I really was mad.
Because I suddenly got up
And threw it straight in his face:
No man deserves to live in the world
If he's such a jerk.

► *So Far, So-So*

So far, so-so. And forgive me for hurrying off.
My eyes are tearing from the cold
And I have a date with two young people
In a cellar some three or four miles from here.
But they are really black as the soil,
Because they eat little and think a lot.

זיי אַרבעטן אויך בײַ אונדזער פאַך.

און מיר לאָזן זיך אַלע וואַקסן בערד.

בײַ זיי וואַקסן שוואַרצע, בײַ מיר אַ רויטע,

נאָר זייערע וואַקסן אַ ביסל גיכער

און בלאָזן זיך שוין ווען עס גייט עס אַ וויכער,

נאָר מײַנע, די רויטע, העַנגט אַ טויטע,

העַנגט אַ טויטע, זאָג איך.

◄ ס'עט זײַן אַזוי

קודם וועט מען דעם ריז דעם רויטן

וואָס אַלעמען וויל ער שלאָגן און טויטן —

אַוועקזעצן עסן אַרבעסשיטן —

אַוועקזעצן עסן אַרבעסשיטן.

דערנאָך וועט מען זײַנע קראָקאָדילן

פרעגן בפרהסיא צי זיי ווילן —

מיט אַלע קליינע קינדער זיך שפילן —

מיט אַלע קליינע קינדער זיך שפילן.

ווילן זיי ווילן — וועט מען אין גאָרטן

אויסלייגן פאַר זיי קאָרטן —

אַ לאַנד ווו ס'איז אייביק פורים דאָרטן —

אַ לאַנד ווו ס'איז אייביק פורים דאָרטן.

האָבן זיי דאָך ליב צו נאַשן,

וועלן זיי לויפן אומגעוואַשן —

אויפצועסן די האָמענטאַשן —

אויפצועסן די האָמענטאַשן.

וועלן קינדער דערווייל זיך אונטעראײַלן,

און צעגליען בײַם פייער אין זייערע הייל'ן —

אַלע בויגנס מיט די פײַל'ן —

אַלע בויגנס מיט די פײַל'ן.

און מיט די העמערלעך זיי צעהאַקן אויף ברעקלעך,

און פון די ברעקלעך אויסשמידן טשוועקלעך —

און אַוועקשיקן קיין כעלם אין פעקלעך —

און אַוועקשיקן קיין כעלם אין פעקלעך.

וועלן כעלמער מיט אַ היטל אַן אַלטן —

כאַפן די זון ווען זי גייט זיך באַהאַלטן —

און צום הימל זי צושלאָגן — וועט זי זיך האַלטן —

און צום הימל זי צושלאָגן — וועט זי זיך האַלטן.

They, too, work in our profession.
And we all let our beards grow.
Theirs grow black, mine is red,
But theirs grow a little faster
And puff up with pride when a wind blows.
Mine, the red one, hangs like a dead one,
Hangs like a dead one, I say.

➤ *So It Shall Be*

First we'll take the red giant who'd beat
Everyone up and force him to sit—
Peapods to eat,
Peapods to eat.

Then we'll demand of his crocodiles
Publicly to put on a smile
And play with the little children a while,
And play with the little children a while.

If they are willing, we will endeavor
To lay out a land of cards so clever,
Where it's Purim forever,
Where it's Purim forever.

The crocodiles, though, love to nosh,
And they'll run off, neglecting to wash
And eat up every homentosh,
And eat up every homentosh.

Then the children will hurry and go
To heat up—so hot that they glow—
Every arrow-and-bow,
Every arrow-and-bow.

And with small hammers they will not fail
To break them to pieces and forge from them nails,
And send them to Chelm in parcels by mail,
And send them to Chelm in parcels by mail.

With an old hat, the Chelmites may
Capture the sun as it's going away,
And tack it to the sky, so it will stay,
And tack it to the sky, so it will stay.

Purim—a festive Jewish holiday commemorating the salvation of the Jews of Persia, as described in the Book of Esther, marked by a light, carnival atmosphere.

to nosh—to snack, especially on sweets.

Homentash—"Haman's Pocket," a triangular cookie with a poppyseed filling, a special Purim treat.

neglecting to wash—a Jew is obliged to wash his hands and say a blessing before eating.

Chelm (pronounced: Khelm)—a proverbial city of lovable fools, famous for their attempts to catch the moon in a barrel of water.

איך און דו — ניט אָומרו און ניט רו,
גרוי און בלאַנד וואָס שפּאַרט זיך צו
איינער צו דעם אַנדערן.

זיך אָנגעטראָפֿן אומגעריכט
ווי בעטלער צוויי מיט שטעקן און לאַמטערן-ליכט —
ביינאַכט ביים וויים וואַנדערן.

ווי בעטלער צוויי וואָס האָבן זיך מיט טאָרבע און מיט וואַסער-קריגל
דערזען ווי אין שפּיגל —
איינער אין דעם אַנדערן.

מען טוט אַ צי אַ ברעם,
דאָס אויג ווערט טריב.
ניט איך האָב דיך פֿיינט —
ניט דו האָסט מיך ליב.

אין "ספּיק-איזי" — דאָס בלומען-מיידל ◄

כאַיעמשמיל מיטן סטייק-מעסער אין האַנט —
טאָנצט און שילט דעם פּרעזיס פֿון לאַנד,
נאָר אַרום זיַין פּנים פֿינצטערט זיַין באָרד
ווי אַ פֿלויט אַרום אַ הייליקן אָרט,
און דאָס בלייכע מיידל וואָס שטופּט די בלומען
זאָגט אַז איר ליבסטער דאָ אויף דער וועלט —
שלאָגט ווען זי ברענגט ניט אַהיים קיין געלט —
דאָס זאָגט זי און שטופּט מיר בלומען.

קען זיַין אַז מען דאַרף טאָקע הייבן אַ פֿויסט
צו ווערן ווי אַ משיח געגרויסט,
נאָר די הורן — תּלמידים מיַינע ביַים טיש,
האָבן פֿיינט ווי איך פֿינצטערניש,
און דאָס בלייכע מיידל וואָס שטופּט מיר בלומען
דאַרף ניט אַפֿילו די זון — ווייַל אַ פֿליך
שיַינט אויך פֿאַר יענעם מער ווי פֿאַר זיך —
דאָס זאָגט זי און שטופּט מיר בלומען.

זאָג איך, מיידל, מען מוז ניט זיַין דוװקא קראַנק
ווי שולמית אין שיר-השירים-געזאַנג,
און מען מוז ניט געבוירן ווערן בלינד
צו ווערן אַ מאַמע וואָס זויגט אַ קינד,

I and you—neither rest nor unrest,
Gray and blond, pressed
To one another.

Met casually, quick,
Like two beggars with lantern and stick—
At night, while wandering.

Like beggers two, with bag and mug,
Who saw their faces in a mirror—
One in the other.

An eye grows dim,
An eyebrow raised above.
Not that I hate you—
Not that you love.

► *In a "Speakeasy"—The Flower Girl*

Chayem-Shmyl, a steak-knife in his hand,
Dances and curses the head of the land,
But his beard is dark around his face
Like a fence around a graveyard.
And the pale girl thrusting flowers at me
Says that her lover who calls her honey
Beats her when she doesn't bring him money—
She says, and thrusts the flowers in my face.

Maybe one has to really raise
A fist—to get, like a messiah, praise;
But the whores—my students at the table—
Hate the darkness as I do,
And the pale girl thrusting flowers at me
Doesn't need the sun—because a bald head
Glows not for itself but for others instead—
She says, and thrusts the flowers in my face.

I say: girlie, for love you don't have to be sick
Like Shulamith in the Song of Songs,
And you don't have to be born blind
To become a mother suckling a child.

Moyshe-Leyb Halpern's
manuscript of "I and You."

נאָר דאָס בלייכע מיידל וואָס שטופּט מיר בלומען
הערט ניט און ווײַזט מיר אָן אויף איר שויס,
פֿון דאָרט — זאָגט זי — קריכט דאָס לעבן אַרויס —
דאָס זאָגט זי און שטופּט מיר בלומען.

זאָג איך, מיידל, דאָס לעבן האָט אַ היים —
אַ שטוב אָן אַ פענצטער מיט וועענט פֿון ליים,
און מען דאַרף ניט — זאָג איך — צו דעם קיין נס
זיך צו ווײַזן אין ווײַסן קלייד פֿון אַ מת.
נאָר דאָס בלייכע מיידל וואָס שטופּט מיר בלומען
זאָגט אַז זי האָט ליב איר קלייד,
ווײַל ס׳איז רויט ווי די פֿאָן פֿון מײַן אָרעמקייט —
דאָס זאָגט זי און שטופּט מיר בלומען.

רעד איך צו איר, ווי צו גאָט, אויף דו —
אפֿשר קענסטו מיר — זאָג איך — שענקען רו,
און צונעמען דעם האָניק פֿון סם,
וואָס ווײַנט אין מיר ווי אַ שטרוי אין ים!
נאָר דאָס בלייכע מיידל וואָס שטופּט מיר בלומען,
זאָגט — אַז בלומען פאַרדופּלטן דעם שווייס
ווען מען נעמט אַרום אַ פֿרוי וואָס איז הייס —
דאָס זאָגט זי און שטופּט מיר בלומען.

◄ מיר די רעוואָלוציאָנערן
אָדער
◄ ס׳אַמעריקע

ער האָט זיך אַזוי לאַנג געענאַרט
אַז ער איז אויואַנגאַרד,
ביז ער האָט זיך אַליין דעם קאַפעליוש פֿון שטרוי
אָנגעצונדן אויפֿן קאָפּ,
און אָט־אַזוי —
מיט אויסגעשפּרייטע הענט
און מיט "געוואַלד, סע ברענט!"
איז ער די טרעפּ אַראָפּ.
איז איטלעכער אין גאַס וואָס האָט אים אָנגעטראָפֿן
מיטגעלאָפֿן —
אויך מיט אויסגעשפּרייטע הענט,
און מיט "געוואַלד, סע ברענט".

האָט לעבן מיר מײַן פֿריינד מיט מויל און אויגן
ווײַט־צעעפֿנטע צו מיר זיך צוגעבויגן
צו הערן וואָס איך זאָג.

But the pale girl thrusting flowers at me
Won't listen, and shows me her lap: no doubt,
From there, she says, life crawls out—
She says, and thrusts the flowers in my face.

Girlie, life has a home, I say,
A house without windows and walls of clay;
And you don't need, I say, any miracles
To show up in the white dress of a corpse.
But the pale girl thrusting flowers at me
Says that she loves her dress, you bet,
'Cause it's like my poverty's banner red—
She says, and thrusts the flowers in my face.

Then I talk to her, as to God, saying Thou—
Couldst thou, I say, grant me some peace
And take away the honey of my poison
Which cries in me like a straw in the sea!
But the pale girl thrusting flowers at me
Says that flowers overpower the sweat
When you take a hot woman to bed—
She says, and thrusts the flowers in my face.

➤ *We The Revolutionaries*
    or
➤ *This America*

He kidded himself for so long
That he was Avant-Garde,
Till he set fire to
The straw hat on his head,
And just like that—
With outstretched arms,
Shouting "Help, fire!"
Ran downstairs.
Then everyone who saw him in the street
Ran too—
With outstretched arms,
Shouting "Help, fire!"

At this, my friend
Leaned over to me,
Eyes and mouth wide open,
To hear what I would say.

האָב איך אַ וואָרף געטאָן דאָס שטיקל קיכל

און אָפּגעוווישט אויף גיך מיט זיך אַ טיכל —

פּנים, שטערן, נאָז —

ביים קאָוועגלאָז,

און אויך אַרויס מיט אויסגעשפּרייטע הענט.

האָט מיך מיַין פריַינד (שפּעטער מיט אַ טאָג)

באַגעגנט

און געפרעגט פאַר וואָס איך האָב זיך ניט געזעגנט,

און פאַר וואָס איך האָב פאַרגעסן —

אין רעסטאָראַן באַצאָלן פאַר מיַין עסן.

האָב איך געענטפערט: "רעוואָלוציאָנערן".

האָט ער אויף דעם אַ לאַך געטאָן

און האָט געזאָגט "גרויסאַרטיק".

האָב איך דאָך שוין געזען אַז ער איז אַ פּאָדליעץ;

האָב איך פאַרשטייט זיך אים דערפאַר דערלאַנגט אַ זעץ

אַזוינעם ווי מען דאַרף —

און אים געלאָזן וויסן קורץ און שאַרף —

אַז מיר זענען שוין מיט אונדזער פריַינדשאַפט פאַרטיק.

◄ שאַלאָמויזן

איך טראַג אַ פאַר אַלטע פאַנטאָפל,

איך טראָג מאַטראָזן-הויזן,

און דער גאַסט מיט די בּרילן לאָזט מיך ניט אָפּ

איך זאָל אים דערציילן פון די שאַלאָמויזן

פון די באַרימטע העלדן שאַלאָמויזן.

די שאַלאָמויזן דינען גאָט ווי מען דאַרף,

און זיי טראָגן רויטע היטלעך.

און זומער פאָרן זיי תּמיד מיט אָקס

און פאַר ווינטער האָבן זיי גרינגע שליטלעך,

פאָרן זיי אין די דאַזיקע שליטלעך.

פון וויַיבער האַלטן זיי קיינער ניט.

און זיי עסן אַלע טאָג ראָסל.

און ווי ייִדן די שמד האָבן זיי פיַינט

אַזוינעם וואָס מען רופט אים אַ יאָסל, חלילה יאָסל,

זיי האָבן איינעם שוין דערהרגעט אַ יאָסל !

זיי לעבן פון דעם וואָס זיי מאַכן שנײ

פון אייער וואָס ווערן צעבראָכן פון צוקער.

און פרעגט זיי אַ פרעמדער דעם וועג צו דער באָד

זאָגט מען נישט דאָ-אַרום, נאָר דורים,

נישט דאָ-אַרום, נאָר דורים.

Then I threw down the piece of cake
And wiped with a handkerchief fast
My face, my forehead, my nose—
Over the cup of coffee—
And ran out, with outstretched arms.
When my friend met me (next day)
And asked why I didn't say Good-bye,
And why I forgot to pay
The restaurant
I answered: "Revolutionaries!"
At this he laughed
And said "Wonderful."
So I saw through him, that he is scum,
And naturally I punched him
As he deserved—
And told him, short and sharp,
That our friendship
Was finished.

➤ *Shalamouses*

I wear a pair of old slippers,
I wear sailor trousers,
And the bespectacled visitor won't let go:
I must tell him about the Shalamouses,
The famous heroes Shalamouses.

The Shalamouses pray to God, as one should,
And wear red hats.
In summer they travel always on wheels,
For winter they have light sleds,
So they travel in those sleds.

They don't think much of women.
And eat chicken soup every day, of course.
And as Jews hate conversion they hate
One who is called Yossel, God-forbid Yossel,
They've already killed one Yossel!

They make a living by making snow
From eggs whipped up with sugar.
And if a stranger will ask the road to the bath,
They won't say there but yonder,
Not there, but yonder.

Shalamouses—a nonsense word in Yiddish, sometimes used for "absurdities," "trifles," "sweet nothings," or whatever a context may invite. The two parts of the word are suggestive of "schlemiel" and an odd plural of "mouse." Perhaps the poem mocks the hero worship of the Soviet Union by the Communists.

Yossel—might perhaps suggest Stalin's first name, Joseph; it is also used as equivalent to "Yoyzl," the Yiddish nickname for Jesus.

פֿאַר נאַכט אָבער זעצן זיי זיך אַרײַן
אין צעריבענע שיסלען קנאָבל,
און זיי ברענען און גיבן אַפֿילו ניט
קיין זיפֿץ פֿון אַזוי פֿיל טראָבל,
פֿון אַזוי פֿיל אומזיסטן טראָבל.

און נאַקעט אַזוי ביז די האַלבער נאַכט
זיצן זיי, מיט רעספּעקט צו מעלדן,
פֿראָסטע שאַלאַמויזן דאַכט זיך, און דאָך —
ס'אַראַ וווּנדערלעכע העלדן.
ס'אַראַ גרויסע העלדן.

◄ מײַן שרײַעדיקייט

מײַן שרײַעדיקייט איז אײַנגעשלאָפֿן איבער מײַנע העלנט
ווי אַ קראַנקער אין מיטן גאַס אין אַ ווינטערנאַכט אויף אַ שטיין,
דאָס ליכט פֿון דער לבֿנה אויף אים אַזוינעם איז געל ווי אויף אַ טויטן,
און בלויז דער ווינט וואָס פֿליט אין דער פֿינצטער פֿון שילד צו שילד —
איבער די אַלטע קליידער-געשעפֿטן — זעט אים —
און די וועלט איז דאָך אַזוי אומענדלעך-רײַך אין פֿענצטער,
וואָס לײַכטן אַרויס אין דער נאַכט — אַנטקעגן רעלסן
בײַ די ברעגן פֿון ים,
פֿון ברעג אַרונטער,
פֿון פּאַלאַצן מיט גאָרטן און צוים אַרום זיך —
און דאָרט איז וואַרעם לײַב אונטער זײַד —
און געלער און אָן ברוינער קוכן צווישן פֿינגער און ציין ווי פֿערל קליינע,
בעת די אויערן הערן ליבע-רייד פֿון מאַן אַדער פֿרוי,
און פֿאַראַן ווײַן-פֿלעשער מיט אַזוינע לאַנגע שמאָלע העלדזער שיינע
און מיט זילבער פֿון אויבן און מיט גאָלד
און בלומען פֿאַר אַזוי פֿיל איבעריק געלט
אויף הערצער — וואָס זענען אפֿשר זייער גוט — ווײַל זיי האָבן ליב.
נאָר ווי פֿרעמד און ווי אָפּגעשיידט זיי זענען פֿון דעם אין מיטן גאַס.
לויט זייער פֿרײַלעכקייט איז ער אין גאַנצן נישטאָ,
אויסגעטראַכט בלויז. אויסגעטרוימט פֿון אַ שרעקנדיקן אין דער פֿינצטער
אין אַ נײַער דירה ערגעץ
איינער אַליין
די ערשטע נאַכט,
שלאָפֿט ער ניט — הערט ער דעם ווינט — מיינט ער, ווער ווייסט וואָס
עס טוט זיך דאָרט ערגעץ אין דרויסן.

At night, however, they sit
In dishes of ground garlic,
And they burn and won't even sigh
From so much trouble, the darlings,
From so much unnecessary trouble.

Naked, they sit until midnight,
I respectfully answer, if anyone queries:
They seem just simple Shalamouses, and yet—
What wonderful heroes.
What great heroes.

➤ *My Crying-Out-Loud*

A manuscript version of the
poem. For the printed version,
see above, *Posthumous Poems I.*

My Crying-Out-Loud fell asleep in my hands
Like a sick man on a stone in a street in a winter night,
The moonlight on his face is yellow as on a corpse
And only the wind roaming in the dark from signboard to signboard
Over the old garment shops will see him—
And the world is so immensely rich in windows
Shining out into the night—onto the rails
At the seashore,
From the shore down,
From palaces encircled in garden and fence—
And inside there are bodies warm under silk
And yellow and brown cake between fingers and teeth like tiny pearls,
While the ears listen to love-talk of a man or a woman,
And there are bottles of wine with such beautiful long slender necks
And with silver on top and with gold
And flowers costing so much unnecessary money
Pinned over hearts—which must be very good—for they love.
Yet how foreign, how separated they are from that man on the street.
To judge by their rejoicing, he does not exist at all,
A mere invention, dreamed up by a scared man in the dark
Somewhere in a new flat,
All alone,
On his first night,
He cannot sleep—so he listens to the wind—and thinks, who knows what
Is going on somewhere outside.

◄ דאָס האָב איך גערעדט צו מיַין איינציקן זון ביַים שפּיל — און מער צו קיינעם ניט

דערווייַל אַ מולטער, איבער קלעצעלעך פיר, דיַין פערד.
פאַר וועמען וואַלגערהאַלץ, פאַר דיר אַ שווערד.
און נאָך איז ניט פון שטאָל, נאָר פון גאַזעט-פּאַפּיר
דער המן-טאַש דאָ אויף דיַין קאָפּ בײַ דיר.
די מאַמע יאָמערט, — פּרעמדע פלעשער קלייַבט ער אויף און טעפּ —
פאַר דיר סאָלדאַטן אויף די טרעפּ.
די מאַמע לייגט אַוועק אַזוי פיל מי —
און דו צעלעכערסט אַלע טאָג די לאַטעס אויף די קני.
און דיַינע שיך — איך שווער עס דיר אַז בעַרן צוויי —
אַפילו הונגעריק, צעעפענען די מיַילער ניט ווי זיי.

נאָר מער פון אַלץ (און וועמען דאָס געפעלט)
אַזוינס-אַ פלאַפּעלט שוין פון איינגענעמען אַ וועלט.
ס׳קעצעל פירט מלחמה מיטן בייַוול-קנויל,
און ער — ווייסט גאָט מיט וועמען ניט! — און קען דאָך צו זיַין מויל
קיין לעפל מיט מיט געקעכץ ניט צוטראָגן אַליין.
שוין אָפּגערעדט פון אָפּראַמען דעם מינדסטן שטיין
וואָס וואַרט אין וועג, פון אונטער קויט און גראָז,
אויף יעדן נאָר וואָס האָט אַ גאַנצע נאָז.

נאָר זאָל שוין זיַין אַז אויסבעטלען דאָס אַלצדינג וואָס מען וויל,
דאַרף קיינער ניט. און ראַנגלען זיך דערפאַר איז אויך אַ שפּיל.
נאָר ווו איז דאָס? — פאַר וואָס זאָל איך ביז בלוט צעקייַלן זיך
מיט דעם שלימזל דאָ געליימט ווי איך?
— און וואָס איז זיג? אַז דער צו העלדישקייט דערווײַלט
איז אויך אַ מת, וואָס פעלט ניט דעם וואָס צײלט.
און ווער באַדאַרף מען זאָל צוריקקומען צו ווייַזן אויף פּאַראַד
אַז מ׳האָט צוויי פיס געהאַט
און מ׳האָט פאַרביטן זיי — די האַץ-האַץ — אויף קוליעס צוויי, ניט וויסנדיק פאַר וואָס? —
דער סוחר שרייַט אַז ער איז דער באַלעבאָס.
און ווייַל מען דאַרף צו די ירידן פון דער וועלט
אַ פרייַען וועג — האָט ער צעשטעלט
האַרמאַטן אומעטום, ווו נאָר עס איז פאַראַן
אַן אָפּהאַלט פאַר זיַין שיף, אַ גרענעץ פאַר זיַין באַן.

און דער וואָס אַרבעט ווײַנט, — אים פעלט דער פּלעדערווייש
וואָס זאָל פון מייַלן-ווייַט, פון רויטשילדס טיש
אַרייַנשאַרן צו אים אין מויל אַרײַן
דאָס עסן מיטן ווײַן.
און אים, דעם קעניג אויפן טראָן
באַדאַרף מען צוהאַלטן די באַק ווען ס׳טוט אים ווײַ אַ צאָן;

So far, your horse is a trough on four blocks.
For others a rolling pin, for you—a sword.
And not yet of steel, but of newspaper
Is the tricornered *homentosh* on your head.
Mama complains: the neighbors' bottles and pots—
For you they are soldiers on all the stairs.
Mama works so hard—and you, every day
You make fresh holes in your kneepatches,
And your shoes—I swear: two bears,
Even when hungry, don't open their mouths like this.

But, above all—and some may like it—
This brat already prattles of conquering the world.
The kitten makes war against a ball of yarn,
And he—God knows against whom he won't!—and he can't even
Put a spoonful of hot food into his own mouth,
Let alone clear the smallest stone
Which lies in wait under dirt and grass
For anyone who still has a nose to break.

Maybe people should not beg for everything they want.
And fighting for it, too, is a game.
But where is it? Why should I get bloodied and beaten
By some schlemiel as clumsy as me?
And what is victory? A man chosen to be a hero
Is also a corpse, and won't be missed by whoever is counting.
And who needs to come back to show at a parade
That he had two legs
And traded them—hop-hop—for two crutches, not knowing why?
The merchant shouts that he's the boss.
And because one needs an open road
To the fairs of the world—he placed
Cannons wherever there is
A bar to his ship, a border to his train.

The working man cries: He lacks a featherduster
To reach miles away, to Rothschild's table,
And shovel into his mouth
Food and wine.
And the king on his throne
Needs his cheek held when he has a toothache;

Part one of a longer poem.

Homentash—a triangular Purim cookie.

— און לערנען אויף אַ האַרף

אַ קרעכץ טאָן ווי מען דאַרף,

ווען ס'טרעפֿט דער הענקער מיט זײַן מעסער-שניט

דעם ווידערשפּעניקער ניט-אַקוראַט אין גאָרגל אין דער מיט.

נאָר דאָ טאַקע — און מיט מײַן גאַנצן בלוט און אָטעם וואָס איז הייס —

איך זאָג זיך אָפּ פֿון אַלץ וואָס העלפֿט דערציִען צו בייז.

און ווי גערעכט עס זאָל ניט זײַן אַנטקעגן האַר דער קנעכט —

גערעכטער מאָרד איז טאָפּלט אומגערעכט !

און קלאָרער נאָך — די שוועראָרד פֿון שייד אַרויס

אפֿילו ווען זי שיצט, ווייל שעכטן בלויז !

און גאָרנישט מער ! איך לייקן ניט — מיט אייגענע צוויי הענט

באַדאַרף מען דאָ ניט בויען פֿאַר זיך קיין תּפֿיסה-ווענט;

און ברויט אַ שטיק איז בילכער פֿון אַ קרוין.

נאָר ווער עס שיקט אונדז שטאַרבן צוליב דעם און רופֿט דאָס לעבנס-לוין:

אים שילט דער פּגר פֿון סאָלדאַט, — דער טויטער בליק

פֿון דעם מאַרטירער — קרבן זײַנס וואָס וויגט זיך אויפֿן שטריק,

און דאָס צו זען איז וויסטעניש גענוג.

און בלויז דער דאָרשטיקער פֿון זין גערירט צעברעכט אַליין זײַן קרוג.

איך ווייס, דײַן אויער איז אַ וואַנט דערווײַיל,

און איך פֿאַר דיר אַ הונט וואָס האַוקעט אויף אַ מײַל.

נאָר כ'האָב דיך ליב — פֿאָרשטטײַסט — איך וויל אַז דו זאָלסט דאָ

אַ קינד אויך האָדעווען ווען איך בין מער נישטאָ.

און שיקן תּפֿילות צו דער הויך

וואָס גרייכן קוימען אױפֿן דאַך, און שרעקן רויך,

דאָס איז מיר פֿרעמד, — און מיט פֿאַרלייגטע הענט

קען שטיין אַ קניאַק אַ וויסטער ווען אַ שיקסע ברענט.

פֿאַר אים דאָס קרעפּלפֿלײש פֿון שור-הבר אינאיינעם מיט אַ מיצווה-קניש

ווען ער וועט זײַן אַ מת אָן צײַן בײַ דעם גן-עדן-טיש.

פֿאַר מיר דײַן וואַקסן דאָ (מײַן לעבן נאָכן טויט)

איז זשאָר פֿון גיהנום אויף מײַן טעגלעך ברויט.

און בעסער לאָז מיך זײַן די בלאָטע וואָס דו האַלטסט,

מיט דײַנע צײַן אין פֿויסטן — ווען דו פֿאַלסט.

און זאָל די זון אַוועקנעמען איר שײַן

פֿון די פֿיר אײלן ערד וואָס זאַפֿן אײַן

דײַן בלוט פֿאַרגאָסן, פֿאַר אומזיסט.

נאָר אַש מײַן איבערבלײַב, וואָס אַרט מיך ווער דו ביסט,

אַז אױיך דער וואָרעם דאָ וואָס וויינט פֿון דר'ערד אַרויף

האָט אָדערן וואָס קניפֿן אים צונויף —

מיט אַלץ אין מיר וואָס קער זיך אָן מיט דיר.

And needs to be taught on a harp
How to groan properly
When the executioner's blade doesn't strike precisely in the middle
Of the rebel's gullet.

But I—with all my blood and warm breath
I reject everything that helps prepare for evil.
No matter how right the slave against his master—
A just murder is doubly unjust!
And clearer yet: the sword out of its sheath,
Even when defending, wants only to slaughter!
And nothing else! I don't deny: With our own two hands
We needn't build a jail here for ourselves.
And bread is better than a crown.
But he who sends us to be killed for it and calls it life's reward—
Is cursed by the cadaver of a soldier, by the dead gaze
Of a martyr—his victim dangling on a rope.
Just seeing this is desolation.
And only a thirsty man who's out of his mind breaks his own jug.

I know, so far your ear is a wall
And to you I'm a dog, barking from a mile away.
But I love you—you see—I want you, too,
To raise a child when I'm no longer here.
And sending prayers upward,
Which reach the chimney on the roof and scare the smoke—
That's not for me. Only a pious character
Will stand with folded hands while a *shikse* is on fire—
Give him the *kreplach*meat of Heaven's Wild Ox and a *mitzvah*-knish
When he is a toothless corpse at Next-World's feast.

Kreplach—dumplings.
Wild Ox—Shor-Ha-Bar*
Knish—baked, filled pastry.

For me your growing here (life after my death)
Is embers from hell on my daily bread.
When you fall down, I wish
I were the mud you clench in your teeth and fists;
I wish the sun would take away its glow
From the six feet of earth that soaks up
Your blood, spilled in vain.

But ashes, my remains, what do I care who you are,
If even the worm crying up from the dust
Has veins that tie him
To everything in me that has to do with you.

ווי ים-גרונט מיט אַ שיף, ווי קבר-ערד מיט גראָז און ווי די שוועל ביַים טיר
מיט יעדן צוויַיג פון בוים, וואָס שטרעקט זיך צו דער זון אינאיינעם מיטן באָרג.
נאָר שלעף דעם הימל פון דער וועלט אַראָפּ און טראָג אים אויפן מאַרק,
וואָס טויג, אַז בלויז דאָס שטיקל ערד וואָס מ'האָט אונדז אָנפאַרטרויט
פאַרסמען מיר אַ אונטער אונדז די קראָפּעווע דאָס ברויט.
מיר, האָס דריַיאייניקער — פלעבייער-פרינץ-פאָעטעט,
מיר, קאַניבאַל דאָ אַ אייביקער ביַי זיך אַליין אין אָטשערעט.
מיר, סטאַדע דאָ מיט העלדזער און מיט קעפ —
ווי טעפּ מיט פלעשער ליידיקע צעשטעלט אויף אַלע טרעפּ.
מיר שפּילכלעך איבעריקע — ווי מיסט פון הויז
אַרויסגעשליַידערט פון מוטערשויס.

און וואָס אַז אָט דאָס אַלץ האָט אויסגעטראַכט
די שרעק וואָס העלפט דער נאַכט
אונדז צוגעווינען דאָ צום לאַנגן לעצטן שלאָף.
וואָס קער זיך אָן דער סוף —
דער וואָרעם אין דער ערד וואָס קריקט פון מת אַרויס
מיט דיר, דעם קינד — אָט ערשט פון מוטערשויס!
און וואָס, אַז אָט דאָס בינטל הויט
דערטראָגט שוין מיט די הענט צום פיסק, דעם אייגענעם, אַ שוואַרץ שטיק ברויט?

ווער דאַרף דאָ אויג, דאָס שליסל-לאָך אין טיר
צום חושך אייגענעם, וואָס רירט זיך ניט אין מיר,
אַפילו ווען איך מאָן
אַ שטויבל פון די טעג וואָס כ'האָב געשטעלט אין קאָן
ביַי אָט דעם קאָרטן-טיש וואָס לאָזט געווינען בלויז:
געבויגנקייט וואָס שטרעקט זיך מער ניט אויס!
ווער דאַרף, איך זאָל געליימט —
ווי אַ געשטאָרבענער אין טויטנהעמד
זיך איַינהערן צום אָטעם מיַינעם — ווינט וואָס נעמט מיך מיט
צו ווערן וואָלקן-בלאָטע אויפן מאַרק וואָס בליַיבט פון יאָר-יריד!

דער בלינדער מיַינט — אוי-וואַ! אַ ראָד די ערד!
און ער, ווי אויף אַ פור אַ ליידיקע, מיט אויסגעשפּאַנטע פערד!
ער מיַינט — גאָט דאַרף אַרויסציַען זיך מיט זיַין געבורטס-פאַבריק פון מוטערשויס,
ווַייל אים האָט מען פאַרגעסן בריל מיטגעגעבן ווען ער איז פון דאָרט אַרויס.
און ווען אים נאָר וויל זיַין שטעקן און ער פאַלט —
באַדאַרף מיט אַלע שטיינער קריג פירן דער וואַלד,
און טעלעגראַפן-סלופּ דאַרף זיַין פאָר אים צו וויַיזן פיַיגן צוויי
פון פיעקעליק אַראָפּ, דעם רעגן מיטן שניי.
און אַלע מיַילער דאָ ווי פענצטער אויסגעבראָקענע — פאַרשטאָפּ,
ווַייל ס'עסט זַיין פיַינט, דער שטאָט-גבאי, וואָרעניקעס פון טאָפּ
און ער אַ הערינג בלויז
מיט זיבן ציבעלעס ווי פויסטן גרויס!

Like the sea-bottom to a ship, like grave-earth to grass, like the doorstep
To every branch of a tree, stretching with the mountains to the sun.
But drag the sky down from the world and take it to the market—
What's the use, if even the piece of earth that we were given
Is poisoned by our feet, like grain by nettles.
We, the trinity of hate—plebs-prince-potentate,
We here, eternal cannibal trapped in his own reeds.
We here, a flock with necks and heads
Like pots and empty bottles on all the stairs.
We useless toys—like trash from a house
Hurled out of mother's lap.

So what if all this was invented
By fear which helps the night
To get us used to the long last sleep.
What does the end—
The earthworm crawling out of a corpse—have to do
With you, the child—just out of mother's lap!
And what if this bundle of skin already
Manages to carry to his own snout a piece of black bread?

Who needs the eye, the keyhole in the door
To my own darkness, which doesn't stir inside me,
Even when I demand
One speck of dust of the days I staked
At this gaming table, where you can win:
The stoop that never straightens out!
Who needs my numbness—
Like a corpse in his shroud
Listening to my own breath—a wind that carries me away
To be the cloud-mud in a marketplace, left over from a yearly fair!

William Gropper: *Next War*, cartoon for the "New York American," May 21, 1934.

The blind man thinks: Oh my! The earth is a wheel!
And he—in an empty wagon with unharnessed horses!
He thinks that God, with his birth-factory, should clear out of mother's lap,
For they forgot to give him eyeglasses when he came out of there.
And if his stick fools him and he falls—
The forest should make war on all the stones.
And a telegraph pole should be there, to give the finger,
From behind the oven, to the rain and to the snow.
For him, stop up all mouths like broken windows,
Because his enemy, the city-boss, eats dumplings from a pot—
While he eats just a herring
With seven onions big as fists!

און פרעג דעם לעמעך, ביי זיין שועסטערקינד, וואָס זעט ער מער,
צו וועלן ווייניקער ווי ער !
דער פענכער דארף אַ טייך צו שפּיגלען זיך.
און איך — מיין בלינדקייט צו דערזען — דארף דיך.
אים גיב אַ קאַנטשיק אַ טאַרנאָדאָ-ווינט צו אָפּשמייסן די פליג
וואָס קלייבט דאָס מיסט אַרום זיין מויל, ווייל זי איז הונגעריק.

דער לעמעך מיינט פאַר אים באַדארף די שטיפמאַמע, די נויט,
באַשמירן מיט אַ קאַלעפל דאָס איינגעמאַכטס צום ברויט,
און שטוף (ווייל ער האָט אָנגעטאָן אַ נייעם לייבצודאַק)
די אוצרות פון דער וועלט ווי קרויט אים אין אַ זאַק.
און ווייל דער רעטעך האָט אַ טשופּיק מיט אַ בויך,
באַדארף ער אויך !
און ווייל די בת-מלכה — זיין גליק,
נישט שפּרייטן זיך ווי שׂימחת-תּורה אויפן טיש אַ קאַטשקע נאָזנדיק,
באַדארף מען ביים בן-מלך (ווי פון אַ קינד די וועש)
אַראָפּכאַפן פאַר אים דעם קאַפּעליוש פון בעש.
און פאַר זיין פערד פאַרויס אַן עמוד-אש דארף ברענען גאַס
מיט ברויט, און הערינג-פאַס.
און אויף דער חתונה ביים קאַטער מיט דער גאַנדז — אַ וואַרע מאַכט;
פאַר אים און פאַר זיין פאָווע מיט די קרומע פיס וואָס ער האָט מיטגעבראַכט.
און טויט דעם שפּילפויגל וואָס נעמט זיך אָן
ווען ער ווייל אויסהאַקן דעם מאַרשאַליק אַ צאָן.
געערכט איז ער — אַז קעז האָט לעכער אויך באַדאַרף מען ניט קיין פלייט
אַנצוטרעטן דער כּלה אויפן קלייד.

און ניט צו דאַרפן גיין אין באָד אַריין
איז בעסער דאָנערשטיק זאָל שבת זיין.
און ניט צו זיין באַק ביים שכּנס בלומענטאָפּ — דער לאָרד
דאַרף צאָלן שטראָף פאַר שאָקלען מיט דער באָרד.

נאָר שווינג אַ דונער ווי אַ גראַגער אין דער פּורים-נאַכט
פון המנען אַ ממזר דאָ, וואָס אחשוורוש האָט נישט אומגעבראַכט —
איז פירער פון דער וועלט. און רישעות — זיין געבאָט —
פירט אויס די פּלוי אפילו דאָ, וואָס וועקט צו זוכן גאָט.
און זון און שטערן דאָ —
אַ זייגער וואָ קיין ווייזער איז נישטאָ.
און ביי דער ערד — געפין די בלינדע קישקע ווו זי איז,
וואָס העלפט איר האַרט מאַכן דאָס מיסט פיס אין זיך — דאָס אייזן פאַר דער שפּיז.
און מיר אַליין (אַ וואָרט מיינס, גיב אונדז קיין גוט אויג)
די הויזן אויף אַ שטעריק און אויפן בויך אַ פויק
און טויטשרעק אייגענער וואָס הייבט זיך אויף מיט דעם וואָלקאַנען-רויך.
און שול און קלויסטער דאָ מיט גאָלד אויף דאַך און טיר

And ask the sucker, his cousin, what more does he see
That he should ask for less!
The bladder needs a river for a mirror
And I—to see my own blindness—need you.
And he wants a tornado as a switch to flog the fly
That eats the dirt around his mouth because it's hungry!

The sucker thinks: for him stepmother Need
Should spread jam on bread with a ladle.
And since he wears a pious undergarment, one must stuff for him
The treasures of the world like cabbage in a sack.
And since the radish has a forelock and a big belly
He needs one, too!
And if the princess—his happiness,
Won't spread her legs like a duck, nose in table, on Simchas Torah,
One must snatch off (like a child's underwear)
One's felt hat to the prince.
And in front of his horses a pillar of fire shall burn the street,
Bread, stock and herring barrel.
And at the wedding of the tomcat and the goose—make way
For him and for his peacock with the crooked legs!
And death to the nightingale that intercedes
When he wants to knock out the jester's tooth.
Right he is—if even cheese has holes, you don't need a flute
To step on the bride's dress.

Arbe'kanfes*—pious undergarment.

And the Sabbath should fall on a Thursday—
So he won't have to go to the bath.
And not his billy-goat at a neighbor's flower-pot—the lord himself
Should pay a fine for shaking his beard.

But swing a thunder like a rattle on a Purim night as much as you like—
A bastard of Haman, overlooked by Ahasuerus,
Is leader of the world. Evil—his commandment—is observed
Even by the flea that wakes you up to seek God.
And the sun and the stars here—
A clock with no hands.
And in the earth—go find the appendix
Which hardens its refuse—the iron for the spear.
And for me (oh, my word, don't cast an evil eye!)—
The trousers on a string and the drum on my belly
And my own death-dread, rising with volcano smoke.
And church and synagogue with gold on roof and door—

Simchas Torah—the last day of Sukkot, the feast celebrating the end of the yearly cycle of Torah-reading in the synagogue.

Sabbath on a Thursday—an allusion to the custom of washing once a week on Friday.

rattle—a noisemaker for Purim to drown out Haman's name.

פֿאַר אונדזער וועלט — צוויי מכות בראַנדיקע, אַ צוגאָב צום געשוויר,
וואָס רופֿט זיך פֿעלקער-שטאָלץ !

און וואַלד גיט בײַטש און תליה-האָלץ,
און פֿאַנען-דראַנג פֿאַר דער מלחמה-שיף וואָס ליגט בײַם פֿרעמדן ברעג
ווי אויף אַ ליבעסבריוו אַ טינטן-פֿלעק.
און פֿאַרלאָמענטן — שמעלץ-אויוונס פֿאַר אונדזער כהן דעם בערזן-לץ.
און ווו אַ קאַלב אַ גאָלדנס שפּרינגט מען אַרום דעם ווי רויכפֿיש אין אַ נעץ,
און פֿעלט אויס ברויט פֿאַר אונדז דער שטיפֿמאַמע דער ערד
פֿאַרבײַט זי דאָס מיט אײַזן פֿאַר דער שווערד.

און שפּיץ פֿון שטיוול ווײַזט דעם וועג פֿאָרויס
צו לעבן ליכטיקן, דאָרט ווו מען שעכט אונדז אויס.
און פֿעלט אונדז האַניק צו דער מאָס
פֿון אָט די בייזקייטן וואָס ברעכן אונדז ווי גלאָז ?
וואַקסט אויס מיט אויגן צוויי, ווי לעכער אויפֿן שנײַ,
דער וועלט-גולם — משיח, וואָס פֿראָוועט טרײַסט-געבורט מיט שאָלעכץ פֿון אַן אײַ.
און אים פֿאַרקויפֿט ווי פֿון אַ קאַלב די הויט
אַ ברודער הײַנט אַ לײַבלעכער צום טויט.

נאָר מעג אַ איינעם משפּטן דאָס פֿינצטערע געשווײַג
פֿון אַ משוגענעם, וואָס היט אַ פֿויגל ווו, וואָס ליגט שוין טויט אין שטײַג.
און מעג זײַן מאַמע וואָס איז טויט (אַפֿילו שוין אויף זײַן חרטה-וועג)
אים נאָכגיין מיט אַ פּרצוף ווי די לעצטע טעג
פֿון ירושלימס בראָך.
און טרעפֿט אים אָן אין צעזאָרס צירק דערנאָך
אַ לײַב וואָס לאָזט נאָך זיך
שיריים ווי אַ רבי גאָטיע-בענדלעך, האָניטשעס פֿון שיך —
דו מיש זיך ניט. דו ווייסט — פֿון זײַנס אַ מינדסטן ריר
שמעקט מער מיט טויט ווי פֿון אַ טויטנצעטל אויף אַ פֿרעמדער טיר
אין אַ מגיפֿה-צײַט. און גרינגער איז
צו לויפֿן דורך אַ פֿעלד אַן אָפֿגעשניטענעם מיט הוילע פֿיס,
צו ראַטעווען פֿון רויבפֿויגל, אַ שמעטערלינג, וואָס פֿליט.

נאָר דער וואָס שוועבט מיט טשוועקעס אין די הענט צו סלופּעס צוגעשמידט
איז אַ פֿאַרלוירענער ! און קלייד אויף אים — אַפֿילו פֿון אַ גאַסנווײַב
איז ניט קיין שטאָפּיק אויף אַ פּלאַש אויף זײַן צעשטאָכן לײַב.
און ניט נאָר בלויז דער וואָלקן אין דער הויך
בײַם שײַן פֿון שׂריפֿה-רויך —
נאָר אויך די וואָנץ אויף אונדז, בײַם ליכט געזען איז רויט
ווי זון פֿאַרטאָג — ווי מאַזל-אונטערגאַנג אויף קינדערהויט !

For our world two searing abscesses, on top of the ulcer
Called nations' pride!

Forests supply whips and gallows-wood
And flagpoles for a warship that lies at foreign shores
Like an inkstain on a loveletter.
And parliaments—melting pots for our priest, the stock-market jester.
Wherever there's a Golden Calf, they dance around it like fish of prey in a net.
And if our stepmother Earth lacks bread for us
She replaces it with iron for a sword.

And the toe of our boots shows the way
To the light of life, where we are slaughtered.
And if we lack the right measure of honey
For this malice breaking us like glass—
Then emerges, with two eyes like holes in snow,
The world-Golem—the Messiah, who celebrates
Consolation-birth with the shell of an egg.
And a brother, flesh of my flesh,
Sells him, like the skin of a calf, to death.

May he be judged by the dark silence
Of a madman who's watching a bird dead in its cage;
May his dead mother (even on his remorse-path)
Follow him with a face like the last days
Of Jerusalem's ruin;
And if afterward, in Caesar's circus,
A lion meets him, who leaves behind
Leftovers like a *rebbe*: underwear bands and leggings—
Don't mix in. His slightest stir
Smells of death worse than a death notice on a door
In time of plague. It would be easier
To run barefoot through a new-mown field
To save a flying butterfly from a preying bird.

leftovers—customarily, a Hassidic rebbe ate first; his leftovers were given to his followers as a special favor.

But the one who hovers, bound to poles, with nails in his hands,
Is lost! The clothes on him—less than on a street-walker:
Not even a bottle-stopper on his pierced body.
And not merely the cloud above
In the gleam of a city fire—
The bedbug on our bodies, too, is red in the light—
Like the sun at dawn, like measle-sunset on baby-skin!

און רעד מיר ניט פון דעם, וואָס שלאָפט מיט קאָפּ אויף שטײן,
און זעט מלאכים ווײַס ווי סמעטענע צו דר׳ערד אַרונטערגײן.
ניט זײ, און ניט די טויב פון נח׳ס מבול, נאָר דער חלף-שניט
וואָס עפֿנט אויף בײַם קאַלב דעם גאָרגל אינדערמיט —
בעט איבער צווישן זיך
דאָס פֿײַער מיטן וואָסער אויף דער קיך.

און סאָזשע — רעשט פון אַלעמגוטן — רייניקט אויס
דער קוימענקערער איבער אונדז, ווי נאָך אַ מת דאָס הויז.
נאָר ער — זײַן בעזעם שלײַדערט ער פון דאַך אַראָפּ,
און ניט ווי דו פון פֿאַרקאַנעס דײַן קאָפּ.

ס׳איז וואָר, איך קען קיין דערווײַל
דיר מיט אַ מעסער צוקוועטשן דעם בײַל,
און שיטן צוקער אויף דער צונג ווען דו האָסט זיך ווי געטאָן
אויף יענעם אָרט, וואָס אויך דער קעניג דאַרף צו זיצן אויפֿן טראָן.

נאָר ניט צו שיקן דיר אַ קאַסטן שאָקאָלאַד
פֿאַרשרײַבט מען דײַן געבורטסטאָג אַקוראַט!
עס זיצט שוין ערגעץ וווּ
בײַ דײַן סאָלדאַטן-ראָק אַ שנײַדערייונג אַ לעמד-וואָוו ווי דו,
און זאָל זײַן האַרץ אים אָנקלאָגן פֿאַר וואָס ער זינגט דערבײַ!
נאָר ווי דאָס זאָל ניט זײַן, פֿאַר ביקסן שמעלצט מען בלײַ,
און ווער סע ווייסט אַז ס׳איז נישטאָ
קיין ווײַזערס אויפֿן וועלטזײיגער פון זון און שטערן דאָ —
דער קען זיך נעמען צײַט
און ווי אַ שטערנזעער פרעמדע וועלט פון ווײַט —
זיך אויסמאָלן זײַן גרוב — מיט בלומען אין אַ ראָד,
ווי בעזעמער וואָס מ׳האָט שוין אָפּגענוצט אין הינטערהויף פון באָד.

נאָר איך — פֿון טויזנט גריבער אָפֿענע אין שלאַכטפעלט ווינט מײַן ווײ,
ווײַל קלאָר איז מיר ווי איינס און איינס איז צוויי:
דער אמת פון דײַן שפיל — אָט נעם אַליין
מיט דײַנע הענט וואָס זײַנען נאָך צו קליין
צו ווי טאָן אויפֿן וואָר — און ווי די מאַמע, טרויבן אויף אַ טאַץ פֿאַר דיר —
לייג אויס די רײַד מײַנע — די שרעק אין מיר.
וואָס רופֿט דיך ווי אַ שטומער פֿון אַ זומפֿ מיט זײַן געלײמט געשרײי.
וואָס וויל איך דען? — דער האָן מיט זײַן געקרײי
וועקט אויף מען זאָל אים שעכטן וועט מען האָבן שמאָלץ!
איך וויל, דו זאָלסט אין וואָרט מײַנעם, דעם שטויבל זאַלץ,
דערזען דעם ים, און זאָלסט אָפּזאָגן זיך פֿליען אויף אַ הײיפיש רײַטנדיק,
נאָך שיפן דאָ, וואָס גייען מיט ברײַט קיין האַצעפלאַץ אָ פֿירן בײַנוול קריק!

And don't tell me about one who sleeps, head on a stone,
And sees angels white as sour cream walking down to earth.
Not they, and not the dove of Noah's flood, but the knife slash
Slitting the gullet of a calf—
Makes peace between
The fire and the water on the stove.

his head on a stone—an allusion
to Jacob's dream.

And soot—the vestige of all happiness—
The chimneysweep will clean it out, like a house after a death.
But he throws his broom down from the roof,
Not like you hurling your head down from fences.

It's true, so far I can
Press your bump with a knife
And pour sugar on your tongue when you get hurt
In that place that even a king needs to sit on his throne.

But it's not to send you a crate of chocolate
That they register your birthday with precision!
Somewhere a tailorboy—one of the Thirty-Six Just, like you—
Already bends over your soldier's tunic—

Thirty-Six*

And may his hump accuse him for singing at his work!
Anyway, they are already melting lead for rifles,
And he who knows that there are no hands
On the worldclock of sun and stars—
May take his time and,
Like a star-gazer observing strange worlds from afar,
Imagine his own pit, with flowers in a circle
Like used-up sweeping-branches in the backyard of a bath.

But I—my pain cries from a thousand open pits in a battlefield,
Because I see as clearly as one and one are two,
The truth of your play. If you wish—
As mama lays out grapes for you on a platter—
With your own hands that are too small
To really hurt, lay out my words—the fear in me
Calling out to you like a mute man shouting from a swamp.
What do I want?—the rooster crowing
Wakes people up to slaughter him for chickenfat!
I want you to see in a drop of salt—my word—
The whole sea; and to refuse to race, riding on a shark,
After ships that carry bread to Hotseplots and bring back cotton!

Hotseplots—a Yiddish
equivalent to Oshkosh; implying
a distant place, the end of the
world.

עס וועט דײַן אונטערגײן
דער פערל אין דער טיפעניש ניט צוגעבן קיין חן,
און וואר סע בענקט נאָך ווינט און אינד־געזאַנג,
קען האַרכן גלאַק און צדקה־פּושקע בײַם לוויה־גאַנג.

און רופט דער פּרעזידענט — דער פּאַטער אַלעמענס, ווייסט אײן גאָט ווי אַזוי,
אים שיק פאַרויס, צו זען, אַז הימל־פלויים און פּנים הונגעריקס איז בלוי,
בײַם שׁונא אויך אין לאַנד! — און אַז אַ טויטנפעלד
איז אומעטום (אויך אָן געהרגעטע) אַ צירונג פאַר דער וועלט.
און די אַלמנות אויך — ווי פּאַסט־פּעקלעך מיט אַ פאַרנאָרעטן אַדרעס
אויף די געלעגערס אין דער נאַכט — דערמאָנען ניט פאַרגעס!
און זאָלן זײַנע לײַט וואָס העלפן די אַלפֿאַנזן לײדיק־גײן —
פֿון זײַנע פּאָנען העמדער נײַען —
פאַר קינדער וואָס שלעפן זיך אָן אָנבײַסן אין חכמה־שטאָל אַרײַן,
צו לערנען זיך (ווי אויף כפרות, עופות דאָ) צום שעכטבאַנק ראוי זײַן.
און ער אַלײַן — קען צו אַ שוסטער דאָ פאַרדינגען זיך.

Chaim Gross: *Roosevelt and Hoover in a Fist Fight*, 1932–33.

Your drowning
Won't add beauty to the pearls in the depths,
And he who longs for wind and song of waves
May listen to bells and charity boxes at a funeral.

And if the President—who is everyone's father,
    only God knows how—
Should call, let him go first, to see
That sky-plum and hungry-face are blue
In the enemy's country, too! And that a deathfield
Is everywhere (even without dead bodies) an ornament for the world.
And the widows—like parcels with blurred addresses
On beds at night—don't forget them either!

And let his men who help the pimps go idle—
Cut up the banners and sew shirts
For children who trudge hungry to the wisdom-stables
To learn (like chickens for the Atonement ritual)
    to be worthy of the slaughter-bank.

chickens for the atonement ritual—on Yom Kippur, a chicken is slaughtered for man's sins.

— רעגירן איז קיין האנטווערק ניט. ס׳איז אלטמאָדיש ווי סקריף אין נייע שיך.
און ניט נאָר קרוינען טויגן ניט, די זון איז דאָ אין קאָפּ זאָל ליכטיק זיין!
און אַ צילינדער לאָזט צומאָל קיין לופטל ניט אַריין —
דאָס זאָגט די מעדיצין,
וואָס היט די פליג אפילו דאָ — עס זאָל פון איר ניט קראַנק ווערן די שפּין,
ווייַל מיר באַדאַרפן שפּינוועב אויף דער וויסנשאַפט ווי צעזאַרס פּאַטריאָט
דאָס חזיר־פלייש אויף דעם מזבח פון יעהאָווא־גאָט.

און בלוט פאַרגאָסנס פאַר אומזיסט קען ווערן אויף העברייער אָפּגעוווענדט.
ער דאַרף נאָר ווי פּילאַטוס וואַשן זיך די הענט,
און עסן (אויב ס׳איז שבת) ביי דיין טיש געפילטע פיש,
וואָס זיינען זיס ווי געסט וװי לאַנג זיי זיינען פריש.

נאָר זאָל ער זיך היטן זיך עס זאָל ביי אים אין האַלדז קיין ביין נישט בלייבן שטיין,
דאָס קען נאָך זיין אַזאַ מין שׂימחה דאָ — ס׳זאָל טאַנצן גיין
דיין פריינד דאָס נעגערל. — ער האָט זיך אויך געפּרייט
װען מ׳האָט פאַרברענגט זיין טאָטן לעבעדיקערהייט —
פאַר צוויי־יאָרן, פאַרביי אַ בעקעריי — האָט אים דער ריח פון ברויט
אַ זעץ געטאָן אין נאָז — האָט ער געזאָגט ״גוטמאָרגן״ צו אַ ווייַסער מויד.

And he can hire himself out to a shoemaker.
Ruling is not a craft. It is old-fashioned, like a squeak in new shoes.
And not only crowns are worthless! The sun is here to bring light into our heads,
Yet a top hat will not let through one drop of air—
Thus says medicine,
Which protects even a fly so the spider won't get sick,
Because we need spiderweb for science, as Caesar's patriot
Needed pork on Jehovah's altar.

pork on Jehovah's alter—a reference to the desecration of the Jewish Temple in Jerusalem by the Romans.

And blood spilt in vain can be diverted to the Hebrews.
All he has to do is wash his hands like Pilate
And at your table eat (if it's the Sabbath) *gefilte fish*,
Which is sweet like guests as long as they're fresh.

But he must watch out not to choke on a bone,
This may bring so much joy—that your friend, the little Negro,
Will go dancing. That's how he rejoiced
When they burned his father alive—
Two years ago, as he walked by a bakery, the smell of bread
Struck his nose—and he said "Good-Morning" to a white broad.

William Gropper: *Fantasy*, 1965.

J. L. Teller

1912–1972

Judd L. Teller, as he signed his name in English, was a versatile writer in several languages and only sporadically a Yiddish poet. Because he was active in Jewish political and social organizations and was a journalist, lecturer, and author of political books, he was hardly considered "a poet." However, the 220 pages of his collected poems published posthumously as *Durkh Yidishn Gemit* (Through Jewish Mood) in Tel Aviv in 1975 show him to be one of the remarkable Yiddish poets of his generation.

Born in Tarnopol in eastern Galicia. Teller experienced World War I, suffering starvation and the fear of changing military powers as described in his autobiographical cycle, "Invasion." His father went to America before the war, and all contact with him was lost for some years. He finally brought his wife and two sons to America in 1921. Teller studied in Hebrew schools in New York, notably the Herzeliya High School and the Teachers' College of what later became Yeshiva University, where his Talmud teachers included Dr. Pinkhas Churgin and Abraham Shauer, the father of painter Raphael Soyer. He graduated from City College and received a Ph.D. in psychology at Columbia University.

A child prodigy and extremely well-read, Teller wrote essays, poems, and stories in both Hebrew and Yiddish. His first book of Yiddish poetry, *Symbols*, was published when he was eighteen years old. *Miniatures* (1934) was in the vein of American Objectivist verse, though more symbolically suggestive and erotically tense than other Objectivist poems. Teller was close to the Introspectivists and published in *In zikh*. His next book, *Poems of the Age* (1940), broke entirely with the poetics of the short, concentrated poem. Under the impact of the impending Holocaust, his tone changed into that of Yiddish Modernist talk-verse, combining personal point of view and moralizing asides with elements of historiosophical essay, intellectual reflection and irony, and autobiographical narrative. Teller combined a close-up but ironic view of the great Viennese figures of psychoanalysis with a historiosophical grasp of the approaching Holocaust. All this was interspersed with sharply observed, metaphorical miniatures that were reminiscent of his early

Judd L. Teller.

poems. After a long period of abstention from writing Yiddish poetry, he came back to it in 1959, encouraged by the editor of the Tel Aviv quarterly, *Di Goldene Keyt*, returning again to shorter, less talkative and more hermetic poems.

Teller was an intelligent and prolific journalist and a sharp polemicist in both Yiddish and English. Among other positions, he served as editor-in-chief of the Independent Jewish Press Service, as political secretary of the American Zionist Organization, as advisor to the Israeli delegation to the United Nations, and, in his last years, was founder and director of the Policy Planning and Research Institute of the Synagogue Council of America. Teller published a number of books in English on historical and political topics: *Scapegoat of Revoution* (1954); *The Kremlin, the Jews and the Middle East* (1957); *The Jews: Biography of a People* (1966); *Strangers and Natives* (1968); and *The People of Yiddish* (1971).

The poems selected here are drawn from the carefully produced posthumous edition.

◄ אָוונט-מאָטיוו

פאַרבענקטע נעז נענען צום ריח פון געעלטערטע רויזן;
עס איז אַן אויסגעבענקטע, געצערטלט שעה —
אַ שעה, וואָס טראָגט אירע אייגענע האָר.
נאָר מאָדנע, ווי בײַ מיר בייגן זיך די קני,
די לאַנדשאַפט שווינדלט דורך פאַר מײַנע אויגן,
ווי אַן איבערגעריסענער פילם.
און מײַן פינטלדיקער בליק שטויסט זיך פּלוצעם אָן אין פּוסטן לײַלעך פון דער נאַכט.
די האַנט זוכט פאַרצווייפלט אַן אָנלען אין דער לופט,
דער קערפער זינקט,
אַלץ ווי אין אַ נעפּל —

ווי ווערטער, וואָס מען כאַפּט-אויף אַ מאָל אין שלאָף — — — —

◄ פיגור

ווינטן וועלן ברעכן שטאַמען
אַרום שלאַנקן מיידל-גאַנג;
דאָס פּנים וועט זיך רײַסן
ווי דורך נעצן;
זון וועט שוידערן
און שויבן וועל בראָזגען אונטער ליכט:
ווער וועט אויפטײַען די פרייד
אין האַרטע און שפּיציקע נאָפּלען?

◄ פעלדז

זון בושעוועט ווי שלאַכט.
מײַן לײַב איז יונג
צווישן פעלדזן.

דאָ האָט האָגל געבלענדט
און פאַרלענדט.

➤ *Evening Motif*

Longing nostrils move
To the smell of aged roses.
Coveted, fondled hour—
Hour that wears her own hair.
Strange, how my knees bend,
The landscape spins before my eyes
Like an interrupted film.
My blinking gaze stumbles suddenly
On the empty sheet of the night.
My hand gropes desperately for support in the air.
My body sinks.
Everything floating in a fog—

Like words overheard in a dream— — —

➤ *Figure*

Winds will crack tree trunks
Around her slender walk.
Her face will emerge
Ripping through meshes.
The sun shudders,
Panes rattle under light:
Who will thaw the joy
In hard, pointed nipples?

➤ *Rock*

Sun raging like a battle.
My body is young
Among rocks.

Here
Hail dazzled
And ravaged.

ביימער — וואַכע פעלן
אין העלע טשאַדן;

שטיין — דיקער
אָפּגעדעקטער דיך —

איינצוזאָסן זיך אין אַלץ,
ווי וואַסער.

◄ רויִנען

טעמפּע, פּלאַכע פּנימער
פון פעלדזן;
ווי פון קראַנקע אויערן
רינען ריטשקעלעך.
דאָ שפּראָצן גראָזן
אונטער חרובע כוואַליעס,
און ביי נאַכט וואיִען שטערן.

◄ אויפן וועג

ווינט שטערט דיין גאַנג
און שטיקט דיך ווי רויך.
פון בערג בלאַנקט
מיט ווייַטער זון און קאַלטע טייַכן.
ביסט איינזאַם
אין שפּעטן ליכט.
אויטאָס שאַרכן שאַרף
ווי בלעטער.

◄ ווינטער-פֿאַרנאַכט

שלאַנקע ייִנגלעך לויפן
אין האַלב-ליכט און שרייַען;
אַרום וואַרעמע, ליכטיקע טורעמס
קלעטערן ווייַזערס, ווי מאַלפּעס.

טעמפּע קולות און שפּעטע זון.
דער פּראָסט קנאַקט האַרט ווי שאָלעכץ,

Trees—alert furs
In bright fumes.

Stone—thick
Uncovered groin.

To bite into it all,
Like water.

➤ *Ruins*

Blunt, flat faces
Of rocks.
Brooks leak
As from infected ears.
Grass sprouts
Under ruined waves.
And at night the stars wail.

➤ *On the Road*

Wind hinders your walk,
Chokes you like smoke.
Mountains gleam
With a distant sun and cold rivers.
You are lonely
In the late light.
Cars rustle, sharp
Like leaves.

➤ *Winter Evening*

Slender boys run
In half-light, shouting.
On warm, shining towers,
Clock-hands climb like monkeys.

Blunt voices and late sun.
The frost cracks hard, like shells.

ערגעץ ווײַט גרװיל מװערן
װי אײַזבערג,
און שױבן פלאַקערן העלער
פון שטרױ.

◄ שטאָט-שאָסײ

דער ווינט טרײַבט שילדן
װי קװאַליעס איבער אונדזערע קעפ;
די זון בראָזגעט, װי גלאָז,
און איז אַ קאַלטע בלענדעניש
צװישן די בײמער.

שײַנען פאַרקאַפן אין װילדװעב;
אױטאָמאָבילן טראָגן זיך
מיט אימפעט, װי אױף גליטש.

ס׳טונקלט. פענצטער זענען אָפן,
און פון ראַדיאָ שרײַט די נאַכט
מיט הײסע קולות.

◄ עטיוד

רױקן איבער שטאָט פאַר נאַכט
װי בלעטער אין װינט;
הינט ליגן פלאַך װי שװעלן.
רעגן-פלעקן אױף די שױבן
װי פון פרישער פאַרב.
אױסשטעל-פענצטער אַנקערן
װי שיפן.

◄ פּײזאַזש

די פײגל רײצט
דער הײסער ריח
פון שטײַפע בערגלעך ערד.

דער פאַרנאַכט איז טעמפ
מיט שפעטע רױקן
איבער דעכער...

Somewhere far away, buildings loom
Like icebergs.
And panes flare up brighter
Than straw.

➤ *City Highway*

The wind chases signboards
Like waves over our heads.
The sun shatters like glass,
Cold dazzle
Between trees.

Carlights surprise in wildweb.
Automobiles race
Impetuously, like ice-skating.

Dusk falls. Windows are open.
From radios, night screams
With hot voices.

➤ *Etude*

Smoke over the city at dusk
Like leaves in the wind.
Dogs lie flat like thresholds.
Rain-spots on windows
Like fresh paint.
Store-fronts anchor
Like ships.

Abraham Walkowitz: *City No. 2.*

➤ *Landscape*

Birds aroused
By the hot smell
Of taut mounds
Of earth.

The evening is blunt,
With late smoke
Over rooftops.

דײַן ריר
צינדט ווילדע שאָטנס אויף די ווענט;
ווינטן לויערן
אויפן קילן, בלויען פלאַם
פון דײַנע נאָפלען.

◄ חיהש

דײַן צאַרטער, ווילדער רײַטער
וואָס קלײדט די שפאָרן
ווי אַ פרוי.

אין פאַרנאַכטן פון רויטלעכע הימלען
און וואַרעמע דעכער,
האָט ער ליב דײַן ברוינע, וואַרעמע פעל,
דײַן האַרטן געבײַן צווישן זײַנע קני,
און שעמט זיך פאַר דער היימישקייט
אין דײַנע גלוסטיקע אויגן.

דורך פײַכטן וואָל, מיט אַ לאַמטערן,
וועט ער שפעט זיך קערן צו דיר;
קניִען פאַר דיר,
ווי פאַר אַ געץ,
מיט אַ זשמעניע היי.

◄ פרוי אין רעגן

אָנמעכטיקע ווענט
און אימפעטיקע פלאַנצן.
פינצטער. וואַרעמע, רוישיקע ריטשקעס
איבער שינדלען און ברעטער.

דו וואַקסט שלאַנק
אין פלוצעמדיקן ווילדן ליכט;
דײַן קלײד וויקלט זיך
ווי בלעך אין פלאַם.

נאַכט. שרײַענדיקע פייגל
און פליִענדיקע בלעטער.

Your stir
Ignites wild shadows on the walls.
Winds lurk
At the cool, blue flame
Of your nipples.

➤ *Animal Mood*

Your gentle, wild rider
Adorns your stirrups
Like a woman.

In evenings of purple skies
And warm roofs,
He loves your brown, warm fur,
Your hard bones between his knees,
And is bashful of the intimacy
In your lusting eyes.

Through damp wool, with a lantern,
He will return to you late,
Kneel before you
As before an idol,
With a handful of hay.

➤ *Woman in Rain*

Languid walls
And impetuous plants.
Dark. Warm, rattling brooks
Over shingles and boards.

You are growing slender
In sudden wild light.
Your dress curls
Like tin in a fire.

Night. Shouting birds
And flying leaves.

גלוסט ◄

צעריײצטע קישנס פײַניקן
אַ מיידלס רויע נאָפלען;
איר מויל איז האַרט ווי פעלדז,
און פײַכט מיט ערשטן נעפל;
די שלײפן שלאָגן טאָם-טאָמס
הייס און טעמפ;
און הענט בריִען ווי קראָפעווע
אויפן נאַקעטן לײַב.

* ◄

אפשר איז עס גאָט
וואָס וואַקסט בײַ מיר אויפן לײַב?

דײַנע קלײנע, שאַרפע צײן
האָבן גאָט געקרייציקט.

גאָט איז די לעגענדע
פון ווײַסן געווינס.
פאַר טאָג בלאַנקט עס ווי שניי פון אַלע דעכער.

נאָר איצט איז נאַכט.
שטערן — שטילע, פלינקע
טריט פון האָרן.

דײַנע זומער-שפרענקעלעך זענען געדיכט
און רייצן ווי דער ריח פון ים.

גאָט איז ניט יונג,
אים שלעפערט דער ריח פון ים.

ווילד געזאַנג ◄

איך וועל דיך נעמען ווילד, ווי פראָסט;
אויסשלאָגן שווייס
אויף דײַן לײַב.

➤ *Desire*

Excited pillows torture
A girl's raw nipples.
Her mouth is as hard as rock
And wet with first fog.
The temples beat tom-tom,
Hot and blunt.
And hands—like nettles—
Sting the naked body.

➤ *

Perhaps it is God
Growing on my body?

Your small, sharp teeth
Crucified God.

God is the legend
Of white conscience.
At dawn—a glitter like snow
On all rooftops.

But now it's night.
Stars—quiet, brisk
Steps of rabbits.

Your freckles are dense
And excite like the smell of the sea.

God is not young,
He is drowsy from the smell of the sea.

Max Weber: from *Shriftn 6*,
Spring 1920.

➤ *Wild Song*

I shall take you, wild as a frost.
I shall make sweat
Break out
On your body.

מיר וועלן זיך טראָגן
דורך בלעגנדיקע טשאַדן,
און דו וועסט מיך זאָפן
ווי רויך.

נאַכט וועט איַילן
מיט כמאַרעס און טיַיכן —
איבער אונדז סטיַיעס
מיט וויסטע געשרייַען.

◄ שפעט-אָוונט

טראָמווייַען לויפן אָפ
ווי הייסע שריפט.
סע איז די פיַיערלעכע שעה
פון טורעם-ציפערבלעטער.

ווי צויגן לויערן אָרעמס אין דער פינצטער,
און טיַיכן פאַרפאַלגן די שטאַמען פון ביימער.

אָטעם איז איצט ווילד
ווי ריח פון ערשטן ברויט,
נאָפלען גליִען און ציטערן
און זענען בלוי פון פראָסט.

פענצטער ברענען שטיל און רויט,
ווי רייַפע פרוכט שפעט-זומער.

◄ דער ריטער זינגט

קראַנקע וואַרצלען זוכן איצט
די וואַרעמקייט פון פיַיכטער ערד;
נאַכט איז עלטער פון געשריי,
פון טיַיכן און פון פייגל.

דו ביסט שלאַנק,
און טראָגסט דיַינע הערנער אין נעפל;
און דיַינע פאַלדן זענען נאָך וואַרעם מיט ווינט.

אין שפעטע נעכט וועל איך בענקען
נאָך דער אָפגעהאַקטער זילב פון דיַינע טריט,
נאָך דיַין קנעכל וואָס איז רויט
ווי די באַק פון אַ קינד.

We shall race
Through dazzling fumes,
And you will sip me
Like smoke.

Night will rush
With clouds and rivers—
Over us, flocks
Cry out bleakly.

➤ *Late Evening*

Tramways run away
Like hot type.
It is the solemn hour
Of tower-clock dials.

Like bitches, arms lurk in the dark.
Rivers torment the tree trunks.

Breath is wild
Like the smell of first bread.
Nipples glow and tremble,
Blue from the frost.

Windows burn, calm and red,
Like ripe fruit in late summer.

➤ *The Knight Sings*

Sick roots grope
For the warmth of wet earth.
Night is older than scream,
Than rivers and birds.

You are slender,
You carry your horns in the fog.
Your folds are still warm with wind.

Late at night I shall long
For the interrupted syllable of your steps,
For your ankle, red
As a baby's cheek.

אויערן וואַכן ווי הינט און ווי שטערן;
האָרכן ווייטן פּליעסק
צווישן ווערטער.
דאָס לײַב רײַסט אָן.
ביימער, שויבן בלענדן מיט פּראָסט.
הערנער שווינדלען, ווי פייגל,
אין טונקל.
שטיבער זענען וואַך ווי אַך ווי דער דרויסן.

לידער פון דער צײַט (1940)

פּסיכאָאַנאַליז

◄ ייִד זיס אָפּענהיימער אויף זײַן ערשטן באַזוך בײַם פּראָפעסאָר זיגמונד פרויד

דאָס ביסטו — דער אייביקער ייִד.
פון עשׂו וויגליד, פון ערלס לעגענדע.
און איך בין דײַן פּלימעניק — ייִד זיס אָפּענהיימער.
ווײַט-זעער, קלאָר-זעער, דורכזעער,
וועסט מסתּמא זאָגן אַז איך — בין גאָרניט איך,
אַז דער וואָס גלוסט צו בעלער און צו שיקסעס
איז ניט — ייִד זיס.

איך בין איצט די שפּיגלפלאַך פון טײַך,
פאַרשלאָפט אין קוסטע-ברעגן.
פון מיר צינגלען קוואַלן,
פייכט-פּלאַנצן און ווערעם.

מײַן ייִחוס: הענדלער מיט ווייץ און גערשטן
וואָס פלעגן גנביש אונטערלייגן
שווערגעוויכט אויף וואָגן.
כ׳ווייס פאַר וואָס.
נאָר ווילסט ניט מישפּטן וואָס גוט און שלעכט איז.
ווילסט דערקענען.

לערנער וואָס האָבן זיך אַרומגעצוימט מיט שטעכיק דראָט,
און, ווי אויפן שפּאַציר-הויף — אַרעסטאַנטן
מיט געפּענטעטע טריט
געהיפעט אין אַ קרײַז פון לאָון.
מיטנטאָג. זון האָט געשרפעט די אויגן.

Ears, alert like dogs and like stars,
Hear a distant splash
Between words.
The body blisters.
Trees and panes dazzle with frost.
Horns flit by like birds
In the dark.
Houses vigilant like fields.

POEMS OF THE AGE (1940)

Psychoanalysis

► *Jud' Süss Oppenheimer on his First Visit with Professor Sigmund Freud*

That's you—the Eternal Jew.
Of Esau's lullaby, of Gentile legend.
And I am your nephew—Jud' Süss Oppenheimer.
You, seer, who can see far, see clear, see through,
You may say that I—am not I,
That one who craves feasts and shikses
Is not Jew Süss.

I am now the mirror-surface of a river,
Languid between bushy shores.
Springs emerge from me,
Water plants and worms.

My pedigree: traders in wheat and barley,
Who would slyly slip
Extra weights onto the scales.
I know why.
But you don't want to judge between good and bad.
You want to understand.

Scholars, who encircled themselves with barbed wire:
Like prisoners in a jail-yard,
They hopped with shackled feet
In a ring of Don'ts.
Midday. The sun seared their eyes.

Jud' Süss Oppenheimer—
Joseph Süss Oppenheimer, or
"the Jew Süss" (1698–1738),
Jewish financier and minister of
the treasury of the Duke of
Würtemberg. He introduced a
strongly centralized system of
taxes to enrich the duke's treasury
and was known for his strict rule
and personal profligacy. After the
duke's sudden death, Jud' Süss
was executed, in an atmosphere
of anti-Semitism. "Jud' Süss" was
popularized in a novel (1925) by
the German-Jewish writer, Lion
Feuchtwanger, and then in an
influential Nazi film (1940).
Teller's poem was published in *In
zikh*, in October 1937.

Eternal Jew—Wandering Jew*.
The Eternal Jew appears as a
bogeyman in Christian folklore.

Esau—twin brother of Jacob,
prototype of the Gentile in
Jewish folklore.

Don'ts—reference to the 365
prohibitory laws of Orthodox
Judaism.

חונפים: געטראָגן די ספר־תּורה
אין פּראָצעסיעס צום בישאָף,
געקעמט דעם שטויב מיט די בערד,
און צוריקגעגאַנגען הינטערוווײלעכץ
מיטן פנים — צו אים וואָס טראָגט דעם צלם.

זיי אַלע — מילדע שאָטנמענטשן,
פונעם גמזו־שטאַם.

און איך בין גמזוס אייניקל.
ער איז געווען אַ שעמעוודיקער ייד
און איצט צינדט ער מרידות אין מײַן חלום,
נוצט מײַן קול פֿאַר זײַנע לעסטער־רייד,
ווײל אויפמאַנען דאָס שײַטל פלייש.

אין בלויע שעהען מיט אַ גוייִשער טאָכטער,
כּישופט ער מיר אַרויס מײַן פֿאַרגואַלדיקטע שוועסטער,
(קעשענעוו, פּראָסקוראָוו, בריסק)
און מײַנע גלידער רײַסן זיך צום שענדן.

מיך שרעקט די ניט־דערזאָגטע זילב,
דאָס וואָס כ׳האָב ניט געאַנט.

ס׳פּרעסט מיך דער חלום, ווי דער ים — די יבשה.
קלאָר־זעער, דורכזעער,
נעם מיך ווי גרויפּן אין פויסט,
ווי אַן איי קעגן ליכט.

מ׳זאָגט אויף דיר אַז בײַ נאַכט
מישסטו קרײַטעכצער אין אָקריפ.
דאָס ביסטו — דער אייביקער ייד.
איך בין ייד זיס אָפענהײַמער,
דײַן פלימעניק.
איש גמזו איז געווען מײַן זיידע.

טײַטשער פון חלומות.
צי פון מיר אַ זאַנג.
פֿאַרזוך מיך
ווי גערשטן אויף ירידן.

Flatterers: they carried the Holy Torah
In processions to the Bishop,
Raked the dust with their beards,
And retreated backward,
Facing him who wore the cross.

They all were gentle shadow-men
Of the Gamzu-tribe.

And I am Gamzu's grandson.
He was a timid Jew—
And now he fires revolts in my dream,
Uses my voice for his profanities,
Wants to collect his pound of flesh.

In blue hours with a Gentile daughter,
He conjures up for me my violated sister
(Kishenev, Proskurov, Brisk),
And my limbs rage to rape.

I fear the unfinished syllable,
Things I have not sensed.

The dream gnaws at me, as the sea at the land.
You, who see clear, see through,
Take me like grains of barley in your fist,
Hold me like an egg against the light.

They say that at night
You mix herbs in a brew.
That's you—the Eternal Jew.
I am Jud Süss Oppenheimer,
Your nephew.
Gamzu was my grandfather.

You, interpreter of dreams.
Pull a stalk out of me.
Taste me
Like barley at the fair.

Gamzu—probably an allusion to Nahum of Gamzu (Gimzo), Rabbi Akiva's teacher. According to legend, he was "blind in both eyes, crippled in both hands, lame in both legs and his body was covered with boils." Yet, at every calamity that befell him, he would say: "This, too, is for the best." (In Hebrew: **Gam zu le-tova**, hence the name, **Gamzu**.)

Kishinev, Proskurov, Brisk—places of famous pogroms that shook the Jewish world in 1903, 1919, and 1937, respectively.

◄ ייִד זיס דערצײײלט װעגן זיי און װעגן זיך

צײַט פון קופערזון, פון הייסן װעלקן.
מײַן פלײצע בענקט שוין װידער נאָכן קרײץ,
די פיאטעס און די דלאַניעס עפענען זיך
װי קנאָספן.

כ'בין ייִד זיס.
אַ שנײַדער מיט אַן עלעגאַנטער טאַליע.
כ'צאַפ גלעזער סאָדע־װאַסער אויף אַ זײַטיק געסל,
כ'שרײַב ניגונים
פון פרײד גרויל בענקשאַפט
װי די געלע לבנה
אין ניו־יאָרקער האַפן.

כ'עס, טרינק, באַנעם ריחות, קולות, נוץ
זײער װאָג און צענטימעטער.

ס'רוישן די שפּאַצירן, אומצוטרוי גרײַפט מיך
פלוצעם אָן, װי װעטער־טויש.
צװישן די צײן קנאַקן זיי ניט יאָדערן,
נאָר טשװועקלעך. מײַן אַקסל נעמט זיך שמוגלען,
ס'פינטלט דאָס אויג און כ'פיל דעם קויטיקן שטראָם
װאָס האָט מיך אַרויסגעכוואַליעט
בײַ גאָלגאָטאַ.

דער מינדסטער שׂינאה־בליק שטויסט מיך אויף שטאָלצן.

מײַן קול שטעלט זיך נביאיש.
די װערטער רײַטן נאַשפיץ מיט רעטאָריק.
כ'זוך אין די קנייטשן אויף מײַן פנים —
די קלײנשריפט פון רמבם, די קלאָרשריפט
פון אַמסטערדאַמער שלײַפער.
כ'זוך מופתים אויפן אייגענעם שטערן.

ס'איז האַרבסט, מיט פאַרבן און מיט זעט.
זײערע פרויען בליאַסקען װי די סערפן.
און לייגן זיך װי תבואה.
יעדע איז פּוטיפרס װײַב. װי יוסף
היט איך מײַנע יונגע פּאָלעס.
כ'פאַרשטעל די גראָבע ייִדישע ליפן,
כ'צי אײַן די לײצעס פון מײַן ייִדישער
מענטשלעכער גלוסטונג,

Time of coppersun, of hot withering.
My back longs again for the cross.
My soles and my palms open up
Like buds.

I am Jew Süss.
A tailor with an elegant cut.
I tap soda-water in a back street.
I write melodies
Of joy horror longing
Like the yellow moon
In the port of New York.

I eat, drink, sense smells, voices, use
Their scales, their measuring tapes.

The promenades are noisy. Mistrust grips me
Suddenly, like a change in the weather.
Between their teeth they crunch not seeds
But nails. My shoulder smuggles me through,
My eye blinks and I smell the dirty stream
That floated me up
At Golgotha.

The tiniest gaze of hatred pushes me onto stilts.

My voice tunes up prophetically.
The words ride proudly with rhetoric.
In the lines of my face I seek
The small letters of Maimonides, the clear writings
Of the Amsterdam lens-polisher.
On my own brow I seek miracles.

Autumn. Autumn of colors, autumn of plenty.
Their women gleam like sickles.
And fall like stalks of wheat.
Each one is Potiphar's wife. Like Joseph
I watch my young coattails.
I cover my thick Jewish lips.
I pull the reins of my Jewish
Human lust

Ben Shahn: *Maimonides with Calligraphy*, 1965.

Maimonides—Moses Maimonides, (1135–1204) Jewish Spanish-Egyptian philosopher, physician, and scientist.

Amsterdam lens polisher—the Jewish philosopher, Benedict (Baruch) Spinoza (1632–1677), supported himself as a lens polisher.

Potiphar's wife—she tried to seduce Joseph in Egypt and, failing, accused him of rape.

און טאַפּ מיט פֿאַרצוווייפֿלטע הענט דאָס לײַב
צי ס׳שפּראָצן ניט פֿון מיר די עקן
און די הערנער פֿון דער
ייִד-לעגענדע.

כ׳בין אַ שנײַדער, צאַפּ סאָדע-וואַסער,
שרײַב ניגונים, און צי צוריק מײַן ייִחוס
ביז אַ טרערנדיקער באָבען.
אָבער וואָס האָבן זיי מיר אָנגעדולט,
אַרײַנגעליאַרעמט
וועגן אַנקער מיט ישו-קרייציקער
און זקני-ציון?

וווּ איז מײַן סוף? און וווּ בראשית
פֿון לעגענדע?
מײַן פֿלייצע פֿילט זיך ניט היימיש
מיט אַ שטול און זוכט דווקא
אַ קרייץ.
צווישן די צײַן האַלט איך טשוועקלעך
גלײַך ווי זיי.

דאָס בין איך, פֿאַרוואָרצלט אין אַלץ
און אין גאָרניט.
ייִד זיס.
אַנדרוגינוס.

◄ בריוו צו זיגמונד פֿרויד

ווי איז געווען דאָס וועטער יענעם טאָג?
מיט וויפֿל פֿאַרבן האָט געברענט די שקיעה?
אין ווין צי אין פּאַריז,
האָבן אין דיר אויפֿגעבליצט
די עשהס און לאָוון
פֿון דײַן פּסיכאָאַנאַליז?

אַ שמאָלע גאַס. ווי דורך אַ ליקע
האָט די זון געקאַפּעט.
פּלוצעם — צעפֿלאָשעטע פֿערד
הינטער דיר.
ביסט געלאָפֿן און אויסגעגאָסן גראָטעסק.
אַזוי האָט אויך געדאַנק
אַנגעפֿלוצעמט אויף דיר.

And feel my body with desperate hands:
Have I sprouted the tails
And the horns
Of the Jew-legend?

I am a tailor, I tap soda-water,
Write melodies, and draw my pedigree
As far back as a tearful grandmother.
Yet why have they cluttered up my head
With deafening shouts:
That I belong with the Jesus-crucifiers,
With Elders-of-Zion?

Elders of Zion—"Protocols of the Elders of Zion," a forged anti-Semitic document purporting to be the records of the "International Jewish Conspiracy," dating from the beginning of the twentieth century.

Where is my end? And where is the beginning
Of legend?
My back does not feel comfortable
With a chair, it goes looking for
A cross.
Between my teeth I hold nails
Just like them.

This is me, rooted in everything
And in nothing.
Jew Süss.
Androgynous.

► *Letter to Sigmund Freud*

How was the weather on that day?
With how many colors did sunset burn?
Was it in Paris or in Vienna
When inside you, like lightning, struck
The Do's and Dont's
Of your Psychoanalysis?

Do's and don'ts—reference to the 613 positive and negative precepts governing all of Jewish Orthodox life.

A narrow street. As through a funnel
The sun dripped.
Suddenly—terrified horses
Behind you.
You ran like a grotesque phantom.
Thought burst upon you
Suddenly like this.

און אפשר גאָר בײַ זיך אין צימער?
די אויגן האָבן געמידט. קינדער האָבן געשריִען
אונטער די פענצטער. אַ קאַטערינטשיק האָט
געצאָפט אַ פאָלקסליד.
דער טאָג איז געווען כמאַרנע און הייס,
מיט לאַנגווײַל און דערווואַרטונג.

װאַסער ניגון האָט זיך דיר דיר געפלאַנטערט
יענעם אינדערפרי? טי-דאַם, דאַם-דאַם, טי-דאַם.
האָט די זייף דיר געביסן די אויגן?

און ווי האָט זיך דיר אויסגעקעמט דער שרינט?
האָסט פאַרגעסן צו באַצאָלן דעם קאָנדוקטאָר.
האָסט אים איבערגעצאָלט
האָסט געגלעט קליניווואַרג איבער די קעפלעך,
מיט צעשטרייטע אויגן אַ פאָרש געטאָן דעם הימל,
און ווײַטער געשפאַנט ווי אַ חסר-דעה.

װאָס האָט זיך דיר געחלומט יענעם פאַרטאָג?
פליגן האָבן געזשומעט אַרום נעץ פון דײַן שלאָף.
די קעלט האָט פאַרשראָקן די קאָלדרע.
פליגן האָבן דיך געקושט ווי צוקער.
דײַן ברודער האָט זיך געפאָרט מיט אַן אָדלער.

זאָג, ווי ביסטו דערגאַנגען צו דער רגע
װאָס האָט געפלייכעט איבער דיר
ווי אַ זוניקער רעגן
אין דײַן זיידנס ערב-פּסח?

◄ זיגמונד פרויד צו צוויי און אַכציק יאָר

פייגל שרײַען מיט דער מאַמעס קול.
דער טאַטע ווואַרפט זיך פאַר די רעדער.
דעם ייִנגל קריכט אַ זשאַבע פון די האָר.
געדענקסט דעם חלום פונעם קליינעם זיגמונד?

איצט צו צוויי און אַכציק יאָר
איז זײַן נאַכט טרוקן און קלאָר
און סקריפּעט מיט שטילקייט.
דער שלאָף אויסגעלײַטערט.
די קאָמפּלעקסן אויסגעריכערט.

Or were you in your own room?
The eyes drooped tired. Children shouted
Under the windows. An organ-grinder
Milked a folk-song.
The day was cloudy and hot,
Full of boredom and expectation.

What melody was tangled up in your head
On that morning? Ti-dam, dam-dam, ti-dam.
Was the soap stinging your eyes?

melody—a Hassidic melody
without words.

And how did the part in your hair go?
You forgot to pay the conductor.
You overpaid him.
You stroked the heads of children.
With vacant eyes you surveyed the sky
And strolled on like a madman.

What did you dream that morning?
Flies buzzed around the net of your sleep.
The cold scared your blanket.
Flies kissed you like sugar.
Your brother copulated with an eagle.

Tell me, how did you reach the moment
That poured down on you
Like a sunny rain
On the eve of your grandfather's Passover?

► *Sigmund Freud at the Age of Eighty-Two*

Published in *In zikh*, June 1938.

Birds scream with mama's voice.
Papa throws himself under the wheels.
A frog creeps out of the boy's hair.
Do you remember the dream of little Sigmund?

Now, at the age of eighty-two,
His night is dry and clear
And squeaks with silence.
Sleep is elucidated.
The complexes smoked out.

יעדע מורא צוגעקייטלט.
יעדער פחד צוגערינגלט.

נאָר אין רינוועס פון נאַכטיקן רוען
רוישט די שרעק פאַרן טויט.
ווי פייגל-פלי, ווי ווינט אין ביימער
האָבן אַלע זי באַנומען,
פּאַטריאַכן, קריגער און קדושים.
דער בלינדער יצחק האָט אפילו רבקהן ניט געטרויט,
דער זקן יעקב האָט קלוג גערעדט,
און אַלט געטרערט,
געוואָלט אויפלעבן אַן אַלטע דיך
מיט יוספס יונגער האַנט.

ס'איז ניט דער טויט. אים דרייסט נאָכצוגיין
האָט ער שוין לאַנג
מיט קופער צוגעפעסטיקט
די שלעסער פון די קני.
ס'איז עפעס אַנדערש, און גלייך אַזוי אַלט.
ביי טאָג האָט ער אַרויסגעקוקט פון פענצטער,
געזען די סאָלוטירנדיקע הענט.
דעם האַקנקרייץ. געשמעקט מיט קלוגער נאָז
דאָס אַלטע ביעזע בלוט
אין יונגע אַריער-שקצים.

Ben Shahn: *Freud*, 1956.

Every fear, chained in.
Every fright, bolted up.

Only in the drainpipes of nightly rest
Clatters the fear of death.
Like birds in flight, like wind in trees
Everyone has grasped it:
Patriarchs, warriors, saints.
The blind Isaac didn't even trust Rebecca,
The old Jacob spoke wisely,
Tearful with age,
Wishing to enliven an old thigh
With Joseph's young hand.

The old Jacob . . . old thigh—cf. Genesis 47:29.

It's not death. To follow death boldly
He had long since
Fastened with copper
The locks of his knees.
It's something else, and just as old.
By day, he looked out the window,
Saw the arms in salute.
The Swastika. He smelled with his clever nose
The old evil blood
In young Aryan *shkotsim*.

Shkotsim*—young Gentile men.

די די האָבן ייִדיש-יאַדיש-עברית אויף. שקצים
נאָמען אַ איז ר׳ וועמען נאָך
חלה. ווי געקנאָטן מצה. ווי געקניט װאָרט דאָס
— הבדלה ווי געפלאָכטן
גוי. עשׂו. ערל.

געגאַמענט, בייזיקײטן אלע חיות, די אָדם ווי האָט, ער
רשׁי אייגענעם אַן געשריבן
עקדת-יצחק. און קין-הבל אויף
פאַנג, הייסער זונס דעם — פאַטריאַרך דעם ווי נאָר
טייטש: עברי פראָסטע דאָס איצט אים שמעקט
גוי. עשׂו. ערל.

רעגן. מיט רוישן רוען נאַכטיק פון רינוועס די
פּאָרטאָג. מיט מורמלען ביימער די
מורא? איז װאָס מורא?
זאַמד. אין אים פאַרשאַרט או צוזוייטן דעם פּלעט מצרי אײן
שפּעטזומער, אין סעדער ווי רייף מוט, עקיבאס נאָר
זיך, באַוועלטיקט
עשאַפט, דעם און שייטער דעם
וועזן גאַנצע דאָס אָן קניפּט
אות. ייִדישן פון פליגל אָן

מער איז זיך באַצווינגען
היפּנאָז. שאַרקאָס ווי

יאָר אַכציק און צוויי צו פרויד זיגמונד
האַנקרייצן, די פון קלעטערט
חזרט:
גוי. עשׂו. ערל. המן.

◄ לעבן פון אַפּ זיך זאָגט שטעקעל װילהעלם

פאַניק שטויביקער אין ביקעס צעווילדעטע ווי האָבן די װאָס די
צוריק. אויף געריסן זיך זייַט, אַ אָן פאַרקערט
שטריק פּאַקנדיקע מיט וועג דעם פאַרלאָפן ער איז
סטאַדע. דער אין אַרייַנגעשמיסן צוריק
פּאַשע, דער פון צוריקקער פאַרנאַכטיקן אין
צינגער, שטומע צווישן העמד לאַנגן אין
הערנער, צעבונטעוועטע איבער בייַטש אַ געווען ער איז
פעלן, פרייכנדיקע פייַכטע אויף האַנט צאַרטע אַ
הײלער. אַ און פּאַסטעך אַ

Shkotsim. Those whose name he carries
Have chewed the word in Hebrew-Joodisch-Yiddish,
Chewed it like matzo, kneaded it like challah,
Braided it like *Havdolah*-candles—
Orel. Esau. Goy.

As Adam named all animals, he named all evils.
He wrote his own Rashi
On Cain-Abel and Isaac's sacrifice.
Yet, as the Patriarch savored his son's fresh game,
He savors now the smell of simple Hebrew-Yiddish:
Orel. Esau. Goy.

The drainpipes of nightly rest clatter with rain.
The trees murmur with dawn.
Fear? What is fear?
One Egyptian kills another and covers him in sand.
Only Akiva's courage, ripe as orchards in late summer,
Masters itself,
The pyre and the gallows
And ties the whole being
To the wings of a Jewish letter.

To overcome oneself is more
Than Charcot's hypnosis.

Sigmund Freud at eighty-two
Climbs out of the Swastikas,
Recites:
Haman. Orel. Esau. Goy.

► *Wilhelm Stekel Gives up Life*

Like wild oxen in dusty panic,
They bolted, raced back—
He headed them off, with waving ropes
He whipped them back into the herd.
In evening return from the pasture,
In his long gown among mute tongues,
He was a whip over rioting horns,
A gentle hand over damp wheezing hides,
A shepherd and a healer.

Matzoh*

Challah*

Hav'dolah-candles*

Orel, Esau, Goy—various epithets for non-Jews.

Rashi*—the most famous and lucid commentary of the Bible.

patriarch—an allusion to the biblical patriarch Isaac, as a blind old man, who had to make do with the smell of game instead of the reality of it.

one Egyptian—Exodus 3:11–12: "... when Moses was grown ... he went out unto his brethren, and looked on their burdens; and he spied an Egyptian smiting a Hebrew, one of his brethren. And he looked this way and that way, and when he saw that there was no man, he slew the Egyptian and hid him in the sand."

A'kiva (Akiva ben Joseph, known as **Rabbi Akiva**)—a rabbinic sage of the first and second centuries, A.D., imprisoned by the Romans after the failure of the Bar Kokhba revolt. Rabbi Akiva embodied the tradition of learning vis-à-vis Bar Kokhba's militarism. He was famous for his contributions to Jewish mysticism; according to legend, he was one of the four who "entered the orchard" of secret lore and the only one who emerged whole.

Charcot, Jean-Martin—a nineteenth-century French neurologist, one of Freud's teachers. Charcot's use of hypnosis stimulated Freud's interest in the psychological origins of neurosis.

נאָר וואָס האָט זײַנע אויגן צעמישט אויפן באַרג-אַראָפ,
אים צעשראָקן ווי אַ שאָף,
ער זאָל זיך טאָן אַ לאָז
איבער קוסט און שטיין,
איבער דראָט,
איבער צאַם נאָך צאַם,
מיט צעקאַליעטשעטע קלאָען אַריבערן לעצטן פּאַרקאַן?
די דעפעש האָט אָנגעזאָגט:
שטעקעל, ווילהעלם, מ.ד.,
מאָרד
דורך אייגענער האַנט.

זײַן צוגעוווינטער גאַנג איז געוועזן איבער הויפן
און בנינים פון שפּיטאָל, דער ריח פון בעז שטענדיק געווירצט
מיט קאַרבאָל. אַ ווילד האַלב-געשרײַ
הינטער גראָטעס
אין אַ שטילן ווײַסן קאָרידאָר.
אין יעדן וואָרט אויף מענטשנס ליפ
האָט ער ווי פרויד
געזען אַ בריק
אויף לויפן אַהער,
אויף לויפן צוריק,
באַשאָף און פאַרניכט,
די זינד
און די שטראָף,
דעם יעגער
וואָס יעגערט אויף זיך,
די וווּנד
און די היילונג.

But what was it
That confused his eyes on the way downhill,
Scared him like a sheep,
To make him plunge
Over bush and stone,
Over barbed wire,
Over barrier after barrier,
Clawing, wounded, over the last fence?
The cable announced:
Stekel, Wilhelm, M.D.,
Murdered
By his own hand.

His usual walk led through yards
And buildings of the hospital, the smell of lilac ever spiced
With carbolic acid. A wild half-cry
Behind bars
In a quiet white corridor.
In each word on a man's lips
He saw like Freud
A bridge
To run there,
To run back,
Create and destroy,
The sin
And the punishment,
The hunter
Hunting himself,
The wound
And the healing.

Raphael Soyer: *Pugnacity*, 1937.

אין יעדן גענעצדיקן שענקער הינטער דער שראַנק,
אין יעדן הכנעהדיקן פּנים ביים שייבל אין באַנק,
געזען אַ מידן באַנאַפֿאַרט
אויף אַן אומעטיק פֿערד
ביי וואָטערלו פֿאַר נאַכט.
ס׳טראַגט יעדער וועזן אין זיך זיין געפֿאַנגענשאַפֿט,
די בראַנד און שאַנד פֿון אַ פֿאַרלוירענער שלאַכט.

ביי די טישלעך אויפֿן טראָטואַר, אין שפּאַציר-
שטראָם אויפֿן בולוואַר, האָט זיין אויג
מיט צער אויסגעטיילט פֿינימער ווי צעשמעטערטע
צען געבאַט, לויט אַ פֿינטל און גרימאַס
דערקענט ווער ס׳איז אונטערן סיני
געווען.

ער האָט געווּוסט און געזאָגט: צו רו דער וועג
איז אָפֿט צוריק, דורך עגל און מן, ים סוף
און פֿלייש-טעפּ, צייכנס אויף טירן און טויט
פֿון בכורים, צו פֿינגער וואָס וווּטיקט
אויף קוילן און קילט זיך
אויף צונג, צו אַלערשטן שטאַמל.

ער האָט אין יעדן גוף דערשנאַפֿט יעקבס
צעקריגטע שטיבער, געלאָקערט אויפֿן
קראַנקנס חלום און געזוכט אין אים דעם
גרוב ווי יוסף ליגט געבונדן, בנימינס
זאַק מיטן פֿרעמדן בעכער, אין יעדער וויג דערשפֿירט
דעם דעספּאָט וואָס וויל צווישן סנאָפּעס
זיין אַן אויסגעטיילטער סנאָפּ.

גוט געדענקט
די פֿאַרדאַכטן און קללות
פֿון יעדן פּאַציענט.
(וואָס גרינטלעכער דאָס היילן
איז שאַרפֿער דער האַס).
אָבער די גורל-שריפֿט אויף דער וואַנט
האָט אָט דעם ייִד
(ווילהעלם שטעקעל,
מ.ד.
פֿלעגט שפּאַצירן אויפֿן פּראַטער, לייענען ״די נייע פֿרייע פּרעסע״,
טרינקען קאַווע מיט דריי שטיקלעך צוקער)

In every yawning barkeep behind the counter,
In every meek face at a teller's window,
He saw a tired Bonaparte at twilight
On a sad horse
At Waterloo.
Every being carries his own prison in himself.
The brand and the shame of a lost battle.

At the tables on the sidewalk, in the strolling
Stream on the boulevard, his eye
Recognized faces like smashed
Ten Commandments, from a wink or a gesture
He knew who had been
At Mount Sinai.

Who was under Mount Sinai—i.e., a Jew. According to Jewish lore, *all* Jews—past, present, and future—were present at Mt. Sinai when Moses received the Torah.

the road . . . backward—events in the life of Moses, in reverse order.

He knew and said: the road to rest
Is often backward, through the calf and the manna, Red Sea
And fleshpots, signs on doors and death
Of first-born sons, to finger that aches
On hot coals and cools
On a tongue, to the primeval stammer.

In every body he sniffed Jacob's
Quarreling houses, he lurked
At the sick man's dream and sought in it
The pit where Joseph lay bound, Benjamin's
Sack with the foreign goblet, in every cradle he sensed
The despot who among the sheaves
Will be the chosen one.

who among the sheaves—allusion to Joseph's dream.

He remembered well
The suspicions and the curses
Of each patient.
(The deeper the healing
The sharper the hatred.)
But the writing on the wall
For this Jew
(Wilhelm Stekel,
M.D.,
Used to stroll on the Prater, read "Die Neue Freie Presse,"
Drink coffee with three cubes of sugar)

Die Neue Freie Presse—a Viennese newspaper, for which Theodore Herzl worked as a journalist.

אָנגעצייכנט ער זאָל זײַן

אַ היילער, אַן אָפּשפּרעכער פֿון

אַנגסט, אַן אָפּטרײַבער

פֿון מורא.

האָט דער קלאָר-פֿאַרשטײער

פֿאַרבלאָנדזשעט אין גאַנג

צווישן טיר און בעט,

זוכנדיק דעם לאָמף-שנור

צו באַלײַכטן זײַן אייגענע שרעק?

נײן. דער אַלטער אָפּשפּרעכער איז פּשוט

געוואָרן מיד, געזען —

דער פֿיבער שטײַגט.

דער טערמאָמעטער פֿלאַצט.

בונט אין דער געפֿערלעכסטער פֿאַלאַטע.

דער וואָנזין שפּרינגט

פֿון יאַק.

יודנצייכן, געטאָ-דראָט, און הענקעלס

איבער לאָנדאָן-בריק.

(ער האָט געשטעלט דעם דיאַגנאָז

נאָך לאַנג צוריק.)

צערייצטער המון אין אַ פֿאַקל-פּאַראַד.

דער פֿאַרשוין

בײַם מיקראָפֿאָן

קווינטשעט:

כ׳האָב מאַכט!

(קליניש-באַקאַנט. שרעק פֿון מאַקבעט

פֿאַר באַוועגלעכע שאָטנס אויף אַ פֿינצ-

טערער וואַנט).

ווילהעלם שטעקעל

איבער זיבעציק

און מיד

(די יאָרן סקריפּען

ווי אַן אַלטער דיל)

טראָאקט:

צײַט צו מאַכן נאַכט.

איין ייד

אויפֿן קרייץ

איז גענוג.

Destined him to be
A healer, an exorcist of
Angst, a purger
Of fear.
Did this lucid understander
Lose his way
Between door and bed,
Groping for the lamp cord
To light up his own fear?

No. The old exorcist was simply
Weary. He saw
The fever rising.
The thermometer bursting.
Mutiny in the most dangerous ward.
Madness leaps
Out of the jacket.

Jew-sign, ghetto-wire and *Henkels*
Over London Bridge.
(He diagnosed it all
Long ago.)

Frenzied crowds in a torch-parade.
The creature
At the microphone
Squeaks:
I have power!
(Clinically known. Macbeth's fear
Of shadows moving on a
Dark wall.)

Wilhelm Stekel
Over seventy
And weary
(The years squeak
Like an old floor)
Thinks:
Time for night.
One Jew
On a cross
Is enough.

אַדלער.
שטעקעל.
פֿרויד.

אַפֿילו די שוועל
האָט ניט געמערקט אײַער אָפּפֿלי
אין דער פֿיַיערדיקער קאַטש
פֿון אַן אורח.
אין אײַערע קאַבינעטן איז געווען
אַ געווייַנטלעכער חצות.
אויפֿן טיש האָט ווי שטענדיק
געפֿינטלט אַ קנויט.
די טעקע אויפֿגעמישט צו אַ נייַ בלאַט.
די פֿעדער,
ווי אַלע מאָל,
פֿייַכט.

אָבער אין דרויסן איז די שרעק גערונען ווי בלוט.
דונערן האָבן געשריִען ווי פֿרעמדע פֿייגל
אויף יענער זייַט באַרג. בליצן האָבן
געפֿלאַקערט ווי ראָש-חודש-פֿייַערן
אויף אַ קאַלטער
פֿעלדזיקער הייך.
אַ, זעער —
ווו זענט איר אָפּגעלאָפֿן מיט די שלאַקסן
אין דער ליַארעמדיקער נאַכט?

ווי אָפּגעזוכטע קעץ האָבן מיר זיך צוריקגעשאַרט
צו די פֿריזבעס פֿון די אַלטע שרעקן,
דערהערט ערגעץ אין אונדז —
ווי אויף אַ שמאָלער פֿאַרנאַכטיקער גאַס —
דאָס ראָשיקע שליסן
פֿון לאָדנס, ריגלען און שטאַבעס,
דערשפֿירט אַז עס בלאָזט אַ לאַנגע דאָרפֿישע ווינאַכט
מיט געפֿאַקטע צערקוועס און צאָרנדיקע שענקען,
און פֿון מורא געמינטערט
דעם אָפֿשפֿרעך-זשאַרגאָן
פֿון אונדזערע באָבעס.

ווו איז דער שנעלוועג
צו חלום, צו וואָר?
דער טייַך איז אריבער די ברעגעס.

Adler.
Stekel.
Freud.

Even the doorstep
Did not notice your flight
In the fiery coach
Of a single letter.
It was a true Midnight   **Midnight***
In your study.
On the desk, as ever,
A wick flickered.
The file open on a new page.
The pen,
As always,
Wet.

But outside, fear ran like blood.
Thunders screamed like strange birds
Beyond the mountain. Lightning
Flared up, like fires announcing a New Moon   **fires announcing**—there was a
On a cold   custom in ancient Israel of
Rocky height.   announcing a new month by
Oh, seers—   climbing a high peak and lighting
Where did the downpour sweep you away   a fire, which was relayed
In the tumultuous night?   thoughout the country.

Like prodigal cats, we crawled back
To the ledges of the old fears;
As on a narrow street at dusk,
We detected somewhere inside us
The hurried closing
Of shutters, bolts, bars;
We felt the blowing of a long village Christmas night
With packed churches and wrathful taverns,
And, out of fear, we revived
The exorcising jargon   **jargon**—a pejorative epithet for
Of our grandmothers.   Yiddish.

Where is the highway
To dream, to reality?
The river overflowed its banks.

די בריק איז אַוועק מיטן טײַך.
די סימבאָלן צעמישט
ווי פֿאַרערגנטע שריפֿט.

דער הימל סליונעט פֿאַראַשטן
איבער זון-פֿאַרשווענקטע אויסגעקערטע גאַסן.
טאַנקען קראָמטשען (ווי ברויט)
טורעמער און מויערן.
שטוקאַס טראָגן זיך אויף יאַגד איבער דעכער.
באָמבעס, ווי שטובהינט, לויפֿן נאָך
אַ בלאָנד קינד איבער בײַטן אין אַ גאָרטן
צווישן ווײַס-געשירצטע באָנעס, וואַסער-
שטיינער, עפֿלביימער.

גערינג.
היטלער.
פּעטען.
זענען דאָס ווערטער פֿון אײַער שרעק-לעקסיקאָן?
וואָס באָדײַט אַ דינע וואָנצע איבער אַ שמאָל מויל?
וואָס באָדײַט דער קרומקרײַץ אויפֿן אײַפֿל-טורעם?
וואָס?

אין וואַלד, דער באָגין ווי אַ דעקרעט:
געשטאַפּאָ.
אָנמעלדונג
דען
יו-
דען,
עט-
צעט...
געהויקערטע ייִדישע זקנים פּעשפּעטען זיך
איבער די אייגענע בערד, זוכן מיט בלינדע
פֿאַרצאַפּלטע הענט מזוזות אויף די ביימער
אין אַ קינעמסלאַנד.

וואָר צי סימבאָל?

איר זענט אַרויס און געלאָזט צעפּראַלט די טירן.
דער ווינט האָט צעבלאָזן פֿון אײַערע טישן
די באַשריבענע פּאַפּירן.
זענט איר אַוועק, ווײַל אויך אײַערע קני האָבן געציטערט
פֿון וווילו-באַקאַנטער יודנשרעק, ווען איר האָט דערזען
דעם פּלאַם פֿון ברעננדיקע שטעט
אויף אײַער שכנס בוינט?

The bridge swept away by the river.
The symbols blurred
Like writings in a rain.

The sky is salivating parachutes
Over sun-bathed, swept streets.
Tanks munch
Towers and walls like bread.
Stukas race, hunting over roofs.
Bombs, like pet-dogs, pursue
A blond child on garden-beds
Between white-aproned nannies, water-
Pebbles and apple-trees.

Goering.
Hitler.
Petain.
Are those words from your scare-lexicon?
What does a thin mustache over a narrow mouth mean?
What does the crooked cross on the Eiffel Tower mean?
What?

In a forest, dawn like a decree:
Gestapo.
Announcement:
Den
Ju-
Den,
Et-
Cet . . .
Hunched old Jews whispering
Over their own beards, seek with blind
Trembling hands a mezuzah on the trees
In No-Man's-Land.

Reality or symbol?

You departed and left the doors ajar.
The wind blew the scribbled papers
Off your desks.
Did you leave because your knees, too, trembled
With the well-known Jew-fear, when you saw
The flame of burning cities
On your neighbor's bayonet?

Me'zuzah*

No-Man's-Land—the border
between Germany and Poland,
where German Jews of Polish
origin were deported by the
Nazis in 1938 and not accepted by
the Poles.

און ווער האָט אײַך געגעבן אויסרײַז-שײַנען?
פֿאָדערט מען אויך דאָרט דעם "יאָד"?

אַדלער.

שטעקעל.

פֿרויד.

דרײַמאָל "יאָד"

אונד דרײַמאָל יודע.

אַ, מײַסטער פֿון הײלן און רכילות.

איזט עס וואַהר,

זאָגט,

אַז דער הער ריבענטראָפּ

אונד דער הער גאָט

האָבן אַ פֿאַקט

אונד אַז די מאַגדאַלען

(לופּעסקו

פֿון נצרת)

מוס גיין?

(די בלעטלעך פֿון נײַעם טעסטאַמענט
כליפּען בײַם ים משומד אין די הענט.)

פּ.ס. ווי גייטס דאָרט מיט דײַטשן לעבנסראום?

◄ פּליטים-ליד

א

ווינער שפּעט-נאָוועמבערדיקער אָוונט
מיט לאַמטערן-שײַן דורך שניי,
מיט ווײַסן נעפּל פֿון דונײַ,
מיט ראָסע-כתב אויף שויבן פֿון פֿאַרנער קאַפֿיי.

פּלוצעמדיקער ווינט אין צעפֿראַלטער טיר.
שטיוול און געבײַזער.
מ׳פֿרעגט אויף מיר.

ווי אַרויסגעשפּאַנט
פֿון רויכנדיקע פֿאַרבן און בראָנדזענער ראַם —
שלײַדערער פֿון פֿלאַם
אונטערן שרײַענדיקן אָדלער פֿון רוים,
וואַרפֿער פֿון שפּיז,
צ׳יער פֿון שווערד
אין נאָמען פֿון קרײץ
און הייליקן גײַסט.
זיג! הייל!

And who gave you exit-visas?
Do they require a "J" there too?

Adler.
Stekel.
Freud.
Thrice "J"
And thrice Jew.
Oh, masters of healing and gossip.
Is it true
That Herr Ribbentrop
And Herr Gott
Concluded a pact
And that Magdalen
(Lupescu
of Nazareth)
Must go?

a "J"—all official documents of Jews were stamped with a "J" in Nazi Germany.

(The pages of the New Testament
Weep in the hands of the convert.)

Lupescu—Magda Lupescu, the Jewish mistress of King Carol II of Rumania, exerted a strong influence on Rumanian public affairs in the 1930s and was vilified by the Rumanian fascists.

P.S. How much *Lebensraum* do they have there?

► *Deportation*

Original title: "Refugee Poem."

I

Late November evening in Vienna:
Lantern light through snow,
White mist over the Danube,
Steam script on windowpanes on Parner Kaffee.

Sudden wind in the opened door.
Boots and angry words.
Asking for me.

As if stepping out
Of smoking colors and a bronze frame—
Flame throwers
Under the screaming eagle of Rome,
Spear hurlers,
Drawers of swords
In the name of the cross
And the Holy Ghost.
Sieg! Heil!

שלאָגט אויס אויף פילדערדיקן מעש דעם גירוש-מאַרש.
איך קום. ער
קומט.
פאַרשווענקט דעם שטראָז מיט שרײַענדיקן, טראָמפלענדיקן פֿעבל.
רײַט אָן מיט זאָטלען און מיט שפֿאָרן.
צינדט די סמאָלע-פֿעסער.
האַלט די פֿאַקלען הויך.
און הייבט די קינדער איבער קעפ
זיי זאָלן זען
דאָס נס.
גיט יעדער בראַוווער האַנט —
אַ שטיין.

פֿאַלט צוריק און שפֿאַלט אַ וועג.
פֿירט זיי דורך
די בלאָנדע
שילטנדיקע
הורן
צום צערעמאָניאַל פֿון שפֿײַען מיר אין פֿנים.

זיי ניוכען און שמעקן און וואָיען ווי די הינט.
ער קומט.
ער
קומט.

אויף בלייכע טרעפֿ
אין בלויען דרויסן,
די לופֿט איז שאַרף,
דער מאַנטל — דין.

איך. ער.
אַהאַספֿער.
לעסטערער און
פֿרעמדער.

נאָטס איך דעם דלות פֿון צווייטן באַצירק,
נאָטס איך דעם שליסל צום מלך אַביונס טיר,
אַבי לאָזט דעכקען.
דער מינדסטער נאָגל,
די געפֿאַלנסטע האָר
פֿרעפֿלען, שעפֿטשען
דעכקען.
און דאָס ביישטידל אַ פֿאָרש טאָן מיט דער האַנט
ווי דער זיידע כסדר בײַם אַריבערגיין די שוועל.

Beat on noisy brass the expulsion march.
I am coming. He
Is coming.
(Flood the highway with a shouting trampling mob.)
(Ride in with saddle and spurs.)
Ignite barrels of tar.
Hold high the torches.
And lift the children over your heads
So they can see
The wonder.
Give every brave hand
A stone.

Fall back and make way.
Lead them through—
The blond
Cursing
Whores—
To the ceremony of spitting in my face.

They sniff and smell and howl like dogs.
He is coming.
He
Is coming.

On pale stairs
In the blue street,
The air is sharp,
(The coat—thin.)

I. He.
Ahaseurus.
Blasphemer and
Stranger.

Go on, take the poverty of the Second district,
Take the key to the door of the Beggar King,
Only let us breathe.
The tiniest fingernail,
Any fallen hair—
Whisper, lisp,
Breathe.
Searching the doorpost with our hand
Like grandfather crossing a threshold.

Ahaseurus*

Second District—the second district of Vienna, on the other side of the Danube, was the center of the Jewish population, especially those of Polish-Galician origin.

Beggar King—in Jewish liturgy, an epithet for a human king as opposed to God, the King on High. In folklore, a reference to a rich man or a dignitary who has lost his possessions; may also refer to the Jews of the Diaspora.

Searching the doorpost—religious Jews, entering a house, are obliged to touch the Mezuzah* attached to the doorpost.

ס׳וואַגלען מיט די אַמסטערדאַמער דרוקער

מיט שירצן אויף די לענדן,

ערשט פון װערקשטאַט אַפּגעטראָטן,

מענדלעסאָן — פון לעסינגס שאַך אַװעקגעריסן.

װי צו תּשליך גייען זיי צום װאָקזאַל.

װי צו תּשליך פליִען שטיינער

איבער זיי.

אַדיע,

אונד גריסע גאָט.

עס גייט אויך אַ פּאָעט

מיט דײַטשן "סיף" אין די יידישע ביינער.

אייביק װידערקול אין סאָסנעדיקע אַלפּן.

מיט װײַנאַכטס גײַסט שמעקט װײן.

טומל אויפן באַנהויף, געדראַנג אין צוג.

די יודען

נאָך לובלין.

ב

לאַנדשאַפט אין װײַסן זאַװערוכעדיקן טשאַד.

די װאַגאָנען זענען אָפּן.

מ׳שנײַדט טרוקן ברויט,

מ׳שײלט האַרטע אייער.

(קינדער פאַרגייען זיך אויפן קול.)

קאָרדאָװער, טאָלעדעער,

גיט נאָר אַ דערצייל,

שאָקלט אויס די מעשיות

װי שטערן פון די בערד.

די יאַזדעס פון מײַן שטאַם.

געגאַן צופוס.

געריטן אויף פערד.

אויף פאַרשװענקטע דעקן

געלעגן געשמידט.

אין יעדן האַפּן געקלונגען מיטן חלפן-בײַטל.

געגליט אין שטעט װאָס שרײַען מיט בײַנאַכטיקן פלאַם

װי קאָמעטן.

שיקסעס דװיגען קאָנען פון דער פלומפּ,

אין שניי װאָליען זיך הינט.

אַ סטאַנציע. אַ ייִשוב.

איר האָט דאָ אַ טײַך, װאָס כדאַי ער זאָל שמעכן.

דער הײַנע, ער רעכנט אַ שיבוש.

אַ האַלב טוץ אייער פאַר אַ ליד.

And straying with us: the Amsterdam printers,
Aprons on their waists,
Just stepped out of their workshops,
Mendelsohn torn away from Lessing's chess.
As to *Tashlikh*, they walk to the station.
As to *Tashlikh*, stones are flying
Over their heads.
Adieu.
Und grüsse Gott.
A poet walking too
With German "syph" in Jewish bones.

Eternal echo in pine-covered Alps.
Vienna smells of the Christmas spirit.
Crowded train. Station. Din.
Die Juden
Nach Lublin.

II

Landscape in white blizzard fume.
The wagons are open.
Cutting dry bread,
Peeling boiled eggs.
(Children in a spell of crying.)
You, from Cordoba, from Toledo,
Come tell your tale,
Shake out the stories
Like stars from your beards.
The voyages of my race.
On foot.
On horseback.
Lying chained
On wave-swept decks.
Clinking the changer's purse in every port.
Glowing in cities that scream flames into the night
Like comets.
Peasant girls drag buckets from the pump.
Dogs wallow in snow.
A station. A settlement.
You have here a river that deserves to be famous.
This Heine, he sells cheap.
Half a dozen eggs for a poem.

Amsterdam printers—Amsterdam was the center of Jewish printing for all of Europe, esp. in the 16th–18th centuries.

Mendelsohn—Moses Mendelsohn (1729–1786), the Jewish-German philosopher, friend of Gotthold Ephraim Lessing, major German playwright and critic.

Tashlikh—the Jewish custom of going to cast away sins in a river on the first day of Rosh Ha-Shana. Since rivers were often in the Gentile part of town, such a walk might lead to trouble.

A poet . . . Jewish bones—possibly a reference to Heine.

Lublin—Lublin Reserve in central Poland was planned by the Nazis to be a concentration area for Jews brought from various countries (before the Final Solution was adopted).

Cordoba, Toledo—centers of Jewish life in medieval Spain.

אין ווינטערדיקער וויסטעניש צלמים אויף קאָשטשאַלן,
בייזע גויים אויף וואָקזאַלן,
ס׳איז אַלץ אַזוי וווייטיקדיק אייגן.

נאָר מיין הויך איז נאָך דאָ אויף דער שויב
פון אַ ווינער קאַפֿע, מיין ליפ איז נאָך דאָ
אויף אַ ווינער גלאָז טיי.
שיקט מיך אָפ מיט טויזנט באַנען
אין געגראַטעוועטע וואַגאָנען.
דורך דער טראַקט פון אייערס אַ טעאַטער,
דורך דער זילב פון אייערס אַ ליד,
וועל איך אויפֿגיין פון דאָס ניי
אין אייער מיט.
אַהאַספֿער, דער אייביקער
ייד.

◄ צו אַ קריסטין

די לופֿט איז קלאָר. דאָס מעבל שטיל.
מיין האַנט, ווי אַ פֿאַרבענקטער פֿויגל
איבער דיינע בריסט.

איך רעד צו דיר פֿאַרטרויטע רייד.
איך בין אַ ייד.
(די שטוב איז אומרויק
און מיט פֿעלנשאַרף.)

מיינע פֿיאַטעס בלוטיקן פֿון ס׳ניי
אויף גלאָז-שפֿליטער פֿון דורות.
(קרייציקן איז גראַד
ניט אונדזער געביט.
צי קאָנען דען סוחרים
אַ טשוואָק אַריינשלאָגן?)

די ראשונים:
בעכער-אונטערווואַרפֿער,
צעפֿליקער פֿון זיידענעם העמדל,
רויבער פֿון תרפים.

מיין גוף —
גנבה.

In winter wasteland, crosses on churches,
Spiteful Gentiles at railway stations,
It is all so painfully familiar.

But my breath is still on a windowpane
Of a Viennese Kaffee, my lip is still
On a Viennese glass of tea.
Send me away on a thousand trains
In barred wagons.
Through the womb of your daughter,
Through the syllable of your song,
I will rise again
In your midst.
Ahaseurus, the eternal
Jew.

➤ *To a Christian Woman*

The air is clear. The furniture still.
My hand, like a longing bird
Over your breasts.

I speak to you confiding words.
I am a Jew.
(The room is uneasy,
With fur-rustle.)

My soles bleed again
On glass splinters of generations.
(Crucifying is not precisely
Our domain.
Would traders know how
To hit a nail?)

The ancestors:
Goblet-smugglers,
Rippers of a silk coat,
Robbers of omens.

My body—
Theft.

Chaim Gross: *Naomi*, 1947

קינבאַקן פון אַ מאָנגאָל.
עשׂוס קול.
נאָר די הענט, אוי ווי די הענט זענען יעקבס
אַ פּראָשעניע אויסצושטעלן.

שטאַם־געדענקעגישן, ווי עשׂר מכּות,
פּייניקן די חושים.
איבער מיין ווינטער שרייען נאָך אַלץ
גאַליצישע סאָוועס,
מאָנען דער באָבעס
שבת־בראשיתדיקע שיסל מיט רייז.
פּורים־צייט, אַז ס'לויפן־אָף די שנײען,
טופען אין מיין בענקשאַפט טומלענדיקע ייִדן
מיט שופליעס, בעזעמער און פּיקעס
פּאַר די טאַרנאָפּאָלער שוועלן.
דער סערעט רעווועט
ווי צום שלאַכטהויז,
פון געזיגמסן לויכטן
סטראָמפעס
ווי קרישטאָלן.

וויפל צייט אַוועקגעהאַקט ווי אייז, אַוועקגעקערט
ווי ברודיק וויַיס?

און דאָס בינדט זיך
(פאַר וואָס)?
מיט קינדער — פילדערדיקע
געצנדינער
אין ניו־יאָרקיש־פאַרנאַכטיקן פּאַרק.
דער באָלעם פליט ווי אַ סימבאָל
אין טונקעלער לופט.
שקיעהדיקע שויבן אין פאַרהויכטע שטאָקן
דערמאָנען קנויט־טשאַד און פאַרקטיקע קאָפּאָטעס,
יאָמערלעכע יעלהס אין אַ דושנער קלויז.

נאָגנדיקע יעלהס פון גערשווינס סאַקסאָפאָן.

דורך די "סיינט־לואיס־בלוז"
זוכט יעקב רחלס לענדן,
אברם גייט ווי אין געשפּאָן נאָך הגרס שווערן גאָנג,
און אַ יונגע מוטער ברענט ווי דער סנה
אין אַ ווייסטער, גלוסטיקער נאַכט,
צווישן איר און איר מאַן —
אַ ים און אַ שלאַכט.

Chins of a Mongol.
The voice of Esau.
But the hands, oh, the hands are Jacob's
To fill out a petition.

Tribal memories, like the Ten Plagues,
Torment my senses.
Galician owls
Still clamor in my winter,
Still demand my grandma's
Genesis-Sabbath bowl of rice.
At Purim time, when the snows melt,
Tumultuous Jews stamp in my longing
With shovels, brooms and picks
Before the thresholds of Tarnopol.
The river Seret roars
As if led to a slaughter-house,
From cornices gleam
Long icicles
Like crystals.

How much time cut-away like ice, swept-away
Like dirty white?

And this ties in
(Why?)
With children—rattling-away
Pagans
In a New York evening park.
The ball flies like a symbol
In dark air.
Sunset panes on misty upper stories
Recall wick-soot and pious black coats.
Wailing laments in a stuffy *shul*.

Heart-rending laments of Gershwin's saxophone.

Through the "St. Louis Blues"
Jacob seeks Rachel's loins,
Abram walks harnessed to Hagar's heavy step,
And a young mother burns like the Burning Bush
In a desolate, lustful night,
Between her and her husband—
A sea and a battle.

the voice of Esau—a reversal of the biblical phrase, "The voice is Jacob's but the hands are Esau's" (Genesis 27:22), which became a proverbial expression indicating Jewish verbal prowess and physical weakness vis-à-vis the Gentiles.

Genesis-Sabbath—the first Sabbath after Sukkot, when the yearly cycle of Torah-reading resumes.

Tarnopol—Teller's Galician hometown on the river Seret. (See the cycle, "Invasion," below.)

אָט דאָס זענען זיי:

די אָבות,

די עמיגראַנטישע אמהות,

שרייען פון מגילות און הגדות,

קלאָגן ייִדיש אויף איעדן לשון.

גויִיש פרויענצימער,

היט זיך פאַר די מאָנסביל

פון אָט יענעם שטאַם

וואָס ווי נאָר אַ הונגער

ציט ער אָפ פון כּנען.

◄ מעדיטאַציע ביי דער סטייוועסענט קירך

דער קלויסטער איז צעבליט מיט גרינס

און איינגעוואָרעמט אין דער לאַנדשאַפט

פון אַ וועלטשטאָט.

קינאָ-שילדן גייען-אויף ווי זעונג.

אַלץ וואָס שטומט און לעבט

איז אַן אָפּבילד פון מיינע

אויפגעוואַכטע חושים.

מיין יעדער גליד איז דורכגעשטראָמט מיט פייער.

דאָס פנים גליט מיט ליבע און מיט מאָרד.

ווער זוכט עס איצט אַ קיום דורך מיין גוף?

איך זוך אַ קרובישאַפט צווישן דער לעגענדע

פון שלאָנגקאַנג, פוטער און פאַרפום,

וואָס מעקלערט ווי די שטאָט,

און מיין פרומער מאַמען

וואָס האָט אָן אַ מאָנסביל אָפּגעוועלקט

די נעכט פון אירע בעסטע צוועלף יאָר.

ווי ספירות טליקען אויף געשטאָלטן.

דאָס ליכטיק-מילדע פנים פון מיין ברודער.

מיין טאַטע, אַ טרוימער און אַ שוועקלינג,

מיט צאָרנדיקן פויסט,

מיט שינאה וועלטן איינצוּוואַרפן,

וואָס פאַר אַ שמייכלדיק וואָרט

צופט ער גראָז פון יענעמס האַנט.

This is how they are:
The fathers,
The immigrant mothers,
Crying out from Megillas and Haggadas,
Lamenting Yiddish in every tongue.

Gentile woman,
Beware the males
Of that tribe
Who, as soon as famine comes,
Flee from Canaan.

555
J. L. Teller

Megillah*—here, an allusion to the five little books of the Bible read publicly on holidays and days of mourning: Song of Songs—on Passover; Ruth—on Shavuot; Lamentations—on Tish'a Be-Av; Ecclesiastes—on Sukkot; Esther—on Purim.

Ha'gadah*

➤ *Meditation at Stuyvesant Church*

The church is blossoming in green,
Nestling in the warm landscape
Of a world-metropolis.
Movie billboards rise like visions.

Mute and living images:
Reflections of my
Awakened senses.
Fire streams in my every limb.
My face glows with love and murder.
Who seeks now to come into being
Through my body?

I look for a link between the legend
Of slenderwalk, fur and perfume,
Selling like the city,
And my pious mother
Who withered without a man
In the nights of her twelve best years.

Figures emerge like the spheres.

The shining gentle face of my brother.
My father, a dreamer and weakling,
With raging fist,
With hatred enough to knock down worlds,
For a smiling word,
He would nibble grass from your hand.

אַלע רעדן איצט דורך מײַנע תנועות
און מײַן גאַנג
און עס רעדט באַצײַטנס שױן דאָס גראָז
װאָס װעט נאָך אַזױ פיל און אַזױ פיל זון-קרײַזן
אױפשפּראָצן פון מײַנעם אַ פאַרװעלקטן פוס.

װער בין איך װאָס פײניקט זיך מיט װערטער
אין שאָטן פון אַ קלױסטער
אין פאַרהילכטער צעפלאַקערטער שטאָט?
מײַנע דורות האָבן געשאָלטן דעם צלם,
געשפּיגן אין גלחס הײליק װאַסער,
בײַ יעדן װעטערטױש דערפילט
די נאָגל-װוּנדן אױף די הענט און פיאַטעס.

אַ שיכּור פון דער באַװערי
שפּאַנט זיכער װי אַ נס
איבער דער גאַס.
בלוטיקט. אפשר איז ער יעזוס
אױפן קרײַץ. און אפשר גאָר
אַ ייִד פון בריסק, פון טשענסטאָכאָװ.

איך טראָג דעם חורבן-גלוסט פון קײלער,
די מורא פון ייִד.
דאָס האָט אַ בתולה פון מײַן שטאַם
פאַרזיגלט אין אַנגסט
דאָס געזיכט פון איר פאַרגװאַלטיקער.

די אױערן זענען דול
פון בין-גערױיש פון גאַסן.
אױף קאָרטן און מזלות
איז שױן אַלץ פאַרצײַכנט.

They all speak through my gestures
And my walk,
And so speaks the grass
That, after so many circles of the sun,
Will sprout from my withered leg.

Who am I, torturing myself with words
In the shadow of a church
In a clamorous, blazing city?
My generations cursed the cross,
Spat in the priest's holy water,
With every weather-change, they felt
Nail-wounds in their hands and feet.

A drunkard from the Bowery
Walks the street,
Confident as a miracle.
Bleeding. Maybe he is Jesus
On the cross. Or maybe
A Jew from Brisk, from Czestochowa.

I carry the slaughterer's lust for destruction,
The fear of a Jew.
It was a virgin of my race
Who sealed in terror
The face of her rapist.

My ears are ringing
With the buzzing of streets.
In cards and stars
It is all written.

Louis Lozowick: *Yellow Moon/
Overhead Wires*, 1967

פֿאַרנאַהמען...צונאַהמען...
געבוירן אין טאַרנאָפּאָל, בײַם סערעט.
אַריבער די רעלסן ליגט זבאַראַזש,
אָן דער זײַט — פּאָדװאָלאָטשיסק,
און אין װאָלאָטשיסק —
דער רוס,
דער מאָסקאַל.
אַז ר׳האָט אין 1914 זיך באַװיזן מיט פֿערד,
צעבראָכענע װעגענער,
באַרװעסע זעלנער
און רײַטער מיט פּיקעס
אױפֿן באַרג-אַראָפּ װאָס פֿירט אין שטאָט אַרײַן,
האָט די מאַמע צעשראָקן די לאָדנס פֿאַרמאַכט.
אױף אַ באַנקבעטל אין פֿינצטערער קיך
האָט זיך צונױפֿגעדריקט דאָס װײַבערש
הױזגעזינד מיט אַ צװײי-יאָריק קינד
און געװאָרט.
װײַטע שׂריפֿות
האָבן דורך שפּאַרעס
די סטעליע געפֿאַרבט.

מײַן ערשט געדענקען איז
דאָס קראַכן פֿון שױבן
בײַם שכן אױפֿן מאַרק.

װי לאַנג איז געװען בײַ אונדז דער מאָסקאַל?
אין קלאָרע אינדערפֿריִען
װאָס האָבן געלױכטן װי דער באָבעס לײַכטער,
װי ייִדישע פֿענצטער דעם ערשטן טאָג פּסח,
פֿלעגן זעלנער שפּיִען אין פּאָמאַדע-שאַכטלען
און שמירן די שיך.

ס׳פֿלעגן זיך בײַטן די מונדירן און די היטלען,
קומען מיט שאַסן אין פֿאָרשטאָט
און אָפּציִען מיט שׂריפֿות אױפֿן מאַרק.
מען פֿלעגט שלעפֿן טױטע פֿון סערעט,
געפֿינען הרוגים אונטער שניי
אין די בערג.

► *A. Passport*

Forename . . . Surname . . .
Born in Tarnopol, on the River Seret.
Over the tracks lies the city of Zbarazh.
To the side—Podvolotshisk,
And in Volotshisk itself—
The Russian,
The Moskal.
When he appeared in 1914 with horses,
Rickety carts,
Barefoot soldiers
And riders with lances
On the slope going down to the city,
My frightened mother locked the shutters.
On a bench-bed in the dark kitchen
The houseful of women
And a two-year old child
Huddled together
And waited.
Through the slits
Distant fires
Dyed the ceiling.

My first memory is
Windows crashing
At a neighbor's in the marketplace.

How long did the Moskal stay in our town?
On bright mornings
That shone like grandma's candlesticks,
Like Jewish windows on the first day of Passover,
Soldiers would spit into boxes of shoe-polish
And smear their boots.

The hats and uniforms would change,
Would come with shots in the suburb
And leave with fires in the marketplace.
People would drag corpses out of the Seret,
Would find bodies under the snow
In the mountains.

This autobiographical cycle evokes images from World War I. Galicia, including Teller's hometowns of Tarnopol and Zbarash, originally a part of Poland, had belonged to the Austro-Hungarian Empire since the eighteenth century. In World War I, the area was overrun by the Russian army. In 1920 it was taken by the Bolsheviks and recaptured by the new Polish independent regime. The towns were populated by Jews, Catholic Poles, and Russian-Orthodox Ukranians.

Podvolo'tshisk—the name indicates a suburb of Volotshisk.

Moskal—a derogatory Polish nickname for the Russians.

ביז היינט גאַלאָפירן אין מיין חלום
טשערקעסן אויף פאַרגע פערד,
פֿאַדקאָוועס זיגלען מיט ווידערקול דעם ברוק,
ס'רייסט אויף אַ בריק און שלעפּט מיט
דעם צוג.

◄   ב.   אַרייַנמאַרש

ווידער יאָגט דער רייַטער אויפֿן זבאַרזשער וועג.
צופוסנס — טאַראַנאָפּאָל.
צוויי בערג, און הינטער זיי — דער סערעט.
די צערקוווע ליגט אין טאָל.
און הינטער מויערן, אין אַ סאָד,
דער מאָנאַסטיר ווו יעזוויטן
ראַנגלען זיך מיט לייב און גאָט.

שפּעטזומער-בלעטער פֿאַלן אויפֿן רייַטערס פּלייצע.
די זון שלאָגט אים אין די אויגן,
פֿלאַטערט פֿון דער פּיקע — ווי אַ פֿאָן.
ער שיסט אַראָפּ אַן עפּל פֿון אַ בוים,
דאָס פֿערדל הירזשעט,
טריטלט אין אַ קרייַז.

ער, איינער — אויפֿן זבאַרזשער וועג.
אין עקשטעאָט ברענען סקלאַדן.
אויף דער בריק — דעם פֿייַנדס שינעלן
ווי אַ פֿאַרלייַגטער שטראָם.

איבער דעכער לויפֿט אַ יינגל.
שאָטנס לויפֿן-מיט מיט ביידן.

און איינער טיילט זיך אויס
און טראָגט זיך באַרג-אַראָפּ.
אַ מענטש פֿאַרפֿלאַקט זיך בייַ אַ פֿלוּיט
צו ווערן שאָטן,
ווערן ברעט.

פֿון צוויי זייַטן ציִען
קריסטלעכע פּראָצעסיעס.
פֿראַוואָסלאַוונע קופּער,
און קאַטויליש גאָלד.
פֿון אַ הילישקע — אַן עדה ייִדן
מיט צעשראָקן ברויט און זאַלץ.

To this day, Cherkesses on steaming horses
Gallop through my dream,
Horseshoes brand the cobblestones with echoes,
A bridge blows up, sucks in
The train.

Cher'kesses—Caucasian people,
famous as horseback fighters,
who served in the Russian army.

► *B. They March In*

Again a rider gallops on the Zbarazh road.
At his feet—Tarnopol.
Two mountains, and behind them—the Seret.
The *tserkov* lies in the valley.
And behind walls, in an arbor,
The monastery where Jesuits
Struggle with flesh and God.

Late summerleaves fall on the rider's shoulders.
The sun strikes his eyes,
Flutters off his lance—like a pennant.
He shoots an apple off a tree,
The horse neighs,
Trots in a circle.

Alone—on the Zbarazh road.
On the outskirts warehouses burn.
On the bridge—the enemy's winter-coats
Like a dammed-up stream.

Over roofs a boy is running.
Shadows are running with both of them.

One breaks away,
Dashes downhill.
A man flattens against a fence
To become shadow,
Board.

From two sides
Christian processions advance.
Orthodox copper,
Catholic gold.
From a side lane—a crowd of Jews
With frightened bread and salt.

דעם שתּדלנס אויגן זוכן שוין
דעם קאָמענדאַנט.

און עס שטראָמען, טופען די חיילות
צום מאַרק, צו די קאַזאַרמעס,
צו דער ברענענדיקער מיל.

די לופט איז האַרב
מיט ליכט, מיט פאַרב
פון ווײַסע, פרישע צלמים
אויף גויישע טירן.
אין אויטאָס זיצן אָפיצירן.
עפּאָלעטן, גרויע שלייפן און לאָרנעטן.
אין די זאָטלען — יונגע לייטענאַנטן.
און נאָך יעדן שטאָלצן פערד —
דאָס פּראָסטע מיליטער.
פורן מיט פּראָוויאַנטן.
מונדירטע מוזיקאַנטן.
און די פאַרמאַכטע וועגענער
פון רויטן קרייץ.

◄ ג.   משפּט

אַ סעפּטעמבערדיקע מילדע זון לאַשטשעט
די קאַכלען אויף בית-מדרש דעכער,
דאָס גאָלד אויף די קאָשטשאָלן.

גויים שוווענקען איבער די טראָטואַרן,
ווי יריד-צײַט אויסגעצירט אין פאַרבן,
באַרג-אַראָפּ
מיט דער פאַנסקאַ
פאַרבײַ די אַלייען,
דורך בלעטער-קופעס און דורך ווינט,
דורך אַ זאַווערוכע פון קאָלירן,
צום ברייטן הויף פון יעזויטן קלויסטער.

דאָרט הילכט אַ מיליטערישער אָרקעסטער.

הינטער בײַמער טאַנצן דאַמען
מיט די לייטענאַנטן.
דער שופט זיצט אין שאַטן:
צעקנעפּלטער מונדיר,
גרויע באַקנבערד.

The petitioner's eyes seek
The commandant.

And the armies stream, stamp
To the marketplace, to the barracks,
To the burning mill.

The air is harsh
With light, with color
Of white, fresh crosses
On Gentile doors.
Officers sit in automobiles.
Epaulettes, gray temples, monocles.
In the saddles—young lieutenants.
And in the wake of each proud horse—
The simple infantry.
Carts with provisions.
Uniformed musicians.
And the closed wagons
Of the Red Cross.

► *C. Trial*

A mild September sun caresses
The shingles of synagogue roofs,
The gold of churches.

As during a fair, in colorful dress,
Gentiles wash the sidewalks
Downhill,
Along Panska Street,
Past the alleys,
Through leaf-heaps and wind,
Through a blizzard of colors,
To the wide yard of the Jesuit cloister.

A military band blares.

Behind trees, ladies dance
With lieutenants.
The judge sits in a shadow:
Unbuttoned tunic,
Gray sideburns.

זיי קומען פון אַ קעלער דורך אַ שווערער טיר,
פינטלען קעגן ליכט
און ניסן ווי די פערד.
מען שטעלט זיי מיט די פלייצעס צו אַ ווייסער מויער.
מען פאַרבינדט זיי די אויגן און מען בינדט זיי די הענט,
מ׳פאַרקעמט זיי די האָר און מ׳צעכראַסטעט זיי דאָס העמד.

עס גייען פרישע יונגען דורך דער שווערער טיר,
די זון איז וואַרעם און דער טויט איז גיך.

ד. ◄   לאַנדשאַפט מיט מיליטער

מ׳פירט אַ שייגעץ מיט דער גאַס,
עס בלענדן אַלע שויבן,
דעם צאַלמייסטערס
בלאַנדער קאָפ
צווישן בלאַנקע זעבלען.

They are coming from the cellar through a heavy door,
Blinking in the light,
Wheezing like horses.
They are stood with their backs to a white wall.
Their eyes are blindfolded, their hands tied.
Their hair is combed and their shirts undone.

Fresh boys walk through the heavy door,
The sun is warm and death is swift.

William Gropper: *The Invaders*,
1942.

➤ *D. Landscape with Military*

They take a fellow through the street,
All the windows are shimmering,
The paymaster's
Blond head
Between shining sabers.

פּיקעס און שינעלן
בײַ דער שראַנק
און אויף דער בריק.
אַ סטאַדע קערט צוריק
אין הייסן שטויב.
הײַזער ציטערן
פון נאָנטע האַרמאַטן.

פון ערגעץ-וווּ אַ כאָפּטע
פרײַלעכע סאָלדאַטן
מיט געוואַנטן, ברויטן,
שאָקאָלאַדן.

אַלע טירן זענען אָפן. אין
אַלע דירות שטייען-אײַן זעלנער,
פוצן ביקסן אויף די פריזבעס,
שפּילן קאָרטן אויף די שוועלן.

פרויען שלאָפן אין די קליידער,
מאַמעס וואַכן איבער טעכטער,
די נאַכט איז טמא מיט קאַזאַרמעשן געלעכטער.

◄ ה.   הינטערן פראָנט

צעטומלטע טעג און גיכע מנינים.
אינדערפרייענדיקער האַנדל
אין האַלב-אָפענע קראָמען.
קינדער קלײַבן קאַשטאַנען
און פּאַטראָנעס.
הינער רײַסן זיך פון זעלנערשע
לאַפּעס,
און ציוויל-לײַט גראָבן שאַנצן
פאַר די כאַטעס.

דער רוס שרויפט אָפּ
די קליאַמקעס פון די טירן,
קאָנפיסקירט די צלמים
און די כתרים.
טײַסטערס זענען פול
מיט ווערטלאָזע פּאַפּירן.
מ׳נעמט מענטשן פון געלעגער
און מ׳ברענגט זיי ניט צוריק.

Lances and overcoats
At the cabinet
And on the floor.
A herd returns
In hot dust.
Houses shudder
From approaching cannons.

From somewhere—a bunch
Of jolly soldiers
With cloth, bread,
Chocolate.

All doors are open. In all
Flats soldiers are quartered,
Polishing rifles on the ledges,
Playing cards on the doorsteps.

Women sleep in their clothes,
Mothers watch over their daughters,
The night is defiled by barracks' laughter.

➤ *E. Behind the Front*

Confused days and hasty *minyans*.
Early-morning trade
In half-open stores.
Children gather chestnuts
And empty cartridges.
Chickens flap in soldiers'
Paws,
And civilians dig trenches
Around their huts.

The Russians unscrew
Brass door handles,
Confiscate crosses
And Torah-crowns.
Wallets burst
With worthless bills.
People are taken from their beds
And are never returned.

וועגט האָבן אויערן
און יעדער שאָטן איז אַ שפּיק.

מ׳טרעט אָפּ דעם מיליטער
די שטובן מיט די בעטן.
אין גרויסאַרטיקע סאַלאָנען
אויף פּליושענע דיוואַנען
לאַכן דינסטן אויף סאָלדאַטסקע שויסן
און צירן זיך
אין אָנגעריובטע גאַרדעראָבן.

◀ ו. אידיליע

דער טאָג איז גרוי ווי די פֿאַרב
פֿון טאַנקען. לאָדנס ווי גאַזמאַסקן
אויף שטיבער. דער שאָסיי —
צעבראָכענע וועגענער און טיפע
גריבער. דרײַ ייִדן מיט טלית-זעק שאַרן
זיך הינטער די געשטעלן אויפֿן
מאַרק. אַ סאָלדאַט זיצט מיט די פֿיס
הינטער זיך און עסט ברויט מיט
מאַרמאַלאַד.

◀ ז. לאַנדשאַפֿט מיט מלחמה

אונדזער בלוט רינט אומעטיק דורך פֿרעמדע קאַנטן
אונטער אַ הייסער זון
וואָס שמעקט הינטיש
פֿאַרגאַסענע פֿעלדזן.
שוואַרצאַפּלען בריט
דער בלענד פֿון טײַכן, שויבן
און אַנדערע גלאַנציקע פּלאַקן.
בלעטער פֿאַלן ווי קופּער.
ביימער שרײַען
מיט פֿייגלשע גאָרגלען.

אויף בערגלעך
פֿון אונטער צוזעריגן-קאַמופּלאַזש
רײַסט זיך דאָס הייסע האָווקען
פֿון מאַשינגעווערן.

Walls have ears
And every shadow is a spy.

People yield to the soldiers
Their rooms and beds.
In splendid salons
On plush sofas
Maids laugh in soldiers' laps
And dress up
In plundered finery.

➤ *F. Idyll*

The day is gray as the color
Of tanks. Shutters like gasmasks
On houses. The highway—
Rickety carts and deep
Craters. Three Jews, tallis-sacks under their arms,
Trudge behind the stands in the
Market. A soldier sits, his legs
Folded under him, and eats bread with
Marmalade.

➤ *G. Landscape with War*

Our blood runs sadly through foreign zones
Under a hot sun
That sniffs like a dog
At the wet rocks.
Pupils are seared
By the dazzle of rivers, windows,
Shiny surfaces.
Leaves fall like copper.
Trees shout
With bird throats.

On hills,
From under the camouflage of branches
Spurts the hot barking
Of machine-guns.

‏דורשטיקע ביקס-

‏רערן

‏ניוכען

‏אין פֿאַרע

‏און שטויב.

‏רויכלעך טאַנצן אום

‏ווי ווײַסע מײַז

‏אין אַ שטײַג

‏פֿון פֿײַער.

‏אַ וואָלקן אין פּאַניק פֿאַרפֿאַלט דעם לאָדן

‏אויף דער זון.

‏קוילן פֿליִען

‏ווי פֿייגל אין מבול.

◄   ‏ח.   אַ קינד זעט

‏מײַן מאַמע בײַ נאַכט אונטערגעוועגנס.

‏זי שמוגלט מאַכאָרקע אין בוזעם, אויף היפטן.

‏אַ צײַט פֿון מרידה און הפֿקר,

‏סאָלדאַטן רײַסן עפּאָלעטן,

‏באַנען לויפֿן און שטעלן זיך

‏אָן חשבון.

‏וואָקזאַלן מיט קולות, געפּאַק און בהלה.

‏די מאַמע אַליין צווישן מאַנסביל.

‏מײַן באָבע באַקט ברויט צום פֿאַרקויפֿן.

‏כ׳זע אברם פֿון אור-כשדים

‏אַ באָרוועסן אין אויוון.

‏מען קלאַפּט אין טיר, מ׳רימעט מיט אַ שטאַבע.

‏אַ נאַכטיק קול רעדט גוייִש.

‏ס׳ענטפֿערט ניט די באָבע

‏און פֿאַרציט דעם קנויט.

‏מײַן ברודער טראָגט קרישן פֿון מאַרק.

‏פּראָסטיקע פֿאַרטאָגן. טעמפּע שאַסן

‏הילכן פֿון עקשטאָט.

‏די זון אײַלט זיך איבער פֿלייטן.

‏דער טאָג איז צעשראָקן

‏און קליין.

Thirsty rifle-
Barrels
Sniff
In steam
And dust.
Puffs of smoke dance
Like white mice
In a cage
Of fire.

A cloud slams in panic the shutter
Of the sun.
Bullets fly
Like birds in the flood.

➤ *H. A Child Sees*

My mother at night on the road.
She smuggles tobacco in her bosom, on her hips.
A time of revolt and chaos.
Soldiers rip off epaulettes,
Trains run and stop
With no reason, no rhyme.
Train stations—noise and baggage and panic.
Mama alone among men.

Grandma bakes bread to sell.
I see Abram of Ur
Barefoot in the oven.
A knocking on the door, the clang of an iron bar.
A voice in the night talks goyish.
Grandma doesn't answer
And turns down the wick.

My brother carries baskets from the market.
Frosty dawns. Dull shots
Echo from the outskirts.
The sun hurries over fences.
The day is frightened
And small.

און אין פֿאַרנאַכט. אַ קינד פֿון אַ יאָר פֿינף.
די סטאַדע לויפֿט מיט הערנער,
מיט שטויב און מרוקעריַי.
די פֿלויטן סקריפּען, ס׳פֿראַלן-אויף די טויערן.
דער פּאַסטעך קומט צו לעצט אין לאַנגן העמד.

שקיעה-וואָלקנס טורעמען זיך
ווי וויַיטע ווילדע שטעט.
דאָרטן ערגעץ איז מיַין טאַטע.

◄   ט.   עמיגראַנטיש

מיַין מאַמע פֿירט מיך איבער גאַסן
פֿון אַ גרױסער שטאָט.
שאַרפֿעדיקער זומערדיקער מיטנטאָג
רײצט מיט לעמאָנאַד, מיט באַרן
און מיט לאָדי.
פּלוצעם — ווי אַ בליץ,
פֿינצטער — ווי אַ בוים אין שטורעם,
שטײגט אויף אַ נעגער —
דער ערשטער אין מיַין לעבן.
קינדער רעדלען גרױסע, דינע רײפֿן.
גערטנער רױשן און טונקלען
הינטער שטאַכעטן.

די מאַמע אײַלט און האַלט מיך
בײַ דער האַנט.
קלאַװיר-שפּיל טראָגט זיך
ווי אַ דינער ריח
צװישן פֿאַרהאַנגען און צוויַיגן.
טראַמװײען-קלאַנג
און עלעגאַנטע פֿערד
אויף אַלע ראָגן.

מיר גייען איבער פּאַסטן, איבער באַנקן,
נאָך פֿרעמדע מאַרקעס,
נאָכן טאַטנס געלטער.
מיַין מאַמעס פּנים אין אַלע ווייזע-אַמטן.
פֿאַר בײַזע פֿליכעס און בײַ שטרענגע טישן
שטופֿט זי מיך פֿאָרױס,
ווי דעם מום — אַ בעטלער.

And at twilight. A child of five.
The herd rushes: horns,
Dust and mooing.
Fences squeak. Gates open.
The shepherd comes last in a long robe.

Sunset-clouds tower
Like distant dream cities.
Somewhere there, my daddy.

➤ *I. Of Immigration*

My mother leads me through streets
Of a big city.
A scorching summer afternoon
Teases with lemonade, pears,
And ice cream.
Suddenly—like lightning,
Dark—like a tree in a storm,
A Negro rises—
The first one in my life.
Children roll big thin hoops.
Behind the palings
Arbors rustle and darken.

Mother hurries and holds me
By the hand.
Piano sounds hover
Like a thin fragrance
Among curtains and branches.
Tram clatter
And elegant horses
On all corners.

We go through banks, postoffices,
For foreign stamps,
For father's money.
My mother's face in all visa bureaus.
At strict desks and angry bald heads
She pushes me forward,
As a beggar would his lameness.

מענטשן חתמעענען
זיגלען פּאַטאַל
ווי גאָט,
ווי שיקזאַל.

פֿאַר נאַכט,
ווען פֿאַרבן-קולות פֿלייצן איבער שטאָט,
אויף אַ קילער, ווייטער גאַס —
מײַן מאַמע מיט פֿאַרשוואָלענע פֿיס,
מײַן האַנט אין אירער
איז מיד.

מיט וויפֿל יאָר צוריק?

יעדער זומער דערמאַנט מיר פֿון דאָס נײַ
די אַנגסטן-פֿריידן
פֿון אַ קליינעם ייִד.

◄ 98 פֿאַרענהייַט

דער הימל איז נאַכטיק און
שווער. מיר זעענען
געאַנפֿלט צו דער ערד
ווי ביימער.
עלעקטרישע שילדן טייען
אין אַ געלן טשאַד און
לאָמפֿן שווימען אום
אין אָפּגעזעצטער לופֿט.
קינדער פֿאַלן אַרויס פֿון
חלומות,
ברייט איז דאָס געזאַנג
פֿון אונדזערע הייזעריקסטע לידער.
אונדזער זומער. אונדזער צייַט.
זקנים זעענען מיד
פֿון ניט פֿאַרשטיין,
פֿון אייגענעם קרוקלען געביין.
ס׳הונגערט דער קנעכט
און צינדט די
גאַרדינען בייַם האָר.

Men sign,
Seal forever,
Like God,
Like fate.

At twilight,
When color-voices flood the city,
In a chilly, distant street—
My mother with swollen legs,
My hand in hers,
Is tired.

How many years ago?

Every summer reminds me anew
Of the anguish-joys
Of a little Jew.

► *98 Fahrenheit*

The sky is full of night
And heavy. We are
Umbilically connected to the earth
Like trees.
Electric signboards melt
In yellow smoke.
Lamps swim
In sediments of air.
Children fall out of
Dreams.
Bread is the tune
Of our hoarsest songs.
Our summer. Our age.
Old men are tired
Of not understanding,
Of their own brittle bones.
The slave is hungry
And sets fire to
The draperies of his lord.

◄ ליד

איך בין היַינט ווי אַ
גרויסשטאָט, אויסטערליש-
צעצונדן, פול מיט
קולות און מיט
סודותדיקע בלוטן.
איך בין היַינט איבלדיק-
צעלויכטן ווי די
שילדן אויף דער טרינק-גאַס,
פול מיט קרימענס,
פענצטער און טומאַנען,
בלענד פון
פלוצעמדיקע באַנען.
פרויען וואַקלען
אויף דער גאַס
און דרייען שליסלען
אַרום פינגער.
בעטן טרעטשען אונטער
זקנים.
קינדער וויינען.
איך בלאָנדזשע אין אייגענעם ליַיב,
בין סותר די אייגענע גלידער.

◄ מינאָר

די נאַכט איז בלוי, און פלעקלעך
וויַיס אויף דער קאַלדרע.
מיַין וויַיב איז פאָרצעלַיי, און איך
ווי האָגל אויף די פענצטער.
אונדזער חלום חזרט איבער
אונדזער טאָג.

איר זענט גערעכט, חברים.
פון איַיך שמעקט די רעוואָלוציע
ווי בראָנפן און ס'דרייט זיך איַיך
אַפילו ניט דער קאָפ.

אַז איַיער שטיין וועט טרעפן
אין מיַין פענצטער
וועט עס מיך אָסור פאַרדריסן.

➤ *Poem*

Today I am like a
Big city, steeped in bizarre
Fires, filled with
Voices and
Mysterious strains of blood.
Today I am disgustingly
Illuminated like the
Signboards in drink-street,
Full of chimneys,
Windows, fogs,
And the dazzle of
Sudden trains.
Women totter
In the street
And twist keys
Around their fingers.
Beds creak under
Old men.
Children cry.
I roam in my own body,
I contradict my own limbs.

➤ *In a Minor Key*

The night is blue, stains
Of white on the blanket.
My wife is porcelain, and I
Am like hail on the windows.
Our dream repeats
Our day.

You are right, comrades.
You smell of revolution
Like brandy and your head
Isn't even dizzy.

When your stone strikes
My window
I shall hardly resent it.

◄ ניו-יאָרקער פּייזאַזשן

א

הויכע כוואַליעס ווינט
שוועַנקען
די גאַסן
און וויגן אונדז
ווי זעגלען
ווי מאַסטן
אויף שפּיגלדיקע
פּלאַכן.
די שטאָט
ווי דער ים
איז אָן ראַנד.
שויבן
שפּריצן
גאָלדענעם
שפּריי.
שטיבער
פֿאַרשווימען
פֿון אויג.
די זון
פֿינטלט
מיט רעגן,
און
פּלוצעם —
טונקל-שטיל
ווי ערב מבול.

ב

איבערנאַכט
האָט דער סעזאָן פֿאַרביטן
זײַן פֿעסטע זומערדיקע שריפֿט
אויף ציטערדיקער האַרבסטשריפֿט,
זאַפֿטיקן גרינעם געפֿליסטער
אויף בײַנערדיקן
געל-בלעטערדיקן
שאָרך.
אַלץ איז אויסגעשיילט
ווי יאָדרעס
און ווי אין מאַרמאָר
אויסגעקריצט

► *New York Landscapes*

I

High waves of wind
Wash
The streets
And rock us
Like sails
Like masts
On mirror
Surfaces.
The city
Like the sea
Has no rim.
Panes
Spurt
Gold
Drizzle.
Buildings
Swim out
Of sight.
The sun
Blinks
Rain,
And
Suddenly—
Dark-still
As eve of the flood.

II

Overnight
The season changed
Its firm summer hand
To quivering autumn writing,
Juicy green whisper
To bony
Yellow-leafy
Rustle.
All is peeled open
Like kernels
And engraved
As in marble

Abraham Walkowitz: *Metropolis*,
1923.

אויף קאַלטער,

קלאָרער

לופֿט.

די זון וואַרעמט זיך

בײַ שפּיצן

און געזימסן.

פֿייגל פֿליִען זי פֿאַרבײַ.

שױבן מײַדן זי.

אַ דונער שלאָגט

מיט האַרטער פֿױסט

אין איר בראָנדזענעם שאַרבן.

ג

אָדלער־בריקן

קלאַמערן די שטאָט

אין וואַכער נאַכט,

קלאָר

און

קרישלדיק

ווי פֿראָסט.

נערוון שוידערן

ווי רעלסן.

פּולסן

פֿילדערן

ווי אונ־

טער־

באַנען.

טריט אין חצות

הילכן ווי געבאַט,

און אָדערן

קאַפּען

ווי קראַנען.

ד

אַן עראָפּלאַן

קריצט

זײַן מאָנאָגראַם

אין שוואַרצן

מירמל

פֿון דער נאַכט.

כ׳בין פֿאַרהילט

אין ליכט און נעפֿל

ווי דער ראָג.

In cold,
Clear
Air.
The sun warms herself
At steeples
And cornices.
Birds fly by her.
Panes elude her.
Thunder pounds
With a hard fist
On her bronze skull.

III

Eagle-bridges
Brace the city
In waking night,
Clear
And
Crisp
Like frost.
Nerves shudder
Like rails.
Pulses
Pound
Like sub-
Way-
Trains.
Steps at midnight
Echo like Commandments,
And veins
Drip
Like faucets.

IV

An airplane
Scribbles
His monogram
In black
Marble
Of night.
I'm covered
In light and fog
Like the streetcorner.

פֿאַרפֿלייצט מיט פּאַניק
ביז די ברעגעס.
גאַטס גיפֿטיקער ביס
גליט אויף מיַין דיך.
די נערוון
ברענען
ווי צעבושעוועטע
מאַרקן.
כ׳שווים אין פּיצלעך שפּיגל
און קען זיך ניט
דערקענען.

ה

די זון רײַסט אויף
אין מיַינע אויגן.
כ׳פֿיל דעם עראָפּלאַן
אין מיַינע אינגעוויידן.
וואַלקנס וויקלען מיך
אין קאַלטע טיכער;
מידע בינען
זשומען
אין די חושים;
ווינטן וואַרפֿן מיך
אויף גליִענדיקע
חלפֿים.
כ׳פֿאַל ווי שטערן,
כ׳צעפֿלי ווי צוויט,
איך בין אין קלעם
פֿון גאַטס געמיט.

ו

עס שנייט
דורך אַלע
מיַינע פּאָרן.
איך גלאַנץ
ווי פֿיַיכטע
אָוונטיקע
טראָטואַרן
צעבליט
מיט שטערן
און פֿאַנאַרן.

Flooded with panic
To the brim.
God's poisonous bite
Glows on my groin.
The nerves
Burn
Like riotous
Markets.
I float in mirror splinters
And cannot
Recognize myself.

V

The sun blows up
In my eyes.
I feel the airplane
In my guts.
Clouds swathe me
In cold shawls;
Tired bees
Buzz
In my senses;
Winds hurl me
On glowing
Knives.
I fall like stars,
I scatter like pollen,
I am in the grip
Of God's mood.

VI

It snows
Through all
My pores.
I glisten
Like wet
Evening
Sidewalks
Blooming
With stars
And lanterns.

שנייען ציִען
ווי מאָטן
צום ליכטקרייז
פֿון מײַן אָטעם.
איך שטיי אין ווײַסער שטילקייט
ביז דער דיך.
אַלע מײַנע פּולסן
שלאָגן
מיט אַ מאָל
ווי זייגערס
און דונערן,
ווי גלאָקן
ערב חגא.

◄ אָקטאָבער

כ׳בין אָפּגעבלעטערט,
און ביז דער דיך
אין קופּעס קרישלדיקן קופּער.
די לופֿט איז טרוקן.
די זון —
פֿאַרגליווערטער סאָק
אויף קאַלטע שויבן.
הויכע גאָרנס שטראַלן
ווי ווײַטע פּלאַנעטן.
דער ווינט איז אויסגעװועפּט.
דער פֿראָסט שפּאַלט די קאָרע
בוירערט אין די פֿאָרן.
בלויז איך, ניט דער בוים,
וועל זיך ניט באַנײַען.

◄ פֿאַנטעזיזם: 1968

אונדזער נאַכטיקער
שאָטן
פֿאַלט
אויף די דילן
פֿון ווײַטע פּלאַנעטן.
מיר פֿרווון די קליאַמקעס
פֿון דער לבנה
און לאָזן אין רוים

Snows gather
Like moths
At the light-ring
Of my breath.
I stand in white calm
Groin-deep.
My pulses
Beat
All at once
Like clocks
And thunders,
Like bells
On Christmas Eve.

➤ *October*

I am unleafed.
I stand—groin-deep—
In heaps of crumbling copper.
The air is dry.
The sun—
Gelled sap
On cold panes.
High stories beam
Like distant planets.
The wind is played out.
Frost splits the bark,
Drills into the pores.
Only I, not the tree,
Will not be green again.

➤ *Pantheism: 1968*

Our night-
Shadow
Falls
On the floors
Of distant planets.
We try the doorknobs
Of the moon
And leave in space—

ווי אין שניי
פֿאַרטאָגיקע סליאַדן,
וואָס פֿירן ניט אין ערגעץ.
מיר זענען ליים און גיפּס
און שם־המפורש.
ליכטיאָרן צעטראָגן
ווי טוי
דעם לײַבשווייס
פֿון אונדזערע מוראַס.

◀ ניו־יאָרק דורך ייִדישן געמיט

די גרויסטשטאָטישע גאַסן
פֿיִערלעך פֿאַרגאַפֿט,
ווי שטיבער וואָס וואַרטן
אויף מאַנסבילשן
צוריקקער
פֿון יום־טובֿדיקן מעריבֿ.
ווינטן נאָגן
ווי חזנישער ציקל.
וואָלקן־קראַצערס פֿלאַקערן
ווי עבֿודה־זהרס
אַנטקעגן אַ זון
פֿון אויסגעשײַערט ייִדיש מעש.
פֿאַרנאַכטיקע פֿאָרכט
פֿאַלט אויף מיר
ווי אַ טלית
און כ׳באַנעם דעם מײן פֿון מײַנע טעג
פֿירקאַנטיק קלאָר
ווי אונטערן יד
פֿון בעל־קורא.

As in snow—
Dawn-traces,
Leading nowhere.
We are clay and plaster
And the Holy Name.
Lightyears scatter
Like dew
The body-sweat
Of our fears.

➤ *New York in a Jewish Mood*

Big-city streets
Gaping solemnly
Like homes waiting
For men's
Return from holiday prayers.
Winds nag
Like a cantor's liturgy.
Skyscrapers aflame
Like pagan worship
Against a sun
Of scoured Jewish brass.
Evening awe
Descends on me
Like a tallis
And I sense the meaning of my days
Like clear square letters
Under the pointing hand
Of a Reader.

Louis Lozowick: *First Avenue Market*, 1934.

Pointing Hand*—a silver pointer in the form of a long hand used to indicate the text in the Bible scroll, written in the holy script of "square letters" and read by the Reader.

זעגלען שווימען אויף די ראַנדן פון דער שקיעה.
וואַסער־קאַטשקעס שנאָבלען קרישקעס
בײַ די ברעגעס.
שטעט, ווי סעדער.
קליינע, באַבלומטע וואָקזאַלן.
קאַפעליעס אין אָוונטיקע גערטנער.
ציפערבלעטער
ווי מזלות
אויף די הייכן.
און אַלץ איז אַרומגעזוימט מיט בערג
און קאַרעקטע שווייצאַרן.

גענוי ווי דאַן. גענוי ווי דאַן.
ווען ביסט געווען
אַן אויסגעחלומט כנען
בײַ מײַנע טויט־געיאָגטע ברידער
און האָסט זיי ניט געלאָזט
די בערג אַריבער.

פון 3 לידער פון קאַשמאַר

◄ מבול

דער מוח איז שוין אָפגעשניטן
פון יבשה.
דאָס לײַב
פלייצט
פאַרפלייצט
און פענטעט
ווי מיט וואַסער־שטריק
די קנעכלען, די קני,
און די דיך
פון לעצטן
קלאָרן געדאַנק.
די שטראָמען זאַמלען זיך
און שטײַגן
צום מוח:
דאָס לײַב
צענעמט אונדז
זין בײַ זין
און שווענקט אונדז אַרויס
צום ים.

Sails float on the margins of sunset.
Water-ducks dive for crumbs
At the shores.
Towns like orchards.
Small, flower-covered stations.
Bands in evening gardens.
Clockdials
Like zodiacs
On the heights.
And all of it is hemmed with mountains
And correct Switzermen.

Precisely like then. Precisely like then.
For my death-haunted brothers
You were
The dream of a Canaan
And didn't let them
Over the mountains.

From **Three Poems of Nightmare**

► *Flood*

The brain—cut off
From the land.
The flesh
Flows
Floods
And shackles
As with water-ropes
The ankles, the knees,
The groin
Of the last
Clear thought.
Streams assemble
And rise
To the brain:
The flesh
Dismembers us
Sense from sense
And drains us out
To the sea.

אונדזער פֿאַרשראָקן קול
טיקט זיך
װי אַ זעגל
צװישן די װאַסער־קאַמען.
דער טאָג איז דין װי גלאָז;
אַ װאָלקן בלוטיקט
אינעם שנאָבל
פֿון דער זון.

◄ חצות

פֿון אַלע בלוט־קאַנאַלן
גײען אױף טומאַנען.
הילן די נאַכט פֿון אונדזער לײב
צעשטערנט מיט יום־טובֿדיקן
גיהנום.
אין דרױסן
דראָזשען
דונערן.
מיר פֿאַרציִען די שטאָרן.
מיר לײענען אונדזערע לײבער
װי ברײל —
אין דער פֿינצטער,
מיט די פֿינגער.
פֿון די פֿאָרן
שלאָגט פֿאַרע.
די לײב־קאַכלען
זענען אָנגעגליט.
די ריגלען שפּרינגען
פֿון הײן.
אונדזער צונױפֿגעפֿאָרט געגליד
אַרױסגעשװענקט
פֿון לײב
צאַנקט
אױפֿן קרײץ
פֿון אַ בליץ.
דער הימל איבער אונדז
צונטער־רױט.
מיר זענען צעפֿראַלט װי דער דרױסן,
פֿאַרקלעמט װי אַ פֿױסט.

Our frightened voice
Ducks
Like a sail
Between water-crests.
The day is thin as glass;
A cloud bleeds
In the beak
Of the sun.

➤ *Midnight*

From all the canals
Of the blood, fogs rise.
They wrap the night of our flesh,
Starred with festive
Hell.
Outside
Thunders
Shiver.
We pull the curtains.
We read our bodies
Like Braille—
In the dark,
With our fingers.
Our pores
Exhale steam.
Our body-bricks
Are glowing.
The bolts burst
From heat.
Our coupled limbs
Swept away
From the body
Flicker
On the cross
Of lightening.
The sky over us,
Scarlet-red.
We are pried open like the outside,
Clenched into a fist.

Malka Heifetz-Tussman

1896–

In recent years, Malka Heifetz-Tussman has become one of the best-known Yiddish poetesses. Though she published individual poems as early as 1919 and participated in some of the best Yiddish journals (e.g., *In Zikh, Tsukunft, Yiddisher Kemfer*, the Warsaw *Literarishe Bleter*, the Toronto *Tint un Feder*, etc.), her first book, *Poems*, did not appear until 1949. Both *Poems* and *Mild My Wild* (1958) were published in Los Angeles; four subsequent books appeared in Israel.

Malka Heifetz was born in a village in Volyn (Russia) where her father was the manager of an estate. She studied with private tutors whom her father hired for his eight children and, later, in Russian schools in the neighboring towns. In 1912 she immigrated to America, where she continued her studies. Her first poems were written in Russian. Among other things, she wrote for an English anarchist journal, *Alarm* (Chicago, 1914). In 1924, she became a teacher in a secular Yiddish school in Milwaukee and attended the University of Wisconsin at the same time. Later she moved to Los Angeles, where she was an elementary and high school teacher and eventually an instructor of Yiddish language and literature at the University of Judaism. At present, Heifetz-Tussman lives in Berkeley, California, where her son is a professor of philosophy. She was awarded the Itsik Manger Prize for Yiddish Poetry in Tel Aviv in 1981.

The poems in this anthology were selected and translated by Kathryn Hellerstein. "Desert Wind" was translated in collaboration with the poetess. "Lord, My God," "Sweet Father," "Forgotten," and "In Spite" appeared earlier in *Journal of Reform Judaism* (Spring 1979).

Malka Heifetz-Tussman.

◄ מיט צײן אין ערד

מײן באק אויף דער ערד
און איך ווייס פאַר וואָס גנאָד.

מיט ליפן צו דער ערד
און איך ווייס פאַר וואָס ליבע.

מיטן נאָז אין ערד
ווייס איך פאַר וואָס גנבה.

מיט צײן אין ערד
ווייס איך פאַר וואָס
מאָרד.

וואָס זשע זיינען ווערטער
אין פאַרגלייך
מיט צײן אין ערד?
וואָס איז געשריי
אין פאַרגלייך
מיט צײן אין ערד?

און גאָרניט איז גענוג,
און גאָרניט איז שיין
און קיין מאָל איז גאָרניט אזוי
אָט אזוי.

איז קלאָר מיר גענוי,
ווייס איך פאַר וואָס
דער מענטש
וואָס גראָבט מיט צײן די ערד
און דער
וואָס רייסט זיך פון דער ערד
ווערט אַלע מאָל,
אוי אַלע מאָל
דאַרפן ווײנען איבער זיך.

➤ *With Teeth in the Earth*

My cheek on the earth
And I know why mercy.

Lips to the earth
And I know why love.

My nose in the earth
I know why theft.

Teeth in the earth
I know why
Murder.

What are words
Compared to
Teeth in the earth?
What is shouting
Compared to
Teeth in the earth?

And nothing is enough,
And nothing is now
And nothing is ever
Like this.

I know clearly.
I know why
The man
Who digs the earth with his teeth
And he
Who tears himself from the earth
Will always
Oh, always
Have to weep for himself.

Max Weber: from *Shriftn 6*,
Spring 1920.

מאַמע מײַנע

אָט שטייען מיר אַרום אונדזער מאַמען.
אַזוי ווי אַ פעדערל איז גרינג אונדזער מאַמע.
ווו נעמט עס אַ גרינגינקע מאַמע
אַזאַ שווערער געוויין?

אַ קלוגשאַפט ווי אַ זון־פלעק
פלאַטערט אויף איר פנים —
פלאַטערט אום צווישן וויעס און איר מויל.
און איר קלוגשאַפט, דוכט זיך,
צײלט אונדז דרײַ מאָל איבער.
און איר קלוגשאַפט, דוכט זיך,
טײַטלט מיט די פינגער:

אָט זענט איר, אָט!
אָט זענט איר מיר — שפּענער.
און ער געווען איז איינער,
איינער — מײַן דעמב.

מילד מײַן וויִן וויילד (1958)

► קנעכטשאַפט

אַ נאַקעט פייגעלע, ערשט פון אײ אַרויס,
האָט אומגערוקט מיר עמעצער אַרײַנגעלייגט אין האַנט.
אין דערשטוינטן שוידער האָט רעפלעקס
אַ בויג געטאָן די פינגער,
אין האַלבקרייַז שטייַף
אַ שיסעלע פאַר פרעמדער, בלויער וואַרעמקייט
פאַרשטאַרט.

אוי, וואָס טוט מען מיט אַ לעבן אין דער האַנט?
ווי האַלט מען דאָס אַ לעבן אין אַ האַנט?
ווי גרויס,
ווי גרויס איז אַ ברעקעלע לעבן?

דאָס קלייניטשיקע פולס אין מײַן האַנט
האָט מיר איבער די שלייפן געשלאָגן,
געשטאָכן די הויט פון מײַן לײַב.

➤ *Her Oak*

For Mother

Eight, we stand around our mother.
Our mother is light as a feather.
From where in such a light mother
Does such heavy weeping come?

Wisdom like a sunspot
Flutters on her face—
Flutters between eyelashes and mouth.
And her wisdom, it seems,
Counts us three times.
And her wisdom, it seems,
Points with her fingers:
Eight, you are eight!
My eight you are—chips.
And he was one,
One—
My oak.

MILD MY WILD (1958)

➤ *Slavery*

A naked little bird just out of the egg—
Someone unexpectedly put it in my hand.
A shudder of amazement, a reflex
Bent my fingers
In a stiff half-circle
Frozen into a bowl
For the strange, blue warmth.

What shall I do with a life in my hand?
How shall I hold a life in my hand?
How big,
How big is a crumb of life?

The tiny pulse in my hand
Throbbed up to my temples,
Stung the skin of my body.

דאָס פיצינקע לעבן אין האַנט
איז גרויס געשטיגן.
געטורעמט איבער מיר האָט מוראדיק
דאָס לעבלעכקייט אין האַנט.

איך בין פאַריאַקט מיט הילפלאָז לעבן אין מײַן האַנט.
דאָס געצאַפּל פון הוילקייט
האָט מיך פאַרקנעכט.
און איך ברעך זיך.

איך   צ ע ב ר ע ק ל   זיך.

◄ ערד-ציטערניש

צוויי בײַזע הענט האָבן מיך פון מאַמען אָפּגעריסן.

איך קניפּ זיך אַרײַן אין מאַמעס צעפלאַטערט קליידל
און הענג איבער אַן אָפּגרונט.
מײַן קליין הענטל רײַסט זיך צו מאַמעס טיכל.
אָט, אָט דערלאַנג איך אירע האָר.
די האָר!
אַ וויכער צערײַסט דעם קנופ און דרײט מיך אַרײַן
אינדערלייידיק.
קליינע פינגערלעך ווי מאָטילן
ציטערן אינדערלופטן:
עלנט, עלנט, עלנט.

עקעלעך פון מאַמעס טיכל
גייען אויס.
פונקען — מײַן מאַמעס האָר
טוקן זיך.
מײַן מאַמע-גאָט האָט מיך אַראָפּגעוואָרפן.
מאַמע-גאָטס פּנים
לעשט זיך.
מאַמעשקייט שווימט אַוועק פון מיר
און איך פאַרגיי זיך אויף אַ פרעמדן אַקסל.
פ ר ע מ ד ן   אַקסל.

The wee life in my hand
Grew big.
The warmth in my hand
Towered over me fearsomely.

I am bound to the helpless life in my hand.
The twitch of nakedness
Enslaved me.
And I broke.

I shattered.

► *Earthquake*

Bad hands tear me from Mama.

I knot myself into Mama's fluttering skirts
And dangle over an abyss.
My little hand tries for her kerchief.
Soon, soon I'll reach her hair.
Her hair!
A whirlwind breaks the knot and spins me
In the void—
Little fingers like butterflies
Trembling in the air:
Forsaken! Forsaken!

The ends of Mama's kerchief
Flicker out.
Sparks—my Mama's hair—
Dive.
My Mama-god has cast me down.
Mama-god's face grows dim.
A Mama-world drifts away from me.
And I sob on a stranger's shoulder.
Stranger's shoulder.

Max Weber: Yiddish text:
Mother Love. 1920. (From
Shriftn 3 Spring 1921)

◄ דיך געזען צווישן ביימער

דו האָסט זיך דערוויַיטערט,
אַוועק.
איך האָב דיך דערזען צווישן ביימער
און דו ביסט שענער,
ביסט שענער נאָך צווישן ביימער.

איך האָב געזען דיַין משוגענעם קאָפּ
צופֿאַלן צו אַ בוים ווי מע פֿאַלט אויף
דער מאַמעס קישן.
פּאַמעלעכקע
געוויגט האָט זיך דיַין קאָפּ
צום טראָפּ
פֿון מיַין אָטעם
און דו ביסט אַזאַ שטילער געוואָרן,
אַזאַ שטילער ביַים בוים.

די שטאָט ביַי נאַכט אָן דיר
איז אַן אָקס אַ שוואַרצער, אַ שטומער
און איך בלאָנקע דורך
די פֿינצטערע שטחים פֿון
מורא.

◄ דונער מיַין ברודער

דונער מיַין ברודער,
מיַין מעכטיקער ברודער,
שטיינער אויף שטיינער געקיַיקלט — דיַין קול.
וואַלדיק און גוואַלדיק דיַין קול.
סאַ פֿרייד דיר ווען דו טוסט די בערגער צעטריַיסלען,
סאַ גליק דיר
ווען דו טוסט צעטומלען די קריכיקע בריאים אין טאָל.

➤ *Saw You Among Trees*

You withdrew,
Departed.
I spotted you among trees
And you were more beautiful,
Yet more beautiful among trees.

I saw your crazy head
Fall upon a tree as one falls
On his mother's pillow.
Slowly
Your head swayed
To the beat
Of my breathing
And you were so quiet,
So quiet by the tree.

The city at night without you
Is an ox, black, mute.
I stray through
The dark distances of
Fear.

Max Weber: Woodcut, from
Shriftn 6, Spring 1920

➤ *Thunder My Brother*

Thunder my brother,
My powerful brother,
Stones rolling on stones—your voice.
Like a forest, forceful, your voice.
What pleasure you take in making mountains rattle,
How happy you feel
When you bewilder creeping creatures in the valley.

אַ מאָל
גאָר אַ מאָל:
דער שטורעם — מײַן טאַטע —
ער איז אױף אַ טונקעלן װאָלקן געריטן,
אױף יענער זײַט סדר-העולם
פֿאַרקוקט זיך אַריבער,
צום תּוהו-ובוהו אַריבער,
דעריבער
איך אױך האָב אַ קול —
אַ קול פֿון אַ מוראדיק ברומען
אין קלעם פֿון מײַן שטומען.
פֿאַראַן מיר געבאָטן
ענגע פֿאַרבאָטן
„דו זאָלסט ניט,
דו זאָלסט ניט״
אַ דונער,
מײַן װילדער, צעלאָזענער ברודער.

אונטער דײַן צײכן (1974)

◄ אַלמנהשאַפֿט

טו עפּעס
מיטן מם אין
„אַלמנה״
ס׳זאָל ניט זײַן
װי אַ
זשוק
װי אַ
מוק

ס׳קריכט איבער מײַן הױט
און גראַבלט
„טױט״
און גראַבלט
„טױט״

טו עפּעס
מיטן מם
אין
אַלמנה

Once
Long ago
The storm—my father—
Rode on a dark cloud,
And stared at the other side of the Order-of-the-Universe,
Across to the chaos.
I, too,
Have a voice—
A voice of fearsome roaring
In the grip of my muteness.

And there are commandments
Forbidding me:
"Thou shalt not,
Thou shalt not"
O thunder,
My wild unbridled brother.

UNDER YOUR SIGN (1974)

➤ *Widowhood*

Do something
With the W in
"Widow"
So it shall not be
Like a beetle
Like a
Gnat

It crawls over my skin
And scratches
"Death"
And scratches
"Death"

Do something
With the W
In
Widow.

ס'פֿאַרנאַכטיקט.
מיר פֿאָרן קורצוועג פֿון מושב חגלה
צו חברים אין קיבוץ המעפּיל.
ס'פֿירט אונדז
שווער סאָפֿענדיק און האָפֿענדיק
אַן אַלטער חצי-אויטאָ — חצי-שלעפּ
איבער רויטע שטיינער,
זאַמד
און הרודעס רויטע ערד.
בײַ די זײַטן —
מידבר, מידבר אונטערטעניק
דעם מידבר-ווינט — דעם ווילדן קעניג.
אַ מורד בבורא-עולם איז דער מידבר-ווינט.
זײַן גיהנום און גן-עדן דאָ
מישט ער אויס צוזאַמען.
ווי גאָט געפֿורעמט האָט
פֿון ערדן-שטויב זײַן מענטש —
אַ זכר און נקבה
אַז פּרוקפֿערן און מערן זאָל זיך זײַן באַשאַף,
פֿורעמט דאָ דער מידבר-ווינט
זײַן אייגענעם באַשאַף.
ער פֿורעמט, פֿורעמט
און אויסגעפֿורעמט האָט פֿון הייסן זאַמד
בלענדנדיקע, ראַזעווע און גלאַטע
ווײַבער-לײַבער.
מיט ווילדער תּאווה
די גופֿים זייערע באַשוווערט,
סימעטריש זיי אַרײַנגעפֿאַסט
אינאַנאַנדער,
צו ליבע לעסבישער זיי אָפּגעגעבן.
און אַזוי פֿאַרמישפּט זײַן באַשאַף
צו אייביקער עקרות
האָט דער מידבר-ווינט דער מורד.
ס'פֿאַרנאַכטיקט.
זונקאָלירן פֿון ניטדאָיִקן באַלײַכט
מיניען איבער ראָזע לײַבער.
ריטעם —
קומט אַ שאַרך פֿון יענעם ריטעם
וואָס פֿון איידער
תּוהו-ובֿוהו אײַנגעצאַמט און אײַנגעשפּאַנט געוואָרן איז
איז סדר.
איך האָב געגאַפֿט און פֿאַר דער שוידערלעכער שיינקייט
די אויגן מיינע האָב איך פֿאַרמאַכט ...

ישראל 1960, פֿאַרשריבן 1973, קאַליפֿאָרניע.

► *Desert Wind*

Dusk comes on.
We take a shortcut from Moshav Hogla
To Kibbutz Hama'apil.
The rickety pickup truck is
Panting, bumping
Over stones, sand and
Clumps of red earth.

Desolate desert—servile to
The mad ruler—the wind.

Desert wind rebels against the Creator.
Here he mingles His paradise and hell:
God formed mankind from
Dust of the earth—
Male and female to be fruitful
And multiply.
Here the desert wind forms
His own creation:
From hot sand he fashions
Dazzling, rosy, smooth
Female bodies,
Makes them heavy with
Passion,
Symmetrically fits them into
One another
And gives them to
Lesbian love—
To eternal barrenness.

Dusk:
Colors of unearthly illumination
Play a strange rhythm
Over those bodies—
An inkling of
That other rhythm
Before chaos was harnessed and tamed
Into order.

I gape
And before the dreadful beauty
I half-close my eyes . . .

Moshav—a cooperative village in Israel.

Kibbutz—a communal village in Israel.

Max Weber: *Shriftn*, 1920.

Israel 1960, written in California, 1973

מײַן פרײַנד — דער דיכטער טעד
איז געקומען זיך געזעגענען.
געקומען זאָגן מיר "שלום".
ער האָט ליב דאָס וואָרט, זאָגט ער מיט התפעלות:
זאָגט מען נאָר שלום
באַדאַרף מען מער שוין גאָר ניט זאָגן.

"איך פאָר פון צײַט צו צײַט זיך מיט זען מיט אַלטע טאַטע-מאַמע
וואָס ווילן אַלץ דאָס אַלטע הויז לעם באַסטאָן
ניט פאַרלאָזן.
אַ הויז אַ גרויס מיט צימערן אַ סך,
מיט קליינע פענצטערלעך,
אַ קעלער און אַ בוידעם
און סקריפענדיקע טרעפ.

גוט אין קעלער אָנצוטאַפן
דעם אַלטן טיש דעם דעמבענעם,
אַ באַנק מיט גראָבע פיס געשניצטע
און גרויסע טעפ טשוגונענע און פאַנען
וואָס די אַלטיטשקע
ווייל זיך נאָך מיט דעם ניט שיידן.
זיי זײַנען, זאָגט זי,
אַ טייל פון איר לעביקייט,
איר פלינקע שוועביקייט ווען
מיט גרויסע הילצענע פאַלאַניקעס
זי האָט געמישט פאַטראָוועס אין די טעפ
און פריילעך איז געווען אַרומצוטאַנצן
אַרום מישפחה און די אָפטע געסט.
דעריבער לאָזט זי ניט פון קעלער קיין זאַך רירן.

כ'נעם אויך דאָס קליינוואַרג מיט.
ס'ווערט דאָס הויז פאַרהיילכט מיט זייער שרײַען
אין טויבע אויערן פון זיידע-באָבע.
באַלד זיי לאָזן זיך צום בוידעם לויפן,
עפענען די קופערטן מיט די ברייטע אײַזן-רייפן
און שלעסער גרויסע וואָס מע קען שוין ניט פאַרשליסן,
נאָר זאָל זיך דאַכטן זיי באַשיצן
אַלטער-אַלטער האָב און גוטס.

די מיידלעך —
זיי כאַפן זיך צו אַלטע קליידער,

My friend, the poet Ted,
Has come to say good-bye,
Has come to say "Shalom."
He likes the word; with enthusiasm he says:
"Say Shalom
And you need say no more.

"From time to time I go visit my elderly parents
Who want never to leave
Their house near Boston.
A large old house with many rooms,
With tiny windows,
A cellar and an attic
And creaking stairs.

"In the cellar it is good to touch
The old oaken table,
A bench with thick, carved feet,
Great cast iron pots and skillets
That my mother
Refuses to part with.
They are, she says,
A part of her liveliness,
Her nimble hovering when
She stirred delicacies in the pots
With wooden spoons
And happily fussed over
Her family and frequent guests.
She won't let anything budge from the cellar.

"I take the kids with me.
The house is deafened by their shouts
In their grandparents' deaf ears.
Soon they set out running to the attic,
Open the trunks with the wide iron bands
And large locks that lock no longer
But still seem to protect
Great-great possessions.

"The girls
Throw themselves upon old clothes,

צו די קרינאָלינען וווּ
דער פישביין שטאַרצט אַרויס פון צעלעכערטן בראָקאַט,
צו די שאַלן מיט די האַנט־געשטריקטע שפיצן.
וואָס נאָר זיי זעען דאָרטן
שלעפּן זיי אויף זיך אַרויף.

אין די האָר פאַרשטעקן זיי זיך גרויסע קאַמען
און בראַשקעס פון פאַרשיידענע קאָלירן
און אוירינגען וואָס באָמבלען ביז
די אַקסלען זיי אַרונטער.
איינע כאַפּט אַ וועֶרטענע מיטן נאָמען טעסי איינגעקריצט
און די צווייטע כאַפּט אַ הימען־ביכעלע
אין פאַרבלאַסטן שריפט.

די ייִנגלעך שלעפּן פון די קאַסטנס
שינעלן און מונדירן מיט גרויסע קנעפ די מעשענע,
צי׳ען אָן אויף זיך די שטײַפע יעגער־הויזן
און שטיוול טרוקענע מיט שפּאָרן,
און אויף די אַקסלען הענגען אָן
שווערדן, שפּיזן, ביקסן אַלערליי —
כלי־זײַן פאַר מלחמה און געיעג,
און מיט רעוואָלווערן אין/די הענט
זיי לאָזן זיך אַראָפּ און הייבן אויף
אַ כמאַרע שטויב פון קרעכצנדיקע טרעפּ.
זיידע, באָבע לאַכן,
ווישן זיך די אויגן
און שאָקלען מיט די קעפּ.

אַזוי פיל געשיכטע, טראַדיציע
אויף אַלטע ביידעֶמער!
און זאָלן קינדער וויסן פון וואַנען
זיי שטאַמען.״

יאָ — האָב איך געזאָגט:
קינדער זײַנען ניט קיין רעטעכער.
קינדער האָבן וואָרצלען טיפע.

איך וועל אויך מײַן קליינוואַרג נעמען,
פירן זיי אין אַלטן הויז.
גוט וועט זײַן אין קעלער אָנצוטאַפּן
מײַן זיידנס שטעגֶנדֶער מיטן אָפּגעבראָכן פיסל,
אַ מצה־שטייסל,
קופּער־פּאַנען וואָס ס׳האָבן באָבעס, מומעֶס
אין זיי אײַנגעמאַכטס געפֿרעגלט.

Crinolines where
The fishbones poke from worn brocade,
Shawls with handmade lace.
Whatever they see there
They pull up.
In their hair they stick combs,
Brooches of different colors,
And earrings that dangle
Down to their shoulders.
One grabs a spindle inscribed with the name 'Tessie,'
And another a hymnal
In faded print.

"The boys drag from the trunks
Military coats and uniforms with big brass buttons.
They pull on tight hunting-trousers,
Dried-up boots with spurs,
And hang from their shoulders
Swords, spears, all sorts of rifles—
Weapons for war and hunting,
And with revolvers in their hands
They descend, stirring up
A cloud of dust from moaning stairs.
Grandfather and grandmother laugh,
Wiping their eyes
And shaking their heads.

"So much history, tradition
In old attics!
Children should know where
They come from."

"Yes," I say,
"Children are not radishes.
Children have deep roots.

"I, too, will take my kids
And travel to our old house.
In the cellar it will be good to touch
My grandfather's lectern with its broken-off feet,
A matzo-grinder,
Copper pans in which
Grandmothers and aunts would make preserves.

אױפֿן בױדעם שטײען שפֿין-פֿאַרװעבטע טשעמאָדאַנעס
מיט גראָבע שטריק פֿאַרבונדן.
די מײדלעך מײַנע װעלן זיך אַ יאָג טאָן
צו דער עלטערבאָבעס זאַכן:
אַ ראָטאַנדע מיט שליאַמעס,
אַ טשיפֿיק מיט אַ שטערן-טיכל,
אַ קרבן-מינחה, אַ שׂרה-בת-טובֿים-תּחינה
און אפֿשר ליגט ערגעץ פֿאַרשטעקט אַ שנירל פֿערל
װאָס געשאָנקען איר דער זיידע צו דער חתונה,
און אפֿשר אירע אױרינגלעך
װאָס זי צו ליכט-בענטשן פֿלעגט אָנטאָן.
אין די הענטלעך װעלן מײַנע מײדלעך נעמען
די לײַכטער זילבערנע נאָך מיטן חלב אין די רערן.

די ייִנגלעך װעלן כאַפֿן זיך
צום עלטערזיידנס חפֿצים:
אַרײַנקריכן אין זײַן סױבלנעם טולופ
װאָס אָנטאָן פֿלעגט דער זיידע װען
ער איז צום ״טשערנאָבילער״ געפֿאָרן.
געפֿינען װעלן מײַנע ייִנגלעך דאָרט
אַ יאַרמלקע, אַן אַרבע-כּנפֿות,
אַ קיטל און אַ טלית,
רבינו תּמס תּפֿילין,
ארץ-ישׂראל-ערד אַ זעקעלע,
אַ חנוכּה-לעמפּל און אַ טאַביק-פּושקעלע,
אַ קידוש-בעכער און אַ תּהילימל,
אַ סאַמעט-מענטעלע פֿאַר דער ״רײניקײט״,
און אױך כּלי-זײַן:
אַ שופֿר װאָס קען הימל שפֿאַלטן
און אַ שיסערל — אַ בשמים-ביקסל.
יאָ. קינדער דאַרפֿן װיסן פֿון װאַנען
זײ שטאַמען.

און טעדי פֿרעגט:
װוּ איז דײַן אַלטע הױז,
דײַן קעלער און דײַן בױדעם?
און איך ענטפֿער ייִדישלעך —
אַ פֿראַגע אױף אַ פֿראַגע:
װוּ איז
דאָס אַלטע הױז מײַן זיידנס?

In the attic, spider webs cover valises
Bound with heavy rope.
My girls will race
To great-grandmother's things:
A woolen cape trimmed with fur,
A white cap with a kerchief,
A *Korbn-Minkhe* and Sarah Bas-Toyvim's litany,
And perhaps, tucked away somewhere, a string of pearls
That grandfather gave her for their wedding,
And perhaps the earrings that she used to wear
For blessing the Sabbath candles.
My girls will take in their little hands
The silver candlesticks with drippings in the sockets.

"My boys will rush to
Great-grandfather's precious things:
They'll slip into the sable overcoat
That grandfather wore when
He traveled to the Chernobyl rebbe.
There my boys will find
A yarmulke, an *arbe-kanfes*,
A white robe and a tallis,
A set of Rabeynu Tam's tefillin,
A small bag of soil from the Holy Land,
A menorah and a snuffbox,
A Kiddush cup and a psalmbook
A velvet mantle for the Torah scroll,
And also weapons:
A shofar that can split the heavens
And a little shooter—a spice-box for the Sabbath.
Yes, children need to know where
They come from."

And Teddy asks,
"Where is your old house—
Your cellar and your attic?"
And I answer in a Jewish way—
A question with a question,
"Indeed, where is
My grandfather's old house?"

Korbn Minkhe—a woman's prayerbook.

Sora Bas-Toyvim's Litany—a collection of prayers for women in Yiddish.

Cher'nobyl rebbe—the head of a Hassidic dynasty in the Ukraine.

White robe (Yiddish: **Kitl**)—worn by men on solemn or festive occasions.

Ra'beynu Tam's tefillin—a special kind of tefillin as prescribed by the twelfth-century sage, Rabeynu Tam.

bag of soil from the Holy Land—dead Jews were buried with their heads on soil from the Holy Land.

◄ אַרויס און אַרײַן

פֿון אינזיך
אַרויס,
פֿון זיך
אַוועק
ווּהין?

קודם
אַרויס פֿון דער ענגשאַפֿט
אין חלל, אין שטח, אין ברייטקייט
פֿאַרברייטן דעם שפּאַן,
פֿאַרלענגען דעם בליק,
צעוויגן דעם גאַנצענעם גוף
אָט אַהער, אָט אַהין —
געראַם!

די פֿינגער —
וואָס ציטערן אַזוי מײַנע פֿינגער
ווי קעצלעך מיט אײגעלעך נאָך בלינדע
פֿאַרוואָרלאָזט אין האַרבסטיקן פֿעלד?
וואָס מאָנען די שפּיריקע פֿינגער?

זיי בענקען:
מיט פֿינגערשע שפּיצן
באַרירן זיי ווילן
אין שפּאַן-אויף-אַ-שפּאַן
די היימישע ענגשאַפֿט
דערפֿילן.

◄ *

מײַן האַר,
איך — דײַן קלײנער גאָרטן
ברענג דיר דאָס גערעטעניש פֿון מײַנע בײטן —
מײַן פֿאַרמעג
צײַטיק צי ניט גאָר צײַטיק —
אַלץ אײנס: דײַן גאָב.
נעם אָן, מײַן האַר, מיט גוטוויליקײט
נאָר ניט מיט פֿײַער.

➤ *Out Of and Back In*

Out
Of the self,
Away
From the self
Where to?

At first
Away from the narrowness
Into void, into space, into expanse—
To broaden the stride,
To extend the glance,
To swing the whole body
From here to there—
Roomy!

My fingers—
Why do my fingers tremble
Like kittens still blind
Abandoned in an autumn field?
What do these sensitive fingers demand?

They long:
With fingertips
They want to touch
In a space you can't turn in—
To sense
The familiar narrowness.

Raphael Soyer: (Untitled),
(no date).

➤ *

Lord, my God,
I—your little garden—
Bring you the harvest of my soil—
My bounty
Ripe or not quite—
All the same your boon.
Accept it, my Lord, benignly
But without fire.

ניט מיט פֿײַער.
ס׳איז דאָך ניט אמת אַז דו האָסט ליב
דעם רויך פֿון פֿעטן קרבן ...
סע איז ניט אמת.
און זע
ווי הכנעהדיק ס׳האָבן מיך געמאַכט
די יאָרן
אַז פֿאַר יעדן טראָפֿן חסד
זאָל איך דאַנקען.
דאַנקען.

◄ טאַטע זיסער

און איך רוף אים
טאַטע זיסער
כאָטש איך געדענק ניט דעם טאַטן.
דאָך עפּעס געדענקט זיך:
אַ דאָרן,
אַ פֿײַער,
אַ דונער,
אַ באַרג
און עפּעס אַ קול.
ווען מיר דאַכט זיך
איך הער זײַן קול
באַלד שרײַ איך:
דאָ בין איך !
דאָ בין איך, טאַטע זיסער!
אַז אַ טאַטע פֿאַרלאָזט
איז ער אַלץ נאָך אַ טאַטע
און איך וועל ניט אויפֿהערן בענקען
און שרײַען
״דאָ בין איך״
ביז ער וועט דערהערן,
וועט זיך דערמאָנען
און רופֿן מײַן נאָמען
און ריידן צו מיר
דורך פֿײַער.

No fire, my God.
It cannot be true that you delight
In the smoke of the fat offering—
Not true!
And see how humble
The years have made me:
That for each drop of mercy
I am thankful.
Thankful.

➤ *Sweet Father*

And I call Him
Sweet Father
Although I don't remember my father.
But I do remember
A thorn,
A fire,
A thunder,
A mountain
And something of a voice.
When I think
I hear His voice
I shout at once
Here I am!
Here I am, Sweet Father!
When a father abandons
He is still a father,
And I will not stop longing
And calling
"Here I am"
Until He hears me,
Until He remembers me
And calls my name
And talks to me
Through fire.

◄ פֿאַרגעסן

האַר פֿון דער וועלט!
בורא-עולם,
איך שטיי פֿאַר דיר
מיט אָפּגעדעקטן קאָפּ,
מיט אויגן ניט פֿאַרשטעלט —
עקשנותדיק
ברייט צעעפֿנט אַנטקעגן דײַן ליכט.
סע ציטערט ניט
אַן איינציק העּרעלע פֿון מײַן ברעם
פֿאַר דײַן גרויסקייט.
מיינע בענטשליכט
איך שטעל אין לײַכטער אַרײַן
הויך און ווירע-גלײַך
זיי זאָלן פֿלעמלען צו דיר
אָן אַ טראָפּעלע הכנעה.
איך שטייג צו דיר
אָן מינדסטן פּחד אין מײַן נפֿש.
כ'האָב לאַנג געשליפֿן מײַן געוואַגטקייט
צו שטעלן זיך פֿאַר דיר
גלײַך-אויף-גלײַך, באַשעפֿער,
און לאָזן מײַנע טענות זיך עפֿענען פֿאַר דיר
גערעכטע
פֿון מײַן מויל אַרויס.

ווייי מיר, ווייי מיר:
איך האָב פֿאַרגעסן!
איך קען זיך ניט דערמאָנען
וואָס איך בין געקומען מאָנען.
איך האָב פֿאַרגעסן,
ווייי מיר.

◄ צולהכעיס

דו זאָגסט:
"דו ביסט ייִד און ביסט דיכטער
און שרײַבסט ניט קיין לידער
פֿון חורבן.
ווי קען דאָס אַ ייִדישער דיכטער
ווען גרויס
אַזוי גרויס איז דער חורבן?"

Master of the world!
Creator,
I stand before You with bared head,
With eyes uncovered,
Stubbornly
Facing Your light.
Not a single hair
Trembles on my brow
Before Your greatness.
I place my Sabbath candles
In candlesticks
Tall and straight as a ruler
So they may flicker toward You
Without a drop of humbleness.
I rise to You
Without the slightest fear.
For a long time I've sharpened my daring
To stand before You
Face to face, Creator,
And to let my just complaints
Open out before You
From my mouth.

Woe is me: I've forgotten!
I can't remember
What I came to demand.
I've forgotten.
Woe is me.

➤ *In Spite*

You say:
"You are a Jew and a poet
And you've written no poems
On the destruction.
How can a Yiddish poet not,
When the destruction is enormous,
So enormous?"

פּשוט:

אױף צולהכעיס די פֿאַרװײסטער.

אױף צולהכעיס װעל איך ניט װײנען בפֿרהסיא.

אױף צולהכעיס

אױף פּאַפּיר ניט אױפֿשרײַבן

מײַן טרױער.

(אַ בושה אױפֿצושרײַבן

"טרױער" אױף פּאַפּיר)

אױף צולהכעיס

װעל איך אַרומגײן אין דער װעלט װי

זי געװען װאָלט מײַנע.

אָודאַי מײַנע !

װעמעס דען ?

װעט מען מיר שטערן,

פֿאַרצױמען מיר די װעגן

װעט זי נאָך אַלץ זײַן מײַנע.

װאָדען — ניט מײַנע ?

אױף צולהכעיס װעל איך ניט יאָמערן

װען אַפֿילו

די ערד פֿון מײַן װעלט זאָל חלילה

מיר װערן די גרײס

װי מײַן זױל װאָס שטײט אױף איר

װעט זי נאָך אַלץ זײַן

מײַנע !

אױ

נאָך װי מײַנע.

אױף צולהכעיס

װעל איך חתונה מאַכן קינדער

אַז זײ זאָלן אױך האָבן קינדער.

אױף צולהכעיס די רשעים װאָס פֿלאָדיען זיך

אין מײַן װעלט

און מאַכן זי מיר

ענג.

Simple:
In spite of the destroyers,
To spite them I will not cry openly,
I will not write down my sorrow
On paper.
(A degradation to write
"Sorrow" on paper.)
To spite them
I'll walk the world
As if the world were mine.
Of course it's mine!
If they hindered me,
Fenced in my roads,
The world would still be mine.

To spite them I will not wail
Even if (God forbid) my world becomes
As big as where my sole stands—
The world will still be mine!

To spite them
I'll marry off my children
That they shall have children—
To spite the villains who breed
In my world
And make it narrow
For me.

Abraham Walkowitz: from
Ghetto Motifs, 1946.

◄ חלום

מויל פון פֿאַרחתמעטן ברונעם
בגוואַלד אויפגעריסן.
איך האָב דאָרט אין זילבערן לויטער
מײַן פּנים געפֿונען.
און איך האָב מײַן פּנים געטרונקען,
געטרונקען,פֿאַרטרונקען
דעם דאָרשט צו מײַן פּנים
אין ברונעם
דערטרונקען.

◄ באַהיט

באַהיט מיך
חלילה כ׳זאָל זאָגן
אַט איצטער
אין רײַפקייט פון יאָרן:
שפּאַן אויס די פֿערדלעך, מיקיטאַ,
איך וויל שוין אין ערגעץ
ניט פֿאָרן.

באַהיט מיך
חלילה
אַזעלעכס כ׳זאָל זאָגן.

◄ אויס און ווידערווערן

ס׳טרעפֿט מיט מיר אַ ״ווערן-אויס״:
פון וועלט אַרויס,
פון זיך אַרויס
אָן שרעק,
אָן פֿרייד,
אָן זיפֿץ, אָן טרער —
אויס.

פלוצלינג
ווי אַ ניַי-געבערן
קומט אַ ״ווידערווערן״,
קומט מיט פֿרומער פֿרייד

► *Dream*

Mouth of the sealed well
Forcibly broken open.
There, in silver clarity
I found my face.
And I drank in my face,
Drank in,
Got drunk on
The thirst for my face
Drowned
In the well.

► *Keep Me*

Keep me
From saying
Right now
In the ripeness of years:
Unharness the horses, Mikita,
I don't want to go
Anywhere.

Keep me
From saying
Such things.

Mikita—a Ukranian name
indicating a coachman in the
poetess' childhood landscape.

► *Out and In Again*

It happens with me that I become out—
Out of the world
Out of self
No fear
No joy
No sigh, no tear—
Out.

Suddenly
Like a new birth
A Becoming-Again
Comes with pious joy

און טרערן
ווי כ׳וואָלט דעם שבת-קודש
אין מיטן-וואָך
אין שטוב ביי זיך דערזעֶן.

און איך בענטש דעם ווידערוועֶרן.
ס׳איז אַלע מאָל מיר ערשטיק-ניי
און שטרענג
און רחמימדיק
און טוט רחמימדיק מיר ווי.

און איך שמייכל (1983)

◀ רודף מיינער

שטילערהייט —
שטילינקערהייט
מיינע רייד,
כּדי
דו זאָלסט זיך אָנשטרענגען
מיך הערן.

מיר איז זייער נייטיק
דו
זאָלסט מיך דערהערן.

דו?
און ווער ביסטו, גערודפטער,
רודף מיינער
דו?
נייג זיך צו מיין שטילקייט צו
און הער זיך צו,
רודף מיינער
דו.

◀ היימלאָז

גאָט
האָט אויפגעבויט אַ וועלט
און
האָט ניט ווו צו נעכטיקן.

And tears
As if in my house I beheld
The holy Sabbath
In the middle of the week.

And I bless the Becoming-Again
Always as new as the first time,
As strict
And merciful—
And mercifully it hurts.

AND I SMILE (1983)

➤ *My Persecutor*

Quietly—
So quietly
My speech,
So that
You shall strain
To hear me.

I need
You to
Hear me.

You?
And who are you, persecuted one,
My persecutor
You?
Bow to my silence
And listen,
My persecutor
You.

➤ *Homeless*

God
Built a world
And
Has no place to stay overnight.

א

‫— — — און איך בין אַנטלאָפן,‬
‫אין מײַן חלום-לאַנד אַרײַנגעלאָפן,‬
‫און דער בײזער חלום‬
‫איז מיר נאָכגעלאָפן —‬
‫אַ יאָר אַ גאַנצן מיך פאַרפאָלגט‬
‫אין מײַן חלום-לאַנד.‬

ב

‫און די גרויסע זין מײַנע‬
‫זיי שרײַבן:‬
‫— — — דו ביסט אַוועק.‬
‫מיר האָבן דײַנע גיכע טריט‬
‫דיר נאָכגעקוקט,‬
‫צום ערשטן מאָל דערזען‬
‫סאַראַ קלייניקע דו ביסט,‬
‫געחידושט זיך‬
‫ווי גיך סע קענען לויפן דײַנע קליינע פיס.‬
‫פאַרלאָזענע‬
‫דיר נאָכשרײַען געוואָלט,‬
‫נאָך איין מאָל אויפכאפן דײַן בליק,‬
‫נאָר דו האָסט זיך ניט אומגעקוקט צוריק...‬
‫איצט‬
‫שוין צײַט:‬
‫קער זיך אום.‬
‫די ווײַט‬
‫וואָס ליגט צווישן אונדז‬
‫איז טויב און שטום‬
‫און דו ביסט דאָרטן‬
‫אויך אַליין.‬
‫קום! דאָרט ווו ס׳זעענען דײַנע זין‬
‫דאָרטן איז דײַן היים.‬

ג

‫אין עראָפלאַן:‬
‫מיט פאַרמאַכטע אויגן‬
‫שטיל אין זיך פאַרטוקט‬
‫אָטעמענדיק טיף אַרײַן-אַרויס,‬
‫טוט מײַן אָטעם פרום אַזוי מתפלל:‬

I

—And I ran away,
Ran into my dreamland,
And the bad dream
Ran after me—
Followed me a whole year
In my dreamland.

II

And my big sons
Write:
—You left.
We watched
Your swift steps,
Noticing for the first time
How tiny you are,
Marveling at
How swiftly your small feet can run.
Feeling abandoned
We wanted to call after you,
To catch your glance once more,
But you didn't look back . . .
Now
It's time!
Return.
The distance
Between us
Is deaf and dumb
And, you, too, are there,
Alone.
Come!
Wherever your sons are,
There is your home.

III

In the airplane:
With closed eyes,
Quiet, sunk into myself,
Breathing deeply in and out,
My breath piously says this prayer:

גיב מיר, טאַטע זיסער,
נאָך אַ פינעף יאָר —
שטילע פינעף יאָרעלעך באַשער,
אַ ביסל רו באַשער.

ד

איצטער
יאָרן זיבן שפּעטער:
איך זע דעם שאָטן פון זײַן בּרעם.
(ווי די וועלט
איז גרויס דער שאָטן פון זײַן בּרעם)
איך זע
דער ״איך בּין״ שמייכלט צו מײַן טרער:
דו גענאַרניצע,
האָסט געוואוסט אַז
דו וועסט וועלן מער

און מער — — —

Sweet Father, give me
Another five years—
Grant me five quiet years,
A bit of rest.

IV

Now
Seven years later:
I see the shadow of His brow.
(The shadow of His brow
Is as wide as the world)
I see
The "I Am" smile at my tear:
You faker,
You knew that
You would want more
And more—

Berysh Vaynshteyn

1905–1967

Berish Vaynshteyn's* first book of poetry, *Brukhshtiker* ("junk"—literally, "broken pieces"), with its rough surface, elliptical and uncouth syntax, Galician dialectical expressions, and rich naturalistic American details in a surrealist composition, was a tour de force of expressionistic poetry about the lower depths of New York.

Vaynshteyn was born in Reyshe (Rzeszow), Galicia. At the age of eighteen he went to Vienna, and at twenty he settled in New York. Like many of his contemporaries, the Holocaust brought him back to writing about his hometown in the old country and its Hassidic milieu. Vaynshteyn's trilogy of epic, book-length poems encompasses his three homelands: *Reyshe* (1947; later translated into Hebrew), *America* (1955), and *In King David's Estates* (1960), which describes Israel as the imaginary biblical land of his childhood and the land in which his children settled.

The poems of *Broken Pieces* (1936) were included in Vaynshteyn's better known book of *Poems* (1949). They were, however, severely edited and lost some of their original roughness as well as a number of important descriptive details (including some ethnic remarks). Here the original text has been restored.

*Also Weinstein.

Berysh Vaynshteyn, 1949.

◄ אינעם באָרט

אויף שטיינערנע דילן ליגן שווערע שטריק מיט שטאָלענע אַנקערס;
קאַסטנס, באַלן און הויכע שטויסן געפּאַקטע זעק.
ס׳ליגן אַנגעוואָרפענע קופערטן מיט רייכע מעשענע שלעסער,
נאָפט-פעסער און גערייפטע הילצערנע פעסער מיט אײַזן-בעטאָן,
און פון די ווענט שלאָגט קילער ריח פון אויסלענדישע סחורות.

ס׳ציִען ברייטע לאַסט-שיפן פון שערבורג און פון האַווער,
מיט טונקעלע, פּראַנצייזישע געזיכטער פון יונגע מאַטראָסן
וואָס זענען פלינק און האָבן גרינגע פיס צו קלעטערן אויף הויכע שטריק.
פון שטענדיקן פאָרן, ווייסן זיי סימנים פון וואָלקנס, שטורעמס און רעגנס,
און קענען רופן סיגנאַלן בײַ נאַכט אין ווינט אויפן ים.

פּעליאַקן, נעגערס, איטאַליענער און שטאַרקע ייִדן לאָדענען סחורות;
זייערע אַקסלען טראָגן שאַרפע האַקנס, אויף די לענדן אַנגעהאָנגען בינטלעך עסנס,
די קליידער זייערע, לעדערנע פאַרטעכער, האַרטע שטרוקסענע העמדער.
די שטאַרקסטע זענען די, וואָס האָבן געשפּאַנטע בײַכער, פעסטע הענט מיט דיקע פינגער;
די הויטן פון זייערע פינגער זענען צעריסן פון שטריק און צענאָגלטע קאַסטנס,
און זענען געל, גראָב, אָפּגעשיילט ווי קלאָאַן פון פערד.

פרעמדלענדישע שיפן פאַראַנקערן דעם באָרט און שפּאַרן פון זיך די וואַסערן אין ווינט.
ס׳שטײַגן אָפּ אויסלענדישע געזיכטער, גערמאַנען און ייִדן מיט אָנגעשראָקענע קינדער,
זייערע קליידער זענען באַהאָנגען מיט אָנגעטשעפּעטע נעמען צו אַ קרוב, צו אַ גאַס,
און די פּנימער שטומען הינטער שטאַכעטן, הינטער שווערער קעלט פון גראַטעס, —
גראַטעס פון דיסציפּלינירטן פּחד פאַר מונדירן און שטרענגען קאַלענדער-גורל.

אויף שטיינערנע דילן ליגן שווערע שטריק מיט שטאָלענע אַנקערס;
היימישע קושין מיט אַנגעוואָרפענע ציגלען פון גרענעצן און לענדער.
אינעם באָרט גלאַנצט דער ברוקיר, אויסגעווינטיקט פון טריט און פראַכט-וועגעלעך.
פונעם האָפן נעפּלט טונקל דער וואָקזאַל, שויבן ווערן אָוונטיק שווער,
און פון די ווענט שלאָגט קילער ריח פון אויסלענדישער סחורה.

► *On the Docks*

The title of the book means
"junk," literally "broken pieces."
We have kept the name, "Junk,"
for the poem of that title.

On stone floors lie heavy ropes with steel anchors,
Crates, bales and high piles of bulging sacks.
Chests with rich, brass locks lie scattered about,
Oil barrels and hooped wooden casks filled with reinforced concrete,
And the walls give off a cool smell of goods from foreign lands.

Wide cargo-ships pull in from Cherbourg and Le Havre
With dark French faces of young sailors,
Agile and light for climbing on high ropes.
Their endless voyages have taught them to read signs of clouds and storms and
    rains,
They know how to call their signals out at night in the winds of the sea.

Poles, Negroes, Italians, and sturdy Jews load merchandise;
Their shoulders carry sharp hooks, on their waists hang bundles of food,
Their clothes: leather aprons, rough burlap shirts.
The strongest have tense bellies, powerful hands with thick fingers,
Their skin, torn by ropes and nailed crates,
Is yellow and coarse, cracking like the hooves of horses.

Ships from foreign places anchor at the docks, thrust the waters into the wind.
Immigrant faces disembark, Germans and Jews with frightened children,
On their clothes hang pinned-on names of a relative, of a street;
The faces are mute behind iron spikes, behind the heavy cold of bars,
Bars of disciplined fear before uniforms and rigid calendar-destiny.

On stone floors lie heavy ropes with steel anchors,
Familiar baskets with scattered seals of borders and countries.
At the docks the pavement is shining, eroded by footsteps and cargo-carts.
From the harbor looms the dark mist of a railway station, panes grow heavy with
    evening,
And the walls give off a cool smell of goods from foreign lands.

◀ מאַטראָסן

מאַטראָסן האָבן אַ האַרץ, וואָס בענקט נאָך באַנען, מענטשן און שטעט;
זייערע אויגן האָבן זיך אין די ווילדקייט פון ים, ווייטקייט פון לענדער.
פאַר בענקשאַפט — הענגען איבער זייערע בעטן בילדער פון האַפנשטעט,
פאַטאָגראַפיעס פון אַ לאַכנדיקער מיידל וואָס איז קלוגער פון אַן עלטערער שוועסטער,
און די מאַטראָסן איז גרינג צו טראַכטן, אויפן געלעגער ווען ס׳לײַב ווערט האַרט,
פון געבלומטע זאָקן-בענדלעך אויף יונגע קני, וואָס שלאַנקען אומרויִק,
און פון פעסטע קאָרסעטן, וואָס מאַכן בריסטיק די צײַטקייט פון אַ מיידלס לײַב.

ערגעץ אויפן ים, זילבערן זייערע פנימער דער לבנה אַנטקעגן אין אַ יום-טוב-נאַכט;
אויסגעזעצט אויפן דיל אין ווײַסע מאַרינאַרקעס, מיט די פיס פאַרלייגט ווי כינעזער
און מיט צעפלאַמטע ליפן, האַרט איינער דעם אַנדערן אַרומגענומען ווי אַ פרוי,
ס׳רײַסן זיך פון זיי ניגונים דורך היייזעריקער לופט, דאָס געדעכעניש צו אַ מאַמע,
וואָס גייט אַרום געבויגן מיט שוועַרע קוישן אויף בײַדע אָרעמס,
האַזירן איבער פרעמדע האַפן-שטעט, די אויגן אויפגעהויבן צום הימל,
און זוכט ס׳פנים פון אַ זון, פון אַ טאַכטער אין אויפגעהויבענעם רויך פון שיפן.

מאַמעס פון מאַטראָסן זענען שוואַכע, נידריקע, וואָס צערטלען די ערד מיט זייערע טריט,
און האָבן אַ טבע צו געבן דער וועלט שטאַרקע זין, געזונטע טעכטער;
די מאַנסבילן זייערע — הויך און ברייט מיט האַריקע הענט,
שוועַרע, רויטע נעז, בײַזע ברעמען און האַרטע, ווילדע בערד.

Louis Lozowick: *Mid Ocean,*
1930.

➤ *Sailors*

Sailors have hearts that yearn for trains and crowds and cities;
Their eyes hold the wildness of the sea, the farness of countries.
Out of longing—over their beds hang pictures of port cities,
Photographs of a laughing girl, smarter than an older sister.
In bed, when the flesh is hard, sailors think with ease
Of flowery garters on young knees, restlessly slender,
And of stiff corsets which make breasty the ripeness of a girl's body.

Somewhere on the sea, their faces silver toward the moon on a holiday night;
Sitting on the floor in white jackets, their legs folded like Chinese,
With hot lips, one hugging the other hard like a woman,
Their melodies break forth through the hoarse air, the memory of a mother
Who wanders around, stooped over, with heavy baskets on both arms,
Peddling through foreign port-cities, her eyes lifted to the sky,
Seeking the face of a son, a daughter, in the rising smoke of ships.

Mothers of sailors are tiny, weak women, caressing the earth with their steps.
They are used to giving the world strong sons and healthy daughters;
Their menfolk are tall and broad, with hairy hands,
Heavy, red noses, angry eyebrows and rough, wild beards.

מאַטראָסן האָבן אַ האַרץ, וואָס בענקט נאָך מענטשן, באַנאַן און שטעט.

אין די שטעט שפּאַצירן זיי אויסגעפּוצט אין רונדע, ווייסע קעלנער,

בלאָע מונדירן און ברייטע, לאַנגע הויזן אויף קליינע פֿיס.

מיט דער ווילדקייט פֿון ים גלוסטן זיי צו מיידלעך מיט שעמעוודיקע אויגן,

וואָס זיצן טיף אין שויס, פֿאַרלייגט אַ פֿוס אויף אַ פֿוס און ציטערן מיט די קני.

הענט וואָס אַנקערן שיפֿן, ליגן שווער אויף אומרויקע מיידלישע היפֿטן,

אויף הייסע אַקסלען און ענגע דעקאָלטן פֿון וואַרעמען, דורכזיכטיקן זייַד;

ווילדע קושן נאָגן די וואַרצלען פֿון זייער בוזעם, די פֿינגער פֿון די הענט,

און קילן דעם בלאָנד פֿון זייערע קני אין אָוונט-שאַרך פֿון יולי-בלעטער.

און ס'בלוטיקט די רייפֿקייט פֿון שיינע טעכטער אין אַ האַפֿנשטאָט.

► מייַן גאַס — שיפּסהעד בעי

רעגן. טונקעלע נאַכט.

ווינטן שוועטקען אָפּ דעם רעש פֿון שווערער נעץ.

רינשטאָקן רוישן מיט שנעלן אָפּפֿלוס איבער נאַבעלן אַספֿאַלט.

אויף נאַסן טראָטואַר גלאַנצט פֿאַרביק אָפּגעשלאָגן ליכט פֿון אויסלאָגן.

אויטאָס טראָגן זיך געשווינד, גליטשיק און גרינג.

נאָך די רעדער יאָגט אויפֿגעבלאָזענער שוים.

רעגן. שאָטנס פֿון אָפּגעשטאָנענע ביימער אויף אָוונטיקע שויבן.

ראָסטיקע פֿעלדער מיט אָנגעוואָרפֿענעם ברוכוואַרג,

און באַן-שינעס מיט שטאָלענער ווייַטקייט.

אויף אויסגעוויוקטע שטרעקעס בלאָטיקן פֿוסגייער,

פֿישערס מיט פֿאַרוואָרפֿענע ווענטקעס אויף אַקסלען,

אין האַרטע רעק, מיט פֿאַרלאָפֿענעם רעגן אויף נאָנטן געזיכט.

פֿון די געסלעך יאָגט שטילע פֿאַרע און רירט דעם פֿראָסט פֿון די שטיינער.

שטיקער אייַז ברעכן זיך נאַכגעביק אונטער די טריט.

פֿון פֿישער-האָפֿן שמעקט נאַסער קוילן-גריז, סמאָלע און צוגעפוילטע קלעצער.

אַ פֿאַרלוירענער ים-פֿויגל באַוועגט די שפּעטע טונקל פֿונעם ברעג.

אין די פֿישער-בודקעס טליִען טריבע לעמפּלעך, קיסלוודיקע נאַכט.

בלעכענע באַליעס מיט אָנגעקלעפּטן בלוט.

טשערפּקע הענט קלאַפּן שווער מיט נאַסע שערן און לאַנגע, ברייטע מעסערס.

שנעקעס מונטערן זיך אויף אייַז, און קלעטערן גרינג איבערן ראַנד פֿון קויש,

ס'שווימען פֿיש, רויִק און סאַרטירט; פֿיאַווקעס — שלאַנק און שוימיק.

רויע פֿישערקעס, דורכגענומען פֿון זאַלץ און ווינט, קעלט און קאַוע,

מיט לאַכעדיקע פֿנימער, און געשפּאַנטע בריסט פֿון וואַרעמע דעקאָלטן,

שייַערן די פֿיש-קלעצער מיט קאַלטן וואַסער און פֿאַרלעשן די בודקעס.

שיפֿן ציִען אָפּ אין דער פֿינצטער פֿון אָוונט-באָרטן און צעוואַרפֿן די וואַסערן.

די כוואַליעס נעמען אָפּ ס'ליכט פֿון מיטגענומענע לאַמטערן,

און צעשווימען דעם ברעג, שטויסן די שיפֿן פֿון די אַנקערס.

Sailors have hearts that yearn for crowds and trains and cities.
In cities they stroll, dressed up in round, white collars,
In blue uniforms, and wide long trousers over thin legs.
With the wildness of the sea they lust for girls with bashful eyes,
Who sit deep in their laps, legs crossed, with trembling knees.

Hands that anchor ships lie heavily on restless hips of girls,
On hot shoulders and narrow cleavages in warm, transparent silk;
Wild kisses gnaw at the roots of their breasts, at the fingers of their hands
And cool off the dazzle of their knees in the evening rustle of July leaves.
The ripeness of beautiful daughters is bleeding is port-cities.

► *My Street—Sheepshead Bay*

Rain. Dark night.
Winds rinse away the noise of heavy wetness.
Gutters clatter in a rush of water over noble asphalt.
Wet sidewalks shimmer colorfully in the reflected light of shop windows.
Cars stream swift, slippery and light.
Whipped-up foam in the wake of their wheels.

Rain. Shadows of bare trees on evening windows.
Rusty fields, cluttered with junk,
And railroad tracks humming with steel distances.
Pedestrians sloshing through drenched wastes,
Fishermen with rods thrown over their shoulders,
In coarse jackets, rain swelling on their faces.
Quiet steam rises from the side-streets and touches the frost of the stones.
Pieces of ice break submissively underfoot.

The fishing harbor smells of damp coal-grease, tar and rotting logs.
A lost sea bird stirs the late darkness of the shore.
In the fishing huts smoulder bleak lamps, December nights,
Tin tubs plastered with blood.
Calloused hands pound heavily with wet shears and long wide knives.
Shrimp clamber on ice, climb easily over the rim of a basket,
Fish swim, calm and sorted; leeches—thin and foaming.

Raw fisherwomen, soaked in salt and wind, cold and coffee,
With laughing faces and taut breasts straining warm bodices,
Scrub the fishboards with cold water and put out the lights in the huts.
Ships depart in the dark from evening docks and plow the waters.
The waves pick up the light of ship-borne lanterns,
Foam up the shore and push the ships off their moorings.

נעגגערס

◀ נעגגעריש דאָרף

ס׳בליט דער הימל קאַלט און אויסגעשטערנט איבער נעגגערישע כאַטעס.
אָפּגערינענע וואַסערן פֿון מילדן שניי, גליווערן דין אין אַייז.
קוימענס שטײַגן רויכיק און טונקל, נאַפֿט-לעמפּלעך באַפֿלעמלען די שויבן,
און דורך די שויבן זינגען נעגגער אין אַ זונטיק, אין נעגגערישן דאָרף.

ס׳איז היימלעך אין נעגגערישן דאָרף אין אַ זונטיקדיקן ווינטער-אָוונט.
שוואַרצלײַב אין היַיסן זײַד, לאָקערן אויף שטראָזן נאָך אַ נעגגער יונג
און אַנטרינען גלוסטיקע מיט געלענדטע היפֿטן פֿון ווילדע הענט,
דורך שכונותדיקע פֿעלדער, וואָס שטייען האַרט און שווער מיט נאָמנטן ווינט.

אין נעגגערישן דאָרף, זענען קלוג די נעגגער וואָס ווייסן שוין פֿון גרויסע שטעט,
וואָס טראָגן קליידער מיט שטאַטישן שניט, און אַ וווּנד פֿון אַ ווילדן מעסער.
פֿון זייערע פֿיס רירט זיך ריטמישער דזשעז, גליטשיק און גרינג איבערן דיל.
נעגגערטעס זעצן זיך שעמעוודיק אויף זייערע קני, מיט אָפֿענע שויסן.

William Gropper: *Migration*,
c. 1932.

► *Negro Village*

The sky blooms cold and starry over Negro huts.
Waters run off the mild snow, freeze thinly into ice.
Chimneys rise smoking and dark, kerosene lamps flicker in the windowpanes,
And through the windows Negroes sing on a Sunday in the Negro village.

A Negro village on a Sunday winter-evening feels like home.
Blackflesh in hot silk, lurking on roads for a Negro boy
And fleeing passionately with swaying hips from frenzied hands,
Through neighboring fields that stand hard and heavy with approaching wind.

In the Negro village, wise are the Negroes who know of big cities,
Who wear clothes of city cut and the wound of a savage knife.
From their feet moves rhythmical jazz, gliding and light over the floor.
Negresses sit bashfully on their knees, with open laps.

אין איטלעכן הויף, פאַר איטלעכער שוועל, ליגן רויִק געלאַסענע הינט,
די העלדזער אויסגעקראָכן, צוגעטשעפּעט צו אַ געפּונענע שטיק בראָקװאָרג;
זיי זענען באַרעמהאַרציק צו אַ דורכגייער און עסן פון אַ פרעמדער האַנט,
און מאַכן היימיש אַ מענטש, װאָס שטעלט זיך אָפּ אַ מאָל ביי נאַכט אין נעגערישן דאָרף.

אין װאַלד, העט הינטערן נעגערישן דאָרף, העט הינטערן נעגערישן צמענטאַש,
טליִען פייערן און שאַטענען אַפּ אויף ברייטע געזיכטער, שװערע קופּערנע הענט.
העק פּאַקען געשמאַק איבער ביימער, אין דורכזיכטיקן רויך,
און ס'ברעכן זיך שאַרפע צװייַען, טרוקן שפּרינגען אָפּ שפּענער אין דער נאַכט.

ס'שטייט אַן אָפּגעאַקערט אַזאַ װי אומעטום, ס'זינקט אַ קלויסטער אַזאַ װי אומעטום.
נאָר אויפן צמענטאַש אַ שװאַרצער קבר, אַ שװאַרצער גלאַט, שװאַרצע מתים.
אַ לװיה מיט אויפגעהויבענע אָרעמס, יעמערט פאַר אַן אָפּן קבר אין יעלהדיקער תפילה,
און קיל שמעקט די צעגראָבענע ערד מיט אַ פריש טרונעלע, מיט אַ פריש געשטאָרבן קינד.

ס'דאָרף טרויערט דורך שיכורת, דורך פּאָרקעט און דורך מילדער שטאַמלונג.
ס'טראָגט קיינער אויף קיינעם נישט קיין קללה, אויף אַלעמענס ליפן אַ שטילע באַגריסונג.
אַ נאָר־תמיד אויפן קייזערװועג לײַטערט "לינקאָלנס" געזיכט אין ליכטיקן טרויער
און ס'קוקן זײַנע אויגן אראָפּ מיט אַזוי פיל באַשערמונג צום נעגערישן דאָרף.

די לבנה גייט אויף אַ צעװאָרפענע אויף די פענצטער, אַ צעװאָרפענע איבער דעכער,
און גרינלעך־קיל, העלן אויף די שויבן; שומיק, װי אָװנטיק װאַסער אין װינט.
דורך אומעטיקע שפּיגלען אנטפּלעקט זיך אויסגעטאָן אַ פלוצעמדיק לײַב,
און ברוינלעך־שװער װערן די שטיבער ענג מיט װאַרעמען נעגערישן ריח.

ס'טאָגט אויף דער מאָרגן איבער מאַגערע פעלדער. קינדער קוויטיקן אין די װויגן.
טויבן רירן זיך פויל, קלאַפּן טרוקן מיט די פליגל און װאַרקען אויף נידעריקע נעסטן.
נעגערישע נאָנאַס אין קליידער אַזעלכע װי װייַסע, עפענען טרויעריק איטלעכנס טיר
און לאָזן נאָך זיך אַ שטיל ביסל עסן, אַ װאַרעם לײַב'ל און אַ געװאַשן העמדל.

פּונעם נעגערישן דאָרף ציִען קאַליקעס, און גייען זיך פונאַנדער אין פרעמדע שטעט.
די װאָס זענען שטום, בלינד, פירן מיט זיך אַ קינד, אַ װײַב, זאָל העלפן בעטן.
און די מיט צערונענע געזיכטער, מיט בלוטיקע אויגן און אויסגעשטאַרצטע ליפן,
צעשטעלן זיך רחמנותדיק אויף די ראָגן, פאַרגייען אין שיכורת און שטאַרבן קלוג.

פאַרטאָגיקער רויך טליִעט אויף אַ שטאָטיש פעלד אין אַ פאַרטאָגיקן דעצעמבער,
פרעמד צעהייצטער רויך פון אַ פרישן נעגעריִונג פון נעגערישן דאָרף.
פון זײַן געצעלט װײַעט צוגעריִרטער פּראָסט, קעלט פון ראָסטיק בלעך,
און אויף אָנגעקליבן האָלץ — טרוקענען קליידער, אַ װעסט און אַ היימיש העמד.

אין שטאָט גייט ער אום און שװערן װינט אַ פאַרלוירענער און קיינעמענס נישט.

In each yard, before each threshold, calm dogs lie quietly,
Their necks bald, tied to a stray piece of scrap.
They are merciful to the passer-by; they eat out of a stranger's hand;
A man who stops at night in the Negro village feels at home with them.

In the forest, far beyond the Negro village, far beyond the Negro cemetery,
Fires smoulder and cast shadows on broad faces, on heavy copper hands.
Axes wave gleefully over trees, in the transparent smoke,
Sharp branches break and slivers splinter dryly in the night.

A cross stands here as everywhere, a church as everywhere.
But in the cemetery a black undertaker, a black priest, black corpses.
A funeral with raised arms, wailing before an open grave in a lamenting prayer,
And a chill smell of dug-up earth with a fresh coffin, the fresh body of a child.

The village mourns in drinking, in awe and in mild stammering.
No one swears at anybody, on all lips a quiet greeting.
A memorial candle on the highway lights up "Lincoln's" face in bright mourning
And his protective eyes look down on the Negro village.

The moon rises scattered on the windows, scattered over the roofs,
The panes light up with a greenish chill, foamy like evening waters in the wind.
In sad mirrors emerges undressed a sudden body,
Brown-and-heavy grow the houses, dense with warm Negro smell.

The morning dawns over meager fields. Babies lie dirty in their cradles.
Doves move lazily, beat dryly with their wings and hum in low nests.
Negro nuns, clad like white ones, sadly open every door
And leave behind them a quiet bit of food, a warm undershirt, a clean blouse.

From the Negro village, cripples trudge off and scatter over alien cities,
Some that are mute or blind take with them a child, a wife, to help them beg.
And those with washed-out faces, with bloodshot eyes and protruding lips,
Stand pitifully at street corners, sink in drinking and die wisely.

➤ *Negro Geo'ge*

Early morning smoke smoulders over a city field in a December dawn,
Alien smoke fueled by a Negro boy fresh from a Negro village.
From his tent blows hoarfrost, the chill of rusty tin;
On a pile of gathered wood, clothes are drying, a vest and a shirt from home.

In the city he walks around in the heavy wind, lost and belonging to no one.

ס׳צעשיטן זיך זײַנע טריט אין שניי, פֿון זײַנע אויגן צעפֿאַלט טריפֿנדיקע קעלט,
און אויפֿן געזיכט טרײבט ס׳ליכט פֿון פֿאַנאָרן, דער רייץ פֿון שויפֿענצטער.
ס׳באַגריסט אים קיינער נישט; מע פֿרעגט זיך בײַ אים אפֿילו אויף קיין גאַס נישט אָן.

אַ צעקנעפֿלטער, אין אַ געפֿונענעם קאַפֿעליוש וואָס אַ זאַווערוכע האָט עמעצן פֿאַרבלאָזן,
שפֿרייַזט ער לעם עלעגאַנטע רינשטאַקן און זאַמלט אָפֿפֿאַל פֿון גערויכערטע פֿאַפֿיראַסן.
און מיט אַ גוט אַ האַרץ צעוואָרפֿט ער זיי אויף הינטער שוועלן וווּ ס׳נעכטיקן בעטלער.
די וואָס זענען וווּנדיק און שלאָף, פֿירט ער צו זיך אַהיים אויפֿן שטאַטישן פֿעלד.

זײַנע ליפֿן זענען טרויעריק ווי ס׳נעגערישע דאָרף און שילטן די שרעק פֿון שטאָט.
ס׳שטומט אין אים ס׳בלוט פֿונעם טאָטן פֿעטערסאָן, די לעגענדע פֿון זײַנע זיידעס.
פֿון זײַן לײַב רירט זיך די בײַטיש, וואָס האָט זײַנע זיידעס אויפֿן מאַרק פֿאַרטריבן,
אין דער זון דעם טויט דערזעןם, און אויף די בײַוול-פֿעלדער שוואַרץ אויסגעשטאָרבן.

ר׳איז מיט גרימצאָרן אין דער שטאָט אַוועק צו געשטאַלטיקן איטלעכן ווי זיך.
זײַנע גלידער רײַסן זיך צו באַשאַפֿן מענטשן טונקעלע ווי זײַן לעגענדע,
שוואַרץ ווי זײַן מאַמע, ווי זײַן שוועסטער, ס׳איז וווּילד אין אים די זרע
צו באַרוכפֿערן אַ פֿרוי אויף צו געברן לײַבער אַ סך פֿאַר אַ שוואַרצער וועלט.

ניו-יאָרק איז אָבער שטאַרקער ווי אַ לעגענדע, אַזעלכע ווי ער שטאַרבן אָן טרויער,
און אויף ס׳נײַ מוז ער טאָגן אויפֿן מאַרק פֿונעם עמעץ וואָס אים דינגען פֿאַר אַ ביסל געקעכץ.
ער ווערט באַרעמהאַרציק צו זײַנע שכנים וואָס שטיַען מיט אים בײַנאַנד אויף דער זון,
און די גלידער זײַנע רײַסן זיך שוין מער נישט אַזוי הייס, נאָר ווערן ווייך מיט גענאָד.

ס׳האָט די שטאָט געשטילט ס׳פֿײַער פֿון זײַנע אויגן און די היימישקייט פֿון דאָרף,
איצט איז ער רחמנותדיק מיט אַ טרויעריק געזיכט, יונג-געשפֿראַכצטע האָר,
און לויטערט ווי אַ לעגענדע מיט אַ פֿאַרהוילענער נקמה פֿאַר די טאָטעס פֿון קאַראָלײַנע.
בײַ נאַכט גייט ער אויף ווי אַ חלום, און זאַלבט זיך פֿאַרן שוואַרצן דערלייזער.

אונטער אַ מאָנטנעם הימל אָן זון, אָן וואָלקנס, מילד מיט שווערן נאַסן שניי;
בלאָטיקן זײַנע העענט אין מיסטגראַבנס. און קאַפֿען אויף אַ נוצלעך שטיק אַלטוואַרג,
אַן איבערגעקליבעניעם שוך, אַ פֿאַרזעענעם מלבוש, אָדער האָלץ פֿון צעגראַבענער ערד.
פֿאַר זײַן געצעלט וואָרטן צענויפֿגעזאַמלטע קליידער, צו דערנערן אַ מענטש פֿון קעלט.

צו זײַן געצעלט אויפֿן פֿעלד, צי׳ען זיך שלעפֿערס, פֿרויען, שוואַרצע און ווײַסע,
און ער האָט פֿאַר זיי קיין גאָט נישט, ער קען פֿון זיי קיין תפֿילה נישט נעמען,
ר׳האָט בלויז דעם גאָב אַוועקצושענקען ס׳ביסל אָפֿגעשפֿאַרט עסן פֿון לײַטיש מיסט.
די רייד זײַנע זענען ווי בײַ אַלע נעגערס, אָן טרייסט, נאָר מיט אַ האַרץ פֿון רחמים.

His steps scatter in the snow, dripping cold falls from his eyes,
On his face glooms the light of lanterns, the tease of shop windows.
No one greets him; they don't even ask him how to find a street.

Unbuttoned, in a stray felt hat that a blizzard blew off somebody's head,
He strides past elegant gutters and collects cigarette butts;
With a good heart, he drops them at back-doorsills where beggars sleep.
Those who are wounded and weak—he takes them home to the city field.

His lips are sad like the Negro village and curse the fear of the city.
The blood of father Patterson, the legend of his grandfather, is silent in him.
His body flinches from the whip that drove his grandfathers to market.
They saw death in the face of the sun. In cottonfields they died out blackly.

Enraged, he went to the city to shape everyone like himself.
His limbs burst to create people dark as his legend,
Black as his mother, as his sister, the seed is wild in him
To fertilize a woman to bear many bodies for a black world.

But New York is stronger than a legend, people like him die without mourning,
And again he must dawn at the market for someone to hire him for a warm meal.
He becomes gracious to his neighbors standing with him in the sun
And his limbs don't burst anymore so hotly but grow soft with forgiveness.

The city cooled the fire of his eyes and his village homeyness,
Now he is full of pity, wears a sad face, young-sprouting hair,
And brightens like a legend with a hidden vengeance for the fathers from
     Carolina.
At night he rises like a dream and anoints himself for the black savior.

Under a murky sky without sun, without clouds, mild with heavy wet snow,
His hands are mud in garbage bins. They dig up a useful piece of junk,
A cast-off shoe, a forgotten garment, or wood from upturned earth.
Before his tent, a heap of clothes waiting to feed a man from the cold.

Drifters, women, black and white, trudge to his tent in the field,
And he has no god for them, he would not take any prayer from them,
He has only the gift of giving away the bit of saved-up food from people's
     garbage.
His talk is like that of all Negroes, with no consolation, but with a heart of pity.

כאָטש די זון וואָס שפּאַרט אָן אויף זײַן געצעלט, איז ווי די זון פון דאָרף

איז עס אָבער די זון, וואָס פירט אים אַרום צווישן מויערן אין דער העלער שטאָט

און פאַרוואַרפּט אים אויף אַ רויישיקן ראָג מיט אַ נאַריש פּנים און בעטנדיקע ליפּן

און די אויגן זײַנע זוכן אַ מענטש פון דער קעלט צו פאַרקריפּן ס'הײמישע העמד.

◄ "לאָנדרי"

קרימענס אין ווײַסן בלעך בלאַנקען מיטאָגדיק אונטער אַ הויכער זון,

און מאַכן סוחרדיק די גאַס, גרויסשטעטיש דעם האָדסאָן און די האָפּנס.

די לאָנדרי בײַם האָדסאָן האָט אַ סך אַזעלכע קרימענס, אַלע רויכערן מיט אַ מאָל,

זיי שרײַען ווילד צו דער גאַס און איבער צעראויכערטע אויסלענדישע באַרטנס.

שווערע פענצטער אויף די שויבן זעצן אויס די פּײכטקייט פון צעפּאַרעטע וועש.

נעגערישע הענט פאַרוואוישן דעם ריח פון ברויד; העמדער ווערן ווײַס און עלעגאַנט.

אונטער שוואַרצע הענט בלאַנדעט ווײַסער די האַרטיקייט פון קראָכמאַליעטע לײַוונט,

בוזעמס בויגן זיך שוואַרץ פון פּרעס און באַריִרן די הייִמישקייט פון פרעמדע וועש.

ס'איז טונקל. ווענט זעגנען שווייסיק-שווער און רינען ווי פעלדזן אין נעפּל.

פאַראַן בלויז ליכט, וויפל ס'שלאָגט צוריק פון ווײַס צעהאַנגענע לײַלעכער.

אינעם ליכט גיסט אויס טונקעלער שווײַס אויף עלבויגנס און געזיכטער.

אויף די שטריק — ווײַסער שרעק; אָפענע אויגן קוקן שטום און ערגעץ נישט.

ברײַטע אויגן, ווילדע נעז מיט נאַז פולע ליפן און דיקע פלײַשיקע לענדן.

אייזנס טראָגן דעם כוח פון נעגערישע אָרעמס, פלינקייט פון יונגע פינגער;

קאָלנערס לויפן אָפּ שטײַף מיט שנעלער פאַרע, ווי וואָרעמער שטויב אין ווינט.

אין האַלבן טאָג מונטערן אויף די וועשערינס טרויעריק און קיל אויף טראָטואָרן.

אין דער שעה פון הויכער זון בענקען זיי רויִק צום נעגערישן דאָרף.

אויף זיי איז שווער צו דערקענען צי די פּנימער זייערע בלײַכן אָדער צערן.

אַז זיי מאָגערן, ווערן ברײַטער נאָך די נעז און שווערער הענגען די ליפן.

נעגערס האָבן אַ טבע צו בײַטן די הויט ווען ס'רינט פון זיי בלוט.

אין טונקעלן אָפּגרונט פון נעץ, פלאַמען קעסלען מיט געשמאַקן גלי און היץ;

נאַקעטע הענט פון הוילע נעגערישע ברוסטן וואַרפן האָריק גענעצטע קוילן.

פון שווערן פײַער גלאַנצן לײַבער דער אָפענער הין אַנטקעגן און בריִען מיט בראָנד.

טרוקן ברעכן זיך דורכגעברענטע הויטן נאָך איטלעכן בויג פון רידל.

וואַרעמע רימענס יאָגן אויף און ווילד שטאָל אויף שטאָל רויטע אַקסלען מיט טריפּן מיט אויל.

איטלעכעס מאָל טריפּט אָפּ אַ פרישער טראָפּן און צערינט איבער שלײַפן פון נעגערס,

און מ'ווייסט נישט צי ס'איז בוימל, צי אויסגעשלאָגענער שווייס וואָס רינט אַזוי,

וואַרעם די גופים גלאַנצן סיווי ווי קופער — ווי די הויט אויף אַלע נעגערס.

Though the sun leaning on his tent is like the sun in the village,
It is still the sun that leads him among walls in the bright city
And throws him into a noisy corner with a stupid face and begging lips,
And his eyes look for a man coming out of the cold to sell him his shirt from home.

➤ *Laundry*

White-tin chimneys shimmer in midday under a high sun,
Make the street commercial, the Hudson and the harbors big-city-like.
The laundry at the Hudson is covered with chimneys, all smoking at once,
They shout wildly to the street and above smoke-filled foreign-import docks.

Heavy windows, on their panes settles the mist of steaming wash.
Negro hands scrub off the smell of dirt, shirts become white and elegant.
The hardness of bleached linen glows whiter under black hands,
Bosoms bend blackly from the irons and touch the homeyness of strangers'
    underwear.

It's dark. Walls heavy with sweat, streaming like rocks in fog.
There is only the light reflected from white hung-out sheets.
In such light, dark sweat pours out on elbows and faces.
On ropes—white fear; open eyes look mutely into nowhere.

Wide eyes, flaring noses over full lips and thick fleshy waists.
Irons carry the force of Negro arms, the agility of young fingers;
Collars run off stiff with fast steam like warm dust in the wind.
At midday the laundresses cheer up, sad and cool on the sidewalk.

In the hour of high sun they long peacefully for the Negro village.
No sign whether their faces have gotten pale or wasted.
When they grow leaner, their noses are wider, lips hang heavier.
Negroes have a habit of changing their skin when they bleed.

In the dark abyss of wetness, cauldrons flame with a zesty glow and heat;
Naked arms from bare hairy chests throw wet coals.
From the heavy fire their bodies gleam against the open heat, seared in the blaze.
Their scorched skins crack dryly after each bow of the shovel.

Above red shoulders warm belts drive wildly over steel and drip with grease;
Fresh drops incessantly drip and spread on the temples of Negroes,
And you don't know if it's oil that flows or sweat that breaks out,
Their bodies glisten anyway like copper—like the skin on all Negroes.

פֿון די קעסלען זידט דער ריח פֿון געטראָגענעם גרעט און ס׳שמעקט פֿון בעט, לײַב.
נאַסע הענט פֿון פרוויען צײַלן פֿאַרזיכטיק פֿײַכטע שטויסן געוואַשענע בונטן.
זײַדענע בלוזן פֿון ווײַסע אַקסלען, פֿון גלאַטע דעקאָלטן און פֿלאַכע בריסט,
טראָגן נאָך שפּורן פֿון איידעלן פֿאַרפֿום, פֿון גלוסט און געפֿלעקטן שאַמפּיין.

אין דער לאַנדרי בײַם האָדסאָן צעפֿאַלט די פֿרישקייט פֿון נעגערישע דאָרפֿס-קינדער.
צו פֿיל היץ צענעמט זייער אָטעם און צעעפֿנט זייער מויל מיט שטילן פּראָכן.
זיי גאָרן נאָך טרייסט, נאָך רחמנות; מיט אַ סך גענאָד בענטשן זיי דעם זיידן פֿעטערסאָן
און זינגען בײַ די פֿרעסאַייזנס די זונטיקדיקע לידער פֿון נעגערישן דאָרף.

אַז שיפֿן טלעיען מיט רויקן רויך און ווײַטן ליכט איבערן שפֿעטן האָדסאָן,
קרײַזן זיי פֿרעמד אַרום אין ווילדע קליידער מיט אויגן וואָס שרעקן די ראָגן,
און נעמען היימלעכקייט פֿון איטלעכער גאַס, פֿון פֿאַנאַרן און פֿרעמדע געלעכטערס.
אַ מאָל שטרעקן זיי די הענט צו פֿאַרבינדן אַ וווּנד פֿון אַ שלעפֿער, פֿון אַ שיכור.

◄ האַרלעמער נעגערס

אָוונטן וואָס פֿאַרגעסן אַ מאָל צו צינדן די שטערן אויפֿן האַרלעמער הימל
רינען אָפּ פֿונעם עלוווייטער מיט טונקעלן רעגן און שטאָלענער פֿוילקייט,
און פֿירן נאַס אַהיים אַ שווערן נעגערישן טאַטן צו זײַן הויזגעזינד;
און אין זײַן שטוב פֿאַרען די וועגנט מיט אויפֿגעלייגטן ריח פֿון געקעכצן.

Ben Shahn: *Sharecropper's
Children on Sunday, Little Rock,
Arkansas*, October 1935.

The cauldrons boil with an odor of worn linens and smell of bed, of flesh.
Wet woman-hands count carefully damp heaps of laundered bundles.
Silk blouses off white shoulders, off smooth cleavages and flat breasts,
Still carry traces of subtle perfume, stains of lust and champagne.

In the laundry on the Hudson, the freshness of Negro village children falls apart.
So much heat weakens their breath and opens their mouths in quiet panting.
They long for comfort, for pity, with lots of mercy they bless their grandfather
    Patterson
And sing over the irons the Sunday songs of the Negro village.

When ships smoulder with peaceful smoke and distant light over the evening
    Hudson,
They circle, alien, in strange clothes, with eyes that scare street-corners,
And take in the homeyness of every street, of street lamps and strangers'
    laughter.
Sometimes they reach out a hand to bandage the wound of a bum, or a drunkard.

► *Harlem Negroes*

Evenings that sometimes forget to light up the stars over Harlem's sky
Stream off the El with dark rain and steel rot
And take a wet heavy Negro father home to his family,
And in his home the walls steam with the inviting smell of cooking.

העכט וואָס ציִען מעבל דורך הויכע פענצטער פאַרציִען ס׳שלאָפצימער מיט ראָלעטן
און גלאָסטן צו ברייַטע בעטן, צו אַ געשפּאָנטן קאָרסעט פול מיט שוואַרץ־לייַב.
אין דער פינצטער בייַ זיי נאַכט זענען בלמילאַ אַלע אַלע לייַבער שוואַרץ און ווילד,
און נעגרעס, צווישן זיך, ווייַסן שוין וועלכעס פּנים פון אַ נעגערטע איז שיין.

פון אַזאַ נאַכט, פון אַזאַ פשוטער גלאָסטונג וואַקסן אויס האַרלעמער נעגער־יונגען;
טעכטער וואָס ווייסן, אַזוי ווי ווייַסע, צו פאַרציִען אַ היפּט פאַר אַ מאַן אין גאַס
און קענען שטייַפן דעם גוף, וואַרפן די ברוסט מיט רייַך אונטער זיידענע בראָזירן
ריטמיש פאַר באַזאַפענע מענער, מיט הייסן געזאַנג פון נעגערישע מעלאָדיעס.

האַרלעמער נעגער־יונגען זענען שטאַטישער ווי אַנדערע פון אומעטום ניו־יאָרק.
זיי זענען בלייַך־הויטיק און טראָגן שטענדיק אַ געפּרעסטע הויז, אַ לאַקירטן שוך,
מאַנזשעטן מיט פערלמוטערנע קנעפּ, פרישע קראַגנס אויף אַ טונקל־געשוירענעם קאַרק,
און אויף די פינגער עלעגאַנטע רינגען, קלוגע מאַנירן נאָך ווייַסער באַהעפּטונג.

◄ לינטשינג

ס׳פאַרציִקן דיך ווייַסע ווילדע העגט, העגט מיט אַ געפּונענעם שטריק,
און ס׳קרייציקט אַ יולי־בוים דייַן נעגערישן אלדז;
אין זייַן שוערער רייַפקייַט, אין זייַן פולער בליונג.
אין דער סאַמער גרינקייַט פון בלעטער איז האַפּטיקער די צווייַג
זי ברעכט נישט אָפּ אונטער דער פעטליע.
דער זון אַנטקעגן קלעקט דייַן האַלדז מיט סמנים פון תּליונס פינגער,
בלעטער שלאָגן אויס ווי טוי ווי אַלעמאָל און רירן זיך לינד ווי אַלעמאָל;
און זיי פילן נישט אַז דאַס טרייסלט זיי אַ ווינט פון אַ געהאַנגענעם.

העכגסט שוואַרץ אין געשיינדענע קליידער.
די שאַנד דייַנע שטאַרבט אָפּ אָפּן און יונג.
גראָב שוערן אַראָפּ די פאַרלאָשענע ליפּן
און פאַר איטלעכנס אויגן שטומט דער בלאָנד פון דייַנע שטאַרקע ציין.

גאָט פאַר וועמען ס׳האָט געטערערט דייַן זינגענדיק געבעט אַזוי טרויעריק,
קען זיך פאַר דיר אַצינד נישט ווייַזן, ס׳שפּאָרן אים די פיס, די צוגענאָגלטע העכט,
ער קען אפילו נישט אַן אויג עפענען מיט אַ טרער נאָך דיר,
אָדער אָננעמען ס׳לעצטע וואָרט דייַנס פאַר אַ ווידוי, ר׳איז אַליין געקרייציקט.

נעגער!
ס׳בליט דייַן גוף אין אַ זומער־טאָג כאַטש דו העכגסט, כאַטש דו זעסט די זון נישט מער.
ס׳ווייַב דייַנס וואָס בעט אויס איר אָוונט אויף אַ זייַטיקער שוועל אין אַ גאַס,
און דעם טאַטן וואָס צײַלט שטיקער חלב איטלעכן פאַרטאָג אין אַ יאַטקע־וואָגן.

Hands that pull furniture through high windows
    pull curtains to close off a bedroom
And lust for wide beds, for a taut corset filled with black-flesh.
In the darkness at night all bodies anyway are black and wild,
And Negroes themselves know which face of a Negress is beautiful.

From such a night, from such a simple passion grow Harlem Negro guys;
Daughters who know, like white girls, how to shake a hip at a man in the street
And can tense their body, thrust a provocative breast under silk brassieres
Rhythmically at drunk men, with the hot song of Negro melodies.

Harlem Negro guys are more city-wise than others of everywhere New York.
They are pale-skinned and always wear pressed pants, lacquered shoes,
Cuffs with mother-of-pearl buttons, fresh collars on a dark-shaved neck,
And on their fingers elegant rings, clever manners after white copulation.

➤ *Lynching*

White wild hands snare you with a stray rope,
And a July tree crucifies your Negro neck,
In its heavy ripeness, in its full bloom.
In the thick of green leaves the branch is more pliant,
It does not break with the weight of a noose.
Your neck with marks of the hangman's fingers—blots in the sun.
Leaves break out in dew and sway gently as ever
And don't feel that they are shaken by the wind of a hanged man.

You hang black in flayed clothes.
Your drooping shame dies open and young.
The extinguished lips sag thickly
And the dazzle of your strong teeth—a mute challenge to all eyes.

Your singing prayer wept so mournfully to God,
But he won't appear to you, his legs burst, his nailed hands,
He cannot even open an eye with a tear for you
Or accept your last word as a confession—He's crucified Himself.

Negro!
Your body blossoms on a summer day though you hang, though you no longer
    see the sun,
Your wife making her evening bed on a back doorstep in a street
Or your father, counting pieces of suet in the morning on a meat wagon.

נעגער, ניט אויף דיר בלויז איז געפאַלן דער גורל פון פאַרלענדונג.
אַ סך, אַ סך, שטאַרבן אַזוי ווי דו, אַזאַ טויט איז איצט אַ מאַדע אַזאַ,
אַזוינאַך שטאַרבט מען היינט אומעטום — — —
אין ווערינג, אין דער לעאָפּאַלד-שטאַט און אין קאַראַליינע.

יונגען פון דער וואָליע

◄ יונגען פון דער וואָליע

יונגען פון דער וואָליע, די שטאַרקסטע אין שטאָט!
פיערדיקע, מיט גרויסע גזשיוועס איבער די אויגן,
און מיט געזונטע קצביש פנימער, אַקסלען וואָס טראַגן געשאַכטענע קעלבער.
פון טרײַבן קעלבער האָבן זיי די האַרטע הענט, פון שינדן נבלות גלאַנצן די קליידער
און שמעקן מיט שעכטהויז, מיט פרישן בלוט, מיט יאַטקע און רויע פלישן.

אין אַ יום-טוב-טאָג האָבן זיי ליב צו פוצן זיך אין זעלנערישע מונדירן,
קורטקעס מיט מעשענע קנעפּ, אויפגעשטעלט די הויכע קעלנער,
און לעדערנע דאַשקעס פאַרריקט אין אַ זײַט אָפיציריש.
רײַטהויזן, לאַקירטע שטיוול, מיט שטילעטן אין די כאַלעוועס,
שפּאַצירן זיי מיט כלות ריטמיש נאָכן קלאַנג פון זילבערנע שפּאָרנס.

מײַלער האָבן זיי, ווי זייערע מאַמעס די פּזשעקופּקעס,
וואָס שליענטשען אָן די קעלטן מיט אויבסט אין מאַרק
און קענען שילטן מיט בייזע קללות.
פון בלאָזן פיערטעפּ האָבן זיי צעפאַדערטע ליפּן;
פון קרישן, זעק און רעגנס פּוילן אויף זיי די קליידער,
און נעגל האָבן זיי שאַרפע וואָס קענען מאַכן ווונדן.

יונגען פון דער וואָליע, פון טאַטעס מיט באַן-פּיאַקערס,
און פערד, וואָס לאָזן זיך אויסגעשפּאַנט אויף פרעמדע לאַנקעס פּאַשען.
פון זייערע רײַד פילט זיך בראַנפן מיט טרוקענעם ריח פון ביליקן טיטין;
און האָבן נישט קיין בושה צו קאַפּען די מאַמע, דעם טאַטן און די שוועסטער,
און צו ווינען מיט ווײַבער פון באַרדעל.
פון צו פיל ווײַבער גייען זיי אַרום מיט נאָכגעלאָזטע טריט,
און פון אויף-זײַן לאַנגע נעכט טריפן זייערע אויגן.

אין פּוילישע ווינטער-נעכט בלאָנקען אום זייערע שוועסטער,
און האָבן ליב די ליבע לעם אַ גאַסן-טייער אונטערן פאַל פון שניי.
פון אַ הפקר-יונג, עפענען זיך זייערע בריסט נאָך זויגנדיקע קינדער,
און ווערן מאַמעס בײַם טרײַבן שיין פון אַ גאַסן-לאָמפּ.

Negro, the fate of destruction fell not only on you.
Many, many die like you. Such a death is now in fashion,
Like this they now die everywhere— — —
In Wedding, in Leopoldstadt and in Carolina.

Guys of the Volye

► *Guys of the Volye*

Volye—a Polish name for a suburb, meaning a free area, out of bounds, beyond the city limits.

Guys of the Volye, the strongest in town!
Fiery guys, with thick forelocks over their eyes,
With ruddy butcher faces and shoulders that carry slaughtered calves.
They have rough hands from porging calves, their clothes gleam from skinning
    carcasses,
They smell of slaughterhouse, of fresh blood, of butchershop and raw meat.

On a holiday they like to dress up in soldier uniforms,
Jackets with brass buttons, raised high collars,
And leather visors tilted sideways like officers.
Jodhpurs, lacquered boots, daggers in the boottops,
They stroll with their brides in cadence to the beat of silver spurs.

Porging—Jewish ritual cleansing of the arteries of slaughtered animals.

They have mouths like their mothers, petty peddlers
Who slump with fruit in the cold marketplace
And know how to swear an evil curse;
From blowing firepots, they have parched lips,
Their clothes rot from baskets, sacks and rain,
And their nails are sharp and can draw blood.

Guys of the Volye, of fathers with carriages that drive to the railroad station
And horses that run free to pasture in strangers' meadows.
Their talk smells of brandy with the dry odor of cheap tobacco;
They are not ashamed to kick their mother, their father, their sisters,
And to sleep with the women of a brothel.
From too many women, their walk is slovenly,
And from being awake long nights their eyes drip.

On Polish winter nights, their sisters wander about
And love the love at a street-gate under falling snow.
From a wanton guy, their breasts open up for sucklings,
And they become mothers in the murky light of a street-lamp.

יונגען פון דער וואָליע, די שטאַרקסטע אין שטאָט:
פֿייערדיקע, מיט גרויסע געשוועס איבער די אויגן,
און מיט געזונטע קצבישע פֿינגער, אַקסלען וואָס טראָגן געשאָכטענע קעלבער.
פון טרײַבען קעלבער האָבן זיי האַרטע הענט, פֿון שינדן נבלות גלאַנצן די קליידער
און שמעקן מיט שעכטהויז, מיט פֿרישן בלוט, מיט יאַטקע און רויע פֿלייש.

◄ שחיטה

קילע ווענט מיט שאַרפֿע שטאָלענע הענגערס.
לאַנגע, שמאָלע בלוטקאַסטנס פֿון רויטן צעמענט.
אויף די הענגערס הענגען קעלבער מיט איבערגעשניטענע העלדזער;
לונג און לעבערס שטאַרן ארויס פֿון אויפֿגעשניטענע בײַכער,
און פֿון די שלייפֿן קוקן די אויגן נאָך אַפֿיר ווי לעבעדיק.
בלוט טריפֿט שנעל; פֿון טריפֿן שלאָגט אַ פֿאַרע.

ס'רײַען פֿליגן אין די ברייטע נאָזלעכער פֿון נבלות,
און די וואָס האָבן אַ האַרץ פֿון אַ קצב שינדן די פֿעל,
טרײַבערן, שנײַדן אויס די אָדערן פֿונעם חלב.
קצבים מיט שווערע שטעקנס שלאָגן די אָקסן איבער די קנאָכנס;
זיי רײַסן אויף די געמבעס, און צײַלן די יאָרן אויף די ציין.
אין שעכטהויז ווימלען די בהמות אַזוי ווי מענטשן;
און דער וואָס שעכט — שטילט דאָס געווײן מיט אַ חלף.

◄ פֿאַרטאָגיקע הינט

הינט פֿון פֿאַרטאָג — מאָגערע, הויכע, שטילע און פֿאַרכטיקע,
וואָס האָבן אַ טבֿע צו גיין אָפֿגעזונדערט אויף אַ געלאָסענעם קײַזער-וועג,
הינט וואָס לעקן אַ מאָל אַ פֿאַרטריקנט בלוט פֿון אַ יאַטקע-וואַנט,
זייערע צונגען זענען הייסע וואָס קענען אויפֿטײַען אַ געפֿרוירענעם קצב-שטריק.

הינט פֿון גלוסט אין זאַווערוכעס, הינט פֿון ווילדן געפֿעכט נאָך אַ ביין,
אויף זייערע רוקנס שײַלן זיך געשלאָגענע פֿעלן, אָפֿגעריסן פֿון ראָסטיק מיסט.
זיי בלאָנקען אַ מאָל מיט אַ ווונדיקן פֿוס אין קעלטן איבער האַרטע פֿעלדער,
מיט שפֿורנדיקע נעז אויף וואַלד-שליאַכן, נאָך די טריט פֿון אַ פֿאַרציקטן יעגער.

אויף טונקעלע טראָטואַרן שוימען זייערע צונגען, די אויגן שטאַרן מיט בליאַסק.
שטײַף לאָקערן די עקן נאָך באַהעפֿטונג צו אַ היימישן הונט ביז ס'לויפֿט אַף די נאַכט.
הינט פֿון פֿאַרטאָג — מאָגערע, הויכע, שטילע און פֿאַרכטיקע;
פֿאַר אַ פֿלוצעמדיקן קלאַפ אין ווינט, לויפֿן זיי געשוווינד אָף אין שרעק.

Guys of the Volye, the strongest in town!
Fiery guys, with thick forelocks over their eyes,
With ruddy butcher faces and shoulders that carry slaughtered calves.
From porging calves they have rough hands, their clothes gleam from skinning
    carcasses,
They smell of slaughterhouse, of fresh blood, of butchershop and raw meat.

➤ *Slaughter*

Chilly walls with sharp steel hooks.
Long, narrow blood troughs of red cement.
On the hooks hang calves with slit throats;
Lungs and livers stick out of cut-open bellies
And from under brows eyes gaze as if alive.
Blood drips fast, steam rises from the dripping.

Flies swarm in the wide nostrils of carcasses.
Men, who have the heart of a butcher, skin the hide,
Porge, cut the veins out of the fat.
Butchers with heavy sticks beat the bones of the oxen.
They rip open their muzzles, and count the years in their teeth.
In the slaughterhouse the cattle cry like people;
And he who slaughters calms the crying with a knife.

➤ *Dogs of Dawn*

Dogs of dawn—lean, tall, quiet and fearful,
Who have a habit of walking apart on a tranquil highway,
Dogs that lick dried blood off a butchershop wall,
Their tongues are hot and can thaw a frozen butcher rope.

Dogs of lust in blizzards, dogs of wild squabbling over a bone,
On their backs, bitten hides are peeling, torn by rusty garbage.
They roam with a wounded leg in the cold over hardened fields,
With tracking noses over forest trails, in the footsteps of an avid hunter.

On dark sidewalks, their tongues foam, their eyes bulge glaring.
Their tails stiffly alert for coupling with a house-dog till the night is over.
Dogs at dawn—lean, tall, quiet and fearful;
From a sudden blow in the wind, they flee in fear.

ווינטער, ווען פרעסט ברעכן דעם גאַנג אין גאַס און לבנה צעגליטשט דעם שניי,
ציט די פֿערע פון זייערע פעלן, ווי פון אַ ווינטער-שויב אין אַ זוניקן טאָג.
פֿאַר טאָג זענען זייערע נעז ווייַס מיט פֿאַרלאָפֿענעם פראָסט און שאַרף נאָך רוי-פֿלייש.
זיי שטאַרבן טראָיעריק — פֿאַרשטאַרט פון קעלט און שטעקנס, אין אַ פֿאַרשאַרטן רינשטאָק.

◄ שעפסן אין ניו-יאָרק

אויף זייערע פעלן קען מען נאָך זען די שטילקייט פון די זוניקע בערג,
און אין די אויגן — דאָס אַנטשווייגענע לשון פון מילדן פֿאַסטעך.
ניו-יאָרקער פראָכט-וואַגנס לויפן מיט זיי גרינג, אָנגעדרענגט און שטום,
די עלדזער אָנגעשפֿאַרט אויף די רוקנס איינער אויפן אַנדערן,
די קעפ וואָלנדיק צו די בייכער געטוליעט פון שרעק פֿאַר ניו-יאָרק.

שטאַריק האַלדזן זיי צו עטלעכע נאָכאַנאַנד לויט דער סטאַדע, לויט דער וואָג.
אָפֿגעשוירן די וואָלן ציטערן זיי קאַלט אין אַ ווייַס שבט איבער מאַנהעטן-בריק;
ס׳ווענדט קיינער נישט אַפֿ אויף זיי קיין אויג אָדער אַ גלעט פון אַ האַנט.
אין געשווינד פון ניו-יאָרק שפירן זיי דעם ווילדן וועג צום שלאַכטהויז,
און שטום צעפֿאַלט שעפסענער גענאָד איבערן אייַלנדיקן וועג צום חלף.

*   *   *

פיר מאָל הונדערט שעפסן העננגען צום דיל אַראָפ, מיט פֿאַרלאָפֿענע עלדזער בלוט.
די ווענט אין שעכטהויז זענען אויפגעלייַכט מיט אָפֿגעשלאַגענער זון,
מעסערס פֿיבערן פֿלינק אין די הענט פון רויט-פֿנימדיקע גויִם;
נאָר פון אַ שעפס שינדן זיי נישט די פעלן נאָכן חלף, זיי הוילן נאָר די בייכער.
היגע קצבים האָבן אויפצוהענגען אַ שעפס, ווי לעבעדיק אין די יאַטקעס.

שעפסן אין ניו-יאָרק קען מען גרינג פֿאַרזען, כאַטש מ׳פֿירט זיי אָפֿענע אַדורך,
ווייַל מערסטנס זענען גרוי, און גרוי בייַט נישט די פֿאַרב פון היגע מויערן.
ניו-יאָרק איז צו גרויס צו טראָיערן נאָך שעפסן, אַפֿילו נאָך רינדער וואָס שרייַען.
ס׳פֿאַלט אימהדיק אויף זיי דער וואונדער פון אַזאַ שטאָט, מיט פחד קוקן די אויגן.
הי, לאָזן זיי נישט נאָך זיך קיין קלאָגנדיקן שטויב, נאָר אַ מעת-לעת פון פֿאַסטעך צום חלף.

In the winter, when frost breaks the steps in the street
  and the moon makes the snow slippery

Steam rises from their hides as from a winterpane on a sunny day.
At dawn their noses are white, puffed-up with frost, and sharp for raw meat.
They die sadly—stiff from cold or from sticks, in a dirt-covered gutter.

New York Everywhere

➤ *Sheep in New York*

This title is from the second
edition; the original title is
"Sheep."

On their hides one can still see the calm of sunny mountains,
And in their eyes the faded language of a mild shepherd.
New York trucks run with them light, crowded and mute,
Their necks leaning on each others' shoulders,
Their woolly heads huddling against bellies for fear of New York.

Ropes tie several necks together, by flock, by weight.
When the wool is shorn, they shiver in a white January over a Manhattan bridge;
No one will turn an eye to them or stroke their backs with his hand,
In the speed of New York they sense the wild road to the slaughterhouse,
And sheep-mercy falls apart silently over the speeding road to the butcher-knife.

* * * * * *

Four times a hundred sheep hang down to the ground, their throats blood-filled.
The walls of the slaughterhouse are plastered with reflected sun,
Knives feverish and nimble in the hands of red-faced men;
But they don't skin the hides of sheep, they merely hollow out their bellies,
Butchers here are in the habit of hanging up a carcass as a live sheep in the
    butchershops.

Sheep in New York are easily overlooked, though they are driven in open trucks,
Because most of them are gray, and gray does not change the color of the walls
    here.
New York is too big to mourn for sheep, or even for cattle that bellow.
The wonder of such a city falls frightfully upon them, their eyes filled with fear.
Here their hooves do not raise dust behind them—one single day from shepherd
    to knife.

◄ מענדזשן סטריט

הי זײַנען אויך פֿאַראַן יונגען אַזעלכע ווי די יונגען אויף דער וואָליע.
כאַטש אין די קליידער זעען זיי אויס לײַטיש, ציכטיק און שלאַנק,
אויף די פֿינגער איידל און האָבן הענט מיט ווייכע גוטע פֿינגער,
וואָס ווילן זיך שפּילן מיט בורשטינענע פּיסטוילן און נישט מיט נבלות.

יונגען פֿון מענדזשן סטריט האָבן אַ האַרץ וואָס לוסט צו הרגענען אַ מענטש;
זיי רעדן שטענדיק פֿון מערדער-בלוט און זענען קלוג צו שטרענגע מונדירן.
אין זייערע טונקעלע שטיבער הענגען נאָך אָפּגעשיילטע בילדער פֿון איטאַליע.
פֿרעמד איז זיי די מאַמעס אייביקער טרויער, דער טאַטע מיט דער היימישער שפּראַך.

זיי זענען יונגען פֿון טאַטעס וואָס ציִען אין מאָרגנס צו די באַרטנס מיט די אַדערדיקע הענט.
אַדער שטייען נאַס אין אויפֿגעגאַפּעטע גראַבנס און וואַרפֿן פֿון זיך רידלס טיפֿע ערד.
מיד ווי די טאַטעס, פֿאַלן די זין לומפּיש אין די קליידער אויפֿן בעט ניו-יאָרק פֿאַר טאָג;
און פֿון זייער שלאָף בלאָזט זיך שוימיק זייערער ריח פֿון געהאַלדזטע פֿרויען.

אַז ס׳ווערן אָוונטיק די שויבן פֿון זייערע שטיבער לאָזן זיך די מאַמעס צו דער גאַס
און וואַרפֿן איבער רײַכע מיסטקאַסטנס ווו ס׳כאַווען זיך קעץ קלוג אויפֿן מיסט.
די טעכטער זייערע האָבן אַ שוואַכקייט צו זײַד און צו יונגען אַזעלכע ווי זייערע ברידער,
וואָס קענען זען בלוט פֿון אַ מערדערס וווּנד רינען אין שיכרות ניו-יאָרק פֿאַר טאָג.

Jacob Riis: *Bandits' Roost, 59½*
Mulberry Street, February 12, 1888.

► *Mangin Street*

Here too there are guys like the guys of the Volye.
Though in their clothes they look decent, clean and slender,
They have gentle faces and hands with soft nice fingers
That want to play with amber pistols and not with carcasses.

Guys of Mangin Street have a heart that lusts to kill a man;
They're always talking of murder-blood and know how to outsmart strict
    uniforms.
Peeling pictures from Italy, still hang in their dark houses.
Alien to them is their mother's eternal sorrow, their father's language from
    home.

They are sons of fathers who plod in the mornings to the docks with thick-veined
    hands
Or stand wet in dug-out pits and throw up shovels of deep earth.
Tired as their fathers, the sons fall ragged in their clothes on the bed in a New
    York dawn;
And from their sleep blows a foamy sour smell of embraced women.

When twilight covers the panes of their houses, the mothers go out to the street
And overturn rich garbage bins where cats feed cleverly in the refuse.
Their daughters have a weakness for silk and for guys like their brothers
Who can see the blood of a murderer's wound run drunkenly in a New York
    dawn.

◀ מענטשן וואָס רעדן צו זיך

אויפן ברעג פון טראָטואָרן גייען זיי אָפּגעזונדערט מיט נאָכגעלאָזטע בליקן
און מיט בינטלעך אונטער די אָרעמס שמייכלען זיי צו די רינשטאָקן ;
זיי וואָגלען אום איבער די פֿקרדיקע הייף און גלעטן קעץ, הינט, אויפן מיסט,
פֿאַר ליבשאַפט קלייַבן זיי פֿאַר זיי שפּייַז און רעדן צו זיי ווי צו מענטשן.

פון שטענדיקן דרויסן זענען די קליידער זייערע פּראָכיק, פֿאַרברענט פון זון,
די פֿינגער שטעכיק פון בערד, פון די קאַפעליושן קריכן אַפיר פֿאַרלעגענע האָר,
אויף ווילד-האָריקע לייַבער טראָגן זיי הוילע בורניסן, אָפּגעריבן אָן קנעפ,
מיט הויכע אָנגעקליבענע קעשענעס — פּודעלעך און נאַרישע שטיקלעך אייַזנס.

אויף קילע אָוונט-טרעפ פון שטילע קלויסטערס דרימלען זיי מיט אָפענע מייַלער
און ס׳פֿאַרעט פון זיי וואָרעם ראַסטיקער ריח פון ברוכוואַרג און הינטערהויפן ;
זייערע עלבויגנס טראָגן נאָך פֿאַרוואָקסענע זיגלען פון אָפּגעטער און פֿאַרליבטע מיידלעך,
מיט די הויטן צעביסן און מיט צעהאַקטע שלייפן שרעקן זיי אַ לייַטישן דורכגייער.

Jacob Riis: *Tramp in Mulberry Street Yard.*

► *People Who Talk to Themselves*

On the shore of the sidewalks they walk apart with downcast eyes,
And with bundles under their arms they smile at the gutters,
They roam over vacant lots, pet cats or dogs in the garbage,
Out of love, they collect food for them and talk to them as to people.

From eternal outside, their clothes get crumbly, scorched in the sun,
Their faces bearded and prickly, from under their hats peeps a stale tuft of hair,
Right on their hairy bodies they wear plain burnooses, frayed, without buttons,
With high pockets filled with boxes and silly pieces of iron.

On chilly twilight steps of quiet churches they doze with open mouths,
Their warm steam has the rusty smell of junk and backyards;
Their forearms still show hair-covered seals of crosses and loving girls,
With their gnawed skins and battered temples they scare a decent passer-by.

א מאָל האָבן זייערע אויגן געגלאָסט, ווען ס׳האָט געבלאָטיקט ס׳ערשטע העמד אויף א פרוי
און נאָכגעגאַנגען דעם ווייב מיט א פאַרשלאָפן קינד ביי נאַכט פון א ווייטן קרוב;
איצט גייען זיי אַרום מיטן פנים צו דער ערד געוואָנדט און גאָרנישט וווּנדערט זיי
אין שיך מיט אָפענע שנירבענדלעך איינעם אַזאָ, איינעם אַזאָ, רעדן צו זיך.

ביי נאַכט זוכן זיי ס׳ביסל היימלעכקייט ביי א שויפענצטער און רעדן צו א לאַמטערן.
אַלע טאָג לויפט אויף זיי אויף א האַרט געשוואָלענער ברעם, א מאָל בלוט איבערגעזיצט.
פליגן, וואָס האָבן פיינט זיסקייט און זשומען בלויז אויף פעלן און קרעץ,
שטעלן זיך אָן אויף זייערע וווּנדן ווען זיי שלאָפן צעלייגט אין דער אָפענער שטאָט.

נאָבעלע פאַרביייגייער טרעטן געשווינד אָפ דעם וועג פון זייער שיכורן שלעף.
ס׳וויינען פון זיי מיידעלעך וואָס זיצן פאַראַקטיק אויף טרעפ מיט לויז צעקאַמטע האָר,
צענומען די פיס, און מיט א ברוסטיקן שרינט וואָס בענקט נאָך א ראַנדעווו.

———   ———   ———   ———   ———   ———

אַזעלכע שטאַרבן א מאָל אויף א שטאָטישער באַנק אָדער אונטערן קלאַפ פון א שילד.

◄ דיוויזשאָן סטריט

קעלערס מיט אָנגעקליבענע סאָרטירטע רעק טריבן פון חלבנע ליכט.
פון די דילן ציט פאַרלעגענער שמאַטע-ריח פון שטויסן געטראָגענע קליידער.
פערד, וועגענער מיט ווייסן שימל אויסגעשפּאַנט אויף אָוונטיקן אַספאַלט.
און ס׳לייגן זיך היימיש די קעץ אויף קאַלטע שויסן פון דורכגייענדיקע שלעפּערס.

לעם שטילע מויערן רינען אָפּ צעוווּנדיקטע מיט פרישן בלוט איטלעכן טאָג;
ביי נאַכט שטייען זיי נאָענט זאַלבעצווייי און קוקן זיך וואַרעם אין די אויגן,
זייערע רעקלעך טראָגן אויסגעוואַלגערטע קניטשן פון קאַסטנס און געזימסן,
די טריט ווייען מיט ראָסט פון שטויביקע שוועלן און נאַקלעסיקע שלעסער.

אויף דער זון שלענטשען נעגערס און פאַרציערעווען רויק אויף זיך די קליידער.
נעגערטעס געלעמטע און בלינדע, וואָס האָבן נישט דעם רייך פאַר א לייטיש נעגער,
טראָגן פון זיי באַהעפטונג און פאַרגייען אין שיכרות מיט אויסגענאַגטן לייב;
ביי טאָג קערן זיי זיך אום מיט צעפאַלענע געזיכטער און פאַרקלערטן שווייגן.

אַז ס׳נעמט טונקעלן אַזא גאַס, ווערן הייס די שוועלן מיט תּאווהדיקע לייבער.
מיידעלעך, וואָס הייבן ערשט אָן רייפן ראַנגלען זיך מיט גלוסט אויף שויסן,
און מיט אויגן יונגן-גלי שטילן זיי די ענט הינטערן העמד פון א יונג.
אַראָפּגעזעצטע שטרויזיאַק אויף צעהאַנגענע באַלקאַנען אַנטפלעקן ווילדע נעכט.

Once their eyes lusted, when a woman's first gown bled,
And they followed their wife with a child gotten at night
    with a stranger,
Now they wander around with their faces to the ground and nothing amazes
    them,
In shoes with untied laces, one of one color one of another, and talk to
    themselves.

At night they look for a bit of intimacy in a shop window and talk to a lamp post.
Every day their brow puffs up, hard and swollen, at times blood over their face.
Flies, that hate sweetness and buzz only on hides and scabs,
Cluster on their wounds when they sleep sprawled out in the open city.

Genteel passers-by quickly give way to their drunken trudge.
Girls avoid them, girls who sit at twilight on stoops with loosely combed hair,
Legs apart and a tight breast longing for a rendez-vous.

— —

People like them die some day on a city bench or under the clatter of a signboard.

➤ *Division Street*

Cellars with collected sorted jackets gloom in tallow candles.
From the floor blows a stale rag-stench of heaps of used clothes.
Horses, wagons with white mould, unhitched on twilight asphalt.
Cats lie down intimately in cold laps of passing tramps.

On quiet walls wounded people drip fresh blood every day;
At night they stand close, two by two, and warmly look in each other's eyes,
Their jackets carry slept-in creases from crates and ledges,
From their footsteps blows the rust of dusty thresholds and neglected locks.

In the sun, slumping Negroes quietly mend their clothes.
Negresses, lame or blind, with no appeal for a decent Negro,
Carry their coupling away and get big with drunkenness in their chewed-up
    bodies;
At dawn they come back with caved-in faces and pensive silence.

When such a street grows dark, the doorsills grow hot with passionate bodies.
Girls, just starting to ripen, struggle with the lust in their laps,
And with young-glowing eyes, they calm their hands under a boy's shirt,
Settled straw mattresses hung out on balconies reveal wild nights.

קעלערס מיט אָנגעקליבענע סאָרטירטע רעק טריבן פון חלבנע ליכט.
אין די שויפענצטער ליגן אויסגעדינטע מונדירן פון באָפעדערטע זעלנערס,
קאַלטע פעלד־פלאַשן און אַלטע ביקסן דערציילן פון צעשאָסענע פעלדער
און אויף די פעלדער זינקען שטעכיקע דראָטן, אָפגעריסענע קעפ און פאַרשאָטענע אויגן.

◄ ברוכוואָרג

וואָרעמער ברוכוואָרג ראָסטיקט אויף זוניקע פעלדער פון אָפגעשטאַנענער ערד.
און צום הייסן ראַסט ביַיגן זיך פאַרטאָען שווײַגנדיקע אײַזן־קלויבערס
אָנגעלענט מיט די האַרטע זעק און ס'רײַסן זיך די העַנט אונטער שאַרפן בלעך;
זשאַווערדיקע שניט צעפאַדערן זײַערע פינגער און ס'געלן די העַנט פון פראָן
און אויף די קליידער גרינט שטילער מאַך, אויף די קעלנער אָפגעטראָגענער גלאַנץ.

אומעטום ווו ס'ליגט אָנגעוואָרפענער ברוכוואָרג וואָקסן גראָזן הויך און ווילד.
נאַס צעקריכן זיך פוילע שלאַנגען אונטער טריט אין אַ רעגנדיקן טאָג.
פעסט אין דער ערד זינקט אַן אָפגעריסן שטיק לאַסט־וואָגאָן, אַ צעבויגענע שילד
און אַ פאַרנאַקלעסיקטער אָפגאַט, וואָס וועקט נישט מער ס'אויג פון אַ דורכגײַער
נאָר אַ זעלטענע תפילה פון אַ שכן ווען ס'שטאַרבט בײַ אים אָפ אַ קינד.

אויף אַזוינע פעלדער קרײַזן אום נעגערישע מאַמעס, ייִנגלעך און נאַרישע טאָטעס
געבויגן אין האַרבסט, אין פראָסט און אין זומער קעגן תמוזדיקער זון;
פאַרנאַקט שמעקן זײַערע העַנט, זײַערע טריט, ווי שטויב נאָך זומערדיקן רעגן
און די שיך מיט צעטראָטענעם ריח פון קוילן־גריז, גלאָז און ווילדע שטיינער;
פון די ליפן רינט אָפ שווערע סליונע, קלעפעכצדיקער שוים און שטילע רייד.

פערד אין מאָגערע פעלן ציען אַלטוואָרג מיט אָנגעשטרענגטן שפאַן אין שקיעה.
קלויבערס אויף די פורן סאָרטירן דעם ברוכוואָרג אין אומגעלומפערטע שטויסן,
אָנגעוואָרפענע דראָט־בינטן ליגן געפרעסט און הויך, און סקריפען זשאַווערדיק.
נאָך די רעדער גייען נאָך לאַנגזאַם שטויביקע שיך, אַראָפגעלאָזטע העַנט
און הייבן אויף אַ נאָגל, אַ שרויף, וואָס צעפאַלט נאָכן טרעש פון האַרטע רעדער.

בײַנאַכט ווערן די חורבות פון ברוכוואָרג אַוטעטיק ווי פעלד, ווי וואַלד,
שטיקלעך וואָס האָבן אין זיך נאָך אַ בליאַסק רײַסן זיך קיל צו דער לבנה.
מ'קען נאָך אָנטאַפן אַ פאַרגעסענעם זאַק, אַ וויכטיק שטיקל אײַזן פון אַ קלויבער
אָדער פאַרבײַגיין אַ קלוג־געלעגער אויסגעבעט פון אַ פאַרבליבענעם מענטש;
וואָס קוקט איבער זײַנע קליידער, פאַרריכט זיך אַ העמד, אַ שיך, אויף אין דער פרי.

שטיבלעך פון קלויבערס שטייען פאַרשלאָגן מיט אַ געפונענעם ברעט, מיט אַ פרעמדער טיר.
אויף די דעכלעך פון אָנגעקליבענעם בלעך ליגט ס'ברייטע ליכט פון אַ חודש־נאַכט.
אויסגעטריקנטע גופים פון דורכגענומענעם ראַסט זוכן נאַכט אויף קאַלטער ערד;
קאָלירטע שויב פון נאָבעלע שכנים מאַכן היימלעך זײַערע אויגן, זײַערע נעכט,
און פון די ליפן רינט אָפ סליונע, קלעפעכצדיקער שוים און שטילע רייד.

Cellars with collected sorted jackets gloom in tallow candles.
In the shop-windows lie served-out uniforms of decorated soldiers,
Cold canteens and old rifles tell of shot-up fields;
And in the fields sink barbed wires, severed heads and mud-covered eyes.

➤ *Junk*

Warm junk rusts on sunny fields of drained earth.
Silent, iron-pickers bend busily in the hot rust,
Burdened with coarse sacks, their hands torn from sharp tin;
Rusty scars crack their fingers, palms yellowed with dust,
Quiet moss greens on their clothes, worn luster on their collars.

Wherever junk is strewn, grass grows high and wild.
Wet, lazy snakes slink off from underfoot on a rainy day.
Sunk solidly in the earth: a severed part of a truck, a bent signboard
And an abandoned god-figure, no longer drawing the eye of a passer-by
But a rare prayer of a neighbor when a child dies in his hands.

Over such fields roam Negro mothers, boys and silly fathers,
Bent in autumn, in frost or in the July sun;
In twilight their hands, their steps, smell like dust after a summer rain,
Their shoes carry the odor of coal-grease, glass and wild stones,
Their lips dribble with heavy saliva, sticky froth and quiet words.

Horses in meager skins pull debris with tense steps into the sunset.
Pickers on the wagons sort the junk into awkward heaps,
Piled-up wire skeins lie pressed and high and grate rustily;
Behind the wheels walk slowly dusty shoes, dangling hands,
Picking up a nail, a screw, dropped by the threshing of heavy wheels.

At night the ruins of junk grow dark like field, like forest,
Pieces with saved up luster rise coolly in the moon.
One can still stumble on a forgotten sack, a picker's important piece of iron,
Or pass by a clever lair made up by a leftover man,
Who checks his clothes, mends a shirt, a shoe, for the morning.

Pickers' huts stand boarded-up with a stray piece of wood, a found door.
On the roofs of gathered tin sheets lies the white light of a mid-month night.
Dried out bodies steeped in rust seek night on the cold earth;
Painted windows of genteel neighbors lend homeyness to their eyes, their nights,
And their lips dribble with heavy saliva, sticky froth and quiet words.

I

בריקן הענגען אָנגעצויגן מיט קילן שרעק אויף שטאָלענע שטריק.
צעהייציטע שיפלעך בײַ די ברעגן שטײַגן מיט צעפאַלענעם רויך
אַ מאָל צו אַ פראָסטיקער לבנה, אַ מאָל צו אַ בראַנדיקער זון,
און שלאָגן אויס מיט הויכן נעפל איבער מאַנהעטן.
ניו־יָארק הייבט אָן טריבן און ס׳פּיַיכט די שטאָט ווי לָאנדאָן.

זומערדיקע דעכער טונקעלן פאַרנע און ס׳גלוטיקן לײַבער אויף שוועלן.
רינשטאָקן פון אָפּגעקילטע טראָטואַרן וואַסערן מיסטיק, שוימיק און שנעל.
און דורך דושנע שויבן צעפאַלן געזיכטער מיט איבערלאָפענעם שווייס,
קינדער ליגן הייס צעבונדן אין ווינדעלעך און פייניקן די מאַמעס בריסט.

די שטאָט רוישט קלאַפטערדיק ווי באַנען דורך וואַלד־שטרעקעס.
ברייטע רעדער הייבן דעם גאָז־ריח פון שטראָצן,
טריט טאַפּיען לויזלעך אין צעלאָזענעם פעך אין אַ זומערטאָג.
און לאָזן נאָך זיך אויפגעבלאָזענע סימנים פון פיס.

גויים מיט דורכגעשווייצטע העמדער צוימען דעם שפאָן פון לאָסט־פּערד,
און פון די וועגענער שווערן אַראָפּ באַלן, געהילץ און פעסער.
נעגערס שטעלן אָן אַקסלען נאָך מעל־זעק, נאָך געזונדענע פליישן;
און ס׳שמעקט פון זיי אַ סך ריחות, בשמים, נאַפט און וואָל־שטאָפן.

דאָמען אויף עלעגאַנטע עוועניוס ציִען דורך זומערדיקע אויסלאַגן
מיט שירעמלעך און לײַכטע טעשלעך אויף נאָבעלע עלבויגנס,
דורך די בלוזעס אָטאָמט קילער פערפּום פון הוילע בריסט.
סוחרים און שאָפערן שטרויכלען ס׳געיעג פון אויסלענדישע רײַזנדערס.

II

גאָסן אונטער שינעס, אונטער אײַזן־באטאָן, ליגן שטעליק האַרט.
פון שווערקייט רירט אַ מאָל די ערד פון אונטער די פיס.
הײַזער גרייכן אָנגעשפּיצטע מיט פּיקטן ליכט אין דער נאַכט;
בײַ טאָג בלאָנקען אויף זיי קופּאָלן פריש ווי זילבער־בלעכנד
און צעשפּריצן די זון אין אויגן און אין שויפענצטער.

פאַבריק־קוימענס שטאָרן פאַרברענט מיט פאַרריכערטע שפּיצן צווישן דעכער.
הײַצערס אין דער זון קלעטערן גרינג מיט אײל־קענדלעך אין די העַנט,
און אין די פאַבריקן לויפן ווינטיקע רימענס אָנגעוואַקסן מיט ווילד־שטויב,
רעדער יאָגן פריש אויף אויסגעאיַילטע אַקסן און רינען אויס מיט בוימל.

ס׳שמעקט וואַרעמער אָפּפאַל פון קליידער־שטאָפן, דאַמף פון פרעס־אײַזנס,
אָרעמס שווייצן אָפ האַריק, און פינגער דורך לײַוונט ציִען קילע שטעך.

I

Bridges hang stretched with cool fear on steel ropes.
Feverish boats at the shores rise in crumbling smoke
Sometimes to a searing sun, sometimes to a frosty moon,
And break out in high fog over Manhattan.
New York grows dim and damp like London.

Summery roofs darken steaming and bodies lust on doorsills.
Along chilled sidewalks gutters flow garbagey, foamy and fast.
And through stifling windowpanes, faces disintegrate in overflowing sweat,
Infants lie hot, bundled in diapers, and torture their mothers' breasts.

The city clamors sweepingly like trains through forest stretches.
Wide wheels raise the smell of gas from the highways,
Steps plod loosely in melted tar on a summer day
And leave behind bubbly footprints.

Men in sweat-soaked shirts rein in the walk of dray horses,
And the wagons are loaded with bales, wood and barrels.
Negroes thrust out their shoulders for flour-sacks, for skinned meat;
And they smell of many odors, spices, kerosene and wool.

Ladies on elegant avenues parade past summery window displays
With little parasols and light reticules on refined elbows,
Through their blouses breathes the chilly perfume of bare breasts.
Merchants and chauffeurs trip up the rush of foreign tourists.

II

Streets under rails, under reinforced concrete, lie steel-hard.
From heaviness, the earth sometimes moves underfoot.
Buildings reach out pointed with humid light into the night;
In the day their cupolas shimmer freshly like silver-dazzle
And spurt sun into eyes and display windows.

Factory chimneys stick out scorched with sooty peaks between the rooftops.
Stokers in the sun climb eaily, oilcans in their hands,
And in the factories windy belts run, overgrown with wild-dust,
Wheels whirl freshly on greased axles and bleed oil.

It smells of warm scraps of cloth-fabrics, steam of iron presses,
Arms sweat hairily, and fingers pull cool stitches through linen.

דערשראָקענע געזיכטער בלייכן אין שטאָל און בלאַנקען מיט קאַלטן גלאַנץ,
און בוזעמס פֿאַר זויגנדיקע קינדער שפּאַרן מיט אָפֿענע וואָרצלען אויף מאַשינען.

פֿון נאָענטן ליכט לייגן זיך וויעס אין קנייטשן מיט ווייכן געשוויילעכץ.
אַנטקעגדיקע פֿענצטער שטייען זומערדיק אָפֿן און לאָקערן מיט העלער בענקשאַפֿט,
הייסע שקיעה אויף די שויבן וועקט לוסט צו דער גאַס, צו אַ קינד אין שטוב.
און נידעריקע וואָלקנס אין דער ווייט גליִען דורכזיכטיק ווי שטיקער פֿעלדזן.

III

גראָב-מאַשינען שטויסן זיך אָן אין פֿונקען און קרישלען מיט נאַסע ערד.
וואַלצן פֿון שוואַרצן שטאָל נידערן זומפֿיק אונטער ריטמישע קלעפּ,
נאָך איטלעכן שטויס שלאָגט צוריק אַן אָפּגעשפּרונגענער עכאָ
און אין אָפּגרונט פּלאַצן די קוואַלן, העלנט שטויבן פֿון ראָסט און צעמענט.

לופֿטציגער יאָגן אַרויף מיט ברעטער, געזימסן און מיט זעקלעך צעמענט
און גראָבע הענט וואַרפֿן זיך פֿלינק אַדורך מיט גליִענדיקע ניטן,
שטריק ציִען עמערס געלאָשענעם קאַלעך, שאַטער און געהאַקטע ציגל,
רויע מויערן טונקעלן קיל פֿון פֿרישן אײַזן, פֿון קאַלעך און געשיילטע ברעטער.

Frightened faces pale in steel and glitter with a cold glow,
And breasts for sucklings lean with open roots on machines.

In harsh light, eyelids squint with creases of soft swelling.
Windows opposite are open with summer and invite with bright longing,
Hot sunset on the windowpanes stirs desire for the street, for a child at home,
And low clouds in the distance glow transparently like lumps of rock.

Louis Lozowick: *Skyscraper,* 1930.

III

Digging bulldozers strike sparks and crumble damp earth.
Pylons of black steel descend swampily under rhythmic pounding,
After every thrust, a rebounding echo bounces back
And springs burst in the abyss, hands are dusty with rust and cement.

Lifts rush up with boards, cornices and sacks of cement
And rough hands nimbly toss glowing rivets.
Ropes haul buckets of burnt lime, gravel and mortar;
Raw walls darken cooly with fresh iron, whitewash and peeled boards.

אָוונטן זידן אין הייסע קעסלען פעך, פינימער נעמען אָן ס'ליכט פון לאָמפן
לענדן, געגורטע אין דראָטן זינקען אין גראָבנס מיט געפאָנצערטע אויגן,
אין די טונעלן שפּאַלטן זיך רערן אונטער גלי און שפּרינגען אַף מיט הייץ,
און פלאַטערדיקע סמאָלע מיט גאַז-פלעשער בליצן אויף אין שנעלן ליכט-בלענד.

IV

אַז די רינשטאָקן שאַרכן מיט פאַלנדיקע בלעטער און שמעקן מיט סכך-ריח;
ביַיגן זיך פלאַמען פון ווינטן צו יינגלישע געזיכטער אויף אָוונטיקע ראָגן,
ס'וואַרעמען זיך בעטלער פון ביַיטאָג, שפּורים פאָריכטן זיך די וווּנדן;
דורך זייערע זומער-קליידער בלאָזט פּראָסטיק טרוקענע קעלט.

באַהויכטע אויסלאָגן פאַרלויפן מיט דינעם פּראָסט און ביַיטן זיך אין וויַיסע ביימער.
די שטראַזן ליגן קאַלט און היממלעך, אין דער קעלטן פלאַטערן שאַלן וואָלנדיק אויף גליטש.
מיידלשע פיס רויִשן שלאַנק מיט ליזשבעס און טראָגן זיך יונג איבער אײז;
זייערע פנימער הייס און גרינג יאַגן מיט צעהיצטע בריסט פון אויפגעבלאָזענע בלוזעס,
ווינטן שאַרפן זייערע אָפענע קני און פון זייער אָטעם שמעקט פּראָסט און גליטש.

פון דעכער שווינדלדען רעקלאַמען מיט וואַרעמע ליכטפאַרבן אויף גאַסן-פּנימער,
שפּעטע טראַמוויַיען רוישן מיט ריינעם קלאַנג און מיט אומהיימלעכן ליכט,
אויסגעשטיַיגטע בלאַנדזשאן איבער עוועניוס מיט אַ גאַסן-נומער אין די פינגער.
פון אַן ערגעצדיקן ראַג ראַטשקעט נאָך אַן אינוואַליד אויף קני צו אַ נאַכט-לוזשי
און נאָך אים אַ געלערנטער הונט, אַ שפּילקאַסטן אויף אַ בלינד וויַיב.

אויף אָוונטיקע שוועלן ליגן שווערע שיכורים מיט בראָנפן צעגאַסענע ליפן.
געהאָרכזאַמע נעגערס שלאָפן אונטער איבערצויגענע רעקלעך געשמאַק אויף געזימסן;
קעלטן קאָרטשען זייערע קני און די אָדערן שוידערן אויף מיט נאַסן קראָמף.
די אין ליַיכטע קליידער, און אָפענע העמדער, וואַרעמען איינער דעם אנדערן,
וואַרפן זיך געהאַלדזטע ענגער צום שלאָפן און זיַין ווי אויף גלוסט.

אָפּגעשלאַסענע סקלאַדן שטייען אָנגעוואָרפן מיט האַלב אויסגעלאָדענע סחורות
און אויף אַ טיש וווּ נאָך ליגט אַן איבערגעלאָזט רעקל, אַ לעדערן פאַרטעך,
קאַסטנס שטייען אויפגעבראָכן און צענאָגלט און באַלן געעפנט מיט צעפאַלענע רייפן.
לאָדנס פון מאַגאַזין-פענצטער הענגען אין שרעק פאַרשפּאַרט מיט ראָסטיקער קעלט.

אין קעלט יעמערן קעץ מיט גרינלעך מיט הייסע אויגן און פאָרן זיך און ווילד אויף טראָטואַרן;
שרעק פון אַ דורכגייער, פון אַ שילד אין ווינט, רייַסט איבער זייער באַהעפטונג.
אין אַזעלכע גאַסן פאַרוואָלגערט זיך שטענדיק אַ יונג מיט אַן אָפּגעקילטער פרוי;
זאַט פון ליַיב, זאַט פון וויַינקעלערס, גייען זיי פאַרשלעפטע, אָפּגעזונדערט אָן רייד.
בעזעמער רירן דעם פּראָסט פון פּאַרטאָג, און אויף שוועלן טאָגן מילך-פלעשער.

Evenings boil in hot cauldrons of tar, faces take on the light of lamps.
Loins, girt with wires, sink into pits with armored eyes.
In the tunnels, pipes crack in the glow and break off hotly.
Leaping pitch and gas-bottles flash in the swift light-dazzle.

IV

When the gutters rustle with falling leaves and smell of broken branches,
Flames of winds bend to boyish faces on evening corners,
Beggars warm up from the day, drunkards lick their wounds;
Through their summer clothes frostily blows a dry cold.

Steamed-up window displays are coated in thin frost and change into white trees.
The streets lie cold and friendly, scarves flutter, woolly, on a skating-rink.
Girls' legs swish slenderly on skates and glide young on the ice;
Their faces warm and easy rush with hot breasts in inflated blouses,
Winds hone their open knees and their breath smells of frost and gliding.

Billboards blink from rooftops with warm light-colors on street-faces,
Late trams rumble with a pure sound and uncanny light,
Last passengers stray in avenues with a street number in their fingers.
From a corner somewhere shuffles a cripple on his knees to a night-lodging
And behind him a trained dog, a music box on a blind wife.

On evening doorsteps lie heavy drunkards with whiskey-puffed lips.
Docile Negroes sleep fast on ledges, jackets over their heads;
Cold curls their knees and their veins shudder with a wet cramp.
Those in light clothes, with open shirts, warm one another,
Throw themselves closer into a hug and fall asleep as in lust.

Locked warehouses are piled with half-unloaded wares
And on a table still lies someone's forgotten jacket, a leather apron,
Crates are broken open, nails bared and bales undone with discarded hoops.
Shutters of store windows hang in fear, bolted up with rusty cold.

In the cold, cats howl with greenish hot eyes and mate wildly on the sidewalk;
Fear of passers-by, of a signboard in the wind, disturbs their coupling.
In such streets a guy strays by with a cooled-off woman;
Sated with flesh, sated with wine cellars, they trudge along, separate, with no
    words.
Brooms touch the frost of morning, and on doorsteps dawn milk-bottles.

◄ האַרלעם — — אַ נעגער־געטאָ

אין האַרלעמער געטאָ, אין אַזאַ גלות,
ווערט אפילו פון גאָט אַ נעגער.
מאָנסבילן ליגן כּנעניש ביי די באָרטנס אַרום
און נעכטיקן אויף נאַסע, אויסלענדישע פּעסער;
רעדן צו די קלעצער, וואָס שלאָגן דעם ברעג.
פֿאַר אַלעמענס אויגן, רויש פֿון פֿלאַמיקן שום
פֿון אַמעריקעס שטאָטנדיקע אינדזעלען,
וואָס דערציילן פֿון קייטן אויף העגנט, אויף פֿיס
אָפּגעפֿירטע — אין אַ הייסן צפון־לאַנד.
טרויעריק און ענלעך איז האַרלעם
צום אָריענטאַלישן ירושלים:
טעכטער אין לעצטן בלוי פון זייער גאַס
וואָרטן מיט אויסגעשטרעקטע כּלים אויף ברויט,
ווי די דינסט־פֿרויען אין שלמה המלכס צײַטן.
אויף אַלע אוונטיקע שוועלן נעגערישע פֿנימער.
די פון הונגער, טראָגן זיך אין פּרעכע טענץ;
וויקלען זיך מיט גלוסט אין די טויערן אַרײַן.

שטילער ברענענדיקער פּראָסט פֿאַר די הײַזער
צײַט פון אָפֿענע נעכט אין זייערע שטיבער אַרײַן.
אַ קאַלטע ווינטער־לבנה אויף די שויבן גרינט,
אַ פּראָסט אויף אַ נעגער־פּענצטער מאָלט די ״ביבל״;
דעם בארוועסן משהן מיט אַ שטעקן דורכן ים;
די לוחות פון גאָטס אויסגעקריצטער חכמה.
קינדער — נעגערישע, פֿלאַקסענע
וואַקסן ווי פון תּנך אַרויס,
ווונדערן זיך אויף דער תּיבה פֿונעם מבול
אויף נחס טויב, אין אַלע זייערע פֿענצטער.

אין אַ נאַכט פון קאַלטער לבנה,
געגליכן איז אַ נעגערישער חצות צו חומש.
לויט די מעשׂיות פון זייערע באָבעס, זיידעס —
אפילו דזשעפֿערסאָן קומט איצט פֿונעם אור!
בלויז ״טאָמס קעבין״ זײַנען ווילדע קאַפּיטלעך.
אײַנגעביבלט אַזוי איז אידערעס נעגעריש הויז,
ווען עס שטייען די שטיבער אין טיפֿן ווײַס
אײַנגעשטילט פון פֿאַלנדיקן שניי.
פֿאַרשניעטע באָבעס שטייען אויף, ווי תּפילות,
און ווײַנען נעגעריש אויף זייערע דורות.

► *Harlem—A Negro Ghetto*

In the Harlem ghetto, in such exile,
Even God becomes a Negro.
Men like Canaanites sprawl on the river banks,
Spend their nights on wet barrels from foreign lands;
Talk to the logs bumping against the shore.
Right before everyone's eyes, noise of the flaming foam
Of America's stately islands,
They tell of chains on arms, on legs,
Carried away—into a hot north-land.
Harlem is sad and is like
Oriental Jerusalem:
Daughters in the last blue of their street
Wait with outstretched plates for bread
Like maidservants in the times of King Solomon.
On every evening threshold, Negro faces.
Some, out of hunger, fling themselves into lewd dances,
Whirl with passion into the gates.

A silent, burning cold before the houses
Moves from the open nights into their homes.
A cold winter moon greens on the windowpanes,
A frost paints the Bible on a Negro window:
The barefoot Moses with a staff through the sea,
The tablets of God's engraved wisdom.
Children—black, soft as flax,
Spring forth from the Torah,
Amazed at the ark from the flood,
At Noah's dove, on all their windows.

In a night of a cold moon
A Negro midnight is like Genesis.
In the stories of their grandmas and grandpas,
Even Jefferson came from Ur!
Only "Uncle Tom's Cabin" is an incredible chapter.
Every Negro home is wrapped up in a Bible
When the houses stand in the deep white,
Put to sleep by the falling snow.
Snowed-in grandmas awaken, like prayers,
In Negro-weeping for their generations.

Excerpt from a longer poem.

"Ghetto" was not a common term for black slums in American cities. Vaynshteyn uses a set of metaphors, projecting Jewish destiny onto the black experience.

◄ **פעלן**

שינד-הייזער אונטערן נאַכטיקן בלייענעם הימל,
רוישן הייס מיט לאַנגע ווילדע מעסערס
און שלאַגן-אויס שוואַרצן שוויים אויף נעגערס,
וואָס שמעקן רוי פון אָקסן און פון פעלן.
אַזאַ ברייטער, דינער שטאָל שינדט די הויטן;
די וואָרעמע פעלן פון שאָף און פון רינדער,
דאָס בלוט ציט אָפּ מילד, ווי אויף אַלע חלפים,
און טאָפּיעט-אָפּ זאַלציק און געשוווינד
פון אַ נבלהדיקן רינד.
נאָך מעת-לעתן ווערן די הויטן האַרטער, שטייפער
און עס וועפט דער ריח אויס פון בלוט.
ביי די שינדערס פאַרחלבט ווערן די הענט
פון שפּרייטן די פעלן אויף דער העלער ערד,
אויף זייערע דיקע פינגער אַ נאַסער ליים געלט.
אויף די וועגענער וואָס ציען פון די שינד-הייזער
און פירן מיט זיך די אָפּגעשונדענע קעלבער,
פאָרן נעגערס אויף די שטויסן צעלייגט
און גליטשן זיך נאָכן ווייכן טרעסט פון די רעדער
און זינגען פון לאַנגווייל היזעריקע לידער.
מיט פלעמלעך אין די הענט, פאָרן זיי אויפן געשפאַן
און שאַרן זיך דורך די נעכט אין גאַרבאַרניעס אַריין,
נעגערס האָבן מורא פאַר שינד, פאַר פאַרצוקונג;
פאַר יעדער זאַך וואָס ציט אָפּ פון חלפים.

◄ **אויף דיין ערד, אַמעריקע**

אויף דיין ערד איז מיר באַשערט צו זינגען דאָס געזאַנג פון דיין לאַנד.
כ'האָב אַזוי פיל מענטשן, אַזוי פיל שיפן אין דיינע ברייטע האָפּנס געזען
און ביי דיינע פעלקער פון לשונות גלערנט זיין אין דער פרעמד,
און אָנגעהויבן פאַרשטיין, אַז כאַטש רייּשע, גאַליציע, איז מיין היים,
איז מיין שטאָט ניו-יאָרק — מיינע גאַסן: דילענסקי, רידזש און פּיט,
און היימישער נאָך ביסטו מיר פון יענעם טרויעריקן טאָג אָן געוואָרן,
ווען כ'האָב אויף דיין ערד, אַמעריקע, געזען מיין טאַטע-מאַמע שטאַרבן.

היימישע טאַטע-מאַמע — אייניקלעך פון אַמסטערדאַמער יידישע וואָגלערס;
פון די אור-זיידעס נאָך פון רזשארזש וואַשינגטאָנס גרויסע צייטן,
וואָס האָבן מיט שרעק איבער מבולדיקע וואַסערן זיך זעגלען געלאָזט
מיט זייערע בענטש-ליכט, טלית, און תפילין פונעם אַלטן האָלאַנד
און פאָרן דאַרן לינקאָלן געבראַכט די חכמה פון "האַלי-מאָזעס",
אויף די באָול — פעלדער צו קענען מילדערן דאָס געוויין פון נעגערס.

Skinning-shops under the night's lead sky
Buzz hotly with long savage knives,
Black sweat breaks out on Negro bodies
That smell raw of oxen and hides.
Such a broad thin steel flays the skins,
The warm hides of sheep and cattle.
The blood runs off gently, as on all slaughterers' knives
And drips salty and swift
Off a cow's carcass.
As days pass, the skins grow harder, stiffer,
The smell of blood evaporates.
The skinners' hands are coated with fat
From spreading the hides on bare ground,
On their thick fingers yellows wet clay.
In wagons that leave the skinning-shops,
Carrying off the skinned calves,
Ride Negroes sprawled on the heaps.
They glide with the soft thrust of the wheels
And in their boredom sing hoarse songs.
With lanterns in their hands, they ride atop the carts
And slither through the nights to tanneries.
Negroes are afraid of skinning, of twisting,
Of any thing that runs off slaughter knives.

➤ *On Your Soil, America*

On your soil I was destined to sing the song of your land.
So many people, so many ships I saw in your broad harbors,
And from the tongues of your nations I learned how to be a stranger
And began to understand that though Rayshe, Galicia is my home,
My city is New York—my streets: Delancey, Ridge and Pitt;
And you became more homey to me since that mournful day
When I saw my father-mother die on your soil, America.

Father-Mother from home—grandchildren of Amsterdam Jewish vagabonds;
Of great-grandfathers, from George Washington's great times,
Who sailed in fear over waters of the flood
With their Sabbath candles, tallises and tefillin from old Holland
And brought to the thin Lincoln the wisdom of "Holy Moses,"
To soften the cry of Negroes in cottonfields.

אַזוי פיל טרויעריקע גאַסן זײַנען אויף דײַן ערד, אַמעריקע, פאַראַן!
אומהיימלעך גייען ייִדן אַרום געבויגענע איבער שטיבער
מיט מיסחרדיקע פעק אויף שווערע, מידע אַקסלען אָנגעהאַנגען
און האַנדלען מיט געוואַנטן, גאָלד ווי אין וואַרשע, ווי אין לאָדזש
אויף די שפּראַכן פון ענגליש, שפּאַניש, איטאַליעניש און ייִדיש.

אין דײַנע פאַרנעפלטע נעכט — אויף די עווענוס, אויף די סקווערן,
קען מען זען ווי עלנט עס קענען זײַן מענטשן אויף דײַן ערד.
דײַנע סוף-חודשדיקע לבנות גייען-אויף דינער און בלאַסער
און גיסן זייער אומעט אויף געזיכטער, אויף שיפורן לײַבער,
ווען דײַן ערד, אַמעריקע, איז אין ווינט, איז אין בלוזן שניי.

ערגעץ אין שווערע ווײַטן, אין בלויע טיפן — אָוועק,
זעגלען די שיפן אויף דײַנע אָוונטיקע, געבויגענע וואַסערן.
אויף די צעהאַנגענע בריק פון מאַנהעטן, ברוקלין, קווינס,
ציִען רינדער מיט חלפים ליכט אויף זיך, צו שחיטה
און מאַכן גרויער נאָך ס׳ביסל עלנט פון דײַן ערד, אַמעריקע.

נעכט רייכערן שטאָטיש און שלאָגן האַרבסטיק פון קאַלטע דעכער.
דער בלוי פון די הימלען ווערט אומעטיק ווי די שטאָט, ווי די שויבן.
לענג-אויס דײַנע וואַסערן — ציִען פלעמלדיקע שלעפּ-שיפעלעך
און שאַרן פון זיך פלאַמיקן שוים, טרייסלען ס׳געהילץ פון די ברעגן.
ס׳האָפענדיקע ליכט פון סקלאַדן ווערט ווינטערדיק און גראַשנדיק;
סמוטנע גייען וועכטערס אַרום איבער דײַנע אויסלענדישע סחורות.

אָוונטיקע באַרטנס וואָס זײַנען פון נעפלען שיפור און טריב.
העל און ברוין-קריטיקע מאַטראָסן שטייען בראָנפנדיק אין די שענקען;
שטייען בײַ די דרימלדיקע "באַרס", מיט אַראָפּגעלאָזטע קעפּ
און רעדן צו די אויסגעוואָעפטע ביר-גלעזער, מיט צעגאַסענע מײַלער.
פון שטריק און פון אַנקערס זײַנען זייערע הענט האַרט און פלינק
און קענען מאַסטן ציִען אין מיטן דער וועלט — אין מיטן ים.

אין נאָוועמבער ווערן אַלע זאַכן דאָ ראָסטיק, ווערן געל.
ייִנגלישע פײַערן סמאָליען פון צענאָגלטע קאַסטנס, ברעטער און קאַנען.
גאָט, סאַראַ בענקשאַפט ס׳קוקט פון פּנימער ייִדישע, נעגערישע, איטאַליענישע.
"איסט-סײַד, וועסט-סײַד" — אומעטום די זעלבע פענצטער, די זעלבע נאַכט.
און שטאַרבט א מענטש אויף דײַן גרויסער, ברייטער ערד, אַמעריקע,
איז ווי ר׳וואָלט דאָ געשטאָרבן אין א סך לענדער מיט א מאָל!

So many sad streets on your soil, America!
Uncanny Jews walk around stooped from house to house
With packs of wares hanging on heavy, weary shoulders
And trade in clothes, in gold, as in Warsaw, as in Lodz,
Twisting their tongues in English, Spanish, Italian and Yiddish.

In your misty nights—on avenues and squares,
One can see how lonely people can be on your soil.
Your moons at months' end rise thinner and paler
And pour their sadness onto faces, onto drunken bodies,
When your soil, America, is in wind, in bare snow.

Somewhere into heavy distances, into blue depths—away,
Ships sail on your dusky, stooped waters.
Over the hanging bridges of Manhattan, Brooklyn, Queens,
Cattle walk to slaughter with the glint of knives in their eyes
And make grayer the loneliness of your soil, America.

Nights fume city-like and blow autumnly from cold roofs.
The blue of the skies grows sad like the city, like the windowpanes.
Along your waters float barges with little lights,
Shove off the flaming foam and shake the wood off the shores.
The harborlight of warehouses grows wintry and poor;
Gloomily, watchmen pace among your foreign wares.

Evening docks—murky and drunken with fog.
Blond and muddy-brown sailors stand in taverns stinking of liquor,
Stand at dreamy bars, with bowed heads,
And talk to emptied beer mugs with dribbling mouths.
From ropes and anchors their hands are rough and nimble,
They can haul up masts in the middle of the world—in the middle of the sea.

In November all things here become rusty, grow yellow.
Boyish fires smoulder with nail-studded crates, boards and tin cans.
God, what a longing looks out of faces, Jewish, Negro, Italian.
"East-Side, West-Side"—everywhere the same windows, the same night.
And when a man dies on your great wide soil, America,
It is as if he died in many countries at once!

H. Leyvik

1888-1962

H. Leyvik* is the pseudonym of Leyvik Halpern, born in Ihumen, a small town in Byelorussia. Though his first published work appeared in America, the experiences of his first twenty-four years in tsarist Russia made a profound imprint on Leyvik's personality and poetic imagination. He was the oldest of nine children who lived in a hut with one small room separated for the parents, "the rest—oven, table, two long benches and a chest, the floor of hard yellow clay." The father, "a cohen and a raging man" with "a fiery red beard," used to beat his children. Though a descendant of a Minsk rabbi and author, he was reduced to being "a girls' teacher," the lowest possible rank in Jewish education; from an epistolary manual he taught servant girls how to write letters in the "servant language," Yiddish.

Beginning at age five, Leyvik received a traditional Jewish education in *heder*. When he was ten, he was sent to the Yeshiva in a larger town, where he spent several years studying from early morning until late at night, sleeping in the yeshiva on a hard bench, and "eating days"—that is, eating intermittently with host families in various private Jewish houses. He was often hungry and ill, suffering for a long period from leg wounds caused by starvation, which he later described vividly in "The Chains of Messiah." The master of the Yeshiva was "an enlightened man": along with the traditional Talmudic education, he provided a supplementary teacher for Hebrew grammar (a secular topic!) who introduced the students to secular books in Hebrew and in Hebrew translation.

During the Revolution of 1905, Leyvik attended illegal assemblies in the forest and joined the Bund, the Jewish social-democratic underground party. The Bund promoted Yiddish as the national language of the masses, opposing the "clerical language," Hebrew. Leyvik, though a cohen, ceased attending synagogue and switched from writing poems in Hebrew to Yiddish.

In 1906 Leyvik was arrested by the tsarist police. He refused the services of a famous Russian defense lawyer and declared at his trial:

*Also Leivick.

H. Leyvik

I will not defend myself. Everything that I have done I did in full consciousness. I am a member of the Jewish revolutionary party, the Bund, and I will do everything in my power to overthrow the tsarist autocracy, its bloody henchmen, and you as well.

The sentence was four years of forced labor and exile for life to Siberia. Leyvik was chained and spent his four years in prison, experiencing hunger strikes and solitary confinement, and witnessing whippings and hangings of political prisoners. In his solitary cell in the Minsk "Tower," he wrote his first dramatic poem, "The Chains of Messiah." Finally, in March 1912, Leyvik's years of forced labor came to an end and he was marched off to Siberia—a march from prison to prison that lasted four months; he then traveled for several more weeks on a prison ship up the river Lena, to the place of his exile, the village Vittim.

Comrades who had escaped to America and joined an organization to aid exiled revolutionaries in Russia sent money to the young poet. Leyvik escaped from Siberia. He bought a horse and sleigh and traveled for several months until he came to a train station; then, after crossing European Russia and Germany, he sailed for America in the summer of 1913.

In America, Leyvik became the most prominent poetic figure in world Yiddish literature. He was hailed as "the greatest Yiddish poet and playwright of our time" (1960). Sublimated suffering, messianic fervor, a mystical tone, and a naive humanism, combined with a Neo-Romantic musicality of harmonious verse lines that were imbued with Russian Symbolism, marked the voice of his poetry. He transformed his father's humiliation and harshness into an apotheosis of a father figure. His childhood sufferings merged with the torments of his prison years and were translated into the language of traditional Jewish mythology. Job, Isaac's sacrifice, the Golem of Prague, the Messiah in chains—all informed the language of his vision, particularly in his poetic dramas. For his readers, the details of Leyvik's biography became part of a symbolic suffering personality. In his verse they could find echoes of Dostoyevsky, messianic yearnings, frustrated revolutionary dreams, and soft individual sensibilities in a harsh world. Such characteristics of a lyrical Neo-Romantic poet assumed a national dimension when the twin concepts of Siberian exile and social revolution—meaningful to a whole generation that revolted against the confining world of Orthodox Judaism—took on the Hebrew form of *"Goles un Geule"* (*Galuth* and *Geulah*), Exile and Redemption.

During the years when he achieved worldwide fame as a poet and his works were translated into many languages, Leyvik worked as a wallpaper hanger in New York. As a contemporary poet observed: "Many of us saw him striding in New York's streets with rolls of wallpaper in one hand and with a brush and a bucket of paste in the other." In 1932 Leyvik was forced to stop work and spend four years in the Spivak sanitorium for tuberculosis in Denver, Colorado. There he created some of his best, almost untranslatable poems, achieving a certain lucid serenity and writing, among other things, a beautiful sequel of "Songs of Abelard to Heloise" and a cycle of poems on Spinoza (the idol of Yiddish intellectuals).

Between 1917 and 1920, Leyvik wrote four apocalyptic, visionary poems reflecting the waves of terrible pogroms in Eastern Europe. One of them, "The Wolf," was rediscovered during the Holocaust as a symbolic presentiment. His poetic drama, *The Golem*, published in 1921, in a period of revolution and messianic ferment, made an enormous impact on Yiddish literature. As the *Lexicon of Yiddish Literature* (New York, 1963) observed:

> People read and re-read it, debated and wrote about the problems of the book: World liberation and Jewish redemption, the role of matter and the role of the spirit in the process of redemption, the Jewish Messiah and the Christian Savior, Maharal and the Golem of Prague, the masses and the individual, creator and creation, Realism and Symbolism—all this was stirred up in the 1920s by Leyvik's *Golem*.

For many, Leyvik occupied the position in Yiddish literature previously granted to I. L. Perets (who died in 1915)—that of a spiritual, charismatic authority, a center of literary conscience, who found a national form for universal content.

In the 1920s, Leyvik published poetry and drama in the Communist daily, *Frayhayt*, and monthly, *Der Hamer*. He visited the Soviet Union and his hometown, Ihumen, and a book of his poetry was published in Moscow, but he was criticized there for his "pessimism." In 1929, when the Communists saw the pogroms against the Jews of Palestine as an expression of Arab revolution, Leyvik and other writers broke with the Communist journals and were branded as traitors. Leyvik voiced the deep concern of Jewish intellectuals for the preservation of ethical values vis-à-vis the idolized Revolution.

Like other writers of his generation, Leyvik was active as an editor and journalist. From 1932 to 1934, he coedited the journal, *Yiddish*. Between 1936 and 1952, Leyvik and Joseph Opatoshu edited eight thick volumes of *Zamlbikher* (Assemblies), bringing together the best Yiddish writers of the time. From 1936 to his death, he was a regular contributor of poems and articles to the New York daily, *Der Tog*.

In 1936, Leyvik represented the Yiddish P.E.N. Club at the international P.E.N. congress in Buenos Aires. In his address, he said: "The main problem of our literature in the twentieth century is how to find a synthesis between the national and the universal. Jew and world—this is the central drama of our lives and our literature." In 1937, Leyvik participated in the World Yiddish Cultural Congress in Paris; he was among the leaders of the cultural organization founded there, YKUF. The highly influential YKUF was molded on the "Popular Front" model, bringing together writers and cultural leaders of the left and the center from all over the world. In 1939, after the Hitler-Stalin Pact, Leyvik broke off relations with the left and resigned from YKUF. In 1958, Leyvik received an honorary doctorate from Hebrew Union College and in 1961, an honorary medal from the National Jewish Welfare Board. He died a year later.

For the last four years of his life, Leyvik was paralyzed and unable to speak. During this time, he became an object of pilgrimage for numerous writers and friends. As the *Lexicon of Yiddish Literature* describes it: "His looks, his behavior with his visitors, the way he hugged and kissed his friends—reminded one of the sufferings of Job, the agony of Isaac's sacrifice; he reminded one of the elder Zosima in Dostoyevsky's *Brothers Karamazov*."

In 1914–15, Leyvik was living in Philadelphia, working in a garment shop and learning to be a cutter and, at the same time, encouraged in his writing by the editor of the Philadelphia Yiddish newspaper. It was here that he wrote his famous poem, "Somewhere Far, Somewhere Far Away," which he considered to be his first authentic poem and which he placed at the beginning of his first book.

Leyvik later described how the poem was created. One cold winter night, after a long day's work in the shop, he returned to his tiny attic room. Lying in bed, by the light of a small gas lamp, he watched a snowstorm and felt "lonely, foreign and forlorn in this big new world":

> All of a sudden, something lights up in you: You are really in America, you are lying in an attic, but outside the window a blizzard howls. . . . And before your eyes you see the Siberian landscape from which you just escaped, the distant white hills of immense Siberia, the snow-covered roads and rivers and forests and mountains; the full, absolute and dazzling whiteness, you may say: *the dazzling purity of the world*. And you are part of this whiteness and purity. . . .
>
> I felt that something yearned-for emerged in me—a new start: going to the whiteness, to the untrodden, forbidden land.

Reflecting further on his poem, Leyvik shifted emphasis from the forbidden land with its unreachable covered treasures to suffering humanity:

> To be the justified and chosen partner of suffering man who can never reach the forbidden treasures—perhaps here lies the secret of true human yearning, the fate of man both in his search for a link to that which we call Creator-God, as well as in his connection with the whole world, with human life and death? Therefore, it is not enough to say that there are treasures, forbidden and covered; a second part is needed:

> Somewhere far, somewhere far away
> lies a prisoner, lies alone.———

◄ ערגעץ ווײַט

ערגעץ ווײַט, ערגעץ ווײַט
ליגט דאָס לאַנד דאָס פֿאַרבאָטענע,
זילבעריק בלאָען די בערג
נאָך פֿון קיינעם באַטראָטענע;
ערגעץ טיף, ערגעץ טיף
אין דער ערד אײַנגעקנאָטענע,
וואַרטן אוצרות אויף אונדז,
וואַרטן אוצרות פֿאַרשאָטענע.

ערגעץ ווײַט, ערגעץ ווײַט
ליגט אַליין אַ געפֿאַנגענער,
אויף זײַן קאָפּ שטאַרבט די שײַן
פֿון דער זון דער פֿאַרגאַנגענער;
ערגעץ וואָגלט וועד אום
טיף אין שניי אַ פֿאַרשאָטענער,
און געפֿינט ניט קיין וועג
צו דעם לאַנד דעם פֿאַרבאָטענעם.

◄ אויף די וועגן סיבירער

אויף די וועגן סיבירער
קען עמעץ נאָך איצטער געפֿינען אַ קנעפּל, אַ שטריקל
פֿון מײַנס אַ צעריסענעם שוך,
אַ רימענעם פּאַס, פֿון אַ ליימענעם קריגל אַ שטיקל,
אַ בלעטל פֿון הייליקן בוך.

אויף די טײַכן סיבירער
קען עמעץ נאָך איצטער געפֿינען אַ צייכן, אַ שפּענדל
פֿון מײַנס אַ דערטרונקענעם פֿליט;
אין וואַלד — אַ פֿאַרבלוטיקט-פֿאַרטריקנטן בענדל,
אין שניי — אײַנגעפֿרוירענע טריט.

► *Somewhere Far Away*

Somewhere far, somewhere far away
Lies the land, the forbidden land,
Silvery blue the mountains
Never trod by man;
Somewhere deep, somewhere deep inside,
Kneaded into the earth,
Treasures are waiting for us,
Treasures covered with dirt.

Somewhere far, somewhere far away
Lies a prisoner, lies alone,
On his head, the glow is dying,
The glow of the setting sun;
Deeply covered in snow
Somewhere wanders a man,
He cannot find a road
To the land, the forbidden land.

On the circumstances of the creation of this poem, see the biographical sketch of Leyvik.

H. Leyvik in chains, on his route to exile in Siberia (photo).

► *On the Roads of Siberia*

On the roads of Siberia
Someone may still uncover a button, a lace
Of my torn shoe,
A leather belt, a shard of a clay mug,
A page of the holy book.

On the rivers of Siberia
Someone may still uncover a sign, a splinter
Of my raft that has drowned;
In the forest, in snow—a ribbon with dried blood,
Footsteps frozen in the ground.

This and the following poem refer to Leyvik's exile to, and subsequent escape from, Siberia.

◄ אין שניי

(פֿראַגמענטן)

I

לאַנגע ווינטערדיקע נעכט,
ווײַסע שטראַלנדיקע טעג,
האָב איך אײַנגעשפּאַנט מײַן פֿערד
לאָזן זיך אין ווײַטן וועג.

הײ און ברויט און ווײַן געקויפֿט,
אײַנגענייט דאָס לעצטע געלט,
אָנגעטאָן זיך אין אַ פּעלץ,
מויל און אויערן פֿאַרשטעלט.

ניט געריִרט פֿון שטוב קיין זאַך,
טיר און לאָדן ניט פֿאַרמאַכט,
צו דער שוועל זיך צוגענייגט
און געזאָגט: אַ גוטע נאַכט.

אָפּגעצייכנט מײַנע טריט,
לעצטע אויף דער פֿרעמדער ערד.
נאָך אַ מאָל: אַ גוטע נאַכט,
און אַ שמיץ געטאָן דאָס פֿערד.

II

איז דער וועג מאָנאַטן לאַנג,
ציט זיך ווי אַ זילבער שנור.
פֿאָר איך מיטן זילבער שנור,
מורמל עפּעס אַ געזאַנג.

אין דעם פּוטער אײַנגעדרייט,
אָפּגעדעקט די אויגן נאָר —
קוק איך ווי די זון גייט אויף,
קוק איך ווי די זון פֿאַרגייט.

און דער שניי — ער פֿאַלט און פֿאַלט —
דעק איך אויף די אויגן צו,
לאָז אַראָפּ דעם קאָפּ און ליג.
און דער שליטן פֿליט און פֿליט.

בלײַבט דאָס פֿערד אין מיטן שטיין —
כאַפּ איך זיך פֿון דרימל אויף,
גיב אַ שמיץ און גיב אַ פֿײַף,
דורך די קלאַפּנדיקע ציין.

(Fragments)

I

Long winter nights,
White, radiant days,
I harnessed my horse
To go far away.

I bought hay, bread, wine,
I put on my fur,
I sewed the money up,
Covered mouth and ears.

I didn't touch a thing,
Didn't close the shutters,
I bowed to the doorstep,
Good night, I muttered.

Last steps on foreign soil,
Last steps in these parts.
Again: Good night to all,
And a lash at my horse.

II

Like a silver string unfolding
For months, the road is long—
I travel with the silver string,
Murmuring a song.

Nestled in my fur,
Only eyes are free—
I see the sun at dawn,
The setting sun I see.

The snow falls and falls—
I cover up my eyes,
I let my head drop,
And the sleigh flies and flies.

When the horse comes to a halt—
I wake up from my nap,
I crack the whip and whistle
With chattering teeth, wrapped.

Leyvik visiting his parents in
Minsk, Byelorussia, 1913, on his
escape route from Siberia to
America (photo).

III

אַ קאַלטער ווינט פֿון צפֿון-זײַט
האָט אָנגעהייבן בלאָזן;
מײַן טרײַער פֿערד האָט מיד צום שניי
זײַן קאָפּ אַראָפּגעלאָזן.

די זײַטן אײַנגעפֿאַלן טיף,
די גאַנצע פֿעל פֿאַרפֿראָרן.
ווער ווייס, צי וועלן מיר נאָך הײַנט
אין ערגעץ ווו פֿאַרפֿאָרן?

אַלץ פֿינצטערער און פֿינצטערער.
דער שניי מיט גלאָז פֿאַרצויגן.
איך גיי צו פֿוס מײַן שליטן נאָך
מיט האַלב-פֿאַרמאַכטע אויגן.

עס שטעכן אין דער פֿינצטערניש
ווי שאַרפֿע נאָדלען שטערן;
עס קלאָגן אין דער וויסטעניש
פֿאַרשנייטע וועלף און בערן.

V

עס ווערן די וואָלקנס צעשוווומען,
עס ווײַזן זיך שטערן נאָך שטערן:
— דער וועג איז אין גאַנצן פֿאַרשאָטן —
ניטאָ ווו דעם שליטן צו קערן.

איך שפּאַן זיך אַליין אײַן צום פֿערד צו,
איך העלף אים צו שלעפּן דעם שליטן.
אַ שלעפּ און אַ פֿאַל צו דער ערד צו,
די פֿינגער — צעבלוטיקט, צעשניטן.

דער הימל אַלץ קלערער און קלערער,
אַ גרויסע לבֿנה אין מיטן;
זיי קוקן זיך צו ווי מיר שלעפּן
אַ ליידיקן הילצערנעם שליטן.

VIII

צו אַ טויער צוגעפֿאָרן,
קלאַפּ איך, רוף:
— כ׳בין דערפֿרוירן, — גוטע מענטשן,
עפֿנט אויף.

III

A cold wind from the North
Began to blow;
My faithful horse dropped his head,
Tired, to the snow.

His sides—sunken to the ribs,
His skin frozen.
Who knows whether we'll reach today
Some place warm and cozy?

The night grows darker and darker.
The snow is hard and glazed.
I walk, with eyes half-hidden,
At the side of my sleigh.

Like sharp stinging needles
In darkness, the stars,
Howling in the wilderness,
Snowed-in wolves and bears.

V

Stars light up in the sky,
The clouds are swimming away;
The road is all covered in snow—
No place to turn the sleigh.

I harness myself with my horse,
I help him to carry the weight;
I pull, and I fall to the ground,
My fingers—bleeding and frayed.

The sky grows brighter and brighter,
The moon—in full display;
They watch how we drag and pull
An empty, wooden sleigh.

VIII

At last, we get to a gate,
I knock, and I freeze:
—I am frozen, good people,
Open, please.

שפרינגען הינט אויף קייטן, בילן,
מענטשן — אויף.
גייען. איינער, הער איך, מורמלט:
— עפן אויף!

שרייט א צווייטער: פריִער פרעג זיך,
וואָס און ווער?
ווּ א וואַנדערער, א שלעפער
קומט אַהער.

מורמלט ווידער איינער: עפן,
פרעג, ניט פרעג . . .
אונדזער מזל שוין: מיר ווינען
אויפן וועג.

IX

ווינען זיך מענטשן אין מיטן דער וועלט,
רויִק און וואַרעם איז זיי.
עסן געפאַנגענע הירשן און פיש,
טרינקען צעגאַנגענעם שניי.

לייגן זיך שלאָפן, ווען ס׳קומט נאָר די נאַכט,
אַלע צוזאַמען אין בעט,
דעקן זיך איבער אַריבערן קאָפ,
שלאָפן אין טאָג אַריַין שפעט.

הוליעט אין דרויסן א צפון-זיַיט-ווינט,
נעמט מען א האַק און מען שפאַלט
שייטלעך נאָך שייטלעך אין אויוון אַריַין,
שייטלעך פון אייגענעם וואַלד.

באַקן זיך פלעצלעך און פרעגלען זיך פיש,
קאָכט זיך א קעסל מיט טיי, —
ווינען זיך מענטשן אין מיטן דער וועלט
רויִק און וואַרעם אין שניי.

Dogs on chains jump and bark,
People wake up.
Steps. I hear someone whisper:
—Open up!

Another voice:—Wait, ask who,
What and where?
Every wanderer and roamer
Comes here.

Then the first:—Ask, don't ask
In the cold . . .
That's our luck: we're living
On the road.

IX

People live in the middle of the world,
Warm in the fire's glow.
They eat their game: deer and fish,
They drink melted snow.

They go to sleep when night falls,
All in one bed,
They sleep late into the day,
With blankets over their head.

And when the North wind roams outside,
They take an axe, don a hood,
And cut chunks and chunks for the oven,
Logs from their own wood.

They bake flat rolls, fry their fish,
Boil tea before they go.
People live in the middle of the world,
Peaceful and warm in the snow.

◄ די געל-ווייסע שײַן

אהינטער ניו-יאָרק פֿאַרקײַקלט זיך די זון,
פֿאַרקײַקלט זיך די זון און לאָמפּן צינדן זיך אָן;
אַז לאָמפּן צינדן זיך אָן פֿאַלט אַ געל-ווייסע שײַן,
פֿאַלט אַ געל-ווייסע שײַן אויף אַלעמען אָן.

און מענטשן נעמען אויף מיט נײַגעריקער פֿרייד
די געל-ווייסע שײַן;
(מענטשן האָבן אַ טיפֿע פֿאַרבאָרגענע אַנונג,
אַז די געל-ווייסע שײַן איז אַן אָפּשײַן פֿון ליכט,
פֿון ליכט, וואָס וועט קיין מאָל נישט אויפֿגיין בײַ נאַכט).
מענטשן קוקן מיט קינדערשער פֿאַרליבטקייט
ווי עס שפּרייט זיך די שײַן אויף שטיין און אַספֿאַלט,
און זעט אויס ווי אַ פֿאַרפֿלייצנדיקער טײַך,
וואָס שלאָגט אַריבער די אייגענע ברעגן.

אין די טריט פֿון די מענער
הערט זיך שוין דער אָנזאָג פֿון דעם קומענדיקן שטורעם,
און די פֿאַלדן פֿון סאַמעט און זײַד
אויף די גלידער פֿון פֿרויען
זענען שוין אָפֿן און גרייט צו פֿאַרנעמען
דעם שום פֿונעם קומענדיקן שטורעם. —
דער שטורעם — ער קומט שוין;
דער שטורעם — ער איז שוין געקומען.

דער פֿאַרפֿלייצנדיקער טײַך פֿון דער געל-ווייסער שײַן
האָט דערגרייכט שוין די קני פֿון די מענער און פֿרויען,
האָט דערגרייכט שוין די אַקסלען פֿון מענער און פֿרויען,
און העכער, און העכער — אַריבערן קאָפּ.

וואָס טוען די מענער און פֿרויען
אויפֿן אָפּגרונט פֿון דער געל-ווייסער שײַן?

זיי שווימען אַרויף און אַראָפּ ווי פֿאַרכּישופֿטע בלינדע געשטאַלטן,
געאָרעמט, געקלאַמערט,
געהילטע אין סאַמעט און זײַד;
און טיפֿער נאָך ווערט די פֿאַרבאָרגענע אַנונג אין זיי,
אַז די געל-ווייסע שײַן איז אַן אָפּשײַן פֿון ליכט,
פֿון ליכט, וואָס וועט קיין מאָל נישט אויפֿגיין בײַ נאַכט.

➤ *The Yellow-White Glow*

Beyond New York the sun rolls down,
The sun rolls down and lamps light up;
When lamps light up, falls a yellow-white glow,
A yellow-white glow falls on all of us.

People greet with curious joy
The yellow-white glow;
(Deep in their bones people know:
The yellow-white glow is a reflection of light,
Of light that never will dawn at night.)
People watch with childish eyes
The glow spreading over asphalt and stone—
And it's like a swelling river
Flooding its banks.

The footsteps of men carry
The sound of the coming storm;
The folds of velvet and silk
On the limbs of women
Open up to absorb
The foam of the coming storm— —
The storm is coming;
The storm is here.

The flooding river of yellow-white glow
Reaches the knees of the men and women,
Reaches the shoulders of men and women,
And higher, higher—over their heads.

What do men and women do
In the abyss of the yellow-white glow?

They swim up and down like enchanted blind figures,
Arm-in-arm, clinging to each other,
Veiled in velvet and silk;
And deep down they know:
The yellow-white glow is a reflection of light,
Of light that will never dawn at night.

אונטער די טריט פון מײַנע פיס,
אין די טיפע טיפעלישן פון דער ערד,
הער איך דאָס אומאויפהעריקע גערוויש־געזאַנג פון מײַן לעבן,
שטראָמענווײַז — אָדערנווײַז.

דער דיקער שיכט ערד, וואָס אונטער מײַנע פיס,
ווערט אַ מאָל דורכזיכטיק ווי אַ געשליפן גלאָז,
און פאַר מײַנע אויגן גיבן אַ בלענד
פאַרבן פון זיבן מאָל זיבן קאָלירן.
ווי איינער, וואָס קוקט אַרײַן אין אַ טײַך
און זעט ווי זײַן לעבן כוואַליעט זיך
צוזאַמען מיט זײַן שטאַנדיקער אָפּשפיגלונג —
אזוי בלײַב איך שטיין אַן אַרײַנגעדרונגענער מיט ביידע אויגן
אינעם דיקן שיכט ערד, וואָס אונטער מײַנע פיס.
און איך זע:
לאַבירינטן געצונדענע
אין פײַערן, וואָס מען זעט נאָר אין אַ חלום;
און איבער זיי, און דורך זיי,
שטראָמענווײַז — אָדערנווײַז.
דאָס לעבן, וואָס מען זעט נאָר אין אַ חלום.

איך גיי אַרום אויף דעם דיקן שיכט ערד,
וואָס אונטער מײַנע פיס,
און טראָג אין זיך די פרייד פון די אונטערשטע טיפעלישן
שטראָמענווײַז — אָדערנווײַז.

◄ נישט געזעטיקטע תּאוות

נישט געזעטיקטע תּאוות ווילן זיך אָנזעטיקן,
אָרעמס ווילן פאַרמאַטערט זײַן,
ליפן זוכן פאַרקלעמונג,
פינגער זוכן פאַרברעכונג,
גרינע פײַערן אין די אויגן גרינען זיך נאָך גרינער,
ווי אויגן פון וועלף אויף געפרוירענע פעלדער,
גרינע אויגן אויף געפרוירענע פעלדער.

ווו איז דער, וואָס דאַרף זעטיקן די תּאוות?
פאַר וואָס קומט ער נישט? פאַר וואָס קומט ער נישט? —
ער האָט צוגעזאָגט, צי ער האָט נישט צוגעזאָגט? —
ער האָט דאָך צוגעזאָגט, ער האָט דאָך צוגעזאָגט.

➤ *Under the Tread of My Feet*

Under the tread of my feet,
In the deep bowels of the earth,
I hear the unceasing clamor of my life,
In currents—in arteries.

Sometimes, the thick layer of earth under my feet
Is translucent like crystal glass,
And the hues of seven times seven colors
Are dazzling before my eyes.
As a man looking into a river
Sees his life swaying on the waves,
Its shadowy reflection—
So I stand, eyes piercing
The thick layer of earth under my feet
And I see:
Labyrinths, burning
With fires that you see only in dreams;
And above them, and through them,
In currents—in arteries,
Life that you see only in dreams.

I roam, the thick layer of earth
Under my feet,
And I carry in me the joy of underground depths
In currents—in arteries.

➤ *Unsatiated Passions*

Unsatiated passions want to be satiated,
Arms wish to be tired,
Lips look for merging,
Fingers long for cracking,
Green fires in the eyes are greening greener,
Like eyes of wolves in frozen fields,
Green eyes in frozen fields.

Where is he who should quell the passions?
Why doesn't he come? Why doesn't he come?
He promised, or didn't he promise?—
He did promise, he did promise.

אָנגעשטרענגטע אויגן — ווי צילנדיקע מעסערס,
אָנגעשטרענגטע אויגן שנײַדן דורך אַלע שויבן,
אָנגעשטרענגטע אויגן נישטערן איבער אַלע וועגן:
דער וואָס דאַרף קומען — פֿאַר וואָס קומט ער נישט?
ער האָט דאָך צוגעזאָגט, ער האָט דאָך צוגעזאָגט.

פֿאַרהאַנגען פֿון צימערן — ווי פֿונאַנדערגעריסענע פֿליגלען,
ווי פֿונאַנדערגעריסענע פֿליגלען פֿון דערקײַלעטע פֿייגל —
און דער טאָג איז נאָך ליכטיק, און דער טאָג איז נאָך פֿרײַלעך —
פֿאַר וואָס פֿאַרגייט ער נישט? פֿאַר וואָס פֿאַרגייט ער נישט?
דינע פֿינגער צִיען זיך נאָך דינער,
דינע פֿינגער פֿירן אויף געפֿרוירענע פֿעלדער —
ווײַסע בעטן — ווי געפֿרוירענע פֿעלדער —
בלויע פֿינגער אויף געפֿרוירענע פֿעלדער.

◄ די קראַנקע פֿייגל

וועק ניט אויף די קראַנקע פֿייגל,
האַלט דעם אָטעם אײַן,
זע, זיי ליגן אײַנגעדרייט אין זיך אַליין,
די שאַרפֿע שנאָבלען ביז די צוגעמאַכטע אויגן
אַרײַנגעגראָבן
אין די פֿעדערן די אויפֿגעשויבערטע.

וואָס דערמאָנען אונדז די קראַנקע פֿייגל,
די שנאָבלען זייערע,
די פֿעדערן די אויפֿגעשויבערטע? זיי דערמאָנען אונדז,
אַז איך און דו,
דערנעענטערטע,
געגאַרטע,
געוואַגטע,
זיצן מיט פֿאַרשטיינערונג אין בליק,
געליימטע,
פֿאַרשעמטע,
און קיינער קומט נישט אונדזער בליק פֿאַרשטעלן,
אונדזער קאָפּ אַראָפּבייגן,
פֿאַרוויגן
ווי זיי — די קראַנקע פֿייגל,
וואָס ליגן אײַנגעגראָבן ביז די צוגעמאַכטע אויגן
אין די פֿעדערן די אויפֿגעשויבערטע.

Strained eyes—like pointed knives,
Strained eyes cut through all the windowpanes,
Strained eyes roam over the roads:
He who should come—why doesn't he come?
He did promise, he did promise.

Curtains in rooms—like wings torn apart,
Like torn-apart wings of slaughtered birds—
And the day is still bright, and the day is still gay—
Why doesn't it set? Why doesn't it set?
Thin fingers grow thinner,
Thin fingers freeze in freezing fields—
White beds—like freezing fields—
Blue fingers in freezing fields.

➤ *The Sick Birds*   First part of the poem.

Do not wake the sick birds,
Hold your breath,
See, they are lying curled up in themselves,
Their sharp beaks
Buried up to their closed eyes
In dishevelled feathers.

What do sick birds remind us of,
Their beaks,
Their dishevelled feathers?
They remind us
That I and you,
Close together,
Who craved,
Who dared,
Sit with frozen looks,
Numb,
Ashamed,
And no one comes to cover our gaze,
To lower our head,
To lull us—
As they would sick birds
Lying buried up to their closed eyes
In dishevelled feathers.

ווער צו אונדז זאָל קומען?
ווער וועט אונדז דערהערן?
אַז די טירן האָבן מיר פֿאַרשלאָסן,
אַז די פֿענצטער האָבן מיר פֿאַרהאַנגען,
אַז די ווערטער אונדזערע,
ווי נאָר זיי נידערן אַראָפּ פֿון צונג,
בלײַבן הענגען איבער אונדזער קאָפּ
אַ רגע, צוויי, און — זע:
זיי גיבן צו דער ערד אַ פֿאַל אַראָפּ
מיט שאַרפֿע שנאָבלען ביז די צוגעמאַכטע אויגן
אַרײַנגעגראָבן
אין די פֿעדערן די אויפֿגעשויבערטע.

▶ איבער די שלאָפֿנדיקע אויגן

איבער די שלאָפֿנדיקע אויגן פֿון אַלע מענטשן —
פֿרעמדע מענטשן אין פֿרעמדע הײַזער —
טראָגט זיך דורך דער באַריר פֿון מײַן האַנט,
פֿון מײַן האַנט, וואָס דעקט צו מײַנע אייגענע אויגן. —
אָנגעגליטע פֿײַערדיקע רינגען
קײַקלען זיך אין געדרײַ,
און מײַנע אויגן ווערן נישט מיד
פֿון צו קוקן אויף זיי.

זע, מענטשן ליגן זיך אין הײַזער און שלאָפֿן.

איך בין זיך מתקנא אָן דער רויִקייט פֿון אַלע מענטשן,
אָן דעם ריטמישן אָטעם, וואָס שלאָגט אַרויס פֿון זייערע הערצער,
אָן דער אידילישער טרייַשאַפֿט צו זיי
פֿון די געמאָסטענע פֿינקטלעכע שעהן —
ווען אויבן איבער זייערע קעפּ,
אָן סדר און אָן אויסרעכענונג,
אין געפּילץ און אין געוויין,
קנאַלן צעשטאָטענע דונערן —
פֿאַרוויסטונג און טויט און פֿאַרלענדונג.

זע, מענטשן ליגן זיך אין הײַזער און שלאָפֿן.

זאָל זײַן אַז איך האָב עס האָב עס אָנגעשיקט, אָנגערייצט
דאָס געפּילץ און געקנאַל,
די פֿאַרוויסטונג און פֿאַרלענדונג — דעם כאַאָס —
אויף מײַנעם און אַלעמענס קעפּ?

Who would come to us?
Who would hear us?
We have locked our doors,
We have curtained our windows,
Our words,
Dropping from our tongues,
Hang over our heads
A moment, two, and—see:
They fall to the ground
With sharp beaks up to the closed eyes
Buried
In disheveled feathers.

➤ *Over the Sleeping Eyes*

Over the sleeping eyes of all the people—
Strange people in strange houses—
Hovers the touch of my hand,
Of my hand that covers my eyes—
Glowing rings of fire
Are wheeling around,
And my eyes are not tired
From gazing spellbound.

See, people lie in their houses and sleep.

I am jealous of the calm of all the people,
Of the rhythmical breathing, swelling from their hearts,
Of the idyllic precision
Of their measured, exact hours—
When over their heads,
With no order and no reckoning,
With a whistle and a whimper,
Spilled thunders are roaring—
Desolation and death and destruction.

See, people lie in their houses and sleep.

Could it be, that I have loosed it myself,
The whistling and roaring,
The desolation and destruction—the chaos—
Brought it down on everyone's heads?

א מאָל, ווען אַ שאָטן פֿון רו

צעשפּרייט זיך אויף איבער מיר —

הער איך אַ פֿליסטער פֿון אַ מידן, צערודערטן קול:

— גענוג, נישט מער.

רייץ מיך נישט מער אויף זיך אַליין,

אויף זיך און אויף דיר.

נעם אַראָנטער דײַן אייגענע האַנט פֿון דײַנע אויגן

און פֿאַרלעש אַלע פֿײַערדיקע רינגען.

די תאווה פֿון אומרו — אין דיר,

כאָס און טויט און פֿאַרלענדונג — ביסטו,

דו — דו — אַליין.

זע, מענטשן ליגן זיך אין הײַזער און שלאָפֿן.

◄ דאָ ווײַנט דאָס ייִדישע פֿאָלק

דאָס טרעמדיקע לעבן אין דער טרעמדיקער שטאָט

ברענט אין ווײַסע פֿײַערן.

און אויף די גאַסן פֿון דער ייִדישער איסט-סײַד

ברענט די ווײַסקייט פֿון די פֿײַערן נאָך ווײַסער.

איך האָב ליב אַרומגיין אין דער ברענענדיקייט פֿון דער ייִדישער איסט-סײַד,

זיך שפּאָרן דורך דער ענגשאַפֿט פֿון געשטעלן און פֿון פּושקאַרטס,

און אָטעמען אין זיך דעם ריח און געזאַלצנקייט

פֿון אַן אָנגעהייצטן נאַקעט-לעבן.

און אַלע מאָל, ווען אין דער ווײַסקייט וואַקסן אויס פֿאַר מײַנע אויגן

ייִדן בערדיקע, אַרומגעהאַנגענע פֿון קאָפּ ביז פֿיס

מיט לאַנגע העמדער מיידלשע און ווײַבערשע;

און ייִדן, אָדער ייִדענעס מיט קראַנקע פֿיגעלעך,

וואָס קוקן מיט פֿאַרבענקטע בעטנדיקע אויגן

אויף אַ קונה צו דערלאַנגען אים אַ מזל-קוויטל;

און ייִדן אויף צווײ-רעדערדיקע שטופֿ-וועגעלעך,

בלינדע קאַליקעס, וואָס זיצן טיף אַרײַנגעזונקען אין די אַקסלען

און זעען מיט די אַקסלען דעם קאָליר און גרייס

פֿון אַן אַרײַנגעוואָרפֿענער נדבה, —

דעמאָלט וועקט זיך אויף אין מיר אַ בענקשאַפֿט אַ באַהאַלטענע,

אַ בענקשאַפֿט נאָך פֿון ייִנגלשדיקע יאָרן,

צו מגולגל ווערן אינעם הינקענדיקן בעטלער,

וואָס פֿלעגט אַרומשפּרינגען פֿון גאַס צו גאַס אין אונדזער שטעטל,

(לוריא איז געווען זײַן נאָמען)

און קלאַפֿן מיט זײַן קוליע איבער טראָטואַרן, שוועלן.

Sometimes, when a shadow of rest
Spreads over me too—
I hear the whisper of a weary, unsettled voice:
—Enough, no more.
Do not incite me against myself,
Against me and against you.
Take your hand off your eyes,
Extinguish all the rings of fire.
The passion for unrest—is in you,
Chaos and death and destruction—are you,
You yourself.

See, people lie in their houses and sleep.

► *Here Lives the Jewish People*   First and last parts of the poem.

The towering life of the towering city
Is burning in white fires.
And in the streets of the Jewish East Side
The whiteness of the fires burns even whiter.

I like to stroll in the burning frenzy of the Jewish East Side,
Squeezing through the crammed stands and pushcarts,
Breathing the smell and saltiness
Of a hot naked life.
And whenever, in the whiteness, before my eyes emerge
Bearded Jews, covered from head to toe
With long hanging gowns for girls and women;
Men or women with sick birds,
Looking up with craving, begging eyes
For a buyer, to offer him a lucky ticket;
Jews in wheel chairs,
Blind cripples, sunk deep in their own shoulders,
Who can see with their shoulders the color and size
Of a flung coin—
Then a hidden nostalgia awakens in me,
A nostalgia buried since childhood:
To be transformed into the limping beggar
Who used to hop from street to street in my hometown
(Luria was his name)
And knock with his crutch on sidewalks and thresholds.

ווער ווייסט, צי זיצט ניט אָפט-מאָל אויפן שטופּווועגל, וואָס מײַנע אויגן זעען,
דער זעלבער בעטלער פון מײַן ייִנגלשדיקער בענקשאפט,
און זעט דורך בלינדע הײַטלעך מײַן פאַרוווּנדערונג? —
דעמאָלט איז די וועלט געוואָרן נישט טורעמדיק,
אָבער ווײַס איז זי געוואָרן אַזוי ווי איצט,
פּיִערדיק און ווײַס ווי איצט.

איך גיי אום שעהנווײַז אין די גאַסן פון דער ייִדישער איסט-סײַד,
און מאָל זיך אויס פאַר מײַנע אויגן אין דער פּיִערדיקער ווײַסקײַט
טױערן פאַנטאַסטישע, קאָלאָנען אויסגעשטרעקטע,
וואָס הייבן זיך פון איבער אַלע צוגעפאַלענע געשטעלן
אַרויף-צו צו די ווײַטע אויסגעלײַדיקטע ניו-יאָרקער הימלען.
טױערן, וואָס איבער אַלע זײַערע געזימסן
הענגען אָנגעגליטע, פונקענדיקע שילדן מיט דער אויפשריפט:
ד אָ   וו ו י נ ט   ד אַ ס   ייִ ד י ש ע   פ אָ ל ק.

. . . .

שטיל. האלבע נאכט.
עס וויינט אין מיר די בענקשאפט פון די ייִנגלשדיקע יאָרן.

Who knows, whether in this wheelchair before my eyes
Does not sit the beggar of my childhood nostalgia
Watching my amazement through blind eyelids?—
Then the world had no towers,
Yet was white as now,
Fiery and white as now.

I walk for hours in the streets of the Jewish East Side
And imagine in the fiery whiteness before my eyes
Fantastic gates, soaring columns,
Rising from all the dilapidated stands
Upward, to the far and empty New York sky.
Gates—on all their cornices
Glowing, sparkling signs, inscribed:
Here lives the Jewish people.

. . . . . .

Silence. Midnight.
My childhood nostalgia cries in me.

Louis Lozowick: *Allen Street*
(El), 1929.

דער וואָלף

(אַ כראָניק. 1920)

א

‏... און עס איז געווען אויפן דריטן פרימאָרגן,
‏ווען די זון איז אויפגעגאַנגען אין מיזרח-זײַט
‏איז פון דער גאַנצער שטאָט שוין נישט געבליבן קיין זכר.

‏און די זון איז געשטיגן אַלץ העכער און העכער,
‏ביז וואַנען זי איז צוגעקומען צום מיטן הימל,
‏און אירע שטראַלן האָבן זיך באַגעגנט מיט דעם רבס אויגן.

‏און דער רב איז געלעגן אויף אַ באַרג אַש און שטיינער
‏מיט אַ צענויפגעעפֿרעסטן מויל און אויסגעגלאָצטע שוואַרצאַפּלען,
‏און אין זײַן נשמה איז געווען שטיל און פינצטער און מער גאָרנישט.

‏און ווען זײַנע אויגן האָבן דערפילט אויף זיך די הייסע שטראַלן
‏האָבן זיי זיך פונאַנדערגעשפּרייט און געקוקט און געקוקט,
‏ביז וואַנען זײַן גוף האָט אָנגעהויבן זיך רירן און אויפקומען.

שׂמח בׂחור בילדותך ויטבך לבך בימי בחורותיך והלך בדרכי

לבך ובמראי עיניך ודע כי על־כל־אלה יביאך האלהים במשפט

Ben Shahn: *Ecclesiastes*, 1966.
Hebrew quote from Ecclesiastes
11:9

H. Leyvik

The Wolf

(A Chronicle, 1920)

Abridged version. Omissions are
marked by lines of dots.

I

. . . And it was on the third day in the morning,
When the sun rose in the East
Not a trace was left of the city.

And the sun rose higher and higher,
Till it reached the center of the sky,
And its rays met the eyes of the Rov.

And the Rov lay on a mountain of ashes and stone,
His mouth clenched and his eyes glazed,
And in his soul, silence and darkness and nothing more.

And when his eyes were touched by the hot rays,
They opened wide, peering and probing,
Till his body began to stir and rise.

Rov*—the spiritual leader of a
Jewish community.

און ווען דער רב האָט זיך אויפגעשטעלט און דערזען,
אַז ער איז איבערגעבליבן איינער אַליין אין אַן אויסגעהרגעטער שטאָט
אָן שולן און אָן יידן און אָן ווײַב און קינדער —
האָט דער רב נישט געוווּסט וואָס צו טאָן.

איז ער געשטאַנען און געטראַכט און געוווּנדערט זיך,
וואָס אים האָט מען אויסגעמיטן און איבערגעלאָזט לעבן.

און ער האָט אָנגעשטרענגט די אויגן און די אויערן
צו דערזען, אפשר קריכט ווער אַרויס פון אונטער די חורבות,
און צו דערהערן אפשר אַ שאָס, וועט ער זיך לאָזן גיין אַהין-צו.

נאָר אומזיסט האָט ער אָנגעשטרענגט די אויגן און די אויערן,
ווײַל עס האָט זיך קיינער נישט באַוויזן פון אונטער די חורבות
און קיין שאָס האָט זיך פון ערגעץ נישט דערטראָגן.

און ער האָט אָנגעשטרענגט נאָך מער די אויגן צו דערזען
כאַטש וועמען נישט איז פון די באַזיגער: —
נאָר אויך די באַזיגער זײַנען נישט געווען צו באַמערקן.
קופּעס אַש, קוימענס, טליִענדיקע פלאַמען,
שטילקייט — און מער גאָרנישט.

איז ער געשטאַנען און די זאַך איז אים געווען זייער קשה,
און ער האָט נאָך מער נישט געוווּסט וואָס צו טאָן.

האָט דער רב זיך גערירט פון אָרט און זיך אַוועקגעלאָזט
זוכן און שאַרן מיט די הענט אין די קופּעס,
צו געפֿינען כאַטש די אברים פון די אומגעקומענע
און ברענגען זיי צו קבר-ישׂראל.

נאָר אומזיסט האָט ער געזוכט און געשאַרט אין די קופּעס,
ווײַל קיין זכר פון קיין אבר איז נישט געווען צו געפֿינען,
ווײַל אַלץ איז געווען אַש און קויל און מער גאָרנישט.

האָט דער רב זיך אַוועקגעזעצט אויף אַן איבערגעקערטן קוימען
און ער האָט אויסגעגאָסן די שיך און געוואָלט זאָגן קינות —
ערשט ער האָט פֿאַרגעסן די ווערטער פון די קינות.

און אַז ער האָט דערפֿילט, אַז ער האָט פֿאַרגעסן אַלע ווערטער,
האָט אים אַ שפֿאַר געטאָן אַ שטראָם פון אונטערן לעפֿעלע;
און אַז דער שטראָם האָט נישט געקאָנט גרייכן צו די אויגן
און געבליבן שטעקן אין זײַן צענויפגעקלעמטן האלדז —
האָט דער רב נאָך מערער נישט געוווּסט וואָס צו טאָן.

And when the Rov stood up and saw
That he remained alone in a slaughtered city
With no synagogues, no Jews, no women or children—
Then the Rov did not know what to do.

He stood there and pondered and was amazed
That he alone was excluded and left alive.

And he strained his eyes and his ears
To see: perhaps someone would crawl out from under the ruins,
Perhaps a shot would echo so he could go toward it.

But he strained his eyes and his ears in vain,
For no one appeared from under the ruins
And no shot sounded from anywhere.

And he strained his eyes even more to see
At least one of the victors—
But the victors, too, were nowhere to be seen.
Heaps of ashes, chimneys, smoldering flames,
Silence—and nothing more.

So he stood there, puzzled by it all,
And once again he did not know what to do.

Then the Rov stirred from his place and went ahead,
Searching and shuffling with his hands in the heaps,
To find at least the limbs of the slaughtered people
And bury them in a Jewish grave.

But he searched and shuffled in the heaps in vain,
For no trace of a corpse could be found,
For all was ashes and coals and nothing more.

Then the Rov sat down on an overturned chimney,
Took off his shoes, prepared to recite laments—
But he had forgotten the words of the laments.

And when it dawned on him that he had forgotten all the words,
A tide rose from the pit of his stomach;
And as the tide could not reach his eyes
And got stuck in his cramped throat—
Once again the Rov did not know what to do.

אַז די נאַכט איז געקומען און האָט צוגעדעקט
די חרובֿדיקע שטאָט מיט אַ גרויסער פֿינצטערניש,
האָט דער רבֿ זיך אויפֿגעהויבֿן פֿונעם קוימען,
אויף וועלכן ער איז נאָך געזעסן,
האָט אַ קער געטאָן זײַן פּנים צו מערבֿ-צו
און מיט די זאָקן אויף די פֿיס זיך אַוועקגעלאָזט גיין
מיט דעם ברייטן שליאַך, וואָס פֿירט אין וואַלד אַרײַן.

דער ברייטער שליאַך איז געוועזן באַדעקט מיט אַלערלײַ חפֿצים,
מיט ביקסן און מיט היטלען און צעבראָכענע רעדער,
און די ערד איז געוועזן צעאַקערט און צעטראַמפּלט
פֿון קוילן און פֿון גראַנאַטן,
פֿון פֿערדישע קאָפּיטעס און חיילישע פֿיס,
און אַרום דעם שליאַך און איבער דעם שליאַך —
פֿינצטערניש און שטילקייט און מער גאָרנישט.

און אַז דער רבֿ איז אָפּגעגאַנגען עטלעכע מײַל,
האָט אַ קאַלטער ווינט אָנגעהויבן בלאָזן פֿון צפֿון-זײַט,
און דער רבֿ האָט דערפֿילט אַ גרויסע מידקייט אין זײַן גוף
און אַ קעלט איבער אַלע זײַנע ביינער.

האָט דער רבֿ זיך אַוועקגעזעצט אויף דער ערד צו אָפּרוען,
און דערנאָך זיך אויסגעצויגן אויפֿן מיטן שליאַך
מיט אָפֿענע אויגן צום הימל.
און דער הימל איז געוועזן הויך און טיף און אויסגעשטערנט
מיט מילי-מיליאָסן שטערן.

און ווי דער רבֿ האָט געקוקט מיט זײַנע אָפֿענע אויגן
אַזוי האָבן די מילי-מיליאָסן שטערן
גענומען רײַסן זיך פֿון זייערע ערטער און דרייען זיך,
און שנײַדן זיך און שלאָגן זיך איינע אָן די אַנדערע
און איבערגעשפּאַלטן איינע די אַנדערע,
ביז זיי זײַנען געוואָרן אײַנגעשלונגען אין דער פֿינצטערניש.

און אַז דער רבֿ האָט געזען ווי זיי ווערן אויסגעלאָשן,
האָט עס אים נישט געאַרט און ער האָט ווײַטער געקוקט.
און אַז איין שטערן, דער לעצטער, האָט זיך אײַנגעעקשנט
און נישט געוואָלט פֿאַרלאָשן ווערן,
האָט דער רבֿ אויסגעשטרעקט זײַן רעכטע האַנט
און געטײַטלט מיט אַ פֿינגער, ביז דער שטערן
איז געוואָרן גרין און געל און רויט,
און אַלץ נישט געוואָלט פֿאַרלאָשן ווערן.

When the night descended and covered
The ruined city with a great darkness,
The Rov got up from the chimney
Where he was sitting,
Turned his face to the west,
And with socks on his feet he abandoned himself
To the wide highway leading to the forest.

The wide highway was covered with a multitude of things,
Rifles and hats and broken wheels,
And the soil was plowed open and trampled
By shells and grenades,
By horses' hoofs and soldiers' feet,
And around the highway and over the highway—
Darkness and silence and nothing more.

And when the Rov had walked several miles,
A cold wind started to blow from the north,
And the Rov sensed a great weariness in his body
And cold in all his bones.

Then the Rov sat down on the earth to rest,
And he prostrated his body on the highway,
His eyes open to the sky.
And the sky was high and deep and full of stars,
Myriads of stars.

And as the Rov watched with open eyes,
Myriads of stars began
Tearing loose from their places and turning and circling,
And cutting and striking each other,
And splitting each other apart,
Until they were swallowed up by the dark.

And when the Rov saw that the stars had gone out,
He did not care and looked on.
And as the last star grew stubborn
And did not want to be extinguished,
The Rov stretched out his right hand
And pointed with a finger, until the star
Became green and yellow and red
And still did not want to disappear.

האָט דער רב אַרונטערגעלאָזט זײַן רעכטע האַנט

און אַרויפֿגעלייגט זי אויף זײַנע ביידע אויגן,

ווײַל עס האָט אים נישט געאַרט מער פֿאַרן לעצטן שטערן.

און די האַנט איז געלעגן אויף זײַנע אויגן,

ביז זי איז אַרונטערגעפֿאַלן אַליין צו דער ערד צו,

ווײַל זײַנע ברעמען האָבן אָנגעהויבן אײַנצודרעמלען.

און ווי נאָר ער האָט אָנגעהויבן אײַנצודרעמלען

האָט זיך געכאַפֿט, אַז ער האָט נאָך נישט געדאַוונט

קיין מנחה און קיין מעריב און נישט געלייענט קיין קריאת-שמע:

און ער האָט זיך אויפֿגעזעצט און געוואָלט נעמען דאַוונען —

ערשט ער האָט דעם נוסח פֿון דאַוונען פֿאַרגעסן.

און אַז ער האָט דערזען, אַז ער האָט אויך דאָס דאַוונען פֿאַרגעסן,

האָט אים אַ שפֿאַר געטאָן אַ צוווייטער שטראָם פֿון אונטערן לעפּעלע,

און אַז דער שטראָם האָט ווידער נישט געקענט גרייכן צו זײַנע אויגן

און געבליבן שטעקן אין מיטן פֿון זײַן האַלדז —

האָט שוין דער רב מער נישט געקענט אויסהאַלטן,

און ער איז אויפֿגעשפּרונגען און גענומען לויפֿן

אַלץ ווײַטער און ווײַטער מיטן ברייטן שלייאַק.

די פּאָלעס פֿון זײַן רבנישן בגד

האָבן זיך צעפֿלאַטערט ווי צוויי שוואַרצע פֿליגל,

און דער ווינט האָט געריסן דאָס שטרײַמל פֿון זײַן קאָפּ,

און דער זאַמד האָט אַרונטערגעשלעפֿט די זאָקן פֿון זײַנע פֿיס.

און אַזוי מיט אַ נאַקעטן קאָפּ און באַרוועסע פֿיס

האָט ער זיך אָפֿגעשלאָגן פּלוצלינג אָן דער שוואַרצקייט

פֿון דעם גרויסן פֿערציק-מײַליקן וואַלד.

און זײַן מוח איז פֿון דעם מיט אַ מאָל אויפֿגעצונדן געוואָרן

און פֿונאַנדערגעעפֿנט זיך אויף צוויי טויערן,

און אַ גרויסע ליכטיקייט האָט אַ שטראָם געטאָן אויף זײַנע אויגן,

און ער האָט דערזען דעם פֿערציק-מײַליקן וואַלד

אויף דורך און דורך פֿון איין עק ביז דעם צווייטן.

און אַז ער האָט דערזען דעם וואַלד אויף דורך און דורך,

האָט זײַן אויג נישט געקאָנט מער אויסהאַלטן

דאָס גרויסע ליכט פֿון דער פֿערציק-מײַליקער רחבות,

און זײַן אָטעם האָט געקלאָפֿט די לעצטע קלעפּ.

און זײַן גוף האָט זיך געצויגן צו דער ערד פֿון בענקעניש.

און דאָס ערשטע מאָל פֿאַרן גאַנצן טאָג

האָט זיך אַרויסגעריסן פֿון זײַן אײַנגעשטיקטן האַלדז

אַ הייזעריקער כריפּ, אַ זכר פֿון אַ קלאַנג,

Then the Rov lowered his right hand
And laid it on both his eyes,
For he did not care anymore about the last star.
And the hand lay on his eyes,
Till it dropped to the earth,
For his brows were falling asleep.

And as he was about to fall asleep,
He realized that he had not yet prayed
The Afternoon Prayer and the Evening Prayer
And had not said the *Shema* on going to bed:
So he sat up and prepared to pray—
But he had forgotten the words of the prayers.

And as he saw that he had forgotten even the prayers,
A second tide rose from the pit of his stomach,
And as the tide again could not reach his eyes
And got stuck in his throat—
Then the Rov could not stand it anymore,
And jumped up and darted away, running
Farther and farther on the wide highway.

The tails of his rabbinical coat
Fluttered like two black birds,
And the wind tore the fur hat off his head,
And the sand pulled the socks off his feet.
And thus, with naked head and bare feet,
He suddenly smashed against the blackness
Of the great, forty-mile forest.
And his brain lit up all at once
And gaped open in two gates,
And a great light flooded his eyes,
And he saw the forty-mile forest
Through and through, from one end to the other.

And as he saw the forest through and through,
His eyes could not bear anymore
The great light of the forty-mile expanse,
And his breath beat its last beats,
And in longing, his body was drawn to the earth.
And for the first time that day
From his stifled throat burst out
A hoarse growl, a vestige of a sound,

Afternoon Prayer, Evening Prayer (Minha, Ma'ariv)—two of the three daily prayers.
Shema* (Hebrew: **Kri'at Shema**)—the declaration of God's oneness, uttered daily before retiring and at the time of one's death.

און נאָך איין רגע — האָט זיך אים געדאַכט —
וועט אָנקומען דאָס אמתע געשריי.

און ער איז צוגעפאַלן מיטן שטערן צו אַ בוים,
און געקלאַפט מיט בײדע הענט אין זיין נאַקעטער ברוסט,
און געשטויסן און געריסן פון זיין אינגעווייד
די נישט אַרויסגעקומענע געשרייען פון זיין בענקעניש.

און ער האָט געוואָלט זיך לאָזן לויפן ווײַטער אין וואַלד אַרײַן,
און ווי נאָר ער האָט איבערגעטראָטן די גרענעץ,
אַזוי האָט ער דערפילט ווי זײַנע פיס ווערן אַרײַנגעכאַפט
און אַרײַנגעפלאַנטערט אין געדיכטע שטעכיקע דראָטן.
און ער האָט נאָך נישט צײַט געהאַט אַרויסנעמען די פיס —
ווי די נעצן האָבן אַרײַנגעכאַפט זײַן גאַנצן גוף,
און אַנידערגעשלײַדערט אים אויף אַלע פיר,
און געצויגן אים און געשלעפט אים און געקײַקלט אים
אַרויף און אַראָפ איבער גריבער און אויסגעקערטע וואָרצלען,
און געריסן שטיקערווײַז פון זײַנע בגדים,
און נאָך דעם — אַז די בגדים זײַנען שוין געווען אַראָפגעריסן —
שטיקער הויט פון זײַן נאַקעטן לײַב.

און אַז דער רב האָט דערזען, אַז ער איז מוטער-נאַקעט,
האָט זיך אַ מאָדנער שמײיכל צעגאָסן איבער זײַן פנים,
און איבער זײַנע ציין איז דורכגעלאָפן אַ שאַרפקײט,
און איבער זײַן צונג אַזאַ געזאַלצענע שפײַעכץ,
און די אונטערשטע ליפ האָט גענומען אַרונטערהענגען.

און אַז ער האָט גענומען אַרויסשפײַען דאָס געזאַלצנס פון זײַן מויל —
האָבן דינע הערעלעך גענומען אַרויסשטעכן זיך
פון אונטער זײַן גאַנצער הויט, אַרויסשפּראָצן און וואַקסן,
און אויסלײַגן זיך רײַענווײַז, רײַענווײַז,
אין איין אָרט גלאַט און צוזאַמענגעפאַלן,
אין אַ צווייטן — אויפגעשטעלט און אויפגעשויבערט.

און אַז דער רב האָט געוואָלט פאַר אימה
פאַרדעקן די אויגן מיט די הענט —
האָט ער דערזען, ווי זײַנע פינגער גיסן זיך צוזאַמען,
און קײַיקלען זיך אויף און פאַרשפיצן זיך
מיט לאַנגע אויסגעבויגענע האַרטע נעגל;
און איבערן רוקן, האָט ער דערפילט, ווי עמעצער טוט אים אָן
אַ צוזאַמענגעדרייטע רײַף און שמידט צונויף
זײַן נאַקן און אַרונטערגעפאַלענע פלייצעס.

And it seemed to him that in another minute
The real shriek would come.

And he fell with his forehead to a tree,
And he beat with both hands at his naked breast,
And shook and tried to tear from his entrails
The muted shrieks of his longing.

And he wanted to run deeper into the forest,
And as soon as he crossed the border-line
He sensed that his legs were caught
And entangled in dense barbed wire.
And he had no time to pull his legs free—
For the nets engulfed his whole body
And threw him down on all fours,
And pulled him and dragged him and rolled him
Up and down over holes and upturned roots,
And ripped swatches off his clothing,
And when his clothes were all torn off—
Strips of skin from his naked body.

And when the Rov saw that he was naked
As a newborn babe,
A strange smile suffused his face,
And a sharpness ran over his teeth,
And salty saliva over his tongue,
And his lower lip hung down.

And as he spat the salt out of his mouth—
Thin hair began to sting and spring up
All over his skin, sprout and grow,
And lay in row upon row,
In one place flat and fallen thick,
In another—standing on end and dishevelled.

And when the Rov, in his fear, wanted
To cover his eyes with his hands—
He saw his fingers merge with each other
And bend and grow pointed
With long, crooked, hard claws;
And over his back he felt as if someone had clasped
An iron hoop and forged together
His neck and his stooped shoulders.

און זײַנע אויערן האָבן אָנגעהויבן זיך ציִען און ארונטערלאָזן זיך,
און די צונג אין זײַן מויל אַרויסשלאָגן זיך פון אונטערן גומען,
און קנוילן זיך און שפאַרן זיך פון צווישן די ציין,
און גליטשן זיך און ארויסשטעקן אַלץ לענגער און לענגער,
און זײַנע אויגן האָבן גענומען אויפלויפן
און דרייען זיך אונטער די ברעמען ווי קײַלעכדיקע רעדלעך,
און צינדן זיך אין פראַסטיקע גרינע פײַערן.

און ער האָט דערזען נאָך אַ מאָל דעם פערציק־מײַליקן וואַלד
אויף דורך און דורך פון איין עק ביזן צווייטן,
און זײַן אָטעם האָט אָנגעהויבן קלאַפן
נײַע, זודיקע, ערשט־געבוירענע קלעפ,
און ער איז אויפגעשפרונגען אויף אַלע פיר
מיט אַן אויפגעשפיצטן, אויפגעשויבערטן רוקן
און האָט זיך אײַנגעגאסן מיט די אויגן אין דער פינצטערניש.

און אזוי ווי אַלע גודערעם וואָלטן זיך אַ ריס טאָן פון זײַן בויך,
אזוי האָט אים אַ שפאַר געטאָן אַ דריטער שטראָם צום האַלדז
און מער שוין נישט געבליבן שטעקן אין זײַן גאָרגל,
און אַ ווילד געבריל האָט זיך צעטראָגן איבערן וואַלד
אַלץ העכער און העכער און וואיִענדיקער,
און אַ פלינקער שפרונג האָט נאָכגעפאָלגט דאָס געבריל —
אַ שפרונג אינעם אויסזען פון אַ האַלבן בויגן.

און אַז דער וואַלד האָט דערהערט דאָס ווילדע געבריל
און דעם פלינקן שפרונג פון אַ חיה —
האָט אים אָפּגענומען פאַר אַ רגע זײַן שטורעמדיקער אָטעם;
און אין אַ רגע שפעטער האָט דער וואַלד
נאָך ברייטער פונאַנדערגעוויגט זײַן שטורעם,
און טיפער און טיפער געצויגן צו זיך,
און שטיקערווײַז געריסן און צעשלײַדערט,
און אַרײַנגענומען צוריק אין זיך און באַהאַלטן אין זיך
דאָס ווילדע ברילנדיקע וואיִען.

און עס איז געווען שטורעם און פינצטערניש און מער גאָרנישט.

ב

און עס האָבן אָנגעהויבן אָנצוקומען אין שטאָט
ארויסגעטריבענע ייִדן פון אַנדערע געגנטן,
און גענומען אָפּבויען צוריק די חרובע הײַזער,
און פריִער פון אַלץ — די קאַלטע שול,
ווײַל פון דער קאַלטער שול זײַנען איבערגעבליבן האַלבע ווענט,
און ווײַל די צאָל פון די נײַע ייִדן איז געווען נאָך קליין
האָבן זיי מער ווי איין שול דערווײַל נישט געדאַרפט.

And his ears grew long and hung down,
And his tongue was loosed from his palate,
And curled and pushed between his teeth,
And lolled out and stretched longer and longer,
And his eyes swelled
And rolled under his brows like round wheels,
And ignited in frosty green fires.

And again he saw the forty-mile forest
Through and through from one end to the other,
And his breath began beating
With new, hot, fresh-born beats,
And he jumped up on all fours,
With a pointed, dishevelled back,
And sank his eyes into the darkness.

And as if his entrails were tearing loose from his belly,
A third tide rose in his throat
And this time did not get stuck in his gullet,
And a wild roar spread in the forest,
Louder and louder and howlier,
And a swift leap followed the roar—
A high, arching leap.

And as the forest heard the wild howl
And saw the swift leap of a beast—
It held for a moment its stormy breath;
And a moment later the forest
Swung its storm ever wider
And sucked in deeper and deeper,
And tore to pieces and scattered,
And engulfed and buried in its depths
The wild roaring howl.

Ben Shahn: Drawing from
Biography of a Painting.

And there was storm and darkness and nothing more.

II

And Jews expelled from other places
Began moving into the city,
And started rebuilding the ruined houses,
And first of all—the Cold Synagogue,
For some walls still remained of the Cold Synagogue,
And since the number of the new Jews was still small
They did not need more than one synagogue.

Cold synagogue—the official, solemn synagogue of a community.

און אַז די שול איז פאַרטיק געוואָרן מיט פענצטער און טירן,
האָבן זיי אַרײַנגעשטעלט אין אָרון-קודש די ספר-תּורה,
די אײנציקע ספר-תּורה, וואָס זיי האָבן אָפּגעראַטעוועט
און געבראַכט מיט זיך פון זייערע געגנטן.

און זיי האָבן ביז שפעט אין דער נאַכט פון מעריב אָן
פאַרבראַכט אין שול און זיך משׂמח געווען.
און זייער שׂמחה איז געווען געמישט מיט צער,
ווײַל זיי האָבן נאָך נישט געהאַט קיין אייגענעם רב,
און נאָך גרעסער איז געווען זייער צער,
וואָס קיין ייִד פון דעם פריערדיקן ייִשוב
האָט נאָך נישט באַוויזן צו אומקערן זיך אַהיים.

און עס איז געווען, אַזוי ווי זיי האָבן זיך משׂמח געווען —
זײַנען זיי אַלע געבליבן מיט אַ מאָל פאַרציטערט,
ווײַל עס האָט זיך זיי אויסגעדאַכט, אַז זיי הערן
אַ ווײַט משונהדיק ווײַנען פון ערגעץ.

און אַז זיי זײַנען געוואָרן שטיל און אײַנגעהערט זיך —
איז זייער שרעק נאָך גרעסער געוואָרן,
ווײַל זיי האָבן געהערט אויף אַן אמת, ווי פון ווײַט, ווײַט
דערטראָגט זיך און דרינגט אַרײַן אין דער שול
אַ לאַנג צעצויגן וואָיען פון אַ חיה.

פון אָנהייב בײַז און ברומענדיק, ווי אין אַ רגע פון פאַרצוקונג,
און נאָך דעם דין און פאַרצווייפלט, ווי דאָס קלאָגעניש
פון אַ הונט וואָס רײַסט-אויף זײַן האַרץ פאַר דער לבנה,
און צום סוף שטילער און שטילער און כליפענדיק,
וואָס דערמאָנט אָן געוויין פון אַ מענטשן.

און אַז די ייִדן זײַנען אַרויסגעלאָפן פון שול
און זיך אײַנגעהערט אין דער האַלב-נאַכטיקער פינצטערניש —
האָבן זיי שוין מער גאָרנישט נישט געהערט,
אַ חוץ דאָס קלאַפן פון זייערע אייגענע הערצער,
און דאָס שאַרכן פון די אָפּגעסמאַליעטע ביימער,
וואָס האָבן אַרויסגעשטעקט פון צווישן די חורבות,
און געשאַטן אין דער נאַכט זייערע לעצטע בלעטער —
ווײַל עס איז שוין געווען האַרבסט אויף דער ערד.

און די ייִדן זײַנען געגאַנגען שווײַגנדיקע צו זייערע הײַזער.
און עס האָט זיך זיי געדאַכט, אַז דער, וואָס האָט אַזוי געוואָיעט,
ליגט פאַרבאַהאַלטן אונטער אַ וואַנט צי אַ קרימען,
און ער איז געוואָרן מיט אַ כּיוון שטיל, ווײַל ער לויערט,
און באַלד וועט ער אַרויסשפּרינגען און אָנפאַלן...

And when the synagogue was finished with windows and doors,
They put the Torah Scroll into the Holy Ark,
The only Torah Scroll that they had salvaged
And brought here from their own places.

And they stayed together in the synagogue and rejoiced.
Till late into the night after the Evening Prayer,
And their joy was mingled with sorrow,
For they did not yet have their own Rov,
And even greater was their sorrow,
That no single Jew from the old town
Had returned home.

And it was in the midst of their rejoicing—
All of a sudden they froze in fear
For they imagined that they heard
A distant, strange wailing from somewhere.

And as they fell silent and listened to the dark—
Their fear grew even larger,
For they could hear, from far, far away
A long drawn-out howl of a beast
Reaching and penetrating the synagogue.

At first, angry and roaring, as in a moment of devouring prey,
Then thin and desperate, as the wailing
Of a dog baring his heart to the moon,
And finally, quieter and quieter and whining,
Like the cry of a human being.

And as the Jews ran out of the synagogue
And listened to the midnight darkness—
They could not hear a thing anymore,
Except for the beating of their own hearts
And the rustling of the scorched trees
Protruding from the ruins,
Scattering their last leaves into the night—
As Autumn descended upon the earth.

And the Jews went silently to their homes.
And it seemed to them that the one who howled so
Was lying hidden under a wall or a chimney,
Lurking, holding his breath,
And soon he would leap out and attack . . .

און אַז די ייִדן האָבן דערזען, װי אױפֿן הימל
איז מיטאַמאָל, װי פֿון אַ קעלער, אַרױסגעקראָכן די לבֿנה
און האָט אױפֿגעדעקט די װײַטקײט, װאָס הינטער אַלע חורבֿות
ביז די קײלעכדיקע װענט פֿון די אײנגעשלאָסענע װעלדער,
װאָס האָבן אַרומגערינגלט די שטאָט פֿון אַלע זײַטן, —
האָבן זײ גאָר פֿון דאָס נײַ דערשפּירט די נאַקעטקײט פֿון די גאַסן
און אַז די חורבֿות זײַנען נישט זײערע,
און אַז דאָ זײַנען זײ פֿרעמדע.

און אַז זײ זײַנען שױן געװען אין די הײַזער בײַ זיך,
זײַנען זײ אַ לאַנגע צײַט נאָך געשטאַנען אין דער פֿינצטערניש,
און מיט מורא אַרױסגעקוקט דורך די שײַבלעך,
װי די װײַסע שײַן פֿון דער לבֿנה װערט װײַסער און װײַסער,
און װי אַלע שפֿאַלטן פֿון די חורבֿות װערן אױפֿגעעפֿנט.

און אַזױ אין שרעק זײַנען זײ דערנאָך אַנטשלאָפֿן געװאָרן.
. . . .

ג

און עס איז געװען אין דער פֿרי, װען די ייִדן
זײַנען אַרױסגעגאַנגען פֿון שול נאָכן דאַװונען,
און אין זײערע הערצער האָט נאָך געקלונגען דאָס שאַלן
פֿונעם אלולדיקן שופֿר, און פֿון זײערע אױגן
האָט נאָך אַרױסגעקוקט דער נאַכטיקער פּחד, —
האָבן זײ דערזען װי פֿון דער זײַט פֿונעם ברײטן שליאַך
מיט שנעלע טריט צו דער שול קומט אָן אַ ייִד,
און זײ האָבן זיך אַלע געלאָזט אים מקבל-פּנים זײַן.

און אַז זײ האָבן דערזען, אַז דער פֿרעמדער איז אָנגעטאָן
אין אַ זײדענעם בגד און רבֿנישן שטרײַמל,
איז צו זײער שׂימחה ניט געװען קײן שיעור,
און זײ האָבן אַלע אױסגעשטרעקט די הענט צו געבן שלום-עליכם.

און אַז דער פֿרעמדער האָט נישט געענטפֿערט אױפֿן שלום-עליכם,
און װי ער האָט געהאַלטן אין גײן צו דער שול צו,
אַזױ איז ער געגאַנגען װײַטער און נישט אָפּגעשטעלט זיך אױף קײן רגע,
און קײן אײנציק װאָרט נישט אַרױסגערעדט פֿון מױל, —
האָבן די ייִדן דערזען ערשט, אַז אױף דעם פֿרעמדנס פֿיס
זײַנען נישטאָ קײן שיך, נאָר צעריסענע זאָקן אַ פּאָר,
און דאָס שטרײַמל איז אײַנגעשמוצט און אױסגעריבן,
און דער בגד צעשניטן אין גװאַלד-ריסן,
און זײַן האָריקע צעבלאָטיקטע ברוסט זעט זיך אַרױס נאַקעט,
און דאָס גאַנצע פּנים איז װי אַרײַנגעזונקען
אין די קנײלן פֿון אַ משונהדיקער צעשװײבערטער באָרד;

And when the Jews saw that in the sky
The moon suddenly climbed out, as from a cellar,
And exposed the expanses stretching beyond the ruins
Up to the walls of the enclosing forests
Which encircled the city from all sides—
Then they sensed anew the nakedness of the streets,
And that these were not their ruins,
And here they were strangers.

And as they came back to their own homes,
They stood for a long time in the darkness,
And looked out in fear through the window-panes,
Watching the white glow of the moon getting whiter and whiter,
And all the cracks in the ruins opening up.

And so in fear they fell asleep.
. . . .

III

And it was in the morning, when the Jews
Left the synagogue after prayer,
And in their hearts still resounded
The Autmun shofar of Elul and their eyes
Still projected the night's fear—
Then they saw a Jew coming from the wide highway
And approaching the synagogue with swift steps,
And they all flocked to greet him.

And as they saw that the stranger was wearing
A silk coat and a rabbinical fur hat,
There were no bounds to their joy,
And they all stretched out their hands to welcome him.

Elul—the Hebrew month preceding the High Holy Days. In this period, Jews prepare for the Day of Atonement, pray for forgiveness, and practice blowing the **shofar***; the period is marked by an autumnal atmosphere.

And when the stranger did not answer their greeting,
And walked on to the synagogue as before
And did not pause for a moment,
And his mouth did not utter a single word—
Then the Jews realized that the stranger's feet
Had no shoes, but only a pair of torn socks,
And his fur hat was dirty and worn,
And his coat was slashed in several places,
And his hairy, blood-covered chest was bare,
And his entire face seemed to be sunk
In the tangles of a bizarre dishevelled beard;

און די ייִדן האָבן דערפילט דאָס אבֿלדיקס, וואָס אינעם פֿרעמדן,
און זיי האָבן זיך דערמאָנט, אַז זיי אַליין זייַנען אויך אבֿלים ווי ער,
און זיי האָבן געקוקט איינער אויף די אַנדערע און גאָרנישט גערעדט,
און מיט נייַגעריקייַט נאָכגעגאַנגען דעם פֿרעמדן צום שולהויף,
און זיי האָבן געהאָפֿט, אַז ער וועט באַלד אַליין אָנהייבן רעדן,
און זיי וועלן הערן פֿון זייַן מויל טרייַעריקע, אָבער חשובֿע רייד.

נאָר דער פֿרעמדער האָט אַלץ געהאַלטן אָפּגעקערט זייַנע אויגן פֿון די ייִדן,
און אַזוי, אויף קיינעם ניט קוקנדיק, איז ער צוגעקומען צו דער טיר פֿון שול
און האָט זי אַזוי ווי אָפּגעשטויסן פֿון זיך און אַרייַנגעטראָטן אינעווייניק,
און אַנידערגעזעצט זיך אויף אַ מיזרח-שטאָט לעבן סאַמע אָרון-קודש,
און אַלץ נישט געעפֿנט זייַן מויל צו אַרויסרעדן אַ וואָרט.

און די ייִדן זייַנען געשטאַנען אַרום אים, און מיט יעדער רגע
געפֿילט אַלץ מער און מער דעם פּחד פֿון זייַן שווייַגן,
ווייַל זיי האָבן ערשט איצט דערזען דעם קאָליר פֿון זייַנע אויגן
און דערהערט דעם שווערן אָטעם פֿון זייַן נאַקעטער ברוסט.
און אין אָנגעזיכט פֿון זייַן שווייַגן האָט די גאַנצע שול
אַנטפּלעקט פֿאַר זייערע אויגן איר קאַלטע נישט-היימלעכקייט:
און ס'איז געוואָרן, אַזוי ווי זיי וואָלטן אַרונטערגעלאָזן די קעפּ
און געשעמט זיך צו קוקן אויף די נאַקעטע ווענט,
און אויף דעם פּראָסטן שראַנקל, וואָס האָט געדינט פֿאַר אַן אָרון-קודש.
און דער פֿרעמדער האָט מיט אַ מאָל זיך אויפֿגעשטעלט און געזאָגט:
— וואָס דאַרפֿט איר? גייט. ס'איז מייַן מיזרח-שטאָט, דעם רבס שטאָט.

און די ייִדן האָבן פֿאַרשטאַנען, אַז ער איז נישט בייַם פֿולן זינען,
און זיי האָבן זיך איבערגעקוקט און נישט געוווּסט וואָס צו טאָן.

און דער פֿרעמדער האָט איבערגעכאַפּט זייער איבערקוקן זיך,
און ער האָט אַראָפּגעוואָרפֿן פֿון זיך דעם בגד,
און גענומען קלאַפּן מיט ביידע פֿויסטן אין האַרצן אַרייַן,
און דורך זייַנע ציין האָבן זיך געריסן כאָרכלענדיקע ווערטער:
— ווער האָט אייַך געהייסן די חורבות צוריק אויפֿבויען?
אַז ס'איז חרובֿ, דאַרף בלייַבן חרובֿ.
און ווער האָט אייַך געהייסן וואָרן מייַנע יורשים?
— גייט ברענגט אַ האַק צי אַ מעסער און טוט מיר מייַן רעכט,
— טוט מיר מייַן רעכט, ייִדן, איך בעט אייַך.

און דער פֿרעמדער איז אַנידערגעפֿאַלן אויף אַ באַנק דער אַ פֿאַרשוויגנדלטער.
ווייַל ער האָט שוין וואָכן-לאַנג ניט אַרויסגערעדט קיין מענטשלעך וואָרט,
און ער האָט אַליין נישט געוווּסט פֿון וואַנען די ווענן די ווערטער קומען,
און עס איז געוואָרן אַזוי ווי עפּעס וואָלט זיך אין אים אָפּגעריסן
און אַרונטערגעפֿאַלן אין אַ גרוב און אויך אין מיטגעשלעפּט.

And the Jews sensed mourning in the stranger,
And they remembered that they too were mourners,
And they looked at each other and did not say a word.
Mystified, they followed the stranger to the synagogue yard,
And they hoped that soon he would start talking
And they would hear from his mouth sad but weighty words.

But the stranger still turned his eyes away from the Jews,
And not looking at anyone, he approached the door of the synagogue
And seemed to push it aside, and stepped inside,
And sat on an Eastern seat, close to the Holy Ark,
And still did not open his mouth to utter a word.

Eastern seat—a place of honor in the synagogue.

And the Jews stood around him, and with each passing moment
They felt more and more the awe of his silence,
For only now did they observe the color of his eyes
And hear the heavy breathing in his naked chest.
And in the face of his silence, the people of the synagogue
Saw before their eyes its cold uncanniness.
And it was as if they bent their heads
And were ashamed to look at the naked walls
And at the simple cabinet that served as a Holy Ark.
And all of a sudden the stranger stood up and said:
—What do you want? Go away. It is my Eastern Seat, the Rov's seat.

And the Jews understood that the man was not in his right mind,
And they looked at each other and did not know what to do.

And the stranger caught their glances at each other,
And he shed the coat from his body,
And hammered with both fists at his heart,
And wheezing words growled through his teeth:
—Who told you to rebuild the ruins?
Once ruined, it should remain ruined.
And who told you to become my heirs?
Go, bring an axe or a knife and give me my just desserts,
My just desserts, Jews, I beg you.

And the stranger fell on the bench and was dizzy,
For many weeks had passed since he had spoken a human word,
And he did not know himself where the words came from,
And it was as if something had been torn inside him
And had fallen into a pit and pulled him with it.

און די ייִדן האָבן געמיינט, אַז ער פֿאַלט אין חלשות,

און זיי האָבן אים אָנגעכאַפּט פֿאַר די הענט און געמינטערט אים;

נאָר דער פֿרעמדער איז באַלד געקומען צו זיך און גענומען רעדן

מיט אַ שלוכצנדיקן קול, אַזוי ווי ער וואָלט וויינען:

— איך בעט אײַך, ייִדן, טוט מיר מײַן רעכט. וואָס עס קומט מיר, —

מיר קומט אַ מיתה-משונה, אַ מיתה פֿון פֿרעמדע הענט;

איך וואָלט אַליין געקאָנט איבערשנײַדן מײַן האָלדז

און אַרײַנשטעכן אַ דאָרן אין ביידע אויגן,

און אָפּהאַקן די הענט און אַוועקוואָרפֿן פֿאַר הינט —

איך טאָר דאָס אָבער ניט טאָן אַליין — אַ צווייטער מוז דאָס מיר טאָן!

איך בעט אײַך, ברענגט אַ האַק און טוט מיר מײַן רעכט.

און אַזוי רעדנדיק איז ער צוגעפֿאַלן צו דער ערד,

און געקלאַמערט זיך אָן די פֿיס פֿון די ייִדן,

ביז וואָנען זײַן געווײַן האָט זיך מיט אַ מאָל אָפּגעריסן,

און זײַן האָלדז האָט זיך גענומען ווערגן פֿון גאָר אַנדערע קלאַנגען.

און די ייִדן האָבן די אַנדערע קלאַנגען נישט געהערט,

און זיי האָבן זיך געבויגן איבער אים און געוואָלט אים אויפֿהייבן,

נאָר דער פֿרעמדער איז געלעגן אַ שווערער און אַן אַראָפּגעזונקענער,

און קיינער האָט אים נישט געקאָנט אַ ריר געבן פֿון אָרט.

און איינער פֿון די ייִדן האָט מיט אַ מאָל אַ שפּרונג געטאָן

און גענומען לויפֿן איבער דער שול מיט גוואַלדיקע געשרייען,

ווײַל דער פֿרעמדער האָט זיך אַרײַנגעביסן אין זײַן האַנט מיט אַלע ציין.

און אַז די ייִדן האָבן דערזען די אײַנגעביסענע האַנט,

האָבן זיי איינער נאָכן צווייטן גענומען אַנטלויפֿן פֿון שול,

און איבערגעלאָזט דעם אַנידערגעפֿאַלענעם פֿרעמדן איינעם אַליין.

און דער פֿרעמדער איז געלעגן אַ לאַנגע צײַט מיטן פּנים אַראָפּ,

די פֿיס אויפֿגעדרייט און די הענט אויסגעשטרעקט פֿאַרויס,

און זײַנע אויגן זײַנען געווען אָפֿן, און די אוירערן אויפֿגעשפּיצט,

און זײַנע אַקסלען האָבן שטיל און שטילער נאָך געצוקט,

און אויף זײַנע ליפֿן האָט געראָט דער שמייכל פֿון זײַן ביס.

. . . .

און אַז זײַן קאָפּ האָט זיך אָנגעהויבן פֿאָרדרייען און אַרונטערהענגען,

און זײַן גומען — צוזאַמענציִען זיך פֿון הייץ און טרוקנקייט,

האָט ער זיך אַרונטערגעלאָזט אויף אַלע פֿיר און געפֿויזעט

און געשאַרט זיך און געקײַקלט זיך איבערן רוקן,

און געשלאָגן מיטן שטערן אָן די ווענט און אָן אַ דיל.

And the Jews thought that he had fainted,
And they held his hands and tried to revive him;
But the stranger soon recovered and began talking
With a whimpering voice, as if crying:
—I beg you, Jews, give me my just desserts, what is due me—
A terrible death is my due, a death by alien hands;
I could have cut my own throat,
And pierced both my eyes with thorns,
And cut off my arms and thrown them to the dogs—
But I must not do it to myself—a stranger must do it for me!
I beg you, bring an axe and give me my just desserts.

And speaking thus, he fell to the ground,
And clung to the feet of the Jews,
Till his crying stopped abruptly,
And his throat choked on very different sounds.

And the Jews did not hear those different sounds,
And they stooped over him and wanted to raise him,
But the stranger lay there heavy and sunken,
And nobody could move him from his place.

And suddenly one of the Jews jumped up
And ran around the synagogue screaming terribly,
For the stranger had plunged his teeth into the man's hand.

And when the Jews saw the bitten hand,
One after the other they fled the synagogue,
And left the stranger alone, lying on the floor.

And the stranger lay for a long time face down,
His legs curled, his arms stretched out,
And his eyes were open, and his ears pricked up,
And his shoulders still twitched quietly
And the smile of his bite rested on his lips.

. . . .

Ben Shahn: Drawing from
Biography of a Painting.

And as his head twisted and hung down,
And his palate was parching with heat and dryness,
He lurched onto all fours and crawled
And crept and tumbled over onto his back,
And banged his forehead on the walls and floor.

און פּויזנדיק אַזוי, איז ער אַרויפגעקראָכן אויף דער בימה,

און דערנאָך אויפן טישל, וואָס אויף דער בימה.

און אויסגעצויגן זיך אויף אים מיטן גאַנצן גוף,

און דער קאָפּ איז אַרונטערגעהאַנגען אין דער לופטן צוזאַמען מיט די אַקסלען.

און זײַנע אויגן האָבן זיך אָפּגעקערט אָן דער זײַט

און זיי האָבן זיך אָפּגעשלאָגן אָן דעם אָרון-קודש, וואָס אַנטקעגן,

און אַ שײַן פון אַ ווײַטער דערינערונג איז דורכגעלאָפן איבער זיי;

און אַז די שײַן איז גלײַך פאַרלאָשן געוואָרן צוריק,

האָבן די אויגן נאָך אַלץ נישט געקאָנט זיך אָפּוועדנן פונעם פרוכט

און זיי האָבן װי נאָדלען געשטאָכן אין דער טיף פון זײַן מאַרך.

און דער פרעמדער האָט זיך אויפגעהויבן, און שווער און געצווונגענערהייט

אַרונטערגעשאַרט זיך פונעם טיש און, נאָך דעם, פון דער בימה,

און מיט אונטערגעבראָקענע קני זיך צוגעשלעפט צו די טרעפ פונעם אָרון-קודש.

און עטלעכע רגעס איז ער געשטאַנען בײַ די טרעפ, און דערנאָך

אַרויפגעקראָכן אין דער הייך און צוגעפאַלן מיטן פּנים צום פרוכת,

און ער איז געשטאַנען אַ לענגערע צײַט אַ פאַרגליווערטער,

און ער האָט געפילט אַ שטעכעניש אין די שליפן, און מער גאָרנישט,

ווײַל אויך אינעווייניק אין אים איז אַלץ געוואָרן פאַרגליווערט.

און ביסלעכווײַז האָט די שטעכעניש אַרומגעכאַפּט זײַן גאַנצן גוף,

און זײַנע הענט האָבן אַרומגעקלאַמערט דעם אָרון-קודש װי צוויי רינגען,

און זײַן קאָפּ האָט זיך אָנגעהויבן גראָבן און אײַנדרייען זיך,

און אַרײַנוויקלען זיך אין די פאַלדן פונעם פרוכט;

און מיטן אייבערשטן טייל פון זײַן מוח, װי אַן אָקס מיט העֿרנער,

האָט ער געשטויסן און געלעכערט אין די טירלעך,

ביז וואַנען די הויט פון זײַן מוח איז אויפגעלאָפן אין בלאָטערן,

און געפלאַצט און פאַרגאָסן מיט בלוט זײַן גאַנצן פּנים.

און אַז זײַנע נאָזלעכער האָבן דערשפירט דעם ריח פון זײַן אייגן בלוט,

האָבן די קולות, וואָס זײַנען געלעגן באַהאַלטן אין זײַן אינעװיניד,

זיך אַ ריס געגעבן און צוגעקײַקלט זיך צו זײַן גאָרגל.

. . . .

און נאָך דעם, אַז ער איז שוין געוואָרן אַרויסגעשפרונגען פון שול,

האָט זיך נאָך איבער אַלע אומגעוואָרפענע בענק און שטענדערס

געטראָגן דער פונאַנדערגעשאָטענער שטורעם פון זײַן וויגין.

ד

און ס'איז שוין געוואָרן מנחה-צײַט, ווען דער פרעמדער

איז געלאָפן פון שול צום שליאַך, וואָס פירט אין וואַלד אַרײַן.

און ווען די ייִדן זײַנען אַרײַנגעקומען און דערזען דעם חורבן

און די דורכגעבראָכענע טירלעך פונעם אָרון-קודש,

און דעם צעפליקטן פאַרבלוטיקטן פרוכת,

האָבן זיי אויסגעבראָכן אַלע אין אַ געוויין.

And so crawling, he climbed up to the *Bimah*,
And then climbed onto the table that was on the *Bimah*,
And stretched his body over it,
And his head and his shoulders hung down in the air.

Bimah—the raised platform from which the Torah is read.

And his eyes turned to the side,
And his looks struck the Holy Ark opposite him,
And a light of a distant memory passed through his eyes;
And as the light faded out in an instant,
His eyes still could not turn away from the *Poroykhes*
And they stung like needles in the depths of his marrow.
And the stranger raised himself, and crept down from the table,
Heavily, as under compulsion, slid down from the *Bimah*,
And with bent knees dragged his body to the steps of the Holy Ark.

Poroykhes*—embroidered curtains covering the Holy Ark that contains the Torah scrolls.

For a few moments he stood at the steps, and then
Climbed up and buried his face in the *Poroykhes*,
And for a long while he stood there transfixed,
And he sensed a stinging in his temples, and nothing more,
For inside him, too, everything was congealed.
And little by little the stinging overran his whole body,
And—like two braces—his hands clasped the Holy Ark
And his head began digging and twisting
And wrapping itself in the folds of the *Poroykhes*;
And with the upper part of his skull, like an ox with his horns,
He pushed and gored the doors of the Ark,
Till the skin of his skull swelled with blisters
And burst open and spilled blood over his face.
And as his nostrils inhaled the smell of his own blood,
The voices that lay hidden in his entrails
Jolted and surged up to his gullet.

. . . .

And later, when he leaped out of the synagogue,
Over all the upturned benches and lecterns
There still hovered the scattered storm of his howl.

IV

And it was just before the Afternoon Prayer when the stranger
Ran from the synagogue to the highway leading to the forest.
And as the Jews entered and saw the desolation,
And the broken doors of the Holy Ark,
And the *Poroykhes* shredded and covered with blood,
They all broke out in a cry.

און אַז זיי האָבן דערזען אויף דער ערד דעם פרעמדנס בגד,
און אים אַליין — נישט, האָבן זיי נישט פאַרשטאַנען וואָס דאָ טוט זיך,
און זייער האַרץ איז פול געוואָרן מיט פאַרגעפילן פון אומגליק.
און זיי האָבן געדאַוונט מינחה און מעריב, און געגאַנגען אַהיים,
און אין דער היים מורא געהאַט צו ריידן וועגן דעם,
כדי נישט צו דערשרעקן די פרויען און די קליינע קינדער.

און צוועלף אַ זייגער ביי אַ נאַכט, ווען אַלע האָבן שוין געשלאָפן,
און אַ דראָבנער האַרבסט-רעגן האָט זיך געזיפט פון די הימלען,
און די אַרומיקע וועלדער האָבן, דורך דער חושכניש,
זיך נעענטער צוגערוקט צו די אויסגעלאָשענע שטיבלעך, —
האָבן אַלע מיט אַ מאָל דורכן שלאָף דערהערט אונטער די פענצטער
דאָס זעלביקע וויאיען, וואָס זיי האָבן געהערט נעכטן.

און אַז ס׳זיינען אַריבער עטלעכע מינוט און דאָס וויאיען
איז געוואָרן נאָך גרעסער און שטאַרקער און נעענטער,
האָבן זיי שוין פאַרשטאַנען, אַז דאָס וויאיעט אַן אמתע חיה,
און נישט אין וואַלד ערגעץ, נאָר טאַקע דאָ אין שטאָט,
און יעדער האָט געמיינט, אַז די סכנה איז אונטער זיינע פענצטער,
און געזוכט צו פאַרהענגען און פאַרקלאַפן אַלע שויבן.
און די מאַמעס האָבן געטוליעט צו זיך די קינדער,
כדי די חיה זאָל נישט דערהערן זייערע קולות;
ווייל אַלע האָבן זיי געמיינט, אַז די חיה לויפט אַרום
פון איין גאַס אין אַ צווייטער און פון איין הויף אין אַ צווייטן.
און מיט איינגעהאַלטענעם אָטעם האָבן זיי זיך צוגעהערט
צו פאַרנעמען אין דער שטילקייט דער חיהס שפרינגענדיקע טריט.

נאָר קיינער האָט נישט געהערט די שפרינגענדיקע טריט,
ווייל די חיה איז נישט אַרומגעלאָפן איבער די הויפן,
נאָר געשטאַנען אויפן מיטן מאַרק, אויף די ווענטלעך פונעם ברונעם,
און מיט אַ פאַרריסענעם האַלדז צו די אויסגעלאָשענע שטיבלעך
געצויגן פון די געדארים אַרויס דאָס משונהדיקע וויאיען.

און ס׳איז נישט געווען קיין אַפרו און קיין איבעררייס אינעם וויאיען.
שעה-איין, שעה-אויס, די גאַנצע צווייטע העלפט פון דער נאַכט,
האָבן זיך געקיילקלט איבער דער שטאָט, דורכן רעגן און דורכן ווינט
די נישט-פאַרמאַטערטע אומגעלומפערטע געשרייען.

און ס׳איז געווען אַ געמיש פון געברול און בילעריי,
פון אויסגעצויגענעם קווייטשען און שטורעמדיקן ברומען,
און אין יעדער ענדערונג פון די קולות האָט זיך געהערט
אַ באַהאַלטענע ארויספאָדערונג, אַ רוף און, מער פון אַלץ, אַ געבעט;
און דאָס לעצטע האָט מער פון אַלץ געשראָקן די הערצער,
ווייל עס האָט דערמאָנט אָן דעם געוויין פון אַ מענטשן.

And when they saw the stranger's coat on the floor,
And that he himself was gone, they did not understand a thing,
And their hearts were filled with premonitions of disaster.
And they prayed the Afternoon Prayer and the Evening Prayer, and went home,
And at home they were afraid to talk about it,
Lest they frighten the women and the little children.

And at midnight, when all were asleep,
And a thin Autumn drizzle sifted down from the sky,
And in the darkness, the surrounding forests
Moved in closer to the darkened huts—
In their sleep, they suddenly heard under their windows
The same howling they had heard the day before.

And as several minutes passed and the howling
Grew larger and stronger and closer,
They understood that it was the howling of a real beast,
And not somewhere in the forest, but here in the city,
And everyone thought that the danger was under his own windows,
And tried to curtain and shutter the window-panes.
And the mothers huddled their children in their laps,
So the beast would not hear their voices;
For they all thought that the beast was roaming
From one street to another and from one yard to the next.
And holding their breath, they listened
To sense in the quiet the prowling footsteps of the beast.

But no one could hear its prowling,
For the beast was not roaming about the yards
But standing in the middle of the marketplace, on the walls of the well,
Its throat stretched out to the darkened huts
And it hauled up from its guts the uncanny howl.

And there was no rest and no break in the howling.
Hour after hour, from midnight till dawn,
All over the city, through rain and through wind,
Rolled the indefatigable, shapeless cries.

And it was a mixture of roaring and barking,
Of drawn-out screeching and stormy bellowing,
And in each turn of the voice was heard
A hidden challenge, an appeal, and above all, a pleading;
Which chilled their hearts more than anything,
For it reminded them of the cry of a human being.

און די, וואָס האָבן געוווינט מיט די פענצטער צום מאַרק,
האָבן געפרווווט אַרויסרוקן די קעפ און אײַנצוקוקן זיך,
נאָר זיי האָבן באַלד אַרײַנגעכאַפּט צוריק די קעפּ.
ווײַל זיי האָבן דערשפירט אויף זיך דורך דער פינצטערניש
דאָס גרינע פײַער פון צוויי וועלפישע אויגן.

און אַז דער וואָלף האָט דערזען די אַרויסגעשטרעקטע קעפּ,
האָט ער אַ ציטער געטאָן מיט זײַן גאַנצן גוף,
און זײַן האַלדז האָט זיך נאָך מער אויסגעצויגן
און פֿאַרגאַנגען זיך אין אַ קאַרכלענדיקן יאָמער.

און ביז טאָג האָט אַזוי אָנגעהאַלטן דער יאָמער.
און אַז דער טאָג האָט אָנגעהויבן אַרויסקריכן
אַ בלינדער און אַ דערציטערטער פון אונטער זײַן באַהעלטעניש,
און דער וואָלף האָט נאָך אַלץ מיט זײַן אויסגעווייעטן האַרצן
נישט דערווואַרט זיך, אַז עמעצער זאָל אַרויסגיין אים באַגעגענען —
איז ער מיט אַ מאָל אַנטשוויגן געוואָרן און אַראָפּגעשפרונגען פון ברונעם
און אַוועקגעלאָזט זיך פײַל-אויסן-בויגן צווישן די חורבות.
. . . .

ו

און אין דער נאַכט פון יום-כּיפּור נאָך כּל-נדרי
זײַנען די ייִדן גאָר אין גאַנצן נישט געגאַנגען אַהיים.
און זיי זײַנען איבערגעבליבן אין שול אויף אַ גאַנצער נאַכט,
און אַרומגערינגלטע מיט ליכט, אין ווײַסע קיטלען אָנגעטאָן,
זײַנען זיי געשטאַנען און תּפילה געטאָן צו גאָט.

און ווען עס האָט זיך דערנעענטערט די צוועלפטע שעה,
זײַנען זייערע געווויינען געוואָרן נאָך העכער און שטאַרקער,
און זייערע הערצער האָבן געקלאַפּט פון אומגעדולדיקן וואַרטן,
ווײַל יעדע מינוט האָט זיך געצויגן ווי אַן אייביקייט.
און זיי האָבן געפילט — און זיי האָבן אַליין נישט געוווסט פאַר וואָס —
אַז אין הײַנטיקער נאַכט ליגט דער באַשײַד פונעם סוד,
און אַז מיט זיי אַליין וועט זיך אָפּטאָן עפּעס אויסערגעוויינלעכס.
און זיי האָבן זיך טיפער געוויקלט אין די טליתים,
אַזוי ווי זיי וואָלטן וועלן באַהאַלטן זיך אונטער זיי.

און ווען עס האָבן גענומען שלאָגן די ערשטע קלעפּ פון צוועלף,
איז זייער געוויין פאַרוואַנדלט געוואָרן אין אַן אמתן שטורעם,
אַזוי ווי זיי וואָלטן וועלן מיט זייערע קולות פאַרטרײַבן,
נישט צולאָזן גאָר נאָענט צו דער שול דאָס אָנקומענדיקע וואָיען.
און אײַנגעגראָבענע אין טליתים, באַגאָסענע מיט וועקסענער שײַן,
האָבן זיי אויסגעזען אַליין ווי שטײַקער אָנגעצוונדענער וואָקס —
און נאָך אַ האַר אַ וועלן זיי זיך צעשפריצן און פונאַנדערשמעלצן זיך.

And those with windows facing the marketplace
Tried to put their heads out and look into the dark,
But they soon pulled their heads back,
For they sensed through the dark
The green fire of two wolf's eyes.

And when the wolf saw the heads thrust out,
His whole body trembled,
And his throat stretched even more
And convulsed in a growling wail.

And the wailing lasted till dawn.
And as the day began to crawl out,
Blind and trembling from its hiding place,
And the wolf's heart, emptied in howling,
Still did not see anybody coming to greet him—
He grew silent all at once and jumped down from the well
And shot like an arrow from a bow into the ruins.
. . . .

Ben Shahn: Drawing from
Biography of a Painting.

VI

And on the eve of Yom Kippur, the Day of Atonement,
After *Kol-Nidre*, the Jews did not go home at all.   **Kol Nidre***
And they remained all night in the synagogue,
Surrounded by candles, dressed in white robes,
They stood and prayed to God.

And as the twelfth hour approached,
Their cries became louder and stronger,
And their hearts beat in impatient waiting,
For every minute lasted an eternity.
And without knowing why, they sensed
That on this night a mystery would be solved,
And something uncanny would happen to them.
And they wrapped their bodies deeper in the tallises
As if they wanted to take refuge there.

And when the first sounds of midnight resounded,
Their crying was transformed into a veritable storm,
As if they wished to chase away with their voices,
To bar the coming howl from approaching the synagogue.
And so, buried in their tallises, suffused in waxen light,
They themselves looked like pieces of burning wax—
One move, and they'd spatter and melt.

און מיט אַ מאָל זײַנען אַלע אַנטשוויגן געוואָרן,

און, אַרויסרוקנדיק די קעפּ פֿון אונטער די טליתים,

האָבן זיי זיך אײַנגעגעסן מיט די אויגן אין דער שטילקייט,

וואָס האָט אַרומגעכאַפּט די וואָנט און סופֿיט פֿון דער שול.

און אַז ס׳איז אַריבער אַ מינוט, און צוויי, און דרײַ — און די שטילקייט

איז נאָך אַלץ פֿון ערגעץ און פֿון קיינעם נישט איבערגעריסן געוואָרן,

האָט זיך אַ שטראָם פֿון שׂימחה צעטראָגן איבער אַלעמענס קעפּ

און זיי זײַנען געשטאַנען ווי אויפֿגעוועקטע נאָך אַ בייזן חלום,

און נישט געגלייבט נאָך אַלץ זייערע אויערן.

אָבער די ווײַזערס פֿון זייגער זײַנען שוין געשטאַנען ווײַט ווײַט פֿון צוועלף,

און דאָס וואָיעניש פֿון דער חיה איז נישט געקומען.

. . . .

און אויף מאָרגן איז דער תענית פֿאַר די ייִדן

דורכגעגאַנגען לײַכט און שנעל, כמעט ווי נישט־באַמערקטערהייט.

און אַז ס׳איז געקומען נעילה־צײַט און די שאָטנס פֿונעם אָוונט

האָבן אײַנגעהילט די שול אין אַ טיפֿער און פֿרײַדיקער טונקלקייט,

האָבן די ייִדן זיך דערפֿילט גרינג און אויסגעלײַטערט,

און זייערע פּנימער האָבן זיך דורכגעקוקט ווי דורך אַ שפּיגל אַרויס;

און זיי האָבן מיט פֿרישע כּוחות געזאָגט די נעילהדיקע תפֿילות.

. . . .

ז

און עס איז געוואָרן, ווען דער בעל־תּוקע האָט צוגעטראָגן צו די ליפֿן

דעם שופֿר, און אַרויסגעשאַלט די נעילותדיקע תּקיעות,

האָט זיך די טיר פֿון דער שול מיט אַ בראַך פֿונאַנדערגעפֿראַלט,

און אין דעם האַרץ פֿון די תּקיעות האָט זיך אַרײַנגעשניטן

אַ דינער אויסגעצויגענער געוואָי.

און איידער נאָך די ייִדן האָבן צײַט געהאַט אַרומצוקוקן זיך,

איז שוין דער וואָלף געשטאַנען אויף די טרעפּלעך פֿון דער בימה,

און מיט גרויסע ברענענדיקע אויגן אײַנגעגעסן זיך אין דעם עולם.

און דער עולם, ווי אַ סטאַדע שאָף, האָט זיך צוזאַמענגעשפּאַרט

אַרום דעם עמוד, ווו ס׳איז געשטאַנען דער בעל־תּפֿילה,

און נישט געקאָנט קיין געשריי טאָן געוויל ס׳האָט אים אָפּגענומען דאָס לשון,

און נישט געקאָנט אַ ריר טאָן מיט קיין אבר אבער צו אַנטלויפֿן.

און דער וואָלף איז געשטאַנען אַ שווייַגנדיקער און געוואַרט.

און מיט אַ מאָל האָט ער זיך אַ ריס געטאָן פֿון די טרעפּלעך,

און אַריבער אַלעמענס קעפּ אַרויפֿגעשפּרונגען אויפֿן בעל־תּפֿילה,

און מיט די פֿאָדערשטע לאַפּעס אָנגעכאַפּט אים פֿאַרן האַלדז,

און אַנידערגעוואָרפֿן אים צו דער ערד און גענומען ווערגן.

And suddenly, they all became still,
And poking their heads out from under the tallises,
With their eyes they clung to the silence
That hung on the walls and ceiling of the synagogue.

And when a minute passed, and two and three and the silence
Was still not interrupted by anyone,
A tide of joy washed over them all,
And they stood there, as awakened from a terrible dream,
And still did not believe their own ears.

But the hands of the clock were far past twelve,
And the howl of the beast did not come.

. . . .

And the next day the fasting was easy
And passed quickly, almost unnoticed.

And when time for *Ne'ile* came, and the evening shadows
Veiled the synagogue in a deep and joyful darkness,
The Jews felt light and purified,
And they looked at each other's faces as at mirrors,
And with fresh strength they prayed the *Ne'ile* prayers.

Ne'ile—the closing prayer
marking the end of Yom Kippur.

. . . .

VII

And it was, when the blower of the horn put the shofar
To his lips, and sounded the blasts of *Ne'ile*,
Then the door of the synagogue burst open,
And a thin, protracted howl
Cut into the heart of the horn's blowing.

And before the Jews could look around,
There stood the wolf on the steps of the *Bimah*,
And he pierced the congregation with his large, burning eyes.
And the congregation crowded like a flock of sheep
Around the pulpit where the Reader stood,
And could not shout because their tongues were frozen,
And could not move a limb to flee.
And the wolf stood silent and waiting.
And suddenly he tore away from the steps,
And over everyone's heads jumped onto the Reader,
And with his front paws, gripped his throat,
And threw him to the floor and began choking him.

און דער עולם האָט פון שרעק גענומען לויפן צו דער טיר,
און שיער נישט איבערגעלאָזט אַליין דעם בעל-תּפילה
אין די לאַפּעס פונעם וואָלף אויף אַ זיכערן טויט, —
ווען איינער פונעם עולם האָט פּלוצלונג געכאַפט אַ שטעגנדער,
און מיט אַ קלאַפּ פון אַ ווינקלדיקער שאַרף
אַ זעץ געטאָן דעם וואָלף איבערן קאָפּ און פונאַנדערגעשפּאָלטן זיַין מוח.
און דער וואָלף האָט זיך אַראָפּגעקיַיקלט פון זיַין קרבן,
און, אַ פאַרגאָסענער מיט בלוט, אַנידערגעפאַלן צו דער ערד.

און דאָמאָלסט האָט דער גאַנצער עולם, אין געפילדער און שטויסעניש,
געכאַפט אַלץ, וואָס עס האָט זיך געמאַכט אונטער דער האַנט,
און געשלאָגן דעם וואָלף איבערן האַלדז און איבערן רוקן,
און געטראָטן מיט די פיס איבער זיַין בויך און זיַינע קני.

און פּלוצלונג האָט ווי פון אונטער דער ערד זיך אַרויסגעריסן אַן אוי,
און אַלעמענס הענט, ווי זיי האָבן געהאַלטן אין פיַיניקן,
זיַינען געבליבן אויסגעשטרעקט אין דער לופטן ווי אָפּגענומענע,
ווייל דאָס שטיק פינצטערניש האָט מיט אַ מאָל זיך אָנגעהויבן צו רירן,
און איבערגעקערט זיך מיט אַן אויפגעעפנטן פּנים אַרויף.
און צוויי מענטשלעכע אויגן האָבן אַרויסגעשיַינט דורך דער פינצטערניש
און רויִק און ליכטיק אַרומגעכאַפט אַלעמען מיט די בליקן.
און דער עולם האָט אויסגעבראָכן אין אַ גרויס געוויין,
ווייל אויף דער ערד, אַ פאַרפּיַיניקטער, אין אַ טיַיך בלוט,
איז געלעגן נישט קיין וואָלף, נאָר אַ ייד אין אַ רבנישן שטריַימל,
און אַלע האָבן דערקענט אין אים דעם פרעמדן אורח.

און דער פאַרפּיַיניקטער האָט זיך אָנגענומען מיט די לעצטע כּוחות
און אָנגעהויבן באַוועגן מיט זיַינע שטאַרבנדיקע ליפן.
און אַלע האָבן דערהערט זיַינע טרייסטנדיקע ווערטער:
— "איצט איז מיר גוט, זייער גוט, — ווייַנט נישט, ייַדן".

און ער האָט אויסגעהויכט זיַין אָטעם.

And in fear, the congregation ran to the door,
And almost left the Reader alone
To suffer certain death in the wolf's clutches—
But one of them suddenly grasped a lectern
And with one blow of a sharp corner
He struck the wolf's head and smashed his skull.
And the wolf rolled off his victim.
And fell to the floor, covered with blood.

And then the entire congregation, in uproar and commotion,
Grasped anything that came to hand,
And struck the wolf in his neck and his back,
And trod on his belly and knees.

And suddenly, as if from under the ground, burst a sigh,
And everybody's hands froze in mid-torture
And remained stretched out in the air, as if paralyzed,
For all at once the piece of darkness started moving
And rolled over turning an open face upward.
And two human eyes shone through the darkness
And their calm and bright gaze embraced them all.
And the congregation burst into great weeping,
For on the floor, tortured, in a river of blood,
Lay not a wolf but a Jew in a rabbinical fur hat,
And they recognized in him the strange visitor.

And the tormented man gathered his last strength
And moved his dying lips.
And they heard his consoling words:
—"Now I feel good, very good,—don't weep, Jews,"

And he breathed his last breath.

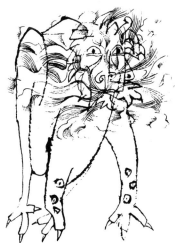

Ben Shahn: Drawing from
Biography of a Painting.

לידער (1932 — 1940)

◄ דאָס שטאַמיקע אין מיר

דאָס שטאַמיקע אין מיר — געזאַנג פון אוראַלטע ביינער ווײַסע,
כ׳בין אַרײַנגעכּישופֿט אין דער ביינערדיקער ווײַסקייט.
קלענער פֿונעם קלענסטן בין איך, אָבער עלטער — אייביק,
היימיש מיטן האַר פון סודותדיקן לעבן.

ווו איז ער, דער אָנהייב מײַנער, וואָס איך האָב אָנגעהויבן?
ווו וועט זײַן דער סוף מײַנער, וואָס איך וועל ענדיקן?
מײַנע אויגן בלאָנדזשען גאָר אַרום איבער העסטער-פּאַרק,
און דאָס האַרץ אין מיר ווערט אויפגעגאַנגען אין גרויסליכקייט.

ווי קום איך אַהער אין העסטער-פּאַרק ניו-יאָרקישן?
איך וועל קומען נאָך אַ מאָל, וועל קומען נאָך אַ מאָל,
צו קוקן אין די שטראַלנדיקע אויגן פון די אָרעמע,
און צו הערן דאָס געזאַנג פון אוראַלטע ביינער ווײַסע.

Abraham Walkowitz: from
Ghetto Motifs, 1946.

POEMS (1932–1940)

➤ *The Sturdy in Me*

The sturdy in me—song of ancient white bones,
I am in the thrall of the bony whiteness.
Smaller than the smallest I am, but older—eternal,
Intimate with the lord of hidden life.

Where is my beginning that I began?
Where is my end that I will end?
Yet, see: my eyes stray over Hester Park
And my heart rises in a great light.

What am I doing here, in New York's Hester Park?
I shall come again, I shall come again.
To look into the radiant eyes of the poor
And to hear the song of ancient white bones.

Poem 3 of the cycle, "My Father."

The title is an ambiguous word, also meaning my stem, my trunk, my race (inside me).

מײַן טאַטנס קבר — נעבן אַן אַלטער מיל
אין אַ קליין שטעטל אין אַ רוסישן,
מײַן מאַמעס קבר — נעבן דער זעלבער מיל. —
אַלטע מיל,
אַלטע מיל, —
שײַן-אױף אין ליכט פון העסטער-פֿאַרק ניו-יאָרקישן.

העסטער-פֿאַרק איז פֿול מיט הענט פֿאַרהאַרעװעטע, ביטחונדיקע,
און הענט פֿאַרהאַרעװעטע טראָגן אױף די דלאָניעס זײיערע
מאָס און װאָג, און דין און פסק, און גורל לעצטן.

װי קום איך אַהער אין העסטער-פֿאַרק ניו-יאָרקישן? —
איך װעל קומען נאָך אַ מאָל און נאָך אַ מאָל —
צו קוקן אין די פֿיערדיקע אױגן פון די אָרעמע,
און צו הערן דאָס געזאַנג פון אוראַלטע בײנער װײַסע.

◄ דאָס הייליקע ליד װעגן הייליקן קרעמער

פֿאַרלאָזן די הייליקע קראָם,
געשטאָרבן דער הייליקער קרעמער,
עס שימלט דער הייליקער שװאָם,
עס זשאַװערט דער הייליקער עמער.
עס װיינען אין הייליקן זאַפֿט
די הייליקע הערינג, טאַראַנען,
אין ניװעץ דער הייליקער נאַפֿט
רינט אױס פון די הייליקע קראַנען.

און דאָס הייליקע צינגל
פון דער הייליקער װאָג —
װיי, װיי, װיי,
שלומערט בײַ נאַכט
און שלומערט בײַ טאָג —
װיי, װיי, װיי.

דורך לעכער פון הייליקן דיל
אױף הייליקע טעלער און טאַצן,
אַ הייליקן גייען קאַדריל
די פֿיסלעך פון הייליקע ראַצן.
דער הייליקער ראַצן-קאַדריל
הילכט אָף ביזן הייליקן בױדעם;
מיט אַ מאָל אין דער הייליקער שטיל —
רייד הייליקע — רייד פון הספדים;

My father's grave—near an old mill
In a small town in a Russian field,
My mother's grave—near the same mill—
Old mill,
Old mill—
Light up in the glow of New York's Hester Park.

Hester Park is full of hands, toiling trusting hands,
And toiling hands carry on their palms
Measure and weight, judgment and verdict, and final destiny.

What am I doing here, in New York's Hester Park—
I shall come again and come again—
To look into the fiery eyes of the poor
And to hear the song of ancient white bones.

➤ *The Holy Song of the Holy Grocer*

The holy store is abandoned,
The holy grocer is dead,
The holy sponge grows moldy,
The holy bucket is rusty.
The holy herrings in a barrel
Cry in the holy brine,
The holy kerosene, in vain,
Runs out of the holy faucets.

And the holy balance
Of the holy scale—
Woe, woe, woe,
Slumbers by night
And slumbers by day,
Woe, woe, woe.

Through holes in the holy floor
On holy plates and platters,
Legs of holy rats
Dance a holy quadrille.
The holy dance of the rats
Echoes in the holy attic;
Suddenly, in the holy calm—
Holy voices—a eulogy:

William Gropper: *Studying*.

אָ, דער הייליקער קונה
פון דער הייליקער וועלט —
וויי, וויי, וויי —
וועט ניט האָבן ווו אויסברענגען
ס׳הייליקע געלט —
וויי, וויי, וויי.

עס שוועבט אויפן הייליקן טאָג
דעם אייבערשטנס הייליקע שליטה;
אין טרויער פון הייליקער קלאָג
באַגלייט ווערט די הייליקע מיטה.
די הייליקע פושקע קלאַפט צו
אין הייליקן טאַקט פון געיאָמער —
מען פירט צו דער הייליקער רו
דעם גוף פונעם הייליקן קרעמער.

און דאָס הייליקע רידל
אין דער הייליקער האַנט —
וויי, וויי, וויי —
גראָבט טיפער און טיפער
אין הייליקן זאַמד —
וויי, וויי, וויי.

◄ ווייסע לבנה

(פון "נעגעריש")

מיר׳ן אַרויסגיין מיט מעסערס, נעגערס,
איבער אַלע גאַסן אָפן,
און דערהיטן די שפעטע רגעס
ווען די ווייסע לבנה גייט שלאָפן.

און מיר׳ן געבן אַ שניט אַ שאַרפן,
אַ ריס טאָן די לבנה און פאַרקאַפן;
אַחוץ אונדז ווער אַנדערש קען דאַרפן
דאָס חיות פון ווייסקייט צו זאַפן.

די בעסטיעס די בלאָנדע שוין וועלקן,
און קוים אויף אַלע פיר זיי קריכן
צו די בריסט פון דער לבנה צו מעלקן
אַ ביסל ווייס פאַר צעטריקנטע פליכן.

Oh, the holy Buyer
Of the holy World—
Woe, woe, woe—
Where will he spend
His holy money—
Woe, woe, woe.

Over the holy day
Hovers God's holy watch;
In sorrow of holy lament
They go after the holy coffin.
The holy alms box beats
To the holy rhythm of weeping—
They are taking to his holy rest
The body of the holy grocer.

And the holy shovel
In the holy hand—
Woe, woe, woe—
Digs deeper and deeper
In the holy sand—
Woe, woe, woe.

The Buyer of the world—
an epithet for God, also meaning
the creator of the world.

► *White Moon*

(from "Negro Poems")

We, Negroes, will go out with knives
In the streets, open and deep,
We shall watch for the late moments
When the white moon goes to sleep.

We shall cut with a sharp stab
And grab the moon that is bright;
If not us, who else would need
To suck the refreshing white?

The blond beasts are withering,
They crawl on all fours ahead—
To the breasts of the moon, to milk
Some whiteness for dry bald heads.

און מיר האָבן צײן װי בײַם טיגער,
און ליפן װי צײַטיקע שװאָמען,
און מיר װײַען און דזשיגען צום זיגער,
װאָס מיר טראָגן אין אונדזערע זאָמען.

מיר'ן אַרויסגײן מיט מעסערס, נעגערס,
און גײן ביז דער לעצטער סכּנה,
און דערהיטן די שפעטע רגעס
צו פאַרכאַפן די װײַסע לבנה.

◄ װאָלקנס אַהינטערן װאַלד

װאָלקנס אַהינטערן װאַלד דערנעענטערן זיך צו די שפיצן פון די בײמער,
שטעכן זיך אַרויף אויף זײ, װי בײַכער אויף אָנגעשאַרפטע שפיזן.
רויט פאַרגיסט זיך די הימל, און עס נידערט אַרונטער אַלײן דער באַשעפער
מיט אַן אויפגעעפנט אויפגעריסן לײַב, אַז עס זעט זיך זײַן גאַנצע אינגעװייד.
עס שמעקט פון אים מיט געזאַלצענער הײ, און עס זידט דאָס געשרײַי פון זײַן װוּנד.
— באַשעפער, זאָג איך, דו גײסט דאָך אָף מיט בלוט. צי שטאַרבסטו, באַשעפער?
אָבער אַנשטאָט צו דערזען אויף זײַן פנים אַן אויסדרוק פון װײטיק צעקרימטן,
דערזע איך גאָר שטילן און װײכן גוטמוט, און אַנשטאָט מיר צו ענטפערן —
לאָזט ער זיך נידערן אַרונטער קמעט ביז צו דער סאַמע ערד צו.
איך גיב זיך אַ ריס צו אים, װײַל אים אָנכאַפן בײַ אַ בערג פון אַ פינגער.
— באַשעפער, זאָג איך, דו פאַרגיסט מיך מיט בלוט, — צי שטאַרב איך, באַשעפער? —
און, װידער, אַנשטאָט מיר צו ענטפערן, ציט ער זיך אויס איבער מיר,
פאַלט צו מיט זײַן פנים צו מײַנעם, אַזוי װי אַ פרוי,
און נעמט אומפירן מיט די ליפן מיט זײַנע איבער מײַן גאַנצן גוף,
און איך פיל אַזאַ הייסן ברי, װי פון אַ לעקנדיקער צונג, איבערן לײַב מיר
גייט אום די צונג און לעקט אָף דאָס בלוט, װי אַ חיה, — אַ מוטער,
װי אַ געװוינערין לעקט אָף דאָס בלוט פון איר נאָר-װאָס געבוירענעם קינד.

איך עפן מײַנע אויגן, איך זע: די זון איז שוין לאַנג אַװעק, און דער װאַלד
האָט זיך צוגערוקט נעענטער צו מיר, װי אַ שומר, און שרײַט מיט פליגלדיקע קולות. —
דער ריח פון גאָטס אויפגעריסן לײַב הערט זיך פון מיר און פון דער ערד אַרום,
ריח פון טראַקט, פון געבורט. — אַט דאָ אין מיטן פון דער װעלט
בײַם ברעג פון אַ װאַלד, האָסטו מיך נאָך אַ מאָל באַשאַפן, באַשעפער,
האָסטו מיך אַ צװייטן מאָל, אַ צװייטן מאָל געבוירן,
געבוירן און איבערגעלאָזט ליגן מיט שפורן פון בלוט אויף מײַן מײַן פנים. —

— באַשעפער — באַשעפער! —

And we have teeth like the tigers,
Lips—ripe mushrooms, take heed!
And we howl and hail the winner
That we carry in our seed.

We, Negroes, will go out with knives
To the last danger. And soon
We shall watch the late moments
And carry off the white moon.

➤ *Clouds Behind the Forest*

Last passage of a long poem of
the same title (1930).

Clouds behind the forest come close to the tops of the trees,
Are impaled on them, like bellies on sharpened spears.
Red fills the sky and the Creator himself descends,
His body torn open, his entrails hanging out.
He smells of salty heat and the scream of his wound is searing.
—Creator, I say, your blood is running out. Are you dying, Creator?
But I do not see on His face an expression of twisted pain,
I see soft and quiet goodness. Instead of answering—
He lowers Himself to the very earth.
I leap to Him, I want to grasp Him by His fingertips—
—Creator, I say, you are covering me with blood—am I dying, Creator?
And again, instead of answering, He stretches over me,
His face covers my face, like a woman,
And his lips begin to move over my whole body,
And I feel the hot breath, like a licking tongue, over my body,
The tongue moves and laps up the blood, like a mother animal,
Like a woman after childbirth lapping up the blood of her new-born infant.

I open my eyes, I see: the sun left a while ago, and the forest
Has moved closer to me, like a guard, and shouts with winged voices.—
The odor of God's torn-open body steams from me and from the earth around,
Odor of womb, of birth.—Here, in the middle of the world
At the shore of a forest, you created me once again, Creator,
For a second time—a second time you bore me,
Bore me and left me lying with traces of blood on my face.— —
                    —Creator—Creator!—

(סאַנאַטאָריע אין קאָלאָראַדאָ)

◄ עפן זיך, טויער

עפן זיך, טויער,
נעענטער זיך, שוועל, —
איך קום צו דיר ווידער,
צימערל-צעל.

מײַן לײַב — פײַער,
מײַן קאָפּ — שניי;
און אויף מײַנע אַקסלען
אַ זאַק מיט געשריי.

אָפּשייד. אָפּשייד.
אויגן. הענט.
אַדיע אויף די ליפן
דערברענט — פאַרברענט.

מיט וועמען צעשיידט זיך?
פון וועמען אַוועק? —
דאָס אייביקע פרעגן
דאָס מאָל ניט פרעג.

אין פײַער, אין פלאַקער
אַרומיקער סטעפ,
און שניי אינעם פלאַקער
אויף בערגיקע קעפּ.

איך לייג צו די פיס דיר
מײַן זאַק מיט געשריי,
לאַנד קאָלאָראַדאָ
פון פײַער און שניי.

► *Open Up, Gate*

Open up, gate,
Threshold, you tell—
I am coming again
To an intimate cell.

My body—fire,
My head—snow;
And on my shoulders
A bag of woe.

Farewell. Farewell.
Hands. Eyes. Bowed.
A goodbye on the lips
Flared—burnt out.

From whom did I part?
Farewell to what past?—
Perennial questions
This time don't ask.

In fire, in flame
The prairie spreads,
And snow in the glare
On mountainous heads.

I bring to your feet
My bag of woe,
Land Colorado
Of fire and snow.

(Sanitorium in Colorado)

Two poems from the cycle
written during Leyvik's stay in a
TB sanitorium in Denver,
Colorado, 1932–1936.

H. Leyvik.

פּשוטע, נאַקעטע רייד.
די וועלט איז אין ווינטער פֿאַרקראָכן:
מיך שרעקט ניט מײַן אייגענער טויט, —
איך האָב מורא פֿאַר דעם טויט פֿון מײַן שכן.

איך פֿאַרנעם זיך מיט אַלץ וואָס איך קען,
אַפֿילו מיט צוטראַכטן גראַמען;
— איך פֿרעג אָט אַזוי בײַ מײַן פּען —
צי ווייס זי פֿון וואַנען מיר שטאַמען?

צי ווייס זי וואָס מיינט אין שפּיטאָל
אַ שכן וואָס גייט אויס דאָ-נעבן?
צי איז ניט דאָס שטאַרבן, צומאָל,
אַ טראָט צו אַ נײַערן לעבן? —

עס האָט ניט קיין ענטפֿער מײַן פּען, —
פֿון וואַנען גאָר זאָל זי עס האָבן? —
דערווײַלע — ביז וואַנען — וואָס — ווען —
מען טראָגט שוין מײַן שכן באַגראָבן.

מען טראָגט אים אויף יענער זײַט שוועל,
און ווי נאָר אַריבער — פֿאַרשוווּנדן,
ס׳איז דאָ אין שפּיטאָל אַ טונעל
מיט דעם טהרה-שטיבל פֿאַרבונדן.

צום שטיבל, דורך שוואַרצן טונעל,
דורך שמאָלע, דורך טיפֿע זיגזאַגן,
מען פֿירט אים אויף רעדלעך שנעל-שנעל,
נאָך שנעלער ווי איך פֿרעג מײַנע פֿראַגן.

דערווײַלע — ביז וואַנען — וואָס — ווען —
מײַן שכן — ער איז שוין אין שטיבל;
און איך שרײַב נאָך אַלץ מיט מײַן פּען,
גראַם שטיבל — פֿאַריבל — מיט איבל.

באַגינען. די וועלט איז פֿאַרשנייט.
די וועלט איז אין ווינטער פֿאַרקראָכן;
מיך שרעקט ניט מײַן אייגענער טויט,
נאָר די ליידיקע בעט פֿון מײַן שכן.

Simple, naked words.
The world in winter's labor;
I am not afraid of my death—
I am scared of the death of my neighbor.

I am busy with all I can do,
I invent rhymes, bad or good;
Just like this, I am asking my pen—
Does it know our roots?

Does it know what it means: in the hospital
A neighbor is dying nearby?
Is not death, perhaps, a step
To new life, a lullaby?

My pen has no answer for me—
How could it? Its face is grave.
Meantime—till we think—what—and when—
My neighbor is carried to his grave.

They carry him over the threshold,
And he disappears, in gloom,
The hospital has a tunnel
Direct to the cleansing room.

cleansing room—a room where corpses are ritually cleansed before burial.

To that room, through a black tunnel,
Through zigzags far below,
They carry my neighbor on wheels
Swifter than I can know.

And before we can think—what—and when—
My neighbor is in that room;
And I am still writing with my pen,
Rhyming: room—gloom—doom.

Dawn. The world snowed in.
The world in winter's labor;
I am not afraid of my death,
But of the empty bed of my neighbor.

אַז איך טראַכט וועגן אונדז — יִידישע פּאָעטן,
אַזאַ צער כאַפּט מיר אַ מאָל אַרום;
עס וויִלט זיך שרײַען צו זיך אַליין, בעטן, —
און דעמאָלט גראָד ווערן ווערטער שטום.

אַזוי משונהדיק זעען אויס אונדזערע לידער, —
ווי זאַנגען, וואָס אַ הייישעריק צעפרעסט;
אַ טרייסט: — צו ווערן זיך אַליין דערווידער,
צו שלײַכן זיך אויף גאָטס ערד, ווי פרעמדע געסט!

דאָס בלוט פון אונדזער ווערט אויף קאַלטע פינגער,
פון פינגער — אויף נאָך קעלטערן צעמענט;
אַ, פאַרשעמטע, לעכערלעכע זינגער,
פאַרוואָרפטע אין פאַרשעמטערע פיר ווענט!

און אַז עס קומט אַן אייגענער, אַ נאָענטער
פון אַ קעלער, צי פון אַ שאָפּ אַרויס, —
זײַן שטומע צונג נאָר אין אונדז דערקאָנט ער,
און אונדזער פּיִערלעכקייט מײַדט ער אויס.

און מיר, ווי קינדישע, פאַרליבטע ריטער,
ווי דאָן קיכאָט, מיט איבערכאַפּטער מאָס,
מיר בלײַבן ציטערן מיט אונדזער ציטער,
אין עלנט, איבער יעדן וואָרט און אות.

און אַ מאָל, ווי קעץ מיט אויפגעריִיצטע גלידער
שלעפן זייערע קעצלעך פאַרוויִרט פון זאָרג, —
אַזוי שלעפּן מיר פאַרן האַלדז אונדזערע לידער
צווישן די ציין, איבער גאַסן פון ניו-יאָרק.

אַז איך טראַכט וועגן אונדז, יִידישע פּאָעטן,
אַזאַ צער נעמט מיך אַ מאָל אַרום,
און עס וויִלט זיך שרײַען צום נאָענטן, בעטן, —
און דעמאָלט גראָד ווערן ווערטער שטום.

When I think of us—Yiddish poets,
A sorrow grabs me—sharp, acute;
I want to scream to myself, to pray—
And just then the words grow mute.

So outlandish is the look of our poems—
Like stalks the locusts have possessed;
One comfort: get disgusted with yourself,
Slink on God's earth, an alien guest!

The blood of our word on cold fingers,
From fingers—to cement, hard and cold;
Oh, ashamed, ridiculous singers,
Squeezed between four disgraced walls!

And if one like us comes, a brother
From a cellar, a sweatshop he's cursed—
He finds in us his own mute tongue
And avoids our solemn verse.

And we, like children, like knights in love,
Like Quixote, doing things unheard,
In loneliness as ever we tremble
Over every letter and word.

Sometimes, like frazzled cats, dragging
Their kittens around, distraught,
We drag our poems between our teeth
By the neck through the streets of New York.

When I think of us, Yiddish poets,
A sorrow grabs me—sharp, acute;
I want to shout to a brother, to pray—
And just then the words grow mute.

Yiddish Writers. On top, from
left: Joseph Opatoshu, H.
Leyvik. Bottom left: A. Leyles.

ממעמקים —
אַ װאָרט אַזאַ.
אַ װאָרט אַזאַ:
פֿונדערטיפֿעניש.
װאָס מיינסטו מיט זיך
פֿונדערטיפֿעניש?
װאָס באַטײַטסטו פֿאַר מיר
פֿונדערטיפֿעניש?
פֿאַר װאָס יאָגסטו מיך,
פֿאַר װאָס פֿאַרפֿאָלגסטו מיך
פֿון קינדהייט אָן,
פֿון חדר אָן,
פֿון װײַסע חצות-נעכט אָן —
פֿונדערטיפֿעניש?

ממעמקים —
איך רוף צו דיר
פֿונדערטיפֿעניש;
איך בעט צו דיר,
איך שטרעק מײַנע הענט צו דיר
פֿונדערטיפֿעניש;
איך װיל זײַן דערקאַנט צו דיר,
איך װיל זײַן נאָענט צו דיר,
איך װיל דיך אָנרירן,
איך װיל דערגרייכן דיך,
איך װיל זיך אױפֿהייבן צו דיר —
פֿונדערטיפֿעניש.

ממעמקים —
װאָס פֿאַר אַ קלאַנג ביסטו?
װאָס טראָגסטו מיט זיך —
פֿונדערטיפֿעניש?
װאָס פֿאַרמאָגסטו אין זיך —
פֿונדערטיפֿעניש?
זאָגסט עס אײן מאָל — זאָג עס נאָך אַ מאָל,
זינג עס נאָך אַ מאָל
און טאָקע נאָך אַ מאָל:
מי —
מאָ —
אַ —
מאָ —
קים —

Mima'amakim—
What a word.
What a word:
Fromthedepths.
What do you mean,
Fromthedepths?
What do you mean to me,
Fromthedepths?
Why are you chasing me,
Why are you racing after me
From childhood,
From *Heder*-school,
From white midnights—
Fromthedepths?

Mima'amakim—
I am calling to you
Fromthedepths;
I am praying to you,
I am stretching my hands to you
Fromthedepths;
I want to be known to you,
I want to be near to you,
I want to touch you,
I want to reach you,
I want to raise myself up to you—
Fromthedepths.

Mima'amakim—
What sound are you?
What do you bring with you—
Fromthedepths?
What do you possess in you—
Fromthedepths?
You're saying it once—
Say it again,
Sing it again,
And then again:
Mi-
   ma-
     a-
       ma-
         kim—

An allusion to Psalm 130:1: "Out of the depths have I cried unto thee, O Lord."

William Gropper: *Prayer Shawl.* 1962.

וועמענס געשריי איז דאָס?

ווער פאַרגייט זיך אַזוי?

וועמענס געזאַנג אַזאַ

פונדערטיפעניש?

זאָגסט עס אײן מאָל —

זאָג עס נאָך אַ מאָל,

און טאַקע נאָך אַ מאָל —

פון —

דער —

טי —

פע —

ניש.

◄ ליד וועגן דער געלער לאַטע

ווי זעט אויס די געלע לאַטע

מיט אַ רויטן, אָדער שוואַרצן מגן-דוד

אויפן אָרעם פון אַ ייד אין נאַציילאַנד —

אויפן ווײַסן פאַן פון אַ דעצעמבער-שניי?

ווי וואָלט אויסגעזען אַ געלע לאַטע

מיט אַ רויטן, אָדער שוואַרצן מגן-דוד

אויפן אָרעם פון מײַן פרוי און זין

און אויף מײַן אײגענעם אָרעם —

אויפן ווײַסן פאַן פון אַ ניו-יאָרקער שניי?

פאַרוואָר —

די פראַגע עגבערט ווי אַ מוק אין מוח,

די פראַגע ווי אַ וואָרעם עסט דאָס האַרץ.

און פאַר וואָס נאָר יוצא זײַן מיט ווערטער?

און פאַר וואָס ניט טאָן די פולע אחדות-פליכט

און אַלײן טאַקע ניט אָנטאָן אויפן אָרעם

די באַשערטע געלע לאַטע מיטן מגן-דוד

לפני עם-וועדה אין ניו-יאָרק ווי אין בערלין,

אין פּאַריז, אין לאָנדאָן און אין מאָסקווע ווי אין וויזן?

פאַרוואָר —

די פראַגע עגבערט ווי אַ מוק אין מוח,

די פראַגע ווי אַ וואָרעם עסט דאָס האַרץ.

ערשטער שניי איז הײַנט אַרויסגעפאַלן,

קינדער טראָגן זיך אויף שליטעלעך איבערן פּאַרק,

און די לופט איז אָנגעפילט מיט פרייד-געשריי. —

האָב איך, ווי די קינדער, ליב דעם ווײַסן שניי,

און באַזונדער האָב איך ליב דעם חודש כיסלו. —

Whose cry is it?
Who convulses in it?
Whose song is it
Fromthedepths?
You're saying it once—
Say it again,
And then again—
Out-
    of-
        the-
            depths.

➤ *Song of the Yellow Patch*

How does it look, the yellow patch
With a read or black Star-of-David
On the arm of a Jew in Naziland—
Against the white ground of a December snow?
How would it look, a yellow patch
With a red or black Star-of-David
On the arms of my wife and my sons,
On my own arm—
On the white ground of a New York snow?
Truly—
The question gnaws like a gnat in my brain,
The question eats at my heart like a worm.

And why should we escape with mere words?
Why not share in full unity
And wear on our own arms
The destined yellow patch with the Star-of-David
Openly, in New York as in Berlin,
In Paris, in London, in Moscow as in Vienna?
Truly—
The question gnaws like a gnat in my brain,
The question eats at my heart like a worm.

Today the first snow descended.,
Children are gliding on sleds in the park,
The air is filled with clamor of joy.—
Like the children, I love the white snow,
And I have a special love for the month of December.

First poem of a cycle, "Poems of the Yellow Patch." The refrain in parenthesis echoes Leyvik's first poem, "Somewhere Far Away."

(ערגעץ ווײַט, ערגעץ ווײַט
ליגט אין שניי אַ געפֿאַנגענער).

אַ גאָט געטרײַער, פֿון אברהם, פֿון יצחק און פֿון יעקב,
שטראָף מיך ניט פֿאַר אָט דער ליבע מײַנער, —
שטראָף מיך יאָ פֿאַר עפּעס אַנדערש, —
שטראָף מיך יאָ, פֿאַר וואָס איך קענט ניט אויס
פֿונעם זעלטענעם ניו־יאָרקער שניי קיין משה,
און פֿאַר וואָס איך מאַך פֿון שניי ניט קיין באַרג סיני,
ווי איך פֿלעג עס טאָן אַ מאָל אין מײַנע קינדער־יאָרן. —

(ערגעץ וואָגלט ווער אום
טיף אין שניי אַ פֿאַרשאָטענער).

שטראָף מיך יאָ און שטאַרק, פֿאַר וואָס איך טו ניט אָן
אויף אַן אמת דעם זעקס־טורעמדיקן מגן־דוד
און דעם קײלעכדיקן אין־סוף פֿון דער געלער לאַטע —
צו דערמוטיקן ישראלן אין דעם הענקער־לאַנד,
און צו לויבן און דערהייבן אונדזער אָרעם
מיט דעם שטאָלץ פֿון אונדזער ייחוס־הערב
איבער אַלע לענדער פֿון דער גאָרער וועלט.
פֿאָרוואָר —
די פֿראַגע עגבערט ווי אַ מוק אין מוח,
די פֿראַגע ווי אַ וואָרעם עסט דאָס האַרץ.

(ערגעץ ווײַט, ערגעץ ווײַט
ליגט דאָס לאַנד דאָס פֿאַרבאָטענע).

(Somewhere far, somewhere far away
lies a prisoner, lies alone.)

O dear God, God of Abraham, of Isaac and of Jacob,
Scold me not for this love of mine—
Scold me for something else—
Scold me for not kneading
This wonderful snow of New York into a Moses,
For not building a Mount Sinai of snow.
As I used to in my childhood.—

(Somewhere wanders a man,
Deeply covered in snow.)

Scold me for not really wearing
The six-towered Star-of-David
And the infinite circle of the yellow patch—
To hearten the sons of Israel in Hangman's-Land
And to praise and raise our arm
With the pride of our ancestral emblem
In all the lands of the wide world.
Truly—
The question gnaws like a gnat in my brain,
The question eats at my heart like a worm.

(Somewhere far, somewhere far away
Lies the land, the forbidden land.)

Louis Lozowick: *Winter Morning*
(New York). 1935.

◄ אין פייער

די לאַנגע, די פינצטערע נאַכט איז פייער.
מיין קאָפּ אויף אַ קישן פון פלאַמיקן פייער.
איך אָטעם אַריין און איך אָטעם אַרויס פייער
דורך אָפענע טירן און פענצטער פון פייער.
מיין האַנט שטרעקט זיך אויס און מאַכט צייכנס אין פייער,
נעמט שרייבן אין פייער מיט פייער אויף פייער.
כ'בעט רחמים, כ'זוך שיצונג פון פייער,
כ'טו תפילה: אַ ראַטעווע, ראַטעווע, פייער!
דערהער איך ווי ס'פלאַקערן קולות אין פייער:

דיין טאַטע בין איך — דיין פאָטער פון פייער,
דיין מאַמע בין איך — דיין מוטער פון פייער,
דיין טאַטע וואָס האָט דיך געיידישט אין פייער,
דיין מאַמע וואָס האָט דיך געזווגן מיט פייער.
געדענקסט דאָך דיין הענג-וויג אויף שטריקלעך פון פייער
אַ מאָל אין אַ שטיבל ביים אויפגאַנג פון פייער;
געדענקסט ווי עס האָבן געפלאַטערט אין פייער
די שטריקלעך, דערלאַנגט צו דער סטעליע מיט פייער,
געדענקסט ווי מיר האָבן פאַרכאַפט דיך אין פייער
און לויפן געלאָזט זיך מיט דיר צווישן פייער,
געלאָפן פון פייער, דורך פייער, אין פייער.
מיר קומען איצט ווידער דיך טוליען צום פייער,
דיך ווידער פאַרוויקלען אין וויקל פון פייער
און ווידער דיך הייבן, דיך טראָגן אין פייער
פון פייער, דורך פייער, צום פייער. — — —

אזוי הער איך קולות אין נאַכטיקן פייער,
ביז וואַנען עס הייבט אָן צו טאָגן מיט פייער,
און וואָס עס קומט נאָך דעם — דאָס ווייס נאָר דאָס פייער,
וואָס צייכנט מיט פייער אין פייער אויף פייער.

◄ אַז מיר האָבן זיך געלאָזן באַרג-אַראָפּ

אַז מיר האָבן זיך געלאָזן באַרג-אַראָפּ
צו דעם וואַסער פונעם טיפן ברונעם,
האָבן זיך צעלויכטן איבער אונדזער קאָפּ
זיבן העלע יום-טובדיקע זונען.

➤ *In Fire*

The long, dark night is fire.
My head on a pillow of flaming fire.
I inhale and exhale fire
Through open doors and windows of fire.
My hand reaches out and makes signs in fire,
Writing in fire with fire on fire.
I ask for mercy, seek defense in fire,
I pray: Oh, save me, save me, fire!
And I hear voices blazing in fire:

    I am your father—your father of fire,
    I am your mother—your mother of fire,
    Your father who made you a Jew in fire,
    Your mother who nursed you, an infant, with fire.
    Remember your cradle, hung on ropes of fire
    Once, in a hut, at the dawn of fire;
    Remember, how the ropes fluttered in fire,
    The ropes reaching the ceiling of fire,
    Remember how we caught you in fire
    And ran with you between fire and fire,
    Ran from fire, through fire, in fire.
    Now we return to hug you with fire,
    To swaddle you again in diapers of fire,
    To raise you again, to carry you in fire
    From fire, through fire, to fire— — —

I hear the voices in nightly fire,
Until the beginning of dawn in fire,
And what will come—no one knows but the fire,
Drawing with fire in fire on fire.

➤ *When We Let Ourselves Run Down-Hill*

When we let ourselves run down-hill
To the water of the deep well,
Seven bright and festive suns
Shone above our heads.

אָון זיי האָבן אונדז געוואַרעמט און געגלעט,
וואָכעדיק געהאַלטן אונדז די אויגן,
ביז אין נאַכט אַריַין, ביז שפּעטסטער שפּעט,
ווען מיר האָבן זיך צום וואַסער טיף געבויגן.

ווען מיר האָבן זיך צום וואַסער צוגעריִרט,
מיט זַיין פרישקייט קוויקן זיך גענומען,
ווען מיר האָבן אַלע מיט איין מאָל דערשפּירט
טעם־גן־עדן איבער אונדזער גומען.

אַז מיר האָבן נאָך דעם אויפן וועג צוריק
באַרג־אַרויף געלאָזט זיך אַלע הייבן —
זַיינען שוין די זונען מער פאַר אונדזער בליק
נישט געהאַנגען פיַיערדיקע אויבן.

בלוי־געדיכטע נאַכט האָט זיך געשפּרייט
איבער מיזרח, מערב, דרום, צפון.
און די זיבן זונען אַלע, מידערהייט,
זַיינען צוגעדעקט געלעגן און געשלאָפן.

אויף די בערג־שפּיצן געלעגן זַיינען זיי
און געאָטעמט באַרג־אַראָפ מיט קורצן אָטעם,
ביז אַ וויַיסקייט, אַ צעזיפטע ווי אַ שניי,
האָט אונדז אַלעמען אין מיטן וועג פאַרשאָטן.

◄ ערשטע גראָזן

ערשטע שטילע גראָזן
האָבן ניט קיין מורא פאַר אַ שטורעם.
לאָמיר זַיין ווי ערשטע גראָזן.

איינער ליגט פאַרלאָזן,
איַינגעדרייט אין רייפן פון יסורים, —
קומען מיר צו דעם וואָס ליגט פאַרלאָזן.

קומען מיר און זאָגן:
ערשטע קליינע גראָזן ווייסן בעסער
ווערטער פון נחמה ווי צו זאָגן.

וואָרעם זיי פאַרמאָגן
רו, וואָס האָט נאָך ניט פאַרזוכט קיין מעסער. —
קאָן דען עפּעס בעסערס ווער פאַרמאָגן?

They warmed us and caressed us,
They kept our eyes awake,
Till far in the night, till late as late,
When we bowed to the water deep.

When we touched the water with our lips,
When we reveled in its delight,
When all at once we savored the taste.
Of Eden on our palate.

And when later, on our way,
We began to climb uphill—
The flaming suns before our eyes
Hung over head no more.

A blue-thick night spread over all—
East, West, South, North.
And the seven suns, exhausted,
All lay concealed, and asleep.

On the mountain-peaks they lay gasping
Breathing down on us,
Till a whiteness, sifted like snow,
Covered us all on the road.

➤ *First Grass*

First silent grass
Has no fear of a storm.
Let us be like first grass.

Someone lies abandoned,
Curled in hoops of pain.
We come to one lying abandoned.

We come and say:
First, low grass knows better
How to say soothing words.

For first grass has calm
Not yet tried by a knife.
Could one have anything better?

נעמען מיר אים אים טראָגן

צו די ערשטע קליינע שטילע גראָזן,

ביז מיר ברענגען אים צו זיי צו טראָגן.

נאַכט. דערנאָך נעמט טאָגן.

דער געטרייסטער ליגט אין ליכט אין ראָזן

מיט די ערשטע גראָזן, ווען ס׳נעמט נאָגן.

◄ יום-טובֿ

(פֿון ״דערמאָנונגען״)

דער טאַטע פֿירט מיך פֿאַר אַ האַנט אין שול.

דער טאָג איז פֿרימאָרגנדיק זוניק,

דער טאָג איז — יום-טובֿ.

מײַן האַנט — אין דער רעכטער האַנט פֿונעם טאַטן;

מײַן האַנט — אַ הענטל,

און דעם טאַטנס — אַ גרויסע, אַ וואַרעמע,

אַ זיכערע אין הייליקייט פֿון רו,

באַשיצט און באַהיט פֿון גאָט ברוך-הוא.

דער טאָג איז — פּסח.

מיר שפּאַנען איבערן פֿרײַען אָפּגעלייידיקטן מאַרק.

דער טאַטע גייט, און איך שפּרינג אונטער.

זײַנע שמאָלע אַקסלען הייבן זיך צום הימל,

זײַן רויטע באָרד שמייכלט צו דער זון.

דער טאַטע גייט, און איך טאַנץ אונטער,

מײַן קליינער שאָטן טאַנצט אַרײַן אין זײַנעם,

מײַן קליינער שאָטן דערגרייכט קוים זײַנע קני.

דער טאַטע איז הײַנט מילד ווי יום-טובֿ.

אַלע קראָמען אין שטעטל — געשלאָסן,

אָבער דער מאַרק אַליין איז רחבותדיק אָפֿן

צו אַלע פֿיר זײַטן.

אַלע שטיבלעך שטייען, אויסגעגלייכט ליכטיק,

געבענטשטע אין חסדיקער רו,

פֿאַרטרויטע אין דער האַנט פֿון גאָט ברוך-הוא,

ווי מײַן הענטל אין דער האַנט פֿונעם טאַטן.

כ׳בין אַלט געווען פֿינף יאָר,

און דער טאַטע איז אַלט געווען — אייביק.

We raise and carry him
To first, low, silent grass,
Till we bring him there.

Night. Then the day dawns.
The calmed man lies in pink light
With the first grass, when the day dawns.

► *Holiday*

   (From "Remembrances")

My father leads me by the hand to Synagogue,
The day is sunny with dawn,
The day is—holiday.

My hand—in my father's right hand;
My hand—a little palm,
My father's—big, warm,
Secure in the holiness of rest,
Watched over by God almighty.
The day is—Passover.

We stride over the open, empty marketplace,
My father walks, and I hop on.
His narrow shoulders lifted to the sky,
His red beard smiles to the sun.
My father walks, and I dance along,
My small shadow dances into his,
My small shadow reaches to his knees.
Today father is gentle like a holiday.

All the stores in town are closed,
But the marketplace is wide open
To all four sides of the wind.
All the huts stand, lighted like equals,
Blessed in graceful rest,
Confided in the hand of God almighty
As my little palm in the hand of my father.

I was five years old.
My father was— —an eternity.

זעקס זײַנען זיי געווען —
זעקס צעטומלטע גבורהדיקע אָקסן.
זעקס נאַרישע אָקסן,
און אפשר נישט קיין נאַרישע גאָר.
וואָרעם אין דער אמתן —
פֿון וואַנען האָבן זיי געקאָנט וויסן
וואָס עס באַטײַט אַן אַרענע
און אַ המון אַ פֿערציק־טויזנט־קעפֿיקער?
וואָס עס באַטײַט און וואָס עס מיינען
טאָרעאַדאָרן,
און רײַטערס,
און שפיזן,
און שווערדן,
און אָפֿענאַרערישע טיכער?

אַפֿילו אַ מענטש וואָלט דאָך קליגער ניט געווען,
ווען מען האָלט אים מעת־לעתן אין דער פֿינצטערניש,
און מען יאָגט אים דערנאָך אַרויף אויף דער אַרענע
אַ באַגאָסענע מיט טראָפֿישן זון־פֿלאַקער,
און מען נעמט אים אַטאַקירן מיט פֿײַלן און מיט פּיקעס,
און מען נעמט רייצן מיט רויטס זײַנע אויגן,
און דער המון לאַכט, רעוועט, פֿאַרקײַכט זיך —
וואָס וואָלט ער דען געטאָן, דער מענטש?

אין דער אמתן, זאָגט אַליין,
וואָס וואָלט אים געבליבן צו טאָן,
אויב נישט אַרומשפּרינגען ווי אויף זודיקע קוילן,
אויב נישט אַרומדרייען זיך אַרום זיך אַליין
און שלאָגן מיטן שטערן אין אַלע צאַמען אַרײַן,
אין אייגענעם פֿאַרשווינדלטן שאַטן אַרײַן,
אין דער אייגענער אַנטלויפֿנדיקער אויסדרוכטעניש.

. . . .

זעקס זײַנען זיי געווען —
זעקס צעטומלטע, גבורהדיקע אָקסן,
אַרומלויפֿנדיקע, צעשוימטע, צעבלוטיקטע, —
און אָט שלעפֿט זיי שוין אַ קייט פֿאַר די פֿיס
פֿון דער אַרענע אַראָפּ,
און זייערע הערנער די אומזיסטיקע שלעפֿן זיך נאָך;

They were six—
Six perplexed heroic bulls.
Six silly bulls,
Or perhaps not so silly.
After all,
How could they have known
What it means: an arena
And a crowd of forty-thousand heads?
How could they have known what it means:
Toreadors,
And riders,
And spears,
And swords,
And deceitful clothes?

Even a man would not have been wiser
If they had kept him for days in the dark,
And then chased him out into the arena
Flooded with tropical sun-blaze,
And then attacked him with arrows and pikes,
And teased him with red,
And the crowd laughs, howls, gasps—
What would he have done, a man?

Really, admit it:
What else could he have done,
If not jump and leap as on red-hot coals,
If not circle around his own body
And strike with his forehead at fences,
And strike his own dizzy shadow,
His own fleeing delusion.

·   Slightly abridged.

Six they were—
Six dumbfounded, heroic bulls,
Dashing, foaming, bleeding—
And now a chain hauls them by the legs
Down from the arena,
And their vain horns drag on;

און די שאַרפֿע שווערד באַמבלט זיך

אן אויסגעלאָשענע אין די הענט פֿון טאָרעאַדאָר,

און דער עולם זיצט אַן אָפּגערעוועטער,

אַ צעקנייטשטער ווי די פֿאַררעטערין — די טוך.

און אויך די זון לעשט זיך אַהינטער דער אַרענע,

אויך די זון שלעפֿט עמיצער מיט אַ קייט

פֿון הימל אַראָפּ,

פֿון הימל אַראָפּ,

אַראָפּ, אַראָפּ.

◄ מקובלים אין צפת

מקובלים

אויפֿגעשטאַנענע אין חלום

שפּאַנען איבער צפת.

האַלבע נאַכט

אין ווייסן נעפּל.

דאָ אַ געסל,

דאָ — אַ גאַס,

דאָ אַ קעלער,

דאָ — אַ טרעפּל.

זינק אַראָפּ

און הייב זיך אויף,

און פֿאַל-צו

צו אַ ניי-געווייסטער שוועל

און — רו.

מקובלים

נעמען זיך אַרום אין חלום,

און זיי לאָזן זיך אַוועק

מיט אַ לכה-דודי-טראָט

לקראת כלה.

ווער עס איז די כלה —

וויסן אַלע.

אָבער ווו איז זי? —

— ווו?

זאָגן אַלע:

גייט, געפֿינט זי,

גייט, געפֿינט די כלה,

גייט און זאָגט איר,

אַז דער חתן איז שוין דאָ —

אַ נתעלה.

פֿון אַ תהומיק טיפֿן סקלעפּ

And the sharp sword is dangling,
Spent in the hands of the toreador,
And the crowd sits howled out,
Crumpled like the traitor—the cape.
And the sun, too, is spent behind the arena,
The sun, too, is being dragged by a chain
From the sky down,
From the sky down,
Down, down.

➤ *Kabbalists in Safed*

Kabbalists
Awakened in a dream
Stroll through Safed.

Half night
In a white fog.
A passage.
A street.
A cellar.
A step.
Sink down
And rise
And fall
To a newly-whited threshold—
And rest.
Kabbalists
Hug each other in a dream,
And abandon themselves
To a step of *Lekha dodi*
Likrat Kala: Go Lover
Toward your Bride.
Who is the bride?—
All know.
But where is she?—
Where?—
They all say:
Go, find her,
Go, find the bride,
Go and tell her
That the bridegroom has arrived—
Has risen.

Safed (Hebrew: **Tsfat** or **Zefat**)—a city in the Galilee and major center of the Kabbalah, especially in the sixteenth and seventeenth centuries.

Lekha dodi likrat kala—a Kabbalist love song to greet the Sabbath, as a lover greets his bride, sung in the Sabbath eve service. The Hebrew words are given here in the Sephardic (and modern Israeli) pronunciation.

איז ער אויפגעקומען —
אַ נתגלה.
און ער וואַרט
אָט-אָ דאָ,
אויף אַ טרעפּ
געפּאַרבט אין ווײַסן בלאָ —
אָט-אָ דאָ.

מקובלים
אויפגעשטאַנענע אין חלום
טאַנצן אַ התעוררי-טאַנץ
לקראת כלה
דער באַגערטער.
און מיט זיי צוזאַמען
טאַנצט דער חתן
איר באַשערטער.
אָט-אָ קומט זי
דורך אין ווײַסן אַ פּאַרדעקטע,
אירע הענט —
צוויי פליגל אויסגעשטרעקטע.
אַלע, אַלע,
אין אַ כתר-רינג געשלאָסן,
טראָגן צו די אָרעמס פון דער כלה
איר באַשערטן, שבתדיקן חתן.

עורי, עורי, —
זינגען אַלע,
טאַנצן אַלע
לקראת כלה;
פון דער הייך — צו לעצטער נידער,
צו דער טיף פון לעכער,
ביז אַרויף-צו, ווידער,
העכער.

מקובלים
אויפגעשטאַנענע אין חלום
שפּאַנען איבער טורעמס און אוהלים,
איבער דעכער —
העכער, העכער, העכער.

From an abyss of a deep cave
He appeared—
Is revealed.
He is waiting
Right here,
On a step
Painted sky blue—
Right here.

Kabbalists
Awakened in a dream
Dance a *hit'oreri* dance—
An Awakening Dance *Likrat kala*—
Toward the bride,
The desired bride.
And with them
Dances the bridegroom,
Her destined man.
Here she comes,
Covered in white,
Her arms—
Two wings outstretched.
And all, and all,
Locked in a Crown-ring,
Bring the destined Sabbath bridegroom
To the arms of the bride.

Uri, Uri—
Awake, awake—
All sing,
All dance
Likrat kala—
Toward the bride;
From high above—to the lowest low,
To the depths of pits,
And upward again,
Higher.

Kabbalists
Awakened in a dream
Stride over tower and tent,
Over roof and spire—
Higher, higher, higher.

painted sky blue—the characteristic color of the walls in old Safed.

crown (Hebrew: **keter**)—in the Kabbalah, the highest of the ten **sefirot** or emanations of God.

אַ חבר־דיכטער האָט גערעדט צו מיר אַזוי צו זאָגן:
מיר זאָלן אַלע אָנשרײַבן דאָס לעצטע ליד.
דאָס ליד אַרײַנטאָן אין אַן אָרון און עס טראָגן
דורך גאַסן וווּ עס וווינט דער אַמעריקאַנער ייד.

מיר וועלן אײַנהילן דאָס ליד אין בלויע טיכער,
און אפשר גאָר עס אײנוויקלען אין פּראָסטן ווײַס,
אין בלעטער־ווײַס פֿון אַלע דיכטערס ביכער,
וואָס ליגן אין די קעלערן — אַ שפּײַז פֿאַר מײַז.

און אויך אין בלעטער־רויט פֿון אָפּגעראַמטע דיכטער,
וואָס וואַלגערן זיך אין תּפֿיסות, צי בײַם ים צפֿון־ים,
צי אפשר שוין געטויטע צו דער גלאַריע פֿון פֿאַרניכטער,
צו נרן פֿון יעדן קין וואָס פֿאַרשטעלט זיך פֿאַר אַ תּם.

און ווער עס האָט נאָר ווען אַ שורה־ליד געשריבן
וועט אונטערהייבן דעם פֿאַרדעקטן אָרון מיט זײַן האַנט,
דערנאָך, דורך גאַסן פֿאַר פּראָצעסיעס צוגעקליבן,
מיט שטאָלצקייט לאָזן זיך צום ענדע־ברעג פֿון לאַנד.

פֿאָרויס וועט גיין דער יינגסטער, אין זײַן האַנט זײַן פֿעדער,
מיט פֿײַערלעכקייט וועט ער זי צעשמעטערן אויף שטיק,
אַ שלײַדער צום אַספֿאַלט, און גלײַך נאָך אים אײדער, —
אַזאַ־אַ מאַרש פֿון איסט־בראָדווי צו ברוקלין־בריק.

פֿון בריק — צו בראָנזוויל, און צו פֿלעטבוש, און צו בראַיטן,
צו קוני־אײַלענד, און צו סי־גייט — צום אַטלאַנטיק־ים,
און אין די ווײַסע קוואַליעס, העט צו אַלע ווײַטן,
אַרײַנוואַרפֿן אין שטורעם־ווירבל אונדזער לעצטן גראַם.

מיר וועלן אַלע שטיין דערנאָך בײַם ברעג אַטלאַנטיק,
און קוקן ווי די קוואַליעס טורעמען אין שוים,
אין צאָרן, צי אין לויב, וואָס דיכטער האָבן אײגנהאַנטיק
אַוועקגעשענקט דעם תּהום דאָס פּלאַטערניש פֿון זייער טרוים.

און נאָך דעם? — נאָך דעם וועלן מיר, צום טרויים געטרײַע,
צעשיידן זיך און אויסזוכן אַ ברוך־שפּיץ פֿון אַ פֿען,
און אָנשרײַבן אַ נײַ געזאַנג — אַ קינה־ליד אויף דער לוויה
און אָנשרײַבן דאָס ליד דאָס התלהבותדיק, מיט העכסטן ברען!

A fellow poet spoke thus to me:
Let us all write our last song.
Let us put the song in a coffin and carry it
Through streets where he lives, the American Jew.

We shall fold the song in blue kerchiefs,
And wrap it, perhaps, in simple white,
In the white of leaves from all poets' books
That lie in cellars—food for mice.

And in the red of leaves from purged poets
Who languish in prisons, or by the North Sea,
Or, perhaps were slaughtered for the glory of destroyers,
For every Cain disguised as a sheep.

purged poets—an allusion to the Soviet Yiddish poets who were purged by Stalin in 1948 (and executed in 1952) and whose fate was not yet clear when the poem was written.

And anyone who's written a line of verse
Will raise the covered coffin with his hands,
And then, through streets selected for processions,
Proudly go to the last shore of the land.

At the head—the youngest, with pen in hand,
He will solemnly smash it to pieces and throw it
To the hard asphalt, and in his wake, the rest,——
Marching from East Broadway to Brooklyn Bridge.

From the Bridge—to Brownsville, to Flatbush, to Brighton,
To Coney Island, to Seagate—to the Atlantic Sea,
And to the white waves, to the distant winds,
Throw into the whirlpool our last rhyme.

Then we will stand at the shore of the Atlantic
And watch the waves tower in foam—
In rage, or in praise for the poets who themselves
Gave to the abyss the flutter of their dream.

And then?—Then, faithful to our dream,
We'll separate and seek a splinter of a pen,
And write a new song—an elegy on the funeral,
And write the song in exultation, as we can!

◄ צו אַמעריקע

שוין איין און פערציק יאָר אַז כ׳לעב אין דײַנע גרענעצן, אַמעריקע,
אַז כ׳טראָג אין זיך די ברכה פון דײַן פרײַהייט, — יענע פרײַהייט
וואָס איז געהייליקט און געבענטשט געוואָרן דורכן קרבן-בלוט פון לינקאָלן,
און דורך די הימנעס פון וואָלט וויטמאַן. זע, ווי אויסטערליש: איך זוך
נאָך הײַנט אַן ענטפער אויף די סתּירות, אויף דער אומרו פון מײַן לעבן,
און כ׳פרעג: פאַר וואָס האָב איך ביז הײַנט נאָך ניט באַזונגען דיך
מיט פרייד, מיט לויב, מיט לויטערער באַוווּנדערונג,

Louis Lozowick: *Brooklyn Bridge*, 1930.

➤ *To America*

For forty-one years I have lived in your borders, America,
Carrying within me the bounty of your freedom—that freedom,
Sanctified and blessed by the blood of Lincoln's sacrifice
And in the hymns of Walt Whitman. See, how strange it is: to this day
I seek an answer to the contradictions, to the unrest of my life,
I wonder, why haven't I sung you, to this day,
With joy, with praise, with pure admiration—

ווי ס׳פּאַסט פֿאַר דײַנע רחבותן, פֿאַר דײַנע שטעט, פֿאַר דײַנע וועגן,
פֿאַר דײַנע פּרעריס און פֿאַר דײַנע בערג און טאָלן: און נאָך מער:
פֿאַר מײַנע קלײַנע וועלט — אַ מאָל אין בראָנזוויל, און אַ מאָל אין קלינטאָן סטריט,
אַ מאָל אין באָראַ־פּאַרק, אַ מאָל אין בראָנקס און אין די הײַטס,
און מער פֿון אַלץ — פֿאַר אַלע מײַנע פֿוס־שפּאַצירן איבער איסט־בראָדוויי, —
די איסט־בראָדוויי וואָס פֿילט אויך הײַנט מיך אָן מיט אויפֿגעהײַיטערטקייט,
מיט היימישדיקער אייגנקייט, ווי נאָר איך שטעל מײַן פֿוס אויף איר אַרויף.

שוין אײַן און פֿערציק יאָר אַז כ׳לעב אונטער די הימלען דײַנע,
שוין העכער דרײַסיק יאָר אַז כ׳בין אַ בירגער דײַנער,
און — כ׳האָב ביז היינט אין זיך נאָך ניט געפֿונען, ניט דאָס וואָרט
און ניט דעם אופֿן ווי אַזוי מײַן אָנקום און מײַן אויפֿקום אויף דײַן ערד
צו מאָלן ברייט־אַנטפֿלעקעריש ווי דו ביסט עס אַליין, אַמעריקע.
ווי נאָר עס איז געקומען וועגן דיר צו רייד, האָב איך געצאַמט
די ווערטער מײַנע, זיי פֿאַרשטײַפֿט אין שטרענגער אײַנגעהאַלטנקייט,
געבונדן זיי אין צימצום־קנופֿן. גאָר מײַן וועלט און גאָר מײַן לעבן
געהאַלטן אונטער סודותפֿולע שלעסער, ווייַט פֿון דײַן צו־אָפֿענער פֿאַרנעמיקייט.
איך זאָג אַצינד דיר אויס: ווען כ׳בין אַרונטער פֿון דער שיף
מיט אײַן און פֿערציק יאָר צוריק, באַרירט דײַן ערד, — האָב איך געוואָלט
מיט מײַנע ליפֿן צופֿאַלן צו איר און קושן זי. יאָ, יאָ, געוואָלט, געזאָלט
און — כ׳האָב עס ניט געטאָן ... אויף דײַן געבענטשטער ערד דערנאָך
האָב איך, אין זכר פֿון מײַן פֿאָטערשער געשטאַלט, געשריבן שולד און בענקשאַפֿט־לידער,
און כ׳האָב צו דער געשטאַלט געזאָגט: נעם־צו אין מײַן פֿאַרשפֿעטיקונג
די קושן וואָס איך האָב, נאָך זײַענדיק אַ קינד, געוואָלט־געזאָלט
און אייביק זיך געשעמט געוועזמט צו געבן דיר... אין גאָר דײַן גרויסקייט
וועסטו, אַמעריקע, געוויס ניט פֿועלן בײַ זיך צו זאָגן
אַז דו ביסט מער, אַז דו ביסט יחוסדיקער, בילכער פֿון מײַן טאַטן.

און אפֿשר וועסטו זאָגן וועגן זיך: איך בין ניט מער, צי בין איך אָבער ווייניקער? —
פֿאַרוואָר — כ׳וואָלט זייער וועלן הערן ווי דו זאָגסט עס.
ווײַל ווען איך בין דער עס, וואָלט עס זײַן אַ באַלזאַם פֿאַר מײַן האַרץ,
און כ׳וואָלט געקאָנט, כאַטש אין דער שקיעה פֿון מײַן לעבן, עפֿענען פֿאַר דיר
די אַלץ נאָך אײַנגעשלאָסענע ווידוויים וועגן דיר, אַמעריקע.
כ׳זאָג נאָך אַ מאָל — איך האָב פּרובירט עס טאָן דורך הונדערטער רמזים
פֿון פֿערז און גראַם, דורך אויפֿברויזן פֿון טראַגיק־דיאַלאָגן,
דורך אויפֿגעהויבֿענע און פֿאַלנדיקע פֿאַרהאַנגען. איך האָב געזוכט
ניט אײַן מאָל און ווי אַזוי אַראָפּצוריַיסן פֿון מײַן אייגן האַרץ דעם פֿאָרהאַנג
צו ווערן אָפֿן און אינטים מיט דיר, אַמעריקע, כאַטש העלפֿט פֿון דעם
ווי כ׳בין אינטים מיט דעם בית־עולמל פֿון קליין איהומען,
וואו ס׳ליגן מײַנע טאַטע־מאַמע די פֿאַרגאַנגענע אין יענע ווײַטע טעג,
אין יענע ווײַטע טעג פֿאַרמבולדיקע פֿון דער ערשטער וועלט־מלחמה:
ווי כ׳בין אינטים מיט די צעגליטע שנייען פֿונעם דערפֿעלע ווײַטים
אויף די אירקוטסק־יאַקוטישע פֿאַרלוירענקײַטן פֿון סיביר;

To match your vast expanses, your cities, your roads,
Your prairies, your mountains and valleys. Even more:
For my own small world—in Brownsville, or on Clinton Street,
In Borough Park, in the Bronx, or on the Heights,
And above all: for all my walks on East Broadway—
That East-Broadway which fills me even now with stirring vitality,
With intimate hominess, as soon as I set foot in her streets.

For forty-one years I have lived under you skies,
For over thirty years I have been your citizen,
And until now I have not found in me the word, the mode
For painting my arrival and my rise on your earth
With strokes as broad and revealing as you are yourself, America.
As soon as speech would shift toward you, I would curb
My words, rein them in with austere restraint,
Bind them in knots of understatement. My whole world and my whole life
I held under secret locks, far from your wide open breadth.
I shall disclose it now: when I got off the ship
Forty-one years ago, and touched your earth—I wanted to
Fall prostrate upon it, kiss it with my lips. Yes, yes, I wanted to, should have,
And—I didn't . . . And later, on your blessed earth
I wrote, in memory of my father's image, songs of guilt and longing.
And I said to that image: accept, though late, the kisses
That I wanted to give—should have given—as a child
And ever was ashamed to give you . . . In all your greatness,
America, you surely will not bring yourself to say
That you are more, that you are privileged above my father.

And maybe you will say: I am not more, but am I less?—
Indeed, I would have liked to hear you say that.
Had I heard this, it would have been a balm to my heart;
Even at the sunset of my life, I could have opened for you.
The still sealed confessions about you, America.
I say again—I tried to do it in hundreds of hints
In verse and rhyme, in the tempests of tragic dialogues,
In raised and fallen curtains. Often I sought a way
To tear down the curtain covering my own heart,
To be open, intimate with you, America, at least half
As intimate as I am with the little cemetery in small Ihumen,
Where my father-mother rest, passed away in those far-off days,
In those far-off days of World War One, before the flood;
As I am intimate with the glowing snows in the village Vittim
On the God-forsaken Irkutsk-Yakutsk expanses of Siberia;

Ihumen—Leyvik's tiny hometown in Byelorussia.

Vittim—the place of Leyvik's exile in Siberia.

ווי כ׳בין אינטים מיט יצחקס גאַנג צום באַרג מוריה און מיט מוטער רחלס קבר.
מיט דודס תפילות און מיט ישעיהס ליכטיקער נבואה,
מיט לעקערטס אויפגעגאַנג אויפן תליה-קנופ און מיט די אויפגאַנג-טענץ פון עין-חרוד. —

איך האָב פּרובירט, — און קלאָר איז, אַז ס׳איז מ יי ן שולד און ניט דיין
וואָס, נאָך מיט דרייסיק יאָר צוריק, האָב איך אונטער דיינע הימלען דיינע
געטרוירערט טיף אין זיך, געקלאָגט זיך אַז איך טראָג מיין ייִדיש ליד
אין אַנגסט, דורך דיינע גאַסן און דורך דיינע סקווערן,
פאַרקלאַמערט צווישן מיינע ציין, ווי ס׳טראָגט אַ קאַץ אַן עלנטע
די קעצלעך אירע, זוכנדיק פֿאַר זיי אַ רו-אָרט אין אַ קעלער ווו; —
אַז ווען איך טראַכט נאָר וועגן מיינע ברידער — ייִדישע פּאָעטן —
נעמט זייער גורל ווי אַ קלאַמער מיך אַרום, און ס׳ווילט זיך תפילה טאָן פאַר זיי,
פאַר זייער מזל, — און גראָד דעמאָלט ווערן אַלע ווערטער שטום.
אווודאי איז עס מיין שולד, און ניט דיין, אויך היינט, ווען נאָכן אָפּגאַנג
פון יענע דרייסיק יאָר טוט טרויערן מיין האַרץ אויף ס׳ניי עלעגיש
וואָס היינט, נאָך מער ווי ווען עס איז, האָט ס׳בייזע מזל
צעשלייַדערט אַלע ייִדישע פּאָעטן איבער ניי-סיבירן,
און אונדזער פּלאַטעדריקע דיכטער-שיף פאַריאָגט אין תהום פון שטורעמס,
אין תהום פון שטורעמס אויף אויף דיינע וואַסערן, אַמעריקע,
אויף טויט-סכנה; און אין דער טויט-סכנה זוך איך ס׳בראַווע ליד
פון בראַוון קאַפּיטאַן אויך היינט. דער בראַווער קאַפּיטאַן זאָל ניט פאַראַטן
זיין גורל-ליד אויך היינט. — — —
דו זעסט — איך בין אַכזריותדיק צו זיך און ווען כ׳זאָג: א ו ו ד א י — איז עס מ יי ן שולד,
ווען כ׳וואָלט געקאָנט אַנשטאַט "אווודאי" זאָגן: אפשר און מסתמא.
איך היט מיך פון צו וואַרפן כאַטש אַ טייל פון שולד אויף דיר, אַמעריקע.
און גאָט אַליין אין הימל איז אַן עדות אַז דו ביסט ניט ראוי נאָך
צו פילן זיך אין גאַנצן ריין פון שולד, אין גאַנצן ווייַס ווי שניי. — — —
דו זעסט — אין דער מינוט וואָלסטו אַליין באדאַרפט צו הילף מיר קומען
און מאַכן גרינג מיר דאָס געפינעניש פון יענע ווערטער,
וואָס טראָגן אי התקרבות, אי צונויפגיסונג און אי געזעגענונג.
צונויפגיסונג מיט אַל דיין שיינקייט און מיט אַל דיין גרויס צעאַטעמטקייט;
געזעגענונג? — וואָס גרעסער די צונויפגיסונג, אַלץ נענטער קאָן קאַן געמאָלט זיין
די רגע פון צעזעגענונג. זי קאָן געשען אין דיינע גרענעצן,
זי קען אָבער געשען אויך ווייַט, מחוץ פון דיינע גרענעצן; —
זי קען מיך אויפהייבן און מיך אַוועקטראָגן צו יענע וווּנדער-ערטער,

As I am intimate with Isaac's walk to Mount Moriah
    and with mother Rachel's grave,
With David's prayers and with the
    bright prophecy of Isaiah,
With Lekert's rise upon the gallows
    and with the dance-of-dawn in Eyn-Harod.—

I tried,—and it is clear: the fault is mine, not yours,
That thirty years ago I mourned under your skies
Deep inside me, lamented that I carry my Yiddish song
In fear, through your streets and through your squares,
Clenched in my teeth, as a forsaken cat might carry
Her kittens, in search of a cellar, a place of rest;—
That when I think of my brothers—
    Yiddish poets—their destiny
Embraces me like a clamp, I want to pray for them,
For their lot—and then all words grow mute.
Certainly, it is my fault, not yours, when even now
After thirty years have passed my heart mourns again,
An elegy on how, now more than ever, the evil lot
Has scattered all Yiddish poets over New-Siberias,
And chased our trembling poets' ship into an abyss of storms,
Into an abyss of storms on your waters too, America,
In death-danger; and in that death-danger I search
    for the brave song
Of the brave captain. The brave captain shall not betray
His song-of-destiny today.— — —
You see—I am cruel to myself when I say:
    It is *certainly* my fault,
If instead of "certainly" I could say "maybe", or "perhaps."
I am trying not to cast part of the blame on you, America.
And may God in Heaven witness that you are not yet worthy
To feel free of guilt, as white as snow—
You see—you yourself should have come to my aid right now,
To ease my task of finding proper words
Expressing intimacy and fusion and farewell.
Fusion with your beauty and your expansive breath;
Farewell?—the stronger the fusion, the closer I can see
The moment of farewell. It may occur within your boundaries,
And it may happen far away, beyond your borders:
It may uplift me and carry me to those wonder-places,

Lekert—Hirsh Lekert (1879–1902), a shoemaker and Bund activist in Vilna who organized an armed attack to liberate political prisoners. He assassinated the Russian governor of Vilna for flogging Socialists after a May Day demonstration and was hanged. Lekert became a hero of the Jewish labor movement and self-defense.

Eyn-Harod—the first kibbutz in the swamps of the Jezreel Valley, famous for its pioneering spirit and collective dances into the night.

Thirty years ago . . . all words are mute—an allusion to the poem, "Yiddish Poets." See above.

Brave Captain—an allusion to Whitman's "O, Captain, My Captain."

ווו כ׳בין נאָך יינגלווייז אַרומגעגאַנגען מיט אברהם אבינו
אַרום באר-שבע, און מיט דודן אַרום די טויערן פון ירושלים,
זי קאָן מיך ברענגען אויך צו הײַנטיקע אַרויפגאַנגען פון ניי-ירושלים.

אויך דו, אַמעריקע, ביסט נאָענט מיט זיי אַרומגעגאַנגען,
אויך דו האָסט אין דײַן האַרץ פאַרנומען גאָטס געבאָט און ברכה
צו זײַן אַ לאַנד וואָס רינט מיט מילך און האָניק,
צו זײַן פילצאָליק ווי דער זאַמד בײַם ים און ווי די שטערן אויפן הימל,
צו זײַן נביאיש פרײַ, ווי ס׳האָבן וועגן דיר געחלומט דײַנע שעפער. —
אָ זאָל דער חלום פון וואָלט וויטמאַן און פון לינקאָלן אויך הײַנט דײַן חלום זײַן!

אין טעג פון עלטער, ווען איך שטיי אין העלן אָנגעזיכט
פון דער, אָדער פון יענער ליכטיקער צעזעגענונג, — דערמאָן איך וויִדער זיך
אָן דער מינוט, ווען כ׳האָב מיט אײן און פערציק יאָר צוריק
דערגרייכט דײַן ברעג, אַמעריקע, און כ׳האָב געוואָלט און כ׳האָב געזאָלט
אַ פאַל טאָן צו דײַן ערד און צופאַלן צו איר מיט מײַנע ליפן,
און — כ׳האָב עס אין פאַרלוירענער צעטומלונג ניט געטאָן, —
דערלויב עס מיר צו טאָן אַצינדערט, — וואָראָהאַפטיק אַזוי ווי כ׳שטיי
אַרומגענומען מיט דער העלקײט פון התקרבות און געזעגענונג, אַמעריקע.

12טער סעפּטעמבער, 1954.

Where as a boy I walked with Father Abraham near
Beer-Sheba, and with David around the gates of Jerusalem,
It may bring me, too, to today's climbing road to New Jerusalem.

You too, America, walked close with them,
You too, have absorbed in your heart God's commandment and blessing:
To be a land flowing with milk and honey,
To be numerous as the sands of the sea and the stars in the sky,
To be prophetic and free, as your Founders dreamed you.—
O, let the dream of Lincoln and Walt Whitman be your dream today!

In days of old age, when I stand in the bright vision
Of one or another shining farewell, I recall again
The moment, forty-one years ago, when I reached
Your shore, America, and I wanted to and should have
Fallen prostrate to your earth and touched it with my lips,
And in confused embarrassment I did not do it,—
Let me do it now—as I stand here truthfully,
Embracing the glare of intimacy and farewell, America.

September 12, 1954

Ben Shahn: *All That Is Beautiful*,
1965. Phrases from *Maximus of
Tyre*: "All that is beautiful. But
for remembrance sake. The art of
Phidias."

Appendixes

I. Introspectivism [Manifesto of 1919]

II. Chronicle of a Movement: Excerpts from Introspectivist Criticism

INTROSPECTIVISM

[Manifesto of 1919]

I

With this collection,[1] we intend to launch a particular trend in Yiddish poetry which has recently emerged in the works of a group of Yiddish poets. We have chosen to call it the *Introspective Movement*, a name that indicates a whole range of individual character and nuance.

We know that introspective poems as such are nothing new. In all ages, poets have occasionally written introspectively; that is, they looked *into themselves*[2] and created poetry drawn from their own soul* and from the world as reflected in it. There are introspective poems in modern Yiddish poetry as well, even though the poets did not use this term.

The difference, however, between us and those other poets, both Yiddish and non-Yiddish, ancient and modern, is that we are dedicated to deepening, developing, and expanding the introspective method.

The world exists and we are part of it. But for us, the world exists only as it is mirrored in us, as it touches *us*. The world is a nonexistent category, a lie, if it is not related to us. It becomes an actuality only *in* and *through* us.

This general philosophical principle is the foundation of our trend. We will try to develop it in the language of poetry.

Poetry is not only feeling and perception but also, and perhaps primarily, the art of expressing feelings and perceptions adequately. It is not enough to say that all phenomena exist to the extent that they enter into an organic relation with us. The poet's major concern is to express this organic relation in an introspective and fully individual manner.

In an introspective manner means that the poet must really listen to his inner voice, observe his internal panorama—kaleidoscopic, contradictory, unclear or confused as it may be. From these sources, he must create poetry which is the result

---

* The Yiddish word *zel*, "soul," is equivalent to Freud's *Seele* and can be translated as *psyche*.

1. This Introspectivist manifesto, written in 1919, was published as the opening of *In Zikh: A Collection of Introspective Poems*, Max N. Maisel, New York, 1920.

2. In the original: "*In zikh*," which gave the name to the journal and the movement, Inzikhism.

of both the fusion of the poet's soul with the phenomenon he expresses and the individual image, or cluster of images, that he sees *within himself* at that moment.

What does take place in the poet's psyche under the impression or impact of any phenomenon?

In the language of our local poets, of the "Young Generation" (*Di Yunge*),[3] this creates a *mood*. According to them, it is the poet's task to express or convey this mood. How? In a concentrated and well-rounded form. Concentration and well-roundedness are seen as the necessary conditions, or presuppositions, that allow the poet's mood to attain universal or, in more traditional terms, *eternal*, value.

But this method, though sufficient to create poetic vignettes or artful arabesques, is essentially neither sufficient nor true. From our point of view, this method is a *lie*.

Why?

Because the mood and the poem that emerge from this conception and this method must inevitably result in something cut-off, isolated, something which does not really correspond to life and truth.

At best, such poems are embellishments and ornaments. At worst, they ring false, because the impression or the impact of any phenomenon on the poet's soul does not result in an isolated, polished, well-rounded, and concentrated mood. What emerges is more complex, intertwined with a whole galaxy of other "moods," of other feelings and perceptions. In the final analysis, concentration and well-roundedness of poetry symbolize the lie, the awesome contradiction between literature and life, between all of art and life.

We Introspectivists want first of all to present life—the true, the sincere, and the precise—as it is mirrored in *ourselves*, as it merges with us.

The human psyche is an awesome labyrinth. Thousands of beings dwell there. The inhabitants are the various facets of the individual's present self on the one hand and fragments of his inherited self on the other. If we believe that every individual has already lived somewhere in one incarnation or another—and this belief is often vividly sensed by each of us—then the number of inhabitants in the labyrinth of the human psyche is even higher.

This is the real *life* of a human being. In our age of the big metropolis and enormous variety in all domains, this life becomes a thousandfold more complicated and entangled. We Introspectivists feel the need to convey and express it.

In what form and shape does this complexity of moods appear?

In the shape of association and suggestion. For us, these two elements are also the most important methods of poetic expression.

Of course, poets of all times have used suggestion and association. The pre-Raphaelite Rossetti and the later Swinburne often used these elements in their work. Yet we want to make association and suggestion the poet's major tools because it seems to us that they are best suited to express the complex feelings and perceptions of a contemporary person.

So much about the introspective method. As for *individual* manner, it is perhaps even more important.

---

3. An Impressionist, cosmopolitan trend that dominated Yiddish American poetry from 1907 to 1919.

Because we perceive the world egocentrically and because we think that this is the most natural and therefore *the truest and most human* mode of perception, we think that the poem of every poet must first of all be *his own* poem. In other words, the poet must in every case give us what he himself sees and as he sees it.

Essentially, this should be self-evident as a prerequisite for any poetry. It should be but is not.

Indeed, most poems, not just Yiddish ones but the majority of non-Yiddish ones as well, lack the full individuality of the poet and hence of the poem, too. In most poems, the poet does not delve deeply enough to see what appears in his own psyche. Perhaps the fault lies with language, which generally works in our lives as a misleading and deceiving category. Be that as it may, we think that, in the great majority of all poetry, the poet is not sufficiently individual. He employs too many stock images and ready-made materials. When the poet, or any person, looks at a sunset, he may see the strangest things which, ostensibly, have perhaps no relation to the sunset. The image reflected in his psyche is rather a series of far-reaching associations moving away from what his eye sees, a chain of suggestions evoked by the sunset. *This*, the series of associations and the chain of suggestions, constitutes *truth*, is life, much as an illusion is often more real than the cluster of external appearances we call life. Most poets, however, will not even focus on what occurs inside themselves while they are watching a sunset but will paint it, search for colors, describe the details, etc. If, in addition, they are subjectively attuned, they will perhaps dip their brush into a drop of subjectivity, into a patch of color of their selves, make a comparison with their own lives, express some wisdom about life in general, and the poem is done.

For us, such a poem is not true, is a cliché. We insist that the poet should give us the authentic image that he sees in himself and give it in such a form as only he and no one else can see it.

If such a poem then becomes grist for the mill of Freudian theory, if it provides traces of something morbid or sick in the poet, we do not mind. Art is ultimately redemption, even if it is an illusory redemption or a redemption *through* illusion. And no redemption is possible in any other way but through oneself, through an internal personal concentration. Only a truly individual poem can be a means of self-redemption.

2

Both the introspectivity of a poem and its individuality must use suggestion and association in order to reach full expression. Now, the individuality of the poem has a lot to do with what is generally known as *form*.

In fact, form and content are the same. A poem that can be rewritten in another form is neither a poem nor poetry. They cannot be separated from one another. To speak of form and content separately is to succumb to the influence of a linguistic fallacy. And if we speak of form as a separate concept, it is merely for the sake of convenience, as is the case with many other linguistic fallacies.

The generally known aspect of form is *rhythm*. Every poem must have rhythm. Rhythm is the mystery of life; art which is no more than an expression of life obviously must also have rhythm. But what kind of rhythm must a poem have?

There is only one answer: it must have the only possible and the only imaginable rhythm. Each poem must have its *individual rhythm*. By this we mean that the rhythm of the poem must fit entirely this particular poem. One poem cannot have the same rhythm as any other poem. Every poem is, in fact, unique.

And if we see, in certain poets, how the most divergent poems are similar in their rhythm, this in itself is the best sign of their lack of productivity and creativity, and also of their lack of genuine sincerity.

We cannot understand how it is possible for a real poet to write one poem about the subway, another about the sand at the seashore in summer, and a third about his love for a girl—all in the same rhythm, in the same "beat." Two of the three poems are certainly false. But, more certainly, all three are false, because if a poet can write three poems in the same rhythm, this is proof in itself that he does not listen to the music in his own soul, that he does not see anything or hear anything with his own eyes and ears.

We demand individual rhythm because only thus can the truth that we seek and want to express be revealed.

This leads us to the question which has recently stirred the consciousness of poets in all languages and not least that of Yiddish poets, the question of *free verse*.

Free verse is not imperative for introspective poets. It is possible to have introspective poems in regular meter. Though regular meter may often appear as a hindrance, a straitjacket, free verse in itself is not enough. We Introspectivists believe that free verse is best suited to the individuality of the rhythm and of the poem as a whole; and for *that* rather than for any other reason, we prefer it to other verse forms.

Hence it is the greatest mistake, even ignorance, to claim (as many do) that it is easier to write free verse than to write in measured meters. If comparison here makes sense at all, the opposite is true. It is easier to write in regular and conventional meters because, after some experience, one acquires the knack and the poem "writes itself." But free verse, intended primarily for individual rhythm, demands an intense effort, a genuine sounding of the inner depths. Therefore free verse more easily betrays the non-poet, revealing the internal vacuum, if that is what is at stake.

When non-poets take on free verse, their situation is no easier than when they wrote iambs, trochees, or anapests. On the contrary, while in the latter case they can perhaps produce a certain musicality and thus create the impression that they are writing poetry, in the former case they are unproductive from the first or second moment, and their failure is exposed.

Only for the real poet is free verse a new, powerful means of expression, a new, wide world full of unexplored territories. For the non-poet, however, free verse is nothing but a mousetrap into which he falls in his first or second line. Let the non-poets beware of it!

We emphasize again that we are not against regular meters as such. Every true poet, Introspectivist or not, may sometimes feel that only in a regular rhythm, in a certain "canonical" meter, can he create a particular poem. It is more correct to say (for poets, it is a truism) that, inside every poet, including Introspectivists, *a certain poem will often write itself* in a regular meter. Then he does not fight it. Then he understands that it had to be like this, that in *this* case, this is the truth, this the individual rhythm.

If we prefer free verse, it is only for that reason. In general, we think that regular meter, the rhythm of frequently repeated beats, adapted itself perhaps to an earlier kind of life before the rise of the big city with its machines, its turmoil, and its accelerated, irregular tempo. That life was quiet and flowed tranquilly—in a regular rhythm, in fact—in beats repeated in short, frequent intervals.

Just as contemporary life created new clothing, new dwellings, new color combinations, and new sound combinations, so one needs to create a new art and new and different rhythms. We believe that free verse is best suited for the creation of such new rhythms. It is like fine, yielding plaster in which the inner image of the poet can find its most precise and fullest realization.

For the same reason, we are not against rhyme. Rhyme has its own charm and value. This is natural. The spirit of creative poets has used it for thousands of years as one of its poetic devices. This in itself is proof enough of its value. We say merely that rhyme is *not* a must. It often sounds forced or leads us on like a delusive, fleeting light. In such cases, rhyme is harmful and best avoided. Rhyme is good only when it is well-placed, when it is woven naturally into the verse. It is unnecessary to seek it, to make an effort to have rhyme at any cost, especially in our time when there is no need to learn poems by heart, when traveling poets do not have to recite their poems to amuse an ignorant or unpoetic audience.

Whenever a poet does feel the call of a wandering troubadour to recite his poems for a more primitive audience, as in the case of the American poet, Vachel Lindsay, the rhyme is well-placed and is good.

As with regular and irregular rhythm, many tend to assume mistakenly that writing without rhyme is easier than with rhyme. This is false. One can easily learn to make rhymes. And while one can sometimes cover with rhyme a trivial mood, which thus acquires the pretension to poetry, such a camouflage has no place in a rhymeless poem. There, one *must* be a genuine poet and a genuine creator. If not, the rhymeless poem will betray it much faster and easier than a rhymed one will.

The music of a poem—no doubt a desideratum—does not depend on rhyme. Rhyme is merely one element of its music, and the least important one at that. The music of a poem must also be purely individual and can be attained without rhymes, which necessarily produce a certain stereotype: after all, rhymes are limited in quantity and quality.

The *individual* sound combination is really necessary; indeed, because of our Introspectivism, we believe it to be unusually important. Not only do we not deny this element in poetry but we try to give it a new impetus, precisely through the individuality of the poem.

The musical and sound aspect of the Yiddish language has been generally neglected by most of our poets. Alliteration as a poetic device has remained almost untouched, although it is strongly represented in our language. As far as we can, we will try to remedy this neglect.

Individuality is everything and introspection is everything—this is what we seek, this is what we want to achieve.

When a certain phenomenon appears to a poet in the shape of colors; when an association carries him away to the shores of the Ganges or to Japan; when a suggestion whispers to him of something nebulous, something lurking in a fragment of his previous incarnation or of his hereditary self—all these are the roads and the labyrinths of his psyche. He must tread them because they are *he*, and only through the authentic, inner, true, *introspective* "I" lies the path that leads to creation and redemption.

3

Once this is accepted, it is self-evident that everything is an object for poetry, that for the poet there is no ugly or beautiful, no good or bad, no high or low. Everything is of equal value for the poet if it appears *inside* him, and everything is simply a stage to his internal redemption.

For us, then, the senseless and unproductive question of whether a poet "should" write on national or social topics or merely on personal ones does not arise. For us, everything is "personal." Wars and revolutions, Jewish pogroms and the workers' movement, Protestantism and Buddha, the Yiddish school and the Cross, the mayoral elections and a ban on our language—all these may concern us or not, just as a blond woman and our own unrest may or may not concern us. If it does concern us, we write poetry; if it does not, we keep quiet. In either case, we write about ourselves because all these exist only insofar as they are in us, insofar as they are perceived *introspectively*.

For the same reason, we do not recognize the difference between "poetry of the heart" and "poetry of the head," two meaningless phrases that belong to the same category of linguistic fallacies mentioned above. If the first phrase implies unconscious creativity and the second *conscious creativity*, then we say that neither we nor anybody else knows the boundary between conscious and unconscious. Certain aspects of the creative process are always conscious and cannot be otherwise. There is no tragedy in that. The modern poet is not, cannot, and should not be that naive stargazer who knows nothing but his little song, who understands nothing that goes on in the world, who has no attitude to life, its problems and events, who cannot even write a line about anything but his little mood, tapped out in iambs and trochees. The contemporary poet is a human being like other human beings and must be an intelligent, conscious person. As a poet, this is what is required of him: to see and feel, know and comprehend, and to see with his own eyes and be capable of expressing the seen, felt, and understood in his own internally true, introspectively sincere manner.

If conscious poetry means the expression of underlying thought in poetry, we see nothing wrong in that, either. A poet need not and must not be spiritually mute. A poet's *thought* is not a drawback but a great advantage. As a poet, as an artist, he must only be capable of expressing his thought in a proper form, of creating from it a work of art. And this depends on just one condition: that the thought should be his own, that it should be the true result of the fusion of his soul and life; and that he should express it in that form, in those very images, in the same true colors and tones as they take shape inside him, as they emerge and permeate him in the labyrinth of his soul. There is no boundary between "feeling" and "thought" in contemporary man or in the contemporary poet. Both are expressions of the same "I"; they are so closely intertwined that it is absurd to wish to separate them.

We make no distinction between intellectual poetry and poetry of feeling. We know of only one distinction: that between authenticity and falsehood, between true individuality and cliché. In the first case, poetry is born; in the second—"mood-laden" as it may be—merely licorice, vignettes, and false tones.

Our relationship to "Jewishness," too, becomes obvious from our general poetical credo.

We are "Jewish poets" simply because we are Jews and write in Yiddish.[4] No matter what a Yiddish poet writes in Yiddish, it is ipso facto Jewish. One does not need any particular "Jewish themes." A Jew will write about an Indian fertility temple and Japanese Shinto shrines as a Jew. A Jewish poet will be Jewish when he writes poetry about "vive la France," about the Golden Calf, about gratitude to a Christian woman for a kind word, about roses that turn black, about a courier of an old prince, or about the calm that comes only with sleep. It is not the poet's task to seek and show his Jewishness. Whoever is interested in this endeavor is welcome to it, and whoever looks for Jewishness in Yiddish poets will find it.

In two things we are explicitly Jewish, through and through: in our relationship to the Yiddish language in general, and to Yiddish as a poetic instrument.

We believe in Yiddish. We love Yiddish. We do not hesitate to say that he who has a negative relation to the Yiddish language, or who merely looks down on it, cannot be a Yiddish poet. He who mocks Yiddish, who complains that Yiddish is a poor and shabby language, he who is merely indifferent to Yiddish, does not belong to the high category of Yiddish poets. To be a Yiddish poet is a high status, an achievement, and it is unimaginable that a person creating in Yiddish should spit in the well of his creation. Such a person is a petty human being and an even pettier poet.

As to Yiddish as a language instrument, we think that our language is now beautiful and rich enough for the most profound poetry. All the high achievements of poetry—the highest—are possible in Yiddish. Only a poor poet can complain of the poverty of the Yiddish language. The real poet knows the richness of our language and lacks nothing, can lack nothing.

Poetry is, to a very high degree, the art of language—a principle that is too often forgotten—and Yiddish poetry is the art of the Yiddish language, which is merely a part of the general European-American culture. Yiddish is now rich enough, independent enough to afford to enrich its vocabulary from the treasures of her sister languages. That is why we are not afraid to borrow words from the sister languages, words to cover newly developed concepts, broadened feelings and thoughts. Such words are also *our* words. We have the same right to them as does any other language, any other poetry, because—to repeat—Yiddish poetry is merely a branch, a particular stream in the whole contemporary poetry of the world.

We regard Yiddish as a fully mature, ripe, independent, particular, and unique language. We maintain that Yiddish separated long ago not only from her mother—German—but also from her father—Hebrew. Everything that ties Yiddish to Hebrew in an artificial and enforced way is superfluous, an offence to the language in which we create. Spelling certain words in Yiddish differently from other words because of their Hebrew etymology is false and anachronistic.[5] All words in Yiddish

4. In Yiddish, the same word, *Yiddish*, means both "Yiddish" and "Jewish."
5. Yiddish, though using the Hebrew alphabet, employs a European-type, close-to-phonetic spelling for words of any origin except Hebrew; the latter preserve their Hebrew, vowelless spelling.

are equal, it is high time to clean out the white basting of Hebrew spelling from certain Yiddish words.

We are not enemies of Hebrew. For us Yiddish poets, there is absolutely no language question.[6] For us, Hebrew is only a foreign language, while Yiddish is *our* language. We cannot forget, however, that Hebrew and Hebraism have kept on disturbing the natural development of the Yiddish word and of Yiddish poetry. We know that, if not for the Hebraism of the Haskalah movement,[7] which later branched out into Zionist Hebraism on the one hand and assimilationist anti-Yiddishism on the other, Yiddish poetry would stand on a much higher level than it does today. We know that if Yiddish poetry had developed normally and naturally from the poet Shloyme Etinger[8] to now, if the natural course had not been interrupted by Hebraism and the Hebraists, there could be no language problem for anyone; it would perhaps never have arisen. The rich Yiddish literature would have nipped it in the bud.

We think, therefore, that one must finally have the courage to sever any tie between our language and any other foreign language. A time comes when a son must break away altogether from his father and set up his own tent. The last vestige of Hebrew in Yiddish is the Hebrew spelling of certain words. This must be abolished. As poets rather than propagandists, we solve the problem first of all for ourselves. We shall spell all Yiddish words equally, with no respect for their pedigree.

These are our views, these are our poetic aspirations in the various realms that must concern a poet in general and a Yiddish poet in particular.

4

Our emergence is not intended as a struggle against anybody or as an attempt to annihilate anyone. We simply want to develop ourselves and take our own road, which is, for us, the truest road.

We come at the right time, at a time when Yiddish poetry is mature and independent enough to bear separate trends and promote differentiation and diversity, instead of straying hesitantly in one herd.

By saying that we come at the right time we admit that everything that has come before us was also at its right time.

Mikhl Gordon, Shimon Frug, Morris Rosenfeld, Avrom Reyzin, A. Liessin, H. Royzenblat—they are all good in their own time, but only *in* their own time.[9] All that was necessary for the development of Yiddish poetry, for its gradual progress

6. An allusion to "the War of Languages" raging at the beginning of the twentieth century, in which Hebrew and Yiddish competed for the title of "the" national language that would dominate Jewish education and culture.

7. The movement of Enlightenment in European Jewish culture, 1780–1880, promoting aesthetic ideals of German or Russian culture, despising Yiddish as a "jargon" and preferring German or Hebrew with Mendelssohn or, with the poet I. L. Gordon, Russian or Hebrew to the language of the masses.

8. One of the few Yiddish poets of the Haskalah, Etinger (1799–1855) was a learned writer who created fine poetry not published in his lifetime.

9. Mikhl Gordon (1823–1890) was a poet of the Haskalah in Lithuania; Shimon Frug (1860–1916), a famous poet in Russian and Yiddish, introduced meters in Yiddish poetry; Morris

was contributed by them and thus made our appearance possible. To this extent, we do not fight against them, we do not try to shout them down. On the contrary, we express our gratitude for their role in our emergence.

Only one representative of the older Yiddish poets has crossed the boundary of his time and is, for us, not merely a precursor but a fellow poet. This is *Yehoash*.[10]. In our view, he is the most important figure in all of Yiddish poetry today. He is a poet who does not stop searching, who has the courage and the talent—we do not know which is more important or more beautiful and greater—to sense at the very zenith of his creativity that this is perhaps not the way and to depart from the well-known path of scanned iambs and trochees to write in new forms and in different modes. Perhaps he should have been the initiator of a new trend in Yiddish poetry and perhaps also, at least in part, of our trend. He did not do this for understandable reasons, and we would like to note that we regard him as one who is close to us.

The development of a new group of Yiddish poets would not have been possible without certain intermediate steps. Art, like life, does not leap but develops gradually. On those intermediate steps, we find the so-called *Yunge* (the Young Generation).

Aynhorn, Menakhem, Mani Leyb, Zisho Landoy, Rolnik, Slonim, Schwartz, Ayzland, M. L. Halpern, B. Lapin—they are all good and good in their time.[11] They have accomplishments, and not only do we not deny that but we understand and readily admit that only because of their work was a further development of Yiddish poetry possible, of which the Introspective trend is an expression.

All these poets led Yiddish poetry out onto a broader road. They brought Yiddish poetry, which was strongly akin to the verse of wedding jesters and rhymesters,[12] closer to art and genuine poetry. In the case of poets like Rolnik or Mani Leyb, one could say that they made Yiddish poetry deeper, though as to the latter, it would be more correct to say finer. Slonim has the accomplishment of showing a sensibility for rhythm and, in part, also for individual rhythm.

The major contribution of the Young Generation, however, is with respect to language. They introduced a certain Europeanism into the language, a greater artistic authenticity, and raised the level of a Yiddish poem. They canceled Peretz's "my song would have sounded differently if I sang for Goyim in Goyish."[13]

Rosenfeld (1862–1923), was a major "sweat-shop poet" in America; and Avrom Reyzin (Abraham Reisin; 1876–1953), A. Liessin (1872–1938), and H. Royzenblat (1879–1956) were major American Yiddish poets at the beginning of the twentieth century.

10. Yehoash (1872–1927), born in Russia, published most of his books in America. He is famous for his classical translation of the Bible into Yiddish.

11. David Aynhorn (Einhorn; 1886–1973), Menakhem (later: M. Boreysho; 1888–1949), Mani Leyb (Leib; 1883–1953), Zisho Landoy (Zishe Landau; 1889–1937), J. Rolnik (Rolnick; 1879–1955), J. Slonim (1885–1944), I. J. Schwartz (1885–1971), R. Ayzland (Iceland; 1884–1955), M.-L. Halpern (1886–1932), and B. Lapin (1889–1952) were American Yiddish poets of or close to the Young Generation. Most of them continued writing poetry simultaneously with the Introspectivists.

12. An allusion to the poetry of the Badkhonim, wedding jesters who extemporated rhymed verse in Yiddish ranging from coarse comedy to national and topical themes. An example is the popular poet Eliokum Zunser (1836–1913), who was active in Russia and America.

13. I. L. Peretz (1852–1915), one of the three Yiddish "Classics," expressed in these lines from the opening of the long poem, "Monish," the inferiority complex of his time about the poverty of the "Jargon," i.e., Yiddish.

There it remained, however. As for content, even the deepest of them stayed on the surface and the finest hit a wall. With all his sensibility for rhythm, Slonim stopped where he should have, and perhaps could have, started. As for language, there too they came to a dead end. The refreshing, enriching, and refined became ossified and degenerated into a fruitless wasteland.

As with the older writers, here too there is an exception—namely, H. Leyvik.[14]

Leyvik is only in part one of the Young Generation. From the first, he introduced so much that is individual—and even profound—that there can be no talk of his stopping, of his having already completed his poetic mission.

We regard him, too, as being close to us.

The Young Generation, as a whole, however—as a group—belong only to their own time. If one wants to characterize their contribution, which we consider finished, it is the contribution of an interim stage, of a bridge to a new poetry—a poetry more independent, courageous, profound, and authentic both in content and in form, to use an old formulation.

5

We would like to add a few comments on the mode of writing, points which can be found in most modern trends, such as, for example, in the American Imagists. We will also remark on the way in which this collection, which we consider the first in a series, was compiled.

Since we see our trend as an expression of a movement toward life, toward life as it is reflected in us—which is real life—we are in favor of making the language of our poems as close as possible to the spoken language in its structure and flow. We therefore abolish any possibility of "inversion," the contortion of the natural sentence structure for the sake of rhythm and rhyme. One cannot and under no circumstances should say "bird thou never wert" or "but not your heart away"[15] or even worse barbarisms. One must write, "you never were a bird," "don't give your heart away," whether there is a rhyme or not, whether it scans or not.

We are against using expressions for their ostensible beauty. There can be no beauty without profound relationship and without authentic meaning.

We strive to avoid banal similes, epithets, and other figurative expressions. Their very banality makes them a lie and we seek, first of all, introspective honesty and individuality.

We try to avoid superfluous adjectives altogether, which add nothing and are merely an unnecessary burden. "Far distance" or "blue distance" or "snowing snow" do not make the distance or the snow different. Instead, it is always better to have an authentic, individual image.

It is always better to use the right word for the corresponding concept, even if it is not "beautiful" according to popular aesthetics. A word in the right place is always beautiful. If anyone has to look it up in the dictionary, this is none of the poet's business.

14. See his poetry in this volume.
15. Here, English equivalents (by Shelley and Houseman) to the Yiddish phrases were used.

As to the composition of this collection, the initiative lies with the signers of this introduction. They invited others after agreeing on the tenets and goals of this trend. We have included here such poems as are more or less close to our position.

All these rules, as it were, were not formulated in advance of the poems. Should anyone think so, he is guilty of an absurdity. The rules, like the whole movement, grew out of poems already written. It cannot be otherwise. If in the process of writing new rules develop, even contradictory ones, we shall record that, too.

The poem creates the rule and not vice versa, and that is why no rule can be considered binding forever.

The number of poems included in this collection does not by any means indicate the relative importance of a poet. Neither does it have to do with whether the poet was one of the initiators. It indicates merely that someone has written more poems.

All participants are equally important.

We know that every poet develops better in solitude than in a group. The eight poets whose works are represented here are very different from each other. If we have decided to appear as a group with a particular name (which, by the way, should not be taken literally), it is because, through this collective separation and delimitation, we hope to enhance the individual development of each one of us.

We have been led to this collective step by the current internal situation of Yiddish poetry—chaotic, faceless, characterless, and increasingly an obstacle to further development.

Jacob Glatshteyn   A. Leyeles   N. Minkov

CHRONICLE OF A MOVEMENT

Excerpts from Introspectivist Criticism

The following passages are what they purport to be—namely, excerpts. Like the "Diary of Fabius Lind," they are a kaleidoscope of reflections and responses on various aspects of art, language, history, the reader, the lot of Yiddish in America, and also on free verse and the creative process. They reflect the multiple concerns and struggles of their authors and the beliefs that fed this poetry and grew out of it. The excerpts are arranged as a chronicle, in chronological order. Centering on the early writings of the young poets who attempted to clarify the principles and attitudes of Introspectivism, they are taken primarily from the critical prose of two poets represented in this anthology, Leyeles and Glatshteyn. The intention is not to show their practical literary criticism or political and social thought and journalism, but rather their reflections on the nature of poetry and its place in this, the historical world.

Most of the excerpts have been selected from twenty years of the journal *In Zikh*, with an emphasis on the founding years. The last sections are from Glatshteyn's first book of criticism, published after the Holocaust and profoundly impressed by it, entitled *In tokh genumen (Sum and Substance: Essays 1945–1947*, New York, 1947, 544 pp.). The titles of the excerpts are either taken from the source (without any claim to represent the whole piece thus titled) or supplied by the editors and put in square brackets (as are all other editorial additions). Ellipses are indicated by three dots in square brackets [. . .].

[1] *[On the Limits of the "Young Generation"]*

In the grayness of New York's lime kiln, in the shadowy shimmer of East Broadway and in the insolent artistic night life of Broadway; here, where everyone "makes a living" *for himself* cut off from any milieu which might look up reverently to the white hands of a poet; here, where a poet walks unnoticed like a shadow through

A front page of *In zikh*, August, 1929.

New York streets, is squeezed in subways and elevateds along with everyone else, returns home soiled at night with everyone else—in this lime kiln, several young people sense instinctively that their own liberation is not with the liberation of the group, that they, as individuals, are still drowning in the bile of their own suffering.[. . .]

   And the young man, cut off from his home, in the smoke of a city which has not yet mixed with his blood, suddenly senses his own personal misfortune and feels that "*I*—am lost forever . . ." (Zisho Landoy).[16]

   16. Landoy (Landau; 1889–1937), a beloved figure and ironic lyrical poet of the "Young Generation" in New York.

And because this was felt instinctively by several young people, it was called a group. And because the older writers were not used to a tone of singing about oneself, they called the group "The Young Generation."[. . .]

The Young were the first to feel the urge not to be men who write literature but men. Here is my book of poems, here I am with all my strengths and weaknesses. But in this respect, they still did not go far beyond their elders.[. . .] Still preoccupied with himself, the Young poet forgot to work on himself, to deepen his insight into himself. Yes, to become a person—not a literature, but an interesting person! With very few exceptions, the Young did not become interesting persons, they remained everyday, average people.[. . .]

The undoubtedly great advantages and innovations of "the Young Generation" and their influence on the development of Yiddish poetry is even now, after a short span of some ten years, no more than material for literary history.[. . .]

And not only in content but in form as well, the achievement of the Young becomes more and more a drawback. From the dry *cholent*-language (Frug's expression),[17] from a broken vessel, the Young undoubtedly created an almost perfect instrument flexible enough for nuances and half-tones. The language became finer, honed and polished. But here too, as in content, they went astray. Mani Leyb[18] has great merits for the Yiddish poetic language. Mani Leyb has achieved a rare subtlety. Mani Leyb's language can bring out a poetic tremor. But this is precisely where Mani Leyb's weakness lies. His polishing of the language led him to overrefinement, as it were. Mani Leyb's language is not alive. His poems grow more and more bookish, material for dreamy girls. [. . .] The linguistic Mani-Leybism in the hands of small, helpless imitators has given birth to a lifeless language, without the slightest breath of the spoken word. With two exceptions— Leyvik with his simplicity and Halpern with his vulgarity, liveliness and boister- ousness—the language of the Young is colorless and dead, though so much has been written about the great merits of the Young who gave us a finer language instrument.[. . .]

The "Young" preached contentlessness and the poetry of bare mood and thus enabled the gray nothings to find a place in Yiddish poetry. [. . .] It reached the point where the less a poem said the higher poetry it became and, if a poem was totally empty, it was crowned as "unmediated" and was called the highest poetry.[. . .] They were scared of a thought. In addition to contentless, a poet was supposed to be thoughtless and, for a while, thoughtlessness and contentlessness ruled in Yiddish poetry.[. . .]

(Jacob Glatshteyn, "A Quick Run Through Yiddish Poetry," *In Zikh*, January 1920.)

[2] *[After World War One]*

In moments of despair, you feel that poetry, even in its newest forms, though the peak of art, is still too weak to express the chaotic, bloody times. But to ignore our time altogether—who has the strength for it? Who can be so heartless?[. . .]

17. Shimon Frug (1860–1916), a Jewish poet in Russia, wrote in Russian and, condescendingly, in Yiddish; he adapted the lower-class spoken Yiddish language to the Russian meters.
18. Mani Leyb (Leib; 1883–1953) was the leading poet of the "Young Generation" in New York.

In our time of millions slaughtered, so many souls wandering without redemption, when science is dumbfounded, the poet is left only with his poetry, only with his art as a lantern in the dark corridors of life's labyrinth. He must turn to himself if he wants to extract some answer from life, a resolution, a consolation.

(Jacob Glatshteyn, "A Quick Run Through Yiddish Poetry," *In Zikh*, February 1920.)

[3] *[Words—The Stumbling Block of Poetry]*

Words are living beings. They have their own history. They have certain associations. And these associations are heavy stones around the thin neck of words.

With time, the human soul has not become more lucid but has grown darker. As the world has more riddles for an adult than for a child, so the entanglement of the world and its phenomena have increased as humanity has become more civilized and developed. Ever darker, more mysterious the soul, too.

And as the soul tried to express itself—and this is the essence of literature and especially of poetry—it had to work with ready-made, *concrete* words, which have a definite meaning and little flexibility, words which are used *not only* for poetry and literature.[. . .]

The materials of the musician and the painter belong only to them. [. . .] But poetry operates with words, the same material which expresses the world of the worker and the peasant, the doctor and the merchant. Words which fill the factory, the observatory, the laboratory, and the kitchen. Words—this is the great stumbling block of poetry. She often hurts herself on them. Gets tangled up in them. Trips over them.

The stumbling block of poetry—but—how great the consolation—the triumph of the poet!

Indeed the material of kitchen and factory and scientific study, but he—the poet—is able to make both music and painting with these words. Able to chase concreteness out of the words. To wipe out the face of tradition which drags along behind. To smooth the contours, hills and trenches of history which they carry.

The poet can neutralize the general and the everyday meaning of language. For him, words can—and *should*—become tones and colors—only.

He is the one who experiences anew the great revolution on earth, when man just began to speak. He discovers anew the joy of self-expression, of being able to convey an internal world in external sounds. He creates always from the beginning.[. . .]

If a poem is not a new act of creation, it sinks under the weight of the stones hung on the words by their past.[. . .]

(A. Leyeles, "Poetic Re-Creation," *In Zikh*, January 1920.)

[4] *Poetic Re-Creation*

Re-creation must seek new forms. New forms are the expression of new content slumbering in the formlessness of chaos, longing there, waiting languidly.[. . .]

The unvanquished wish to cast off the mountain of lies heaped up by an external, alien world; the drive to break all the fetishes which populate the external, alien world and are imposed on your soul; the desire to cut off the thread of tradition, tradition of words, tradition of art, etc., which has become a burden; the imperative to break out of whatever was stuck on you, was hung on you, heaped on you—this is the imperative of re-creation.

The ability to find a proper expression for all this, relying on nothing, not recognizing any rules—this is the meaning of the new forms and of the new rhythms.

If the internal world is a chaos, let the chaos be *given*. There is nothing to be afraid of. The chaos will not come as a shapeless piece of darkness anyway. For a poet, it will naturally take on certain, appropriate forms—and it will be a re-creation. This is how the world was created:

From an internal drive of someone's chaos to express himself, to break out, to find redemption and some kind of appropriate form.

(A. Leyeles, "Poetic Re-Creation," *In Zikh*, January 1920.)

[5] *"Jewish Art"*

Mr. Nigger[19] has gone off on a sandy road with his articles about "Jewish Art."[. . .]

When one says "Jewish Art," with the emphasis on the second word, I know what it is. I feel then that I draw not only satisfaction but excitement when I observe the emergence of an independent Yiddish literature, a genuine poetry, real art, regardless of all impediments, regardless of the absolute lack of suitable milieu, of a loving stimulation and encouragement.

But if they say to me: "Jewish Art," with the emphasis on the first word, I don't know what it is at all. Even more, I feel some kind of instinctive peril from such an emphasis.

Is there a Russian Art? A German? English? French?

Only insofar as one emphasizes the *second* word. Then it is the sum of Russian, French, German, English artists, or—since we are speaking here primarily about literature—writers. To that extent, one can and should speak about a Yiddish literary art, i.e., as a sum of Yiddish writers.

I do not pretend to be naive. I know what Mr. Nigger means. He speaks of the inner content of this literature and he wants Yiddish literature to have an explicit, inherently Jewish content.

But what does this mean? An idea? A mission? Does Mr. Nigger want Yiddish literature to have a missionary function? For example, something that would in its essence substitute religion for the world, and especially for us?

From the way Mr. Nigger conceives the concept of Jewish Art, it seems that this is what he means and this is a mistake. A basic, dangerous mistake.[. . .]

19. Sh. Nigger (1883–1955) was the pseudonym of the dominant Yiddish literary critic in America.

Literature is *art*. And art has its own laws, the highest of which is—art itself. Art is *only* an expression of life and can have no other relation to life. It can be neither life's chambermaid nor life's mistress. It cannot serve as spiritual guide and cannot teach how to behave in life. It can only be an expression of the feelings, thoughts, impressions, moods, and opinions of a certain number of individuals. In other words:

It can only be art.[. . .]

Literature is not prophecy, not general redemption, not social politics and not national politics.[. . .]

Revolution and pogroms can be "themes" for literature. But the revolution itself is ever loftier, the pogroms still more shattering, tragic than the greatest work of art about them.[. . .]

The smallest Jewish pogrom, one brutally murdered Jew, one humiliated and violated woman can influence a person and a Jew, changing his mood and stirring up his soul more than ten books. All this, real life, is much more terrifying than Lamed Shapiro's story, "The Jewish Kingdom," and all that is said in it.[20] And if all this can change nothing, then a work of art can certainly change nothing. "The Jewish Kingdom" is only the artistic expression of the impact which the Jewish tragedy made on Shapiro the artist. This expression is a genuine work of art and that is all that is demanded of a book. From this point of view, there is actually no special Jewishness in this work. The strength of the book is in its art. Because it is art, it is Jewish anyway. It is Jewish also because it is written by a Jew and in Yiddish.[21] There cannot be and should not be any other Jewishness.

(A. Leyeles, "Jewish Art," *In Zikh*, March 1920.)

[6] *[Poetry—A National Art]*

In the February issue of the monthly English literary journal, *The Dial*, James Oppenheim has an interesting article arguing that poetry is becoming more and more the characteristic national art of America. He claims that while fiction, the novel, and the short story can be considered the national art of Russia, for example, in America this place is occupied by the half-lyrical, half-narrative poetry.[. . .]

There is, undoubtedly, much truth in the arguments of the Jewish-American poet. They also suggest the idea that poetry may become—perhaps is presently becoming—the national art of the Jews, because the same factors which have inhibited fiction, the novel, and the short story from becoming the national American art are at work among our people too.

No doubt the Jews are a highly pronounced nationality, not less but more so than the Russians or French. But while there is an internal factor which makes poetry the national American art, with the Jews, the same result stems from an external factor. With the Americans, the dominant fact is that they are a composite nation, a mixture of many and varied nations and bloods. With the Jews, however, the fact that they are scattered over the whole world, strewn among many peoples,

20. L. Shapiro (1878–1948), a Yiddish fiction writer in New York, became famous with his stories based on the pogroms in Russia in 1905.

21. Here, as elsewhere, it is impossible to translate the identity of the two notions, "Yiddish" and "Jewish," in the author's argument, since in the original only one word is used for both.

linked to each other by all kinds of fates, makes poetry, with its broader possibilities for a scattered, more chaotic, more abrupt and momentary expression, more fitting to our spirituality, more capable of becoming our national art.

Perhaps that is why we have seen such an upsurge of poetry lately among Jews all over the world at the expense of prose.

("Poetry—the National American Art," in "Reflections," *In Zikh*, March 1920.)

[7] *Poetry and Language*

Mr. Oppenheim indicates [in the abovementioned article in *The Dial*] that the new American poetry starts with Walt Whitman. Whitman launched the new era by renouncing the canonized poetic language which had dominated British poetry and whose tradition was omnipotent in America as well. Whitman took the simple American language of conversation as a basis for his creation and thus caused a rupture between domestic and British poetry.[. . .]

We Jews also have a "canonical poetic language" in some sense. This is the language of the folk song. Most older poets have used this language, whether labeling their poems as folkloristic or not. The "Young" went one step further but they too created a "canon," a kind of sugar-coated refinement.

We, the Introspectivists, want the *spoken* language, but the spoken language of the more intelligent, more conscious part of the Jewish people. Not the tradition of folksiness and not the "hothouse" language of the Young, but the language of the conscious Jewish intelligentsia.

("Poetry and Language," in "Reflections," *In Zikh*, March 1920.)

[8] *The Dear Reader*

Does Yiddish literature have—a reader? We admit that this species is a great mystery for us. Often it seems that there is no reader and that whoever reads a Yiddish literary work is himself a kind of literary Marrano. He writes for himself clandestinely and waits for an opportunity to emerge into the world.[. . .]

Yiddish literature, Yiddish poetry already has writers. What is lacking, however, is the reader, and this is especially true for Yiddish poetry.

("Reflections," *In Zikh*, June 1920.)

[9] *Free Verse*

Each of the cited elements of musicality in poetry is important in itself. When one poet succeeds in combining all the elements at once, a wonderful effect emerges, a musicality which is—it seems to me—richer, more impressive than actual music because it is a music not of neutral sounds but of living words of the human language. It speaks, therefore, more directly, more enchantingly and, at the same time—more mysteriously. Only rare poets have reached that level. Sometimes Coleridge in England, sometimes Verlaine in France, sometimes Balmont and Bryusov and occasionally Sologub in Russia, sometimes Dehmel in Germany and, above all, the American Edgar Allan Poe.[. . .]

Free verse is needed only because it gives the poet a greater possibility to express a complex internal life and in the most individual, most fitting way for him.

All the meters are little, simple, even single-toned arias. When you read a somewhat longer poem in the same rhythm, it becomes monotonous and ugly. Many poets sense that and, in their longer works, change the rhythm in various passages. Nevertheless, no great variation is possible there. Neither does it help the monotony of individual passages.

Free verse is what is called in music a fugue or, better, a symphony. It does not consist of one often-repeated, simple and monotonous air but of various airs blended together, of various interwoven voices and tones.[. . .]

Aside from that, in free verse it is possible to introduce the so-called dis-harmony which makes the poem richer, even truer, more responsive to con-temporary psychic experiences.[. . .]

In this sense, all former and familiar devices may help: the old rhythms (but differently and unexpectedly combined), alliteration, even rhyme. All this must be subordinated to the natural, inner rhythm, the rhythm of the individual, experi-enced mood, vision, emotion; the natural rise and fall of a mood as well as the natural rise and fall and the natural *flow* of language and of human breathing.

Then, and only then, can free verse truly become a new poetic instrument full of the broadest possibilities, rich with the finest, most subtle and individual nuances and shades.

In free verse, the individual *line* too acquires a new value, a new life. In the old verse, the line is conditioned by the meter or—even more often—by the rhyme. As a result, the length of the line is often quite arbitrary. Frequently, it is "padded" with superfluous material.[. . .] In free verse, such poetic "license" has no place. There is no place in it for superfluities. Every line must be in its place, a full line—according to the inner rhythm of the whole poem, according to the poetic sense, and according to the individual breath of the poet.

(A. Leyeles, "Free Verse," *In Zikh*, July 1920.)

[10] *[Verslibrisme—Expression of a New Content]*

Verslibrisme is assumed to be an innovation in form. In reality, it is an expression of a new content. The new content is the modern life of the modern man, who is breaking away from the old idyllic world, from the old provincialism and small-town atmosphere. And I do not mean only field and forest and river and flowers and grass and moon. Not only "nature." A modern poet can write about these things too. It is only that he will write about them *differently*. The modern poet may not write one poem about steam and electricity, about airplanes and radios. He may write about trees and grass—and still be modern. Modern because he will be *different*. Broader and more universal, stronger and more energetic, more chaotic and kaleidoscopic. The machine and the dirigible are merely external signs of the broader horizons of modern man. For art, such external signs are trifles. What is important for art is the new, inner feeling that is created, the new music that stirs in the world, the new, *all-uniting* rhythm which vibrates in it.

Verslibrisme is the expression of this newness, of Modernism in this sense. Free verse achieves two goals at the same time. First, it is a wonderful confirmation of

Nietzsche's sentence that, for the true artist, the essence of art is where the layman sees or hears only "form." In other words, it confirms the absolute identity—for the artist—of form and content. Second, it provides the linguistic, acoustic, and visual means to express the broader universal breadth with which the modern world increasingly lives.

(A. Leyeles, "Two Years," *In Zikh*, July 1922.)

[11] *[Poetry—Chaotic, Kaleidoscopic]*

We, Inzikhists, Introspectivists, tossed in, among others, the terms: *kaleidoscopic, chaotic*. Nothing has baffled and frightened more than these. How come? And where are "concentration," "crystallization," "consolidation"? How can art exist without them?

But again and again, we must repeat that the modern poet is much less interested in questions of aesthetics and ethics than in the fullest expression of his "I," of his inner world, which is also his world-system, the expression of his relation to world and life.

To give oneself. But what is he? What is his "I"?

I am I and not I—at the same time. I am, was, will be—at the same time. I am part of the whole and the whole—at the same time. I am a piece of formed chaos, the whole primeval chaos and the whole eternal form—at the same time. So I see the world and I see myself—at the same time. I express myself and express the world—at the same time.

This is our introspectivist "chaos," our kaleidoscopic vision. And tone and sound and color and rhyme and regular meter and *vers libre*—all these are the means which the introspectivist poet uses to achieve, to give expression to himself and simultaneously to the world. In other words, to create his world-system.

Therefore, there is no forbidden object for him, no definite, dogmatic form, no impossible connections. Therefore, he is simultaneously at the Ganges and at the Hudson, in the year 1922 and in the year when Tiglathpileser conquered and terrorized a world. Therefore, the Introspectivist is chaotic and kaleidoscopic.

(A. Leyeles, "Two Years," *In Zikh*, July 1922.)

[12] *[Scare Points and Exclamation Points]*

Paul Laurence Dunbar sang of the deep black misfortunes of his race in small, beautiful, and moving poems; and, among us, our misfortune is smeared all over with scare points and exclamation points.

(Jacob Glatshteyn, "A. Leyeles," *In Zikh*, January 1923.)

[13] *The Problem of the Reader*

The problem of the reader does not exist for us. We have long ago despaired of the possibility of having what is called a readers' circle for the new Yiddish poetry. In any case, not here in America. Perhaps such an animal does exist in Poland. Perhaps also in Russia. In America—nonexistent. Perhaps the reader of modern Yiddish literature will come later. Hope can never harm. Now he doesn't exist and perhaps cannot exist. Here there is no young Jewish intelligentsia that would be interested in literature, much less in Yiddish literature. The Yiddish reader is found primarily among the workers. And they—they are still stuck with Edelstadt[22] or with those who came after him, singing about their poverty and about the "shining tomorrow."

If the shlemiel "Modernism" ever does go astray among "the workers' ranks," it happens through the medium of the ultraproletarian press, and there "innovation" is understood only from the point of view of revolution, the red banner, and toil. When I read the poems in the columns of that press, when I sometimes read an apology for the "new poetry," I am filled with pity for the poor poets of poverty. Vulgarity, tastelessness with no redeeming feature, perhaps except for stupidity— this is defended, this is submitted to the weary worker as the new art, the poetry of *revolt*.[. . .]

Outside of the proletarian press and the proletarian reader with the pseudo-new poetry that is bred there, there is absolutely no reader for the new Yiddish poetry in any other circles; and—we don't care.

("Reflections," *In Zikh*, January 1923.)

[14] *Tradition*

We have no tradition, I mean the Inzikhists. It is hard to point out the threads that tie us to previous periods of Yiddish poetry.[. . .]

We have no tradition. Our roots perhaps barely touch the roots of previous Yiddish poetry. It is, however, false to assume that our tradition is non-Jewish poetry. Surely, we are similar to the new trends and movements that can be found among poets of other languages. Certainly, there is a more direct relation between an Introspectivist and a German Expressionist or English Vorticist than between us and most Yiddish poets of the previous periods.

But this direct relation is *all of Modernism*, the whole *difference* of contemporary poetry, of contemporary art in general.

The Inzikhists came, throwing overboard the tradition of Yiddish poetry. We simply ignored it. The impulse was a purely poetic one, the same as that of all poets the world over. Hence the authenticity of the Inzikhist poems from a purely poetical, artistic point of view, but also—and this is inevitable—the impression of foreignness in the eyes of those who regard Yiddish poetry *merely* as a part of Jewish culture, who are looking for thread-weaving, who emphasize, throughout, the word "Jewish."

Perhaps we are—my dear friends and even dearer enemies, in case the following words make your blood boil, you are most cordially invited to observe the conditionality of my phrase, the "perhaps"—the first real Yiddish poets in the sense that we don't know any other impulses outside of purely *artistic* ones—in Yiddish. In the first period, "Jewishness" dominated our poetry; in the second period, poets strayed among various alien motifs, borrowed with more or less skill; only in our period is there pure, unadulterated poetry in Yiddish. That means—perhaps the first true Yiddish poetry.[. . .]

22. David Edelstadt (1866–1892), one of the founders of Yiddish proletarian poetry in America, was a beloved figure among Jewish workers.

We have no tradition. We have found very little that could serve as tradition for us. The tradition begins perhaps with us, strange as it may sound. It is certainly not our wish—but observe how poems are being written nowadays, how they *try* to write. Isn't it following the ways of the hardly four-year-old Inzikhist "tradition"?

("Reflections," *In Zikh*, March 1923.)

[15] *[Art and the Fourth Dimension]*

In his book *Tertium Organum*, the Russian mystic and mathematician Ouspensky has immensely elevated the value of art as one of the keys to understanding the riddle of world and life. Studying our capacity to grasp the external phenomena surrounding us, he came to the conclusion that, as long as we think and feel three-dimensionally, i.e., as the world *appears* and not as it *is*, we will never understand it. He indicates that, in art, we may perhaps see a hint of the "language of the future" which will help us to overcome the limitation of the three dimensions. Because what is the language of art?[. . .] The strange adjectives, metaphors, and other figurative devices express the poet's striving to convey what he senses about the world, for which language has as yet no proper words. There are no words because there are no concepts yet. But there already are sensibilities and vibrations in the poet—who is a human type of a higher psychic organization—which he seeks to convey. He is still seeking in the dark. He is still groping with blind fingers. He is still a jabbering baby. But it is a jabbering not on the threshold of the three-dimensional world known to us—as in the case of the baby—but on the threshold of a four- and more-dimensional, true world, not yet known to us.[. . .]

To the real world, the phenomenal world, i.e., the world of appearances, Ouspensky (like many philosophers before him) opposes the noumenal world, the world of whatever is *behind* appearances. He says: Everything has a soul, something that is behind the appearance, and truth is certainly *behind* appearances. From the same wood, we make a cross, a mast, and a gallows. All three are *wood*, but what a difference between the three![. . .]

In this sense, I understand the formula, "art for art's sake." Armed with his intuition, the modern artist does not want to know any tasks or goals other than art because he knows that, for him, art is the only road to arrive at the truth, to see the world in its real light, and to understand his own relation to the world.

(A. Leyeles, " 'Art for Art's Sake,' " *In Zikh*, May 1923.)

[16] *[Rhythm—the Inner Essence of the Poem]*

Rhythm is what actually makes the poem. When a poem has an "impact" on the reader, it is primarily due to its rhythm. How often does a reader of a good poem feel that he would not be capable of explaining what the poem actually means, what the poem wanted—and nevertheless he feels something that grips him and carries him away. This was achieved by the rhythm.

What is rhythm?

It is *not* the singsong, not a "mellifluous grammar," not the well-measured feet. It is the inner essence of the poem, which often has nothing to do with the words or even with the images. It is the "inexplicable," which the poet himself could not have understood and which the reader will misunderstand if he tries to analyze and explain it.

It is the sensing—through sound and combination of sounds, through associations, suggestions, and word-colors—of something that cannot be expressed in any other way. It is a kind of psychic, intuitive onomatopoeia, the attempt—mostly unconscious—to convey the vibrations of his soul in a given case, under specific circumstances, in a definite situation.[. . .]

And this is the mark of various gradations of poets, from the barely poet to the genius poet. Monotonous rhythm is the best sign of the small, the flat, the trivial—the three-dimensional and maybe only two-dimensional poet. A poet who senses the fourth dimension, the world of the true realities, the noumenal world—he is rich in rhythms, in nuances of rhythms. Only through wide variation of rhythms, rich in number and nuances, can we, three-dimensional men, reach the true and unique rhythm of the world, the cosmic rhythm which is "the song of the universe." [. . .]

Monotonous rhythm in a poet is a sign that he resides on one plane, in one particular corner, and his corner is small and meager. He may write about a thousand things, but in truth they are copies of only one thing, reproductions of one cliché.[. . .]

Multiplicity of rhythms means growth, and growth is *life*. Multiplicity of rhythms expresses the drive to break out of the myriad of illusions which the phenomenal world has spun around us. It is a many-faceted and multirunged ladder to the "noumen" of things. Monotonic rhythm is the decline into *one* illusion, the unwillingness and, more correctly, the *inability* to break out of your own illusion.

This is "mood," "feeling," "heart," and other such things.[. . .]

"Poetry of feeling" and "poetry of thought," to the extent that they exist, are both results of monotonous rhythm, and vice versa. Both are rhythmical monotone, both are little, confined illusions. Only in the melting of thought and feeling under one immense tension, resulting in a chemical fusion that is unlike either of them—artistic, creative intuition—only there is the truth, the truth which is absolutely unavailable to the dualist who is divided himself and seeks justification by dividing others.[. . .]

Words, ideas, content, images by themselves have no independent meaning in a poem. They exist only to serve. They help to create rhythm. When the poet succeeds in combining words, both in the associations and suggestions that they evoke and in their sound; when he succeeds in bringing them into the necessary relationship with all musical elements of the poem, including rhyme or meter; when the images and "ideas" that he invests are in the same relationship to those elements—then, as a result, we have the rhythm of a poem, the "form" of a poem, the soul of a poem—the poem.

(A. Leyeles, "Rhythm, Form, Technique," *In Zikh*, June 1923.)

[17] *[Form and Technique]*

If we understand that the main thing in a poem is its rhythm, we must also understand that there cannot be a bad "form" with a good "technique," or vice versa. The rhythm emerges as a result of the absolute mutual concurrence and fusion of all poetic elements. Hence, it would be unimaginable to have *one* good element with a bad overall result. If the overall rhythm of the poem is bad, there can be no "good" technique, because then the technique will be unsuitable: ergo—bad. The same is true for the opposite. There can be no good "form" (rhythm) along with bad "technique." If technique is a poetic element, and if it is bad, unsuitable, then the rhythm cannot be good either.

Technique in poetry is an empty sound. If, by this, you understand the *knowledge*, for example, that a sonnet has fourteen lines and the ability to assemble fourteen lines, then you are very naive—to put it mildly. The only meaning that the word "technique" can have in poetry is *integrity*, the impression that the poem *had to be* in such a mold and not otherwise. But this integrity is the result of a good *beginning* of the poem, of the immediate, directly and intuitively found mold, which emphasizes the *fullness* of rhythm even more. And that means that technique is, at most, an element of form, and therefore one cannot make a logical sentence: "Bad form—good technique," or vice versa. There does not and cannot exist in poetry such a thing as the difference—and certainly not the opposition—between form and technique.

(A. Leyeles, "Rhythm, Form, Technique," *In Zikh*, June 1923.)

[18[*Gentiles and Yiddish Literature*

That Yiddish literature is still an unknown and almost outlandish thing among the Gentiles is well known. Almost every article about Yiddish that appears in the local English press is an offense to every Yiddish writer. Articles about Yiddish literature have recently appeared in *The Nation* and *The Bookman* which one is ashamed to read. It is hard to imagine so much idiocy collected in one place on any other subject. Who are those Jewboys who assume the right to "describe" us? Who are those Jewish scribblers who supply information about us to those who are ignorant on the subject of American Yiddish literature?

On reflection, one must conclude that the Americans themselves are also to blame. One may expect from *The Nation*, for example, a more responsible relationship to the literature of a people who have created so much here in America. No other immigrant group has built an original, independent, and in more than one aspect American literature in the course of some thirty years than we Jews. Yet *The Nation* gets away with the silly cliché that every ex-reverend can supply. It is irresponsibility of the highest degree.

Recently, the *In Zikh* had its own experience with Gentile colleagues.

The American journal, *Poetry*, got hold of an issue of *In Zikh*. And this is what the editors wrote to us:

"Unfortunately we cannot read your journal. We would like to know in what language it is printed. Is it Chinese?"

Poetry is published in Chicago. Several Yiddish daily newspapers are printed in Chicago. Yiddish periodicals, collections, books are published there. There are certainly also Chinese laundries in Chicago, and the lady-editors of *Poetry* have probably seen a ticket from a Chinese laundry in their lifetime. And, after all that—not to mention that an intelligent person may know the difference between the way Chinese and Yiddish look—to ask whether a Yiddish journal is Chinese does not reflect very positively on the intelligence of the *Poetry* people.

But after all, this is not important.

What is important is: How long will Yiddish literature be unknown among Gentiles? How long will they think of us—in literature—as Hotentots?

A self-respecting Yiddish literature can react to this phenomenon in two ways.

First, it can ignore the external world altogether and wait until the weight, the importance and inner value of our work forces the Gentiles to see us, to consider us and ask pardon for past misrepresentations.

Second, it can inform the non-Jewish journals that all they have printed about Yiddish thus far is false, silly misrepresentation and it can undertake the translation of the best, most characteristic Yiddish works, thus forcing them to have respect for Yiddish.

("Reflections," *In Zikh*, July 1923.)

[19] *[Rhyme]*

We often use rhyme but it is interesting how we employ it. In the old, rhymed poetry, rhyme came as something that must come, that the reader was *expecting*. Therefore it played such an important role. Therefore it is the main element in folk poetry. Therefore it is the *only* safe haven for all small poets and for those great ones who are tired of searching, who have become prematurely pessimistic and who want to lull their conviction in the vanity-of-vanities of life with the ring of rhyme. For them, it is rest. Pause. Achievement.

For us—who have adopted free verse as the main mold of poetic creation—rhyme comes not as an expectation but as a surprise. It comes suddenly. A halt in mid-leap. The leap into the unknown. For us, rhyme is preparation, not rest. For us, it is not denial but confirmation of belief in ever newer and broader possibilities of the world, of a world of which we can only have premonitions but which is not yet opened to our senses.

(A. Leyeles, "Whither Yiddish Poetry?" *In Zikh*, August 1923.)

[20] *[Anglo-American Free Verse and Us]*

There is no need to deny. We have adopted free verse under the influence of American-English poetry. But this was no more than borrowing a shell, a mold. What was actually molded in language was completely and authentically our own, so much so that the mold itself has become different, absolutely authentic and independent.

I read English poetry in free verse, I compare their free verse with ours. And I maintain, with no hesitation whatever, that our free verse is better, more masterful, more rhythmically lucid and more profound, natural, and imperative in its sound and in its flow. It may seem immodest, but I sincerely believe that the free verse of the Introspectivists is now perhaps the best in all languages.

(A. Leyeles, "Whither Yiddish Poetry?" *In Zikh*, August 1923.)

I saw the exhibit of Archipenko's sculpture and painting. I have the highest respect for sculpture. When I hear the word "creativity," my brain immediately sees a man hammering chips of marble or kneading pieces of clay. All of Archipenko's work is pure experiment. I was terribly interested. Every piece of bronze, brass, silver, gold—Archipenko experiments a lot with metals—every block of wood and marble breathed with creative youthfulness. "To hell with all accepted laws. To hell with all perceived beliefs about the nature of sculpture. I, the creator, experiment and here is my world. That's how it is—and that's how I like it." [. . .]

One should write poems as Archipenko hews, hones, assembles, and forges. Always to experiment and to try to master everything. The most classical forms and the freest. The most formal sonnets and rondeaux and the barely noticeable, barely separated-from-prose *vers libre*. To sink your teeth in every metal, in every ore and wood of the world, and extract from the formlessness the fullest unique form of your will. To combine everything in one, to play the full symphony of the meaningful sounds of language and then scatter them again. To pull out one detail and shed the most blinding light on it—to extract its primeval meaning and sense.

To experiment, only to experiment in poetry. To fight against the biological imperative of stasis. To tear up all webs of the established. To shoot the word through with the gunpowder of youth, to hold it shimmering as Archipenko holds the ore of his Egyptian Head.

(A. Leyeles, "Impressions and Expressions," *In Zikh*, November 1928.)

[22] *[The Law of Bipolarity]*

The same writers who perceived America and expressed it in poem, novel, drama, turned to Jewish history and sought characters and situations there for their contemporary and even "American" ideas. . . . Between the turn to history and the focus on New York and on American landscapes (the chronology is unimportant, it was mostly simultaneous), there is a deep internal relationship. The law of bipolarity. The most dedicated verslibriste will suddenly turn to the most confined, classical forms.

(A. L——s, "A Melancholy Dialogue," in "Reflections," *In Zikh*, October 1935.)

[23] *New Forty-four*

Let us start with a dry report.
In the last month, *In Zikh* received new subscribers as follows:

from New York	—	24
from Boston	—	20
from Chicago	—	17
from various other cities	—	3

Altogether, 44 subscribers.
It is not a bad record at all for one month, after the first appeal to our readers to help us enlarge the journal to 48 pages.

Along with the increase in single-issue sales, it shows clearly that there is a contingent of readers for a modern, independent literary journal in Yiddish. We have *underestimated* that reader and we apologize. With pleasure!

(*In Zikh*, November 1935.)

[24] *Topic: Yiddish Literature and the World*

The orphaned isolation of Yiddish literature is a problem that keeps swimming up to the surface. Jews are a world-people in every sense. Yiddish is a world-language in its scope, and yet even Bulgarian or Catalan looks more courageously, with more dignity straight into the eyes of the external world. It is certainly an abnormal situation. It stamps a seal of inferiority on us. We ourselves feel pretty uneasy about it. And never more uneasy than when we happen to meet representatives of other literatures.

I know this from personal experience. When I was in Berlin some thirteen years ago, I did not want to meet the Jewish-German poetess, Else Lasker-Schiller. I knew her poems quite well. She, however, had no inkling of Yiddish poetry. Meeting under such circumstances was not attractive to me. Rather than be in an apologetic situation ("you know, I too write poems"), I preferred not to see the poetess at all, even though her exotic work did have an attraction for me.

What Yiddish writer has not felt such an uneasiness at one time or another?

They don't know us because Yiddish literature, notwithstanding its full growth for the last half-century, is a "closed book" for the non-Jewish outside—in the literal sense of the words.[. . .]

The scandal of the fate of Yiddish in the English world is formidable, especially in America.

In America, a great literature was created in half a century. In the last thirty years, a large part of the best that modern Yiddish literature can show has emerged here. And still—what do our neighbors know about us? Absolutely nothing. If anybody ever writes anything about Yiddish in an English journal, it is grotesque, shameful for him and for us, too. There have been such examples in *The Nation, The Bookman*, and other places. Why? Because the Jews who have written those things did not have the slightest respect for Yiddish, because they themselves looked down on Yiddish, because they—one thing follows from another—did not even bother to study the subject that they presented to the outside world.

It is one of the most annoying, if not outrageous chapters of American Jewish history—this attitude of our own "brothers," I respectfully submit, to the Yiddish language and to everything connected with it. My hands itch to take a swipe at this gang of yesterday's "East Siders." God helped them to learn English and now they establish a veritable "theoretical, scientific" justification for the "truly American" anti-Semitism. Assimilation, assimilators? It is too dignified a word for these characters, the assorted "Broadway Jews" who peddle various wares among the "Goyim" and, God help us, sometimes even Yiddish—"as background." We know where it comes from, where he came from, this most repulsive type of Jew that you can imagine. It is mostly *the second generation*, the children of immigrants, who were born here. The homes of this generation were mostly illiterate, bereft of culture, primitive in every sense. When such homes sometimes got a Yiddish newspaper, the newspaper itself spoke of Yiddish with the greatest contempt, presented the knowledge of English as the highest ideal, *making it* in English as the peak of good fortune. Where, then, could the second generation learn respect for themselves as Jews and for everything that relates to Yiddish?

So, though one can know precisely the source of this annoying phenomenon, the annoyance still rankles. The pettiest Jewish scribbler in English, the lowest reporter on an English newspaper feels sky-high above Yiddish—whether it's the Yiddish press or the demanding, original Yiddish literature.[. . .]

So many years in America, such a fine literature created here, and we remain strangers to our neighbors as if we had lived in Siam or had written in some Eskimo dialect.

It is an anomaly. It should be different, become different. We must get out of our isolation. We must put an end to the situation in which, at the meeting between a Yiddish and an American writer, it is "self-evident" that the Jew should have read *all the works* of the American and just as "self-evident" that the American should have no idea whether the Jew writes mezuzahs, checks or, indeed, "real literature"— something like himself.

A change will come not through back doors and various janitors and matchmakers. It will come only as Joseph Millbauer did it with a number of Yiddish poems in French [in his anthology, *Yiddish Poets Today*]—through personal interest, respect and—most important—love.

And in the meantime, we must wait with dignity.

(A. L——s, "Reflections," *In Zikh*, March 1937.)

[25] *[Poems in Time]*

There are poems that can be written by the dozen not because they are so bad but because they are the product of an open poetic faucet. In such poems, time plays no role. They are, I would say, poems in space but not in time.[. . .]

In A. Leyeles's book of poems [*Fabius Lind*], something happens from the first page to the last and we get an impression not of a collection of poems but of a great human document, of metamorphoses, pain, transformations, elation, and achievement over a range of a lived piece of life in terms of the creeping time.[. . .]

And because *Fabius Lind* is a book of time in the most authentic sense of the word, it became a book of our time, not through consciously written time poems but through a sensibility which caught everything that has hovered over us from 1927 to 1937. In this book, ten years in the life of a highly cultured, unsettled, searching, refined Jew were fixed forever. For me, Leyeles's ten years are also—and primarily—ten Jewish years. Leyeles's book is a national book in the best sense of the word.[. . .]

The name "Fabius Lind," with its externally foreign sound, is symbolic of the sum total of all foreignness which the modern poet has absorbed in order to enrich what is originally Jewish, inherited. The sound "Fabius Lind" is intimately bound up with the new form and with the renewed content. It is just such a phase in the history of Yiddish poetry as the Jewish-sounding names of the past: Mendele, Sholem Aleichem, Yitskhok Leybush, Avrom, and Moyshe-Leyb.[23]

(Jacob Glatshteyn, "The Image of Fabius Lind," *In Zikh*, April 1937.)

[26] *[The Ghetto of Yiddish Literature]*

I do not know if there is a better parallel to ghetto life than writing Yiddish. Imagine a Jewish store in a thoroughly Jewish neighborhood; sometimes a Christian customer may wander in. But no "Aryan" will cross the border of Yiddish writing—it is a purely Jewish territory.[. . .]

Speaking about living spiritually among ourselves, about the narrow walls of Jewish cultural community, about the fear of Jewish narrowness, we must remember that, if Dickens, with all his English peculiarity, meant *the World* for the English, Mendele, Sholem Aleikhem, and Peretz always meant *Ghetto* for us. No matter through how many translators we spoke to the "Aryans," our classical Yiddish literature still meant a spiritual wall around our own lives. But within these confines, a language and an artistic consciousness flourished.[. . .]

It seems that the Yiddish writer, and especially the American Yiddish writer, has developed immunity to the fear of ghetto and decline. In the twenty years that I have had the opportunity to do literary work among Jews and with Jews, I have incessantly heard the voice of Jewish undertakers behind my back whispering in my ear: Your language is dying, your readers are dying out, where is your youth, you yourself are fading away. We Jewish writers went around in circles between Yiddish East Broadway walls and Yiddish undertakers.[. . .]

I just cannot be afraid of the word "Ghetto," because both economically and culturally, for me, ghetto means the greatest part of my life. The coercion to see my own brother, hear his language, see myself in my own national mirror is, for me, no coercion.

(Jacob Glatshteyn, "By Ourselves," *In Zikh*, May 1938.)

[27] *[Free Verse and the Wise Prosaic Smile of Yiddish]*

Whitman went far away from Shelley and Keats—from song to the rhythm of human speech. Free verse is the measured human breath of speaking, shouting, or solemn recitation.[. . .]

Later came the Imagists and, following Whitman's free verse, imposed on it a new constraint. They deepened but also narrowed Whitman's undisciplined music. With the freedom they won, they came back, via another road—almost to old-fashioned poetry—to the condensation and compression of words, whose main function is to be sparing and not wasteful. The Imagists created little models in which images were supposed to be as authentic as the words expressing them. In its essence, this new art was condemned to become small art. It was so precise that, in

23. Here Glatshteyn refers to the pen names or first names of Abramovitch, Rabinovitch, Peretz,

its airiness, it created stiffness. In the hands of the Imagists, the new, hot-breath music of Whitman jelled into small, cooled molds which roused amazement but did not stir the blood.

It became clear that the Imagists, who were smaller poetic figures than Whitman, were afraid to rely on the broad saying alone or on the pulse of the spoken word. They tried to restrain themselves so as not to fall into prose. Whitman was not afraid of prose, he took pieces of prose and set them in a festive order. The Imagists knew that they would fail in Whitman's breadth, therefore they felt better in the new artistic confinement, which was often narrower than the narrowest sonnet.

The Inzikhists who introduced free verse into Yiddish poetry brought with it the triumphs and failures of the new poetic weapon. Often, they too sacrificed content on the road to Imagist precision because they too were looking for possibilities of a new music in Yiddish that would not depend on rhyme or measured syllables. A new prosody was created in Yiddish which is still awaiting study, especially with regard to the new musical territories that it has uncovered.

Many Inzikhists have realized that they condemn themselves to barrenness and sterility and often to the grotesque if they keep looking only for the visual word. Often, clusters of images emerged that obfuscated the inner face of the poem. Yiddish free verse was much more difficult than English. Rhyme and the natural rhythm of rhymed, measured lines could still veil the open face of Yiddish. But free verse could not cover the wise prosaic smile of the clever tongue.

(Jacob Glatshteyn, "Once Again—Form and Content," *Sum and Substance: Essays, 1945–1947*, New York, 1947, pp. 374–378.)

[28] *[Unpoeticalness]*

Every genuine poet longs for unpoeticalness. Poeticalness is limited and definitive. Poetry even has a limited selection of words and a limited scale of moods. When a poet thinks of poetry, he thinks in terms of tradition, of the past and of all that past generations of poets have struggled for and achieved. When a poet longs for poetry, he longs for style, but when he longs for nonpoetry, he longs for the newest and widest impossibilities. A real poet longs for dry words because wet words just ooze feeling. A wet word usually means a ready-made "poetical" word, and poets avoid such words. Genuine poets love human speech. They love to create beauty from plebian unbeauty, from stubborn, blue-collar words that do not easily succumb.

(Jacob Glatshteyn, "Marianne Moore," *Sum and Substance: Essays, 1945–1947*, p. 410.)

[29] *[In the Face of the Total Destruction]*

What is poetry? In the face of the total destruction of a people, of the systematic and cold establishment of ovens and gas chambers, of the slaughter of whole Jewish families, the erasing of whole Jewish genealogies, whole family chronicles—what is literature? Is poetry the attempt to smuggle it in or to conjure it into fourteen lines of a sonnet or is it shouting, wailing, and howling and walking from yard to yard to rouse all the shuttered windows?

(Jacob Glatshteyn, "Ada Jackson," *Sum and Substance: Essays, 1945–1947*, p. 420.)

[30] *[A Whole Poetry Has Become Monotonic and Monothematic]*

Every Jewish poet knew that he could not possibly have the words for the events and that he would not know how to arrange the poor words that he did have. There is a banal expression, "to hammer out feelings," but such a hammering would be grotesque with respect to the feelings. It would mean a top hat on an ash-covered head. In such a case poetic control, which is nothing more than poetic good behavior in public, would be a smooth hairdo and a modulated voice putting a tragicomic question mark on all the mourning and all the wailing. The poet knew all those dangers but he had no other way out.[...]

The poets of our time have been cursed with being poets of the time—and ours is a time beyond the strength of flesh and blood. The Yiddish poet of our time knew that when he wrote poems of the time, he wrote temporal poems, but not to write poems at all would be a luxury of restraint. To wait with each poem until things settle down would have meant to be a poem-professional in mid-destruction. And here we felt like sitting in stocking feet with the whole people and saying elegies.[...]

I am talking of the collective stammer in the heat of the moment which is what Yiddish poetry of our time appears to be. The question is how many individual poems can be saved from this huddled mumbling, and how many will at least be rewarded with the holy anonymity of a poem in the prayerbook.[...]

Whether we want it or not, a collective prayerbook is emerging. And if the Jewish prayer ceremony is not to become stagnant water, it will have to open a little door for the poem of our time, which is much more topical than an "appropriate" chapter of Psalms or an unearthed phrase from Isaiah. The Jewish prayerbook cannot live all the time with the past and remain alive.[...]

Only those poems of our time which are collective and pious and not insistently individual have good chances of remaining. If they do not remain as particular artistic achievements, together they will become the weeping of an epoch. And perhaps from the togetherness, the word will emerge which the separate poem was unable to attain. And only those poems that bow their proud heads and merge into the general crucible of our enormous calamity will achieve in the ensemble if not artistic at least national purpose. This is the sense of the whole, essentially senseless tangle. A whole poetry has become monotonic and monothematic. The times have made Jewish monotheism into monothemism; but precisely in this singing together or, better, wailing together, lies a kernel of light and a promise for tomorrow.

(Jacob Glatshteyn, "The Hard Road," *Sum and Substance: Essays, 1945–1947*, pp. 424–427.)

Ahaseurus 1. Persian King in the Book of Esther.
2. See Wandering Jew.

Arbe'kanfes—Pious undergarment (Hebrew: *arba kanfot*). A sleeveless undershirt with four fringed corners worn by pious Jews.

Borscht Soup made of beets ("red borscht") or cabbage, a staple of Jewish and Eastern European diet. A rich borscht would have pieces of solid food or an "eye" of a hard-boiled egg swimming in it.

Challah Braided egg-bread, made especially for the Sabbath and festive occasions.

Echod (Hebrew: *Ekhad*) One, oneness, the ultimate attribute of God in Jewish belief; uttered daily in the Shema.

Eternal Jew See Wandering Jew.

Ge'more (Hebrew: *Gemarah*) The main body of the Talmud, discussions of the Mishnah, encompassing law and legend. In Yiddish parlance, *Gemore* stands for the whole Talmud. Gemore-teaching represented a second level of education, after the Torah, which was taught in the *heder*.

Golem 1. A soulless creature, created by magical means (e.g., the Golem of Prague).
2. Dummy.

Goy   Gentile (frequently with negative overtones), often indicating the peasant population surrounding Jewish towns in Eastern Europe.

Hagadah   (Yiddish:*Ha'gode*) Liturgical text read at the family Passover Seder.

Hanukah lamp   A nine-branched candelabrum used to celebrate the eight days of Hanukah.

Hav'dolah candles   (Hebrew: *Havdalah*) Special braided candles for the ceremony marking the end of the Sabbath.

Heder   (or *Cheder, Kheyder*) Primary Jewish school, providing all-day education for Jewish boys from the age of three or four.

Holy Ark   The cabinet holding the Torah scrolls in the synagogue.

Kaddish   1. Memorial prayer for the dead. 2. An orphan.

Kasha   Buckwheat groats, a coarse porridge, mainstay of the Jewish and Eastern European diet.

Kiddush cup   A goblet used to make the blessing over wine.

Kol-'Nidre   The opening prayer of Yom Kippur. The solemn, sad melody of Kol-Nidre was considered a masterpiece of Jewish music.

Kreplach   Dumplings.

Landsman   A fellow townsman encountered in a new place.

Leviathan—Great whale. Reserved as food for the righteous in the world to come.

Matzo   (Hebrew: *Matzah*) Unleavened bread, eaten during the eight days of Passover.

Megillah   1. See Scroll.
2. One of the five little books of the Bible: Song of Songs, Ruth, Lamentations, Ecclesiastes, and Esther.
3. Long-winded discourse, long story.

Menorah   A seven-branched candelabrum, used in the synagogue. (In America, used also for Hanukah lamp).

Mezuzah   A small container that holds a Bible verse and is attached to every doorpost.

Midnights, Midnight Vigil   (Hebrew: *Hatsot, Tikun Hatsot*) Midnight prayers, especially Hassidic, reading hymns and lamentations on the destruction of the Temple and *Galuth Ha-Shechinah* (Exile of the Shechinah, emanation of God).

Midrash   A literary genre including homiletic interpretations of the scriptures.

Minyan   Ten adult male Jews, the minimum for congregational prayers; hence, the smallest number of people constituting a community.

Mishnah   Collection of oral laws that forms the basis for the discussions of the Talmud. A Mishnah-Jew is a simple man who can read the Hebrew Mishnah but not the Aramaic Talmud.

Pious undergarment   See Arbekanfes.

Pointing Hand   (Hebrew: *Yad*) A silver pointer used to read the Torah scrolls in the synagogue.

Po'roykhes—Curtain   (Hebrew: *Parokhet*) Embroidered curtains covering the Holy Ark that holds the Torah scrolls in the synagogue.

Rabbi, Reb   "Mr."—a title of respect or deference for a man, used with his first name.

Rashi   Acronym of Rabbi Shlomo Yitzkchaki, Rashi, of Troyes (1040–1105), the most famous, lucid, and systematic commentator on the Bible and the Talmud. His commentary became a mainstay of Jewish education, and the word *Rashi* became synonymous with commentary, explication.

Rebbe   Leader of a Hassidic sect, charismatic heir of a dynasty.

Rov   (Hebrew: *Rav*) Spiritual and legal leader of a Jewish community (American: rabbi), ordained on the basis of study.

Scroll—Megillah   The Bible is written on parchment scrolls.

Shaytl   Ritually prescribed wig worn by Orthodox married women.

She'ma, She'ma Yis'roel   The credo of the Jewish people, asserting the unity of God. The Shema is repeated before retiring and must be said before dying.

Shikse   Gentile maiden (sometimes used with negative overtones or as a symbol of sexual attraction).

Shkotsim(plural of *Shegets*)   Young Gentile men (with overtones of uneducated, unmannered ruffians).

Shofar   Ram's horn blown as a trumpet, especially during the Days of Awe and the High Holidays that follow.

Shor-Ha-Bar—Wild ox.   Promised to the righteous in the world to come.

Shtshav   Sorrel soup.

Shul   Synagogue.

Spice-box   Used in the Havdalah service, marking the end of the Sabbath.

Tallis   (Hebrew: *Tallith*) Prayer shawl worn by men, white with dark stripes.

Talmud   Comprehensive, multivolume basic book of Jewish law, comprising the Hebrew Mishnah, the Aramaic-Hebrew Gemarah (discussions of law and legends), and commentaries.

Tefillin—Phylacteries. Small black leather cubes containing Bible verses attached with leather straps to the forehead and left arm for morning prayer.

The Thirty-Six Just   (Hebrew: *L"V* = 36; *Lamed-Vov Tsadikim*) According to legend, thirty-six righteous Jews live secretly among us and are the guarantors of the world's existence. The expression, "One of the thirty-six (*Lamed Vovnik*)," is used to indicate a saintly person.

Torah, Torah Scroll   The Pentateuch.

Torah crown   Silver crown on top of the Torah scroll.

Wandering Jew—Eternal Jew, Ahaseurus.   Legendary

character doomed to live until the end of the world because he taunted Jesus on the way to the Crucifixion. The Wandering Jew later became a symbol of the "eternal" existence of the Jews, doomed to wander from exile to exile, and was adopted in modern Jewish literature as well.

Yarmulke Skullcap, worn by men as a head cover.

Yom Kippur The Day of Atonement, holiest day of the Jewish calendar.

Page 28, Raphael Soyer: *In a Jewish Cafe*, 1925. Watercolor and pencil on paper, 21³/₄ × 19³/₈″. Hirshhorn Museum and Sculpture Garden, Smithsonian Institution.

Page 31, "'Kibetzarnie' Literary Cafe." Cartoon by Joseph Foshko. Standing, in center: Sholem Ash, to his right: Joseph Opatoshu, Moyshe-Leyb Halpern. (YIVO, group 249)

Page 33, The "Young Generation," 1915. *Sitting* (from left): Menakhem Boreysho, Avraham Reyzin, Moyshe-Leyb Halpern; *Standing*: A.M. Dilon, H. Leyvik, Zisho Landoy, Reuven Ayzland, A. Raboy; On the wall: Shalom Ash, I.J. Schwartz, Peretz Hirshbeyn, J. Opatoshu; Above: J. Rolnik. (YIVO, group 303 or 224)

Page 36, The Introspectivists, 1923. *Sitting* (from left): Jacob Stodolsky, Jacob Glatshteyn, Celia Dropkin, N.B. Minkov; standing: A. Leyeles, B. Alquit, Mikhl Likht. (YIVO, group 343)

Page 55, Max Weber: *Grand Central Terminal*, 1915. Oil on Canvas, 60 × 40″. Thyssen-Bornemisza Collection, Lugano, Switzerland.

Page 59, Raphael Soyer: *Reading from Left to Right*, 1937. Oil, 26¹/₂ × 20¹/₂″. Collection of Whitney Museum of American Art. Gift of Mrs. Emil J. Arnold in memory of Emil J. Arnold in honor of Lloyd Goodrich. Acq. #74.3.

Page 71, Joseph Foshko: *A. Leyeles*, 1939.

Page 73, A. Leyeles at the offices of "Der Tog." (YIVO)

Page 75, Ben Shahn: *The Alphabet of Creation*. 1957. Serigraph in black, 31¹/₄ × 22″. New Jersey State Museum Collection, Trenton. Anonymous Donor.

Page 77, Louis Lozowick: *Hebraica I*. Courtesy Mrs. Adele Lozowick.

Page 79, Ben Shahn: Figure from *The Alphabet of Creation*. Collection of Mrs. Bernarda Shahn.

Page 81, Joseph Foshko: Title page of *Labyrinth*, 1918.

Page 91, Chaim Gross: Sketch for *Bareback Riders*, 1960. Pencil, 11¹/₂ × 27¹/₂″. Chaim Gross Collection.

Page 93, Adrian Lubbers: *Exchange Alley*, 1929. Lithograph on paper, image: 16⁹/₁₆ × 4³/₄″. National Museum of American Art, Smithsonian Institution, Museum Purchase, 1973.24.3.

Page 99, Max Weber: *Rush Hour, New York*, 1915. Oil, 36¹/₄ × 30¹/₄″. National Gallery of Art, Washington; Gift of the Avalon Foundation.

Page 103, Joseph Foshko: Illustration to "In the Subway." (from A. Leyeles, *America and I*, 1963)

Page 107, Joseph Foshko: Illustration to "Evening." (from A. Leyeles, *America and I*, 1963)

Page 127, Georgia O'Keeffe: *Radiator Building, Night, New York*, 1927. Oil, 48 × 30″. The Alfred Stieglitz Collection, Carl Van Vechten Gallery of Fine Arts, Fisk University, Nashville, Tennessee.

Page 137, Max Weber: Woodcut, from *Shriftn* 6, Spring 1920.
The woodcuts and linoleum blocks by Max Weber reproduced in this volume were originally published in the Yiddish literary journal *Shriftn*, which was dominated by the writers of the Young Generation, in the years 1919–1926. As Weber's biographer noted: "the reproductions in *Shriftn*, printed in black ink on off-white paper, were the exact size of the original prints and were characterized by a delicacy and fine clarity of line and form, particularly evident when compared with the later, flatter, and more heavily inked reproductions in *Primitives* (1926)." (Daryl R. Rubenstein, *Max Weber; A Catalogue Raisonné of his Graphic Work*, University of Chicago Press, 1980). As Rubenstein points out, "there is no record that Weber titled any of his relief prints." Subsequent identifying titles were of two kinds; A "Jewish" and a cosmopolitan label, sometimes attached to the same figure (e.g. Rabbi Reading/Pensioned, or Rabbi/Face with a Beard).

Page 139, Louis Lozowick: *Subway Construction*, 1930. Courtesy Mrs. Adele Lozowick.

Page 141, Ben Shahn: *Bulletin Board*, c. 1953. Brush drawing, 9¹/₂ × 6″. Private Collection.

Page 143, Louis Lozowick: *Nuns on Wall Street*, 1941. Courtesy Mrs. Adele Lozowick.

designer: Randall Goodall   **photo researcher:** Lindsay Kefauver   **Yiddish compositor:** Mac Shaibe, Tel Aviv
English compositors: Trend Western, Los Angeles, and Context, Berkeley   **English text:** ITC Galliard
printer: Malloy Lithographing   **binder:** John H. Dekker & Sons